Dictionary of Criminal Justice

George E. Rush
California State University
Long Beach

ALLYN AND BACON, INC.
BOSTON   LONDON   SYDNEY   TORONTO

Second printing . . . September, 1978
© Copyright 1977 by Allyn and Bacon, Inc.
470 Atlantic Avenue, Boston, Massachusetts 02210.

Printed in the United States of America.

Library of Congress Cataloging in Publication Data

Rush, George Eugene, 1932–
    Dictionary of criminal justice.

    Criminal justice, Administration of—Dictionaries
I. Title.
HV6017.R87   364'.03   77-8235
ISBN 0-205-05814-0
ISBN 0-205-05815-9 (pbk.)

The author would like to thank copyright owners and publishers for allowing the following sources to be used in this book.

The Administration of Justice, Second Edition, by Paul B. Weston and Kenneth M. Wells, copyright © 1973, pp. 267–274. Reprinted by permission of Prentice-Hall, Inc., Englewood Cliffs, New Jersey.

Automatic Data-Processing Systems, Second Edition, by Robert H. Gregory and Richard L. Van Horn. Copyright © 1960, 1963 by Wadsworth Publishing Company, Inc., Belmont, California. Reprinted by permission of the publisher.

Dictionary of American History, by Michael Martin and Leonard Gelber. Reprinted by permission of Philosophical Library, Inc. Copyright © 1966 by Philosophical Library, Inc.

Dictionary of American Politics, Second Edition, permission granted by Edward C. Smith and Arnold Zurcher. Copyright © 1968, Harper & Row (Barnes & Noble Division).

Dictionary of Criminology, by Richard Nice. Reprinted by permission of Philosophical Library, Inc. Copyright © 1965 by Philosophical Library, Inc.

iv

Consulting Editors
for the
Allyn and Bacon
Criminal Justice Series

Vern L. Folley
Chief of Police
Bismarck, North Dakota

Donald T. Shanahan
Associate Director, Southern Police Institute
and University of Louisville

William J. Bopp
Director, Criminal Justice Program
Florida Atlantic University

Dictionary of
Criminal Justice

Other Sources

Bridgewater, William, editor. *The Columbia-Viking Desk Encyclopedia*, New York: Viking Press.

Fox, Vernon. *Introduction to Corrections*. Englewood Cliffs, New Jersey: Prentice-Hall, Inc., 1972.

Goldfarb, Ronald L., and Singer, Linda R. *After Conviction*. New York: Simon and Schuster, 1973.

Mannheim, Herman, editor. *Pioneers in Criminology*. New Jersey: Patterson Smith Publications, 1972.

Palmer, John W. *Constitutional Rights of Prisoners*. Cincinnati, Ohio: The W.H. Anderson Co., 1973.

Rubin, Sol. *Law of Criminal Correction*, Second Edition (Student Edition). St. Paul, Minn.: West Publishing Co., 1973.

Scott, Sir Harold, editor. *Crime and Criminals*. New York: Hawthorne Books, Inc., 1961.

Sills, David, editor. *International Encyclopedia of Social Sciences*. New York: Macmillan & Co.

Sutherland, Edwin H., and Donald R. Cressey. *Principles of Criminology*, Sixth Edition. Philadelphia: J.B. Lippincott Co., 1960.

Abbreviations of Sources

PC	*Pioneers in Criminology*
POC	*Principles of Criminology*
TDIAS	*Terms and Definitions for Intrusion Alarm Systems*
TDPPC	*Terms and Definitions for Police Patrol Cars*

Preface

The criminal justice student, researcher, or practitioner continually meets in his or her endeavors certain words, names, court cases, phrases, and terms that by their selective nature, have special meaning.

Dictionary of Criminal Justice is intended to compile in one reference volume information that could otherwise be found only by tedious search through a myriad of interdisciplinary literature.

As such, this book satisfies a long-recognized need. This ready-reference volume will enable the teacher as well as student, practitioner, and layperson to quickly pinpoint the object of search, whether it be a name, place, event, court case, or term. The scope goes far beyond conventional coverage as political, sociological, and criminal justice institutional apsects are included.

This dictionary covers the terms used in the wide spectrum of law enforcement, courts, probation, parole, corrections and cites cases, names and places particular to each area.

To reduce the overall length of the dictionary, crossreferences have been minimized by listing most multiple-word entries under their first word. In some cases, it is necessary to look under the more important word to find the desired entry.

Wherever appropriate, definitions provided by generally recognized sources such as *Terms and Definitions for Police Patrol Cars* (TDPPC) are used to avoid proliferation and duplication.

Simply stated, *Dictionary of Criminal Justice*, although not comprehensive, combines the medical, legal, forensic, sociological, anthropological, psychological, and selected management terms *commonly* used in the broad, interdisciplinary field of criminal justice.

Acknowledgements

This dictionary is the fulfillment of an ambition seeded in undergraduate school, but not attempted until successfully completing a Ph.D. program at Claremont Graduate School in 1975. The one-year effort was a task in which certain graduate students at California State University at Long Beach assisted in preliminary research. These students, to whom I am grateful, are Wayne A. Schapper, Richard (Sam) Bass, Trish Lancaster, Richard Barlow, and Jeanne K. Raines. The author wishes to acknowledge his indebtedness to Mary J. Lively who edited, sorted, compiled, typed, and provided encouragement in distressing times.

Finally, this book is dedicated generally to the criminal justice field and specifically to my wife Heather.

Dictionary of Criminal Justice

A

abandon: (1) to forsake one's interest in property (2) to desert

abandonment: (1) the relinquishment of a claim or privilege (CDTP) (2) in marine law, the relinquishment by the insured to the underwriters of what may remain of the property insured (CDTP)

abandonment of wife: deserting his wife by a husband without reasonable cause, or neglecting to provide for her support (CDTP)

abate: (1) to terminate; to decrease (CDTP) (2) quash, beat down, or destroy (CDTP)

abduction: (1) generally defined as the taking of a female, man's wife, child, or ward, without her consent, or consent of parents or guardian, by fraud and persuasion, or open violence, for the purpose of marriage or prostitution (Created by statutes in many states.) (CDTP) (2) unlawfully taking away any maid, widow, or wife, contrary to her will. At common law a taking for money and a marriage or defilement are essential to the completion of the offense. *See also* seduction (CDTP)

abductor: one who carries away a child, a ward, a wife, etc., by fraud, persuasion or open violence (CDTP)

aberrations: optical defects in a lens which cause imperfect images (MPPF)

abet: encourage or incite; often applies to aiding an individual in the violation of a law

abettor: one who aids, abets, or instigates (CDTP)

abeyance: a state of suspension; being undetermined. In expectation (CDTP)

AB Inconvenienti [*Lat, lit "from inconvenience or hardship"*]: a term applied in those cases where from inconvenience or practical impossibility the prosecution can't establish a fact which is part of the prosecution

AB Initio [*Lat, lit "from the beginning"*]: refers to the first act or to the beginning of a state or condition (A void marriage is of no affect ab initio.)

abjuration: the renunciation under oath of one's citizenship or some other right or privilege (DAP)

abjure: to renounce or abandon by or upon oath (CDTP)

able (code): a word formerly authorized for the letter A in transmitting messages when a possibility of a misunderstanding existed. The following are the formerly authorized code words (now replaced by Alpha): Able, Baker, Charlie, Dog, Easy, Fox, George, How, Item, Jig, King, Love, Mike, Nan, Oboe, Peter, Queen, Roger, Sugar, Tare, Uncle, Victor, William, X-ray, Yoke, and Zebra. *See also* Alpha (code) (DWMT)

Abelman v. Booth: a case involving a State's attempt to release an abolitionist editor held by a federal marshal for violating a federal law. In its opinion, 21 How. 506 (1859), the Supreme Court held that when a person is legally in federal custody for a federal offense and this fact has been made known to State authorities by proper return on a writ of habeas corpus, the State is barred from proceeding further, federal authority being exclusive (DAP)

abort: failure to accomplish a mission for any reason other than enemy action. It may occur at any point from initiation of operation to destination (DWMT)

aborted firing: a firing which is cut off either manually or automatically after the firing command has been given, but before ignition has been initiated (DWMT)

abortion: the unlawful destruction, or the bringing forth prematurely, of the human fetus before the natural time of birth. (53 L.R.A. 327) To procure an abortion is to cause or procure the miscarriage or premature delivery of a woman (CDTP)

abortive trial: a trial terminated before reaching a verdict

abrasions: marks on emulsion surfaces, which appear as pencil marks or scratches. Usu. caused by pressure or rubbing (MPPF)

abridge: to shorten; to shorten by deleting words without changing the meaning

abrogate: to abolish or nullify

abscond: to leave one's usual residence or to conceal oneself, usu. in order to to avoid legal proceedings

absolute address: actual location in storage of a particular unit of data; an address expressed as a number that the control unit can interpret directly (ADPS)

absolve: to free from guilt or obligation

abuse: to treat improperly or ill use. To injure (CDTP)

accelerator: the alkali added to a developing solution to increase the activity of a developing agent and swell the gelatin, thus shortening developing time (MPPF)

acceptance inspection: an inspection of a vehicle by its owner or designated representative to determine: (1) whether a new vehicle being delivered satisfies the terms of the sales contract, has been properly serviced, and has no apparent manufacturing defects; or (2) whether maintenance or repairs contracted for on an existing vehicle were properly performed (TDPPC)

access control: the control of pedestrian and vehicular traffic through entrances and exits of a protected area or premises (TDIAS)

access mode: the operation of an alarm system such that no alarm signal is given when the protected area is entered; however, a signal may be given if the sensor, annunciator, or control unit is tampered with or opened (TDIAS)

accessory: (1) a person who helps a criminal either before or after he commits a crime but is not present at the crime (TDPPC) (2) an added part, component, or assembly that does not replace an existing item of standard equipment (TDPPC)

accessory after the fact: every person who, after a felony has been committed, harbors, conceals or aids a principal in such felony, with the intent that said principal may avoid or escape arrest, trial, conviction or punishment, having knowledge that said principal committed or was charged with such felony. (Cal. P.C., Sec. 32.) One who, knowing a felony to have been committed, receives, relieves, comforts or assists the felon (CDTP)

accessory before the fact: one who helps another to commit a crime but is absent when the crime actually is committed

access time: time required to read or write a character, word, or field in a particular location. Frequently used to mean average access time for all locations in a particular storage unit (ADPS)

accident or misfortune: a person is not criminally liable for an accident happening in the performance of a lawful act with due care (CDTP)

accomplice: one who aids another in committing a criminal offense

accumulator: (1) a register in the arithmetic unit in which operands are placed and in which arithmetical results are formed; also used for logical-arithmetic operations and for intermediate storage (ADPS) (2) a circuit which accumulates a sum. For example, in an audio alarm control unit, the accumulator sums the amplitudes of a series of pulses, which are larger than some threshold level, subtracts from the sum at the predetermined rate to account for random background pulses, and initiates an alarm signal when the sum exceeds some predetermined level. This circuit is also called an integrator; in digital circuits it may be called a counter (TDIAS)

accuracy: the degree of correspondence between data, files, and outputs and the true results obtainable by extremely careful data gathering and processing. Accuracy is measured in terms of either the number of items that are different or the amount of difference between the calculated and true result (ADPS)

accuracy of fire: the precision of fire expressed by the closeness of a grouping of shots around the

center of the target (DWMT)

accuracy of firearms: the accuracy of firearms depends upon many contributing conditions. The barrel must be as nearly perfect as mechanical skill can make it. It must be of uniform size of bore its entire length, and the grooves of the rifling must be of uniform width and depth throughout without any defects whatever. The fit of the bullet is next in importance. The bullet must be of correct size (diameter), hardness, density, lubrication, etc. The powder charge must be exactly the same for any given cartridge, and same lot of powder must be used. The primers must have a uniform amount of priming composition (CDTP)

accusation: accusations of guilty conduct may be made by complaints or affidavits, sworn to by injured persons or by police officers. This is true especially in the case of minor offenses. Accusations of felonies are made by indictments found by grand juries or by informations filed by prosecuting attorneys generally following preliminary examinations in magistrates' courts (CDTP)

accusation, modes of: the prosecution of a person charged with crime may be either: (1) upon an indictment or presentment upon oath by a grand jury; (2) upon a coroner's inquisition in cases of homicide where this is authorized by law; (3) upon an information preferred by the proper prosecuting officer without the intervention of a grand jury; (4) upon a complaint or information made under oath by a private person (CDTP)

accusatory stage: the part of a police investigation that is carried out once suspects have been indicated

accused: the defendant in a criminal case; prisoner or defendant

acetate base: the term used to designate a photographic film base composed of cellulose acetate. Also referred to as safety base because of its noninflammability (MPPF)

acetic acid (HC$_2$H$_3$O$_2$): the acid widely used in short stop baths to stop the action of the developer before negatives or prints are placed in the fixing bath. Often used in fixing baths (MPPF)

acetone (dimethyl ketone): a highly volatile, inflammable liquid, solvent for nitrocellulose, etc.; used as ingredient of film cements (MPPF)

achromatic lens: a lens which is at least partially corrected for chromatic aberration (MPPF)

acid fixing bath: a solution of hypo to which has been added an acid (usually acetic acid) for the purpose of maintaining the hypo at the proper acidity (MPPF)

A.C.L.U.: American Civil Liberties Union

acquiesce: to agree; to accept or comply by silence (CDTP)

acquit: to legally absolve a person from an accusation of criminal guilt

acquittal: a release or discharge (as from an accusation), especially by verdict of a jury

Acrol: Eastman Kodak Company trademark for Amidol (MPPF)

acronym: a word formed from the first letters or syllables of the successive parts of a compound term. An example is the word "radar," which was derived from "radio detection and ranging" (DWMT)

act and intent must co-exist: the criminal intent or negligence must unite with the overt act, and they must concur in point of time (CDTP)

actinic light: light which is capable of causing photochemical changes in a sensitive emulsion. Blue and violet are the most actinic of the visible light rays (MPPF)

action: (1) a lawsuit; a proceeding taken in a court of law. A *civil action* is taken to enforce or protect the rights of an individual; a *criminal action* is taken to punish

an offender (2) the operating mechanism of a weapon (3) the processing steps to take when the related conditions are satisfied (ADPS)

active intrusion sensor: an active sensor which detects the presence of an intruder within the range of the sensor. Examples are an ultrasonic motion detector, a radio frequency motion detector, and a photoelectric alarm system. *See also* passive intrusion sensor (TDIAS)

active restraint system: an occupant restraint safety device which requires the user to perform some act or action to make the device effective *See also* seat belt assembly, lap belt, and shoulder harness (TDPPC)

active sensor: a sensor which detects the disturbance of a radiation field which is generated by the sensor. *See also* passive sensor (TDIAS)

act of God: an inevitable event, one which occurs without human aid or intervention (e.g., hurricane, flood, or tornado) and for which, therefore, no one is to be blamed. On this ground carriers are released from liability for loss, and a person is in some cases discharged from his covenant or contract

act of Providence: an accident against which ordinary skill and foresight could not provide (CDTP)

acts and declarations of conspirators: when two or more persons conspire to commit any offense, everything said, done, or written by one of them in the execution or furtherance of their common purpose is admissible as against each of them. But statements of one conspirator as to measures taken, or acts done, not in the execution or furtherance of such common purpose, are not admissible as such as against any of the others unless made in their presence. So a confession made by one conspirator after the conspiracy was ended is not admissible against another, when not made in his presence, or if he denies its truth   (CDTP)

acts of state legislatures: state legislatures, unlike Congress, have inherent power to declare acts criminal and to impose penalties for their violation. Their power, however, in these respects, is not absolute. Their enactments must not conflict with any provision of the U.S. Constitution, or of the state constitution, or with any valid act of Congress   (CDTP)

acts of territorial legislatures: territorial legislatures are created by Congress, and their powers are limited to those conferred upon them by that body. Their legislative power shall extend to all rightful subjects of legislation not inconsistent with the Constitution and laws of the United States   (CDTP)

acts prohibited by statute: as a general rule where an act is prohibited and made punishable by statute only, the statute is to be construed in the light of the common law and the existence of a criminal intent is to be regarded as essential, even when not in terms required   (CDTP)

actuator: (1) a trigger mechanism that slides forward and back on some kinds of automatic weapons and prepares each round to be fired (DWMT) (2) a manual or automatic switch or sensor such as holdup button, magnetic switch, or thermostat which causes a system to transmit an alarm signal when manually activated or when the device automatically senses an intruder or other unwanted condition   (TDIAS)

actus [*Lat*]: an act or action

ad alium diem: at another day   (CDTP)

Adamsite [*Diphenylaminechlorarsine chloride, DM*]: this war gas (also a mob- and riot-control gas) has a very rapid rate of action. Only about 1 minute is required for temporary incapacitation. It causes the same symptoms as diphenychloroarsine (DA), but the effects develop more slowly. Also called a "sternutator" or "sneeze gas," it was developed at the end of WWI (by Roger Adams, an American)   (DWMT)

Adams v. New York, 192 U.S. 585, 48 L. Ed. 575, 24 S. Ct. 372 (1904): the Court, in a unanimous opinion by Mr. Justice Day, refused to explicitly overrule the *Boyd* holding, but the Court limited that decision to the facts in the case. Hence, for all practical purposes the Court returned to the common-law rule of admissibility on search and seizure (See *Boyd* v. *U.S.*)   (ILECJ)

Adams v. Williams, 407 U.S. 143, 32 L. Ed. 2d 612, 92 S. Ct. 1921 (1972): Mr. Justice Rehnquist's opinion holds, 6–3, a known informer's tip is sufficient to support a stop-and-frisk (Acting on a tip supplied moments earlier—about 2:15 a.m., in a high crime area—by an informant known to him, a police officer asked Williams to open his car door. Williams lowered the window, and the officer reached into the car and found a loaded handgun—which had not been visible from the outside—in Williams' waistband, precisely where the informant said it would be. Williams was arrested for unlawful possession of the handgun. A search incident to the arrest disclosed heroin on Williams' person—as the informant had reported—as well as other contraband. That part of Mr. Justice Douglas' dissent should be noted, in particular, which says the officer made the arrest and search without first determining whether Williams had a permit to carry the handgun.)   (ILECJ)

Adamson v. California, 353 U.S. 46, 91 L. Ed. 1903, 67 S. Ct. 1672 (1947): Mr. Justice Reed, for the Court, held (in a 5–4 opinion) that a state constitutional provision, or statute, that allows the prosecutor or the court to comment on the failure of a defendant to testify is not unconstitutional as an abridgment of his privilege against self-incrimination under the Fifth and Fourteenth Amendments. (This decision is so rich in the history of the Constitution, the Bill of Rights, and the Fourteenth Amendment—especially Mr. Justice Frankfurter's concurring opinion—that it should be read to gain a better insight into the relationship between the Bill of Rights and the Fourteenth Amendment.) This case, in essence, reiterated earlier rulings, such as *Twining* v. *New Jersey* and *Palko* v. *Connecticut,* that the due-process clause of the Fourteenth Amendment does not extend to State courts the procedural limitations of the first eight amendments (ILECJ)

adapter: a part or piece designed to permit parts of different sizes or shapes to be fitted together. In weapons use, for example, there are adapters that permit the use of ammunition other than that for which designed for a particular piece (DWMT)

adapter back: a supplementary back for view cameras permitting the use of smaller film or plate holders than the size for which the camera was designed (MPPF)

adapter ring: a device designed to permit using filters, supplementary lenses, etc., of a single diameter with several lens mounts whose diameters differ (MPPF)

Addams, Jane: founder of Hull House, in Chicago, a pioneer settlement house which concerned itself with the problems of the poor, the immigrants, and other components of the urban problem (DC)

Adderly v. Florida, 385 U.S. 39, 17 L. Ed. 2d 149, 87 S. Ct. 242 (1966): the Supreme Court affirmed the convictions by a 5–4 vote in an opinion by Mr. Justice Black holding that the Florida trespass statute was sufficiently specific to sustain a conviction, that it was evenhandedly applied, and that as applied it infringed no First Amendment rights since the state could "preserve the property under its control" for its lawfully dedicated use (In this decision the Court for the first time upheld convictions of participants in a peaceable civil rights demonstration.) (ILECJ)

addict: applying oneself habitually —thus, a narcotic addict is one who habitually uses narcotics (CDTP)

additive process: pertains to color photography; it is the production of color by the superposition of the separate primary colored lights on the same screen. Yellow, for example, is a mixture of red and green light rays in the proper proportion (MPPF)

address: a label consisting of numeric or alphanumeric characters which identifies a storage location, register, or device containing data (ADPS)

address, assigned: during the compiling phase, the absolute address that is associated with an address label written in a source program (ADPS)

address, effective: the address obtained by combing the contents of a specified index register with the address in an instruction (ADPS)

address, relative: a label used to identify a word in a routine or subroutine with respect to its position preceding or following other instructions in that routine or subroutine. A relative address is translated into an absolute address during an assembly or compiler run by introducing a specific starting address for the subroutine within the main routine (ADPS)

address, symbolic: a label assigned to a selected word in a routine for the convenience of the programmer. The label is independent of the location of a word within a routine; it identifies the field of data to be operated on or the operation to be used rather than its storage location. Before the program is executed, the symbolic address is converted to an absolute address (ADPS)

addressing: method of identifying operands in storage (ADPS)

addressing, field: the right-hand character position of an operand is used as its address in selected-length field storage; the left-hand character position is used for instructions (ADPS)

addressing, indirect: the address in an instruction referring to a location that contains the *address* of the operand instead of the operand itself; may be carried through two or more stages (ADPS)

address modifier: a plus (or minus) number added to (or subtracted from) the address of an operand to get a shifted-address for a character-addressable machine; the result is to shift the operand to left or right respectively (ADPS)

add-to-storage logic: processor logic designed to add any operand in storage to any other; an accumulator, as such, is not available (ADPS)

adeia: method of pardoning offenders used in ancient Greece

ad hoc: to this. Respecting this, particularly (CDTP)

ad hoc committee: a committee established for the purpose of investigating or otherwise handling a specific matter. Both houses of Congress establish numerous ad hoc committes. Generally an ad hoc committee is created as a temperary sub-committee of a standing committee. A well-known ad hoc committee in the U.S. Government was the original Committee on Un-American Activities

ad interim: in the meantime (CDTP)

adipocere: a waxy substance into which a cadaver that has been exposed to moisture over a long period of time is converted

adjournment: termination of a session or hearing or postponement to some other time or place

adjudge: to rule upon judicially; to grant through a judicial process

adjudication: (1) the process of judicial settlement (2) the settlement reached through the judicial process

adjust: to correct the elevation and deflection of a weapon so as to place the center of impact on the target (DWMT)

adjustable steering wheel: an option which provides the capability of changing the position of the steering wheel on the steering column to locate the wheel in a more favorable position for different size drivers (TDPPC)

ad litem: during the pendency of the action (CDTP)

adminicular evidence: auxiliary or supplementary evidence, such as presented for the purpose of explaining and completing other evidence (Chiefly used in ecclesiastical law.) (CDTP)

administration of criminal justice: the latter includes also the following subjects: criminal procedure, police organization and administration, prosecution, accusation, the defense of accused persons, the organization of courts, pleadings, arraignment and trial, evidence, judgment and sentence, appeals, probation, parole, pardon, penology and prison administration, juvenile courts, special procedures for crime prevention, and laws designed to change social and industrial conditions in order to prevent crime. The federal government also has an elaborate system of administration of criminal justice (CDTP)

administration, letters of: instrument by which an administrator is authorized to have charge of the goods and chattels of a party who has died without appointing an executor (CDTP)

administrative courts: (1) specialized courts in western Europe that are organized in a separate hierarchy, that apply administrative law, and that have jurisdiction over all cases in which the government or officers of the government are concerned. Sometimes the judges also have some executive functions. Generally administrative courts have a reputation for fairness in protecting the interests of citizens, for rendering speedy justice, for invalidating administrative orders which lack proper statutory authority, and for granting compensation for injuries suffered at the hands of officers or employees of the government (DAP) (2) those courts not created under Art. III of the Constitution which are usually called legislative courts (DAP)

administrative law: a branch of public law that deals w/the various parts of the executive branch of the government. It is concerned w/setting up such agencies and delineates their powers and duties

administrative vehicle: an unmarked police vehicle used to transport administrative personnel (TDPPC)

administrator [m], **administratrix** [f]: one to whom letters of administration have been granted by a court and who administers an estate

admiralty: the court dealing with maritime questions; the branch of law administered by such courts

admiralty jurisdiction: the authority to try cases arising under maritime law. It is concerned with wartime captures, collisions, piracy and lesser crimes, and torts on the high seas and on navigable lakes and rivers; also with contracts for shipments of goods, insurance, and wages of seamen. It is not concerned with crimes and other incidents committed on board ships while they are in port. Original jurisdiction in admiralty cases is exercised by federal district courts acting as admiralty courts (DAP)

admissible: capable of being admitted; in a trial, such evidence is that which is allowed by the judge to be introduced into the proceeding

admission: (1) the act by which attorneys and counselors become officers of a court and are licensed to practice law. The requirements for admission to the bar vary greatly in different states (2) a voluntary statement or acknowledgment, made by a party, that is admissible in evidence against that party (3) an express or implied acknowledgment that an allegation in the pleading of the opposing party is true

admission, civil and criminal cases: there is no distinction between civil and criminal cases in respect to the use of admissions. In general the rules of evidence in criminal and civil cases are the same. Whatever the agent does within the scope of his authority binds his principal, and is deemed his act. Difficult questions sometimes arise in civil cases where two persons are jointly charged with the commission of crime. One of the accused may make statements respecting the crime which would be strong evidence as to its commission. How far such statements are admissible against the other who is charged with the crime must then be determined. In cases where conspiracy is charged the admission of one of the accused may become, by reason of the other proof in the case, admissible against the other. By themselves, and without other proof, they are not admissible; but, if the proof shows the existence of the conspiracy, statements as to details of the crime charged made in pursuance of the object of the conspiracy by one of the parties become admissible against the other. (McKelvey Evidence, 151) In cases of a joint crime, such as fornication or adultery, which cannot be committed except by the concurrent act of two parties, the rule is the same as in cases of conspiracy (CDTP)

admissions and declarations by defendant: declarations made by the defendant, or by a third person by his authority, if relevant, are admissible against him, but they are not admissible in his favor (CDTP)

admitting to bail: allowed to go free on putting up cash, or giving bond (CDTP)

admonish: to advise or warn in a friendly manner

adolescence: the age between puberty (14 for males, 12 for females) and majority (21)

adsorption: the process whereby the surface of a solid may attract and hold firmly the molecules of another gaseous, liquid, or dissolved substance. The most effective adsorbents are therefore finely divided and/or porous, so that their surface area is large in relation to their gross bulk (FS)

A.D.T.: American District Telegraph Company

adult: any person 21 years of age or older

adulteration: debasement by foreign mixture. Generally applied to food or drink (CDTP)

adultery: voluntary sexual intercourse between a married person and someone other than his spouse. It is made punishable by fine and imprisonment by the statutes of most of the states, and it is a generally recognized ground for an absolute divorce

Adurol: a form of hydroquinone, which is used as a developing agent. Chemical name is mono-bromo-hydroquinone (MPPF)

Ad valorem: according to the value (CDTP)

adversary: an opponent, as in a legal action

adversary proceeding: a legal proceeding involving contesting or opposing parties

adverse: opposed to; an adverse witness is one called by the opposite party, or a person's own witness if he is hostile (CDTP)

advise: to give legal advice or counsel

advocate: the attorney who speaks or writes in support of a client's cause

aerial perspective: an impression of depth or distance in a photograph by means of progressively dimin-

ishing detail due to aerial haze (MPPF)

aero: applied to a lens, camera, or film intended for use in photography from aircraft (MPPF)

Aethelbert, King of the Kentings: authored the earliest written Anglo-Saxon laws (circa 600 A.D.)

affiance: to assure by a pledge, such as a mutual promise or agreement between a man and a woman that they will marry

affiant: a person who constructs and signs an affidavit

affidavit: written statement made under oath, usually before a notary public or other authorized person

affiliated: to be intimately connected or associated with (CDTP)

affinity: (1) a relationship between individuals through marriage, distinguished from consanguinity, blood relationship (2) the chemical attraction of one substance for another. Sodium sulfite has an affinity for oxygen, thereby reducing oxidation of the developing agent in a developer (MPPF)

affirm: make a positive statement of a fact (CDTP)

affirmance: a pronouncement that the case was rightly decided by the Court from which the appeal was taken (CDTP)

affirmation: positive declaration or assertion that the witness will tell the truth. An affirmation is not made under oath

affirmative: declaratory of what exists; opposed to negative (CDTP)

affray: in criminal law, the fighting of two or more persons in some public place to the terror of the people. It differs from a riot in not being premeditated (CDTP)

afocal: applied to a lens system which has both foci at infinity; afocal systems include certain wide angle and telephoto attachments for lenses which do not change the lens extension (MPPF)

aforethought: premeditated. Thought of beforehand (CDTP)

after officer gains legal access: where an officer, without a warrant, gains legal access to accused's house his removal of articles of evidence therefrom has been held not to constitute an illegal search under statutes requiring search warrants or warrants of arrest for a search of a dwelling. However, where an entrance is effected upon a mere pretext, a seizure of contraband goods therein is unlawful (11 Fed. 2d 892)   (CDTP)

against whom admissible: a confession is only admissible against the person who made it. A confession by one defendant is not competent evidence against his co-defendant (150 U.S. 93)   (CDTP)

age: with children under the age of 14 it must be shown affirmatively that they are of sufficient capacity to know that the act is wrong. At common law children under 7 years were incapable of committing crime   (CDTP)

agent: one who acts for or in the place of another by authority from him   (CDTP)

agent provocateur: (1) an unofficial police agent who associates with politically disaffected groups or persons suspected of crime to win their confidence or encourage them to resist authority and commit illegal acts, and subsequently informs on them (DAP) (2) an undercover man hired by one nation to encourage disaffected elements of another nation's citizenry to commit acts of sabotage, sedition, or treason (DAP)

agent's liability for his own acts: an agent, if of sufficient mental capacity, is criminally liable for his acts, though they are committed by command of his principal, and in the course of his principal's business (19 N.E. 405)   (CDTP)

age of consent: the youngest age at which a female may consent to sexual intercourse without making the man liable to a rape charge; in most states the age of consent is 18

age of maximum criminality: that chronological age period in a person's life during which, judging from criminal statistics, he is most likely to get into conflict with the criminal law. In the case of serious offenses against property (robbery, burglary, larceny), the 16 to 20 year age span seems to fall in this category, a slightly higher age group leading in offenses against the person. Offenses against public order are most common in the third decade of life. The uneven quality of American statistics makes positive assertions difficult. However, in some foreign countries, England for instance, the highest offense rates for serious crimes seem to lie in the early adolescent period. Generally speaking, crime rates decline after the age of 20 and very rapidly after the age of 40   (DOS)

agglutinin: antibody substance in the blood which causes a clumping of blood cells or bacteria in liquid suspension. This property is used (e.g., in a crime laboratory) in blood typing

aggravated assault: an unlawful attack by one person upon another, usually with an additional criminal motive besides inflicting severe bodily injury

aggravation: (1) any action or circumstance which increases the magnitude of a crime or its penalties (DAP) (2) any action or circumstance which intensifies the seriousness of a dispute and makes its solution more difficult (DAP)

aggression: the attempt by one state to impair another state's political sovereignty or territorial integrity by forcible means devoid of moral or legal justification (DAP)

aggressive patrol: a controversial police practice involving the saturation of a high-crime area with policemen who stop, question, frisk, and search pedestrians and motorists, often at random, in an effort to confiscate weapons and/or to prevent crimes

aggressor: a person who initiates a quarrel or fight, often through an unprovoked attack

agitation: (1) the procedure used in processing to bring fresh solution in contact with the emulsion. This may be done by moving the material in the solution, as in tank development, or by moving the solution itself, as in tray development. Agitation may be either constant or intermittent. Agitation is necessary to assure uniform development results (MPPF) (2)(a) an attempt to stir up popular enthusiasm and support for some political nostrum or cause (b) sustained and persistent effort (sometimes considered subversive) that threatens to upset the status quo (DAP)

Agnew, Spiro Theodore [*1918-*]: born in Baltimore on Nov. 9, 1918, Agnew, whose Greek father had shortened the family name from the original Anagnosto- polous. In 1966 elected Governor of Maryland. Elected to vice-pres- idency in 1968 on the ticket with Richard M. Nixon; reelected in 1972 with Nixon, but on Oct. 10, 1973 he resigned the vice- presidency amid charges of illegal financial dealing while in office in Maryland. He pleaded no contest to charges of federal income tax violations and was found guilty (*Webster's American Biographies*)

agnomen: a nickname or additional name

Aguilar v. Texas, 378 U.S. 108, 13 L. Ed. 723, 84 S. Ct. 1509 (1964): a divided Court applied the same standards for obtaining a search warrant to the states as those applicable to the federal government (ILECJ)

Ah Sam, 41 Cal. 645 (1871): this is a classic California case in the form of motions (AOJ)

aid: to assist. To get together with

aid and abet: to assist in the com- mission of a crime through words, acts, presence, or other encourage- ment and support

airbag: a type of passive vehicle occupant restraint system in which a bag is inflated between the occupants and the dashboard and steering column to minimize personal injury in the event of a front-end collision (TDPPC)

air bells: small bubbles of air which attach to the surface of an emul- sion and leave a small area unaf- fected by the solution. Can be removed by vigorous agitation (MPPF)

air cushion: *See* Airbag (TDPPC)

air gap: the distance between two magnetic elements in a magnetic or electromagnetic circuit, such as between the core and the arma- ture of a relay (TDIAS)

air gun: a rifle or gun operated by compressed air rather than a power charge. It was invented in Germany, and the first examples date from the late 16th century (DWMT)

air rifle: a rifle that utilizes com- pressed air to propel a projectile (DWMT)

air spring: a component of the suspension system which utilizes confined gas to assist in absorbing and damping the effect of road shocks on the vehicle (TDPPC)

alarm: an alarm service or an alarm signal (TDIAS)

alarm circuit: an electrical circuit of an alarm system which produces or transmits an alarm signal (TDIAS)

alarm condition: a threatening con- dition, such as an intrusion, fire, or holdup, sensed by a detector (TDIAS)

alarm device: a device which signals a warning in response to a alarm condition, such as a bell, siren, or annunciator (TDIAS)

alarm discrimination: the ability of an alarm system to distinguish between those stimuli caused by an intrusion and those which are a part of the environment (TDIAS)

alarm line: a wired electrical circuit used for the transmission of alarm signals from the protected premises to a monitoring station (TDIAS)

alarm signal: a signal produced by a control unit indicating the existence of an alarm condition (TDIAS)

alarm state: the condition of a detector which causes a control unit in the secure mode to transmit an alarm signal (TDIAS)

alarm station: (1) a manually actuated device installed at a fixed location to transmit an alarm signal in response to an alarm condition, such as a concealed holdup button in a bank teller's cage. (TDIAS) (2) a well-marked emergency control unit, installed in fixed locations usu. accessible to the public, used to summon help in response to an alarm condition. The control unit contains either a manually actuated switch or telephone connected to fire or police headquarters, or a telephone answering service. *See also* remote station alarm system (TDIAS)

alarm system: an assembly of equipment and devices designated and arranged to signal the presence of an alarm condition requiring urgent attention, such as unauthorized entry, fire, temperature rise, etc. The system may be local, police connection, central station or proprietary (For individual alarm systems *see* alphabetical listing by type, e.g., intrusion alarm system.) (TDIAS)

Albastone: a commercially prepared material for casting footprints and similar indentations used by some investigators instead of plaster of paris

albumin paper: sensitive paper, usually printing-out paper, in which the silver salts are suspended in albumin instead of gelatin; sometimes spelled "albumen" paper (MPPF)

alcohol: one of a class of chemical compounds containing a *hydroxyl* radical (one oxygen and one hydrogen atom) attached to a open carbon-atom skeleton. The best known is *ethanol* (or ethyl alcohol), the alcohol present in intoxicating liquors. Another is *methanol* (methyl alcohol; wood alcohol) (FS)

alcoholism: the pathological disorder caused by excessive indulgence in alcoholic beverages

Alcoholism, National Committee on: organized in 1944, this committee supplements the work of Alcoholics Anonymous by studying alcoholism as a disease, by encouraging analysis of its workings, and by disseminating information on the subject

alias: (1) applied to a writ issued where one of the same kind has been issued before in the same case (2) a false name (CDTP)

alias dictus: in its common use this term is contracted to "alias" and means "otherwise called" (CDTP)

alias writ: a second writ issued in the same cause, where a former writ of the same kind has been issued without effect (CDTP)

alibi: a type of defense to a criminal prosecution that proves that the accused could not have committed the crime with which he is charged, since evidence offered shows that he was in another place at the time

alidade: an instrument for determining direction consisting of a rule and sighting device; used in sketching, especially large outdoor areas

alien: foreigner; a foreign-born resident of this country who has not become a naturalized citizen

alienate: to transfer property or a right to another

alienist: a specialist in the study of mental disorders

aliens and suspected enemies: the protection afforded by the Fourth Amendment applies to all persons within the jurisdiction of the United States (C.J. 56, 1166) (CDTP)

align: (1) to bring into line, such as the front and rear sights of a gun

(DWMT) (2) placing operands within words so that operations can be performed correctly—for example, shifting numbers to put the units values (and others) in corresponding positions before adding (ADPS)

alimony: the allowance made by court order to an individual for support from the spouse. When the award is made during the pendency of a suit and includes money for support as well as for preparation of the suit, it is called "alimony pendente lite"

aliquot: a precisely known proportional part, from the analysis of which the composition of the whole can be calculated (FS)

aliter: [Lat]: otherwise

alkali: a substance with basic properties which can neutralize acid. An example of an alkali which is commonly used in developing solutions is sodium carbonate. Alkalies are often referred to as "accelerators or activators" (MPPF)

allegation: an assertion of what a party to an action expects to prove

allege: (1) to assert; to set forth (2) to plead (CDTP)

allocution: a prisoner's answer (which is recorded in the trial proceedings) to the court's query as to whether or not judgement should be pronounced against him if he is convicted

allonge: an addition, or rider, to a bill of exchange or promissory note

alloy: two or more metals mixed by fusing

Almeida-Sanchez v. United States, U.S. 266, 37 L. Ed. 2d 596, 93 S. Ct. 2535 (1973): search of an automobile more than 20 mi. from the Mexican border, without either a search warrant or probable cause to believe there was evidence in the automobile, is not a border search (ILECJ)

alopecia: baldness

Alotis, 60 Cal. 2d. 698 (1964): this is the leading case on the discre-

tionary power of a sentencing judge in granting probation, despite the fact a deadly weapon was involved in the commission of the crime (AOJ)

Alpha (code): an authorized word for the letter A, used in transmitting messages when a possibility of a misunderstanding exists. It supersedes the old *Able* code. The following are authorized code words: Alpha, Bravo, Charlie, Delta, Echo, Foxtrot, Gold, Hotel, India, Juliet, Kilo, Lima, Mike, November, Oscar, Papa, Quebec, Romeo, Sierra, Tango, Uniform, Victor, Whisky, X-ray, Yankee, and Zulu. *See* Able (code) (DWMT)

alphabet: sets of letter symbols—for example, a through z—used to form words. More broadly, any set of symbols used to represent data (ADPS)

alphanumeric a coding system capable of representing alphabetic characters, numerals, and other symbols (ADPS)

altercation: a fracas, fight, fuss, noisy quarrel

alternative writ: a writ granted on ex parte affidavits and requiring the person to do a certain thing or show cause why he should not be compelled to do so (CDTP)

alternator: a device which transforms a portion of the mechanical power output of a vehicle's engine into electrical power to operate the electric components of the vehicle. An alternator performs the same function as a generator but maintains a higher electrical output at vehicle engine idle speed (TDPPC)

alveoli: the ultimate tiny air spaces in the lungs through the walls of which gases and vapors are exchanged between the breath and the blood (FS)

Alyeolar air breath alcohol system: trade name of a device to test the breath to ascertain blood alcohol content

AM: amplitude modulation. A type of radio transmitting wave. This is the conventional type of transmitting wave and is more susceptible to static interference than is FM, frequency modulation, which has little or no static problems (LEV)

A.M.A.: American Medical Association

amanuensis: one who copies a written document (CDTP)

amatol: a high explosive made of a mixture of ammonium nitrate and trinitrotoluene (TNT). There are two main types, classified according to the percentage ratio of ammonium nitrate to TNT: 50:50 amatol, which is capable of being melt-loaded or cast, and 80:20 amatol, which must be consolidated by pressing and extruding. This explosive has approximately the same force as TNT and has been used as the bursting charge for projectiles and bombs when toluene, used in the manufacture of TNT, was in short supply (DWMT)

ambidextrous: able to use left hand as well as right (CDTP)

ambiguous: doubtful or uncertain (CDTP)

ambuscade: a surprise attack upon an enemy; an ambush

ambush: a place of concealment from which a surprise attack can be made; a trap (DWMT)

amendment or alteration of warrant: search warrants are of such grave importance that they may be amended, if at all, only by the officer issuing them, and then only in conformity with affidavits or depositions upon which they are based. A warrant is invalid if amended by the executing officers, even upon the consent of the issuing officer or upon a telephone conversation from him. Nor can even the issuing officer himself amend the warrant unless the affidavit itself were so amended as to conform to the proposed change or unless the original affiant performs some corporal act which would constitute an oath (149 Mass. 323) (CDTP)

amentia: in medical jurisprudence, insanity or idiocy

American Bar Association (ABA): a national organization of attorneys with headquarters in Chicago, Ill. To carry out its program of serving the interests of the legal profession, it is organized in many sections and several committees of members and issues a monthly journal (DAP)

American Bar Foundation (ABF): a research wing of the ABA

American Civil Liberties Union (ACLU): an organization devoted to defending Civil Rights guaranteed in state and federal constitutions. Its services are available to clients upon request, or are voluntarily donated by the legal staff of the Union. Outstanding leaders include Roger Baldwin, Osmond K. Fraenkel, and Arthur Garfield Hayes. It was founded in New York City in 1920, and became famous because of its defense of John T. Scopes in 1925. National headquarters: 156 Fifth Avenue, New York, N.Y. 10010 (DOAH)

American common law: similar in most respects to the English common law. Insofar, however, as the latter is inapplicable to our conditions and surroundings it is not a part of our common law. On the other hand, it includes some usages adopted by the colonists, some English statutes in force when they settled in this country, and a few enacted afterward and before the Revolution. The Supreme Court of the United States has decided that English statutes which were enacted before the emigration of our ancestors, and which were in force at that time, and which are applicable to our conditions and surroundings, constitute a part of our common law. (8 U.S.L. Ed. 311) The common law of many states is expressly defined by an act of the legislature. In some states there are no criminal offenses except those expressly declared by statute. In the absence of evidence of the contrary, the courts of any state presume that the common law prevails in the sister states. Federal courts have no common law jurisdiction in criminal cases (CDTP)

American District Telegraph Company (ADTC): a company operating nationally in the burglar alarm field. It utilizes various protective devices on business houses to detect unauthorized entry into premises and activate alarms (LEV)

American law: the written instrument agreed upon by the people of the Union or of a particular state, as the absolute rule of action and decision for all departments and officers of the government in respect to all the points covered by it, which must control until it shall be changed by the authority which established it, and in opposition to which any act or ordinance of any such department or officer is null and void (CDTP)

American Law Institute (ALI): a national association of prominent lawyers and legal scholars who voluntarily draft model laws, such as the *Model Penal Code*

American Medical Association (AMA): a national organization with headquarters in Chicago, Ill., composed of state and regional medical societies, which represents the professional interests of the bulk of American physicians and seeks to establish standards for drugs and therapeutic devices and to influence legislation and opinion on health-care matters (DAP)

American Municipal Association: a federation of State leagues of municipalities with headquarters in Chicago, Ill., and Washington, D.C. The local leagues provide consultant services on problems of municipal government and some issue periodicals and other publications (DAP)

American Protective Association: a secret anti-Catholic and anti-

foreign organization founded in Iowa in 1887 (DAP)

American Society for Industrial Security: 404 NADA Bldg., 2000 K. Street, N.W., Washington, D.C. 20006. Telephone number—(202) 338-7676. National Organization of Industrial Security Officers (LEV)

amicus curiae: a friend of the court. Usually a lawyer who volunteers to assist the court (CDTP)

ammeter: an instrument that indicates in amperes the rate at which the battery is being charged or discharged (TDPPC)

ammonal: a high-explosive mixture made of ammonium nitrate, TNT, and flaked or powdered aluminum. When used as a bursting charge in projectiles, it produces high temperature and a bright flash on detonation. It was a widely used shell filler in WWI (DWMT)

ammunition: (1) a generic term which includes all manner of missiles to be thrown against an enemy, such as bullets, projectiles, rockets, grenades, torpedos, bombs, and guided missiles with their necessary propellants, primers, fuze detonators, and charges of conventional explosives, nuclear explosives, and chemical and other materials (DWMT) (2) material used in charging firearms, including powder, shot, primers, and cartridge cases (CDTP)

amnesia: loss or impairment of memory. May be result of organic physical causes or psychological factors (LEV)

amnesty: a pardon granted by the government to one accused or convicted of crime, particularly a political crime (LEV)

amortization: partial payments of principal and accrued interest at stated intervals for a definite time, at the end of which the indebtedness will be extinguished (CDTP)

amphetamine: Benzedrine sulfate, a synthetic drug; central nervous system stimulant; causes local constricting effect on mucous membrances. Can be taken orally as a white powder or by injection when in solution   (LEV)

ampule: a small sealed flask which usually contains one dose of a hypodermic medicament (CDTP)

anaemia: lack of blood corpuscles, or blood coloring matter   (CDTP)

anaerobic: of organisms which can live, or processes which can occur, in the absence of air (oxygen)(FS)

anaesthesia: loss of sensation due to disturbance of the nerve function (CDTP)

anaesthetic: an agent used to remove the sensation of pain. It may be local, such as novocaine, procaine, or cocaine; or general, such as ether, chloroform, nitrous oxide or ethylene; or spinal (CDTP)

analgesia: loss of pain sensation (CDTP)

analgesic: a drug which relieves pain or kills pain   (LEV)

analysis: the process of breaking up a chemical compound and recognizing its individual constituents (CDTP)

anamorphic: a lens or optical system in which the magnification is different in two planes at right angles; used in wide-screen movie processes to "squeeze" a wide image into standard format and to "unsqueeze" it in projection on a wide screen   (MPPF)

anaphia: the absence of the sense of touch   (CDTP)

anaphrodisia: absence of sexual desire; impairment of the ability to engage in sexual intercourse

anarchism: the political philosophy that equality and justice may be obtained only through the abolition of the state and its organs. It opposes capitalism and free enterprise. In the United States, anarchists exercised some influence in the trade union and radical political movement in the last third of the 19th century. Anarchists were accused of perpetrating the Haymarket affair in Chicago in 1886, leading to the arrest of seven anar-

chists and the ultimate execution of four of them. An anarchist assassinated President McKinley in 1901. Sacco and Vanzetti, two anarchists, were arrested in 1921 and executed in 1927. . . (DOAH)

anarchist: one who proposes the violent overthrow of the government; one who advocates a lack of government

anarchy: the absence of law or supreme authority

anarchy, criminal: advocacy of the overthrow of any authorized government or the assassination of any of its executive heads (CDTP)

anastigmat: a lens which has been corrected for astigmatism, and therefore focuses vertical and horizontal lines with equal brightness and definition. Anastigmat lenses are also free from other common aberrations   (MPPF)

anatomy: the structure of the body and its parts   (CDTP)

androgynous: having the characteristics of both sexes; hermaphroditic

angle finder: a viewfinder containing a mirror or prism so that pictures may be taken while aiming the camera sideways (MPPF)

angle of view: the angle subtended at the center of the lens by the ends of the diagonal of the film or plate   (MPPF)

angstrom unit (AU): a unit of length equal to one ten-thousandth of a micron. Commonly used as a method of expressing length of light rays   (MPPF)

anhydrous: refers to chemical salts which contain no water of crystallization. Identical in meaning with "desiccated"   (MPPF)

aniline (anilin): a coal tar derivative used as a basis for many dyes. It can also be produced by the reduction of nitrobenzene   (MPPF)

anilingus: licking the anus of another person, producing sexual excitement   (LEV)

animus: state of mind, intention, or will, often ill-will

animus furandi: intention of stealing

annihilate: to absolutely destroy; totally destroy (LEV)

Anno Domini (A.D.) [*Lat, lit in the year of the Lord*]: referring to dates since the birth of Christ

annul: to invalidate, void, or cancel (The marriage was annulled.)

annulment: the act, by competent authority, of canceling, making void, or depriving of all force (DOAP)

annunciator: an alarm monitoring device which consists of a number of visible signals such as "flags" or lamps indicating the status of the detectors in an alarm system or systems. Each circuit in the device is usually labelled to identify the location and condition being monitored. In addition to the visible signal, an audible signal is usually associated with the device. When an alarm condition is reported, a signal is indicated visibly, audibly, or both. The visible signal is generally maintained until reset either manually or automatically (TDIAS)

anomalies: abnormalities associated with criminal constitutions and believed to be causal correlates (DOS)

anomalies, physical: the physical stigmata which Cesare Lombroso held would identify the criminal. It was Lombroso's contention that criminals were born, not made, and evidence of criminality could be seen in the peculiar shape of various parts of the face and head particularly. Although the theory has been discredited, it has been revived in recent years by a small group of physical anthropologists (DOS)

anomalous plea: partly affirmative and partly negative (CDTP)

anomaly: abnormality or deviation

anomie: a state of normlessness, of uncertainty of goals, purposes, identities, roles, procedures, and norms necessary for a properly ordered society to function

anonymous: having no name known or acknowledged (An un-signed letter or note is anonymous.)

Ansco Color: an integral tripack natural-color film which can be activity processed (MPPF)

answer: a defense in writing by the defendant to charges contained in a bill or complaint filed by the plaintiff against him (CDTP)

answering service: a business which contracts with subscribers to answer incoming telephone calls after a specified delay or when scheduled to do so. It may also provide other services such as relaying fire or intrusion alarm signals to proper authorities (TDIAS)

antagonize: to make one feel unfriendly; to create an enemy; to arouse ill feeling (LEV)

ante [*Lat*]: before

antecedent: prior to; preceding (CDTP)

ante litem: before suit (CDTP)

ante mortem: before death (CDTP)

ante mortem statement: *See* dying declaration

antenatal: before birth (CDTP)

antenuptial: before marriage (CDTP)

ante partum: before childbirth (CDTP)

anterior: before, in relation to time or space (CDTP)

anthropometry: the study of the measurements of the human body for the purpose of comparison; also known as the Bertillon system

anthropophagy: eating the flesh of another, either bitten off or sliced from the body (LEV)

antibiotic: a substance produced by or derived from living organisms, such as yeast or molds, which will kill or slow the growth of germs (bacteria) (LEV)

antidote: an agent to neutralize a poison or counteract its effects (CDTP)

anti-halation backing: a coating, usu. gelatin, on the back of a film, containing a dye or pigment for the purpose of absorbing light rays, thus preventing the reflection from the back surface of the film base (MPPF)

anti-lynch bills: federal bills which have attempted to provide the protection of the U.S. courts against attempts at illegal lynching. In over 99 percent of all lynching cases there have been no arrest, presentments, or court convictions. In 1922 the Dyer Anti-Lynch Bill was passed in the House, but was rejected by the Senate. Thereafter successive attempts to legislate against this evil failed. In 1937 alone 59 anti-lynch bills were introduced in Congress, all unsuccessful. By 1955 no such legislation had secured the approval of both houses of Congress despite its advocacy by the last five administrations. These bills have consistently been opposed on state's rights grounds (DOAH)

antimony: used to alloy lead in bullets for hardening the projectile (CDTP)

Antiracketeering Act: a law of Congress, June 18, 1934, which made it a criminal offense to interfere with foreign or interstate commerce by violence, threats, coercion, or intimidation (DAP)

anti-theft alarm system: a system which may be installed on a vehicle to attract attention, usu. by activating an audible and/or visual alarm, when an attempt is made to gain access to, or to start the vehicle, by means other than the normal door and ignition key (TDPPC)

antithesis: contrasting or opposing idea; directly opposite (LEV)

antitrust law: federal and state law which forbids the formation and operations of monopolies and combines which adversely affect commerce (LEV)

anus: the inferior opening of the alimentary canal; the fundament (CDTP)

anvil: a piece of metal in the primer cup, of a cartridge, which when struck by the firing pin activates the priming material (LEV)

Apalachin Meeting: a meeting of high officials of the Cosa Nostra held at Apalachin, New York in 1957. The meeting was interrupted by law enforcement officers who obtained the identity of several persons in attendance (LEV)

apathy: indifference to matters; complacence; showing no interest or feeling (LEV)

aperture: an orifice or opening (CDTP) in cameras, the aperture is usually variable, in the form of an iris diaphragm, and regulates the intensity of light which passes through a lens (MPPF)

aperture sight: an irregularly shaped adjustable mechanical item usually integral to a rear sight. It functions as a peephole through which the sight at the opposite end of a gun is brought into view in aiming at a target or object (DWMT)

apex: (1) the uppermost point or tip (2) the highest or culminating point

aphasia: the loss of speech

A-pillar: the forward-most vertical structural member of a car that supports the windshield, front door, and roof. Also known as A-post (TDPPC)

aplanat: a lens of the rapid-rectilinear type, sometimes better corrected for spherical aberration, but not for astigmatism (MPPF)

apochromatic: refers to lenses which are most completely corrected for chromatic aberration. These lenses focus rays of all colors to very nearly the same plane (MPPF)

apoplexy: a sudden loss of consciousness, usually followed by paralysis (CDTP)

apparent danger: used with reference to the defense of self-defense to justify a killing as necessary for self-preservation

appeal: a case carried to a higher court, in which it is asked that the decision of the lower court in which the case originated be altered or overruled completely

appeal bond: the bond posted by the party which appeals (appellant) guaranteeing to pay damages and costs if he fails to go forward prudently with the appeal (LEV)

appearance: coming into court by parties to an action (CDTP)

appellant: the individual who carries an appeal from one court to another

appellate: relating to appeals; person who appeals to a higher court; appeal from the decision of the lower court to a higher court

appellate court: a judicial tribunal which reviews cases originally tried and decided by inferior tribunals. The appellate court acts without a jury and is primarily interested in correcting errors in procedure or in the interpretation of law by the lower court (DAP)

appellate jurisdiction: the authority of a superior court to review and modify the decisions of an inferior court.

appellee: the party in a lawsuit against whom an appeal is taken; also called the "respondent"

appendant: annexed or appended to something superior and passing with it (CDTP)

application for search warrant: before a valid search warrant may be issued there must be an application therefore under oath or affirmation in proper form, showing probable cause for the issuance of the warrant, in the manner required by statutory and constitutional provisions; there must be a particular description therein of the place to be searched and the thing to be seized (C.J. 56, 1211) (CDTP)

application for writ—by whom: a person unlawfully restrained of his liberty may apply for the writ to secure his own release; or, if he is unable to do so, or is not permitted to make the application, a relative or friend may make application for him. (38 Amer. De. 644) In such a case, however, there must be a showing, to the satisfaction of the court, that the person himself is unable to make the application, or that the application is made in his behalf. A writ may be issued at any period of an imprisonment which is wrongful. Application may be made: (1) by the person imprisoned (2) by another for him. The writ is used principally to obtain a review of: (1) the legality of an arrest or commitment (2) the regularity of extradition process (3) the right to or amount of bail (4) the jurisdiction of the court imposing a sentence. The writ commands the person detaining the relator to bring him before the court and show the reason of the imprisonment (CDTP)

applications study: design of a system and related procedures plus development of equipment specifications to perform a certain data-processing job (ADPS)

appose: to examine an officer with reference to his books (CDTP)

apprehend: to make an arrest on a charge of crime (CDTP)

apprehension: the capture or arrest of a person on a criminal charge (CDTP)

approver: one who confesses his crime and at the same time accuses others to save himself; otherwise called state's evidence (CDTP)

appurtenance: a right (such as a right-of-way) attached to something else; an accessory or adjunct

Aquinas, St. Thomas [*1224-1274*]: St. Thomas, a Dominican priest, developed a complete moral system in which he analyzed the nature of the human acts of reasoning and will and related them to virtues and vices. He emphasized popular participation in government, the necessity of a well-ordered society, the advantages of a unified rule, and the evils of tyranny. His most important work was "Summa Theologica," a systematic exposition of theology on philosophical principles

arbitration: the hearing and determination of a cause between parties in controversy by a person or persons chosen by the parties (CDTP)

arbitrator: the person chosen by parties who have a controversy, to determine their differences, private judges (CDTP)

arch: a fingerprint pattern. The ridges come in from one side, do not recurve, and go out the other side. The ridges make an upward thrust at or near the center of the pattern. There are two kinds: plain arch where the upthrust is smooth and gradual and the tented arch where the upward thrust is sharp (LEV)

archives: records preserved as evidence; public papers and records (CDTP)

area, delinquency: an area of a city marked by an abnormal delinquency rate as compared to other areas of the city of similar size and population. Such areas are often located in zones of transition, and are marked by industrial buildings, waterfronts and railroad yards, deteriorated buildings. . . . (DOS)

area, metropolitan: a region including a large concentration of population together with the surrounding areas where the daily economic and social life is predominantly influenced by the central city (DOS)

area protection: protection of the inner space or volume of a secured area by means of a volumetric sensor (TDIAS)

area sensor: a sensor with a detection zone which approximates an area, such as a wall surface or the exterior of a safe (TDIAS)

areas in storage: characters, fields, or words in processor storage assigned for the following purposes in a program: editing, printing, punching, read-in, constants, working, and write-out (ADPS)

Argersinger v. Hamlin, 407 U.S. 25, 32 L. Ed. 2d 530, 92 S. Ct. 2006 (1972): the court holds, 6-3, through Mr. Justice Douglas, that all defendants facing a possible jail sentence are entitled to be represented by legal counsel in their trial, and that the State must provide a lawyer if the defendant wants one and cannot afford the cost (Three concurring opinions were filed.) (ILECJ)

aristocracy: a government ruled by a class (CDTP)

Aristotelianism: the philosophy of Aristotle became the philosophical basis of Christian theology through the writings of St. Thomas Aquinas

Aristotle [384-322 B.C.]: a student of Plato, Aristotle wrote in one of his treatises ("Politics") that the political community is the source and sustainer of human life; however, the highest good for man is found not in political life, but in theoretical inquiry and contemplation of truth

arithmetic and logic unit: part of a processor that performs the arithmetical operations of adding, multiplying, etc., and the logical operations of comparing one number or name with another (ADPS)

arithmetic operation: addition, subtraction, multiplication, and division (ADPS)

armor-piercing (AP): said of ammunition, bombs, bullets, projectiles, and the like; designed to penetrate armor and other resistant targets (DWMT)

armor-piercing bullet: a bullet having a hard metal core, a soft metal envelope, and a bullet jacket. When the bullet strikes armor, the envelope and jacket are stopped, but the armor-piercing core continues forward and penetrates the armor (DWMT)

armor-piercing incendiary (API): armor-piercing projectiles specially designed to set fires after piercing armor (DWMT)

armor-piercing incendiary tracer: an armor-piercing projectile fitted with a tracer for spotting (DWMT)

armor-piercing sabot (APS): a type of projectile which is armor-piercing and which incorporates a sabot (DWMT)

armor-piercing tracer (AP-T, APT): an armor-piercing projectile fitted with a tracer for spotting (DWMT)

armor plate: a plate of armor. The French made practical use of naval armor during the Crimean War of 1855. It was made of iron. By 1876 iron gave way to plates of steel or steel-faced iron (DWMT) Armpriester v. U.S., 256 F. 2d 294 (C.A.Va. 1958): in this case, information which would have been inadmissible on the issue of guilt was presented during the sentence hearing. Although the Court affirmed on the grounds that the information did not prejudice the defendant, it stated that it would not condone evidence obtained illegally, "even for the limited purpose of determining the sentence" (ILECJ)

armory: (1) a place or building where arms are stored or where drills and reviews are held (DWMT) (2) aboard ship, a compartment where small arms and light machine guns are stowed and serviced (DWMT) (3) formerly, a place or building where arms were manufactured (DWMT)

arms: weapons of offense or defense. Generally speaking, objects of any kind that may be used as weapons (DWMT)

arms chest: a box or case used as a portable locker for holding or transporting small firearms (DWMT)

aromatic: a technical term of organic chemistry, applied to compounds in which the carbon-atom skeletons form closed rings having a certain type of interatomic bonding, and of which *benzene* is the prototype (FS)

arraign: to bring a person before a court to answer a charge

arraignment: the pleading process; legal proceeding at which formal charges are read, the defendant is notified of his rights, and a plea to the charges requested

arraignment and trial: the law regulates the procedure according to which the defendant is brought into court, informed of his rights and placed on trial, as well as the familiar routine of selecting a jury, making the opening statements, introducing evidence, arguing the case to the jury, instructing the jury and receiving the verdict (CDTP)

array: the group of persons summoned into court for jury duty; the order in which these people are ranked in the jury box

arrest: the legal detainment of a person to answer for criminal charges or (infrequently at present) civil demands upon him. Constitutional limitations prevent detention under false or assumed authority and harrassment of persons without warrants properly issued. *See* habeas corpus (DAP)

arrest by officer without warrant, when lawful: a peace officer may, without a warrant, arrest a person: (1) when the person to be arrested has committed a felony or misdemeanor in his presence. In the case of such arrest for a misdemeanor, the arrest shall be made immediately or on fresh pursuit (2) when the person to be arrested has committed a felony, although not in the presence of the officer (3) when a felony has in fact been committed, and he has reasonable ground to believe that the person to be arrested has committed it (4) when he has reasonable ground to believe that a felony has been or is being committed and reasonable ground to believe that the person to be arrested has committed or is committing it (CDTP)

arrest by private person, when lawful: a private person may make an arrest: (1) when the person to be arrested has in his presence committed a misdemeanor, amounting to the breach of the peace, or a felony (2) when a felony has been in fact committed and he has reasonable ground to believe that the person to be arrested has committed it (CDTP)

arrest by warrant: a warrant is a

writ or precept, issued by an authorized magistrate, addressed to a proper officer requiring him to arrest the body of an offender, or suspected offender, therein named, and bring him before a proper magistrate, to be dealt with according to law   (CDTP)

arrest upon hue and cry: is an old common law process of pursing with horn and with voice all felons and such as have dangerously wounded others. The hue and cry could be raised by officers or by private persons or by both. The officer and his assistants have the same powers, protection and indemnity as if acting under a warrant   (CDTP)

arrest upon order of magistrate: when an offense is committed in the presence of a magistrate, he may, by an oral or written order, command any person immediately to arrest the offender, and may thereupon proceed as though the offender has been brought before him on a warrant of arrest (CDTP)

arrest without warrant, by officer: any peace officer may arrest without a warrant under the following circumstances: (1) by verbal direction of a judge or justice of the peace: (a) for a felony or breach of the peace committed in the presence of the judge or justice, (b) for any offense committed in the presence of the judge or justice in court (2) without any direction, but of his own accord: (a) for a felony committed or being attempted in his own presence or view, (b) for a misdemeanor committed in his own presence or view, provided the arrest is made during its commission, or immediately afterwards, (c) on a reasonable charge by another that a felony has been committed by the person arrested, (d) on his own reasonable suspicion that a felony has been committed, and that the person arrested is guilty, though in fact no felony has been committed at all, (e) he may re-capture a prisoner who has escaped from lawful custody, whether before or after conviction   (CDTP)

arrest without warrant by private person: a private person has the same authority as an officer to arrest without a warrant, except that, where he arrests on suspicion for a felony, the felony must have in fact been committed by someone   (CDTP)

arsenic: a poisonous chemical element which in combination with other chemical elements makes poisonous drugs. White arsenic (arsenic trioxide) is one such compound   (LEV)

arson: the malicious burning of buildings and other property

arsonist: a criminal who burns property with lawless and malicious intent   (CDTP)

art: to induce; incite; instigate
        (CDTP)

arte: forced; compelled; constrained   (CDTP)

artery: (1) a blood vessel which carries blood from the heart to various parts of the body (LEV) (2) a means of transportation such as a main highway   (LEV)

article of merchandise: any goods, ware, work of art, commodity, compound, mixture or other preparation or thing, which may be lawfully kept, or offered for sale   (CDTP)

articles disclosed in progress of search: wherever, during the progress of a bona fide search for other commodities illegally possessed, whether with a search warrant or not, discovery is made of legal evidence of the possession of another thing, the possession of which is unlawful, the thing so found may be seized (8 Fed. 2nd 202)   (CDTP)

artifice: trickery

artificer: skilled craftsman

artificial: having an existence presumed in law only; as a corporation   (CDTP)

artisan: one skilled in a trade or craft

Aryan Brotherhood: a group of white prisoners that originated in

San Quentin. These men form an elite caucasian prison gang that exists throughout the California prison system. They can be identified by the tattoo A.B.

ASA (American Standards Association): this organization has arrived at numerical ratings for film emulsion. Most light meters, exposure meters, use this rating in calculating their devices (LEV) For example, Kodak Royal Pan Film has an ASA rating of 400   (MPPF)

ascetism: refraining from sexual involvement   (LEV)

asexualization: a term synonymous with sterilization   (CDTP)

Ashcraft v. Tennessee, 322 U.S. 143, 88 L. Ed. 1192, 64 S. Ct. 921 (1944): with Mr. Justice Jackson dissenting, the Court held that a confession obtained under *aggravating circumstances* (inherent coercion), coupled with unnecessary delays in arraignment, is involuntary, and inadmissible in a state court under due process of the Fourteenth Amendment (Thus the Court coined the "inherently coercive" rule as a substantial equivalent of the "civilized standards" rule that had been created in *McNabb*.) (ILECJ)

as is: a purchase and acceptance without guarantees   (CDTP)

asphyxiate: to kill or make unconscious through interference with normal breathing

asportation: taking and carrying away (If the defendant having taken possession of the goods, has not moved them, there is lacking the asportation necessary to constitute larceny.)   (CDTP)

assassination: (1) the murder of a high public official, whether by one person acting alone or in a conspiracy with others. Four Presidents—Lincoln, Garfield, McKinley, and Kennedy—have been assassinated. Since the latter's assassination such an act has been made a federal crime (DAP) (2) any murder in which the distinguishing feature is resort to treachery or stealth (DAP) The

word comes from "hashshashin" —those addicted to hashish. It originally meant a member of a secret order of Mohammedans, who committed secret murders while under the influence of hashish   (LEV)

assault: an unlawful attempt to hurt another person physically. *See* assault and battery

assault and battery: an unlawful touching of the person of another by the aggressor, or by some substance put in motion by him   (CDTP)

assaulting federal officers: whoever shall forcibly resist, oppose, impede, intimidate, or interfere with any federal officer, U.S. Marshal, or deputy U.S. Marshal, special agent of the division of investigation of the Department of Justice, post office inspector, secret service operative, any officer or enlisted man of the coast guard, any employee of any U.S. penal or correctional institution, any officer of the customs or of the internal revenue, any immigrant inspector or any immigration patrol inspector, while engaged in the performance of his official duties, or shall assault him on account of the performance of his official duties, shall be fined not more than $5,000 or imprisoned not more than three years, or both. If a dangerous or deadly weapon is used the fine will not be more than $10,000 or imprisoned not more than 10 years, or both. Whoever shall kill any of the above-mentioned Federal Officers shall be punished as provided under section 275 of the Criminal Code. Every person guilty of murder in the first degree shall suffer death, murder in the second degree, imprisoned for not less than 10 years and may be imprisoned for life. Voluntary manslaughter, imprisoned not more than 10 years. Involuntary manslaughter, imprisoned not more than 3 years, or fined not more than $1,000, or both   (CDTP)

assembly: the meeting of a number of persons in one place and for a common object (CDTP)

assembly routine: a routine that, before the desired processing starts, converts a source program in mnemonic instructions and symbolic addresses into a machine-language object program. Since the conversion is on a one-for-one basis, assembly-level languages facilitate programming but give the programmer no leverage (ADPS)

assets: all property both real and personal (CDTP)

assign: to transfer to another; to designate for a specific purpose (CDTP)

assignation: an assignment (CDTP)

assignation house: a house of ill fame kept for the meeting of lewd people of both sexes; a brothel (CDTP)

assignee: (1) one to whom a transfer is made (2) one appointed to act for another

assignment: (1) a transfer of property (2) a duty or job delegated by authority

assignor: one who makes an assignment to another

assistance, writ of: a writ from the court of chancery, in aid of the execution of a legal judgment, to put the complainant into possession of lands adjudged to him

assisting officer in making arrest: an officer authorized to make arrests may call upon private persons to assist him, and they are bound to do so, provided they act in his actual or constructive presence (CDTP)

association, differential: the distribution of a person's associations in a manner different from those of other persons; generally stated as an hypothesis of criminal behavior namely, that a person who develops criminal behavior differs from those who do not develop criminal behavior in the quantity and quality of his associations with criminal patterns and in his relative isolation from anti-criminal patterns, and that differential association with these criminal and anticriminal patterns is therefore the cause of criminal behavior. According to this hypothesis, either the techniques, motives, rationalizations, and other elements are learned exclusively in association with criminal patterns, or, if learned in part in other kinds of association, are combined and organized in association with criminal patterns (DOS)

assumpsit: suit incurred through the breach of a simple contract (LEV)

assumption: (1) the pretension of having or possession (CDTP) (2) the taking on in appearance, but not in reality (CDTP)

astigmatism: a lens aberration in which both the horizontal and vertical lines in the edge of the field cannot be accurately focused at the same time (MPPF)

asylum state: the State in which a fugitive from justice from another State, which is demanding his return, is found (CDTP)

asymmetrical (non-symmetrical): applied to a lens having differently shaped elements on either side of the diaphragm, or both (MPPF)

asympotic: mathematically, of a line to which another continually approaches without ever meeting it. Loosely and by analogy, of a continued gradual without actual meeting (FS)

asynchronous (processor): that portion of processor operations in which performance of the next command is started by a signal that the previous command has been completed. Synchronous processors, on the other hand, have a fixed time cycle for the execution of operations (ADPS)

at common law: an unreasonable search at common law is a search which is unreasonably oppressive in its general invasion of the liberty of the citizen (116 S.E. 495)

(CDTP)
at maturity: at the due date (CDTP)

atropine: a poison found in the nightshade plant and in the seeds of the jimson weed. Respiratory paralysis is the cause of death (LEV)

Attaché: a member of the diplomatic staff of his nation, by reason of expert qualifications, stationed in a foreign country (LEV)

attachment: taking into custody of the law a person or property of one already before the court, or of one whom it is sought to bring before it (CDTP)

attainder: the annihilation of all civil rights and privileges which in early English law followed a condemnation for treason or felony. The person attainted forfeited all property and lost all capacity to inherit or transmit property to his descendants; nor could he appear in court or claim the protection of law. In the United States "no attainder of treason shall work corruption of blood or foreiture except during the life of the person attainted." A bill of attainder, which is prohibited by the Constitution, is a legislative condemnation without the formality of a judicial trial (DAP)

attaint: convict of a crime. A writ to inquire whether a jury has given a false verdict (CDTP)

attempts: an attempt to commit a crime is an act done with intent to commit that crime, and tending to, but falling short of, its commission. (1) The act must be such as would be proximately connected with the completed crime (2) There must be an apparent possibility to commit the crime in the manner proposed (3) There must be a specific intent to commit the particular crime at the time of the act (4) Voluntary abandonment of purpose after an act constituting an attempt is no defense (5) Consent to the attempt will be a defense if it would be a defense in case the crime

were completed, but not otherwise. All attempts to commit a crime, whether the crime be a felony or misdemeanor, and whether it be such at common law or by statute, are misdemeanors at common law (54, Pac. 209) (CDTP)

attest: to bear witness and testify under oath or signature

attestation: the act of verifying or affirming, orally or in writing, the genuineness or validity of some legal document, such as a will or an affidavit (DAP)

attorney at law: an officer in a court of justice who is employed by a party in a cause to manage it for him (CDTP)

attorney general: (1) the head of the Department of Justice and a member of the President's cabinet who gives legal advice to the President and heads of departments, supervises district attorneys and U.S. marshals, oversees criminal investigations, and has charge of cases in which the Government is involved. He may appear in court, but rarely does so (DAP) (2) the chief legal officer of a State who advises State and local officers, who may appear in cases in which the State is sued by another State, but who usually lacks the power to supervise locally elected prosecutors (DAP)

attorney general, state: the chief legal officer of the State representing the state in civil and under certain circumstances, in criminal matters. He furnishes legal advice to the governor and State departments (LEV)

attorney in fact: a private attorney; one who is authorized by his principal to do a particular act (CDTP)

Attorney, United States: the chief law officer (federal) in the Federal Judicial District. He represents the U.S. Government in civil and criminal matters. He is under the direction of the U.S. Attorney General, who heads the U.S. Department of Justice. The U.S. Attorney usu. has assistants who aid him in performing the duties of the office   (LEV)

Attorney General, United States: as a member of the President's Cabinet, he heads the U.S. Department of Justice. He is appointed by the President. He is the chief legal officer of the Federal government, representing the national government in civil and criminal matters. He also gives legal advice to other Federal agencies and the President. This post was created by 1879 Judiciary Act   (LEV)

Auburn System: a prison system or procedure first started in Auburn State Prison in New York in 1816. It demands silence on the part of the inmates. The prisoners were assigned to individual cells at night and forced to work in silence during the day   (LEV)

audible alarm device (1) a noise-making device such as a siren, bell, or horn used as part of a local alarm system to indicate an alarm condition (TDIAS) **(2)** a bell, buzzer, horn, or other noisemaking device used as a part of an annunciator to indicate a change in the status or operating mode of an alarm system   (TDIAS)

audimeter: instrument attached to radios in private homes to detect every time the set is turned on and off and to indicate the station to which the radio is tuned. Used as a measure of radio listening habits of population   (DOS)

audio frequency (sonic): sound frequencies within the range of human hearing, approximately 15 to 20,000 Hz   (TDIAS)

audio monitor: an arrangement of amplifiers and speakers designed to monitor the sounds transmitted by microphones located in the protected area. Similar to an annunciator, except that supervisory personnel can monitor the protected area to interpret the sounds   (TDIAS)

audio surveillance: a surveillance by listening. This may be by wiretapping or the use of electronic eavesdropping equipment to pick up conversations of persons. The courts have put restrictions on these types of activities [Reference: Katz v. U.S. 389 U.S. 237 (1967) on use of electronic eavesdropping.]   (LEV)

audita querela, writ of: a remedial writ which sets aside execution or the judgment because of some injustice performed by the party obtaining same and which could not be pleaded at the time of the trial. An arrest of judgment   (CDTP)

auditing: examination of source data, methods of processing, and contents of reports to draw conclusions about the validity of the system and credibility of reports; auditors use many sources of information and various techniques for verification   (ADPS)

audit trail: the path left by a transaction when it is processed; consists of the original document, entry in a transaction list, posting to a file record, and inclusion in a report. Auditors use the audit trail of a transaction for determining the validity of records   (ADPS)

Augustus, John: founder of the probation system in the United States. In 1841 he became the first probation officer, with supervision over minor offenders

aural: having to do with the sense of hearing or the ear   (LEV)

authenticate: to render authentic   (CDTP)

authentication: communication security measure designed to prevent fraudulent transmissions   (DWMT)

authentic document: a document bearing a signature or seal attesting that it is genuine and official   (DWMT)

authority: (1) the power or right conferred on a person by another to act on his behalf **(2)** a public officer or body having certain powers of jurisdiction **(3)** constitutions, statutes, precedent cases, opinions of text writers, and other material cited in arguments

authorize: to empower; to give a right to act   (CDTP)

authorized access switch: a device used to make an alarm system or some portion or zone of a system inoperative in order to permit authorized access through a protected port. A shunt is an example of such a device   (TDIAS)

authorized arrest in unauthorized manner: the fact that an authorized arrest is made in an unauthorized manner will render the officer or person arresting liable, but will not affect the state's right to detain the accused   (CDTP)

authorized dealer: a facility that has been franchised or otherwise designated to sell and service an automotive manufacturer's products   (TDPPC)

authorized service agency: a facility that has been franchised or otherwise designated by an automotive product manufacturer to service and maintain its products   (TDPPC)

autocracy: a government of a monarch unlimited by law; self-rule   (CDTP)

autoeroticism: self-induced sexual gratification or feelings, such as masturbation   (LEV)

autofocal: self-focusing; applied to enlargers which keep the image in focus when changing the degree of enlargement by raising or lowering the head   (MPPF)

automatic: said of a firearm that employs either gas pressure or force of recoil and mechanical spring action for ejecting the empty cartridge case after the first shot and loading the next cartridge from the magazine (DWMT)

automatic feed mechanism: a mechanism in an automatic gun that puts fresh cartridges into the chamber, ready for firing (DWMT)

automatic fire: continuous fire from an automatic gun, lasting until the pressure on the trigger is released. Automatic fire differs from semiautomatic fire of automatic weapons and from single-shot fire of hand-loaded weapons, in both of which a separate trigger pull is required for each shot fired

(DWMT)

automatic gun charger: a gun charger that includes a mechanism for the clearance of gun stoppages and the retention of the breech mechanism to the rear of the gun receiver   (DWMT)

automatic data-processing system: a system that makes maximum use of an electronic data processor and related equipment for processing data   (ADPS)

automatic parking brake release: a device which provides for release of the parking brake without effort by the driver when the vehicle is placed in gear   (TDPPC)

automatic pistol: a pistol capable of automatic or, more commonly, semiautomatic fire   (DWMT)

automatic programming: a way of writing programs based on a problem-oriented language and a translator routine for translating this language to machine language   (ADPS)

automatic rifle: a rifle capable commonly of either semiautomatic or full automatic fire   (DWMT)

automatic sight: a gunsight, especially a telescopic sight, by means of which the alignment of the laying points or telescope on the object to be hit brings the gun into the proper position as to elevation and direction   (DWMT)

automatic transaction recorder: system for recording several of the facts about a transaction with minimum manual input. For example, in a job shop the recorder will pick up the worker and job identification from plates or cards and the start-stop times from a built-in clock, so that only the quantity completed is punched into the keyboard or set up in dials for recording   (ADPS)

automatic weapon: specifically, as used in reference to antiaircraft artillary, any weapon of 75mm or smaller   (DWMT)

automobile theft: the stealing of an automobile or motor vehicle. Under state law it is theft or theft of a motor vehicle. Under federal law it is violation to transport, or cause to be transported, from one state to another, knowing the vehicle has been stolen   (LEV)

automotive engineer: an individual specifically trained or educated in the field of land vehicle design, development, manufacture, maintenance, use, and performance   (TDPPC)

automotive safety inspection: A function assigned to some law enforcement agencies or authorized inspection stations in support of State and local ordinances in which automobiles or other vehicles are inspected for required equipment and safe operating conditions   (TDPPC)

autonomous: self-governing

autonomy: the quality of being self-governing or self-directing

autopositive: applied to a film or paper which renders a positive image when exposed to a positive, or negative image when exposed to a negative, when processed in a single development stage. Distinguished from *direct positive* which produces such images by reversal processing procedures   (MPPF)

autopsy: examination and dissection of a dead body to discover the cause of death

autoradiograph: an image produced on a film or plate by radiations from a radioactive subject in close contact with the emulsion (MPPF)

autoradiography: a method of showing radioactivity, or radioactive sites, in an object by allowing it to act on a piece of X-ray film in contact with it (FS)

autosadism: sexual satisfaction obtained by pain to one's self, self-inflicted   (LEV)

autrefois convict or acquit: a plea made by a defendant that he has previously been tried and convicted or acquitted of the same offense   (CDTP)

auxiliary lens: a lens element which is added to the regular camera lens to shorten or increase its focal length   (MPPF)

auxiliary transmission cooler: an auxiliary heat exchanger that provides cooling in addition to that normally provided for the automatic transmission fluid (TDPPC)

avow: (1) to state openly (LEV) (2) acknowledge (LEV) (3) openly admit membership or association with something   (LEV)

avowtry: adultery   (CDTP)

axiom: in logic, a truth which is self-evident   (LEV)

axis of lens: an imaginary line passing through the center of a lens and containing the centers of curvature of the lens surfaces   (MPPF)

azeotrope: a mixture of liquids of a composition such that it has a constant boiling-point lower or higher than that of any other mixture of the same components (cf. eutectic), and hence distils without change of composition   (FS)

azimuth: a direction expressed as a horizontal angle usually in degrees or mils and measured clockwise from north. Thus azimuth will be true azimuth, grid azimuth, or magnetic azimuth, depending upon which north is used (DWMT)

azimuth circle: an instrument for measuring azimuths. It is a graduated circle and may be mounted on a sight or a gun carriage   (DWMT)

B

B.A.C.: blood alcohol content

back focus: a trade term often used to designate the distance between the back surface of the lens and the surface of the focusing glass when the camera is focused at infinity. This dimension is used in determining the length of the camera bellows suitable for a given lens (MPPF)

back, revolving: a camera back which can be revolved so that either a vertical or horizontal picture may be obtained. Usu. found in the heavier types of cameras, such as press or view cameras (MPPF)

back, swinging: a camera back which can be swung through a small arc so that the divergence or convergence of parallel lines in the subject can be minimized or eliminated (MPPF)

background: generally that part of a scene beyond the main subject of the picture (MPPF)

backing cloth: an adhesive fabric, used to strengthen a photographic print to withstand handling (MPPF)

bad check passer: one who passes worthless checks with the intent or tending to defraud others (CDTP)

bad tendency test: a rule enunciated by the Supreme Court in *Gitlow* v. *New York*, that a legislative body may suppress speech which tends to spread revolutionary doctrines, even though danger of resulting armed uprising or other violence is remote (DAP)

bag, changing: a light-proof bag equipped with openings for the hands, in which films can be loaded or unloaded in daylight (MPPF)

bail: security guaranteeing that a defendant in a criminal proceeding will appear and be present in court at all times when his presence is required (CDTP)

Bailey, F. Lee [(*1933-*), *Lawyer*]: born in Waltham, Mass., on June 10, 1933. While in law school he organized and ran a detective agency, and the investigative experience he gained from it was later as valuable as his formal education in his chosen field of criminal law. He made himself an expert in the electronic techniques used in criminal investigation and in polygraphy ("lie detecting"). It was as an authority on polygraphy that he was originally called into his first major case, that of Dr. Samuel Sheppard of Cleveland, who had been convicted in 1954, amid blaring publicity, of murdering his wife. Bailey helped to force a review of the trial all the way to the Supreme Court, which ruled in 1966 that the pretrial publicity may have prejudiced the jury. In a retrial, completed in 1966, Bailey secured Sheppard's acquittal and thus became one of the country's leading trial lawyers. Employing tactics that bordered at times on the flamboyant, Bailey was on a few occasions censured formally for his trial conduct, but his method of tirelessly pursuing every possible line of investigation and legal action made him one of the most sought-after legal defenders in the country (*Webster's American Biographies*)

bailiff: an officer of the court who executes arrest process; a courtroom attendant; a sheriff's officer

bailiwick: the territorial jurisdiction of a sheriff or bailiff

bake off: to fire unintentionally. It refers to the fact that an automatic or semiautomatic weapon gets very hot when it is fired. If a cartridge remains in the chamber, the heat of the metal can cause it to fire. The bolt of the weapon should be cleared to avoid this problem. "Cook off" has the same meaning   (DWMT)

ball: (1) a bullet for general use, as distinguished from bullets for special uses such as armor-piercing bullets, incendiary bullets, high-explosive bullets, etc. (DWMT) (2) a small-arms propellant which is oblate spheroidal in shape, generally a double-base propellant. The word "ball" is a carryover from a time when most projectiles were spherical in shape   (DWMT)

ball ammunition: non-armor-piercing small-arms ammunition in which the projectile is solid. It is intended for use against personnel or light material or for training purposes   (DWMT)

ball cartridge: a term used in the military service applied to a round of small-arms ammunition consisting of a cartridge case, a primer, powder, and a solid bullet
                    (DWMT)

ball joint: an assembly of two members consisting of a ball on one and a socket on the other to permit movement of the front wheels for steering   (TDPPC)

ballistics: the science or art that deals with the motion, behavior, appearance, or modification of missiles or other vehicles acted upon by propellants, wind, gravity, temperature, or any other modifying substance, condition, or force. The study is divided into external ballistics and internal ballistics   (DWMT)

ballistic table: a table of figures regarding the flight of a given projectile, such as range, angle of departure, time of flight, angle of fall, muzzle velocity, and so forth
                    (DWMT)

ballistic test: a trial of ordinance, projectiles, armor, or powder to determine suitability for acceptance. It is also called a "proof test"   (DWMT)

ballot: the paper used in the act of voting   (CDTP)

Bancroft, Edward [(*1744-1821*), *secret agent*]: born in Westfield, Mass., Jan. 9, 1744, Bancroft received little or no formal education. Possessed of an adventurous and inquiring spirit, he was for a time a sailor, and then a settler in Dutch Guiana (Surinam). At length he moved to England, where, having acquired an education, he became a physician. He wrote numerous articles about America for the *Monthly Review* and published several books, including *Essay on the Natural History* of Guiana, 1769, and *Remarks on the Review of the Controversy between Great Britain and Her Colonies*, 1769. After the outbreak of the Revolution he volunteered his services as a spy to Benjamin Franklin, who was then representing the American colonies in Paris, and he subsequently formed a close association with Franklin's colleague, Silar Deane. Through Deane he was paid by Congress for his work as a confidential agent. At the same time he was in the pay of the British government, to whom he sent, through his fellow spy Paul Wentworth, details of the various French-American agreements and treaties and advance notice of the movement of supplies, ships, and troops from France to America. He was never discovered by Franklin or Deane. After the war, he remained in England and interested himself in the manufacture of textile dyes, making some notable discoveries. He died in Margate on Sept. 8, 1821
(*Webster's American Biographies*)

bandit: an outlawed, desperate robber distinguished from the garden variety by his guerrilla tactics
                    (CDTP)

banditry: consistent and organized robbery and other forms of theft with violence; especially, such behavior when committed by persons who reside in mountainous or other sparsely settled regions
                    (DOS)

banish: to compel by authority to leave one's domicile

banishment: the sending away of a criminal from his dwelling-place

bank robbery, the first: occurred Sat., March 19, 1831, when two doors of the City Bank, Wall Street, New York City were opened by duplicate keys and the bank was robbed of $245,000. Edward Smith, an Englishman (alias Jones, alias James Smith, alias James Honeyman), was indicted by the Grand Jury and arraigned May 2, 1831, at the Court of General Sessions. On May 11, 1831, he was sentenced to five years at hard labor at Sing Sing. Over $185,000 of the loot was recovered (FAMOUS)

bankruptcy: the conditions of a person when a court has determined that his property is to be administered for the benefit of his creditors. Under its power to pass uniform laws on bankruptcy, Congress enacted statutes which were in effect 1800-1803, 1841-1843, 1867-1878, and since 1898. When there is no federal law on bankruptcy, the States may legislate providing they do not impair the obligation of a contract. At present a person may file a voluntary petition of bankruptcy, listing his assets and liabilities, or he may be forced into bankruptcy on petition of his creditors. In either case his assets are disposed of by an officer appointed by the court, his creditors are paid pro rata, and he is discharged from further obligation. In 1933 special provision was made by law to facilitate the reorganization of railroads and other corporations which were in financial difficulties   (DAP)

bar: (1) the railing separating the judge, counsel, and jury from the general public (DAP) (2) the whole body of attorneys and counselors who have been admitted to practice in a court. Cf. bench   (DAP)

barat: to quarrel   (CDTP)

barbiturate: various derivatives of barbituric acid, usually those with a sedative or hypnotic effect

bargain, implicit: a sentencing practice by which the defendant pleads guilty and throws himself on the mercy of the court, with the implied understanding that he will receive a lighter sentence than if he pleaded not guilty and demanded trial

barndoor: folding wings used in front of studio spotlights to aid in directing the light, and to shade portions of the subject from direct illumination   (MPPF)

Barnes, Harry Elmer (*1889-   *): a vigorous profilic writer, editor, and college teacher who was particularly active in the 1920s and 1930s. His major causes were prison reform as exemplified by his *Evaluation of Penology in Pennsylvania* (1922), *The Story of Punishment* (1931), and *Prisons in Wartime* (1944), and opposition to war shown in his *Immediate Causes of World War* (1926) (DC)

barometer: an instrument that measures air pressure and serves to indicate weather changes

barratry: the criminal offenses of exciting groundless quarrels or lawsuits

barrel: a metal tube fastened to the action of a weapon. The barrel may be rifled, or it may have a smooth interior surface (bore)   (DWMT)

barrel assembly: the barrel of a gun with the parts necessary to attach it to the rest of the gun   (DWMT)

barrel distortion: a term applied to the barrel-shaped image of a square object, obtained when the diaphragm is placed in front of a simple convex lens   (MPPF)

barrel life: as applied to small-arms and automatic weapons, the number of rounds which may be fired through a barrel at a particular firing schedule before the barrel becomes unserviceable. Barrel life varies with the firing schedule   (DWMT)

barrel shank: the threaded portion of a barrel encircled by the re-barrel time: time of the movement of the bullet from the time the hammer falls until the bullet reaches the muzzle of the gun (LEV) (DWMT)

barricade: a fortification, often in a street. It is made in haste of trees, earth, overturned vehicles, or anything else that will obstruct (DWMT)

barrier: something which acts as a barricade or which separates people or things; an object or structure which restricts the free movement of people (LEV)

Barron v. Baltimore, 7 Peters 243 (1833): this is, historically, the leading case restricting the powers of the federal government regarding acts of local government. In 1833, the U. S. Supreme Court was of the opinion that the first eight amendments to the Constitution of the United States were limitations on the powers of state or local governments. The Court noted that these constitutional amendments were enacted to guard against the abuse of power by the federal government and contained no expression indicating an intention to apply them to state governments. However, the essence of this decision contributed, in 1868, to the passage of the Fourteenth Amendment with its due process and equal protection clauses (AOJ)

Barrow, Clyde (1909-1934): born in Telice, Texas, 1909, this famous American bank robber and murderer became a legend in his own lifetime through the violent crime spree he committed with his brother Buck and his partner, Bonnie Parker. He was killed at the age of 25 with Bonnie by Texas Rangers. Bonnie and Clyde have since become immortalized in American folklore and movies

bar sight: the rear sight of a firearm. It consists of a movable bar with a notch or peep (DWMT)

barter: the exchange of one article or commodity for another. (CDTP)

baryta: a treated emulsion of barium, sulfate. It is commonly used, in the manufacture of photographic paper, to coat the paper stock before the light-sensitive emulsion is coated. It provides a white surface and keeps the light-sensitive emulsion from being partially absorbed by the paper base (MPPF)

Bass, Sam [(1851-1878), outlaw]: born near Mitchell, Indiana, on July 21, 1851, Bass was orphaned by the time he was thirteen and received little or no schooling. At eighteen he began to roam, moving to St. Louis, to Mississippi, and then to Denton, Texas, working at various jobs from millhand to deputy sheriff. . . . [In] Deadwood, South Dakota, Bass, Bud Collins, and their gang began preying on stagecoaches and in Sept. 1877, at Big Springs, Neb., they took $65,000 in gold and other valuables from a Union Pacific train. Four more train robberies in the region around Dallas followed in quick succession. The Texas Rangers finally persuaded one of Bass's men, who had been captured, to serve as an informant; with his aid a trap was ready when an attempt was made to rob the bank at Round Rock and in the gunfight that ensued, Bass was mortally wounded, dying 2 days later on July 21, 1878, his 27th birthday (Webster's American Biographies)

bastard: one born of an illicit connection and before the lawful marriage of its parents (CDTP)

bast fibres: fibres occurring beneath the bark or outer layer of plant stems; some (flax, jute, hemp, etc.) are used in making fabrics or cordage (FS)

batch processing: collection of data over a period of time for sorting and processing as a group during a particular machine run (ADPS)

baton: a law enforcement officer's night stick; a "billy stick" (LEV)

battered child syndrome: deliberate injury of children by adult brutality. Majority of victims under

three years of age. Injury caused by parents or custodians (LEV)
battery: (1) any unlawful beating or use of force upon an individual (2) the frizzen in a flintlock, the steel or iron plate against which the flint strikes to make the sparks (CDTP)
battery compartment shield: an item of equipment that protects the battery from damage by engine heat. Also known as heat shield (TDPPC)
battery cup: the small cup which contains the primer (CDTP)
Baumes laws: the restrictive penal legislation sponsored by a committee of the New York State Senate of which Sen. Caleb H. Baumes was chairman. These laws, enacted in 1926, provided an increase in penalty with each successive offense and an automatic life sentence for the fourth offense whether known at the time of conviction or discovered after sentence. The term "Baumes laws" has been widely applied to similar habitual offender laws subsequently enacted in other states (DOS)
bawdy house: a house appropriated for the purpose of prostitution (CDTP)
bayonet: an edged steel weapon with a tapered point and a formed handle designed to be attached to the muzzle end of a rifle, shotgun, or the like. Bayonets were first introduced in Bayonne, France, in the 17th century, and the earlier forms were made to be fitted into the bore of a musket or rifle (DWMT)
bayonet knife: an edged steel weapon with a tapered point and a formed handle for overhand or underhand gripping. It is designed for use as a hand weapon, for general-purpose use in the field, or as a bayonet when attached to the muzzle of a carbine, rifle, or the like. The blade is less than twice the length of the handle, and it is usu. without a blood groove (DWMT)
bayonet lock: a means of quickly attaching or removing a lens from a camera by turning through only part of a revolution (MPPF)
bayonet lug: a projection on a weapon for engaging a slot on a bayonet (DWMT)
bayonet scabbard: a leather or metal case for carrying a bayonet (DWMT)
B&E: breaking and entering
bead: a system of high-strength wires, embedded in the inner ring of a tire, which anchors the ply chords, holds the tire to the wheel, and maintains the airtight seal (TDPPC)
bead, sight: the name given the small knob mounted at the muzzle end of the barrel of a firearm to serve as a front sight (DWMT)
beam divergence: in a photoelectric alarm system, the angular spread of the light beam (TDIAS)
beam test: a microscopic examination of crushed marihuana as a means to identify it (LEV)
Bean, Roy [(1825?-1903) frontier figure]: born in Mason County, Ky., about 1825, Bean worked at various jobs, sought gold in the West, and traded in Mexico before eventually making his way to Texas about 1875 and settling in San Antonio. In 1882 he moved to a barren spot known as Vinegaroon on the lower Peco River and opened another in the series of saloons he had been operating for construction men working on the Southern Pacific Railroad. He soon became, more or less officially, the local justice of the peace. He held court sessions in the saloon, where he dispensed rough and ready justice and hung up a sign designating him "the law west of the Peco," a phrase that became a part of Western legend (Webster's American Biographies)
beat: the area usually assigned to a foot patrolman to cover and be responsible for (LEV)
Beauharnais v. Illinois, 343 U.S. 250, 96 L. Ed. 919, 72 S. Ct. 725 (1952): Justice Jackson's dissenting opinion makes it plain that the Fourteenth Amendment

does not incorporate the First. (Later Court decisions seem to recognize this principle. The states under the due process clause of the Fourteenth Amendment still have more extensive powers over speech, press, and assembly than the federal government.) (ILECJ)

Beccaria, Marchese De (Cesare Bonesana) (*1738-1794*): one of the founders of the classical school of criminology, Beccaria wrote an essay on crime and punishment which led to major changes in European criminal laws. Besides denouncing torture and excessive use of the death penalty, he further argued that the penalties should equal the offenses, and that certainty of penalties is more effective as a deterrent than severity

bed: the base of a camera, usually carrying the focusing guide rails (MPPF)

Beer's law: the optical density of a colored solution is proportional to the concentration of the light-absorbing substance (MPPF)

before whom returnable: in the absence of statutory restriction, search warrants may be made returnable before the justice of another district than that of the one issuing the warrant, or before any court having jurisdiction to deal with the matters involved (CDTP)

behavior modification: a method of treatment of offenders, based on the belief that all behavior is learned and that socially acceptable behavior can be learned as a replacement for deviant behavior

bell: or swell of the muzzle, so called because the muzzle flares out in the shape of a bell (CDTP)

bellows: a folding tube of the accordion type which permits movement for focusing between the back of the camera and the lens and which collapses when the camera is packed. The camera bellows is usually made of leather or black cloth. Modern miniature cameras have a helical-threaded

metal tube in place of a bellows (MPPF)

bellows draw: the maximum extension of a camera bellows (MPPF)

belly gun: a handgun having a short barrel, the principal use of which is for close range firing (LEV)

belted ammunition: cartridge ammunition arranged in a belt for use in a machine gun (DWMT)

belted ball: a bullet with a raised band or belt around it. It was used in a rifle that had rifling consisting of two wide grooves (DWMT)

belted bias ply tire: a bias ply tire which contains two or more additional layers of ply cords in the form of belts placed between the body plies and the tire tread. Material used in the belt cords may be rayon, fiber glass, steel, or other high-strength material. *See also* bias ply tire (TDPPC)

belted case: a cartridge case with a band or belt just ahead of its extractor groove. It is used to seat the cartridge in the chamber (DWMT)

belt-fed: the term describing an automatic weapon that is supplied by cartridges from a feed belt (DWMT)

Benanti v. United States, 335 U.S. 96, 2 L. Ed. 2d 126, 78 S. Ct. 155 (1957): the Court through Chief Justice Warren held that Section 605 of the Federal Communications Act "contains an express, absolute prohibition against the divulgence of intercepted communications" in a federal prosecution. (States continued, nonetheless, to admit wiretap evidence despite the fact such evidence was the fruits of a violation of federal law. In *Benanti* the Chief Justice cast doubt on the continued viability of the silver platter doctrine in search cases by referring to the matter as an "open question." This view was approvingly quoted three years later in *Elkins* when the Court overruled the silver platter doctrine.) (ILECJ)

bench: (1) to place a firearm, not in

use, on a bench, table, or other suitable object ("Unload your pistol and bench it.") (LEV) (2) the place where the judges sit in court; the collective body of judges sitting as a court (LEV)
bench parole: probation
bench seat: a seat in a vehicle which extends from one side of the vehicle to the other without a break in the seat portion. The seat back may be divided (TDPPC)
bench warrant: a warrant issued by a judge for the apprehension of a person either on a charge of contempt or for a criminal offense (CDPT)
beneficiary: one who receives a benefit or is designated to receive a benefit in the future (CDTP)
Benjamin, Judah Philip [(*1811-84*) *Lawyer and Confederate statesman*]: He served on the U.S. Senate, where he defended Southern policies. Known in the North as "the brains of the Confederacy" he served the South as its attorney general, secretary of war, and secretary of state. When the South was defeated, he escaped to England where he continued to practice law.
Bentham, Jeremy (*1748-1832*): one of the founders of the classical school of criminology, Bentham stated that the amount of pain caused by punishment should be in exact proportion to the amount of pain caused by the commission of the crime. His pleasure-pain theory further states that punishment should be strictly utilitarian and enforced for the greatest number of people, not merely for the purpose of vindictive satisfaction
Benton v. Maryland, 395 U.S. 784, 23 L. Ed. 2d 707, 89 S. Ct. 2056 (1969): in the Court's last decision of the 1969 Term, the Court through Mr. Justice Marshall held, 6-2, that the Double Jeopardy Clause of the Fifth Amendment is applicable to the states through the Due Process Clause of the

Fourteenth Amendment [The decision overruled *Palko v. Connecticut*, 302 U.S. 319, (1937), one of the Court's earlier landmark decisions. The Double Jeopardy prohibition "represents a fundamental idea in our constitutional heritage," Mr. Justice Marshall said. "*Palko*," he continued, "represented an approach to basic constitutional rights which this Court's recent decisions have rejected."]   (ILECJ)
Benzedrine: a trade name for a chemical which causes shrinkage of nasal cavity membranes. It is one trade name for amphetamine which is also a stimulant (LEV)
Benzidine Test: a preliminary chemical test for blood. If the test is negative the presence of blood is eliminated. If it is positive the stain may be blood, but the laboratory should conduct further tests to determine definitely if blood is present   (LEV)
bequeath: to give personal property by will.   (LEV)
bequest: the gift of property by will or testament   (LEV)
Berger v. New York, 388 U.S. 41, 18 L. Ed. 2d 1040, 87 S. Ct. 1873 (1967): the Court (5-4), held New York State's permissive wiretap statute to be "too broad in its sweep resulting in a trespassory intrusion into a constitutionally protected area and is, therefore, violative of the Fourth and Fourteenth Amendments" [The Court pointed out that since *Mapp* (1961), "the Fourth Amendment's right of privacy has been declared enforceable against the States through the Due Process Clause of the Fourteenth Amendment." The decision did not outlaw wiretapping. It simply struck down New York's permissive wiretap statute as unconstitutional. There is an implication in the decision that a statute can be drafted that would meet constitutional requirements.]   (ILECJ)
Bertillon, Alphonse (*1883-1914*): a

French criminologist, Bertillon is considered the creator of forensic science. He devised the first scientific system for the identification of the person, based upon measurements of the body. Bertillon also developed a system of forensic photography using standardized photos of full face and profile

Bertillon method of identification: a system of determining whether an individual under investigation is the same individual as one whose anthropometric measurements are on record. It was invented by Alphonse Bertillon and applied to the identification of criminals when he was made head of the Paris police department in 1883. It consisted of a series of measurements of certain parts of the body, of standardizing the photograph, of noting peculiar markings, and of so classifying the data as to make easy the location of thousands of records. His method is based on the observation that physical maturity fixes the skeletal dimensions for life. It has been widely superseded by the fingerprint method, because Bertillon's method is not adapted to immature persons, is often unreliable for adult women, marks can be altered, and facial expression in the photograph changes often with age (DOS)

best evidence rule: one coming into court must bring the best evidence available to prove the questions involved in the case. If a written document is involved it is the best evidence and must be produced unless it is shown it has been lost or destroyed (LEV)

bestiality: sexual relations between a human being and an animal

Betts v. Brady, 316 U.S. 455, 86 L. Ed. 1595, 62 S. Ct. 1252 (1942): in a 6-3 decision, the Court held that a state-court indigent defendant in a noncapital case has no right to appointed counsel under the Amendment's due process clause. (During the reign of *Betts* the Court made it clear that denying a defendant the assistance of his own counsel in any case, at any stage, in any issue, constituted a per se violation of "fundamental fairness.") (ILECJ)

between-the-lens: a shutter located between the front and back elements of a double lens (MPPF)

beyond a reasonable doubt: a legal term used relative to proof by evidence. In cases where the state (prosecution) uses direct evidence (in whole or part) as proof of the offense the evidence must convince the jury (the judge if no jury is used) of the guilt of the accused "beyond a reasonable doubt." *See* doubt, reasonable (LEV)

bias: favor or support a given point of view; preference or prejudice (LEV)

bias ply tire: a tire in which the cords in the plies crisscross the center line of the tire at an angle which is substantially less than 90 degrees. Cords may be arranged in two or more (even number) plies depending, in general, on the strength desired in the finished tire. Materials used in body cords include nylon, rayon, and polyester. *See also* belted bias ply tire (TDPPC)

bid: a formal or informal proposal, submitted by a vendor or supplier in response to a purchase request, that specifies the terms and conditions under which he will provide a requested product, material, or service (TDPPC)

bid proposal: a solicited or unsolicited proposal by a vendor to supply products, materials, or services (TDPPC)

biennial: happening once in two years (CDTP)

bifid: separated into two parts (CDTP)

bifurcation: the dividing or forking of one line into two or more branches. A term used in describing fingerprint patterns. *See* fingerprints (LEV)

bigamy (or polygamy): is a statutory and not a common law crime. It is committed where one, being legally married, marries another person during the life of his or her wife or husband. The statutes generally except from their operation a person whose husband or wife has been absent for a certain number of years without being known by such person to be living within that time   (CDTP)

big bertha: a custom-made camera, ususally consisting of a 4 x 5 or 5 x 7 Graflex body combined with a powerful telephoto lens. Most important feature is its lens. It is a very bulky camera   (MPPF)

big brother plan: a plan for reducing juvenile delinquency by securing the cooperation of recognized community leaders to act as "big brothers" to boys who appear before the juvenile court. The plan aims to organize the economic and social resources of the community to assist boys who need a helping hand and a little practical guidance in growing into self-respecting manhood. The service is entirely voluntary on the part of the men of the community, but the success of the plan is almost impossible to determine since adequate records of their work are seldom maintained   (DOS)

big fix: an arrangement between political machines and the underworld for the nonenforcement or partial enforcement of laws relating to bootlegging, racketeering, and other forms of organized crime and vice   (DAP)

bilateral: relating to, or having two sides   (CDTP)

bill of attainder: a legislative act declaring an individual guilty, without trial, of a crime, such as treason

bill of exceptions: a written statement of objections or exceptions taken by either side (or party) on the court's rulings or instructions during a trial. These are used as an integral part of the record when the case is appealed and are used by the appellate court in reaching its decision ("When the judge ruled against the motion of the defense attorney he reserved a bill of exceptions.")   (LEV)

bill of exchange: a written order by one person to another requiring the person to whom it is addressed to pay a certain sum on demand or at a fixed date (CDTP)

bill of indictment: a document, usually prepared by the prosecutor, charging a person with the commission of a crime, which is furnished the grand jury for their consideration. If the latter finds there is sufficient grounds to support the charge they return it with the endorsement "true bill," if not they endorse it with the words, "not a true bill"   (LEV)

bill of lading: a written account of goods issued by a carrier to the consignor consisting of a receipt for the goods, and an agreement to deliver them at the place directed   (CDTP)

bill of pains and penalties: a legislative conviction similar to an attainder, except that it imposes a penalty of less than death. It is prohibited in the United States   (DAP)

bill of particulars: an amplification of the proceedings designed to make more specific the allegations appearing therein   (CDTP)

bill of rights: a brief statement of certain fundamental rights and privileges which are guaranteed to the people against infringement by the government. The English Bill of Rights from which some provisions of American bills of rights have been derived is a statute of Parliament passed in 1689. The Virginia Bill of Rights, 1776, incorporated some common law principles. The first ten amendments to the Constitution of the United States, popularly called the Bill of Rights, were added to the Constitution in 1791 after State ratifying conventions had objected to the absence of such guarantees in the original document. They were originally limitations on the federal government only (*see Barron* v. *Baltimore*). Beginning in 1925, many of the substantive provisions of the federal Bill of Rights have also become limitations on State governments by judicial interpretation. A bill of rights is nearly always the first article of a State constitution (DAP)

bill of sale: a written document transferring the rights to and interest in personal chattels (CDTP)

binary-coded alphanumeric: a scheme for representing all alphabetic characters, digits, and special symbols in binary notation. The use of six bits for each character is common since $2^6 = 64$, which is generally adequate for the alphabet involved (ADPS)

binary-coded decimal: a system for representing *each* decimal digit by a code written in binary notation. Among the several systems are the 8-4-2-1 and the Excess-3 schemes (ADPS)

binary number: a number with the base 2 having the following positional values: 64, 32, 16, 8, 4, 2, 1, 1/2, 1/4, 1/8, etc. (ADPS)

Binet Test: a method of determining the mental age of a child, by asking him a series of questions considered proper for normal children of his age and grading him accordingly (CDTP)

bio-assay: the estimation of the amount of potency of a drug or other physiologically active substance by its action on a suitable living organism (FS)

birefringence: the property whereby some fibres, natural crystals, and certain constituents of living tissues have two *refractive indices*, and so split a ray of light passing through them into two (FS)

birthmark: a disfiguration, discoloration, or abnormal blemish on the skin at the time of birth (LEV)

bisexuality: the playing the role of the male and female simultaneously. A person often does not consciously realize the roles being played. It has been said that no one is completely free of this dual role playing (LEV)

bit: a binary digit; hence, a unit of data in binary notation; abbreviated from *binary digit* (ADPS)

Bivens v. **Six Unknown Named Agents, 403 U.S. 388, 29 L. Ed. 2d 619, 91 S. Ct. 1999 (1971):** Mr. Justice Brennan for the Court, 6-3, held that an apartment dweller has a federal cause of action for damages against federal narcotics agents who allegedly violated the Fourth Amendment by entering his apartment without a warrant and arresting and searching his apartment without probable cause. (The various opinions contain a wide range of commentary why the search and seizure exclusionary rule has failed to effectively deter illegal police practices, and suggest possible alternatives to replace the rule.) (ILECJ)

black body: a theoretically perfect radiator, having no power of reflection (MPPF)

Black Guerrilla Family: a prison gang formed at San Quentin by the late George Jackson. This violent group is the predominant black organized gang in the California Prison System today

Black Hand: an organization which obtains money unlawfully by threats and violence committed against the victim (CDTP)

blacklist: a list of the names and other identifying data of prominent union leaders, organizers, and members. Such a list was used before the 1930s by anti-union business firms in their attempts to prevent the employment of such persons. The enactment of the Wagner Act has rendered the blacklist unworkable (DOAH)

blackmail: the extortion of money from a person by threats of accusation or exposure. See extortion (CDTP)

black market: illegal, questionable, or unethical sales, including sale of stolen or government rationed items, or items which are in much demand and in short supply (LEV)

blackout: applied to photoflash lamps, a lamp having a visually opaque coating transmitting only infrared radiation, and used for photography in total visual darkness   (MPPF)

Black Panther Party: a black prison gang formed by Huey Newton. Today they are a nonviolent political black group based in Oakland, California

blade sight: a type of thin front sight or post sight   (DWMT)

blank ammunition: a cartridge or shell loaded with powder but not with a bullet or projectile. It is used in training, in signaling, and in firing salutes. The powder charge is held in place by a wad crimped in the open end of the case. When a blank is fired, the wad can injure persons in front of the gun   (DWMT)

blank warrants: signed by the issuing officer who authorizes the executing officer to put in anything he sees fit are insufficient, as are all blanket forms of search warrants which are general in their terms authorizing a search in the broadest terms   (CDTP)

blasphemy: at common law—maliciously reviling God or religion. Many of the States have enacted statutes regarding blasphemy
(CDTP)

bleacher: a chemical compound, usually containing potassium ferricyanide, employed for bleaching or dissolving silver images. Bleachers are used in both reversal and toning processes   (MPPF)

bleaching: the first step in the intensification of a negative is to bleach the negative until it appears white when viewed from the back of the film or plate. After bleaching, the negative is redeveloped. It is also necessary to bleach bromide prints before toning or developing them into sepia and white prints   (MPPF)

bleeder: sufferer from hemophilia   (CDTP)

blemish: a defect or abnormality evidenced by disfiguration, particularly of the skin; blot, stain
(LEV)

blisters: small bubbles forming under an emulsion due to the detachment of the emulsion from its base. Blisters are caused by some fault in processing   (MPPF)

block: a group of words, fields, or data elements transferred as a unit for input and output purposes
(ADPS)

blocked: the arrangement of records in blocks for input and output. Generally two or more data records are placed in a block on tape, depending on the length of records and blocks. *Blocking* is the combining of two or more data records into one block for writing on tape. *Deblocking* is the separation of blocked records preparatory to processing. *Unblocked* data records are recorded as individual blocks on tape   (ADPS)

blocked up: applied to highlights in a negative which are so overexposed or overdeveloped that no detail is visible   (MPPF)

blocking factor: the number of data records that can be contained in a given block on tape   (ADPS)

blocking out: painting out undesired background area on a negative   (MPPF)

blockmark: a mark placed in storage to indicate the end of a block of data to be written on tape for a processor that handles variable-length blocks on tape   (ADPS)

blood feud: a quarrel between families or clans

bloodless emergency: an emergency situation confronting a police officer where the subject is not involved in violence such as accidents, shootings, or fights. Bloodless emergencies may be responses to mental cases, victims of drugs or alcohol, or suicidal patients
(LEV)

Bloom v. Illinois, 391 U.S. 194 (1968): this decision restricts the summary power of the judiciary to act in contempt cases and holds that the right to trial by jury in serious criminal contempt cases in state courts is constitutionally guaranteed (AOJ)

blowback: escape, to the rear and under pressure, of gases formed during the firing of a gun. Blowback may be caused by a defective breech mechanism, a ruptured cartridge case, or a faulty primer (DWMT)

blowback action: an action in a weapon that utilizes the pressure of the propellant gases to force the bolt to the rear, independently of the barrel, which does not move relative to the receiver. The gases, produced by the propelling charge, act against the cartridge case, which in turn acts to force the bolt to the rear. A weapon which employs this method of operation is characterized by the absence of any breech-lock or bolt-lock mechanism (DWMT)

blow-forward action: an action in a weapon that utilizes the pressure of the propellant gases to force the barrel forward from a standing breech to open the action and eject the fired case. A spring brings the barrel back to firing position and also reloads and cocks the gun. Typical of this action is that of the Borchardt pistol, the forerunner of the Luger (DWMT)

bludgeon: a short stick, with one thick, heavy, or loaded end, used as an offensive weapon; hence, any clublike weapon (DWMT)

blue laws: (1) a puritanical code regulating public and private morality in the theocratic New Haven colony during the 17th and 18th centuries (DAP) (2) any laws prohibiting athletic contests or the opening of stores and theaters on Sunday, race-track betting, or any similar activity usually regulated by individual conscience. Recently the Supreme Court, as a protection of religious freedom, has exempted businessmen who observe a Sabbath day other than Sunday from the obligation to obey Sunday-closing laws (DAP)

blue-ribbon jury: a special jury composed of persons belonging to the upper economic and social strata which might be empaneled in New York counties having a population of one million or more. Such juries were abolished by law in 1965 (DAP)

Blue Sky Law: legislation to protect innocent people from being sold securities (stock) by fraud (LEV)

bluing: the colored finish of the metal parts of guns in various shades of blue, black, and brown, produced by artificially rusting the metal (CDTP)

B.N.D.D. (BNDD): Bureau of Narcotics and Dangerous Drugs

board of pardons: a State board, having various official designations, which acts alone or with the governor in granting executive clemency to criminals or advises the governor in the exercise of that function (DAP)

Board of Parole: an eight-man board in the Department of Justice which grants or revokes all paroles of federal prisoners. If authorized by a court, the board determines the date of a convicted person's eligibility for parole (DAP)

board of review: an administrative appeals board which, after hearing evidence, determines whether an assessment, action, or decision of an officer was correct (DAP)

Bodin, Jean (*1530–1596*): a French philosopher, Bodin, in *Six Livres de la Republique*, attempted to construct a systematic scientific approach to politics. He felt that the government should be guided by virtuous activity, which would eliminate corruption, and establish laws which would provide a majority of the people with good lives

body: the exterior of a vehicle which houses the engine, passengers, and/or cargo (TDPPC)

body armor: equipment to protect the wearer against attacks from blows, hurled objects, knives, bullets, and other weapons (LEV)

body fluids: fluids of the body including blood, urine, saliva (LEV)

body guard: a device to protect occupants of the driver's seat in a car from attack by persons in the rear of the vehicle (LEV)

body lean: the tendency of the body of a vehicle to roll about its longitudinal axis during a change in direction (TDPPC)

body-on-frame: a method of automobile construction in which the body and frame are fabricated in two separate assemblies. The body is bolted to the frame which is the primary structural unit of the vehicle (TDPPC)

body type: the passenger or cargo compartment of a vehicle which often indicates the number of doors, seats, roof construction, or intended use. Also referred to as body style (TDPPC)

bogus: not genuine; fake; false; not what it purports to be. (LEV)

BOI: Bureau of Identification

Bolshevism: belief in the overthrow by force of the institution of private property and capitalism (CDTP)

bolt: (1) the sliding part in a breechloading weapon that pushes a cartridge into position and holds it there when the gun is fired. It may also be called the "breechblock" (DWMT) (2) the short arrow shot from a crossbow. The tip was often made of steel and of square section, either pointed or blunt. Most bolts had flights of wood or leather (DWMT)

bolt action: a rifle action in which a lever-operated bolt extends from the breechblock (DWMT)

bolt mechanism: the mechanical assembly in a bolt-action gun that includes the moving parts which insert, fire, and extract a round of ammunition (DWMT)

bomb: nonmilitary or homemade infernal machine. They follow no definite plan of construction and are extremely dangerous, may be detonated by one or more of several means. First consideration should be to clear the area of people who would be hurt by the explosion and then give attention to doing something to prevent property damage. The army has trained personnel who are qualified to cope with the problem (LEV)

bomb mattress: the name given to a bomb suppression device sold by Federal Laboratories, Inc. (LEV)

bona fide: in good faith; honestly, without fraud or unfair dealing; genuine

bond: (1) a pledge of money or assets of value offered as bail by an accused person or his surety to secure the former's temporary release from custody. Bond is forfeited if the conditions of bail are not fulfilled. (DAP) (2) an evidence of indebtedness (which may or may not be negotiable), issued to long-term creditors by governments or corporations (DAP) (3) a binding legal claim or covenant (DAP)

bond method: the Premium Bond Lottery of England. Only the 4 percent interest goes into the lottery. Prizes are tax-free (LEV)

bond or recognizance, the: cannot be taken unless authorized by law, and when authorized, it must be taken in the manner and form prescribed by law. If unauthorized or illegally taken, or if it is not in proper form, it is generally void (CDTP)

bondsman: a person bound by a writing obligatory for the performance of the act of another (CDTP)

Bonger, Willem Adriaan (*1876–1940*): a Dutch criminologist, it was due to him that criminology in Holland became a separate field of science. His small classic, *An Introduction to Criminology*, was a great success. Even today there is no other textbook which gives such a complete survey of criminology so compactly. Through this book and his doctor's thesis, *Criminality and Economic Conditions*, Bonger had a great influence on American and English authors (PC)

Bonneville, Arnould de Marsangy (*1802-1894*): Arnould Bonneville de Marsangy was an influential voice in the field of criminal legislative reforms in the France of the mid-nineteenth century. Jurist by profession, his innovative ideas on many criminological problems led the *Encyclopedia of the Social Sciences* to include him as a reformer and a social scientist. Born in Mons, Belgium, of French parents, in March 1802, Bonneville was a descendant of an ancient noble family. He studied law in Paris, and had a distinguished career as prosecutor, president, judge at Versailles, and imperial councillor at Paris   (PC)

bonus: a sum given, or paid, over and above what is actually payable   (CDTP)

booby trap: an explosive charge such as a mine, grenade, demolition block, shell, or bulk explosive fitted with a detonator and a firing device, all usu. concealed and set to explode when an unsuspecting person touches off its firing mechanisms by stepping upon, lifting, or moving a harmless-looking object. Also often used as a verb   (DWMT)

boodle: money accepted or paid for the use of political influence; bribe money. The term originated in New York City about 1883   (DAP)

book: (1) betting operation, "making book," operated by a "bookie" (LEV) (2) A document in a jail or law enforcement agency on which information is recorded concerning persons who have been arrested—"police blotter" (LEV) (3) the act of entering information on the police blotter or book   (LEV)

bookie: a person who operates a racing "book"; one who takes illegal bets on horse races   (LEV)

bookmaker: (1) a bookie (2) one who takes bets of sporting events and races   (LEV)

bookmaking: the practice of receiving and recording bets made

on the results of horse racing and other sporting events; often illegal

boom: a stand, usually on wheels, having an extension arm on which a microphone or lamp may be attached   (MPPF)

booster spring: a device installed on the springs or shock absorbers that acts to compensate for an overload which would cause the springs to sag and the vehicle to assume a non-level attitude. Also known as a helper spring, or overload spring   (TDPPC)

Booth, John Wilkes [(*1838-1865*) *actor and assassin*]: born in 1838 near Bel Air, Md. Booth was a son of Junius Brutus Booth and a brother of Edwin Booth. After the fall of Richmond and General Lee's surrender at Appomattox, Booth decided on assassination, enlisting one accomplice to murder Vice-President Andrew Johnson and another to kill Secretary of State William H. Seward. On the evening of April 14, 1865, Booth ascended the stairway to the President's box at Ford's Theater and shot Lincoln in the head. He leaped to the stage crying "Sic sempre tyrannis! The South is avenged!" and escaped through the rear of the theater. His accomplices were unsuccessful in their assassination attempts, although Seward was badly beaten. Booth was not located until April 26, when he was found hiding in a barn near Bowling Green, Va., and was either killed by his captors or died by his own hand; the facts have never been ascertained (*Webster's American Biographies*)

bootlegger: one who sells or carries around for sale intoxicating liquor in violation of law   (CDTP)

bootlegging: illegal manufacture, transportation, and/or sale of intoxicating liquor

bootstrap: the use of prior steps to advance operations at the next stage; for example, a few instructions entered through the console can cause a processor to start reading a load routine which then

takes over to read the remainder of the load routine and the whole program (ADPS)
bore: the gun barrel diameter. Same as the gage (LEV)
boresight: an instrument inserted in the bore of a gun to align its axis with its sights (DWMT)
boresighting: the process by which the axis of a gun bore and the line of sight of a gunsight are made parallel or are made to converge on a point. The term may be used in reference to any weapon and its sight (DWMT)
borstals: the English institutions which are organized for the treatment and treasuring of youthful offenders. Eleven in number, these institutions provide special care for the varying types of offenders. Four of the borstals are walled, four are open, one is for boys who have broken parole (designated as "revokees") and one for the especially difficult problem cases (DOS)
borstal system: the halfway house in Europe. Devised there and used to reorient persons recently released from prison or hospital (for drugs or alcohol, etc.). *See* halfway house (LEV)
Boston Massacre: the name applied to the killing of five men and the wounding of others when British troops fired into a crowd of men and boys in Boston. The "massacre" occurred in 1770 as a result of the quartering of two regiments of troops in Boston, sent to protect British officials in executing the Customs Acts. John Adams acted as counsel for the British in the trial that followed. The British officer in command was acquitted, though accused of giving the order to fire. Two British soldiers were given light sentences for manslaughter. It is one of a series of occurrences developing colonial resistance to Parliamentary policy on the eve of the American Revolution (DOAH)
Boston Police Strike: a strike of 75 percent of the Boston police force

on Sept. 9, 1919. The immediate cause was a refusal of the police commissioner to recognize the policemen's union. Governor Coolidge was requested to intercede after the outbreak of the strike but refused. Mayor Petes then brought in sections of the militia which broke the strike. Coolidge followed this act by commanding the police commissioner to assume charge, and called out the entire state guard, after order had already been established. His often-quoted declaration that "there is no right to strike against the public safety by anybody, anywhere, anytime" projected him into the national limelight as a supporter of law and order. This resulted in his consideration by the Republican party as an outstanding candidate in the convention of 1920 (DOAH)
bottomry: a contract by which a ship is pledged as security for a loan
bounce light: flash or tungsten light bounced off ceilings or walls to give the effect of natural or available light (MPPF)
bounty: a reward or premium, usually offered as an inducement for some act
Bovee, Marvin H. (*1827-1888*): anti-capital punishment crusader, who, beginning his career as a Wisc. legislator, carried his campaign to abolish the death penalty to N.Y., Ill., Mass., and elsewhere, his speeches and legislative labors resulting in various reforms (DC)
bowie knife: a single-edged utility and fighting knife named after Col. James Bowie (d. 1836), who made such knives popular (DWMT)
Bow Street Runners: a unit of the police force as organized in the London, England, metropolitan area in the last half of the 1700s, by John and Henry Fielding. They were also known as "Thief Takers." They operated out of the Bow Street station. Some called this unit the first detective squad

as their function was to get to the scene of the crime quickly and investigate the case (LEV)

bowstring: the string of a bow (DWMT)

box camera: an inexpensive camera, boxlike in form, with either few or no adjustable controls; also referred to as a "simple camera" (MPPF)

Boxer cartridge: the first center-fire metallic cartridge to be used successfully. This cartridge, consisting of a coiled brass case with an iron head and an anvil primer and containing a roundnose lead bullet, was developed in the 1860s by Col. Edward M. Boxer, of England (DWMT)

Boxer primer: a primer in which the anvil is an integral part of the primer assembly. It is favored in the United States over the Berdan primer (DWMT)

boxlock: a pistol or gun action in which the lock mechanism is contained within the frame (DWMT)

box magazine: a boxlike device that holds ammunition and feeds it into the receiver mechanism of weapons (DWMT)

box respirator: a gas mask having a mask that covers the face and a chemical-filled box that filters the air breathed by the user (DWMT)

boycott: the organized effort of a combination to cause loss or injury to a person, by coercing others against their will to withdraw from him their beneficial business intercourse by threats to cause them damage or loss unless they do so (CDTP)

Boyd v. United States, 116 U.S. 616, 39 L. Ed. 746, 6 S. Ct. 524 (1886): the Court, through Mr. Justice Bradley, held that there was a link between the Fourth and Fifth Amendments so that one became definitive of the other, and one test of the reasonableness of a search was whether or not its object was to uncover incriminating evidence. (The decision stands out as the Court's first authoritative utterance on searches. The *Boyd* holding created

much confusion in lower courts until it was "vitually repudiated" 18 years later in *Adams* v. *New York*.) (ILECJ)

B-pillar: counting from the windshield, the second vertical structural member of an automobile body that forms the door pillar at the rear of the front door and supports the rear door and roof, except in hardtop or convertible body styles. Also known as B-post (TDPPC)

Brady v. U.S., 397 U.S. 742 (1970) (together with McMann v. Richardson, 397 U.S. 759, and Parker v. North Carolina, 397 U.S. 790): the decisions in these three cases on guilty pleas in the same term of the Supreme Court attach paramount significance to the presence of counsel for the defendant during the pleading process. This is a fine review of the plea of guilty as a rational choice over going to trial in certain instances (AOJ)

brake: *See* disc brake *and* drum brake (TDPPC)

brake area: *See* brake lining area (TDPPC)

brake failure warning light: a red indicator located at the driver's position that illuminates when a hydraulic-type failure has occurred in the braking system (TDPPC)

brake lining area: the surface area of the friction material which seats on the braking surface when the brakes are activated (TDPPC)

brake lock-up: the condition existing when the wheels stop rotating during braking as a result of the application of excessive pressure on the brake pedal. Also called wheel lock-up (TDPPC)

brake loss: a reduction in, or complete loss of, braking effectiveness. *See also* fade (TDPPC)

brake pedal reserve: the distance remaining between the floor board and the brake pedal when maximum force has been exerted on the brake pedal (TDPPC)

brake recovery: the return of full brake effectiveness after a temporary reduction due to heat or water fade (TDPPC)

brake system: a combination of one or more brakes and their related control devices that retards, stops, or prevents a vehicle from moving (TDPPC)

branch: (1) a subdivision of any organization (DWMT) (2) a geographically separate unit of an activity which performs all or part of the primary functions of the parent activity on a smaller scale. Unlike an annex, a branch is not merely an overflow addition (DWMT) (3) an arm or service of the Army (DWMT) (4) See jump (ADPS)

Brandeis, Louis Dembitz (1856–1941): an Associate Justice of the U.S. Supreme Court. Tried to reconcile the developing powers of modern government and society with the maintenance of individual liberties and opportunities for personal development (EWB)

Brandenburg v. Ohio, 395 U.S. 444, 23 L. Ed. 2d 430, 89 S. Ct. 1827 (1969): Chief Justice Warren in a per curiam opinion that overrules Whitney v. California, 274 U.S. 357 (1927), finds the Ohio Criminal Syndicalism Act (Ohio Rev. Code, section 2923.13) unconstitutional and unconstitutionally applied to the appellant, a leader of a Ku Klux Klan group (The First Amendment bars laws prohibiting the "advocacy" of force or lawlessness that is not directed to inciting or producing imminent lawless action and not likely to incite or produce such action. Merely urging the moral propriety or even the moral necessity of a resort to force is distinguished from preparing a particular group for violent action. Justices Black and Douglas concur: the "clear and present danger" test should not be applied in First Amendment interpretations, they declare.) (ILECJ)

branding: marking with a symbol or letter to signify ownership

brass knuckles: a weapon worn on the hand to strike with, so constructed that the metal instead of the knuckles hit the intended object (CDTP)

breach: violation of an obligation or of the law (LEV)

breach of peace: a violation of the public tranquility and order. The offense of breaking or disturbing the public peace by any riotous, forcible, or unlawful proceeding (CDTP)

breach of trust: the willful misappropriation by a trustee of a thing which has been lawfully delivered to him in confidence (CDTP)

break alarm: (1) an alarm condition signaled by the opening or breaking of an electrical circuit (TDIAS) (2) the signal produced by a break alarm condition (sometimes referred to as an open circuit alarm or trouble signal, designed to indicate possible system failure) (TDIAS)

breaking: a forcible breaking, removing, or putting aside of something material which constitutes a part of a building and is relied on as a security against intrusion; a forcible entering of a building (CDTP)

breaking doors: forcibly removing the fastening or entering through the door of a house so that a person may enter (CDTP)

breaking doors, etc.: an officer, if, after notice of his purpose and authority, is refused admittance, may break an outer or inner door or window of a house, for the purpose of executing a warrant, or of making a lawful arrest without a warrant, or to liberate himself or another who, having entered to make an arrest, is detained therein. A private person may so break into a house, to prevent a felony, or to arrest a person for a felony actually committed by him, but not to arrest a suspected felon. Either an officer or a private person may so break into a house to arrest a person who has escaped from lawful custody (CDTP)

breakpoint: a point in a program at which a processor may be made to stop automatically for a check on the progress of the routine. A con-

ditional breakpoint permits the programmer to control operations by means of a switch setting and to continue the program as coded, if desired conditions are satisfied (ADPS)

Breathalizer: name of a commercial product (device) to test the breath of a suspected drinker and arrive at a determination of the blood alcohol content of the person (LEV)

breathing: movement of a projected picture upon the screen due to buckling of the film in the projector (MPPF)

breath testing equipment: equipment designed to test the breath of a person to determine the blood alcohol content of the person. There are several such devices manufactured commercially. Some of the manufacturers of such equipment may be determined from trade publications (LEV)

breech: (1) the rear-end of the gun barrel; the place where the ammunition is loaded into the barrel (LEV) (2) rear part of a firearm, behind the bore (CDTP)

breechblock: the steel block against which the barrel or bore, of a breech-loading gun, closes to prevent the escape of the explosive charge. The firing pin functions through the breechblock. Imperfections (marks and small ridges) on the face of the breechblock are imparted to the softer metal of the cartridge case or shell when the gun is fired, thus making identification possible by a laboratory examination to establish that such cartridge or shotgun shell was fired in a particular weapon (LEV)

breech face: the face or flat surface of the breechblock (LEV)

breech loader: an early developed rifle of the United States, A gun where ammunition is inserted in the barrel at the breech end as contrasted to the muzzle loader, where the ammunition is loaded through the front end or muzzle of the barrel (LEV)

Breed v. Jones, — U.S. —, 44 L. Ed. 346, 95 S. Ct. 1779 (1975): juvenile proceedings are radically changed by a unanimous opinion by Chief Justice Burger which holds that after a transfer hearing (waiver of jurisdiction) double jeopardy can be invoked insofar as a subsequent criminal trial in adult court. The Court's ruling in effect requires the transfer hearing be held prior to the adjudicatory hearing, whether the transfer is ordered or not. (It compels the juvenile courts to reassess their conduct, which courts have frankly become somewhat "sloppy" in their procedures because of their "parental" posture whereupon they operated on the principle "we can do no wrong because we are thinking first and foremost of the child.") (ILECJ)

bribe: a price, reward, or gift or favor bestowed or promised with a view to pervert the judgment or corrupt the conduct of a judge, witness, or other person (CDTP)

bribery: the action of giving, receiving, or offering money or other reward for the purpose of influencing the action of an officer, voter, or any other person entrusted with a public duty; usually prohibited by law under penalties which in some States may include the disfranchisement of a voter convicted of bribery (DAP)

bribery of United States Officer to influence his decision or action [*Federal Pen. Code, Sec. 39.*]: Maximum fine three times the value of amount of money or property offered and maximum jail sentence three years (CDTP)

bridge: fingerprint ridge pattern or configuration where two main ridges are joined by a connecting ridge (LEV)

brief: a summary of the law relating to a case, which is prepared by the attorneys for both parties to a case and given to the judge

brightness range: variation of light intensities from maximum to minimum. Generally refers to a subject to be photographed. For example, a particular subject may have a range of one to four, that is, four times the amount of light is reflected from the brightest highlight as from the least bright portion of the subject   (MPPF)

brilliance: a term denoting the degree of intensity of a color or colors   (MPPF)

brilliant: a term used in referring to the tone quality of a negative or print   (MPPF)

Bristow, Benjamin Helm (*1832-1896*): an American lawyer, Kentucky unionist, and federal official, as U.S. Attorney in Kentucky, he fought the Ku Klux Klan, and as U.S. Secretary of the Treasury, he crushed the Whiskey Ring.   (EWB)

Brockway, Z. E.: as the first superintendent of Elmira Reformatory in New York in 1876, Mr. Brockway was responsible for the first use of the indeterminant sentence in the United States. As the method of release from the indeterminant sentence, Brockway introduced the use of parole

broker: an agent who transacts business for others   (CDTP)

bromide paper: a photographic printing paper in which the emulsion is made sensitive largely through silver bromide. Bromide papers are relatively fast and usually printed by projection (MPPF)

bromoil: a process for the making of prints in permanent oil pigments on the base of a bromide print   (MPPF)

brothel: a house appropriated for the purpose of prostitution   (CDTP)

Brown v. Illinois — U.S. —, 45 L. Ed. 2d 416, 95 S. Ct. 2254 (1975): the Court held through Justice Blackmun that the mere giving of the warnings required by Miranda v. Arizona, 384 U.S. 436, does not dissipate the taint of a defendant's illegal arrest and render admissible statements given after the arrest   (ILECJ)

Brown v. Maryland, 12 Wheat. 419

(1827): a case in which the Supreme Court developed the original-package doctrine, declaring that so long as an imported commodity remained in the container in which it had been imported, State tax and police regulations could not apply to it   (DAP)

Brown v. Mississippi, 297 U.S. 278, 80 L. Ed. 682, 56 S. Ct. 461 (1936): in this first state-confession case to go to the Supreme Court of the United States, the Court held that the use by the state of an obviously coerced confession violated the petitioner's due process rights under the Fourteenth Amendment. (The main emphasis was not on police misconduct—albeit that was shocking—but on an abuse of discretion by the trial judge in permitting the confession to be introduced.)   (ILECJ)

Bruton v. United States, 391 U.S. 123, 20 L. Ed. 2d 476, 88 S. Ct. 1620 (1968): overruling Delli Paoli v. United States, 352 U.S. 232, Mr. Justice Brennan, writing for the majority, held that a confession of one defendant cannot be used at a joint trial in which it might prejudice a codefendant ("Because of the substantial risk that the jury, despite instructions to the contrary, looked to the incriminating extrajudicial statements in determining petitioner's guilt, admission of Evans' confession in this joint trial violated petitioner's right to cross-examination secured by the Confrontation Clause of the Sixth Amendment," said the Court.)   (ILECJ)

Bryan, William Jennings (*1860-1925*): an American lawyer, editor, and politician, he was the Democratic Party's Presidential nominee three times and became secretary of state. Called the "Great Commoner," Bryan advocated an agrarian democracy   (EWB)

buccal intercourse: act of using the mouth on sex organs   (LEV)

buccal onanism: fellatio   (LEV)

buck and ball: a cartridge with a round ball and three buckshot (CDTP)

bucket shop: a place in which individuals bet on the fluctuations of the stock market

buckshot: small lead bullet, or large shot, usually a sporting load (CDTP)

buffer: (1) a solution of salts, etc., so formulated that the effects of adding small quantities of acid or alkali are neutralized, and such additions do not change the P_H (FS) (2) device for compensating for differences in speed between two devices to permit them to operate together (ADPS)

bug: (1) to plant a microphone or other sound sensor or to tap a communication line for the purpose of surreptitious listening or audio monitoring; loosely, to install a sensor in a specified location (TDIAS) (2) the microphone or other sensor used for the purpose of surreptitious listening (TDIAS)

buggery: sodomy

building security alarm system: the system of protective signaling devices installed at a premise (TDIAS)

bulb: shutter setting in which the leaves remain open as long as the button is depressed and close as soon as the button is released; marked "B" on cameras (MPPF)

bulk storage: large-volume storage used to supplement the high-speed storage; may be addressable, as with disks and drums, or nonaddressable, as with magnetic tapes. Also called "secondary" and "external storage" (ADPS)

bullet: a projectile made for firing in a rifle or pistol. It is that part of a cartridge which is discharged or fired from a firearm. It is usu. made of lead. The types of bullets include: (1) connelures: has grooves around it for lubricant or for crimping; (2) flatpoint: has a flat nose. The "wadcutter" used for target practice is of this type; (3) hollow-point: has hollowed nose which causes the bullet to flatten or mushroom on impact; (4) metal-cased: has a jacket of metal covering the nose; (5) soft-point: has a metal case except for the nose which is of lead (LEV)

bullet group: the grouping of bullet holes in a target from one weapon fired from one place. Variations are due to improper aim or to ballistic differences (DWMT)

bullet jacket: a metal shell surrounding a metal core, the combination constituting a bullet for small arms. The jacket is either composed of, or coated with, a relatively soft metal such as gilding metal which engages the rifling in the bore, causing rotation of the bullet (DWMT)

bullet mold: an implement into which molten lead is poured to cast bullets (DWMT)

bulletproof: resistant to bullets or rifle fire. Said of a bulletproof shelter or bulletproof glass (DWMT)

bullet-proof equipment: equipment in the nature of armor, shields, or garments which protect the user from firearms bullets. Much research has been done in recent years to develop such equipment. The International Chiefs of Police Association has arranged with the National Bureau of Standards to operate a testing laboratory to test police equipment. Information on the merits of equipment can be obtained through this source (LEV)

bullet-proof glass: glazing material designed to resist or prevent the passage of ballistic projectiles (TDPPC)

bulletproof vest: a vest made of steel chain, plates, or some other impenetrable material used to protect a man's torso from small-arms fire and shell fragments (DWMT)

bullet shell: an explosive bullet with a bursting charge in a tube (CDTP)

bullhorn: an electric megaphone (DWMT)

bullion: uncoined gold or silver in

the mass   (CDTP)
bull's eye: the center of the target, a shot which hits the center
                            (CDTP)
bunko game: act or trick contrived to gain the confidence of the victim who is then defrauded. This form of theft is handled by a special investigative unit in most police departments
bunko operator: a criminal who resorts to tricks and devices known as "bunko games" in unlawfully obtaining property from others
                            (CDTP)
Burdeau v. McDowell, 256 U.S. 465, 65 L. Ed. 1048, 41 S. Ct. 574 (1921): the federal rule of exclusion was held to be "a restraint upon the activities of sovereign authority and . . . not . . . a limitation upon other than governmental agencies." (This principle reflects the long-held historic-constitutional doctrine that the Bill of Rights bound only officers and agents of the federal government.)
                            (ILECJ)
burden of proof: duty of establishing the existence of fact in a trial in court   (CDTP)
bureaucracy: government or other organizations characterized by a hierarchy of officials
Bureau of Narcotics and Dangerous Drugs [BNDD]: formed April 8, 1968 by a merger of the Bureau of Narcotics of the U. S. Treasury Department and the Bureau of Drug Abuse Control of the Department of Health, Education, and Welfare. It is a part of the U.S. Department of Justice. The address is: Bureau of Narcotics and Dangerous Drugs, U.S. Department of Justice, Washington, D.C. 20537. BNDD has regional offices and laboratories strategically located throughout the nation   (LEV)
burglar: one who commits burglary
                            (LEV)
burglar alarm (B.A.) pad: a supporting frame laced with fine wire or a fragile panel located with foil or fine wire and installed so as to

cover an exterior opening in a building, such as a door, or skylight. Entrance through the opening breaks the wire or foil and initiates an alarm signal. See also grid
                            (TDIAS)
burglary: in criminal law, is the breaking and entering the house of another in the nighttime, with intent to commit a felony therein, whether the felony be actually committed or not. To constitute the crime: There must be an actual or constructive breaking, and an entry. The house broken and entered must be the dwelling house of another. An outhouse within the curtilage is regarded as part of the dwelling house. Both the breaking and the entry must be in the nighttime, and both must be with the intent to commit a felony in the house. Burglary is a felony at common law
                            (CDTP)
burglary, safe: the illegal entry of a safe. Several methods are used by safe burglars. Some of these are: "blowing"—the use of explosive; "peeling"—peeling the safe back until entry is gained, usually by manipulating the locking device; "punching"—the use of a punch to force the locking mechanism; "ripping"—using a device working on the principle of a can-opener and ripping open parts of the safe; "drilling"—drilling holes in the safe at pertinent points and either forcing the locking mechanism or actually gaining access to the inside chamber of the safe by reaching through the hole; and "burning"—gaining entry by use of a flame cutting torch or thermal burning bar   (LEV)
burglary tools: tools which are suitable for gaining illegal entry to a safe. The possession of such tools are illegal in many states, but the intent to use them to commit a crime must also be shown. The courts have held that it is immaterial that the tools might also be used for lawful purposes   (LEV)
burn: a lesion caused by heat, elec-

tricity, chemicals, and friction. Classified as, first degree, where only the superficial layer of skin is involved, such as ordinary sunburn; second degree, where the deeper layer of skin is involved; third degree, where all layers and possibly the underlying muscles and tendons are involved. Its healing may result in scar or a pigmented area   (CDTP)

burned out: applied to an overexposed negative or print lacking in highlight detail   (MPPF)

burnese: a powder high in cocaine content used by many drug addicts

burning in: a method of darkening parts of a print in which certain parts of the image are given extra exposure while the rest of the image is protected from the light   (MPPF)

business application: a closely related set of activities that are treated as a unit—for example, each of the following: customer accounting, inventory control, or order entry and sales may be treated as a unit for conversion to automatic data processing and operation   (ADPS)

business data processing: processing of data for *actual* transactions—purchases, sales, collections—involving file processing, calculations, and reporting; also includes processing *planned* transactions for budgeting and operating control purposes. Characterized by large volumes of input and output with limited amounts of computation during processing   (ADPS)

business swindler: one who counterfeits business methods in his practices of fraud   (CDTP)

bust: to arrest   (LEV)

butt: the rear end of a rifle stock or spear. It is also a term used to describe the mound of earth used as a backing for a target   (DWMT)

butt plate: the metal plate on the butt   (CDTP)

butterfly: silk gauze or scrim on a frame, used to soften or diffuse a highlight, or to cast a soft shadow on some part of a picture or photo   (MPPF)

buttock: the prominence on the back of either hip region   (CDTP)

C

CA: abbreviation for Circuit Court of Appeals, Federal. The letters are followed by the designation for the Circuit, i.e., CA5 = 5th Circuit; CADC = the District of Columbia Circuit Court   (LEV)

C—4: "plastic" explosive; a high explosive   (LEV)

cabinet camera: an automatic camera, usu. operated by a coin-slot device; occasionally combined with an automatic developing machine   (MPPF)

cabinet-for-safe: a wooden enclosure having closely spaced electrical grids on all inner surfaces and contacts on the doors. It surrounds a safe and initiates an alarm signal if an attempt is made to open or penetrate the cabinet   (TDIAS)

cable release: a flexible shaft for operating the camera shutter   (MPPF)

cache: a hidden quantity of materials or items   (LEV)

cadaver: a corpse; dead body   (CDTP)

cadence: a standard time and pace set in marching   (DWMT)

Cady v. Dombrowski, 413 U.S. 433, 37 L. Ed. 2d 706, 93 S. Ct. 2523 (1973): the Court in this 5-4 opinion distinguishes between the search of a home and the search of an automobile, and allows more latitude in respect to the search of an automobile. ("Where, as here, the trunk of an automobile, which the officers reasonably believed to contain a gun was vulnerable to intrusion by vandals, we hold that the search was not 'unreasonable' within the meaning of the Fourth and Fourteenth Amendments.")   (ILECJ)

Caesarean section or operation: the taking of a baby from the uterus of its mother by cutting through the abdominal wall and the wall of the uterus. Its name is derived from the belief that Julius Caesar was delivered by this means   (LEV)

caffeine: a stimulant drug present in coffee or tea   (CDTP)

Cain: farmer son of Adam and Eve, known as world's first murderer for killing of brother Abel

Caldwell, Charles (*1772-1853*): an American doctor, Caldwell wrote *Elements of Phrenology*, the first American textbook on the concept of the relationship between head conformations and personality characteristics of individuals

calendar: the list of cases arranged for trial   (CDTP)

caliber: a term that derives from the Latin *qua libra*, "what pound," first applied to the weight of a bullet and then to the diameter. The bore diameter is measured in hundredths of an inch. Twenty-two caliber is a gun barrel measuring 22/100 of an inch in diameter. This term is similar to gage, which is used in shotguns but the latter is arrived at in a different manner. *See* gage

calibrated speedometer: an instrument that indicates the speed at which a vehicle is moving and that is certified as to accuracy   (TDPPC)

California emissions package: a special automobile emission control system designed specifically to meet the emission standards set by the State of California   (TDPPC)

California v. Byers, 402 U.S. 424, 29 L. Ed. 2d 9, 91 S. Ct. 1535 (1971): in this 4-4 decision by Chief Justice Burger the Court held the Fifth Amendment's self-incrimination clause neither vitiates a California statute that requires a motorist involved in an accident to stop and identify himself nor requires a restriction on the prosecutorial use of the information that the statute compels a motorist to supply. (Mr. Justice Harlan finds that the statute in fact does involve self-incrimination. However, he is "constrained to hold that the presence of a 'real' and not 'imaginary' risk of self-incrimination is not a sufficient predicate for extending the privilege against self-incrimination to regulatory schemes of the character in this case." The *Marchetti-Grosso* line of cases—gamblers' wagering stamps—are distinguished from the present case.)   (ILECJ)

call letters: the letters and/or numbers assigned to police radio transmitters and/or transceivers, fixed or mobile   (LEV)

call signals: coded signals used by law enforcement to transmit short messages by radio or other means of communication where speed and confidentiality are needed. *See* signal, ten-dash   (LEV)

Camara v. Municipal Court, 387 U.S. 523, 18 L. Ed. 2d 930, 87 S. Ct. 1727; See v. Seattle, 387 U.S. 541, 18 L. Ed. 2d 943, 87 S. Ct. 1737 (1967): speaking for a six-justice majority, Mr. Justice White's opinion held that health and fire inspectors are no longer entitled to search a home or business without warrant or consent. (Frank v. Maryland, 359 U.S. 360, was expressly overruled. The two cases establish a diluted-probable cause standard for such search warrants so it can be said that probable cause to issue a warrant exists if reasonable legislation or administration standards for conducting an inspection of the area are satisfied. Note should be taken, moreover, that the decisions hold that different official intrusions upon privacy not directed at obtaining criminal evidence constitute "searches" for Fourth Amendment purposes, but are not subject to the same probable cause standards as the ordinary search in criminal cases.) (ILECJ)

camera, pinhole: a camera which has a pinhole aperture in place of a lens (MPPF)

camera angle: the point of view from which a subject is photographed (MPPF)

camera obscura: a darkened room in which an image is formed on one wall by light entering a small hole in the opposite wall (MPPF)

Cameron v. Johnson, 390 U.S. 611, 20 L. Ed. 2d 182, 88 S. Ct. 1335 (1966): the Court held 7-2 that while picketing cannot be made a crime, blocking the entrance to a public building can constitute a criminal act (ILECJ)

Camorra: an underworld, secret, criminal organization which arose in the city of Naples in 1830 and continued to thrive until about 1922. While the Camorra was identified with the underworld of Neapolitan life it also had contacts with civil, political, and religious authorities during its varied career. It represented a nineteenth-century version of an entrenched "racket" protected by civil and political authorities (DOS)

camouflage: disguise; to conceal the ordinary appearance or hide by a counterfeit appearance (CDTP)

cancel: (1) to annul (CDTP) (2) to blot out or obliterate (CDTP)

candid photography: a term applied to pictures taken without posing the subject. The object is to catch natural expression (MPPF)

candle: a unit of luminous intensity; approximately equal to the intensity of a 7/8-inch sperm candle burning at 120 grains per hour (MPPF)

candle-meter-second: a unit of exposure consisting of the light from a standard candle burning for one second at a distance of one meter from the photographic plate (MPPF)

candlepower: luminous intensity expressed in terms of the standard candle (MPPF)

canister: (1) a special short-range antipersonnel projectile designed to be fired from guns, both artillery and small arms. It consists of a casing of light sheet metal, which is loaded with preformed submissiles such as small steel balls. The basing is designed so that it opens at, or just beyond, the muzzle of the gun. The submissiles are then dispersed in a cone, giving effective coverage of the area immediately in front of the gun. Another term for canister is "case shot" (DWMT) (2) in certain special types of projectiles, the subassembly or inner container in which the payload is contained, such as canister or smoke (DWMT) (3) that part of a gas mask containing a filter for the removal of poisonous gases from the air being inhaled (DWMT)

canister cartridge: a cartridge assembled with a projectile consisting of a light metal case filled with steel balls, steel fragments, or steel slugs. When fired, the projectile breaks upon leaving the muzzle of the weapon, and the contents scatter in the manner of a shotgun cartridge (DWMT)

canister shot: See canister, sense 1 (Canister shot was first used in about 1400.) (CWMT)

cannabism: poisoning with hemp or hashish (CDTP)

cannelure: (1) a groove in a bullet that contains a lubricant or into which the cartridge case is crimped; a groove in a cartridge case providing a purchase for the extractor; extractor groove (DWMT) (2) a ringlike groove in the rotating band of a gun projectile to lessen the resistance offered to the gun rifling and to prevent fringing. (DWMT) (3) a ringlike groove cut into the outside surface of a water-cooled machine-gun barrel into which packing is placed to prevent the escape of water from the breech end of the water jacket (DWMT) (4) the grooving of a blade to lighten it without impairing its stiffness (DWMT)

cannibalize: to remove serviceable parts from one item of equipment in order to install them on another item of equipment (DWMT)

canon: a standard or principle accepted as fundamentally true and in conformity with good usage and practice (LEV)

Canons of Police Ethics: standards, principles, and policies governing the conduct of law enforcement officers. It was adopted by the IACP at its 1957 conference. It embraces the following areas of conduct: Article 1. Primary responsibility of job; Article 2. Limitations of authority; Article 3. Duty to be familiar with the law and with the responsibility of self and other public officials; Article 4. Utilization of proper means to gain proper ends; Article 5. Cooperation with public officials in the discharge of their authorized duties; Article 6. Private conduct; Article 7. Conduct toward the public; Article 8. Conduct in arresting and dealing with law violators; Article 9. Gifts and favors; Article 10. Presentation of evidence; Article 11. Attitudes toward profession (ILECJ)

cap: (1) a container for fulminate or other explosive used to ignite the powder for percussion guns (CDTP) (2) the cover for a gun part such as the grip or butt (CDTP)

capacitance: the property of two or more objects which enables them to store electrical energy in an electric field between them. The basic measurement unit is the farad. Capacitance varies inversely with the distance between the objects, hence the change of capacitance with relative motion is greater the nearer one object is to

the other (TDIAS)

capacitance alarm system: an alarm system in which a protected object is electrically connected as a capacitance sensor. The approach of an intruder causes sufficient change in capacitance to upset the balance of the system and initiate an alarm signal. Also called proximity alarm system (TDIAS)

capacitance sensor: a sensor which responds to a change in capacitance in a field containing a protected object or in a field within a protected area (TDIAS)

capacitor: an electrical circuit element consisting of one or more pairs of plates separated by some insulating material; sometimes called a condenser but the term capacitor is preferred since it is more specific (MPPF)

capacity, system: the power of a system to store data in files, accept transactions, process files, and furnish results (ADPS)

capias [Lat, lit that you take]: a generic name for writs (usually addressed to the sheriff), ordering the arrest of the person named

capias ad respondendum, writ of: a writ issued to the sheriff commanding him to seize the body of the defendant for failure to appear in answer to a summons (CDTP)

capias pro fine: a writ for the arrest of a person who had not paid a fine (CDTP)

capital crime: any crime punishable by death.

capital offense: capital crime

capital punishment: See punishment, capital

capitulate: to draw up an agreement; to surrender conditionally (CDTP)

capped bullet: a bullet having a protective cap of harder metal on its nose (DWMT)

capper: (1) a person employed by an attorney to solicit business (CDTP) (2) Captain: An administrative title or rank, above that of lieutenant and below that of major. Depending on the organizational structure of the agency, the captain usu. has command over a company, shift, special operation or detail   (LEV)

caption: title or heading of a document   (CDTP)

caption and direction: captions or directions are essential parts of search warrants and were held so at common law. Requirements that the caption run in the name of a state or government must be met, and in some jurisdictions a caption with the name of the state is held not to run in the state's name although the opposite is held in other jurisdictions (consult statute). The warrant must be directed to some peace officer or officers having authority to execute the warrant, the direction being to officers of the same state in the county in which it is issued for service; and hence, a warrant directed to any sheriff, marshal, or policeman without specifying the county is invalid unless statutes provide otherwise, and where the statute requires the direction be "to the sheriff of the county or to any constable or marshal of the town or city," a direction to "any constable" is insufficient. Under the federal practice the warrant must be directed to an officer or class of officers any one of whom is authorized to execute it (300 Fed. 21)   (CDTP)

capucine: a band holding the barrel of a gun or pistol to the stock   (DWMT)

carat: a weight of four grains

carbine: a rifle of short length and light weight. It was formerly used chiefly by cavalry and mounted infantry, but in recent years has been used extensively by service troops and others. In the 17th century, carbines were sometimes smoothbores of a type later called "musketoons"   (DWMT)

carbine butt: a detachable buttstock that can be attached to a pistol so that the weapon can be used as a carbine   (DWMT)

carbineer, carabiniere: a term derived from the French *carabinier*, or cavalry soldier armed with a carbine. In modern Italy a *carabiniere* is a policeman   (DWMT)

carbolic: a poisonous acid; Phenol   (CDTP)

carbonates: a term applied to certain alkaline salts, such as potassium carbonate and sodium carbonate, used as an accelerator in a film developer   (MPPF)

carbon monoxide poisoning: the result of the inhalation of the odorless poisonous element contained in illuminating and exhaust gases of automobiles or incompletely oxidized coal in a dampered furnace. The victim is profoundly unconscious, the skin is red, and breathing deep and noisy. The pulse is full and rapid (CDTP)

carbon process: referring to a process using a printing paper, the final image of which depends on the thickness of the gelatin layer in which finely ground carbon or other pigment is suspended   (MPPF)

carbro process: a combination of the carbon and bromide methods for making a print   (MPPF)

cardiac: relating to the heart: A sufferer of heart disease   (CDTP)

cardinal points: in a thick lens or lens system, the two principal points, the two nodal points and two focal points   (MPPF)

Cardozo, Benjamin Nathan (*1870–1938*): an associate justice of the United States Supreme Court from 1932 to 1938. He interpreted law according to its effects on society

card punch: a device for punching data in cards. Examples are: simple hand punches, keyboard print-punches, paper-tape-to-card converter punches, and high-speed punches for magnetic-tape-to-card conversion, or for direct output from the processor   (ADPS)

Cardwell v. Lewis, 417 U.S. 583, 41 L. Ed. 2d 325, 94 S. Ct. 2464 (1974): in a plurality opinion, 5–4, with Mr. Justice Powell concurring to reach the result, the Court held police may search an impounded vehicle following the owner's arrest for murder (ILECJ)

carnal: pertains to "actions of the flesh"; sensual; sexual   (LEV)

carnal abuse: an act of debauchery of the female sexual organs by those of the male which does not amount to penetration

carnal knowledge: sexual intercourse

carnally know: sexual bodily connection. Generally applied to the act of the male in sexual intercourse in violation of law (CDTP)

carousal: a loud or boisterous drinking incident   (LEV)

carrier current transmitter: a device which transmits alarm signals from a sensor to a control unit via the standard ac power lines   (TDIAS)

carrier ring: a ring that carries the breechlock of a gun when it is withdrawn from the breech and swung out of the way during loading   (DWMT)

Carroll v. United States, 267 U.S. 132, 69 L. Ed. 543, 45 S. Ct. 280 (1925): in a 7–2 opinion Chief Justice Taft held that a moving vehicle can be stopped, and searched on probable cause that at the time it is carrying contraband or other illegally possessed goods. (The Chief Justice brought out that there "is a necessary difference between a search of a store, dwelling house, or other structure in respect to which a proper official warrant readily may be obtained, and a search of ship, motor boat, wagon, or automobile, for contraband goods, where it is not practicable to secure a warrant because the vehicle can be quickly moved out of the locality or jurisdiction in which the warrant must be sought.")   (ILECJ)

carry: (1) digit to be added to the next higher column when the sum of digits in one column equals or exceeds the number base (ADPS) (2) process of forwarding the carry digit (ADPS) (3) to hold a

weapon or standard in such a way that it is practically vertical at the right side. The term was once used in commands such as "carry arms" or "carry sabers" (DWMT)

cartridge: (1) a light-tight container which may be loaded with film in the dark and placed in the camera in daylight (MPPF) (2) the container for an explosive charge which may or may not include the bullet. The modern cartridge is placed in the gun, ready to fire, but the early cartridge was broken and the contents emptied into the chamber or barrel   (CDTP)

cartridge belt: a belt having loops or pockets for cartridges or clips of cartridges   (DWMT)

cartridge box: a leather box used to carry cartridges. It is suspended by a strap or worn on the belt. Cartridge boxes were displaced by the cartridge belt   (DWMT)

cartridge case: (1) a container used to hold the propelling charge. In fixed ammunition it also holds the projectile and a primer (DWMT) (2) a metal container for the explosive charge   (CDTP)

cartridge clip: a metallic device used to contain rifle or pistol cartridges for ease of loading into a rifle or an automatic pistol   (DWMT)

cartridge link: a unit part of a link belt by means of which ammunition is fed into automatic weapons   (DWMT)

case: a lawsuit or item of legal work. A case previously decided is a precedent case and a case on which a lawyer or judge is presently working is a problem case.

case law: judicial precedent generated as a by-product of the decisions which courts have made in resolving unique disputes, as distinguished from statutes and constitutions. Case law concerns concrete facts. Statutes and constitutions are written in the abstract

cassette: a film cartridge or magazine   (MPPF)

Cassidy, Butch (Robert Parker) (*1866–1908*): together with Harry

Longbaugh ("The Sundance Kid") he formed an outlaw gang that robbed trains and banks throughout the Southwest. While in the United States, he established the Hole-in-the-Wall, a vast mountain fortress which protected outlaws from law officials. He was reported to have been killed by Bolivian soldiers in San Vicente

cast: (1) to mold; to take the impression of certain objects and markings by use of a substance which will harden and retain its shape. Used in law enforcement to record in physical form such things as footprints in soil, tire impressions, tool marks, etc. Many casting materials are used. Plaster of paris is one commonly used for casting impressions in soil. A material called "moulage" is used where fine detail is needed and the surface is rigid (LEV) (2) the physical object or reproduction made by casting (LEV)

castrate: to remove the testicles or ovaries. (CDTP)

casus: a case; an event; a happening. (CDTP)

catalepsy: an abnormal condition where a physical posture is maintained and the muscles become rigid; usu. the subject loses consciousness. This is common in cases of hysteria and schizophrenia (LEV)

catalysis, catalyst: a catalyst is any substance which promotes a chemical reaction by its presence without itself being used up in the reaction. This effect is called *catalysis* (FS)

catch: a part of the mechanism for holding another part in a desired position, as the bayonet catch, safety catch, locking catch, etc. (CDTP)

catch lights: the small reflections of a light source, found in the eyes of a portrait subject (MPPF)

catheter: a slender, flexible instrument used to insert into body passages to examine or drain. Usu. refers to the instrument used to pass through the uretha to drain urine from the bladder (LEV)

caucus: a local political meeting (CDTP)

causa: (1) a suit or action (CDTP) (2) a cause (CDTP) (3) a reason (CDTP)

causa causans: the immediate or operating cause

causal: relating to cause, or being in the relation of a cause

causa mortis: in anticipation of death (CDTP)

causation, multiple, theory of: the theory that no one "cause" in any process leading to a given event is the sole cause thereof; a further theory that many factors have interacted to produce the actual result at any given moment; that at a given moment many factors in any given situation are interacting in a field from which the succeeding situation-process will be derived, and that many separable factors may be indispensable to a given effect but produce their unique resultant situation-process only when thus combined in this particular and unique configuration (DOS)

cause: the matter for decision in the court (LEV)

cause, challenge of jurors for: each side in a trial (prosecution and defense) have the right, prescribed by law, to challenge prospective jurors (veniremen) for cause, such as prior convictions, unsound mind, kinship to one of the parties, bias or prejudice, etc. If the court agrees with the challenge the prospective juror will not be allowed to serve on the jury. *See* challenge of jurors (LEV)

caveat: a formal notice given by a party interested to a court or judge against the performance of certain judicial acts (CDTP)

Caveat Emptor [*Lat, lit let the buyer beware*]: the use of this formula under certain legally qualified conditions enables the seller to decline legal responsibility for the quality or quantity of his ware. It does not, however, apply to the question of the title of property   (DOS)

cavere: to beware; to take care; cautious   (CDTP)

cease-and-desist order: an order issued by an administrative agency to an individual, firm, or corporation requiring that a particular fiscal or business practice be discontinued, and continuing in effect until reversed by a court of competent jurisdiction—commonly used by agencies charged with the regulation of business, as the Federal Trade Commission, a State public service, or railway, commission   (DAP)

celluloid: a transparent film made from cellulose nitrate   (MPPF)

cellulose nitrate: any of several esters of nitric acid used as explosives or propellants and produced by treating cotton or some other form of cellulose with a mixture of nitric and sulfuric acids. It is also called "nitrocellulose"
(DWMT)

Celsius: the preferred name of the Centigrade thermometer scale
(MPPF)

censorship: examination by a public authority of any printed matter, telephonic or telegraphic dispatch, wireless dispatch or broadcast, or dramatic or similar spectacle, prior to publication or transmission, with a view to making such deletions or revisions as the preservation of military secrets, public morality, the interests of religion, or some other consideration may require. Except in time of war or national emergency, governmental agencies in states with an English common-law background rarely exert a censorship over printed matter or over instrumentalities for transmitting intelligence. In this respect they differ sharply from the governments of many contemporary states and particularly from authoritarian governments under which censorship is constant and

universal. Liberals have always regarded the absence of public censorship as a basic condition for the exercise of the twin rights of freedom of speech and the press, and as necessary to the maintenance of popular government
(DAP)

censure: the formal resolution of a legislative, administrative, or other body reprimanding an administrative officer or one of its own members for specified conduct
(DAP)

census: a periodic enumeration of the population of a political unit. The data secured ordinarily include not only the simple number of persons, but also facts concerning sex, age, race, and a variety of other characteristics which may be very inclusive. The oldest continuous genuine census in the world is that of the United States, which was inaugurated at the beginning of its independent national life in 1790, and has been conducted regularly at ten-year intervals ever since   (DOS)

census tract: a relatively small, permanent, homogenous area, having a population usually between 3,000 and 6,000, into which certain large cities (and sometimes their adjacent areas) have been subdivided for statistical and local administrative purposes through the cooperation of a local committee and with the approval of the U.S. Bureau of the Census. In 1940 there were 60 American cities with census tract systems   (DOS)

center-fire: when said of a cartridge, one having the primer in the center of the base of the case. When said of a firearm, one using center-fire cartridges. Center-fire is contrasted to rimfire, in which the primer is in the rim of the base of the case   (DWMT)

Centigrade scale: (1) a temperature scale in which 0 degrees represents the ice point and 100 degrees the steam point. Celsius is now the preferred term in technical use (MPPF) (2) to convert to Fahrenheit from Centigrade use the formula: Centigrade reading X 9/5 plus 32 (LEV)

centimeter: one-hundredth of a meter; 2/5 of an inch or 0.3937 inch. An inch is the equivalent of 2.540 centimeters (CDTP)

Central Intelligence Agency (CIA): an agency created by the National Security Act of 1947 to coordinate intelligence services of federal agencies, to evaluate and interpret intelligence relating to national defense, and to make such intelligence available, when appropriate, within the Government. It operates under the direction of the National Security Council (DAP)

central pocket loop: a fingerprint pattern. Consists of at least one recurving ridge or an obstruction at right angles to the line of flow, with two deltas, between which, when an imaginary line is drawn, no recurving ridge within the pattern area is cut or touched. It is classified as a whorl (LEV)

central station: a control center to which alarm systems in a subscriber's premises are connected, where circuits are supervised, and where personnel are maintained continuously to record and investigate alarm or trouble signals. Facilities are provided for the reporting of alarms to police and fire departments or to other outside agencies (TDIAS)

central station alarm system: an alarm system, or group of systems, the activities of which are transmitted to, recorded in, maintained by, and supervised from a central station. This differs from proprietary alarm systems in that the central station is owned and operated independently of the subscriber (TDIAS)

centrifuge: an instrument for rapidly separating the constituents of a suspension of a solid in a liquid, or of one liquid in another with which it is immiscible (e.g., blood, milk, muddy water), by whirling it round in a suitable container, so that separation by centrifugal force is much faster than it would be by gravity alone (FS)

Cepa Paper: a Kodak trade name for a tough tissue paper for diffusion purposes or vignettes (MPPF)

certified: authenticated; testified to in writing (CDTP)

certified check: a check issued by a bank which insures that the account on which it is drawn has sufficient funds to cover the check, i.e., the bank certifies the check will be honored (LEV)

certified copy: a copy to which is added a certificate under hand and official seal of the public officer authorized to certify same (CDTP)

Certiorari [Lat, lit to be more fully informed]: (1) an original writ or action whereby a cause is removed from an inferior to a superior court for review. The record of the proceedings is then transmitted to the superior court (2) a discretionary appellate jurisdiction that is invoked by a petition for certiorari, which the appellate court may grant or deny in its discretion. A dominant avenue to the United States Supreme Court

cestui que trust: person for whose benefit a trust is created; a beneficiary under a trust (CDTP)

chaining: (1) for some processors, instructions in sequence that have sequential addresses (the address register contains the address of the next operand wanted after the preceding instruction is executed) can be "chained" together and the operand address(es) omitted (ADPS) (2) printed listings of transactions each of which contains a reference to the preceding transaction for the record involved; may also have an index to the most recent transaction for every record in the file (ADPS)

chain of command: the administrative arrangement (order) of officials of an agency through which orders or instructions are passed

(downward or upward)   (LEV)
chain reaction: a reaction (often explosively rapid) in which the energy liberated by the reaction of the first few molecules serves to "trigger off" the reaction of others, and so on progressively until all of the available material has reacted   (FS)
challenge: an objection taken by either party to one or more or all of the jurors who are to try a person accused   (CDTP)
challenge of jurors: action on the part of either side of a trial by jury of the prospective jurors (veniremen) to prevent the venireman from serving on the jury. There are two kinds: Peremptory—no reasons must be given for objecting to the prospective juror—the number allowed to each side is fixed by law, and Challenge for Cause—the reason for objecting to the person as a juror must be given (such as prior conviction, kinship to parties, bias or prejudice, etc.). No limit is placed on the number to be so challenged. See peremptory challenge; cause, challenge of juror for
                                (LEV)
chamber: (1) any of the compartments in the cartridge cylinder of a revolver (DWMT) (2) to insert a round of ammunition in the chamber of a firearm or gun (DWMT) (3) the enlarged or diminished rear part of a cannon which holds the powder (DWMT) (4) in certain types of old ordinance, a detachable device which contained the charge. It was inserted at the breech of the weapon   (DWMT)   (5) in military mining, a cavity for a powder charge. It is located in a mine shaft or gallery   (DWMT)
chamber pressure: pressure created in a gun's chamber by the expanding gases of the propellant charge
                                (DWMT)
chambers: the official private office or quarters of a judge. The office of the judge when he is not in the court room   (LEV)

Chambers v. Maroney, 399 U.S. 42 (1970): a U.S. Supreme Court landmark case on searches of automobiles, holding that if the officer has probable cause to believe that a car contains evidence of crime and the car is mobile he may search the car at the scene or move it to the police station and search it there, in both instances without a warrant. If he impounds the car he should obtain a search warrant   (LEV)
champerty: the carrying of a suit in the name of another, but at one's own expense, with the view of receiving as compensation a certain share of the avails of the suit
chancery procedure: formerly the procedure in Chancery Courts where the King's representative (the chancellor) presided in cases in which were involved certain persons, usually women or children, who were unable under existing laws to protect themselves. Today such procedure has been adopted by the juvenile court in assuming the guardianship of the delinquent child and a protective interest in his welfare
                                (DOS)
change file: a list of the transactions effectively processed against a master file   (ADPS)
change of venue: a suit which is initiated in one county or district may be changed to another county or district for trial purposes (e.g., the Angela Davis trial and John Linley Frazier trial, transferred from the county of initial jurisdiction to the County of Santa Clara)
changes, pending: transactions not successfully processed against the file because of mistakes in data, program errors, records not yet established or already deleted from file, account "frozen," or record was moved within the file and, therefore, was not available in the expected sequence (ADPS)
channel: a path along which data, particularly a series of digits or characters, may flow or be stored

either in a particular set of equipment or a communication network. In storage that is serial by character and parallel by bit (for example, a magnetic tape or drum in some coded decimal processors), a channel comprises several parallel tracks (ADPS)
Chaplinsky v. New Hampshire, 315 U.S. 568, 86 L. Ed. 1031, 62 S. Ct. 766 (1942): the Court held unanimously that states may "punish 'fighting words'." (ILECJ)

character: (1) evidence of the character of a person is admissible in the following cases: *a.* the fact that the defendant has a good character for the trait of character involved in the crime charged may be shown, but the state cannot show that he has a bad character, unless his character is itself a fact in issue, or unless evidence has been given that he has a good character, in which case evidence that he has a bad character is admissible; *b.* the character of the .deceased as a violent and dangerous man may be shown in prosecutions for homicide, on the question whether the defendant acted in self-defense. The term "character" as used in the rules above stated means "reputation" as distinguished from "disposition"; *c.* a witness may be impeached by proof of his bad character for truth and veracity and a witness who has been impeached may be to a degree rehabilitated by proof that his reputation for truth and veracity is good; *d.* in crimes where character is an element, for example, in some sex crimes, the prosecution must prove that the female was of previous chaste character (CDTP) (2) one of a set of elementary symbols, such as those corresponding to the keys of a typewriter. The symbols may include decimal digits 0 through 9, the letters A through Z, punctuation marks, operation symbols, and any other single symbol that a processor can read, store, or write (ADPS) (3) a binary representation of such a symbol. A correct representation of a character in any media is a *valid* character, whereas a combination of bits or punches not representing an accepted character is called *illegal.* For example, in punched-card code, the 0 and 2 punch represent S, a legal character, but the 2 and 3 punch are invalid because they do not represent a character (ADPS)

character evidence: in a criminal trial it is evidence introduced to show good or bad character of the accused. Stress is on the moral qualities of the person. The law in some states provides that no matter how good the character of an accused is it will not in itself be a bar to conviction if the violation is proven beyond a reasonable doubt. (LEV)

characteristic curve: a curve plotted to show the relation of density to exposure. Sometimes referred to as the H and D curve (MPPF)

character reader: a device for scanning and identifying characters on documents that can also be read by people. *Magnetic-ink* readers work with specially-shaped characters printed in metallic ink that is magnetized before reading. *Optical* readers use ordinary-shaped characters printed in ordinary inks (ADPS)

charge: (1) a given quantity of explosive either by itself or contained in a bomb, projectile, mine, or the like or used as the propellant for a bullet or projectile (DWMT) (2) that with which a bomb, projectile, mine, or the like is filled, as a charge of explosive, thermite, etc. Also called the "fill," "filler," or "filling." (DWMT) (3) in small arms, a cartridge or round of ammunition (DWMT) (4) to fill with a charge (DWMT) (5) to place a charge in a gun chamber (DWMT) (6) the act of rushing toward an enemy; an attack (DWMT) (7) facts or alleged facts, pertaining to an accused, in a complaint, information or indictment (LEV) (8) instructions on the law given to a jury by the trial judge which the jury should follow in arriving at the verdict (LEV)

charging: the process of formal criminal accusation usually involving the prosecutor and sometimes a grand jury. The term is also used to mean the judge's instruction of a jury on matters of law

chart: a drawing or sketch showing the location of objects and items and the relationship one to another in a crime scene or other place pertinent to an investigation (LEV)

charter: written grant or privilege (LEV)

Chase, Salmon Portland (1803–1873): American statesman. U.S. Senator from Ohio (1849–55, 1861); anti-slavery leader. U.S. Secretary of the Treasury (1861–64); responsible for national bank system (estab. 1863). Chief Justice of the United States after 1864. His dissenting opinion in Slaughterhouse Cases subsequently became accepted position of the courts as to restrictive force of Fourteenth Amendment. Presided fairly over impeachment trial of Pres. Johnson. Chase earnestly sought the presidency four times, but was never nominated (CVDE)

Chase, Samuel (1741–1811): American Revolutionary patriot, signer of Declaration of Independence, Associate Justice of U.S. Supreme Court (1796–1811). Impeached in 1804 on charge of political partiality, but acquitted (CVDE)

chaste: innocent of voluntary unlawful sexual intercourse. In the seduction statutes it means actual virtue in conduct and principle; one who is not chaste but reforms becomes chaste under these statues

chastity: purity from all unlawful intercourse (CDTP)

chattel: item, article, or piece of personal property that is somewhat transferable

chattel mortgage: a mortgage on chattels, usually as security for the payment of a debt

cheating: the fraudulent pecuniary injury of another by some token, device, or practice calculated to deceive (CDTP)

cheating at common law: a cheat at common law is the fraudulent obtaining of another's property by means of some false symbol or token, such as, when not false, is commonly accepted by the public for what it purports to represent; provided the act does not amount to a felony, the crime is a misdemeanor (CDTP)

cheating by false pretense: obtaining property by false pretenses, not amounting to a common law cheat, is not a crime at common law, but is generally made so by statute. The statutes generally define the crime substantially as the knowingly and designedly obtaining of the property of another by false pretenses, with intent to defraud. (1) The pretense must be a false representation as to some part or existing fact or circumstance, and not a mere expression of opinion or a promise. (2) It must be knowingly false. (3) It must be made with intent to defraud. (4) Some cases hold it must calculated to defraud. (5) It must deceive and defraud; that is, it must be believed, and the property must be parted with, because of the representation (CDTP)

check: (1) an order in writing on a bank for the payment of a definite sum of money (CDTP) (2) a means of verifying the accuracy of data transmitted, manipulated, or stored by a unit or device in a processor (ADPS)

check, mathematical: a check making use of mathematical identities or other properties—for example, checking multiplication by verifying that $A \cdot B = B \cdot A$ (ADPS)

check, summation: a redundant check in which groups of digits are summed, usu. without regard for overflow, and that sum checked against a previously computed sum to verify accuracy (ADPS)

check digit: a check scheme that attaches one or more extra digits to a word according to certain rules so that, if any digit changes, the mistake can be detected (ADPS)

checkering: roughening of the wood on a gun for ornamentation or to give the hand a better grip on its surface (CDTP)

checks, fraudulent or worthless: bank checks which are not honored (paid) by the bank on which drawn, usu. because of insufficient funds which the maker (or drawer) has on deposit. There are "NSF" (not sufficient funds) checks and "no account" checks (where the maker does not have an account at the bank). In such cases the law usu. requires that fraudulent intent be shown. This may be proven by the method of operation of the check passer. In "NSF" cases it may be established by writing the maker of the check a registered letter demanding that the check be made good. If the check is not redeemed within a specified number of days the presumption of fraudulent intent is created by law. Many techniques are used by "professional" worthless check passers. Their operations are widespread and their annual "take" runs into the millions of dollars. *See* national fraudulent check file (LEV)

cheek-piece: a portion of the stock of a long gun for supporting the face in the proper position for aiming (CDTP)

chemical agent: a solid, liquid, or gas which through its chemical properties produces lethal or damaging effects on man, animals, plants, or material or produces a screening or signaling smoke (DWMT)

chemical ammunition: any ammunition, such as bombs, projectiles, bullets, flares, and the like, containing a chemical agent or agents. Such agents include war gases, smokes, and incendiaries (DWMT)

chemical grenade: the general term for any hand grenade or rifle grenade charged with a chemical agent (DWMT)

chemical operations: the employment of chemical agents (excluding riot-control agents) (1) to kill, or incapacitate for a significant period of time, man or animals and (2) to deny or hinder the use of areas, facilities, or materials (DWMT)

chemical spray: aerial release, or a device for aerial release, of liquid war gas for casualty effect or of liquid smokes for aerial smoke screens (DWMT)

Chemical Transportation Emergency Center: *See* CHEMTREC. (LEV)

CHEMTREC (Chemical Transportation Emergency Center): operated by the Manufacturing Chemists Association. Information involving hazardous chemicals in an accident may be obtained by dialing (toll-free) number (800) 424-9300. District of Columbia callers dial 483-7616 (LEV)

chevron: a type of insignia, often in the shape of a V, that indicates rank, class, length of service, etc. (DWMT)

Chicago Boys' Court: this court was established in 1914 as the first special court for minor boys, ages 17 through 20, who were over the age for juvenile court jurisdiction. (LCC)

Chicago Seven, the: the trial of David T. Dellinger, Thomas E. Hayden, Rennard C. Davis, Abbott Hoffman, Jerry C. Rubin, Lee Weiner, and John R. Eroines on the charge of crossing state lines to incite riots in 1968 (at the time of the Democratic National

Convention). On Feb. 18, 1970 the first five listed persons were found guilty. All seven plus two attorneys were sentenced on contempt of court due to their actions during the trial   (LEV)

chicanery: strategem; trickery. Sharp practice   (CDTP)

chief, case in: the case in chief is the principal cause of action against a person. The main body of evidence used for the purpose of proving a defendant guilty (LEV)

chief, declaration in: a statement for the principal cause of action (LEV)

chief, examination in: the first questioning of a witness by the side which called him as a witness (LEV)

chief justice: the official head of a collegially organized court of justice. The Chief Justice of the Supreme Court of the United States presides over the hearing of cases and over meetings of justices for the purpose of reaching decisions; assigns the writing of opinions to different justices who voted with him in making up the majority in deciding a case, himself taking his turn; appoints members of the Court to consider revisions of the rules of procedure; and performs other administrative duties. He presides over the Senate when the President or Vice President is impeached. The following named jurists have held office: John Jay, 1789-95; John Rutledge, 1795-96; Oliver Ellsworth, 1796-1800; John Marshall, 1801-35; Roger B. Taney, 1835-64; Salmon P. Chase, 1864-73; Morrison R. Waite, 1874-88; Melville W. Fuller, 1888-1910; Edward D. White, 1910-21; William Howard Taft, 1921-30; Charles E. Hughes, 1930-41; Harlan F. Stone, 1941-46; Fred M. Vinson, 1946-1953; Earl Warren, 1953-1968; Warren Burger (1969-   )   (DAP)

child: a person under the age of puberty. A child under the age of 7 years is usu. not capable of committing crime. A child of the age of 12 years is presumed to be incapable of crime unless it can be proved the child has sufficient mental capacity to know the wrongfulness of the act charged (CDTP)

child molester: one who injures or has questionable sexual dealings with a child. The child molester who is a sex deviate is called a pedophile. The molested child may be subject to rape, sodomy, indecent exposure, or murder. The pedophile preys on children. *See* pedophilia   (LEV)

children's courts: special courts established to solve the unusual legal and judicial problems of juvenile delinquency. Although a considerable body of protective legislation for the administration of juvenile crime was enacted in the Jacksonian period, it was not until the late 19th century that special children's tribunals were founded to handle such cases. In 1877 Massachusetts and New York provided for separate judicial terms for children's cases. In 1899 special children's courts were set up for the first time in Illinois and Colorado. It had now come to be accepted that juvenile lawbreakers were to be considered apart from adult criminals, and subject to the special guardianship and administration of children's courts. The juvenile court in Denver, Col., presided over by Judge Ben Lindsey, achieved national fame after 1901. In 1906 a children's court was established in Washington, D.C. by Congress. Thereafter, such courts were set up in most of the states of the Union. A system of jurisprudence developed which emphasized informal procedures, separate hearings, psychiatric care, and probation and parole provisions. The medical and psychological sciences have contributed much to the concepts of prevention, therapy, and penology   (DOAH)

chilled shot: hard shot (for shotguns, etc.) made with a lead and antimony alloy (LEV)

Chimel v. California, 395 U.S. 752, 23 L. Ed. 2d 685, 89 S. Ct. 2034 (1969): Mr. Justice Stewart held, 6-2, that a search incident to a lawful arrest in a home must be limited to "the area into which an arrestee might reach in order to grab a weapon or other evidentiary items." Such a search, the majority says, does not include drawers or other closed or concealed areas in the same room, nor does it include adjacent rooms [*Chimel* expressly overrules *Harris* (1947), and *Rabinowitz* (1950) that permitted more latitude as to the permissible area of a search. *Chimel* also lends force to the view that *Cooper* v. *California* does not overrule *Preston* (1963). *Chimel* speaks of "homes." But some courts apply the rule to other places such as automobiles. Consult the prosecutor, or local police legal advisor.] (ILECJ)

chloral hydrate: a sleep-producing drug, white and crystalline in form. Sometimes referred to as "knock-out drops" (if in solution) (LEV)

chloride paper: a photographic printing paper in which the emulsion is made sensitive largely through silver chloride. Usu. chloride papers are printed by contact and require comparatively longer exposure than bromide or chlorobromide paper (MPPF)

chloro-bromide paper: a photographic printing paper used basically for enlarging. Its emulsion contains a mixture of silver chloride and silver bromide (MPPF)

chloroform: a volatile liquid, the fumes of which are an anesthetic. Not presently used much for this purpose by the medical profession. Composed of chlorine, hydrogen, and carbon. Now used as a constituent of liniments. Overdose of the vapors is poisonous (LEV)

choke: (1) to stop breathing by stricture or pressure upon the throat (2) the muzzle end of the gun barrel of a shotgun is made smaller than the remainder of the barrel so as to regulate the density of the shot pattern—control the spread of the shot as they travel through and leave the gun barrel. The common types are the following: full choke, modified choke (LEV)

chose in action: a thing in action; the right to receive or recover a big debt or damages by action at law (CDTP)

christian name: the baptismal name distinct from the surname (CDTP)

chromatic aberration: a defect in a lens which prevents it from focusing different-colored light rays in the same plane (MPPF)

chromatograph: an instrument used in a crime laboratory to analyze gaseous substances, or compounds which can be readily converted into gases (LEV)

C.I.A.: Central Intelligence Agency

cinching: tightening a roll of film by holding the spool and pulling the free end; invariably results in parallel scratches or abrasion marks (MPPF)

cipher: any cryptographic system in which arbitrary symbols represent units of plain text of regular length, usu. single letters, or in which units of plain text are rearranged, or both, in accordance with certain predetermined rules (DWMT)

circle of confusion: an optical term describing the size of an image point formed by a lens (MPPF)

circle of illumination: the total image area of a lens, only part of which is actually used in taking a picture (MPPF)

circuit: a division of the state or county appointed for a judge to visit for the trial of causes (CDTP)

Circuit Court of Appeals: a part of the judicial system of the United States (Federal Courts) known as the U.S. Court of Appeals. There is one for each of 11 districts in the United States (LEV)

circumstances: the facts surrounding an event or deed

circumstantial: depending upon incidents other than the main fact; pertaining to circumstances (LEV)

circumstantial evidence: evidence from which a fact is reasonably inferred, although not directly proven

circumvention: the defeat of an alarm system by the avoidance of its detection devices, such as by jumping over a pressure sensitive mat, by entering through a hole cut in an unprotected door, or by keeping outside the range of an ultrasonic motion detector. Circumvention contrasts with spoofing (TDIAS)

citation: an order, issued by the police, to appear before a magistrate or judge at a later date, usu. used for minor violations since it avoids the taking of suspect into immediate custody

cite: (1) to summon (2) to read or refer to (legal) authorities, in support of a position

citizen's arrest: the arrest of a person by a citizen (not a law enforcement officer) for a felony, without a warrant. A citizen is not authorized to make an arrest by means of a warrant of arrest. In some common law states (if not changed by statute) an arrest for a breach of the peace committed in his presence can be made by a citizen (LEV)

city council: the principal deliberative body of a municipal corporation with power to pass ordinances, levy taxes, appropriate funds, and generally oversee city government (DAP)

city court: a court which tries persons accused of violating municipal ordinances and has jurisdiction over minor civil or criminal cases, or both (DAP)

city manager: an official employed, usually for an indefinite term, by a commission or by a mayor and council to be in charge of the enforcement of ordinances and the construction, maintenance, and administration of all municipal works and services (DAP)

civil: distinguished from criminal; pertaining to a legal matter, pertaining to something noncriminal in nature. Pertaining to the personal or private rights of an individual; pertaining to legal action in court to enforce private or personal rights. (Proceedings in court are usu. criminal or civil. A suit for personal injury is a civil action.) (LEV)

civil action: a law suit on a noncriminal matter (LEV)

civil case: a judicial proceeding to enforce a private right or to obtain compensation for its violation; distinguished from a criminal case (DAP)

civil commotion: a serious and prolonged disturbance of the peace not sufficient to amount to insurrection (DAP)

civil-criminal courts: civil courts are established for the adjudication of private wrongs. Criminal courts are charged with the administration of the criminal laws in which public offenders are tried

civil disobedience: the collective application against the government of the techniques of passive resistance and non-cooperation, such as picketing, boycotting, refusal to pay taxes, and peaceable demonstrations. Its most extensive development occurred in India under the leadership of Mahatma Gandhi (DAP)

civil disorder: disturbance of the peace by a person or persons evidenced by refusal to obey or comply with the law. Many participants are motivated by moral causes or convictions and their actions are symbols of resistance to existing laws and government. Frequently the acts are in violation of criminal laws. Some have called the violent acts "criminal disorder" or "criminal disobedience" (LEV)

civil law: the codified law derived from Roman Law. It is written law classified as to subject matter, with doctrines applicable to all types of disputes or questions. Although distinguished from the English common law which is based principally on precedents and judge-made decisions, Roman civil law also makes use of precedents based on custom and legislation. The civil law derives from the Roman codes, particularly the Corpus Juris Civilies, and has been transmitted chiefly through French law. Civil law is also distinguished from criminal law and is that branch which concerns suits between one person and another. Such suits may relate to a contract, damages, torts, real estate transactions, domestic relations, and many other issues. The rules of procedure in civil law provide for a "judgment" in a case at law or a "decree" in an equity case (DOAH)

civil liability for wrongful searches and seizures: in general, while a search under a valid warrant does not constitute a trespass, a violation, without reasonable ground, of the right of the citizen to security against wrongful search and seizure gives him a right of action. An action may, as the circumstances require, be brought against the officer issuing the invalid warrant, the officer or officers making the wrongful search or seizure, or other persons participating therein (CDTP)

civil liberty: (1) liberty as defined by law; specifically: personal security and the peaceful enjoyment of property and other lawful rights which result from the existence of organized government, as distinguished from the supposed liberty of a state of nature (DAP) (2) freedom from interference or exactions of government officers which violate the constitution or laws of the country (DAP)

civil process: official orders, and documents issued by or under the authority of a court when handling civil matters such as sum-monses, subpoenaes, injunctions, eviction orders, etc. The police officer should be familiar with these as he may be called upon to aid in serving. See legal points (LEV)

civil rights: Those liberties possessed by the individual as a member of the state; especially: those liberties guaranteed to the individual against encroachment by his government. In this latter sense, civil rights are enumerated in the bills of rights of federal and State constitutions and include both substantive rights, such as freedom of speech, press, assembly, or religion; and procedural rights, such as protection against unreasonable searches and seizures or against punishment without a fair trial. The most important civil right is embodied in those clauses in State and federal constitutions which prohibit government from depriving anyone of life, liberty, or property without due process of law. Twice found in the federal Constitution, this clause imposes a limitation upon the States as well as Congress. Of somewhat less importance is the equal-protection clause of the Fourteenth Amendment which limits State action. By its interpretation of these two clauses the Supreme Court of the United States largely determines the scope of civil rights in America. Recently interest in civil rights has been directed toward legislation by Congress and State legislatures to secure certain liberties of the individual against encroachment by other individuals and groups, and to prohibit discrimination by them on account of race, color, religion, or membership in labor unions (DAP)

Civil Rights Act, the: a law of Congress in 1856 designed to protect the rights of freedmen. It attempted to nullify the black codes by defining citizenship and safeguarding civil rights, providing for its terms to be enforced in the federal courts. Although vetoed by President Johnson on March 27, it was enacted over his veto on April 9th. Ultimately its provisions were embodied in the Fourteenth Amendment (DOAH)

Civil Rights Act of 1875: a law of Congress passed on March 1, 1875. It was designed to protect all citizens in their civil and legal rights irrespective of "nativity, race, color, or persuasion, religious or political." The law guaranteed the full and equal enjoyment, to all persons within the jurisdiction of the United States, of the accommodations, advantages, facilities, and privileges of inns, public conveyances on land or water, theatres, and other places of public amusement. It imposed a fine for violation of not less than $500 nor more than $1000 or imprisonment for 30 days to one year. The district and circuit courts of the United States were given exclusive jurisdiction in trial of violations. The Act was tested in the U.S. Supreme Court in 1883. See Civil Rights Cases (DOAH)

Civil Rights Act of 1964: the most potent legislation in this area since the end of the Civil War. Provides equal rights for all citizens in voting, education, public accommodations, and in federally assisted programs. The Act provides for strict enforcement through the Department of Justice and other federal agencies (DOAH)

Civil Rights Cases: a series of five cases tried by the U.S. Supreme Court in 1883 as tests of the constitutionality of the Civil Rights Act of 1875. In each case a [black] had been denied some accommodation or privilege in violation of the Act. The Court held that the rights which the law attempted to protect were social rather than civil rights, and that the Congress therefore had no jurisdiction over these matters. The Court's decisions virtually terminated Congress' efforts to enforce the civil liberties guarantees of the Fourteenth Amendment (DOAH)

civil service: refers to the entire corps of personnel of governments, excluding military and top administrative and judicial officers. Also known as the public service. This is not to be confused with the term "merit system" which refers specifically to the method of appointing civil servants through competitive examination. The federal civil service is the largest body of employees under a single employment head in the United States today. During WW II there were approximately 3,800,000 personnel employed by the United States government (DOAH)

Civil Service Commission: See Pendleton Act

civil service reform: attempts to introduce a merit system into the public service. The first public demands for civil service reform were made in the 1830s as a reaction to the spoils system of the Jacksonian period. In 1853 a system of examinations was established by Congress, but was generally unsuccessful. In 1871 the President was authorized to set down a general system of personnel appointment on the basis of merit and fitness. Its failure led to the first comprehensive national program of merit system examinations in the passage of the Pendleton Act in 1883. This was supplemented in 1903 by the Civil Service Rules and Orders drawn up by President T. Roosevelt. Thereafter, legislative amendments and executive orders extended the scope of the Pendleton Act by increasing the number of classified occupations and eliminating patronage appointments. In the states civil service reform was inaugurated by the enactment in 1883 in New York of the Civil Service Act. Massachusetts (1884), Wisconsin and Illinois (1905), Colorado (1907), New

Jersey (1908), Ohio (1912), and California and Connecticut (1913), had established civil service regulations before World War I, either by legislation or constitutional provisions. Subsequently, six other states put such programs into effect. In this period approximately 500 cities established similar merit system programs (DOAH)

civil suit: legal process before a court, historically in equity, to recover property, maintain a right or privilege, or satisfy a claim (DAP)

clairvoyance: a power attributed to certain persons of discerning objects not normally perceptible, of reading thoughts, etc. (CDTP)

clandestine: surreptitious; concealed

Clark, Tom Campbell (*1899-*): a member of the U.S. Supreme Court from 1949 to 1967, Clark was on the Warren Court during the years of the major civil rights decisions; he presided on such major cases as *Mapp* v. *Ohio* and *Baker* v. *Carr*

classical penal theory: the theory advanced by 18th century jurists and philosophers, notably Beccaria (Italian), Bentham (English), and Feuerbach (German) holding that punishments for crimes should be meted in an exact fashion according to the degree of seriousness of the offense. This theory was widely incorporated in penal laws and still operates in Europe and America in the majority of the provisions for convicting and sentencing criminals adjudged guilty (DOS)

classification and particular writs: under the old English practice, writs were divided into original and judicial writs; but in modern times, original writs have fallen into disuse, and most of them abolished; and in the later practice, writs are divided into original, of mesne process, and of execution; and from the standpoint of their effect upon the property affected, it has been said that writs may be divided into those pointing out, and those not specifically pointing out, the property to be seized. (C.J., vol. 71) (CDTP)

classification of crimes: crimes at common law are divided into treason, felonies, and misdemeanors. Some jurisdictions have a fourth classification of minor or petty offenses, less than misdemeanors, sometimes described as those of which magistrates have had exclusive summary jursidiction, also as police regulations. (258 U.S. 250) (CDTP)

classifications of prisoners: the process, usu. referred to as diagnostic classification, through which a new prisoner is classified according to educational, vocational, treatment, and security needs for proper placement in treatment programs

Clayton Act: purports to exempt labor organizations and their legitimate concerted activities from the provisions of the Sherman Act, and to narrow the jurisdiction of the Federal Courts in labor disputes (CDTP)

clear-and-present danger rule: a rule of constitutional interpretation formulated by Justice Holmes in Schenck v. U.S., 249 U.S. 47 (1919), that in prosecutions for seditious utterances in which statutory encroachment on freedom of speech is pleaded in defense, the question which the court must decide is "whether the words used are used in such circumstances and are of such a nature as to create a clear and present danger that they will bring about the substantive evils that Congress has a right to prevent" (DAP)

clearing block: a wooden block placed in the action of an automatic weapon to prevent its closing and to show that the gun is unloaded (DWMT)

clearing house: a place where there is conducted the business of clearing checks and drafts for banks and adjusting balances between such banks (LEV)

clemency: power granted to the executive branch of government, usually residing with the President or Governor. The power of clemency is the power to grant mercy to one accused or convicted of a crime. It includes the power of pardon, commutation of sentence, reprieve, and amnesty (LCC)

clergy, benefit of: a practice of the middle ages by which the individual who utilized it was able to avoid criminal prosecution by having his case transferred to the ecclesiastical court (LCC)

CLETS: California Law Enforcement Telecommunications Systems (LEV)

client: one who consults an attorney (LEV)

clinical camera: a camera especially designed for use in hospitals and clinics (MPPF)

clinical conditions: medically approved facilities of a hospital, clinic, laboratory, or doctor's office, and activities carried on by approved medical personnel. In the *Schmerber* case the court held that the taking of a blood specimen from an unwilling subject so it could be tested for alcohol content was satisfactory inasmuch as it was done under clinical conditions [Ref.: Schmerber v. California, 384 U.S. 757 (1966).] (LEV)

clip: a device to hold cartridges for insertion into some rifles and automatic pistols (DWMT)

closed-breech action: a system in a firearm in which the bolt or breechblock is closed, with a cartridge seated in the chamber immediately in front of it (DWMT)

closed circuit system: a system in which the sensors of each zone are connected in series so that the same current exists in each sensor. When an activated sensor breaks the circuit or the connecting wire is cut, an alarm is transmitted for that zone (TDIAS)

closed end lease: a type of lease contract which requires periodic payments to the lessor covering equipment cost, financing costs, and profit for a fixed period of time at the end of which the lessee's financial obligation ceases. *See also* open end lease (TDPPC)

closed shop: a situation where the employer, by agreement, hires only union members in good standing as employees. If no such union members are available at a given time, also by agreement, the employer may hire nonunion workers on condition they apply for and become members of the union immediately (LEV)

clue: a thing or information which is apparently pertinent to the solution of a case (crime) (LEV)

clumping: relates to the effective increase in grain size in the emulsion due to the partial overlapping of grains of silver (MPPF)

clutch head screw: a mounting screw with a uniquely designed head for which the installation and removal tool is not commonly available. They are used to install alarm system components so that removal is inhibited (TDIAS)

CN: a lacrimator chemical most commonly used in "tear gas" and in aerosol irritant projectors. The chemical name is Chloroacetophenone (LEV)

Coast Guard Jurisdiction: that commissioned, Warrant, and petty officers of the coast guard are hereby empowered to make inquiries, examinations, inspections, searches, seizures, and arrests upon the high seas and the navigable waters of the United States, its Territories, and possessions, except the Philippine Islands, that nothing herein contained shall apply to the inland waters of the United States, its territories, and possessions, other than the Great Lakes and the connecting waters thereof (CDTP)

coating lens: a thin, transparent coating applied to a lens to reduce surface reflection and internal reflection; also cuts down transmission of ultraviolet rays, acting

somewhat like a haze filter
(MPPF)

COBOL: *C*ommon *B*usiness *O*riented *L*anguage; an English-like programming language designed primarily for business-type applications and implemented for use with many different data processors   (ADPS)

coca leaves: leaves of the coca plant, grown in Peru and Java, which contains cocaine   (CDTP)

cocaine: a stimulant drug obtained from coca leaves; a white, bitter, crystalline substance. It is rigidly controlled by law   (LEV)

cock: (1) the movable portion of the firing mechanism corresponding to the hammer on modern guns (CDTP) (2) to place the cock in position ready to fire   (CDTP)

cocking indicator: a pin that projects from certain rifles and automatic pistols to indicate that the hammer is cocked   (DWMT)

cocking lever: a lever for drawing back (sometimes also for lowering) the striker or hammer of an automatic firearm or the mechanism of a bomb-release gear
(DWMT)

cocking piece: the rearward extension of a striker or firing pin on some guns. It is pulled back to cock the gun   (DWMT)

cocotte: prostitute

code: (1) a system of rules for using a set of symbols to represent data or operations (ADPS) (2) a body of law covering one general subject established by the legislative authority of the state (CDTP) (3) (*In Roman-law countries*) a systematic statement of the body of the law enacted or promulgated by the highest authority of the state, on which all judicial decisions must immediately be based (DAP) (4) (*in the United States*) a private or official compilation of all permanent laws in force consolidated and classified according to subject matter. Such compilations of national laws are the *Revised Statutes of the United States,* first enacted in 1874, and *A Code of the Laws of the United States.* Many States have published official codes of all laws in force, including the common law and statutes as judicially interpreted, which have been compiled by code commissions and enacted by the legislatures. American codes lack the permanence and authority of European codes because of the volume of new statutes and of judicial decisions, each of which, under common law principles, constitutes a precedent for the decision of later cases
(DAP)

code, instruction: the symbols, names, and descriptions for all the operations that a processor executes   (ADPS)

Code, International: a code of words, used in law enforcement, to clarify letters of the alphabet when spelling orally, as by telephone or radio. [The code words are as follows:] A = Alpha, B = Bravo, C = Charlie, D = Delta, E = Echo, F = Foxtrot, G = Golf, H = Hotel, I = India, J = Juliette, K = Kilo, L = Lima, M = Mike, N = November, O = Oscar, P = Papa, Q = Quebec, R = Romeo, S = Sierra, T = Tango, U = Uniform, V = Victor, W = Whiskey, X = X-ray, Y = Yankee, Z = Zulu
(LEV)

code, machine: the code that the processor hardware was built to interpret and execute   (ADPS)

code, multi-mode: the character represented by a pattern of bits, holes, etc., depends on whether the device is in the "letters" or "figures" mode. Corresponds roughly to the upper and lower case characters on a typewriter obtained by use of the shift key
(ADPS)

code, numeric: a code in which the symbols used are all numerals. Four and six-bit codes for electronic equipment; five-, six-, seven-, and eight-channel code for punched-paper-tape; and Hollerith code for punched cards   (ADPS)

Code, the: Cosa Nostra or Mafia

laws, rules, and regulations (internal) by which the organization operates inside the families, between families, and throughout the organization   (LEV)

code check: determination that the character representation is in the "legal" set of characters for the machine being used and that fields have valid characters—that is, numerics are not in alphabetic fields, and vice versa   (ADPS)

code for computer: to express a program in a code that a specific computer was built or programmed to interpret and execute, or in a code that can be translated into machine code (ADPS)

Code Napoleon: the codification of French private substantive law prepared at the instance of Napoleon Bonaparte. It became widely accepted as a model among Latin peoples   (DAP)

code of ethics: written rules, regulations, and/or standards of conduct for members of groups of people engaged in given professions or occupations. Doctors, attorneys, and others have these. One of the codes of ethics for law enforcement is the Law Enforcement Code of Ethics which was adopted by the IACP at its 1957 conference. It has also been adopted by many other law enforcement associations and other organizations (LEV)

code word: a word which has been assigned a classification and a classified meaning to safeguard intentions and information regarding a classified plan or operation (DWMT)

coded-alarm system: an alarm system in which the source of each signal is identifiable. This is usually accomplished by means of a series of current pulses which operate audible or visible annunciators or recorders or both, to yield a recognizable signal. This is usually used to allow the transmission of multiple signals on a common circuit   (TDIAS)

coded cable: a multiconductor cable in which the insulation on each conductor is distinguishable from all others by color or design. This assists in identification of the point of origin or final destination of a wire   (TDIAS)

coded transmitter: a device for transmitting a coded signal when manually or automatically operated by an actuator. The actuator may be housed with the transmitter or a number of actuators may operate a common transmitter (TDIAS)

codefendants: more than one person jointly charged for the same crime   (LEV)

codeine: a derivative of opium. It is similar to morphine but not as strong in its effect. It is a crystalline alkaloid   (LEV)

codicil: an addition to a will, either to add to, to take from, or to alter the provisions of the will

coding siren: a siren which has an auxiliary mechanism to interrupt the flow of air through its principal mechanism, enabling it to produce a controllable series of sharp blasts   (TDIAS)

coerce: to restrain or constrain by force, especially legally or morally (CDTP)

coercion: (1) the use of force to compel performance of an action (DAP) (2) the application of sanctions or the use of force by government to compel observance of law or public policy   (DAP)

coercion—married women: if a married woman, in the presence of her husband, commits an act which would be a crime under other circumstances, she is presumed to have acted under her husband's coercion, and such coercion excuses her act (38, N.W. 503), but this presumption may be rebutted if the circumstances show that in fact she was not coerced   (CDTP)

cognizance: judicial notice of a matter; recognition or notice; the power or jurisdiction given to courts by law   (LEV)

cognomen: a man's family name; a surname

cohabitation: living together as husband and wife; refers to having the same habitation, a habit of visiting, or remaining for a time; there must be more than mere meretricious intercourse

cohesion: attraction that unites bodies (LEV)

cohort analysis: the study over a period of time of a number of persons possessing some common characteristic. *See* tracking

coition: sexual intercourse

coitus: sexual intercourse

coitus a tergo: coitus from the rear (LEV)

coitus inter femora: sexual act performed between the thighs of the participant (LEV)

Coleman v. Alabama, 399 U.S. 1, 26 L. Ed. 2d 387, 90 S. Ct. 1999 (1970): Mr. Justice Brennan's principal opinion, in a case in which the defendant had been charged with assault with intent to murder, held that a preliminary hearing, if held, is a "critical stage," and an indigent defendant has a constitutional right to the appointment of counsel under the Sixth and Fourteenth Amendments. (Only Mr. Justice Marshall joined Mr. Justice Brennan. Six Justices wrote separate concurring and dissenting opinions. There was a vacancy on the Court at the time.) (ILECJ)

collage: a composite photograph made by pasting up a number of individual prints (MPPF)

collate: to produce a single sequence of items, ordered according to some rule, from two or more similarly ordered sequences. The final sequence need not contain all of the data available in the original sets. If, for example, two sets of items are being matched, items that do not match may be discarded (ADPS)

collateral: on the side of a subject (CDTP)

collateral facts: facts not directly connected with the matter in dispute (CDTP)

collateral security: a security in addition to the principal or original security (CDTP)

collating sequence: the sequence of special symbols, letters, and numerals to which the binary values, ranging from 000000 to 111111, are assigned by the equipment designer. The collation table value for each character determines the results of making comparisons—smaller, equal, or larger—and the sequence when sorting (ADPS)

collective bargaining: the determination of the terms and relationships of employment, jointly arranged by an employer and the freely chosen representatives of his employees. Although inhibited by the application of the common law doctrine of conspiracy to labor organizations, collective bargaining was a typical instrument of union negotiation as far back as 1794 when the local unions of printers and cordwainers in New York and Philadelphia practiced it. Today labor organizations bargain collectively on an industry-wide basis. The National Labor Relations Act protects most industrial employees in the exercise of this right. Other federal and similar state legislation guarantee collective bargaining for additional categories of workers (DOAH)

Collective Labor Agreement: a bargaining agreement as to wages, hours, and conditions of work, entered into by employees, most often organized into a labor union on the one side, and an employer or a group of employers on the other side, being designed to stabilize an industry and its labor conditions (CDTP)

collimate: to produce parallel rays of light by means of a lens or a concave mirror (MPPF)

collimating lens: a lens so adjusted as to produce a parallel beam of light (MPPF)

collinear: the line-to-line relation existing between the corresponding parts of the object and its image formed by a lens   (MPPF)

collodion: a transparent liquid obtained by dissolving pyroxylin in a mixture of equal parts of alcohol and ether. It is used as the vehicle for carrying the sensitive salts in the wet-plate process   (MPPF)

colloid: substances of large molecular weight, such as starches, gums, and proteins, which form amorphous solids and dissolve or disperse in water to form "gooey" solutions   (FS)

collusion: an agreement between two or more persons to defraud a third person of his rights or to obtain an object forbidden by law   (CDTP)

colony, penal: a secluded area, generally a distant island outside the nation proper, or occasionally a remote part of the nation, where criminals are sent upon conviction of crimes, usually those within special categories. In effect, sentence to a penal colony involves virtual banishment   (DOS)

color: the sensation produced in the eye by a particular wave length or group of wave lengths of visible light   (MPPF)

color-bearer: a person who bears the colors (the Flag)   (DWMT)

color blind: (Chromatodysopia) (1) total or partial inability to perceive colors independent of the capacity for distinguishing light, shade, and form. Generally thought to be due to inefficiencies of the retinal cone receptors (CDTP) (2) applied to an emulsion sensitive only to blue, violet, and ultraviolet light   (MPPF)

color contrast: a property by which the form of an object can be recognized by its variation in color, whether or not the brightness of all parts of the object is equal   (MPPF)

color guard: a guard of honor which carries the colors of an organization   (DWMT)

color sensitivity: the response of a photographic emulsion to light of various wave lengths   (MPPF)

colored-marker projectile: a projectile loaded with a charge primarily of organic dye and provided with a burster charge. Upon impact the projectile is ruptured, and the dye is dispersed and vaporized by the heat of explosion. The dye then resolidifies in the air, forming a colored smoke cloud which serves as a marker and/or target indicator   (DWMT)

colored smoke: colored-smoke munitions are made in several forms, including projectiles, bombs, grenades, and candles. They may be employed as signals, target markers, zone-identification markers, and so forth. Distinctive smoke colors are red, green, yellow, and violet   (DWMT)

colorimeter: a device used to determine the exact color of a substance, especially when compared with known standards. It is used in the police laboratory in color analysis   (LEV)

colors: the flag or ensign flown by a ship or by military organizations such as infantry regiments. Cavalry banners are called "standards"   (DWMT)

Colquhoun, Patrick (1745–1820): a British magistrate, Colquhoun published Treatise on the Police of the Metropolis, a book which contained discussions of various forms of criminal behavior. He recommended a register of offenders, communication improvement between city and rural magistrates, and the creation of a centralized, trained, vigilant, and active police body

Colt, Samuel (1814–1862): American inventor of a breechloading pistol (patented 1835), which became so popular that Colt grew to be a generic term   (CVDE)

Colt .38 cal. Army, Navy, Marine revolver: the predecessor of this model, in .41 cal., introduced the swing-out cylinder with simultaneous ejection and was the model from which the modern Colt design stemmed. This arm was produced from 1889 through

1908. In 1889 it became the standard sidearm of the U.S. Navy, and in 1892 it was adopted as standard for the U.S. Army. The New Army and New Navy Models differed only in markings and stocks. The New Marine Corps Model was introduced in 1905 and differed only in having a rounded butt. With 6-inch barrels the overall length of these weapons was about 11 inches. The cylinder capacity was six cartridges, and the weight was about 34 oz. This revolver fired the .38 Long and Short Colt, a cartridge that came into considerable disrepute during the war in the Philippines (1898–1900) because of its inability to stop savage Moros (DWMT)

Colt .38 cal. automatic pistol Type 1899: a U.S. service pistol weighing 2 lb. 6 oz. and having a length of 6 inches. The magazine held seven rounds of .38 cal. rimless ammunition. This weapon should not be confused with the .380 cal. pistol by Colt (DWMT)

Colt .380 cal. automatic pistol: a U.S. service pistol weighing 1 lb. 7 1/2 oz. The overall length is 6 3/4 inches, and the barrel length is 3 3/4 inches. The magazine holds seven rounds of .380 rimless ammunition (DWMT)

Colt .45 cal. Double Action Army revolver: this was Colt's first heavy-frame double-action revolver. It was manufactured from 1877 to 1909 and had an overall length (with a 7 1/2-inch barrel) of about 12 1/4 inches. A 4 3/4-inch and a 5 1/2-inch barrel were also standard. The cylinder capacity was six cartridges, and the approximate weight was 39 oz. With the trigger guard made larger and with a longer trigger (to permit use with a gloved hand), this weapon was also known as the "Alaskan Model" and the "Philippine Model" (DWMT)

Colt .45 cal. Government Model 1911, 1911A1: this weapon evolved from an older .45 automatic called the "Old Model" or "Military Model." The M1911, as it was called, met the requirements of the U.S. Government competition of 1911, which called for a weapon that was simple, could be completely disassembled without tools, used a heavy bullet, and had good reliability under unfavorable service conditions. The M1911 weighs 39 oz. and has an overall length of 8.62 inches and a barrel length of 5 inches. The magazine has a capacity of seven cartridges. A few minor changes were made in 1921, and the weapon became the M1911A1. It is also a standard arm of the Mexican Army (DWMT)

Colt .45 cal. New Service revolver: this weapon was introduced in 1897 and not discontinued until 1943. With a 4 1/2-inch barrel, it had an overall length of 9 3/4 inches and weighed 39 oz. From 1917 to 1918 some 150,000 of this model were produced to fire the .45 ACP cartridge. Three-shot half-moon clips were used (DWMT)

Colt .45 cal. revolver Model 1917: a double-action revolver with an overall length of 10.8 inches and a barrel length of 5.5 inches. The weight of the weapon is 2.5 lb., and the cylinder has a capacity of six cartridges. This weapon is the New Service Model adapted in 1917 to take .45 ACP rimless cartridges. It has a muzzle velocity of 830 fps. Colt manufactured 151,700 of these revolvers (DWMT)

Colt .45 cal. Single Action Army revolver: introduced in 1873, this model, with slight modifications in caliber, is also referred to as the "Frontier" or the "Peacemaker." It has an overall length of 13 inches, a 7 1/2-inch barrel (other barrel lengths are 4 3/4 and 5 1/2 inches), and a weight of about 40 oz. The cylinder capacity is six cartridges. This same model was also manufactured to shoot a large number of cartridges, including

.32/20, .38 Special, .357 Magnum, .38/40, .44 Special, and, at one time, .45 ACP   (DWMT)
coma: (1) a lens aberration in which a coma or pear-shaped image is formed by oblique rays from an object point removed from the principal axis of the lens (MPPF) (2) a state of profound unconsciousness in which the patient cannot be aroused. This may be due to a poison, alcohol, diabetes, brain injury, or kidney disease   (CDTP)
comatose: similar to coma; afflicted with coma   (LEV)
combination: a combination lock, especially the outward portion of it   (LEV)
combination print: a composite print made from several negatives (MPPF)
combination sensor alarm system: an alarm system which requires the simultaneous activation of two or more sensors to initiate an alarm signal   (TDIAS)
comity: the practice by which one court follows the decision of another court on a like question, though not bound by the law of precedents to do so
command: in accordance with statutory requirements the warrant must command the officer or officers to execute the warrant by searching for personal property and make a return thereon with inventory of goods seized, and it is void if it does not command such officer to bring such goods or other personal property before the judge or justice issuing the warrant or some other judge, justice, or court designated in the statute having cognizance of the case   (CDTP)
commend: to compliment, praise or express pleasure concerning another's actions, or deeds   (LEV)
commercial law: this branch of law embraces those divisions which relate to the rights of property and relations of persons engaged in commerce   (CDTP)
commission: (1) a warrant, usually issued by the chief executive, which confers the powers and privileges of an office upon a person newly appointed to it (DAP) (2) a body of three or more officials who collectively discharge the duties of an administrative agency   (DAP)
Commission, the: the National Council of the Cosa Nostra. It governs conditions which will exist between and among families as well as between the Cosa Nostra and others   (LEV)
commission of inquiry: a board composed of members of the legislature, administrative officials, nonofficial members, or a combination of two or more of these groups, appointed to investigate and report on a particular problem   (DAP)
Commission on Civil Rights: a federal agency of six members, established by law on Sept. 9, 1957, which investigates and reports upon charges that citizens, and esp. minority groups, have been deprived of their civil and political rights and of equal protection of the laws, or that they are being discriminated against by other citizens and by public authority. The commission makes recommendations to Congress and the President to remedy such conditions (DAP)
commissioner: (1) a member of certain independent federal agencies, of certain State boards, of the principal county board, or of the governing board of a city under the commission form of government (DAP) (2) part of the title widely used for heads of national bureaus and State and municipal departments   (DAP)
Commissioner of Deeds: an officer authorized to administer oaths in all cases where no special provision is made by law   (CDTP)
commit: (1) to violate the law (2) to officially order the admission for safe-keeping of an insane person to a jail or mental institution   (LEV)

common gambler: a person who is the owner, superintendent, or agent of a place for gambling; or who engages as dealer, gamekeeper, or player in any gambling game (CDTP)

common language: a single code used by several different devices—for example, typewriters, calculators, and transmitters—manufactured by different companies (ADPS)

common law: in its origins the law common to all the people of England as it arose out of the decisions of the king's judges. Since it was not statute law it went through many historical changes, being broadened by local custom and judicial interpretation. As transferred to the colonies, the doctrines of the common law came to mean a fundamental law protecting the people against the oppressive acts of government. The federal nature of the United States government after 1789 implied that the principles of the common law were reserved to the states since Congress could exercise only delegated powers which were enumerated in the federal Constitution. In the growth of American constitutional law these principles have been modified by legislative revision and judicial decision. Among the better-known aspects of the common law are the rights set forth in the Declaration of Independence, the civil liberties guaranteed by the Bill of Rights, and other inherent doctrines protecting life, liberty, and property (DOAH)

common-law marriage: See marriage, common law

common nuisance: a nuisance which affects the public in general (CDTP)

communicate: to talk; to convey messages from one person to another; to transmit information in such fashion as to be understood by people receiving it; to make oneself understood (LEV)

communication channel: messenger, voice, mail, telegraph, telephone, and microwave available for transmitting business data over short or long distances (ADPS)

communications carrier: a function provided by a vehicle equipped with radio communications (TDPPC)

communism: a system of social organization involving common ownership of the means of production, and in which goods are held in common (CDTP)

community-based corrections: includes any form of correctional treatment (e.g., halfway houses or parole) that deals with the offender in society, as opposed to out of society (e.g., in an institution)

community property: property acquired, during marriage, by either husband or wife or both, except that which is acquired as separate property by either spouse (LEV)

community relations: the sum total of individual contacts by members of an organization; working with and being a part of the community. It is organizationally a non-line function. Although some departments have a public relations section or department, such work would not be limited to the personnel of that section or department (LEV)

commutation: a lessening of a sentence prescribed by a court

commutation laws: See good-time allowance

compare: to examine two numeric data items to find if one is equal to, smaller, or larger than the other. To examine two alphabetic data items to find if one is the same, earlier, or later than the other in the collating sequence (ADPS)

comparison microscope: a microscope having two objectives, i.e., the part of the microscope nearest the object being viewed. Each objective views a different object, the images being magnified and by prisms brought into focus in a single (or double) eye piece. It is usu. found in a crime laboratory and is used, among other things, for examining markings on bullets to determine if the markings on two bullets can be matched so as to determine if they were both fired from the same weapon (LEV)

compensation: recompense; to pay for debt owed, or for damage caused (LEV)

competency: capability; in evidence, written or other evidence proper to be given as to persons; the ability to act such as to be a witness (CDTP)

competent evidence: that which the very nature of the thing to be proven requires, as, the production of a writing where its contents are the subject of inquiry; evidence which the law declares admissible (CDTP)

compiler: See routine, compiler

complaint: (1) the charge made before a proper officer that an offense has been committed by a person named or described (2) under modern rules of civil procedure, a pleading that must be filed to commence an action

complementary colors: a color is complementary to another when a combination of the two produces white light (MPPF)

complex: mental process patterns and man's environmental reactions. It involves instincts and learning. With instincts as a basis it is man's reaction to the environment about him (LEV)

complexion: the color of the skin, especially of the face, used as a factor in describing a person (i.e., complexion: ruddy) (LEV)

comply: to carry out orders; to act according to instructions (LEV)

composition: (1) an agreement between a debtor and his creditors, by which the latter agree to accept a certain proportion of their debts in satisfaction of the whole (2) (in photography) the bal-

ancing of shapes and tones to produce a pleasing effect (MPPF)

compound shutter: a trade name for an American (or German) shutter similar to the Compur, except that its slow speeds are controlled by means of a pneumatic piston retard instead of a gear escapement (MPPF)

compounding a crime: the offense of accepting a bribe to not prosecute a crime

compulsion: an abnormal urge to execute an act without the desire to do it. The individual cannot stop it at his will. It is based on an underlying unconscious motive (LEV)

compulsive neurosis: obsessive ideals and desires to do complicated and senseless acts, manifested by psychoneurosis (LEV)

compulsory: enforced; obligatory (CDTP)

Compur Shutter: a trade name for a between-the-lens shutter containing independent mechanisms for time (and bulb) exposures and for instantaneous exposures varying from 1 second to as high as 1/500 of a second (MPPF)

compurgation: a primitive form of defense against an accusation of crime, whereby the accused tried to establish innocence by bringing into court a sufficient number of persons who by oath testified to their belief in the innocence of the defendant. It used to be commonly assumed that the jury system arose out of this procedure (DOS)

computer: any device capable of accepting data, applying prescribed processes to them, and supplying the results of these processes. The word "computer" usually refers to an internally stored program data processor; the term "processor" is preferable for business applications (ADPT)

Comstock, Anthony (1844-1915): American moral crusader. Secured New York state and federal legislation against obscene matter.

Organized New York Society for the Suppression of Vice (CVDE)

concave: a surface which is hollowed out or curved inward (LEV)

concave lens: a lens having one or two concave surfaces (MPPF)

concavo-convex lens: a lens having one concave and one convex surface (MPPF)

conceal: to hide or cover up. (LEV)

concealed weapon: a weapon concealed from the ordinary view of others. This may be a gun, knife, or other dangerous weapon. In some states it pertains to concealment on or about the person and constitutes a violation of the law if any part of the weapon is concealed (LEV)

conchoidal: a conchoidal fracture is one resulting in a smooth, generally curved, and sometimes slightly fluted surface, as with glass or pitch (FS)

conclusive evidence: that which is incontrovertible, either because the law does not permit it to be contradicted, or because it is so strong and convincing as to overbear all proof to the contrary and establish the proposition in question beyond any reasonable doubt (CDTP)

concubinage: informal marriage; cohabitation.

concubine: the woman in an informal marriage, who lives with a man without a legal marriage

concur: to agree (LEV)

concurrence of act and intent: to constitute a crime, act and intent must concur. Not only must there be both an act and an intent to constitute a crime, but the act and intent must concur in point of time. (95 U.S. 670) An intent to do a prohibited act, abandoned before the act is done, is not punishable, even though the act should subsequently be committed (CDTP)

concurrent: to operate or run at the same time. When used in reference to sentences imposed upon one convicted of crime, it means he serves all sentences simultaneously or at the same time. If he should be sentenced on two charges and receives five-year sentences on each charge, to run concurrently, he satisfies both after five years imprisonment. As it pertains to jurisdiction of investigating agencies or the courts, it means each has joint jurisdiction, i.e., each agency has jurisdiction over the matter or subject (LEV)

concurrent jurisdiction: authority shared by two or more legislative, judicial, or administrative officers or bodies to deal with the same subject matter (DAP)

concurrent writs: several writs running at the same time for the same purpose (i.e., arrest) of one person, whose whereabouts are unknown, or for service on persons (such as codefendants)

condemn: (1) to find guilty or sentence (2) to judge unfit or unsafe (3) to set apart for public use

condemnation: (1) a judicial proceeding in which private property is taken for public use under the power of eminent domain and compensation to the owner is determined (DAP) (2) the judgment by which property seized for violation of revenue or other laws is declared forfeited to the state (DAP) (3) the determination of a court that a ship is unfit for service, or was properly seized and held as a prize (DAP)

condenser: an optical system in projection printers used to collect the divergent rays of a light source and concentrate them upon the objective lens (MPPF)

condition: (1) an expression that, taken as a whole, may be true or false. A *simple* condition has only one element—for example, "if account balance exceeds credit limit, reject customer's order." A *compound* condition has two or more elements—for example, "if account balance exceeds credit limit but account is current and the new order will not cause balance to exceed twice the credit

limit, then accept order." (ADPS)
(2) the result of a test—for example, greater than, negative overflow (ADPS) (3) a value that an item may have   (ADPS)

condition-name: a name assigned by the programmer to denote one of a number of values that an item of data can assume   (ADPS)

conditional pardon: one to which a condition is annexed   (CDTP)

conditional release: the release of a prisoner on condition that he comply with certain requirements. If the person does not adhere to such requirements he may be put in prison or jail again   (LEV)

conditions of criminality: to render a person criminally responsible for the commission of a common law crime, four conditions of criminality are as follows: (1) the person must be of sufficient age; (2) he must have sufficient mental capacity; (3) he must act voluntarily; (4) he must have criminal intent   (CDTP)

condone: to overlook certain things being done or said. To tacitly agree with things done or said   (LEV)

Condorcet, Marquis de (*1743–1794*): a French philosopher, Condorcet felt that man would eventually progress to ultimate perfection in enlightenment and virtue and would then have no need for police. However, since that state had not yet been reached, Condorcet believed that laws should be centered around the good citizen. His concept of prison was one of the first models to include rehabilitation

cone: the reduction of diameter in a barrel where the chamber joins the bore   (CDTP)

confabulation: the telling of experiences as having actually happened when as a matter of fact the experiences were imaginary—found in psychopaths   (LEV)

confederate: an accomplice, associate; one engaged in activities with others   (LEV)

Confederation, the: the name used to signify the national criminal cartel—organized crime, dominated by the Italian Cosa Nostra. *See* Mafia   (LEV)

confess: to make a statement against interest, involving oneself in crime and other misconduct   (LEV)

confession: a statement, usually recorded, by a person who admits violation of the law; an admission of criminal violations. A confession must be given voluntarily, without force, threats, promises, or coercion being used by the officer receiving the confession. Under the *Miranda* ruling the person being interviewed must be specifically warned of his specific constitutional rights and the suspect must specifically and intelligently waive such rights before incriminating statements, made by him in response to questions, can be admitted in evidence   (LEV)

confidence game: the obtaining of money or property by means of deception, through the confidence a victim places in the swindler

confidential: (1) not freely divulged (LEV) (2) (in government service) information and material, particularly as pertains to defense, the disclosure of which could be against the best interests of the nation   (LEV)

confidential communications: statements made by one person to another when there is a necessary relation of trust and confidence between them, which the person receiving them cannot be compelled to disclose (e.g., the statements made by a husband to his wife or a client to his attorney)

configuration, machine: the pattern of equipment making up a system: size of storage, number of tape units and input-output channels, printer and speed, etc.   (ADPS)

confinement: the incarceration of a person in a place of detention. This may be one accused of crime or one who is believed to be a necessary party to a witness. In its broadest sense it may apply to depriving a person of his freedom of action   (LEV)

confinement, congregate: a method of imprisonment characterizing the early jails of Europe and of this country before the reforms introduced into the Walnut Street Jail of Philadelphia in 1790. Before this change was undertaken the prisoners were allowed to associate day and night. Owing to serious abuses the change in the Walnut Street Jail consisted of keeping the more hardened inmates in separate cells without work, but allowing the others to be lodged in dormitories and to work together in common workshops. Afterwards the term was applied to the Auburn system in contrast with the Pennsylvania or separate system   (DOS)

confinement, solitary: the most severe measure of prison discipline now current in most prisons. It consists of placing the prisoner in a special cell with little light, usu. with only a board or the floor on which to sleep, a ration of bread and water, and sometimes a chain upon the prisoner to restrict his movements. But such measures are becoming less common as prison discipline becomes better understood   (DOS)

confiscated vehicle: a vehicle that has been acquired by an authorized law enforcement agency because its owner has either temporarily or permanently surrendered his right of ownership by violation of an ordinance or law which provides for confiscation   (TDPPC)

confiscation: the seizure of private property by the government without compensation to the owner, often a consequence of conviction for crime or participation in rebellion, or because possession of the property was contrary to law, or because it was being used for an unlawful purpose   (DAP)

conflict of interest: the situation that arises when an officer, in the discharge of his public duties, has to administer, decide, or vote on some matter in which he, or a member of his family, has a private pecuniary interest. Anticipating such a situation, high public officials, upon being elected or appointed, sometimes divest themselves of stock or other forms of ownership in private companies or place their property in the hand of trustees. Legislation regulating conflict of interest has been little developed   (DAP)

conflict of laws: (1) different provisions of two or more laws, each of which may properly govern a particular situation (DAP) (2) private international law   (DAP)

confrontation: a meeting arranged between a witness and an accused for purposes such as identification or determining objections by the witness to the witness

congress: the U.S. Senate and House of Representatives

conjugal: pertaining to the state of marriage or marital relations   (LEV)

conjugal visitation: overnight visitation between inmates of a correctional facility and their spouses, either in facilities set up in the institution or through furloughs granted to the prisoners

Conley, 64 Cal. 2d 321 (1966): this decision in the California courts delineates the idea of diminished responsibility because of intoxication in certain crimes requiring specific intent. A great deal of the discussion is in support of the "condition" precept of Robinson v. California, 370 U.S. 663 (1962), in which the U.S. Supreme Court established new concepts of drug addicts as sick persons   (AOJ)

connivance: (1) guilty knowledge of, or assistance in, a crime (2) consent, express or implied, by one spouse to the adultery of the other

consanguinity: kinship; blood relationship, distinguished from relationship through marriage (affinity)

conscience money: funds paid into a public treasury by persons who feel that they have cheated the government in tax payments or otherwise (DAP)

consecutive: one following another; one after the other; successive. In the sentencing of a criminal offender for more than one offense the court may make the sentences consecutive, i.e., to operate consecutively. In such a situation the offender must complete one sentence before he starts the next. Three five-year consecutive sentences means an ultimate prison term of 15 years (unless, of course, he is paroled or otherwise released) (LEV)

consent: the voluntary yielding of the will to a proposition made by another. In a rape case if consent is given as the result of threats, fear, coercion, trickery, or fraud it is not valid consent, i.e., it is not lawful consent. If the female is below an age specified by law, is mentally deficient, or is drugged or intoxicated to the extent that she is incapable of resisting or of understanding the nature of the act, the consent is not deemed lawful (LEV)

consent, implied: consent which is not expressly given but which is inferred from actions or which is prescribed by law. Several states have laws which provide that when the operator of a motor vehicle obtains a driver's license he waives his right to object to an intoxication test if he should at a later date be charged with driving while intoxicated. This is generally referred to as the "Implied Consent" Law (LEV)

consent search: voluntary consent on the part of the legal possessor of premises or movables for such to be searched. A person, place, or movable may be lawfully searched by an officer of the law if the possessor gives his free and voluntary consent. By possessor is meant the owner if he possesses the premises to be searched or the person who

has the legal right to possess same. The owner of a hotel cannot give consent to search the room of one who is renting the room. It is good procedure to obtain such consent in writing (LEV)

conservatism: (1) general and uncritical opposition to change of any sort (DAP) (2) a reasoned philosophy, associated with the English writer Edmund Burke, directed toward the control of the forces of change in such a way as to conserve the best elements of the past by blending them into an organic unity with new elements in an ever-evolving society (DAP)

consideration: inducement for making a contract (LEV)

console: equipment that provides for manual intervention and for monitoring processor operations (ADPS)

consolidated laws: a compilation of all the laws of a State in force arranged according to subject matter. *See* code (DAP)

conspiracy: a combination or agreement between two or more persons to do an unlawful act, whether that act be the final object of the combination, or only a means to the final end, and whether that act be a crime, or an act hurtful to the public, a class of persons, or an individual. The offense is usually divided into three heads: (1) where the end to be attained is in itself a crime; (2) where the object is lawful, but the means by which it is to be attained are unlawful; (3) where the object is to do an injury to a third person, or a class, though, if the wrong were inflicted by a single individual, it would be a civil wrong, and not a crime. An overt act is generally necessary. Conspiracies are misdemeanors, unless made felonies by statute (CDTP)

conspiracy laws: state legislation in the first half of the 19th century which held illegal combinations of persons whose activities were considered conspiracies against the public interest. These acts were applied to the activities of labor organizations which were considered such combinations. The attempts of workers to organize and use such unions in enhancing their economic status were thus considered illegal. Following the decision of the Massachusetts Supreme Court in 1842 in the case of *Commonwealth* v. *Hunt* the conspiracy laws were rendered inapplicable to labor unions

(DOAH)

constant: a value used without alteration throughout a program

(ADPS)

constant ringing drop (CRD): a relay which when activated even momentarily will remain in an alarm condition until reset. A key is often required to reset the relay and turn off the alarm   (TDIAS)

constitution: the fundamental law of a state, consisting of: (1) the basic political principles which ought to be followed in conducting the government; (2) the organization of government; (3) the vesting of powers in the principal officers and agencies; (4) limitations on the extent of, and methods of exercising, these powers; and (5) the relationship between the government and the people who live under it. The constitution may be simply an uncollected body of legislative acts, judicial decisions, and political precedents and customs, like that of the United Kingdom, or, at the other extreme, a single document drafted and promulgated at a definite date by an authority of higher competence than that which makes ordinary laws, like constitutions in the United States. It may be endorsed by the courts as superior to statutes which conflict with it, as in the United States and a few other countries, or its preservation may be entrusted to the political authorities. In the latter case, which is still the usual one in Europe, a written constitution stands as a convenient standard by which the people may judge the conduct of their govern-

ment and the degree of its respect for their liberties. Constitutions are sometimes classified as *written* or *unwritten,* according to whether or not their written material is presented in consolidated and systematic form, or as *flexible* or *rigid,* according to whether they can be amended by legislative enactment or require a more complicated procedure of proposal and ratification by different authorities. *See* state constitution (DAP)

constitution court: (1) a court created by or under a specific authorization of a constitution (DAP) (2) (in the federal judicial system) a court, established under Article III of the Constitution, whose judges are entitled to tenure during good behavior and to salaries that can not be decreased. The U.S. Supreme Court of Appeals and District Courts were created as constitutional courts, and the same rank was accorded by Congress in 1946 to the Court of Claims, the Court of Customs and Patent Appeals, and in 1956 to the Customs Court, all three of which previously had been legislative courts   (DAP)

constitutional guarantees: formerly, but few trial privileges were given to persons accused of crime. They were not permitted to have counsel and often were practically debarred the right to make a defense. Presumption of guilt and burden of proof were against them. The trial was purely an ex parte proceeding and in many cases all that remained to be done after the indictment was found was to inflict the penalty. The accused might not see or know who were the witnesses against him or even know the nature of their testimony, and was not permitted compulsory process to procure the attendance of witnesses in his behalf. Such procedure often led to great injustice and was subject to intolerable abuse by persons of influence and authority in the country from which our jurisprudence is derived.

Owing to this historical experience, these subjects are now controlled by constitutional provisions in this country   (CDTP)

constitutional law: the body of legal rules and principles, usually formulated in a written constitution, which define the nature and limits of governmental power as well as the rights and duties of individuals in relation to the state and its governing organs, and which are interpreted and extended by courts of final jurisdiction exercising the power of judicial review   (DAP)

constitutional rights: the rights of citizens as guaranteed by the United States Constitution. See Bill of Rights   (LEV)

constitutionalism: the doctrine that the power to govern should be limited by definite and enforceable principles of political organization and procedural regularity embodied in the fundamental law, or custom, so that basic constitutional rights of individuals and groups will not be infringed (DAP)

constructive contempt: a contempt committed out of the presence of the court and which does not involve a failure to comply with an order to appear in court or other official judicial body as ordered by the court. See contempt (LEV)

constructive intent: transfer of intent. If a person intends to do an illegal act and in attempting to carry it out he injures someone else, it is said to be constructive intent. For example, if A intends to shoot and kill B but in shooting at B he hits and kills C, the shooter by law is held to have intended to do what happened. See intent   (LEV)

contact: (1) each of the pair of metallic parts of a switch or relay which by touching or separating make or break the electrical current path (TDIAS) (2) a switch-type sensor (TDIAS) (3) one who is known to the officer and from whom information or services may be expected; a source of

information   (LEV)

contact device: a device which when actuated opens or closes a set of electrical contacts; a switch or relay   (TDIAS)

contact print: a photographic print on which the image or picture is the same as on the negative from which it is made; a one-to-one size photograph. It is made by placing the light-sensitive print paper against the negative and exposing the negative to light   (LEV)

contact printer: a box or machine providing a light source and a means for holding the negative and the sensitive material in contact while they are exposed to this light source   (MPPF)

contact surveillance: the use of tracer preparations which will adhere to the hands, clothing, etc., of a suspect when he comes in contact with it   (LEV)

contacted microphone: a microphone designed for attachment directly to a surface of a protected area or object; usu. used to detect surface vibrations   (TDIAS)

contactless vibrating bell: a vibrating bell whose continuous operation depends upon application of an alternating current, without circuit-interrupting contacts such as those used in vibrating bells operated by direct contact
(TDIAS)

contemporaneous: occurring at the time of the happening of something else. In an arrest it is something which happens at the time of the arrest, or which occurs soon thereafter as part of a continuous, uninterrupted lawful investigation   (LEV)

contempt: willful disregard or flouting of an authority, such as a court

continuance: adjournment or postponement of a case or action before the court to a certain date or indefinitely   (LEV)

continuous crime: a crime consisting of continuous violations, such as possession of stolen property or carrying a concealed weapon. The statute of limitations does not begin to operate on such a crime until the person discontinues the acts constituting the violation (LEV)

contraband: goods the possession of which is illegal; especially smuggled goods

contract: a legally enforceable agreement between two or more parties under the terms of which, for valid consideration, the parties agree to perform some act or refrain from performing some act (DAP)

contract system: a system of employment of prison labor in which an employer contracts for the use of prisoners at or near the prison but food, clothing, and general supervision are provided by the prison. The system began at the end of the 18th century and for a time was the most popular form of prison labor. Opposition of the labor unions and of private manufacturers and the obvious abuses caused by unscrupulous prison officials led to the rapid decline of the system. Less than 1 percent of all prisoners are now employed under this system. In spite of all objections no other system of prison labor has succeeded in providing such a large volume of work under disciplined conditions as the contract system. A return to it, however, is improbable (DOS)

contractual rights: property or other rights secured under a contract. The courts afford protection for such rights, an action for damages being available to an injured party under a contract against the other party or parties thereto who have failed to fulfill their covenanted obligations. Equity also offers remedies, such as a writ of specific performance, to secure the fulfillment of contractual rights. Contracts, and rights thereunder, are protected by the contract clause of the U.S. Constitution as well as by the due-process clauses of the Constitution against impairment by State legislatures; but contractual rights are safeguarded no more than other rights against the exercise of a State's prerogatives of eminent domain, taxation, and the police power (DAP)

contrast: subject contrast is the difference between the reflective abilities of various areas of a subject. Lighting contrast is the difference in intensities of light falling on various parts of a subject. Inherent emulsion contrast is the possible difference between the maximum and minimum densities of the silver deposits with a minimum variation of exposure. It is determined by the manufacturer. Development contrast is the gamma to which an emulsion is developed. It is controlled only by the developer, time, temperature, and agitation (MPPF)

contrast filter: a color filter so chosen as to make a colored subject stand out very sharply from surrounding objects (MPPF)

contrast paper: photographic paper having a contrasty emulsion in order to produce good prints from soft negatives; also called hard paper (MPPF)

contrasty: having a great difference between tones; sometimes applied to a print having mostly black and white, lacking in middle tones, correctly called chalky (MPPF)

contravention: (1) a process of social interaction midway between competition and conflict, consisting of a wide range of activities from mere withholding of cooperation to reproaching, disparaging, thwarting, betraying, or conniving against another, but always falling short of the use of violence or the threat of violence (2) in the French penal code offenses are divided into crimes, delits, and contraventions in the order of their diminishing seriousness. This classification does not correspond exactly with that of the English common law—treason, felony, and misdemeanor. Under French law contraventions are violations of police regulations (DOS)

contrectation: preliminary sex play (LEV)

contributory negligence: an old common-law rule that any lack of care on the part of an injured employee relieves the employer of liability for damages, which has been modified by statute in most States in favor of a rule of comparative negligence by which the employer is relieved of responsibility only in proportion to the relative negligence of himself and the employee (DAP)

control, internal: the procedures used within an organization to achieve accuracy at each state of processing to ensure adherence to policies and to make reports conform to reality (ADPS)

control, operating: the system used to obtain information about events as they occur, process them against files containing the results of previous events, draw conclusions about developments, make decisions, and implement the decisions. Closed-loop control relies upon equipment and excludes people. Open-loop control uses people in some stage of the control process—most frequently for appraisal and decision-making. Real-time control (also called "on-line" control) is comprehensive enough and operates quickly enough to permit control of a process while it is going on (ADPS)

control counter: a counter built into the control unit of a processor and used for sequencing instructions to be executed. It normally contains the address of the next instruction to be performed, but its contents can be changed by means of conditional or unconditional jump instructions (ADPS)

control field: the field used to edit data before output for printing. For example, $$$Z,ZZ9.99 will result in the insertion of a "$", a

"," and a "." as well as the suppression of leading zeros in the number 0000345678 to give an edited field such as $3,456.78 (ADPS)

control sequence: normal order of selection of instructions for execution. In some processors, one of the addresses in each instruction specifies the control sequence. In most processors, the sequence is consecutive except when a jump is made (ADPS)

control unit: (1) the portion of the hardware of an automatic digital processor that directs the sequence of operations, interprets coded instructions, and initiates proper commands to the circuits to execute instructions (ADPS) (2) a device, usually electronic, which provides the interface between the alarm system and the human operator and produces an alarm signal when its programmed response indicates an alarm condition. Some or all of the following may be provided for: power for sensors, sensitivity adjustments, means to select and indicate access mode or secure mode, monitoring for line supervision and tamper devices, timing circuits, for entrance and exit delays, transmission of an alarm signal, etc. (TDIAS)

contumacious: wilfully disobedient to an order of a court (CDTP)

contusion: a bruise on some part of the body; an injury where the skin is not broken (LEV)

conversion: taking the property of another and using same for [one's] own benefit (CDTP)

converter: a device for transferring data from one storage medium to another—for example, from punched cards to magnetic tape (ADPS)

convertible lens: a lens containing two or more elements which can be used individually or in combination to give a variety of focal lengths (MPPF)

convex: the opposite of concave;

curved outward; applied to a lens which is thicker in the center than at the edges (MPPF)

convey: to pass title to property (LEV)

conveyance: (1) a means of transportation such as an automobile, taxi, or bus. (2) (law) a written instrument transferring property or title to property, between persons (LEV)

convict: (1) to find guilty (2) a person found guilty of a crime or misdemeanor (3) any person confined to a state or federal prison under sentence of more than a year for the commission of crime. The term does not apply to persons confined in city and county jails (DOS)

convict labor: work performed by inmates of penal institutions either under contract with private parties or directly for the State, the products of which were forbidden in interstate commerce by an act of Congress effective in 1934 (DAP)

conviction: the result of a trial when the defendant is found guilty

convoy: an escort; to accompany others (LEV)

cool blood: crime not committed in a fit of anger, used in homicide cases in which there is an absence of emotion or violent passion (The crime was executed in cold blood.)

Coolidge v. New Hampshire, 403 U.S. 443, 29 L. Ed. 2d 564, 91 S. Ct. 2022 (1971): this important decision, 5-4, by Mr. Justice Stewart raises four search and seizure issues, and the opinions are subject to several interpretations, and as an "explication" they leave much to be desired. Consult the prosecutor, or local police legal advisor, and act accordingly. The author's interpretation is that (1) the only way of following *Coolidge* is to secure a warrant whenever possible, (2) if there is any question, *Coolidge* settles any controversy that when a warrant is issued it must be by "a neutral magistrate," (3) *Coolidge* limits *Chambers* on automobile searches, and (4) "plain view" is stated unequivocally, in at least the plurality part of the opinion, as restricting warrantless seizures. (Chief Justice Burger, dissenting, says that, "This case graphically illustrates the monstrous price we pay for the Exclusionary Rule in which we seem to have imprisoned ourselves." Mr. Justice Black in his dissent declares that "there is no exclusionary rule in the Fourth Amendment, if it is properly construed...." Mr. Justice Harlan concurs with Mr. Justice Stewart because he feels bound by *Mapp*. However, he begins his opinion by stating that both *Mapp* and *Ker* should be overruled.) (ILECJ)

cooling time: the time necessary to recover "cool blood" after excitement

Cooper v. California, 386 U.S. 58, 17 L. Ed. 2d 730, 87 S. Ct. 788 (1967): in this 5-4 opinion, the Court held that a search of an automobile is reasonable when by statute it is impounded for the purpose of forfeiture as it relates to the transportation of contraband, narcotics, alcohol, and unregistered firearms. (Mr. Justice Douglas, in his dissent, said he felt the Court's opinion either "overrules *Preston* sub silentio," or "that when the Bill of Rights is applied to the states by reason of the Fourteenth Amendment, a watered-down version is used.") (ILECJ)

coordinate method: a system commonly used in sketching to show the relative positions of one point to another (LEV)

coprolalia: medical term for using obscene language; it may occur suddenly in a normal person, possibly indicating mental instability

coprophilia: defecation involved in producing sexual gratification; interest in feces in an abnormal way (LEV) copulation: the act of uniting in sexual intercourse (CDTP)

copy board: a board or easel to which photographs or other originals are fastened while being copied (MPPF)

copyright: an exclusive right granted by law to an author or artist to publish or reproduce his work for a term of years. Holders of copyrights may protect themselves against infringement in the courts. In the United States a copyright runs for 28 years and may be renewed for another 28 years; thereafter the copyrighted work is held to be in the public domain. An international convention to which most of the states of the world adhere prevents infringement by the nationals of one state of the copyrighted productions of nationals of another state (DAP)

copyright law, the first: securing benefit of copyright was passed May 15, 1672, by the General Court of Massachusetts assembled in Boston, Mass., which granted John Usher, a book seller, the privilege of publishing on his own account a revised edition of *The General Laws and Liberties of the Massachusetts Colony.* It was ordered "that for at least seven years, unless he shall have sold them all before that time, there shall be no other or further impression made by any person thereof in this jurisdiction." The penalty for violation of the copyright was treble the whole charges of printing and paper (FAMOUS)

copyright law (state), the first: was "an act for the encouragement of literature and genius," passed during the session of the General Court of Assembly of the Governor and Company of the State of Conn., held in Hartford, Conn., Jan. 8–Feb. 7, 1783. The law gave authors sole right of publication for 14 years with power of renewal. Massachusetts passed a law March 17, 1783, for a 21-year period. Both laws extended rights only to other states having reciprocal legislation (FAMOUS)

copyright law (United States), the first: was an act (1 Stat. L. 124) "for the encouragement of learning by securing the copies of maps, charts, and books to the authors and proprietors of such copies during the times therein mentioned." The bill was signed by the Speaker and the President of the Senate, May 25, 1790, laid before President George Washington on May 27, 1790, and signed May 31, 1790. Rights were granted only to citizens of the United States, a policy which continued until 1891. Protection was extended over a 14-year period, renewal rights being granted only if the author was still alive (FAMOUS)

coram nobis [*Lat lit before us*]: formerly a manner of appeal; applied to writs of error

core: a formation or character detail in fingerprints used in classifying the pattern. It is the approximate center of the pattern area. It is placed upon or within the innermost looping ridge (LEV)

Corex: a trademark of the Corning Glass Works for a type of glass which is highly transparent to ultraviolet light (MPPF)

corned powder: when gunpowder is ground, moistened, and formed into grains, it is called "corned powder." If it is left dry, the resultant dustlike material is called "serpentine powder" (DWMT)

cornering: the handling characteristics of a vehicle during an abrupt change of direction (TDPPC)

coroner: an official who performs specified duties in regard to investigating death cases where there are questionable circumstances or where the deceased was unattended by a physician at the time of death. This office originated in England in the 12th century and was adopted in most states in the United States. Usu. there is one per county. He is elected. The qualifications for one seeking this position differ by statute among the states. In some states the coroner has been replaced by a medical examiner, who must be highly trained in the medical field (LEV)

corporal punishment: physical punishment

corpse: dead body, commonly of a human being.

corpus delicti: the substance of the crime—composed of two elements: (1) the act and (2) the criminal agency producing the act. In a homicide case it must be shown that a human was killed and that the killing was done illegally. In a suicide or accidental death the proof of corpus delicti is not satisfied   (LEV)

correctional client: a person convicted of a crime and sentenced to correctional treatment—both prisoners and parolees would be included

correctional institution: an institution such as a prison that is concerned with rehabilitation rather than punishment

correctional officer: prison guard

corrections: the study of convicted criminals and their rehabilitation

corroborate: to confirm, to "back up" someone's statement; to make it stronger   (LEV)

corroborating evidence: additional evidence confirming that already given

corrosion: damaging change inside the gun barrel caused from chemical reactions of the residue of ammunition fired in the gun or from other chemicals. Proper cleaning and oiling will prevent much of this   (LEV)

corrupt: to break the morals and character of someone; to taint; to make the honest dishonest (LEV)

corrupt practices acts: a series of state and federal laws enacted after 1890 for the purpose of eliminating political practices deemed undesirable. These laws attempted to eliminate bribery, illegal registration, and padded voting, and placed limitations upon contributions to and expenditures by political parties. The first state law was passed in New York in 1890, and was shortly followed by similar legislation in California, Colorado, Kansas, Massachusetts, and Michigan. By 1952 all the states had such legislation. These laws vary in content, some applying merely to primary or other nominating activities, while others apply to elections and/or nominations. Because of their ambiguous phraseology and the lack of enforcement measures, these acts have never been fully successful. Evasions by individuals and lobbying organizations, coupled with machine control of municipal and state politics, have rendered them ineffective. Their general provisions include clauses requiring publicity on campaign finances, identification of donors, and penal provisions concerning violations   (DOAH)

corruption of blood: the legal consequence, under the old common law of conviction of treason or felony, according to which the person so convicted could neither possess nor transmit by inheritance any property, rank, or title
(DAP)

cosmopolitanism: a philosophy or way of life which tolerates and attempts to understand other ideals and institutions in addition to one's own and which rejects intense local attachments and narrow patriotism in favor of more general, and even universal, cultural and political values   (DAP)

cost: the outlay for data, equipment, or operations. Relevant cost concepts are average, fixed, marginal, and replaceable   (ADPS)

Costello, Frank (*1891–*): a New York gambler and racketeer, Costello is a major influence in Cosa Nostra activities on the East Coast

counsel: legal assistance from one trained in law; an attorney (LEV)

count: (1) to state or plead a case (2) each separate offense in an indictment

countenance: to tolerate or approve

of

counterfeiting: the making of imitation money and obligations of the government. Counterfeiting is a federal violation of the law. Primary investigative jusrisdiction is in the U.S. Secret Service, Department of the Treasury   (LEV)

county: a geographical and political division of the state, in all states except Louisiana, where such is called a parish   (LEV)

county court: a body formerly composed of all the justices of the peace within a county which was both the chief county administrative board and a court inferior to the circuit court. At present it may have purely administrative, or purely judicial functions, or combinations of both, depending on the laws of particular States   (DAP)

coupled rangefinder: a rangefinder connected to the focusing mechanism of the lens so that the lens is focused while measuring the distance to the subject   (MPPF)

court: the judicial branch of the government. The official body or agency which dispenses justice. The meeting of persons, by authority of law, for administration of justice   (LEV)

court, adolescent: an experimental court designed to deal with persons between the age of 16 (when the jurisdiction of the juvenile court ends) and 18 or 21, when moral responsibility seems to have matured. The procedure follows the same informal pattern as the juvenile court, and probation and other protective services are used extensively. Chicago and New York have experimented with this type of court but opinions differ as to its value   (DOS)

court, canonical: the ecclesiastical court of the Middle Ages to which criminal cases and cases involving domestic and marital law were referred   (DOS)

court, criminal: a court where criminal, as opposed to civil, cases are tried

court, domestic relations: a court having jurisdiction over cases involving strained relations between husband and wife, such as desertion and neglect, as well as cases of juvenile delinquency. In the latter cases, parent-child relationships are recognized as basically important in producing the delinquency and similarly significant in working out any effective adjustment or plan of treatment for the child. The general philosophy underlying the organization of such courts for dealing with delinquency is to the effect that the family is a unit and that the adjustment is frequently a family rather than an individual problem. Domestic relations courts exist only in our larger cities where sufficient cases arise to warrant a separate court   (DOS)

court, inferior: a court of primary and/or limited jurisdiction. It tries cases of a minor nature. It is generally not a court of record, i.e., no record of the proceedings is made (unless worked out by the parties). It usu. tries only misdemeanor cases, holds preliminary hearings or examinations. It acts as a committing agency for higher courts. Such courts include: Justice of the Peace, Police Courts, Mayor's Court, and Municipal or City Courts   (LEV)

court, juvenile: a court dealing with youthful offenders or juvenile dependents and with adults who contribute to the delinquency of children. In most states the jurisdiction of such courts is limited to children under sixteen; a few have jurisdiction over cases under 18, and California has jurisdiction over young persons under 21. In general, capital offenses of juveniles may be transferred to the regular criminal court, however. Juvenile delinquents are considered wards of the court and are presumed to be treated as children needing help rather than as guilty persons requiring punishment. Hearings are usu. private, and there is generally no trial, although a number of states paradoxically allow a trial if demanded by the child's parents or his "next friend" (DOS)

court, magistrates: in most cities, the lowest court of original jurisdiction in criminal cases. Suspects apprehended by the police are first arraigned in magistrates court. Here evidence is examined. If in the mind of the magistrate the evidence is sufficient, the suspect is bound over for the grand jury or some other specialized court, and bail is set to insure the suspect's appearance at trial. If the offense is a minor one such as violation of a city ordinance the magistrate may have the power to make a judgment and set the penalty (DOS)

court, specialized: a court which has jurisdiction over special types of criminal civil suits. For example, the Morals Court, the Juvenile Court, the District Court, the Appellate Court, are specialized courts (DOS)

court, supreme: the court of last resort—highest court, found in the federal system and in each state as a part of the state system. In the states it is preceded by the name of the state (LEV)

court house: the building at the county seat which houses the principal offices of county government and provides quarters for courts (DAP)

court-martial: a tribunal in one of the armed services composed of officers and enlisted men, which tries armed forces personnel or other persons accused of violating military law. A *general court-martial* of five or more persons, a judge advocate, and a defense counsel may try any offense. *Special* and *summary courts-martial* have limited jurisdiction. In the American armed services, a court-martial verdict may, in some instances, be appealed to the U.S. Court of Military Appeals, which is composed of civilian judges, but not to the civil courts (DAP)

court-martial trial, the first: was held Aug. 24, 1676, in Newport, R.I., by Governor Walter Clarke, Deputy Governor John Crayton, and assistants. Edmund Calverly was the Attorney General. Quanpen, an Indian sachem also known as Sowagonish, was found guilty of participation in King Philip's War against the colonists and ordered shot on August 26. Others who had participated in the war were sentenced to various penalties (FAMOUS)

court-martial trial, the first in the United States at which enlisted men were allowed to sit as members of the court: was convened Feb. 3, 1949, at Fort Bragg, N.C., and consisted of four sergeants and five officers. Rudy F. Johnson, 19, was convicted of escaping from the guardhouse and sentenced to six months at hard labor and fined $50 a month for six months. On the same day, a trial was held at First Army Headquarters on Governors Island, N.Y. It consisted of three sergeants and five officers. Private Thomas F. Quinn of Brooklyn, N.Y., 21, was convicted of absence without leave and theft of government and private property and sentenced to one year at hard labor and a dishonorable discharge (FAMOUS)

court of appeals: a judicial tribunal whose jurisdiction is usually limited to the consideration of points of law in cases already tried and decided by courts of original jurisdiction. In New York, Kentucky, and Maryland it is the name of the highest State court. In about one-fourth of the States and in the federal judicial system it is the name of an intermediate court (DAP)

court of chancery: a court of equity. Formerly existed in England and still exists in some states in the United States for those courts having general equity powers (LEV)

court of claims: a special federal or State court with jurisdiction to hear and decide cases concerning certain carefully defined classes of pecuniary claims against the Government. *See* U.S. Court of Claims
(DAP)

court of claims, the first: was established by an act "to establish a court for the investigation of claims against the United States" (10 Stat. L. 612), signed Feb. 24, 1855, by President Franklin Pierce. It required the appointment of three judges with life tenure by the President with the consent of the Senate. President Pierce appointed Isaac Blackford of Indiana and John James Gilchrist of New Hampshire on March 3, 1855. The judges received $4,000 annually. The court was organized May 11, 1855, with Judge Gilchrist as presiding judge. It was reorganized by act of March 3, 1863 (12 Stat. L. 765). Until March 3, 1887, it was the only court in which cases could be prosecuted against the government
(FAMOUS)

court of common pleas: a court of original jurisdiction for trials according to common law

court of equity: a court which administers justice according to the principles of equity

court of errors and appeals: in New Jersey (and formerly New York), the court of last resort

court of general jurisdiction: a court of original jurisdiction. A trial court (usually a court of record) having jurisdiction over most criminal and civil matters arising in its territorial jurisdiction (LEV)

court of general sessions: in certain states, a court of general original jurisdiction

court of original jurisdiction: trial court. Court of general jurisdiction; usually has jurisdiction to try all cases brought before it. It often hears cases appealed to it from an inferior court—such appeals are heard *de novo*, i.e., all over again   (LEV)

court of primary jurisdiction: a court which has authority to hear (try) cases at the point of origin
(LEV)

court of record: a court which exists independently of the magistrate who presides over it, which keeps a permanent record, which may punish contempt by fine or imprisonment, and to which writs of error or certiorari may be directed. Courts of justices of the peace, and municipal, police, and probate courts are not of record unless so designated by statute
(DAP)

Court of Star Chamber: an English court originally created to prevent the obstruction of justice in the lower courts. Its powers were expanded to an unreasonable degree, and it was finally abolished

courtroom demeanor: actions and statements of a person while in court. This includes testimony, conduct, and personal appearance in the courtroom. It is important for the officer to give thought and preparation to this part of his work. He should: (1) know the facts of the investigation conducted by him—review notes and reports prior to trial; (2) dress appropriately; (3) talk at a voice level so as to be heard by all in the courtroom; (4) be frank and truthful in his testimony; (5) maintain poise and composure
(LEV)

courtroom disruptions: courtroom misconduct which disrupts the orderly proceedings of the court. The U.S. Supreme Court has ruled that the judge may take one or more of three steps to insure orderly conduct in court: (1) warn the defendant (if he is the unruly one) and then exclude him from the courtroom and proceed with the trial; (2) bind and gag him; (3) cite him for contempt of court [Illinois v. Allen. 397 U.S. 337 (1970)] *See* unruly persons
(LEV)

courts, federal: the courts established or provided for by Article

III of the federal Constitution, and established by Congress under its delegated powers. As defined by the U.S. Supreme Court these include the constitutional courts, such as the U.S. Supreme Court, the Courts of Appeal, and the District Courts as well as the special or legislative courts customarily established by Congress by virtue of its powers under Article I, Section 8 of the Constitution
(DOAH)
courts, state: the various judicial systems in the 50 states. Authorized under the Tenth Amendment of the federal Constitution they are established by the state constitutions or state legislation. Three features are common to the organization of all state court systems. Each state has a high court of appeals (usually a Supreme Court), a level of courts of original and general jurisdiction commonly called district or county courts, and at the bottom a tier of justice of the peace courts, including a miscellany of municipal, police, and magistrate courts for the trial of minor civil and criminal cases. Some states have an additional group of intermediate courts of appeal. All states have varying specialized courts for the administration of estates, wills, domestic relations and children's problems, juvenile delinquency, and small claims (DOAH)
courts, trial: courts that have the authority to conduct trials and all the business relating to them
covenant: legal undertaking or promise (LEV)
cover: something behind which a person may place himself so as to be less visible and also be protected from gunfire or other means of injury (LEV)
covering power: the capacity of a lens to give a sharply defined image to the edges of the sensitized material it is designed to cover at the largest possible aperture (MPPF)

covert: (1) hidden or secret, not overt (2) sheltered (A covert woman is under the protection of her husband.)
coverture: legal status of a married woman (LEV)
Cox v. Louisiana, 379 U.S. 536, 13 L. Ed. 2d 471, 85 S. Ct. 453 (1965): the Court said: "We emphatically reject the notion urged by the appellant that the First and Fourteenth Amendments afford the same kind of freedom to those who would communicate ideas by conduct such as patrolling, marching, and picketing on streets and highways, as these amendments afford to those who communicate ideas by pure speech. . ." (ILECJ)
Cox v. New Hampshire, 312 U.S. 569, 85 L. Ed. 1049, 61 S. Ct. 762 (1941): the Court held unanimously that states may regulate parades as an incident to regulating streets for traffic purposes (ILECJ)
crash truck: specialized firefighting apparatus designed to handle fire and accidents involving aircraft. May also refer to special apparatus used to control serious vehicle fires on highways (LEV)
credibility: trustworthiness, believability; the dependability of the testimony (LEV)
credible: believable, trustworthy, reliable (LEV)
credit card: a card issued by a company authorizing the named holder to purchase merchandise and/or services on credit and pay later (LEV)
crim. con.: abbr. for criminal conversation: adultery
crime: a violation of the criminal law, i.e., a breach of the conduct code specifically sanctioned by the state, which through its legislative agencies defines crimes and their penalties, and through its administrative agencies prosecutes offenders and imposes and administers punishments. The term crime is often carelessly and erro-

neously used to designate any kind of behavior as injurious to society, even though not defined by the criminal law   (DOS)

crime, capital: an offense where the punishment may be death, regardless of whether or not the death penalty is actually inflicted. It remains so even where juries are given the option of imposing life imprisonment instead of death as the penalty. Capital crimes are usually not bailable. The number of offenses regarded as capital has been sharply reduced in modern times   (DOS)

crime, causes of: imputed agents or forces determining violations of law. The causes of crime have never been satisfactorily isolated. When used to explain the incidence of crime in general or of certain classes of crimes, the imputed causes of crime are more likely to describe factors of greater or lesser risk for individuals getting acted upon officially. When used to explain the behavior of a single individual, causes represent the attempts to factorize individual cases by ordinary qualitative analysis or clinical diagnosis. The search for causes of crime or of criminal behavior has been fraught with the difficulty of isolating the differential impact of situational factors on varying mental and physical constitutions. It has also been fraught with the difficulty of demonstrating that such and such combination of factors apply to delinquents rather than to nondelinquents or to delinquent behavior rather than to non-delinquent behavior   (DOS)

crime, companionate: a crime committed jointly by two, or occasionally more than two, persons against a third party. Companionate crime is differentiated from organized crime, in that the former is occasional and generally involves only one offense, while the latter is consistent and habitual behavior. It is differentiated

also from such behavior as fornication or gambling in that it has a victim, while fornication and gambling have no third party who is a direct victim   (DOS)

crime, etiology of: the study of the causes of criminal behavior by the case study or clinical method, usually proceeding from the study of individual cases. Isolation of a factor connected with crime in general, by statistical or observational methods, would be conceived as contributing to a study of general causes rather than to etiology of crime   (DOS)

crime, multiple causes of: opposed to the conception of a single cause of crime, such as heredity, feeble-mindedness, poverty, and so on, multiple causes imply that several factors are at work cumulatively to produce crime. The efficaciousness of the conception of multiple causes of crime becomes more apparent in the study of individual cases than in the study of crime in general. Multiple causes can include one dominant factor and two or three minor factors, or they can merely include several reinforcing factors without reference as to which plays the major role. There are limits to the multiplicity of causes. In the clinical or individual case approach, insistence that there are more than four or five causative factors in any case usually means that the clinician or researcher has seized upon factors not fundamentally or directly related to the course of behavior. In the study of general causes of crime by mass statistics or general observation, the inclusion of almost any and all kinds of causes is almost as bad as the fixation on one cause. Everything under the sun cannot be included under multiple causes, unless we desire to discover some very remote and very indirect connections with crime which are not at all causative. Many of the indirect factors related to crime by contingency methods are likely to be risk factors rather than causative factors (DOS)

crime, organized: crime which involves the cooperative effort of two or more criminals in the broadest sense of the term. All degrees of organization may be involved, from the loose informal type to a rather strict institutionalized kind like that of any business organization, or from an organization involving only a few persons to one involving hundreds (DOS)

Crime Control Digest: a bi-weekly publication reporting current items of interest in the field of criminal justice published by *SCI/Tech Digests*, Inc., National Press Bldg., Washington, D.C. 20004 (LEV)

crime gradient: a concept adopted by some criminologists in the study of the ecological distribution of crime. It designates the profile of a curve based on the crime rates of consecutive geographic areas located along a straight line (DOS)

crime index: another name for a *modus operandi* file. The method of the crime is described (LEV)

crime insurance: the Housing Act of 1970 provides government assistance (financial) to those in high crime areas who cannot otherwise buy crime-loss insurance at reasonable rates (LEV)

crime pact, the first interstate: was effected between New York and New Jersey and signed Sept. 16, 1833, in New York City by Benjamin Franklin Butler, Peter Augustus Jay, Henry Seymour, Theodore Frelinghuysen, James Parker, and Lucius Quintius Cincinnatus Elmer. Article 6 related to criminal process for New Jersey and article 7 for New York. The New Jersey legislature ratified the pact on Feb. 5, 1834. The pact was ratified by act of Congress, June 28, 1834 (FAMOUS)

crime prevention commission for interstate cooperation, the first: was the New Jersey Commission on Interstate Cooperation, established by Senate Joint Resolution No. 3, introduced and sponsored by Senator Joseph Gustave Wolber. The joint resolution was passed and signed March 12, 1935, by Governor Harold Giles Hoffman and the commission was immediately organized with Judge Richard Hartshorne as the first chairman. The commission consisted of 15 members, 5 each appointed by the Senate, the Assembly, and the Governor. The commission was responsible for developing cooperation between states on various problems such as crime control, motor vehicles, conflicting taxation, labor problems, agriculture, etc. (FAMOUS)

crime scene: the place or area where a crime was committed. It is important that certain things be done as soon as possible concerning a crime scene, after the police arrive: (1) it should be protected to avoid disturbance or damage to evidence; (2) photographs should be made if practical; (3) it should be sketched and charted; (4) it should be systematically and thoroughly searched; (5) detailed notes should be taken of all facts (LEV)

crime scene sketching: the drawing and charting of a crime scene showing the relative positions of objects, one to another (LEV)

Crime Statistics: a nationwide compilation of crime statistics, based on law enforcement information furnished by local agencies, is prepared and published annually by the FBI in "Crime in the United States," Uniform Crime Report, available through the U.S. Government Printing Office, Washington, D.C. 20402 (LEV)

crime surveys: surveys made with reference to the nature and extent of crime, penal law enforcement, and the administration of criminal courts. The *Report of the National Commission on Law Observance and Enforcement* is the most notable survey made in the U.S. Other surveys include the *Missouri Crime Survey* and the *Illinois Crime Survey* (DOS)

crimes known to the police: reports to police that crimes have been committed. Index currently in use to determine the amount and rates of crime in the United States (DOS)

criminal: a person who has committed a crime. Statistically, a person who has been convicted of a crime. The attempt to include in the concept of "criminal" only those who have committed crimes of a more serious nature, or crimes involving extreme moral turpitude, or persons whose motives are distinctly evil has no basis in science and can lead only to confusion (DOS)

criminal, born: a concept formulated by Lombroso in accordance with which certain persons are biologically so constituted that they must of necessity be criminals. A hereditary criminal (DOS)

criminal, endogenic: a term used by European criminologists to denote a type of offender whose criminality is determined mainly by hereditary and constitutional (both physical and mental) factors (DOS)

criminal, exogenic: used by European criminologists to designate a type of offender whose etiology is determined primarily by situational factors (DOS)

criminal, pathological: a criminal who deviates from the mentally normal type. There are no generally accepted classifications of the mentally abnormal types. The following simple classification, however, is frequently used: mental defective or feebleminded, psychotic or insane, and psychopathic. The latter is the most difficult to define. It includes those criminals who are neurotic, epileptic, and who are judged to possess either a post-encephalitic or a psychopathic personality. Encephalitis is a disease resulting from lesions in the central nervous system. It makes for lethargic and irritable behavior. It also retards learning. The chief characteristic of a psychopathic personality is the deeply disturbed emotional life. There is no standard method of diagnosing a personality as psychopathic. A comparison of psychiatric reports on the psychopathy of criminals shows wide variations in the conclusions as to the proportion of criminals so characterized (DOS)

criminal, white-collar: a person of the upper socioeconomic class who violates the criminal law in the course of his occupational or professional activities; the state, insofar as it reacts against white-collar crimes, generally does so through bureaus and commissions rather than through the police and the criminal courts. A wealthy confidence man, who is a part of the underworld, would not be a white-collar criminal, because he does not have the esteem of the law-abiding community. A wealthy and esteemed business man who commits murder in connection with a "love-triangle" would not be a white-collar criminal (DOS)

criminal action: the accusation, trial, and punishment of a person charged with a public offense. It may be prosecuted by the state as a party itself or by the state at the instance of an individual, to prevent a crime against his person or property

Criminal Appeals Act: an act of Congress, March 2, 1907, which allows the United States to appeal to the Supreme Court in a criminal case when a lower court, without having placed the defendant in jeopardy, has held that a federal statute is unconstitutional (DAP)

criminal behavior: usu. synonymous with crime or violation of criminal code. However, usage places the emphasis on violating behavior whether known or unknown to authorities. As a form of violation, it is akin to violations of all codes or rules: those of family, church, school, labor unions, and various associations. The thing which makes behavior criminal is that the offense against code becomes reportable to the governmental or state authorities (DOS)

criminal biology: the scientific study of the relation of hereditary physical traits to criminal character, i.e., to innate tendencies to commit crime in general or crimes of any particular type (DOS)

criminal career: a career involving habitual crime or devoted to crime as a means of livelihood (DOS)

Criminal Charge: a criminal accusation, through a written complaint, an indictment, or information which is then acted upon in prosecution

criminal constitution: the innate traits of an individual that predispose him to criminal conduct or a life of crime (DOS)

criminal conversation: Adultery; illegal sexual relations with a married woman (LEV)

criminal culture: an integrated set of overt practices and ideas characteristic of a group of people and in conflict with the criminal law; a particular criminal act may be supported by, and be a part of, the criminal culture, which would include similar acts by other members of the group, and for all of these acts rationalizations, evaluations, and codes of behavior in agreement with the criminal acts; in contrast, embezzlement and murder are often committed without the support of any criminal culture (DOS)

criminal fence: a person or firm that makes a business of trading in stolen commodities, either exclusively or more often in connection with a legitimate business. A receiver of stolen goods may make trade in such goods a business, in which case he would be a fence,

or he may receive a stolen commodity and use it for his own purposes, in which case he would not be a fence; every fence is a receiver, but not every receiver is a fence (DOS)

criminal identification: the recording of significant physical characteristics of individual criminals, especially fingerprints, for rapid and permanent identification (DAP)

criminal insane: the legal term for the state of mental derangement which accompanies or induces the commission of a crime and prevents the criminal from knowing the criminal nature of the act committed. The basic test of insanity is the knowledge of right and wrong; thus mental defect is often confused with mental deficiency. Greater interest in the mental processes of those who commit crimes led to a direct challenge of the traditional legal interpretations of insanity as a defense in criminal cases (DOS)

criminal intelligence: any information concerning alleged criminals. The information is not always found to be true through public proceedings or a guilty verdict

criminal intent: the intent to do an act the results of which are a crime or violation of the law. There is general intent and specific intent. Some statutes require the existence of specific intent, some require only general intent and if no intent is set forth in the description of the crime by law no intent is required but the doing of the act is sufficient (LEV)

criminal justice: in the broad meaning of the phrase criminal justice refers to the machinery, procedures, personnel, and purposes which have to do with the content of the criminal law and with the arrest, trial, conviction, and disposition of offenders. The administration of criminal justice thus involves the penal code, the police system, the prosecutor's office, courts, penal institutions, probation, parole, and the officials charged with administering their defined duties   (DOS)

criminal justice, mortality of: surveys, in the form of statistical data, which serve as guides in the analysis of procedural and administrative steps in the administration of criminal justice. Such data on crime cases and prison population reveal the strength or weakness in the various agencies of justice   (DOS)

criminal law: the branch of jurisprudence which deals with offenses committed against the safety and order of the state   (DAP)

criminal man: the conception of the criminal as an individual possessing distinctive physical or psychical characteristics   (DOS)

criminal maturation: the development of a criminal in the established techniques, attitudes, and ideology of criminal behavior; this phrase is based on the assumption that development in criminal behavior follows a standardized pattern analogous to physiological development with advancing age   (DOS)

criminal offense: an offense against a sovereign state, and includes both crimes and misdemeanors. The term has been defined by statute as consisting in a violation of a public law, in the commission of which there shall be a union or joint operation of an act and intention, or criminal negligence, and also as any offense, as well a misdemeanor as a felony, for which any punishment by imprisonment or fine, or both, may, by law, be inflicted   (CDTP)

criminal organization: the structure of relationships between persons and groups which makes the commission of crime possible and which facilitates avoidance of the legal penalties. This structure may be loose, informal, and decentralized, or it may be explicitly institutionalized and centralized. Also, any group of persons who systematically devote themselves, as a

collective unit, to the commission unit, to the commission of crime   (DOS)

criminal procedure: the legal methods used in the apprehension, trial, prosecution, and setting the punishment of criminals

criminal procedure, law of: the law dealing with all facets of the procedures followed in taking an offender into custody through the final court proceedings. Arrest, search and seizures, methods of legally charging the offender with crime, arraignment, trial, and sentencing are included   (LEV)

criminal proceeding: a procedure instigated to prevent a crime or to try and punish the individual who has committed a crime

criminal prosecution: the trial procedure in a criminal court

criminal responsibility: criminal liability for an offense. To be so liable the person committing the act must have done so of his own free will and volition; he must have the capacity for distinguishing right from wrong; and he must have the ability to foresee the evil consequences of his act. The presence of these conditions constitutes responsibility; hence, liability and punishability. On the other hand, certain circumstances may negate responsibility under the criminal law. These are principally: (1) Infancy. Under the common law children under seven years of age are regarded as not being responsible. A like presumption holds for children between seven and fourteen years of age, except that in such cases the presumption may be overcome by evidence. At fourteen years of age under the common law a child becomes fully responsible for his acts. However, it may be added that in most states statutory provisions have given to the juvenile courts jurisdiction over the criminal or delinquent acts of children including those who are beyond the age of fourteen. The maximum age for such juvenile court jurisdiction varies among the states from fifteen to twenty-one years. But it is to be noted that in most states for grave crimes the juvenile courts may waive jurisdiction, thus making children liable to the penalties imposed in the criminal courts; (2) Insanity. A second exemption from criminal responsibility, and hence from liability, is on grounds of insanity. This is interpreted by the courts to mean that he is incapable of making moral distinctions between right and wrong, or of knowing the evil consequences of his acts. The existence or non-existence of insanity is a matter of evidence at the time of trial, and the issue is determined by the trial jury. If an insanity plea is sustained, the accused person is held not responsible and therefore not liable to punishment; (3) Intoxication. Ordinarily, intoxication provides no exemption from criminal liability, though it may reduce the degree of responsibility which a drunken person may be assumed to have had at the time of his offense, and, hence, lessen the severity of his punishment (DOS)

criminal saturation, law of: a theory developed by the Italian criminologist Ferri. The gist of it was that each society has the number of criminals which the particular conditions in that society produce. "As a given volume of water at a definite temperature will dissolve a fixed quantity of chemical substance and not an atom more or less; so in a given social environment with definite individual and physical conditions, a fixed number of delicts, no more and no less, can be committed" (DOS)

criminal statistics: the tabulated numerical data found in the official reports of agencies which deal with the apprehension, prevention, and treatment of offenders against the criminal law. The unit of tabulation may be the case, the offender, or the offense. A common classification of criminal statistics distinguishes between police, judicial, and penal statistics. In the United States the term is generally inclusive; on the continent of Europe it is ordinarily used to designate only the tabulations based on the characteristics of the offender, as distinguished from statistics of criminal justice, and statistics of penal institutions (DOS)

criminal syndicalism: a legal phrase of American law to describe the advocating of the unlawful destruction of property, or an unlawful change in its ownership; a doctrine and practice attributed to the Industrial Workers of the World, a labor organization, and embodied in many state statutes aimed to curb their activities, adopted from 1917 to 1924 (DOS)

criminal tendencies: classifiable behavior tendencies which, if not recognized or checked, may end in the ultimate commission of a criminal act or acts; behavior tendencies which under certain conditions can be expected to develop into a delinquent or criminal pattern; tendencies toward criminal behavior (DOS)

criminal tribes: tribes with a culture which sanctions behavior toward non-members of the tribe which is prohibited by the laws of the state to which the tribe belongs (DOS)

criminalist: a scientist trained to perform crime laboratory functions and relate the findings to criminal investigations (LEV)

criminalistics: the science of crime detection, involving the application of chemistry, physics, physiology, psychology, and other sciences.

criminate: to accuse of a crime

criminology: the scientific study of crime and criminal behavior, which often views crime as a social phenomenon and is concerned with finding causes for criminal behavior

crimping: the end of the cartridge

case or shotgun shell is crimped inward at the end holding the bullet or shot, so as to hold in position (LEV)

criterion: (1) a value used for judging, as in determining whether a condition is true or false (2) a rule or test for making a decision (ADPS)

Critical Stage: one or more points in the criminal justice process that are viewed by the courts as crucial to the outcome of a case

criticize: to make a statement of a critical nature concerning something or someone. ... It may be constructive or destructive criticism. The CADC (Circuit Court of Appeals, Washington, D.C.) on June 19, 1970 ruled in the case of *Minard* v. *Mitchell* that an officer has the constitutional right to criticize the operations of his department and no punitive action could be taken against him for it (LEV)

Crofton, Sir Walter: director of the Irish prison system in 1846. Crofton improved upon the ticket-of-leave system established by Alexander Maconochie by including provisions for revocation of the ticket-of-leave if conditions were violated. He also included provisions for supervision by police officials (LCC)

crop: to trim or cut away the unnecessary portions of a print to improve composition (MPPF)

cross alarm: (1) an alarm condition signaled by crossing or shorting an electrical circuit (2) the signal produced due to a cross alarm condition (TDIAS)

cross-examination: the questioning of a witness by the party opposed to the party which called the witness for direct examination

cross fire: two or more intersecting lines of gunfire (DWMT)

cross hair: an inscribed line or a strand of hair, wire, silk, or the like used in an optical sight for accurate sighting (DWMT)

crossing target: a moving target that crosses the line of sight at any angle. In firing at a crossing target, the firer must aim ahead of, or lead, the target so that the paths of the target and bullet will meet (DWMT)

crossover: an insulated electrical path used to connect foil across window dividers, such as those found on multiple pane windows, to prevent grounding and to make a more durable connection (TDIAS)

cross-projection: a method of sketching the details of a room where the walls and the ceiling are shown (drawn) as if they were on the same plane as the floor. This method gives a clear understanding of the scene, especially if evidence is found on the walls or ceiling (LEV)

cryptanalysis: the study of encrypted or coded texts; the steps or processes involved in converting encrypted text into plain text without initial knowledge of the key employed in the encryption (DWMT)

cryptographer: one who solves or deciphers cryptograms or decodes any secret communications (DWMT)

CS: a chemical agent used as tear gas. Chemical name is orthodchlorbenzalmalononitrile. It is newer than CN and has replaced the latter in some instances (LEV)

cubic inch displacement: the total displacement of an internal combustion engine measured in cubic inches (TDPPC)

culpable [*fr Lat culpa, blame*]: blamable but not necessarily criminal

culpable negligence: acts of negligence, where the doing or failure to do results in injury or death to persons and for which the person is held criminally responsible; act which is done carelessly and foreseeably would result in death or injury to other persons. No intent needs to be proven in such cases (LEV)

culprit: one who has violated the law but has not been convicted. He may still be sought for the crime or may have been legally charged with the crime but not tried (LEV)

cumulative: additional, increasing

cunnilingus: licking, sucking, or mouthing the female sex organ by a male or female (LEV)

Cupp v. Murphy, 412 U.S. 291, 36 L. Ed. 2d 900, 93 S. Ct. 2000 (1973): the court in a 7–2 opinion held that scrapings can be taken from a suspect (exigent circumstances) where probable cause existed to arrest although the arrest did not take place until about a month later (ILECJ)

curative statute: a law, retrospective in effect, which is designed to remedy some legal defect in previous transactions and validate them (DAP)

curb weight: the total weight of a vehicle including a full load of oil, coolant, and fuel but without any passengers or cargo (TDPPC)

curfew offenses: violations of a curfew

Currens, 290 F 2d 751 (1961): this decision establishes new standards of legal insanity and new horizons for diminishing criminal responsibility because of insanity at the time of the commission of a crime (AOJ)

cursive writing: hand writing, contrasted to hand printing (LEV)

curtain aperture: the slit in a focal plane shutter which permits the light to reach the film. The slit may be either fixed or variable (MPPF)

curtilage: the ground within a wall around a house or building

curvature of field: the saucer-shaped image of a flat object formed by an uncorrected lens (MPPF)

custodial care: the care afforded in institutions to socially incompetent persons who need close supervision or require personal assistance in performing elemental human functions (DOS)

custodial officer: one charged with the keep, safety, and/or detention of persons in a prison, jail, or hospital (LEV)

custody: the basic function of correctional institutions. Custody involves maintaining the security of the institution to ensure against escapes from the facility and crimes within it. The primary techniques of custody are controlling the movements of prisoners and providing for their segregation from other prisoners when necessary (IC)

custody, close: constant supervision of the prisoner on the assumption that he will not only run away if the opportunity is offered, but will make the opportunity (DOS)

custody, maximum: care in that type of prison which provides the maximum security—high walls, tool-proof bars, numerous guards, rigid discipline, etc.—for the most hardened prisoners, e.g., Alcatraz among the U.S. institutions (DOS)

custody, medium: care in an institution for prisoners with a type of physical plant less strongly built and equipped [than a maximum-custody facility] and intended to house the less hardened and dangerous criminals, and to give them more freedom of movement and greater self-direction (DOS)

custody, minimum: care of prisoners in an institution built, equipped, and guarded with the least possible restraint required to keep them safely, and to allow the greatest possible freedom. Such an institution is exemplified by some of the camps and farms, by some reformatories, or by honor dormitories within an institution (DOS)

custody, protective: detention by the police of persons essential to the prosecution of justice presumably in order to prevent reprisals against them by criminal elements for their part in furthering the investigation of crime (DOS)

customary law: law derived from long-established usages and customs; distinguished from written law (DAP) cut film: a flexible transparent base, coated with a sensitized emulsion and cut in sheets of various sizes. Often referred to as sheet film (MPPF)

cyan: a blue-green (minus red) color (MPPF)

cyanide gun: a device used for propelling hydrocyanic acid into the face of a murder victim. The acid vaporizes, causing death quickly, which resembles a heart attack (LEV)

cycle: to repeat a set of operations a prescribed number of times including, when required, supplying necessary address changes by arithmetical operations, by an index register, or in other ways (ADPS)

cyclic rate: the rate at which a succession of movements repeats itself, applied especially to the rate of fire of an automatic weapon; the maximum rate of fire for a given automatic weapon (DWMT)

cylinder: (1) the rotating chambered breech of a revolver. A swing-out cylinder is one that swings out for easier loading (ADPS) (2) (data processing) for disk units with multiple read-write heads, all of the data tracks under the read-write heads can be accessed without mechanical movement of the heads. If each disk surface has one read-write head, the tracks under them can be thought of as a *cylinder* consisting of one track from each disk (DWMT)

cylinder stop: the recesses in a revolver cylinder that are engaged by a lever to stop rotation and properly align the cylinder with the barrel (DWMT)

Czolgosz, Leon (*1873-1901*): an American anarchist, he shot and killed President William McKinley in Buffalo on Sept. 6, 1901. He felt that the President was "an enemy of the good working class" and must be executed. He was adjudged and electrocuted in New York Auburn Prison

D

D.A. (District Attorney): may also be called Prosecuting Attorney, Prosecutor, County Prosecutor. This official is elected to office by the people of his district. He represents the people (state, county, etc.) in prosecution of criminal offenders (LEV)

dactyloscopy: (1) fingerprints as a means of identification (LEV) (2) the study of fingerprints and their use as a means of identification (LEV)

dag: an early name for a short pistol, esp. a wheel lock (CDTP)

daguerreotype: an early photographic process which employs a silver-coated plate sensitized with silver iodide and silver bromide. After long exposure, the plate is developed by subjecting it to the mercury vapor (MPPF)

daily reports: a report, made daily, recording the work done by the officer during that day (LEV)

damages: compensation which the law will award for injury done. (CDTP)

Damascus barrel: a barrel that is produced by welding two or more rods or wires of iron or steel together, rolling them into a ribbon shape, and then wrapping the ribbon around a mandrel. The ribbon is then welded, and the tube is finished inside and out (DWMT)

Damascus steel: a hard, elastic steel once highly regarded for the production of sword blades. Like the steel in Damascus barrels, it is made by welding various strips of iron and steel together and then folding and refolding them. The material is characterized by wavy surface patterns (DWMT)

Dampier, William (*1652-1715*): English seaman and buccaneer, born in Somerset. Dampier had already done some buccaneering when he joined a big expedition preparing to leave Jamaica in 1680. With seven ships the buccaneers sailed to Darien, Panama, and then set off overland across the isthmus. After various hardships and adventures Dampier returned to England in 1691 and wrote an account of the expedition, *A New Voyage Round the World*, which became a best-seller   (CC)

D and D: drunk and disorderly

dangerous weapon: a weapon that is capable of producing a fatal wound

dangerousness: the term used to denote the seriousness of various offenses or offenders. It usu. refers to physical threat or harm rather than theft or property damage

dark current: the current output of a photoelectric sensor when no light is entering the sensor   (TDIAS)

darkroom: a room for photographic operations, mainly processing, which can be made free from white light and is usu. equipped with safelights emitting non-actinic light   (MPPF)

darkslide: a British term for a plate holder or a sheet-film holder   (MPPF)

data: figures, words, or charts that refer to or describe some situation   (ADPS)

data collection: incoming data. It is either added to a file on a real time basis or is stored for later file update on a batch basis   (LEV)

data density: the number of characters that can be stored per unit of length, area, or volume. Specifically, for magnetic tape, the number of bits in one row per inch of tape where one bit in each row across the tape makes up a frame representing one character   (ADPS)

data description: an entry in the data division of a COBOL program describing the characteristics of a data item in terms of level, name, length, and alphanumeric content   (ADPS)

data division: a division of a COBOL program describing the characteristics of data: files, records, and data elements   (ADPS)

data element: a group of characters that specify an *item* at or near the basic level. An *elementary* item—for example, "month,"—contains no subordinate item. A *group* item—for example, "date," which consists of day, month, and year—contains items that may be used separately and therefore treated as elementary items   (ADPS)

data item: a unit of data that can be identified by a name or combination of names and subscripts   (ADPS)

data origination: the steps used for obtaining data at the points where events occur. The operations may be manual or mechanical and the data may be obtained in a form that requires conversion or that is directly usable for further processing   (ADPS)

data processing: rearrangement and refinement of data into a form suitable for further use; often involves file processing to update files for transactions that occur   (ADPS)

data system redesign: stresses redesign of files, inputs, data flows; outputs and management procedures are viewed as fixed. New equipment is introduced when warranted   (ADPS)

date: a date placed at the foot of an affidavit for a search warrant is considered part of it, and is sufficient as alleging the time. Too, where the affidavit is incorrectly dated, by an oversight, as of the day after the date in the warrant, it being shown that the warrant was based on such affidavit, the affidavit need not be amended, and in like manner an error in dating the affidavit as of a date long before the date of the warrant and the date it was executed is amendable and will not invalidate the warrant; and, where the affidavit is not dated at all, but a search warrant issued thereon is dated, the warrant and affidavit being on the same paper, the defect does not invalidate the warrant, nor is it error on the trial to permit the judge who erroneously fixed the date to testify to the true date. (269 S.W. 748) (CDTP)

Daugherty, Harry M. (*1860-1941*): U.S. Attorney General (1921-1924). Accused of taking part in the scandal concerning the oil lands at Teapot Dome. The case was dismissed   (CVDE)

Davis, David (*1815-1886*): Associate Justice of U.S. Supreme Court (1862-1877). His decision in *ex parte Milligan* (1866), denouncing arbitrary military power, became a bulwark of civil liberty in the U.S. Helped manage Lincoln's campaign for presidency   (CVDE)

Davis v. Mississippi: a landmark case holding that fingerprints taken as a result of an illegal arrest were inadmissible in evidence. 394 U.S. 721 (1969)   (LEV)

Davis v. North Carolina, 384 U.S. 737, 16 L. Ed. 2d 895, 86 S. Ct. 1761 (1966): in a 7-2 decision the Court held that the original "voluntariness" test will apply to cases arising before *Escobedo* was decided. (This decision is significant in that it shows the *Johnson* decision did not foreclose a person from seeking a reversal of a conviction on the grounds an involuntary confession had been used against him at the trial.)   (ILECJ)

day in court: the right of a person to appear in court and be heard concerning his complaint or his defense

daylight: the light of day caused by the sun as opposed to that of the moon or artificial light   (CDTP)

daylight loading: any arrangement

on a camera, a film magazine, or a developing tank permitting insertion of film in daylight without the use of a darkroom or a changing bag   (MPPF)

day-parole: *See* work release

days of grace: certain days allowed for the payment of a bill or note or contract in addition to the time contracted for in the bill or note   (CDTP)

daytime: (1) that part of the day when there is enough light to see by (LEV) (2) (law) a "rule of thumb" criteria is that it is daytime when there is enough natural light to recognize a person's features at a distance of ten yards. This becomes important in connection with searches where the law and the search warrant specifies search during the daytime   (LEV)

daytop village: a program for rehabilitating drug addicts. *See* therapeutic community   (LEV)

dead body: a corpse. The body of a human being deprived of life, but not yet entirely disintegrated. A dead-born child is to be considered as if it had never been conceived or born.   (CDTP)

dead-born: an infant born dead. Legally such a child is considered never to have existed   (LEV)

dead letter: acts which have become obsolete by long disuse   (CDTP)

dead on arrival (D.O.A.): dead on arrival at a hospital   (LEV)

deadly weapon: a weapon capable of inflicting a fatal wound

death: condition of being dead; stopping of the functions of the vital organs permanently. With the advent of vital organ transplants by surgery the point of death has become a legal question upon which there is much discussion

death penalty: *See* capital punishment

death warrant: a written order (warrant) issued by the legally authorized executive official (usu. the Governor) setting the place and time for executing one sentenced to death by the court (LEV)

death watch: special guarding of a prisoner condemned to die, to prevent his escape or suicide (LEV)

debauchery: excessive hedonistic pleasure; usu. excessive sexual indulgence

debris: trash, rubbish, worthless fragments or parts resulting from the destruction of something (LEV)

Debs, Eugene V. (*1855-1926*): American Socialist leader. Advocate of industrial unionism and a pacifist; imprisoned 1895 for violating injunction in strike at Pullman, Ill., and in 1918 under Espionage Act. Presidential candidate five times. Widely revered as martyr for his principles (CVDE)

debt: something owed; an obligation

debtor: one who owes another

debtor, mortgage: one who gives a mortgage on property to secure a debt owed to another (LEV)

debug: to test a program by running it with test, simulated, or live data on a processor to find whether it works properly, and, if mistakes are revealed either in the final answer or at various stages of processing, to discover the source and make corrections (ADPS)

decapitate: to behead; to cut off the head (LEV)

decedent: one who has died, esp. one recently dead (LEV)

deceit: fraud or trickery; misrepresentation of facts

deceive: mislead; defraud; cheat (LEV)

decelerometer: a device for measuring deceleration in connection with brake testing (LEV)

decentralized data processing: processing data at many (or perhaps only one) locations for an organization that is decentralized managerially, geographically, or both (ADPS)

decimal: (1) pertaining to the number 10 (ADPS) (2) a number system whose base is the quantity 10; a system of notation utilizing ten symbols, 0,1, . . . 9 (ADPS)

decimal number: a number with the base 10 having positional values of 1000, 100, 10, 1, 1/10, 1/100, 1/1000, etc. (ADPS)

decimal point: the separating mark "." between the positional values of 1 and 1/10. The *actual* decimal may appear in data and is usually wanted in output for "display" purposes. If the actual decimal point is retained in data, it occupies an actual space in storage and precludes arithmetical operations (ADPS)

decimeter: a measure of length: 1/10 of a meter (MPPF)

decipher: to determine the meaning of; to decode; to arrive at the meaning of secret characters (LEV)

decision: (1) (data processing) a. in management, a conclusion arrived at after consideration b. in programming, a choice between alternatives depending on prior conditions and use of specified parts of the program (ADPS) (2) a court order, decree, or judgment on a question of law or fact. It differs from an opinion in that the latter is the basis of the decision (LEV)

decision plan: the system used for making managerial decisions; consists of rules prepared in advance or developed ad hoc and applied by men, machines, or some combination. Systems include the exception principle, internal decision, variable processing, manual intervention, and adaptive plans (ADPS)

decision table: organized tabular representation of relationships between variables, sets of conditions, and the related sequences of action that make up rules (ADPS)

deckle edge: a rough or irregularly trimmed edge on a sheet of paper (MPPF)

declaration: a statement

declaration of intention: a necessary step in the procedure of an alien becoming an American citizen. In this step he renounces allegiance to his native country and expresses his intention of becoming a citizen of the United States   (LEV)

declarations of persons other than defendant: declarations by the persons other than the defendant cannot be proved: (1) unless they are part of the res gestae, or (2) unless they are admissible as dying declarations, or (3) unless they are admissible as declarations by authority of the defendant, or (4) unless they are admissible as evidence given in a former proceeding   (CDTP)

declaratory judgment: a judicial declaration in an actual controversy of the existing rights of parties under a statute, contract, will, or other document, without executory process granting relief, but binding upon the parties. It is not necessary to show that any wrong has been done, as in action for damages; or that any is immediately threatened, as in injunction proceedings. In most States and territories, and in federal courts since 1934, this remedy has been made available by statute as a means of ascertaining the rights of parties without expensive litigation, though the courts tend to construe these statutes narrowly   (DAP)

declaratory statute: a statute designed to remove doubts as to the meaning of the law on some particular subject   (DAP)

decline: to refrain; turn down a proposition; refuse   (LEV)

decontamination: the process of making any person, object, or area safe by absorbing, destroying, neutralizing, making harmless, or removing chemical or biological agents or by removing radioactive material clinging to or around it   (DWMT)

decoration: a medal or ribbon awarded an individual for exceptional courage, skill, or meritorious achievement   (DWMT)

decoy: (1) one whose role is to lure a person into a situation where he may be the victim of a crime; one who assumes a role to divert attention away from another (LEV) (2) to lure   (LEV)

decree: a judgment of a court

deduce: to reach a conclusion or arrive at an answer by reasoning   (LEV)

deface: to disfigure, mar, or alter the face or surface of something; to obliterate, alter, or destroy such things as inscriptions, writings, etc.   (LEV)

de facto: (1) actually; in fact (DAP) (2) pertaining to a condition of affairs actually existing. Cf. de jure   (DAP)

defamation: the act of defaming another. Generally it is a violation of the criminal law and is the grounds for a civil action   (LEV)

defame: to make slanderous statements about someone; to maliciously publish or express to any person, other than the one defamed, anything which tends to (1) expose any person to hatred, contempt, or ridicule or (2) expose the memory of one deceased to such things; to injure the good name or reputation of another. The legal definition of defamation will differ among the states (LEV)

default: (1) fail to appear in court at an appointed or certain time. (He lost the case by default.) (LEV) (2) failure to pay a debt or obligation when due   (LEV)

defeat: the frustration, counteraction, or thwarting of an alarm device so that it fails to signal an alarm when a protected area is entered. Defeat includes both circumvention and spoofing   (TDIAS)

defendant: the individual charged in a criminal case; the person against whom relief or recovery is sought in a legal action or suit

defense: (1) the party (or his attorney) against whom an action in court is brought—civil or criminal. Under the adversary system used in our judicial system the two parties in a criminal action are prosecution and the defense (LEV) (2) that which is offered or pleaded in denial of the charge against the accused (LEV)

Defense, Department of: headed by the Secretary of Defense, it is an executive branch of the U.S. Government (LEV)

defense attorney: the lawyer representing the defendant in a criminal action

defense counsel: counsel for the defendant; an attorney who represents and aids the defendant. The courts have held in recent years that the defendant has the right to counsel, either employed by the defendant or appointed by the court, to represent the defendant at each critical stage of the prosecutive procedure, as guaranteed by the Sixth Amendment of the U.S. Constitution (LEV)

defense of accused person: it is a universal principle of criminal law in the United States that a person accused of crime is entitled to the advice of a lawyer and to be represented by him on his trial. In felony cases this principle is carried further, and in many states counsel is provided without cost for a defendant who is too poor to employ a lawyer. In most of the states such counsel is appointed by the judge in the court where the defendant is standing trial. Some jurisdictions have an officer, known as a public defender, who represents impecunious defendants (CDTP)

defensive driving: driving a motor vehicle so as to avoid accidents even though other drivers may be at fault (LEV)

defensive tactics: knowledge and skill in techniques used to defend oneself against physical injury (LEV)

defer: put off; postpone

deferred sentencing: a system in some states, provided by law, where the person convicted of a crime may be placed on probation immediately following the conviction or after he has served a term of imprisonment (LEV)

deficiency judgment: a creditor's claim against a debtor for that part of a judgment debt not satisfied by the sale of the mortgaged property. Example: A owes B $1,000.00 secured by a mortgage on property of A. A defaults in payment of the debt. B obtains a judgment, forecloses and the mortgaged property is sold according to law for $900. The difference—$100—is still owed by A and is covered by a deficiency judgment (LEV)

defile: (1) to make unclean (CDTP) (2) to corrupt the chastity of the virtuous (CDTP)

definite sentence: a sentence that includes a specific period of imprisonment

definition: the clarity, sharpness, resolution, and brilliancy of an image formed by a lens (MPPF)

definition of crime: a crime is an act injurious to the public, forbidden by law, and punishable by the state by fine, imprisonment, or both fine and imprisonment, through a judicial proceeding in its own name. The elements of crime are so variable that it is impossible to give any definition in short scope which will be correct both inclusively and exclusively. As each state is an independent unit in the making and enforcing of criminal law, the laws of the particular state must be examined to determine the criminal character of any act. (210 S.W. 18) (CDTP)

defraud: to cheat or deprive another

defunct: (1) dead (CDTP) (2) extinct (CDTP)

degenerate: (1) one who is morally degraded (LEV) (2) morally bankrupt (LEV)

degree: (1) a relative ranking of things or events; relative quantity or importance. In criminal law, the ranking of crimes according to seriousness (LEV) (2) a scholastic rank of attainment (LEV)

dei gratia: by the grace of God (CDTP)

de jure: (1) by right, according to

law (DAP) (2) pertaining to a situation which is based on law, or right, or previous action. *Cf.* de facto (DAP)

delay: continue; postpone, put off, as in the action of the court or its orders (LEV)

delegate: to give someone authority to represent the *giver* in performing certain acts (LEV)

deliberately: intentionally, "in cold blood"

deliberation: the action of a jury in determining the guilt or innocence, or the sentence, of a defendant

delineate: to illustrate or explain by sketching, drawing, or charting (LEV)

delinquency: (1) failure of an individual to perform a socially designated task; violation of a social obligation (DOS) (2) used in juvenile court law to define juvenile offenses which come under the jurisdiction of the court. The juridically accepted distinction between a "criminal" act and a "delinquent" act is inherent in the theory that juveniles are not motivated by the same responsible considerations as are assumed to actuate adults. Legally and sociologically the distinction is justified by a recognition of the need for differential treatment of juvenile offenders. *Cf.* criminal responsibility; delinquency, juvenile (DOS)

delinquency, juvenile: the antisocial acts of children or persons under age. Such acts are either specifically forbidden by law or may be lawfully interpreted as constituting delinquency. In most states, all offenses committed by children under 16 are considered delinquency. A few states extend the term to include the offenses committed by those under 18. California extends the term to include offenders under 21 (DOS)

Delinquency law (State), Child, the first: was passed April 28, 1909, by Colorado. It defined as guilty, persons "who shall encourage, cause or contribute to the delinquency, neglect or delinquency of

a child" (FAMOUS)

delinquent: (1) a person guilty of antisocial conduct which generally speaking is considered less serious than the type of misconduct designated as "criminal" (2) in American penology the term "delinquent" usu. refers to the juvenile offender whose misconduct is an infraction of the law. Such conduct is generally considered less offensive than an adult's misconduct because of the child's immaturity and the unfortunate environmental circumstances which so frequently occasion his behavior (DOS)

delinquent, defective: a delinquent who has some defect in his physical or mental equipment. Generally speaking, the term refers to delinquents who are feebleminded or otherwise mentally incompetent; hence incapable of assuming responsibility for their conduct (DOS)

delinquent child: a person of no more than a specified age who has committed antisocial acts

delirium: a condition of extreme mental and muscular excitement (CDTP)

delirium tremens: a disorder of the nervous system involving delirium and tremors caused by excessive continued indulgence in alcohol

delit: a grade of crime. American criminal law has followed the English common law in dividing crimes into treason, felonies, and misdemeanors. The Continental European Codes use a different although roughly comparable classification. In the French *Code Penal* crimes are classified as *crimes* (felonies), *delits* (indictable misdemeanors), *and contraventions* (violations of police regulations). The Italian *Codice Penale* uses *delitti* for felonies and *contravenzioni* for misdemeanors. The German *Strafgesetzbuch* employs *Verbrechen* (felonies), *Vergehen* (the French delits and American misdemeanor), and *Ubertretung* (violation of police regulations) (DOS)

deliver: (1) to rescue or set free (2) to aid in the birth of a baby (LEV)

delivery, writ of: a writ of execution employed to enforce a judgment for the delivery of chattels. It commands the sheriff to cause the chattels mentioned in the writ to be returned to the person who has obtained the judgment; and, if the chattels cannot be found, to distrain the person against whom the judgment was given until he returns them (CDTP)

delta: a formation or character detail in fingerprints used in classifying the pattern. It is that point on a ridge at or nearest the point of divergence of two typelines, and is located at or directly in front of the point of divergence (LEV)

delusion: medically, belief in something or someone that does not exist

demented: mentally deranged; insane; crazy (LEV)

dementia: mental deterioration, having symptoms of apathy, impairment of memory, confusion, and lowering of will-power and reasoning power (LEV)

Demerol: a synthetic equivalent of opiate drugs. Controlled by federal law (LEV)

demi: half; partial (CDTP)

demise: the transfer or conveyance of an estate to another (CDTP)

democracy: a form of government in which the nation's (or state's) power resides in the people. If it is participated in directly by all the people it is a pure democracy. If the people give the power to representatives to speak for them it is representative democracy (LEV)

demographic: pertaining to the statistical study of the dynamic changes in population, such as births, deaths, marriages, health, etc. (LEV)

demography: the statistical analysis and description of population aggregates, with reference to distribution, vital statistics, age, sex, and civil status, either at a given time, or over time (DOS)

demonism: the belief in the existence of spirit beings, and the attendant practices of magic for the control or appeasement of such beings. The spirit beings may exist in a variety of imagined forms, such as goblins, ghosts, genii, witches, plant and animal spirits, and a host of the lesser deities, which are either benevolent or malevolent, as the case may be (DOS)

demonology: the systematic study of demonism (DOS)

demonstration: a display of feelings, manifested by parades, meetings, exhibiting placards, shouting, speeches, sit-down actions, etc. (LEV)

demonstrative evidence: evidence which speaks for itself, such as real or physical evidence. Evidence which the jury can see and use in arriving at a conclusion without the necessity of explaining the nature of the evidence. A gun in a murder case would be an example (LEV)

demoralization: loss of personal integrity or of group morale, as process or as condition; disintegration of an habituated scale of values, ideas, definitions of situations, and conceptions of role. A demoralized family, for example, may retain its socio-legal pattern, or its members may be abandoned or deserted or divorced, or in custody, or non-wedlock relations may distort it; the essential thing in loss of group morale (social demoralization) is that solidarity has given way to individualism of ends. In societal demoralization the unity of an entire community, institution, or nation is threatened. Personal demoralization, on the other hand, involves loss of integrity, dissociation, fantasy-thinking, self-deception, fear and furtivity, cumulative dishonesty, maladjustment, internal and external conflict, eventual loss of status and role, and personality breakdown. Distinguished from delinquency, a situation-process which may or may not demoralize the person   (DOS)

demotion: a reduction in rank or position   (LEV)

demur: object; take exception   (LEV)

demurrage: (1) detention of a vessel or car beyond time allowed for loading or unloading (2) payment for such detention   (CDTP)

demurrer: plea for the dismissal of a suit on the grounds that, even if true, the statements of the opposition are insufficient to sustain the claim

denature: (1) to change the nature of (2) to render unfit for eating or drinking   (CDTP)

Dennis v. United States, 341 U.S. 494, L. Ed. 1137, 71 S. Ct. 857 (1951): the court approved the trial judge's instructions to the jury that the charged teaching and advocacy to overthrow the Government had to "be of a rule of principle to incite persons to such action, all with the intent to cause the overthrow or destruction of the Government of the United States by force and violence as speedily as circumstances will permit." (Chief Justice Vinson commented: "No important case involving free speech was decided by the Court prior to *Schenck* v. *United States.*" However, there are two great prior occasions when the scope of the First Amendment's proscription was debated: See *ex parte Jackson* and *Abrams* v. *United States.* (ILECJ)

denounce: attack or condemn; accuse someone of wrongdoing; to inform on someone   (LEV)

de novo: as new; anew; all over again. When an appellate court reviews a case of an inferior record (which is not a court of record) the case is heard *de novo,* i.e., it is tried again in its entirety (LEV)

dense: very dark; applied to a negative or positive transparency which is overexposed, overdeveloped, or both   (MPPF)

densitometer: a device for measuring the density of a silver deposit in a photographic image. It is usually limited to measuring even densities in small areas   (MPPF)

density: a term used in expressing the light-stopping power of a blackened silver deposit in relation to the light incident upon it   (MPPF)

deny: refute; claim a statement is untrue; contradict   (LEV)

Department of Justice: the legal department of the federal government created by a law of June 22, 1870, expanding the office of the Attorney General, which furnishes legal advice and opinions to the President and heads of other federal departments and represents the Government in legal matters concerning taxes, lands, monopolies and trusts, immigration and naturalization, civil rights, internal security, and other civil and criminal proceedings. The Department directs and supervises the work of the Federal Bureau of Investigation, the U.S. Marshals and District Attorneys, the federal penal institutions, the Pardon Attorney, and the Parole Board and conducts all suits in the Supreme Court in which the United States is a party   (DAP)

Department of the Treasury: a department of the federal government, created Sept. 2, 1789, which superintends and manages national finances and is especially charged with improvement of public revenues and public credit. It analyzes taxing policies, collects customs duties and internal revenue taxes, is responsible for borrowing, paying off, and refunding long- and short-term debts, continually studies the flow of lending, enforces export controls, registers and licenses vessels engaged in foreign and domestic commerce, administers the narcotics laws, coins money, prints paper money and postage and other stamps, suppresses counterfeiting and violations of the revenue laws, investigates thefts of government property, and, through its Secret Service Division, protects the person of the President (DAP)

deployment: (1) the act of extending battalions and smaller units in width, in depth, or in both width and depth to increase their readiness for contemplated action (2) in naval usage, the change from a cruising approach or contact disposition to a disposition for battle (3) in a strategic sense, the relocation of forces to desired areas of operation (4) the designated location of troops and troop units as indicated in a troop schedule (DWMT)

deponent: (1) one who makes a deposition (CDTP) (2) one who testifies or swears to the veracity of certain facts; an affiant

deport: (1) to banish; to return a person to the country from which he came (2) to behave (CDTP)

deportation: the forcible return by public authority of an alien to his country of origin, or, rarely, some other foreign jurisdiction. The process is particularly exemplified in connection with the administration of the United States immigration statutes. The grounds of deportation are of two main classes: (1) immoral, criminal, or politically prohibited behavior on the part of the alien, or (2) becoming an economic charge upon the public from causes existing prior to the arrival of the immigrant (DOS)

deposit: (1) to place or leave (2) to lodge for safekeeping or as a pledge (CDTP)

deposition: sworn testimony obtained out of court (LEV)

depraved: wicked; perverted (LEV)

depravity: want of virtue; extreme wickedness; defying of moral sense (CDTP)

depressant: a drug which has a calming effect on the nervous system of a person; a sedative; a tranquilizer. The barbiturate family of drugs is most frequently encountered in this category. Some of the more common barbiturates are: *Pentobarbital, Secobarbital, Amobarbital, Phenobarbital.* Alcohol is also a depressant (LEV)

depressed area: any defined area in which economic activity and employment are at a noticeably lower level than elsewhere and which, therefore, may be considered eligible for assistance under legislation to combat poverty and blight (DAP)

deprive: to take away something a person has the right to; to dispossess (LEV)

depth of field: the distance measured between the nearest and farthest planes in the subject area which give satisfactory definition (MPPF)

depth of focus: the distance which a camera back can be racked back and forth while preserving satisfactory image detail in focal plane for a given object point (MPPF)

depth perception: the ability to determine the distances of things seen with the eyes (LEV)

deputy: a substitute; a person duly authorized by an officer to exercise some or all of the functions pertaining to the office, in the place and stead of the latter (CDTP)

deputy sheriff: one appointed to act in the place and stead of the sheriff in the official business of the latter's office. A general deputy or "undersheriff" is one who, by virtue of his appointment, has authority to execute all the ordinary duties of the office of sheriff, and who executes process without any special authority from his principal. A special deputy, who is an officer pro hac vice (meaning for this one particular occasion), is one appointed for a special occasion or a special service, as, to assist in keeping the peace when a riot or tumult is expected or in progress. He acts

under a specific and not a general appointment and authority
(CDTP)

derangement: insanity

derelict: abandoned; deserted
(CDTP)

deringer, derringer: a small pocket pistol originally made by Henry Deringer, of Philadelphia, but copied by many others   (DWMT)

derivative evidence: evidence obtained as the result of information obtained by a previous act or statement, such as search of premises which furnished leads upon which the later evidence was found. The same would hold where a statement or confession is the basis of obtaining the derivative evidence. If the first acts were illegal then the derivative evidence comes into "the fruit of the poisonous tree" category and is inadmissable. *See* fruit of the poisonous tree   (LEV)

dermis: the skin   (CDTP)

derogatory: bad; degrading; disparaging   (LEV)

Descartes, René (*1596-1650*): a great French philosopher, Descartes was one of the fathers of modern philosophy with his doctrines of Cartesian coordinates and Cartesian curves and was also the founder of analytical geometry. He devoted himself chiefly to the problem of the relation of body and soul, and of matter and mind. His writings influenced most other rationalists, including Leibniz, Spinoza, Malebranche, and many others

description: as in the case of search warrants, the books and papers of which production is compelled, must be specifically described so that they may be identified. A subpoena duces tecum may be of such broad and sweeping character as to come within the meaning of unreasonable searches and seizures as in an order throwing open all the records of a party, without any provision for protection against an investigation not cover-ed by the order. The question of whether the demand so exceeds the limits of proper investigation as to amount to unreasonable search is always a judicial one
(CDTP)

description of hotel: a description of the premises to be searched merely as a named hotel at a particular place is not specific enough, as a hotel may contain many rooms and many innocent people who would be subject to search   (CDTP)

description of things to be seized: the search warrant must particularly describe the thing to be seized, and failing to do so is void. While descriptions must necessarily vary according to the nature of things, generally a minute and detailed description is not necessary, but it must be so definite that the officer will not seize the wrong property, and will be sufficient if it enables the officer to identify the specific property sought, or to locate it with reasonable certainty. (138 Miss. 788)
(CDTP)

desecrate: to desanctify; to profane; to degrade something sacred   (LEV)

desegregation: in the *Brown* v. *Board of Education of Topeka* case, Chief Justice Warren of the Supreme Court read the unanimous opinion of the Court (1954) which declared that segregation of children in public schools solely on the basis of race, even though physical facilities and other "tangible" factors are equal, deprives such children of equal educational opportunities. Later, in 1955, the Court decreed that the implementation of this decision was to be assumed by the lower federal courts which were to supervise and enforce desegregation within a reasonable time. In *Bolling* v. *Sharpe* (1954) the Court also ruled, unanimously, that segregation deprives children of due process of law under the Fifth

Amendment   (DOAH)
desensitizer: an agent, usually a chemical solution, for decreasing the color sensitivity of a photographic emulsion to facilitate developing under a comparatively bright light. The emulsion is desensitized after exposure
(MPPF)
desert: (1) to abandon (LEV) (2) to leave one's post of duty without authority or permission   (LEV)
desertion: (1) abandonment of duty in any of the armed services without leave and without intention of returning (DAP) (2) abandonment of one of the partners in marriage by the other without prior arrangement for the discharge of responsibilities, such as financial support or the care of the home and children   (DAP)
desiccated: a term applied to chemicals in which all moisture has been eliminated   (MPPF)
design approach: the view that the designer takes of the restraints on the design process; his freedom may range from nearly none to almost carte blanche to design whatever seems most useful for the organization   (ADPS)
desist: cease doing something(LEV)
Desist v. United States, 394 U.S. 244, L. Ed. 2d 248, 89, S. Ct. 1030 (1969): the Court held, 5–3, through Mr. Justice Stewart, that Katz does not apply retroactively even to a case that was on direct appeal when Katz was announced. (The whole question of the "retroactivity of decisions of constitutional dimension should be rethought," Mr. Justice Black urged in his dissenting opinion.) (ILECJ)
desperado: a criminal; a lawbreaker; generally denotes a dangerous outlaw; one who is desperate enough to cause harm if encountered
(LEV)
desuetude: state of disuse   (CDTP)
DETAB–X: Decision Tables, Experimental; a programming language that combines decisions tables with COBOL   (ADPS)
detachment: (1) a part of a unit

separated from its main organization for duty elsewhere (2) a temporary military or naval unit formed from other units or parts of units   (DWMT)
detail: to assign men to a particular duty. Also, the men assigned to the duty. The term once referred to the written list of orders or exercises for the day, either for the entire command or for a part of it   (DWMT)
detain: to stop someone and prevent his freedom of action for a period (usually a short period) of time; to interfere with one's freedom of movement or actions
(LEV)
detainer: an instrument filed by one state or jurisdiction to retain a prisoner in another jurisdiction so that he can answer a criminal charge by the filer of the detainer
detection range: the greatest distance at which a sensor will consistently detect an intruder under a standard set of conditions
(TDIAS)
detective: usu. a plainclothes officer engaged in investigating civil and criminal matters
detective camera: an early name for what is now called a candid camera.   (MPPF)
detective vehicle: an unmarked vehicle used for law enforcement activities which may be equipped with a communication radio, portable flashing lights, a siren, or other items   (TDPPC)
detector: (1) a sensor as those used to detect intrusion, equipment malfunctions or failure, rate of temperature rise, smoke, or fire (2) a demodulator, a device for recovering the modulating function or signal from a modulated wave, such as that used in a modulated photo-electric alarm system
(TDIAS)
detention: the state of being detained. See detain   (LEV)
detention, juvenile: the function of providing custody and supervision of children whose cases are pending in the juvenile court to assure

their appearance at the time of their hearing. Various types of place are now in use for such a purpose, including the children's own or boarding homes, jails, special detention homes maintained by the juvenile courts, or miscellaneous places, such as hospitals, almshouses, or police lockups, as the court may designate (DOS)

detention, preventive: *See* preventive detention

detention, protective: based on a policy of social defense or of protection, some countries and states have attempted to keep the defective, habitual, and unimprovable offenders in custody for an indefinite or life period after they would qualify for release if they had been ordinary offenders. Such an extended stay is in part accomplished by delaying the granting of parole or refusing parole. It is also accomplishable by use of third- and fourth-time offenders acts, under which a prisoner may be detained for periods up to life. But these laws have never been put into effective operation by judges. In some European countries, protective detention for habitual and abnormal offenders was written into laws of social defense. But even in these countries very few cases are handled under this measure for social defense (DOS)

deter: to prevent a person from an act by threat or warning, or, as in penology, by example (DOS)

deterrence: in corrections, the deterrence of crime is the prevention of future crime. Specific deterrence posits that the criminal to whom the treatment is applied will refrain from committing crimes in the future because of our treatment. General deterrence reflects the belief that because of the treatment we apply to a specific individual, a group of potential criminals will refrain from committing crimes. A major rationale for capital punishment

has been its supposed general deterrent effect (LCC)

detonate: to explode suddenly and violently (DWMT)

detonating agent: an explosive which is extremely sensitive to heat and shock and which is normally used to initiate a secondary high explosive. It is capable of building up from a deflagration to detonation at an extremely short distance and in a very short period of time (DWMT)

detonating fuze: a fuze designed to initiate its main munition by a detonating action, as compared with the ignition action of an *igniting fuze*. This type of fuze is required for adequate initiation of a high-explosive main charge. *See* igniting fuse (DWMT)

detonator: an explosive train component which can be activated by either a nonexplosive impulse or the action of a primer and which is capable of reliably initiating high-order detonation in a subsequent high-explosive component or train. When activated by a nonexplosive impulse, a detonator includes the function of a primer. In general, detonators are classified in accordance with the method of initiation, such as percussion, stab, electric, flash, etc. (DWMT)

detoxification center: a facility equipped to detain and treat alcoholics with medical services and therapy by psychologists and psychiatrists and to provide for aftercare of such patients (LEV)

develop: (1) to work out by steps and in detail (2) to create or bring into being (3) to process exposed film (LEV)

developer: a solution used to make visible the latent image in an exposed emulsion (MPPF)

developing agent: a chemical compound possessing the ability to change exposed silver halide to black metallic silver, while leaving the unexposed halide unaffected (MPPF)

developing-out paper: a printing paper in which the image is made visible by developing in a chemical solution (MPPF)

development by inspection: development of negatives or prints by inspection, depending on the operator's judgment as to when development is complete (MPPF)

devest: to strip; to deprive (CDTP) *See* divest

deviate: a person who is abnormal or different from the usual person (LEV)

devise: to give or bequeath by will (CDTP)

devisee: person to whom a devise is made. (CDTP)

dexedrine: a stimulating drug, often prescribed for weight reducing, considered potentially dangerous but not physically addicting (LEV)

dextroamphetamine sulfate: a stimulant—a member of the amphetamine drug family, in orange-colored, heart-shaped tablets known as "hearts," "oranges," or "dexies" (LEV)

diabetes: a disease characterized by frequent and excessive urination. "Sugar diabetes" is the most dangerous form. This is caused by improper secretion of insulin by the pancreas resulting in the inability of the body to properly utilize sugars. The condition may result in a semiconscious or dazed condition or becoming fully unconscious (diabetic coma). The officer may confuse a person in this condition with one caused by intoxication with drugs or alcohol (LEV)

diabetic coma: unconsciousness resulting from sugar diabetes (LEV)

diagnosis: the determination of the nature of disease (CDTP)

diagnostic routine: a specific routine designed to locate either a malfunction in the processor or a mistake in coding (ADPS)

dial (safe): a graduated circular, movable plate, which is an outward part of a combination lock used on "combination" padlocks and safe locks (LEV)

dialysis: a process whereby substances having small molecules or ions (e.g., most salts) can be separated from a solution also containing colloids by allowing them to diffuse into water through the pores of a membrane (frequently cellophane) too fine for the colloids to pass through (FS)

diaphragm: a device for controlling the amount of light which passes through a lens. It is usu. an iris diaphragm but may be in the form of slotted discs of fixed sizes (MPPF)

diapositive: a positive image on a transparent medium such as glass or film; a transparency (MPPF)

diatoms: various species of minute, single-celled, water-living organisms with silica "skeletons" which show a fine structure characteristic of the species (FS)

dichotomy: a division into two parts or lines. In charting the organizational structure (chain of command) of a police agency from the chief downward there is a dichotomy when "line" and "staff" are shown (LEV)

dichroic fog: a two-colored stain observed in film or plates. Appears green by reflected light and pink by transmitted light (MPPF)

Dickens, Charles (*1812-1870*): one of the world's greatest novelists, this English writer used his books as a method of exposing abuses in all areas of society. Through such classics as *Great Expectations* and *Oliver Twist*, Dickens was responsible for enlisting public criticism against such conditions as the prisons, schools, hospitals, and the government. His criticism of society was largely moral, for he believed that the abuses were caused by cruelty, selfishness, and hardness of heart

dicta: an opinion of the court upon some question of law not necessary to the decision of the case being considered (CDTP)

dictum: (1) formal statement made by a judge (2) a statement or opinion by the judge on some legal point other than the principal issue of the case.

die: a tool or instrument usually made of steel or other hard substance with which letters or numbers are stamped on objects made of metal or other hard material. They are usually used to identify such items through the letters or numbers   (LEV)

dies: a day   (CDTP)

dies non: a day on which the courts do not transact any business, as Sundays and legal holidays(CDTP)

diethyltryptamine: a chemically prepared hallucinogenic drug; the street name is DET

differential pressure sensor: a sensor used for perimeter protection which responds to the difference between the hydraulic pressures in two liquid-filled tubes buried just below the surface of the earth around the exterior perimeter of the protected area. The pressure difference can indicate an intruder walking or driving over the buried tubes   (TDIAS)

diffraction: an optical term used to denote the spreading of a light ray after it passes the edge of an obstacle   (MPPF)

diffusion: the scattering of light rays from a rough surface, or the transmission of light through a translucent medium   (MPPF)

digest: (1) a summary (2) an orderly compilation   (CDTP)

digital computer: a computer capable of accepting and operating on only the representations of numerals or letters coded numerically. More broadly, a digital computer handles numerals, letters, or symbols represented as discrete items of data, as opposed to measurements   (ADPS)

digital read-out speedometer: a speedometer which presents on its face only those numbers (digits) that show the speed at which the vehicle is moving   (TDPPC)

digitalis: a drug used as a heart stimulant   (CDTP)

dilatory: (1) for the purpose of delay; causing delay or postponement (2) (law) for the purpose of

causing delay or to gain time or to postpone a decision   (LEV)

dilatory exceptions: those exceptions and motions filed for the purpose of retarding progress of the case but which do not tend to defeat the charges   (LEV)

diligence: doing of an act or acts with all practical expedition, with no delay   (CDTP)

diligent: perseveringly attentive; not careless or negligent   (CDTP)

dimethyltryptamine: DMT—an hallucinogenic drug   (LEV)

din: a European system of measuring film speed; little used in this country   (MPPF)

dionine: an opium derivative; a narcotic or habit-producing drug   (CDTP)

diopter: a measure of lens power; the reciprocal of the focal length of the lens in meters   (MPPF)

diphenylamine test: the test to determine the presence of gunpowder residue on the hands of a person suspected of having fired a handgun. The hands of the suspect are coated with melted paraffin, which is removed after cooling and the chemical diplenylamine is used on the inside of the paraffin "glove" removed from the suspect's hands. It is also called the "paraffin test." It is not considered reliable   (LEV)

diphenylaminechloroarsine: a solid material that is dispersed by heat to produce an aerosol causing skin and eye irritation, chest distress, and nausea. In popular usage, "adamsite." One of the "vomiting gases," it is relatively nontoxic   (DWMT)

diphenylchloroarsine (DA): this war gas (also a mob- and riot-control gas) has a very rapid rate of action. Effects are felt within two or three minutes after one minute of exposure. It causes irritation of the eyes and mucous membranes, viscous discharge from the nose similar to that caused by a cold, sneezing and coughing, severe headache, acute pain and tightness in the chest, and nausea and vomiting. In moderate concentrations the effects last about 30 minutes after an individual leaves the contaminated atmosphere. At higher concentrations the effects may last up to several hours   (DWMT)

diphenylcyanoarsine (DC): this war gas (also a mob- and riot-control gas) has a very rapid rate of action. It causes the same symptoms as DA, but is more toxic   (DWMT)

diplomatic: having tact or skill in dealing with people   (LEV)

diplomatic immunity: the exemption under international law of a foreign diplomat, his entourage, and the premises they occupy from taxation, civil suits, criminal process, searches and seizures, and the obligation to appear as witnesses in court in the state to which the diplomat is accredited or through which he may be traveling   (DAP)

dipsomania: an uncontrollable craving for alcoholic beverages

direct action: resort to intimidation or violence (as a sit-in, street demonstration, or riot), in order to overawe the authorities, seize power, or obtain some other political objective   (DAP)

direct contempt of court: any contempt committed in the presence of the court or the failure to comply with a summons, subpoena, or order to appear in court. See contempt of court   (LEV)

direct evidence: testimony or other proof that expressly or straightforwardly proves the existence of fact

direct examination: initial examination of a witness by the party who calls him

direct finder: a viewfinder through which the subject is seen directly, such as the wire finder on various cameras   (MPPF)

direct positive: a positive image obtained directly without the use of a negative   (MPPF)

directed verdict: an order or verdict pronounced by a judge during the trial of a criminal case where the evidence presented by the prosecution clearly fails to show guilt of the accused   (LEV)

direction line: one of the elements in the walking picture. It is the indication of the direction in which the walker is moving. See walking picture   (LEV)

directive: an order or instruction issued by a superior to a lesser administrative official   (DAP)

disability: (1) legal incapacity which may result from infancy, insanity, or some act in contravention of law (2) lack of legal qualifications to hold office, such as want of sufficient age or period of residence, the holding of an incompatible office, foreign citizenship, and, for the presidency, foreign birth   (DAP)

disarm: to remove the detonating device or fuse of a bomb, mine, or other piece of explosive ordnance or otherwise render it incapable of exploding in its usual manner   (DWMT)

disarmament: the reduction of a military establishment to some level set by international government   (DWMT)

disassemble: to take apart a firearm in order to clean or repair it   (DWMT)

disc brake: a type of braking system in which brake pads are applied against a disc-like steel surface to retard, stop, or prevent a vehicle from moving   (TDPPC)

discharge: (1) the release of an individual from custody, from legal obligations, or from the jurisdiction of some tribunal (DAP) (2) the release of a committee from further consideration of a matter submitted to it by a legislative body which has the effect of bringing a matter to the floor (DAP) (3) separation from military service (DAP) (4) the firing of a weapon

disciplinary punishment: punishment to ensure compliance with the rules of a correctional facility

discipline: (1) the maintenance of

order and decorum in any organized public body (DAP) (2) the maintenance of the authority of an administrative superior over a subordinate. (DAP) Generally thought to be either in one of two forms; positive (example) or negative (punishment)

disclaimer: a denial; disavowel (CDTP)

disconnector: the device in an automatic pistol that ensures that firing will not take place until the action is completely closed. It also prevents the firing of more than one shot for each pull of the trigger (DWMT)

discourteous: rude, impolite

discovery: *See* right of discovery

discreet: diplomatic; prudent; tactful (LEV)

discretion: the authority to choose among alternative actions

discretionary funds: action funds (15 percent of total action grant appropriation under section 306) of the Omnibus Crime Control and Safe Streets Act of 1968, which the Law Enforcement Assistance Administration can allocate to grantees by discretion (LEV)

discrimination: unfair treatment or denial of normal privileges to persons because of their race, color, nationality, or religion. Discrimination may be by private persons, or by public authority in unequal statutes or partiality in law enforcement. Its worst manifestations have occurred in employment, education, housing, transportation, and access to public accommodations. Antidiscrimination laws are designed to create equality of treatment and to remove legal protections (as in housing) from agreements to continue private discriminations (DAP)

disfranchisement: (1) state action depriving a designated class or an individual of the privilege of voting, as by imposing new requirements, such as a literacy test; or as a consequence of conviction

for felony or bribery; or because of the neglect or refusal of election officers to register otherwise qualified voters (DAP) (2) any act of discrimination or intimidation by private persons which has the practical effect of preventing exercise of the suffrage—usu. used colloquially (DAP)

disguise: (1) to change appearance so as not to be recognized (LEV) (2) alter the usual appearance of something (LEV)

dishonest: not honest; prone to cheat, lie, or steal (LEV)

disinter: to remove from the grave; exhume (LEV)

disk: a circular metal plate with magnetic material on both sides, continuously rotated for reading or writing by means of one or more read-write heads mounted on movable or fixed arms; disks may be permanently mounted on a shaft or, as a package, they may be removable and others placed on the shaft (ADPS)

dismiss: to end the case in court; to terminate the charges against the accused (LEV)

disorder: riotous behavior; confusion of actions; disturbance of the peace (LEV)

disorderly conduct: a term of loose and indefinite meaning (except as occasionally defined in the state's statutes), but signifying generally any behavior that is contrary to law, and more particularly such as tends to disturb the public peace or decorum, scandalize the community, or shock the public sense of morality (CDTP)

disorderly house: a house in which people live, or to which they resort, for purposes injurious to public morals, health, convenience, or safety (CDTP)

disorderly person: one guilty of disorderly conduct; many states have laws defining who are disorderly persons, such as beggars, tramps, persons who desert their family, etc. (CDTP)

disperse: (1) to break up and/or scatter in different directions

(2) to cause to become spread widely

dispersion: the separation of light into its component colors created by passing white light through a prism (MPPF)

display: visible representation of data on a console, in a printed report, or by other means (ADPS)

display, direct: television-like tubes that display various alphanumeric or graphic results from a processor for viewing or photographing for the record. More simply, a desk set on which selected facts—for example, availability of a seat for a desired airflight—may be viewed (ADPS)

disposition: the outcome or culmination of a criminal case, i.e., charges dismissed, found not guilty, guilty, the sentence pronounced, etc. (LEV)

disqualification: depriving one from participating in a proceeding, due to a condition or some irregularity. A juror, because of prejudice or bias, may be disqualified from serving on the jury. A judge may disqualify himself from conducting a trial because of personal relationship to one or more of the parties or because of bias or prejudice (LEV)

disruptive defendant: See courtroom disruptions (LEV)

dissent: (1) the opinion of a judge or judges, on a multi-judge court, giving a minority view of all or some part of the majority holding in the case being decided (LEV) (2) the expression of a judge who does not agree with the verdict of the majority of the court (LEV) (3) disagree, object, disapprove (LEV)

dissident: (1) differing; not in accord with existing policy, rules, or laws; opposing; dissenting (LEV) (2) one who disagrees with existing laws, rules, etc. (LEV)

dissolve: to annul or set aside an order such as an injunction (LEV)

dissuade: to persuade an individual not to perform an act

distance meter: an instrument used for estimating the distance to a particular object. Also known as a range finder (MPPF)

distinctions between a crime and tort: a crime is a wrong which affects the community in its social aggregate capacity. A tort is a wrong apart from contract, which affects persons in their individual capacity. The former is a public wrong, whereas the latter is a private wrong. In the case of a crime the wrongdoer is liable to a criminal action by the state; whereas in the case of a tort he is liable only to a civil action by the person injured (CDTP)

distortion: defects caused by uncorrected lenses, resulting in images that are not the proper shape (MPPF)

distress: the taking of a person or chattel out of the possession of a wrongdoer, into the custody of the party injured, to procure satisfaction for the wrong done (CDTP)

district attorney: a locally elective State official who represents the State in bringing indictments and prosecuting criminal cases; called also the prosecuting attorney or State's attorney. See U.S. Attorney (DAP)

district court: in the federal court system it is the court of original criminal jurisdiction and a court of record. One such court is located in each federal judicial district and the court has jurisdiction over matters of that district. Several states have district courts which are courts of original jurisdiction. The district over which they have jurisdiction may be composed of one or more counties. They are similar to county courts in other states (LEV)

distringas writ: a writ issued to the sheriff to seize the goods of the defendant and also the defendant from time to time so that the sheriff will have the person when the time comes for him to appear (CDTP)

disturb: agitate; disarrange; create disorder; upset the peace and tranquility (LEV) disturbance of public meetings: at common law it is a misdemeanor to disturb an assemblage of persons met together for any lawful purpose, particularly meetings of a distinctly moral or benevolent character   (CDTP)

disturbing the peace: a criminal charge for interfering with the peace, quiet, orderliness, and tranquility of a community   (LEV)

divergence: ridge pattern in fingerprints. The spreading apart of two ridges which have run parallel or almost parallel   (LEV)

diversion: a decision or program designed to direct offenders from official processing to less formal, less adversary, and noninstitutionalized community-based settings

divert: to turn aside   (CDTP)

divest: strip; rid; free; force to give up; denude; unclothe   (LEV)

division: (1) the parts in which a COBOL program is organized. Identification division provides information to identify the source and object programs. Environment division specifies the equipment to use for translating and running a program. Data division contains entries to define the nature of the data to be processed. Procedure division consists of the processor program to be run with data (ADPS) (2) organizational sub-group   (ADPS)

Division of Investigation: an act was passed by Congress June 18, 1934, empowering certain members of the Division of Investigation of the Department of Justice to serve warrants and subpoenas issued under the authority of the United States; to make seizures under warrant; and to make arrests without warrant for felonies committed where the person making the arrest has reasonable ground to believe that the person so arrested is guilty of such felony and where the person is liable to escape before a warrant can be obtained, but the person arrested shall be immediately taken before a committing officer   (CDTP)

divorce: the dissolution or partial suspension by law, of the marriage relation   (CDTP)

divorces in foreign countries: an act was passed by Congress in 1939, "To prohibit the use of the mails for the solicitation of the procurement of divorces in foreign countries" and making the penalty $5,000 or imprisonment for not more than five years, or both. This applies to any kind of solicitation, including printed cards, circulars, letters, books, pamphlet advertisements, or any kind of notice, giving or offering to give information concerning where or how or through whom a divorce may be secured in a foreign country   (CDTP)

Dix, Dorothea L. (1802-1887): institutional reformer. Her eloquent and detailed memorial to the Legislature of Massachusetts (1843), condemning contemporary attitudes toward and lack of proper care for the insane, began a career which left a trail of new and reorganized hospitals, houses of refuge, and prisons, in this country and abroad   (DC)

Dixie Mafia: a term applied to a group of criminals, connected through a loose confederation, operating in the South   (LEV)

DM: a basic chemical element used in tear gas   (LEV)

DMT: dimethyltryptamine—an hallucinogenic drug found in the seed of certain plants native to the West Indies and parts of South America   (LEV)

D.O.A. (DOA): dead on arrival (at a hospital)

D.O.B. (DOB): date of birth

docket: a formal record of court proceedings   (CDTP)

document: an official paper, deed, manuscript, or any other written or inscribed instrument which has informational or evidentiary value   (DAP)

document examiner: one who is an expert in the field of handwriting, handprinting, typewriting, inks, indented writings, etc.   (LEV)

documentary evidence: evidence

supplied by papers, books, etc.
(CDTP)

documents, readable: papers containing data about transactions, or, loosely, any report written, typed, printed, or imprinted that people can read (often called "hard copy"); also includes printed or interpreted cards and punched-paper tape   (ADPS)

dodge: to shade a portion of the negative during printing (MPPF)

dodging: the process of holding back light from certain areas of sensitized material to avoid overexposure of these areas (MPPF)

Doe, Charles (*1830-1896*): appointed at the age of 29 as Associate Justice to the Supreme Court in New Hampshire, Charles Doe served in that capacity from 1859 to 1874 and as Chief Justice from 1876 until his death in March of 1896. He was mainly remembered for substantial accomplishments in the field of evidence and procedure as well as his work with Isaac Ray in formulating the New Hampshire Rules. Long before Cardozo and Pound made their pleas for the integration of law and science Doe had been the first judge to insist that the law should collaborate with science, particularly in the field of criminal responsibility
(DC)

domain: (1) territory (including air space) over which sovereignty or public authority is exerted (DAP) (2) a landed estate   (DAP)

domestic: household; home (LEV)

domestic relations court: (1) a judicial tribunal of interior grade, usually part of a system of municipal courts, the jurisdiction of which extends typically to matters concerned with family support and the care of children (DAP) domestic relations court, the first: was established in Buffaio, N.Y. in 1909 by Simon Augustine Nash, Judge of Police Court, who privately heard domestic relations cases in his chambers instead of in open court.

Chapter 570, Laws of New York State, approved May 29, 1909, established the City Court of Buffalo, and the domestic relations division was opened January 1, 1910   (FAMOUS)

domicile: the permanent place of residence of a person or the place to which he intends to return even though he may actually reside elsewhere. The legal domicile of a person is important since it, rather than the actual residence, often controls the jurisdiction of the taxing authorities and determines where a person may exercise the privilege of voting and other legal rights and privileges   (DAP)

domineering: arrogant; haughty; despotic   (LEV)

don, the: synonymous with "boss" in the Cosa Nostra   (LEV)

donatio mortis causa: a gift by a person expecting to die (CDTP)

door cord: a short, insulated cable with an attaching block and terminals at each end used to conduct current to a device, such as foil, mounted on the movable portion of a door or window   (TDIAS)

door trip switch: a mechanical switch mounted so that movement of the door will operate the switch   (TDIAS)

dope: any drug that causes stupification   (CDTP)

Doppler effect (shift): the apparent change in frequency of sound or radio waves when reflected from or originating from a moving object. Utilized in some types of motion sensors   (TDIAS)

Dorian love: the love for young males   (LEV)

dormant: sleeping; inactive (CDTP)

dorsal: the back or spine portion of the body   (LEV)

dot: (1) a very short ridge in a fingerprint pattern (LEV) (2) *See* microscopic dot   (LEV)

dotage: the mental weakness of old age   (CDTP)

double action: a method of fire in a revolver and in old-style rifles and shotguns in which a single pull of the trigger both cocks and fires

the weapon (DWMT)
double-circuit system: an alarm circuit in which two wires enter and two wires leave each sensor (TDIAS)

double drop: an alarm signaling method often used in central station alarm systems in which the line is first opened to produce a break alarm and then shortened to produce a cross alarm (TDIAS)

double exposure: the intentional or unintentional recording of two separate images on a single piece of sensitized material (MPPF)

double extension: a term used to describe the position of a camera bellows. A double extension bellows has an extended length of about twice the focal length of the lens being used (MPPF)

double image: a blurred picture, caused by movement of the camera or of the subject during exposure (MPPF)

double jeopardy: putting a person on trial for an offense for which he has previously been properly indicted and a jury has been empaneled and sworn to try him, provided that the jury has not disagreed or been discharged because of the illness of a juror or other sufficient reason—prohibited by the Fifth Amendment. The purpose of the prohibition is to prevent repeated harassment of an accused person and reduce the danger of convicting an innocent one. A federal prosecutor may not appeal from a verdict of not guilty, but a State may make such an appeal if substantial errors are shown. There is no double jeopardy when a convicted person appeals to a higher court; nor when State and federal governments prosecute separately for different offenses arising from the same act (DAP)

double loop: a fingerprint pattern. Also known as twin loop. It consists of two separate loop formations, with two separate and distinct sets of shoulders and two deltas. It is classified as a whorl

(LEV)

double-park: to park a vehicle alongside another which is in a space specified for parking (LEV)

double printing: printing from two or more negatives to make one picture; for example, to use a second negative to print clouds into a landscape (MPPF)

double time: a rate of marching at 180 steps per minute, each step being 3 ft. in length; also the command to march at this rate. It was formerly called "double-quick" (DWMT)

double weight (DW): the heavier weight in which photographic papers are supplied (MPPF)

doubt: uncertainty of mind or the absence of conviction

doubt, reasonable: the state of mind of jurors, in which, after the comparison and consideration of all the evidence, they cannot say that they feel an abiding conviction, to a moral certainty, of the truth of a criminal charge against a defendant

Douglas v. California, 372 U.S. 353, 9 L. Ed. 2d 811, 83 S. Ct 814 (1963): the court held 6-3 that there is an absolute right to the assistance of counsel to make a first appeal under the equal protection clause of the Fourteenth Amendment (ILECJ)

down-time: the period of time that a processor is malfunctioning because of equipment failure (ADPS)

DP: data processing

draft: (1) (law and commerce) a bill of exchange; a written order to a person, bank, etc., for the payment of money to another; a check (LEV) (2) (military) selection of men for compulsory military service (LEV)

draft riots: the first draft riots occurred in New York City July 13–16, 1863. The riots could not be put down by the local authorities, resulting in the dispatch of federal troops by President Lincoln. The riots expressed the anger of the draftees who could not avail themselves of those provisions in the draft act which allowed persons to escape conscription by the payment of money or by obtaining substitutes to serve for them. One thousand persons were killed and property damage was estimated at more than $1,500,000 (DOAH)

drag factor: *See* friction, coefficient of (LEV)

dragon's blood: a resin used as an etching resist (MPPF)

Dramamine®: drug used to relieve or prevent seasickness

drawee: the person to whom an order or a bill of exchange is addressed, who is requested to pay the amount indicated thereon

drawer: the person making an order or a bill of exchange

drawing and charting: *See* sketching

dress: to arrange troops in exact lines at spaced intervals

drift: (1) a term in ballistics which denotes the lateral deviation of the flight of the bullet from a vertical plane coincident with the axis of the bore from which the bullet is fired. The cause of this drift has never been satisfactorily explained but is probably due to the varying density of the atmosphere (CDTP) (2) a controlled four-wheeled slide around a turn. Also, the tendency of an unsteered automobile to deviate from a straight line when travelling on a level surface (TDPPC)

drift method: safe burglar's technique for opening a safe. A tool known as a drift punch is used to drive the lock spindle into the safe (LEV)

drill: exercises for instructing troops, consisting of the manual of arms, marching, and other repetitious exercises for discipline or training (DWMT)

drill method: the drilling of holes at strategic points on a safe, thus allowing manipulation of the locking bars and opening of the safe; a procedure used by safe burglars (LEV)

driving while intoxicated: operating any motor vehicle while under the influence of liquor or narcotics

drop: (1) *See* annunciator (TDIAS) (2) a light indicator on an annunciator(TDIAS) (3) as applied to a gunstock, it means downward bend (CDTP)

drop bed: a camera bed which may be lowered to avoid interference with the view of a wide-angle lens (MPPF)

drop front: a type of rising front which permits lowering the lens below the center of the film (MPPF)

drop shot: soft shot, usu. made with lead (LEV)

drown: to suffocate as the result of liquids in sufficient quantities gaining entry to the breathing passages to produce a lack of oxygen to the vital organs of the body (LEV)

drownproofing: a technique for water safety whereby a person allegedly can avoid drowning for a long period of time without overexertion. Developed by Fred R. Lanque (LEV)

drug: (1) a substance employed in medicine for the treatment of disease (CDTP) (2) a narcotic (CDTP)

drug abuse: (1) the improper use of legal drugs (2) the use of illegal drugs (LEV)

drug addict: one who has become addicted to the use of drugs. *See* addiction (LEV)

drugs, controlled: the drugs which are subject to legal restrictions, such as provided by Drug Abuse Control Amendments of the Food, Drug, and Cosmetic Act (federal). They are known as depressant, stimulant, and hallucinogenic drugs. This category is also covered by the state legislation (LEV)

drugs, dangerous: drugs, other than the hard narcotics, which have proven harmful, if used other than as prescribed by a reputable physician. These drugs have been regulated by law—federal and state. *See* depressants, stimulants, hal-

lucinogens   (LEV)
drum brake: a type of braking system in which the brake lining material is applied against the interior surface of a cylindrical steel housing to retard, stop, or prevent a vehicle from moving   (TDPPC)
drunk drivers: automotive drivers driving while intoxicated   (LEV)
drunkard: one who is habitually drunk; a "common drunkard" is sometimes legally defined as a person who has been convicted of drunkenness a certain number of times over a specific period of time
drunkenness: voluntary drunkenness furnishes no ground of exemption from criminal responsibility, except: (1) where the act is committed while laboring under settled insanity, or delirium tremens, resulting from intoxication; (2) where a specific intent is essential to constitute the crime, the fact of intoxication may negative its existence; (3) the fact of intoxication may be material, where provocation for the act is shown; (4) no criminal responsibility attaches for the acts committed while in a state of involuntary drunkenness, destroying the reason and will   (CDTP)
dry firing: aiming, cocking, and squeezing the trigger of an unloaded firearm   (DWMT)
dry mounting: a method of cementing a print to a mount by means of a thin tissue of thermoplastic material. The tissue is placed between the print and the mount and sufficient heat applied to melt the tissue   (MPPF)
dual citizenship: citizenship both of the United States and of a state. The Fourteenth Amendment of the U.S. Constitution says, "All persons born or naturalized in the United States, and subject to the jurisdiction thereof, are citizens of the United States and of the State wherein they reside"   (LEV)
dual exhaust: a two-pipe system for conducting the exhaust combustion gases from the engine exhaust

manifold to points external to the vehicle   (TDPPC)
duces tecum [*Lat, lit bring with you*]: a writ that requires a party who is summoned to appear in court to bring with him some document or piece of evidence to be used or inspected in court
ducking stool: a stool or chair in which common scolds were formerly tied and plunged into water. It is mentioned in the Domesday Book, and was extensively used throughout Great Britain from the fifteenth to the beginning of the eighteenth century. The last recorded instance of it was in England in 1809   (DOS)
dud: explosive munition such as a bomb or shell which has not been armed as intended or which has failed to explode after being armed   (DWMT)
due process: legal restrictions confining the government "within the limits of those fundamental principles of liberty and justice which lie at the base of all our civil and political institutions," Hurtado v. California, 110 U.S. 516 (1884); practically equivalent to the English term "law of the land." Originally derived from the common law and directed in England to restraining the executive from using arbitrary methods of depriving persons of life, liberty, and property, its later development has been nearly parallel to changes in popular attitudes concerning the importance of individual liberties. In America many of the restrictions were embodied in separate articles of State and Federal bills of rights. The phrase "due process" appears in the Fifth Amendment as a limitation on the federal government and in the Fourteenth Amendment as a limitation on State governments, and its meaning has been expanded by judicial interpretation to include both procedural limitations and limitations on the substance of the laws themselves. Procedural due process was defined

by Daniel Webster as a procedure "which hears before it condemns, which proceeds upon inquiry, and renders judgement only after trial"; it governs both judicial and administrative procedures. Substantive due process, developed by the Supreme Court since 1856, means that the courts will refuse to enforce arbitrary or unjust provisions of statutes under which a person is tried. The court has used the due-process clause both to strengthen other guarantees in the Constitution and as a reservoir of fundamental principles of liberty and justice from which it has at different times drawn such widely different concepts as freedom of contract, the unconstitutionality of continuing to segregate [black] and white school children in the District of Columbia [Bolling v. Sharpe, 347 U.S. 497 (1954)], and the assimilation of most of the first eight amendments to the Constitution into the Fourteenth Amendment, thereby prohibiting the infringement of their provisions by State authorities. Some decisions under substantive due process have led to criticism in some quarters that the Supreme Court has usurped the functions of the legislature   (DAP)

due process of law: (1) the right of an accused individual and the safeguards provided him; (2) the legal methods of conducting a criminal trial

duel: a combat with weapons between two persons. The term may apply to any such combat but, more especially, to prearranged combats in which a ritual of performance controls the behavior of the participants and their accessories   (DOS)

dueling: the fighting of two persons, one against the other at an appointed time and place, upon a precedent quarrel. A misdemeanor at common law, to challenge another to fight a duel, or to be the bearer of such challenge, or to provoke another to send a chal-

lenge. To constitute the crime, no actual fighting is necessary. If the duel takes place and one of the parties is killed, the other is guilty of murder, and all who are present abetting the crime are guilty as principals in the second degree. It is immaterial that the duel is to take place in another state. (8 N.C. 487; 58 Ga. 332)   (CDTP)

dum: while   (CDTP)

dumdum, dumdum bullet: a bullet that flattens excessively on contact; a kind of expanding man-stopping bullet. The name derives from Dumdum, India, where such bullets were first manufactured. The use of this type of bullet is forbidden under international law   (DWMT)

dummy: an artificial address, instruction, or other unit of data inserted solely to fulfill prescribed conditions (such as word length or block length) without affecting operations. A dummy instruction may be converted to an instruction and executed in a later cycle   (ADPS)

dump: to record the contents of internal storage at a given instant of time, usually to help detect program mistakes or errors, or to remove a program and data from the processor to permit running another program   (ADPS)

Duncan case: a decision of the United States Supreme Court holding that where state statutes provided maximum penalties of two years imprisonment and/or a fine of up to $300.00 it was serious enough to entitle the defendant to a jury trial, even though the offense was a misdemeanor under state law and did not involve imprisonment at hard labor [Duncan v. Louisiana. 88 S. Ct. 1444 (1968)]   (LEV)

duplicator: a split lens cap used to photograph a person twice on a single film without a dividing line between the two exposures   (MPPF)

Duquenois reaction: a chemical test for identifying marihuana   (LEV)

duress: unlawful constraint or influence used to force an individual to do some act that he otherwise would not do; compulsion; coercion

duress alarm device: a device which produces either a silent alarm or local alarm under a condition of personnel stress such as holdup, fire, illness, or other panic or emergency. The device is normally manually operated and may be fixed or portable   (TDIAS)

duress alarm system: an alarm system which employs a duress alarm device   (TDIAS)

Durham rule: a legal rule or test dealing with the mentally ill and their responsibility for crime. Under this rule, handed down by a United States Circuit Court in 1954, a person is not held responsible for his criminal act if a mental disease caused him to commit the crime [Durham v. United States, 214 F. 2d 862 (D.C. Cir. 1954)]   (LEV)

Durkheim, Emile (1858-1917): French sociologist. He held that religion and mortality originate in the collective mind of society. He used anthropology and statistics to support his theories. Durkheim's eminence in the field of criminology rests upon his broad approach to antisocial behaviour. Scholars before and after him have attempted to find the cause for crime in external factors as in natural forces, climate, economic conditions, density of population, or certain ecological areas. In contrast to these Durkheim maintained that if an explanation is to be found "it is necessary to look for an explanation" in the very nature of society. He indicates that crime is found in all societies, "Crime is normal because a society exempt from it is utterly impossible." The "fundamental conditions of social organization logically imply it." Crime is not due to any imperfection of human nature or society any more than birth or death may be considered abnormal or pathological. It is all a part of the totality of society. "A society exempt from it [crime] would necessitate a standardization of moral concepts of all individuals which is neither possible nor desirable." Punishment in such a society is only to the degree that it sustains and reinforces the collective conscience. Punishment, therefore, is a mechanical reaction to preserve solidarity. Individuals are but the instruments of society who "strike back" at the offender without any sense of justice or immediate utility. In spite of the crudeness of the method it is a "veritable act of defense" to destroy that which appears to be a menace. Punishment "is a defense weapon which has its worth." The wrongdoer is punished in order to make certain that the act may be considered as abhorrent to the minds of all men. In turn, this preserves the moral ideal of the people. Without punishment no man would know whether acts were "good or bad"   (PC)

duty after arrest: an officer or private person, after making an arrest, must, without unnecessary delay, take his prisoner before a magistrate for examination, but a private person may, if he chooses, deliver his prisoner to an officer   (CDTP)

DWBA: direct wire burglar alarm   (TDIAS)

D.W.I.: driving while intoxicated. A first offense is sometimes referred to as "D.W.I. I" and a second offense as "D.W.I. II"

Dyer Act: the federal law dealing with the interstate transportation of stolen motor vehicles; more commonly referred to as the ITSMV: Interstate Transportation of Stolen Motor Vehicles   (LEV)

dyes, sensitizing: dyes used to extend the color sensitivity of an emulsion. Applied during the manufacture of emulsions to obtain selective sensitivity to colored light   (MPPF)

dying declaration: or ante-mortum statement. One made by a person under belief that he is about to die. The declaration must be a statement of fact as to how he came by his injuries, and it must appear that the deceased expected to die and was without hope of recovery. Such evidence is admissible only in homicide cases (CDTP)

dynamite: a high explosive consisting of nitroglycerin and/or nitroglycol and/or ammonium nitrate and other materials with or without an inert base, packed in cylindrical paper cartridges or in bags. It is set off by a detonator and is used for general blasting purposes (DWMT)

dynamite, military: a blasting explosive in cartridges especially suitable for use in military construction, quarrying, and service demolition work. It has good storage stability, is rifle-bullet insensitive, and can be detonated when wet (DWMT)

dynamite bomb: a bundle of dynamite sticks used as a bomb (DWMT)

E

ear print: the imprint of the ear, showing its structure and contour. Can be made by inking the ear, as in fingerprinting, and pressing cardboard or paper against it, thus transferring the imprint (LEV)

Earp, Wyatt (*1848-1929*): born in Monmouth, Illinois, on March 19, 1848, later moved to Iowa and by 1864 to California. He became a stagecoach driver and later a buffalo hunter. He was also a small-time professional gambler by the time he settled in Wichita, Kan., in 1874. In 1876 he moved to Dodge City, a relatively wide-open cattle town, where he served two terms as assistant marshal, in 1876 and in 1878-79. He was closely associated with Bat Masterson, another gambler, who was for a time sheriff of Ford County. ... Late in 1878 Earp left Dodge for Tombstone, Ariz., where recent silver strikes promised opportunity. He worked for a time as a Wells Fargo messenger while his brother Virgil became marshal. Earp had a falling out with a gang led by Ike Clanton in 1881 and the disagreement soon threatened to erupt into gunplay. Virgil Earp deputized Wyatt and another brother Morgan, and the three, together with "Doc" Holliday, forced a showdown with the Clantons on Oct. 26, 1881, at the O.K. Corral; when the shooting ended, Billy Clanton and Frank and Tom McLowry were dead and Ike Clanton and Billy Claiborne had escaped. The gun fight aroused a considerable portion of the Tombstone citizenry, who strongly suspected it had been little more than murder; Virgil Earp was quickly discharged as marshal. Wyatt wandered north to Colorado in 1882 and traveled widely, later returning to California, where he lived out his last years on the income from mining and real-estate interests. He died in Los Angeles on Jan. 13, 1929 (Webster's American Biographies)

earshot: distance a sound can be heard (LEV)

easel: a device to hold sensitized paper in a flat plane on an enlarger. Generally includes an adjustable mask to accommodate different sizes of paper (MPPF)

Eastman Gang: an Irish-organized gang that dominated the Bowery and East River Area of New York City around the turn of the century. They lost power after their leader, Edward Monk Eastman, went to jail on a robbery and assault charge

eavesdropping: clandestine (usu. secret) hearing of a conversation that was not intended for the hearer. Wiretapping, and the use of electronic "bugs" to hear (and/or record) private conversations, is often referred to as "electronic eavesdropping" or "electronic surveillance" (LEV)

ebriety: drunkenness (CDTP)

ecology: the study of spatial-functional areal patterns that arise and change through processes of ecological interaction. The study of relations between organisms and their habitats specifically, in anthropology, of the adaptation of human cultures to their geographical environments (DOS)

EC smokeless powder: an explosive powder used chiefly in blank cartridges; also called "EC blank fire," "EC blank powder," and "EC powder." EC powder is used in some .22 cal. and shotgun ammunition and was formerly used in fragmentation grenades (DWMT)

ecstasy: a mental state in which there is exhilaration. A rapturous expression, and loss of pain sense (CDTP)

ecstasy intoxication: the period of time when a sadist attains the peak of his emotional reaction from his acts (LEV)

edit: (1) to arrange or rearrange information for the output unit of the processor to print. Editing may involve deletion of unwanted data, and application of standard processes, such as zero-suppression (ADPS) (2) to examine raw data to check or improve their accuracy and relevance before keypunching (ADPS) (3) to examine data during the input operation or at other stages of processing for completeness and correctness (ADPS)

Edmunds Act: passed by Congress in 1882. It provided for the regulation and restriction of Mormon polygamy in Utah. Under the law Mormons, to a great degree, were excluded from local offices, and many were indicted and punished for polygamous practices (DOAH)

E.D.P.: electronic data processing. System of storing and retrieving information by computer (LEV)

effect of admission: the effect of an admission is dependent: (1) upon whether or not it is satisfactorily proved; (2) in what way it may be explained or limited by the party who has made it. There is a distinction between admission and the proof of an admission. Until it is clearly proven that an admission has been made it can have no effect (CDTP)

effect of joining in criminal purpose: where several persons join in the execution of a common criminal purpose, each is criminally liable for every act done in the execution of that purpose, whether done by himself or by his confederate (CDTP)

effect of repeal of statutes: except in jurisdictions where neither English nor American common law is in force, the general rule is that, if a penal statute is repealed without a saving clause, there can be no prosecution or punishment for a violation of it before the repeal. The repeal of an existing statute or law under which a proceeding is pending puts an end to the proceeding, unless it is saved by a proper saving clause in the repealing statute. Even when the statute is repealed after the accused has been convicted, judgment may be arrested, and if an appeal from a conviction is pending when the statute is repealed, the judgment of conviction must be set aside and the indictment quashed. But a repeal after final judgment of the appellate court will neither vacate the judgment nor arrest the execution of the sentence (CDTP)

effective aperture: the diameter of the lens diaphragm as measured through the front lens element; the unobstructed useful area of a lens; it may actually be larger than the opening in the lens diaphragm, owing to the converging action of the front lens element   (MPPF)

effective range: the maximum distance at which a weapon may be expected to fire accurately to inflict casualties or damage (DWMT)

effects: personal estate or property. (142 Pac. 256-258) In Cotton v. Com., 254 S.W. 1061, declared that it has not been decided whether "Effects" in the Federal Constitution and "Possessions" in the state provision include like or different kinds of property, but that it may be said that they have the same essential meaning   (CDTP)

effeminate: womanly; having womanly traits   (LEV)

effeminated man: homosexual male who plays the passive role. Such a person feels and acts in the role of being a woman   (LEV)

efficiency: as applied to shutters, the percentual relationship between the total time a shutter remains open (counting from half-open to half-closed position) and the time required for the shutter to reach the half-open and the fully closed positions   (MPPF)

efficiency of a lens: the ratio of the light actually transmitted by a lens to that incident to it (MPPF)

efficiency report: a performance evaluation report; personnel performance report   (LEV)

effigy: the image or representation of a person   (CDTP)

efflorescence: the process by which a chemical salt loses its water crystallization upon exposure to air   (MPPF)

E-field sensor: a passive sensor which detects changes in the earth's ambient electric field caused by the movement of an intruder. *See also* H-field sensor   (TDIAS)

e.g.: exempli gratia; meaning, for the sake of the example (CDTP)

Egan's Rats: an old-line criminal gang in St. Louis, the Rats were organized by Jellyroll Egan. They eventually became an Irish-organized crime gang that was the forerunner to St. Louis's modern-day Cosa Nostra

egress: (1) to go out of a structure or building (LEV) (2) the means of exit from an enclosure, such as a building   (LEV)

ejaculation: emission of seminal fluid; sexual climax by the male   (LEV)

ejectment: dispossession; expulsion; removal   (LEV)

ejector: a device in the breech mechanism of a gun, rifle, or the like which automatically throws out an empty cartridge case or unfired cartridge from the breech of receiver   (DWMT)

Ektalith: Eastman Kodak trademark for a diffusion-transfer system of producing lithographic plates   (MPPF)

elect: to choose

election law (federal), corrupt practices: The first was passed Jan. 26, 1907 (34 Stat. L. 864). It prohibited corporations from contributing toward campaign funds in national elections of President, Vice President, senators, and representatives. An act passed March 4, 1909 (35 Stat. L. 1088), effective Jan. 1, 1910, further prohibited national banks and corporations to contribute campaign funds in connection with any election to any political office   (FAMOUS)

election law, the first: was passed May 22, 1649, by the General Court in Warwick, R.I. and provided that "no one should bring in any votes that he did not receive from the voters' own hands, and that all votes should be filed by the Recorder in the presence of the Assembly." A committee of four freemen was authorized to determine violations of the law and "to examine parties and to present to this court what they find in the case"   (FAMOUS)

elective franchise: the right of a qualified voter to cast his ballot in an election authorized by law   (CDTP) elector: (1) one who is legally qualified to vote; a voter (LEV) (2) one who has been chosen by the people to be a member of the Electoral College and thus to formally elect the president and vice-president of the United States (LEV)

electrical: related to, pertaining to, or associated with electricity (TDIAS)

electrical system: those components of a vehicle that use and/or supply electrical power; i.e., battery, alternator, ignition system, horn, wiring, and lighting system (TDPPC)

electrocute: to kill by electricity (LEV)

electrocution: a method of capital punishment alternative to beheading, hanging, etc., based upon the theory that it is less painful, more certain, and less liable to accident than the older methods. It is administered by strapping the convict to a heavy chair wired to conduct an electric current of high voltage to electrodes applied one to the head and another to the lower leg of the prisoner (DOS)

electromagnetic: pertaining to the relationship between current flow and magnetic field (TDIAS)

electromagnetic interference (EMI): impairment of the reception of a wanted electromagnetic disturbance. This can be caused by lightning, radio transmitters, power line noise, and other electrical devices (TDIAS)

electromechanical bell: a bell with a prewound spring-driven striking mechanism, the operation of which is initiated by the activation of an electric tripping mechanism (TDIAS)

electron: the negatively charged particle of an atom (LEV)

electron microscope: an optical device which produces a greatly magnified image of small particles by using a beam of electrons (LEV)

electronic: related to, or pertaining to, devices which utilize electrons moving through a vacuum, gas, or semiconductor, and to circuits of systems containing such devices (TDIAS)

electronic data-processing system: a machine system capable of receiving, storing, operating on, and recording data without the intermediate use of tabulating cards. The system is also able to store internally at least some instructions for data-processing operations, and to locate and control access to data stored internally (ADPS)

electronic eavesdropping: listening and/or recording sounds (conversations) clandestinely or where such information or conversations may be pertinent to an investigation. A type of audio surveillance (LEV)

electronic fuze: a fuze, such as a radio proximity fuze, set off by an electronic device incorporated in the fuze (DWMT)

electronic surveillance: See electronic eavesdropping

eligible: suitable; fit to be chosen (CDPT)

Elkins v. United States, 364 U.S. 206, 4 L. Ed. 2d 1169, 80 S. Ct. 1437; Rios v. United States, 364 U.S. 253, 4 L. Ed. 2d 1688, 80 S. Ct. 1431 (1960): the 5-4 Elkins decision overturned the so-called "silver platter" doctrine: the rule that evidence of a federal crime which state police come upon in the course of an illegal search for a state crime may be turned over to federal authorities so long as federal agents did not participate in the search but simply received the evidence on a "silver platter." (The Court used its inherent supervisory power to regulate the use of evidence in federal courts in reaching its decision with the result the decision does not turn on constitutional question. *Elkins*, for the present, recognizes the principle laid down in *Burdeau* v. *McDowell* though there is a drift away from it as is manifested in a number of state court decisions since 1964) (ILECJ)

Elon: Kodak trademark for a popular developing agent (MPPF)

else-rule: a catch-all rule in decision tables to handle the conditions not covered by explicit rules; written by leaving all conditions blank ("irrelevant"). Action taken may be to halt processing, note the condition, or to correct the situation and continue processing (ADPS)

elude: to escape, dodge, or slip away from (LEV)

emancipate: to set free (CDTP)

emancipation: rendered free or set at liberty by [one's] parents, guardian, or master

embalm: to chemically treat a corpse to prevent decay (LEV)

embargo: (1) an edict of a government prohibiting the departure or entry of ships (CDTP) (2) any prohibition imposed by law on commerce (CDTP)

embassy: the official residence or official establishment of an ambassador in a foreign country (LEV)

embezzler: one who fradulently appropriates property or money with which he is intrusted (CDTP)

embezzling government munitions, clothing, army, navy goods, etc.: maximum fine $500 and maximum jail sentence two years (Fed. Pen. Code, Sec. 36) (CDTP)

embezzling U.S. money or property: maximum fine $5,000, maximum jail sentence five years, or both (Fed. Pen. Code, Sec. 47) (CDTP)

embolism: blocking of a blood vessel by a mass such as a clot or other substance (LEV)

embossing: the process by which the central portion of a print is depressed, leaving a raised margin (MPPF)

embracery: consists in the attempt to influence a jury corruptly to one side or the other, by promises, persuasions, entreaties, entertainments, etc. (CDTP)

embryo: the human fetus in its first

three months of life (CDTP)

emergency vehicle: any vehicle such as a patrol car, van, station wagon, or tow truck, which is equipped to respond to emergency situations common to police operations (TDPPC)

emetic: drug or treatment that causes vomiting (LEV)

emigrate: to leave one's country or region to take residence in another country or region (LEV)

eminent domain: the power of a government to take private property for public purposes. This power is considered an attribute of sovereignty and is deemed justifiable when necessary for the proper performance of governmental functions. The power may be properly delegated to the subdivisions of the government, to public utilities, and even to businesses not affected with public interest when the seizure is considered essential for public use. The only limitations on eminent domain are that the property must be taken for a public use and that a fair compensation must be paid for it. The Fifth and Fourteenth Amendments of the U.S. Constitution establish the right and the limitations of eminent domain (DOAH)

emission standards: a set of values which prescribe the limits on the amount of hydrocarbons, carbon monoxide, and nitrogen oxides which a vehicle may emit (TDPPC)

emolument: profit or compensation from office or employment

empathy: understanding of another's feelings and motives (LEV)

empirical: based on experience and observation; based on established facts (LEV)

employee: any person in the service of another under a contract for hire, express or implied, oral or written (CDTP)

employer: a person who hires and supervises others to perform service for him in the operation of his business under an agreement to pay them wages   (CDTP)

emulsion: the light-sensitive layer, consisting of silver salts suspended in gelatin, which is spread over a permanent support such as film, glass, or paper   (MPPF)

emulsion speed: the spread of an emulsion (sensitivity) in reacting to light. It is usu. stated as a factor or number, either by ASA rating or values assigned by the light meter (exposure meter) manufacturers   (LEV)

enact: to legislate; to make into law by a legislature or other such body   (LEV)

enclosure: a fingerprint term describing a ridge line separation (bifurcation) which later meets again to form an enclosure   (LEV)

endanger: cause danger to   (LEV)

ending ridge: a ridge, in a fingerprint pattern, which ends abruptly   (LEV)

end-of-file: special symbols and a trailer label indicate end of a file. Several short files can be recorded on one tape, whereas a long file may extend over several reels—a multi-reel file. Automatic procedures are used to finish processing when the end of a record file on tape is reached   (ADPS)

end-of-tape: a reflective spot or other indicator is placed near the physical end of the tape to signal the end. Automatic procedures are used to handle tapes when the physical end of an input or output tape is reached   (ADPS)

endorse, indorse: (1) write one's name and/or instructions on the back of a check (LEV) (2) to approve of something or a person   (LEV)

endothermic: of a chemical reaction which absorbs heat   (FS)

energy: (1) the force or power of a charge (CDTP) (2) the energy of a bullet is the measure of work it can do. This term is largely used in physics and applied mechanics, and is expressed in foot pounds. The formula is $E = \frac{1}{2}\ w/g\ v^2$ in which w is the weight of the bul-

let in pounds; g, the acceleration of gravity, 32.17; and v, the velocity of the bullet in feet per second. To reduce the weight of a bullet in grains, to pounds, divide its weight by 7,000. As there are several constants in this formula, where a number of energy computations are to be made the operations can be simplified by multiplying the weight of the bullet in grains by the square of its velocity and dividing this product by 450,240   (CDTP)

enforcement: an action or process to compel observance of law or the requirements of public policy   (DAP)

Enforcer, the: in the organizational structure of the Cosa Nostra, the one who uses force or fear to maintain internal discipline and security to threaten or use physical force against persons in order to achieve goals of the organization. The "strong-arm" man   (LEV)

engine emissions: by-products of engine operation, such as heat, vaporized unburned fuel, and exhaust gases. Included in such by-products are hydrocarbons, carbon monoxide, carbon dioxide, nitrogen oxides, and water vapor   (TDPPC)

English common law: the basis of the English common law is immemorial usage and custom, and not legislative enactment. For this reason it is often called the "Unwritten Law." The generic term "Common Law" has been well defined as "those maxims, principles, and forms of judicial proceedings, which have no written law to prescribe or warrant them, but which, founded on the laws of nature and the dictates of reason, have, by usage and custom, become interwoven with the written laws; and, by such incorporation, form a part of the municipal code of each state or nation"   (CDPT)

Enoch Arden law: a statute granting permission to remarry without fear of legal penalty to a person whose spouse has been absent usually for seven successive years (in New York, five) and is presumed dead (DAP)

entail: a principle of law originating in medieval England which provided that, upon the death of the owner of an estate, the entire estate was bequeathed to his heir, and subsequently to an established line of legatees. The system was imported into the British colonies where it was met with great resistance because of its undemocratic features. Virginia took the lead in abolishing entail in 1776, and was followed by other states. By the Jeffersonian period entail had disappeared from the United States (DOAH)

entitle: to give a right or title to (CDTP)

entrance delay: the time between actuating a sensor or an entrance door or gate and the sounding of a local alarm or transmission of an alarm signal by the control unit. This delay is used if the authorized access switch is located within the protected area and permits a person with the control key to enter without causing an alarm. The delay is provided by a timer within the control unit (TDIAS)

entrapment: a defense to criminal responsibility that arises from improper acts committed against the accused by another, usu. a police undercover agent. When police encouragement plays upon the weaknesses of an innocent person and beguiles him to commit crimes he normally would not attempt, it can be deemed improper as entrapment and the evidence excluded under the exclusionary rule

entry: (1) actually entering a building by going inside; permits any part of his body to enter the building, or causes the entry of any instrument or weapon held in his hand (CDTP) (2) a notation written in a stub of a row or in a cell of decision table. Any row must be in the form of either a

limited entry or an extended entry (ADPS)

entry, illegal: the unlawful entering of any house, building, or structure, with the intent to commit a crime (LEV)

enure: to take effect (CDTP)

environment division: the division of a COBOL program in which the programmer lists the features of the equipment needed to run a program: input-output devices, storage size, etc. (ADPS)

enzymes: the constituents of living matter which act as catalysts for the chemical processes of life (FS)

eonism: the desire to wear clothing of the opposite sex (LEV)

epaulet, epaulette: an ornament or badge worn on the shoulders of uniforms. It usually consists of a strap ending in a fringed pad (DWMT)

epidermis: the outer layer of skin (LEV)

epilepsy: a chronic disease characterized by seizures of convulsion, unconsciousness, frothing at the mouth, and in its later stages associated with mental disturbances (CDTP)

episode: an incident or a series of incidents closely related (LEV)

equal protection: a requirement of the Fourteenth Amendment that States must give equal treatment under the law to all persons. For many years the Supreme Court sharply limited the effectiveness of this clause. In the Civil Rights cases, 1883, it held that the clause prohibited only discrimination by private individuals and groups. In *Plessy* v. *Ferguson*, 1896, the Court approved the segregation of different races if equal accommodations were provided; but until the 1930s it rarely reviewed lower court decisions to determine if separate accommodations were in fact equal. In *Brown* v. *Board of Education*, it held that segregated schools were inherently unequal. Other decisions voided State laws discriminating between persons in employment, transportation, housing, and access to public accommodations and places of amusement. But in matters not concerned with race or nationality, classifications may still be made by State legislatures if they are reasonably adapted to the accomplishment of proper governmental objectives (as protection of health, safety, morals, or general welfare), and if all persons falling within a given class are treated alike. Thus State laws may discriminate between residents and nonresidents in access to State privileges, between chain stores and department stores in the rate of taxation, and between residential and commercial districts in zoning regulations because of a reasonable relation to the State's police power. To prevent discrimination by private persons several States have enacted civil rights laws requiring equal treatment for all persons regardless of race, color, creed, or nationality in employment, lodging houses, conveyances, amusement centers, and other places of public accommodation   (DAP)

equipment: all articles needed to outfit an individual or organization. The term refers to clothing, tools, utensils, vehicles, weapons, and other similar items. As to type of authorization, equipment may be divided into special (or project) equipment, equipment prescribed by tables of allowances, and equipment prescribed by tables of organization and equipment   (DWMT)

equipment carrier: the function of a patrol car in providing for the transportation of various items required by an officer to carry out law enforcement duties. This equipment may include weapons, emergency lights, communication equipment, rescue equipment, firefighting equipment, warning devices, and other miscellaneous items   (TDPPC)

equipment for law enforcement, testing: See laboratory, law en-

forcement standards

equitable: fair, unbiased   (CDTP)

equitable action: one founded on an equity or cognizable in a court of equity; an action arising, not immediately from the contract in suit, but from an equity in favor of a third person, not a party to it, but for whose benefit certain stipulations or promises were made (109 U.S. 194)   (CDTP)

equitable right: a right enforceable in a court of equity   (CDTP)

equity: a branch of remedial justice which arose perhaps by the 12th or 13th century in England, when petitions to the King for relief from the positive and rather inflexible rules of the common law were referred to the Lord Chancellor; hence the name "chancery" which is used for an equity court. Much of the substance and procedure of equity was derived from civil and canon law. Abstract principles of justice, or natural law, guided the judge in deciding each suit. In time equity developed its own precedents. Procedure in equity is relatively simple. An attempt is made to present the whole case, with all possible grounds for decision, to a court; and for that purpose all individuals having an interest may be summoned as parties even after the beginning of a case. The court has a considerable choice of remedies in "commanding what is right and prohibiting what is wrong." The most important are the requirements of specific performance, and preventive justice by means of the injunction. Separate equity courts, once the general rule, now exist in only a half-dozen States. In most States both common law and equity are administered by the same judge in the same case; but in others separate proceedings must be held for law and equity cases, even though the same judge may preside over both   (DAP)

equity jurisdiction: the jurisdiction belonging to a court of equity, but more particularly the aggregate of those cases, controversies, and occasions which form proper subjects for the exercise of the powers of a chancery court (CDTP)

equity of redemption: (1) the interest which a mortgagor retains in the property mortgaged (CDTP) (2) the right of the mortgagor of an estate to redeem the same after it has been forfeited, at law, by a breach of the condition of the mortgage, upon paying the amount of debt, interests, and costs (236 Pac. 725-726) (CDTP)

equivalent: equal in worth, power, effect (CDTP)

equivocate: (1) to conceal the truth (CDTP) (2) use ambiguous words (CDTP)

erosion: the wearing away of the inside of the gun barrel from repeated firing of the weapon (LEV)

erotic: involved with sexual love; arousing sexual love (LEV)

erratic: irregular, unpredictable, not according to the usual or expected (LEV)

erratum: an error (CDTP)

error: the difference between an accurate quantity and its calculated approximation. *Errors* occur in numerical methods; *mistakes* are human blunders that occur in programs, coding, data, transcription, and operating; *malfunctions* occur in equipment operations (ADPS)

error tape: a tape used for writing out errors in order to correct them by analysis after printing or further machine processing (ADPS)

escape: the departure or deliverance out of custody of a person who was lawfully imprisoned, before he is entitled to his liberty by the process of law. Escapes are either voluntary or negligent. The former is the case when the keeper voluntarily conceded to the prisoner any liberty not authorized by law. The latter is the case when the prisoner contrives to leave his prison by forcing his way out, or any other means, without the knowledge or against the will of his keeper. Prison breach is the breaking and going out of his place of confinement by one who is lawfully imprisoned. Rescue is the forcible delivery of a prisoner from lawful custody by one who knows that he is in custody (CDTP)

Escobedo v. Illinois, 378 U.S. 478, 12 L. Ed. 2d 977, 84 S. Ct. 1758 (1964): "We hold only," concluded the Court in its 5-4 opinion, "that when the process shifts from investigatory to accusatory and its purpose is to elicit a confession—our adversary system begins to operate, and, under the circumstances here, the accused must be permitted to consult with his lawyer" [The construction of the bridge that led to *Miranda v. Arizona* was begun in Gideon v. Wainwright, 372 U.S. 335 (1963), and completed in *Escobedo.]* (ILECJ)

escrow: where the delivery of a deed is made to a third person, to hold till some condition be performed on the part of the grantee (CDTP)

espionage: in law the act of covertly obtaining for a foreign government a military secret, in time of war or peace. Also used to cover practices in industrial strife by which one side obtains by covert methods information held secret by the other (DOS)

espionage, industrial: agents or paid representatives of one company or industry who obtain secret information about another. This may be accomplished by putting an agent into another company as an employee (LEV)

Espionage Act: passed by Congress in 1917. It prescribed a $10,000 fine and 20 years imprisonment for interfering with the recruiting of troops or the disclosure of information dealing with national defense. Additional penalties were included for the refusal to perform military duty, the advocacy to treason, or the resistance to laws. The Act was attacked as unconstitutional, but its enforcement nevertheless resulted in many arrests and imprisonments. Notable among these were the arrests of Eugene V. Debs, former Socialist Party candidate for the presidency who was sentenced to a ten-year jail term, and Socialist Congressman Victor Berger who was sentenced to 20 years. The latter's paper, the *Milwaukee Leader*, was denied the use of the mails. Some 450 conscientious objectors were sentenced to military prisons   (DOAH)

esprit-de-corps: the "spirit of the body" or the group; morale or loyalty. The fidelity attitude of members of a group for one another and for the group interest
(DOS)

Esquirol, Jean Etienne (*1772 – 1840*): a French psychiatrist and pupil of Pinel, Esquirol worked hard for the reform of mental institutions and for sympathetic treatment of the criminally insane. In his chief work, *Des maladies mentales*, he was one of the first men to emphasize the role of emotions as a source of mental disturbances

establishment: (1) an organization or agency (LEV) (2) (militant group term) the present order of society—government, agencies, organizations; the system   (LEV)

esters: a class of compounds each formed by the combination of an alcohol and an acid. They have two-word names, the first word indicating the alcohol and the second the acid—e.g. ethyl acetate. Usually liquids with a strong, characteristic, often fragrant, smell. However, fats are also esters
(FS)

Estes v. Texas: *See* Estes scandal

Estes scandal: the rigging of cotton acreage allotments and contracts for storing government agricultural surpluses by Billie Sol Estes, a Texas manipulator. His indictment in 1962 was followed by the resignation of two federal of-

ficials, Republican charges of corruption, and his own conviction for swindling. His conviction was later set aside by the Supreme Court in Estes v. Texas, 381 U.S. 532 (1965), because at the preliminary hearing and, to a lesser degree at the trial, the bright lights, numerous strands of television cable, and activities of representatives of news mediums, which were excessive in relation to the public's interest in the news, had prevented a sober search for the truth and so had denied Estes a fair trial   (DAP)

estop: to legally stop or prevent someone from doing something
(LEV)

estoppel: an impediment or bar by which a person is precluded from alleging or denying a fact in consequence of his own previous act
(CDTP)

et [Lat]: and

et al [*Lat*]: abbreviation of "et alii," and others

et cetera (etc.): and so forth; and other things   (LEV)

ethanol: grain alcohol, ethyl alcohol in alcoholic beverages $(C_2 H_5 OH)$ (LEV)

ether: a volatile drug used for general anesthesia   (CDTP)

ethics: standards of moral and official conduct; a system of morals. *See* code of ethics, canons of police ethics   (LEV)

ethyl alcohol: grain alcohol; the kind of alcohol used for drinking. *See* alcohol, ethanol   (LEV)

et scq., et sequitur [*Lat*]: and the following

et ux [*Lat*]: and wife

eunuch: a castrated male human being

eutectic: the melting- or freezing-point of any element or compound is lowered by the presence of another in solution. Hence if two substances A and B are miscible in all proportions, the melting-point of A is progressively lowered by the increasing addition of B, and similarly composition will therefore have a minimum melting-point: this is the *eutectic* mixture. There may also be eutectic mixtures of more than two components. *Cf.* azeotrope (FS)

euthanasia: the theory or practice of "mercy deaths"—permitting physicians or other socially authorized persons to give a lethal dose of medicine to persons painfully and incurably ill or hopelessly defective from birth. At present this theory is opposed to the law and the medical code of ethics; but a sample poll has shown that some 46 percent of the people giving opinions favored euthanasia under government supervision (DOS)

evacuate: to bodily vacate a place or structure; to move out of (LEV)

evacuation: (1) the process of moving any person who is wounded, injured, or ill to or between medical treatment facilities (DWMT) (2) the clearance of personnel, animals, or material from a given locality (DWMT) (3) the controlled process of collecting, classifying, and shipping unserviceable or abandoned material, U.S. and foreign, to appropriate reclamation, maintenance, technical intelligence, or disposal facilities (DWMT)

evacuee: a civilian removed from his place of residence by direction for reasons of his own security or because of the requirements of the situation (DWMT)

evasive: (1) elusive (LEV) (2) acting to avoid capture or injury (LEV)

ever-widening circle search: a method of searching a crime scene where the searcher starts at a focal point, at or near the middle of the area, and searches the area by traveling in widening circles. This may be used in an indoor or outdoor crime scene (LEV)

event: any action that gives rise to data that affects the contents of the files of a business—for example, purchase, shipment, or sale (ADPS)

event chain: a trace of the series of

actions—preparing documents, processing data, and updating files—that results from one initial event (ADPS)

evict: to expel one legally from a place or structure, such as a tenant (LEV)

eviction: expulsion of an occupant (LEV)

evidence: any species of proof, or probative matter, legally presented at the trial of an issue, by the act of the parties and through the medium of witnesses, records, documents, concrete objects, etc., for the purpose of inducing belief in the minds of the court or jury as to their contention (CDTP) (2) the rule is: that the testimony of accomplices will, if otherwise sufficient, alone support a conviction, provided the jury believes it. (243 Fed. 300) Where drug is delivered at agreed price, payment by purchaser is not necessary to complete offense of illegal sale. (279 Fed. 12) Evidence obtained by a state officer in searching the person of a defendent arrested without a warrant is admissable in a federal court. (282 Fed. 261) Where defendant claimed no interest in the drugs found in his room, it was competent for the government to introduce evidence that list found in his possession contained names known to the witness to be drug addicts. (284 Fed. 567) Conviction for unlawful sale of narcotics sustained evidence that informer entered defendant's home and purchased morphine with marked money and that upon a search of the house narcotics were found there, being sufficient to take case to jury. (82 Fed. 2nd 638) Evidence to attempt to sell sufficient (6 Fed. 2nd 48) (CDTP)

evidence, associative: the establishment of a link between the accused and the crime scene by information obtained from physical evidence found at the crime scene and that found on the accused or in places traceable to him (LEV)

evidence, circumstantial: evidence which does not directly prove pertinent facts but from which the pertinent facts can be inferred or deduced (LEV)

evidence, competent: evidence which is furnished by a person competent to testify; infants, insane people, and laymen seeking to testify in areas of specialized knowledge where they have no expert knowledge are examples of incompetent persons (LEV)

evidence, corroborating: evidence that strengthens or supports other evidence; evidence which corroborates other evidence (LEV)

evidence, derivative: See derivative evidence

evidence, direct: evidence which proves the facts in dispute directly, without an inference or presumption being drawn from any other set of circumstances. Contrasted with circumstantial evidence (LEV)

evidence, hearsay: "second-hand information"; facts which the witness did not personally acquire through his five senses, but are what another witness told him. It is generally not admissible in court, but there are exceptions. See hearsay (LEV)

evidence, inflammatory: See evidence, prejudicial

evidence, material: material evidence must relate to the facts in issue and must also be important enough to warrant its use. Materiality of evidence pertains to its importance (LEV)

evidence, opinion: conclusions drawn from a set of facts or circumstances which is offered in trial by a witness. It is usually inadmissible on the part of a layman. There are exceptions, one of which is testimony by an expert after he has been duly qualified before the judge (LEV)

evidence, prejudicial: evidence which is so shocking to the senses of a juror that it may unduly sway his attitude toward one of the parties in a criminal trial; inflam-

matory evidence (LEV)

evidence, relevant: relevant evidence is that which relates to or bears directly upon a fact in issue in the case, and proves or tends to prove the truth or untruth of the fact (LEV)

evidence aliunde: See extraneous evidence

evidence given in former proceeding: is admissible for the purpose of proving the matter stated in a later stage of the same proceeding, under the following circumstances: (1) when the witness is dead, (2) when he is insane, (3) out of the jurisdiction, (4) cannot be found within the jurisdiction, (5) provided the person against whom the evidence is to be given had the right and the opportunity to cross-examine the witness in the former proceeding (CDTP)

evidence rule, best: See best evidence rule

evidence wrongfully obtained: the fact that articles or admissions were wrongfully obtained from the defendant does not render them inadmissible in evidence (CDTP)

evident: clear to the understanding and satisfactory to the judgment; manifest; plain; obvious; conclusive (CDTP)

evidentiary items: items connected with a crime, but not as contraband, fruits or instrumentalities of the crime, or weapons. See mere evidence (LEV)

ex [Lat]: from

examination: the preliminary hearing before the magistrate of the evidence against one accused of crime (CDTP)

examination, cross-examination: witnesses examined in open court must be first examined in chief; they may then be cross-examined, and then re-examined. The examination and cross-examination must relate to facts in issue or relevant thereto; and in most states the cross-examination must be confined to the facts to which the witness testified on his examination in chief. The re-examination must be directed to the explanation of matters referred to in cross-examination, and if new matter is, by permission of court, introduced in re-examination the adverse party may further cross-examine upon the matter (CDTP)

examining trial: *See* preliminary hearing

excepted positions: three categories of positions in the civil service which it is impracticable to fill by competitive examinations in the usual form, such as: *a*. those for which no suitable written examination can be prepared; *b*. those requiring persons whose competence is best attested by experience, previous publications, and letters of recommendation from competent observers; and *c*. those of a confidential or policy-determining character   (DAP)

exception: formal notification of the court that the party objects to its action, during a trial, in ruling on a request or objection of the party taking the action (exception)   (LEV)

exception-principle system: an information system that reports on situations only when actual results are outside a "normal range"; results within normal range are not reported   (ADPS)

exceptions: (1) in cases of libel and nuisance the principal is liable, under certain circumstances, for the acts of his agents or servants upon the ground of his negligence in failing to exercise proper control of them (CDTP) (2) under some statutes the principal is liable for prohibited acts, notwithstanding that they are done by his agents or servants without his authority or contrary to his instructions   (CDTP)

excess-3 code: a binary-coded decimal system that represents each decimal as the corresponding binary number plus three. For example, the decimal digits 0, 1, 8, 9 are represented as 0011, 0100, 1011, 1100, respectively.

The 9's complement of the decimal digit corresponds (also in Excess-3 Code) to the 1's complement of the four binary digits   (ADPS)

exclusionary rule: legal prohibitions against the prosecution (government) using evidence illegally obtained (as by illegal search and seizure). Prior to *Mapp* v. *Ohio* (1961) several states, by law, had exclusionary rules which precluded the use of such evidence. After *Mapp* all states were prohibited from the use of such evidence   (LEV)

exclusion of evidence to contradict answers to question testing veracity: when a witness under cross-examination has been asked and has answered any question which is relevant to the inquiry only so far as it tends to shake his credit by injuring his character can evidence be given to contradict him in the following cases: (1) if a witness is asked whether he has been previously convicted of any felony or misdemeanor, and denies, or does not admit it, or refuses to answer, evidence may be given of his previous conviction; (2) if a witness is asked any question tending to show that he is not impartial, and answers it by denying the facts suggested, he may be contradicted   (CDTP)

excrement: fecal matter; dung; stool   (LEV)

exculpate: to exonerate; to clear of blame or guilt; to prove innocent   (LEV)

exculpatory: tending to clear from guilt, blame, or involvement in an offense; nonincriminating. *Cf.* inculpatory   (LEV)

excusable homicide: when committed by accident and misfortune   (CDTP)

ex delicto [*Lat*]: from the crime

execute: (1) to carry out (LEV) (2) to put into effect (LEV) (3) to inflict the death sentence   (LEV)

execution: (1) a judicial writ directing an officer to carry out the judgment of a court of law

(DAP) (2) enforcement of the judgment, especially of the death penalty following conviction of a capital crime and sentence by a court of law (DAP) (3) rendering valid a legal document by signing and delivering it (DAP)

execution and return of warrant: a research warrant is executed by making the search directed, the authority of the officer in such search being named within the four corners of the instrument, so far as the place to be searched and the time and manner of the execution of the warrant are concerned; and hence, a warrant cannot be extended beyond the privileges granted in its issuance; thus, for example, a warrant issued by a justice of the peace to search premises in the justice's district and county will not, where the premises so designated are divided by the county line, authorize a search of buildings or places in the county other than where issued. Where the warrant is valid, the officers have, of course, a lawful right to enter. While it may be necessary for the officers making a search to have a search warrant, where the warrant is in the officer's coat, on the premises, a few feet from the dwelling being searched, it is sufficiently in the officer's possession. (208 N.W. 260) (CDTP)

execution of the warrant: (1) it can only be executed by the officer to whom it is directed either by name or by description of his office; (2) it cannot confer authority to execute it on one officer, where a statute provides for its execution by another; (3) unless a statute so allows, it cannot be executed outside the jurisdiction of the issuing magistrate or court; (4) where the warrant is necessary, it must be in the possession of the officer at the time of the arrest; (5) it must be returned after the arrest (CDTP)

executions, gangland: killings which are ordered and carried out by gangsters (CDTP)

executive clemency: authority and power given to certain executive authorities of the government, such as the Governor, to set aside a court judgment of sentence. This power is granted by law, usu. the Constitution (LEV)

executive routine: a routine designed to process and control other routines (ADPS)

executor [m.], executrix [f.]: an individual appointed in a will to carry out its provisions

executory process: proceedings whereby, by previous agreement of the parties involved, mortgaged property may be seized and sold without going through the procedure of citing the mortgage debtor into court and obtaining a judgment against him. It is an expeditious way of foreclosure and sale of property on which a mortgage or privilege exists (LEV)

exemplar: a known specimen of evidence to be used by experts for comparison with other (questioned) evidence (LEV)

exempli gratia [Lat]: for the sake of example

exempt: free from (CDTP)

exemption: the right given by law to a debtor to hold a portion of his property free from liability to execution at the suit of a creditor, or to distress from rent (CDTP)

ex facie [Lat, lit from the face]: apparently; evidently. A term applied to what appears on the face of a writing (CDTP)

exhaust: to use up; to develop fully and completely (LEV)

exhibit: an item of evidence; an item obtained in an investigation, particularly one which is to be used as evidence; a physical object offered in evidence during a trial (LEV)

exhibitionism: the exposing of one's (private parts) to obtain sexual gratification (LEV)

exhibitionist: a person who has an impulse to show the sex organs to a member of the opposite sex (CDTP) exhumation: disinterment; removing from the earth of something that has been buried, esp. a human corpse.

exhume: disinter; to recover a dead body which has been properly buried (LEV)

exit: a possible outcome from comparing items of numeric data—equal to, smaller than, larger than, or zero, negative, positive—or from comparing alphabetic data items: same, earlier, or later. An outcome from checking the truth of a condition statement: yes or no. Each outcome may be used to send program control to a different, appropriate subroutine (ADPS)

exit delay: the time between turning on a control unit and the sounding of a local alarm or transmission of an alarm signal upon actuation of a sensor on an exit door. This delay is used if the authorized access switch is located within the protected area and permits a person with the control key to turn on the alarm system and to leave through a protected door or gate without causing an alarm. The delay is provided by a timer within the control unit (TDIAS)

exitus: death (CDTP)

ex officio [Lat]: by virtue of the office

exonerate: to prove not guilty; acquit; to clear of blame or fault (LEV)

exonerate bail: releasing a surety on bail bond (CDTP)

exothermic: of a chemical reaction which produces heat (FS)

expanding bullet: a bullet with a soft nose, such as a dumdum, designed to flatten out when it hits its target (DWMT)

ex parte [Lat.]: one-sided. From the side of one party only; requested by and/or done for one party only. "The order was issued ex parte by the court." This means the court did not have an adversary hearing before issuing the order. The court only heard one side of the question or matter before issuing the order (LEV)

ex parte Hull, 312 U.S. 546 1941: in this case, the court ruled that an inmate's right to apply to a federal court may not be abridged or impaired by a state or its officers. This ruling has been extended by the courts to include any legal material forwarded to the court

expatriation: the act of voluntarily leaving one's country, or abandoning allegiance to one's country

expert: one who is specially qualified in a field or subject matter. This may be the result of education, training, or experience (LEV)

expert evidence: testimony given in relation to some scientific, technical, or professional matter by experts (CDTP)

expert testimony: when there is a question as to any point of science or art, the opinions upon that point of persons specially skilled in any such matter may be given. The words "science or art" in the above rule include all subjects on which a course of special study or experience is necessary to the formation of an opinion. The opinions of experts as to a matter of common knowledge are not admissible, for the jury are as well able to judge of such facts without the aid of the expert opinion. Where a witness possesses knowledge, not of the facts of the case but of a trade, science, art, beyond that of the average person he may give his opinion based upon such special knowledge so that the jury may have this knowledge in arriving at a verdict (CDTP)

expertise: special knowledge concerning a thing or subject; expertness in a special field (LEV)

expiation: a theory of the purpose or punishment for crime based originally upon the belief that crime aroused the anger of the gods against the whole group, and that the only way to mollify that anger was to destroy the offender. Latterly the term has been widened in its meaning to include the turning away of the offender. As thus used it is almost synonymous with retribution (DOS)

expire: (1) to come to an end, as in a lease contract (LEV) (2) to die (LEV)

explicit: plainly shown; spelled out in detail; not vague (LEV)

explode: to detonate; to set off explosives (LEV)

explosive: a substance or mixture of substances which may be made to undergo a rapid chemical change, without an outside supply of oxygen, with the liberation of large quantities of energy generally accompanied by the evolution of hot gases. Explosives are divided into two classes—high explosives and low explosives—according to their rate of reaction in normal usage (DWMT)

explosive bullet: a bullet which contains an explosive and is detonated on contact with its target or via a time fuze. Such bullets were banned for small arms by international agreement in 1868 (DWMT)

explosive D: so called from the initial of Col. B. W. Dunn, the inventor. Also called "dunnite." A high explosive consisting mainly of ammonium picrate. It is used in some armor-piercing projectiles because of its comparative insensitivity to shock and friction (DWMT)

explosive ordnance: ordnance material which normally contains or consists of explosives, for example, bombs, mines, torpedoes, missiles, and projectiles (DWMT)

explosive-ordnance-disposal unit: personnel with special training and equipment who render explosive ordnance safe (such as bombs, mines, projectiles, and booby traps), make intelligence reports on such ordnance, and supervise the safe removal thereof (DWMT)

explosive train: a train of combustible and explosive elements arranged in order of decreasing sensitivity inside a fuze, projectile, bomb, gun chamber, or the like.

The function of the explosive train is to accomplish the controlled augmentation of a small impulse into one of suitable energy to cause the main charge of the munition to function (DWMT)

ex post facto [*Lat*]: after the fact

ex post facto law: a law declaring an act illegal which was legal when committed. Article 1, Section 9 of the Constitution of the United States forbids Congress to enact ex post facto laws. Article 1, Section 10, of the Constitution places the same prohibition upon the state legislatures (DOAH)

exposure: (1) act of exposing. In photography, the time and extent of light entering the lens (lens opening) in relation to the illumination of the subject (exposure time) (LEV)

exposure meter: a device for measuring and registering the amount of light and correlating this information so as to show the correct exposure for the film being used. It is sometimes called a light meter (LEV)

express bullet, express rifle: originally referred to a bullet or rifle with a long range and low trajectory; sometimes refers to the use of a light explosive bullet of large caliber (CDTP)

expropriation: action by the state, under its sovereign power, to take over property for the use of the people (public use). This is under the power of eminent domain. Reasonable compensation must be made for the property so appropriated (LEV)

ex pueris [*Lat*]: from childhood

expunge: to physically destroy information in files, computers, or other depositories

ex rel [*Lat, lit by or on the information of*]: in case titles, it designates the individual for whom the government or public official is acting

extended entry: a notation other than a limited entry with part of the condition or action written in the cells—for example, less than, greater than, or equal to an amount; excellent, good, poor, none, any (ADPS)

exterior: the outward side of a body or structure (LEV)

exterior ballistics: the branch of ballistics which deals with the motion of the projectile while in flight (DWMT)

exterminate: to kill; to eradicate by killing; "stamp out" (LEV)

external: outside; exterior (LEV)

externally stored program: instruction routines set up in wiring boards or plugboards for manual insertion into small-scale processor (ADPS)

extinguish: to put out a light or fire; to cause a fire to go out (die out) (LEV)

extortion: the unlawful taking by any officer, by color of his office, of any money or anything of value that is not due him, or more than is due, or before it is due. The distinction between "bribery" and "extortion" consists in the former, the offering a present, or receiving one if offered; the latter, in demanding a fee or present, by color of office. Extortion in many jurisdictions is the unlawful obtaining of property by force or fear by any person with the consent of the victim. Sometimes called blackmail (CDTP)

extortion by means of telephone, etc.: an act was passed by Congress May 18, 1934 (S. 2249) applying the powers of the Federal Government, under the commerce clause of the Constitution, to extortion by means of telephone, telegraph, radio, oral message, or otherwise. That whoever, with intent to extort from any person, firm, association, or corporation any money or other thing of value, shall transmit in interstate commerce, by any means whatsoever, any threat to injure person or property, reputation of any person alive or deceased, kidnap, accuse of crime, any demand or request, ransom or reward for the release of any kidnaped person, shall upon conviction be fined not

more than $5,000 or imprisonment for not more than 20 years, or both (CDTP)

extract: (1) to obtain certain specified digits from a machine word (ADPS) (2) to replace contents of specific columns of another machine word, depending on the instruction (ADPS) (3) to remove from a set of items of data all those items that meet some arbitrary condition (ADPS)

extractor: a device in the breech mechanism of a gun, rifle, or the like for pulling an empty cartridge case or an unfired cartridge out of the chamber (DWMT)

extradition: the procedure by which a person who commits a crime in one jurisdiction and flees into another can be followed and arrested in the latter with its consent. (1) *Interstate extradiction.* The Constitution of the United States, several acts of Congress, and the statutes of the several states provide that a person charged with a crime in one state who flees from that state into another may be extradited to the former. In order to be extradited the person: (a) must be judicially "charged" with a crime in the demanding state; (b) must not be charged with a crime against the state to which he was fled; (c) must have been in the demanding state in order to have "fled from justice." (2) *International extradition.* By treaties between the United States and most foreign countries provision is made for the extradition of fugitives from justice in specified cases. The several American states cannot act in this matter (DOS)

extrajudicial: out of the ordinary course of law. Made out of court, e.g., an extrajudicial statement (CDTP)

extralegal: outside or beyond the scope of law (DAP)

extraneous: not belonging to the matter in hand (CDTP)

extraneous evidence: in reference to any writing, extraneous evidence is not derived from anything to be found in the document itself

extraterritorial operation: a crime is essentially local, and is the creature of the law which defines or prohibits it; it is an offense against the sovereignty, and can be taken notice of and punished only by the sovereignty offended. Accordingly, the general rule is, that the laws of a country do not take effect beyond its territorial limits, because it has neither the interest nor the power to enforce its will. However, mere physical presence, citizenship, or residence within the state is not always essential in order to render one amenable to its laws and subject to its prosecution; and among the exceptions to the general rule are the cases in which a person, being at the time in one state or country, does a criminal act which takes effect in another (CDTP)

extreme range: the greatest range of a weapon, e.g., the greatest distance a gun will shoot (DWMT)

extremist group: a group or organization, the avowed purpose of which is to bring about some change in our government functions and in society by radical, disorderly, and/or violent methods (LEV)

extrinsic evidence: external evidence; facts other than those contained in the body of an agreement, document, etc.

eyepiece: that part of a microscope, containing lens, which is nearest the eye. (The other end is called the objective.) (LEV)

eyeshot: a distance where things can be seen; range of sight for the eyes (LEV)

eyewitness: a witness who saw the things happen about which he is testifying; one who witnessed the crime or event (LEV)

F

F.A.A. (FAA): Federal Aviation Administration

face value: (1) the value shown on the face (LEV) (2) in the case of bond—the nominal value (LEV) (3) the apparent value of a statement (LEV)

facsimile: exact copy

fact: a thing done; an actual occurrence

factor: a cause, determinant, or necessary condition of an event or change. Less commonly the word is used to designate a component of a situation, whether with or without reference to its causal significance. Classifications of factors vary with the frame of reference. Thus, we may subsume causal factors under the three categories of culture, hereditary or original nature, and physiographic environment; or under the specialized group interests (in the sense of goal-centered activities) found in a situation; or again under the specified categories of behavior and experience, as thought, feeling, action, attitude, purpose. Factors as components are illustrated, in addition, by types of interaction in a social situation— competition, conflict, cooperation, etc.; or, in terms of personnel, by the roles of the individual, the primary group, and special public or integrative organization sharing in a common undertaking (DOS)

factorial analysis: the breakdown of a situation or phenomenon into its factors, as for example, into the underlying cultural, hereditary, and geographic determinants. A factorial analysis may follow a single approach or, instead, a combination of two or more approaches, such as are indicated under *factor*. The latter would be a polydimensional analysis. Where interest centers on the elements rather than the determinants of a situation, componential analysis is a suitable designation (DOS)

factory data collection: devices placed throughout a factory for workers to report production by inserting plates or cards representing themselves and their jobs and by keying in the quantity completed. The data are transmitted to a central compiler that records them and picks up the start-stop times from an internal clock (ADPS)

fade: a temporary reduction of brake effectiveness due to loss of friction between the braking surfaces as a result of excessive heat build-up during extended or hard use of brakes (TDPPC)

fade out: disappear from sight or sound (LEV)

Fahrenheit: a scale for measuring temperature, where water freezes at 32° and boils at 212° under normal atmospheric conditions (LEV)

fail safe: a feature of a system or device which initiates an alarm or trouble signal when the system or device either malfunctions or loses power (TDIAS)

faint: (1) swoon, lose consciousness (LEV) (2) timid, cowardly (LEV)

fair comment: a word used in libel cases, pertaining to statements made by a writer in an honest belief of their truth although they in fact are not true

fair trade laws: state laws passed under the authorization of the Miller-Tydings Act for the purpose of allowing manufacturers of branded products to establish minimum resale prices. The laws required all retailers to sell at the established price when the manufacturer contracted with one of them to do so. By 1952, 45 states had passed fair trade laws over the opposition of consumer groups who charged that they increased the cost of living and tended toward monopoly control. Congress never passed a federal resale maintenance law despite efforts since 1914 to accomplish this. The first such law was passed in California in 1931. In May, 1951 the United States Supreme Court ruled that the Miller-Tydings Act did not give manufacturers the right to enforce retail price maintenance on noncontracting retailers in products moving in interstate commerce. By eliminating this "non-signer clause" fair trade laws were left toothless. Immediately afterwards four bills were introduced in the House of Representatives as amendments to the Miller-Tydings Act for the purpose of restoring this type of state legislation in interstate commerce. On July 14, 1952 Congress passed the McGuire Fair Trade Bill, restoring the right of manufacturers and wholesalers to set the price of brandname products at retail, even though the goods are shipped across state lines. The act restored the "non-signer" clause in state fair trade laws, which provide that a manufacturer must sign with only one retailer in a state to fix the price for the entire state. All states except Vermont, Missouri, and Texas, and the District of Columbia had fair trade laws in 1952 (DOAH)

fait accompli: an action which is regarded as completed and therefore not subject to further negotiation (DAP)

fake: fraudulent; fictitous; forged (LEV)

false: not true; not real (LEV)

false alarm: an alarm signal transmitted in the absence of an alarm condition. These may be classified according to causes: environmental, e.g., rain, fog, wind, hail, lightning, temperature, etc.; animals, e.g., rats, dogs, cats, insects, etc.; man-made disturbances, e.g., sonic booms, EMI, vehicles, etc.;

equipment malfunction, e.g., transmission errors, component failure, etc.; operator error; and unknown (TDIAS)

false alarm rate, monthly: the number of false alarms per installations per month (TDIAS)

false alarm ratio: the ratio of false alarms to total alarms; may be expressed as a percentage or as a simple ratio (TDIAS)

false arrest: unlawful physical restraint of an individual liberty; such restrictions may occur in prisons, jails, or other maximum security facilities

false impersonation: also called personation. To impersonate another falsely and to demand or obtain something of value for oneself or someone else is a federal violation and a state violation (LEV)

false imprisonment: (1) detention under false or assumed authority or because of a miscarriage of judicial procedure (DAP) (2) any unlawful restraint of a person's liberty (DAP)

false pretenses: false representations and statements made with fraudulent design to obtain money, goods, wares, or merchandise with intent to defraud. The distinction between "larceny" and "false pretenses" is that in larceny the owner of a thing has no intention to part with his property, although he may intend to part with possession, while in false pretenses, the owner does intend to part with the property, but it is obtained from him by fraud. (43 Cal. App. 696; 185 Pac. 686) (CDTP)

falsify: to make false statements or representation; to lie (LEV)

family disturbance: domestic quarrel, fight, or noisy problem (LEV)

fanatic: full of wild and extravagant notions; affected with inordinate zeal or enthusiasm, esp. of a religious nature

Faretta v. California, ——U.S.——, 45 L. Ed. 2d 562, 95 S. Ct. 2525 (1975): Justice Stewart speaking for the Court held, 6–3, that the Sixth Amendment guarantees the right of self-representation to a state criminal defendant who voluntarily and intelligently waives the right to the assistance of counsel and who insists on conducting his own defense (ILECJ)

fascism: an autocratic form of centralized government which oppresses opposition and rigidly controls finance, commerce, and industry. It can become a dictatorship (LEV)

fatal: causing death; deadly; resulting in death. (LEV)

fatality: the death of a person (LEV)

Fay v. New York, 332 U.S. 261 (1947): this decision details New York's law for empaneling a "blue ribbon" trial jury in complex and important criminal actions. It also is a fine discussion of "impartial" means for selecting trial juries (AOJ)

FBI (the Federal Bureau of Investigation): a federal government bureau in the Department of Justice charged with the investigation of all violations of federal laws and other matters in which the federal government may have an interest. It was organized originally to give the Department of Justice a permanent investigating staff of its own. It remained a relatively obscure bureau until the reorganization of 1924 gave it better personnel and added functions. The increase in the number of federal crimes has increased the jurisdiction of the FBI. When racketeering became prevalent in the late 1920s the two-fold job of suppressing interstate crime and recapturing the lost prestige of the forces of law and order fell on the FBI. The Bureau also maintained one of the most extensive criminal identification divisions in the world, with extensive files on national and international criminals. During the emergency of WWII, the FBI was charged with the investigation of individuals and organizations believed to be engaging in un-American activity, and of applicants for important governmental posts (DOS)

FBI Laboratory: the crime laboratory of the Federal Bureau of Investigation. The facilities are available, without charge, to all duly constituted state, county, and municipal law enforcement agencies of the United States and its territorial possessions. Examinations are made with the understanding that the official investigation contains evidence of a criminal matter and that the laboratory report will be used only for official purposes related to the investigation or a subsequent criminal prosecution (LEV)

FBI National Academy: a training school for the law enforcement officers conducted by the Federal Bureau of Investigation through its Washington, D.C. headquarters (LEV)

F.C.C. (FCC): Federal Communications Commission

F.D.I.C.: Federal Deposit Insurance Corporation

feasance: a doing; the doing of an act; a performance. See malfeasance, misfeasance, and nonfeasance.

feasibility study: preliminary process of determining the over-all suitability of data processors to specific operations; involves both technical and economical considerations (ADPS)

Federal Alcohol Control Board: an agency created by Congress in 1933 for the purpose of regulating the branding and grading of alcoholic beverages and for the dealing generally with the new problems of interstate liquor traffic raised by the Twenty-first Amendment. It was authorized to establish proper business standards for the liquor industry and foster fair trade methods in the interests of producers and consumers. The agency was later reorganized into the Federal Alcohol Administration (DOAH)

Federal Aviation Act: a law enacted by Congress in 1968. Paragraph 902 of the Act makes it a crime for persons to board an aircraft operated by an air carrier with a concealed weapon. Certain law enforcement officers, such as municipal, state, and federal, are exempted (LEV)

Federal Aviation Administration (FAA): formerly the Federal Aviation Agency, it is an agency of the United States Department of Transportation. Its functions are to issue and enforce safety regulations of airmen as well as the manufacturing and operations of aircraft and air navigation facilities (LEV)

Federal Communications Commission: an independent federal agency which regulates interstate communications and their facilities, i.e., telephone, telegraph, cable, radio, and television (LEV)

federal crimes: acts which are violations of federal laws (LEV)

Federal Deposit Insurance Corporation: a federally created corporation established under the Banking Act of 1933 to provide insurance for deposits in member banks. Banks insured by FDIC are under federal jurisdiction where crimes are involved relative to the bank. Thus such crimes as bank robbery, embezzlement, and theft are federal criminal violations (LEV)

Federal Firearms Act: a law of Congress, June 30, 1938, which forbids any unlicensed person to ship firearms or ammunition in interstate commerce and subjects such shipments to numerous restrictions (DAP)

Federal Kidnapping Law: See Lindbergh Law

Federal Motor Vehicle Safety Standards (FMVSS): mandatory vehicle performance, design features, and objectives established by the National Highway Traffic Safety Administration of the Department of Transportation to enhance vehicle and occupant safety (TDPPC)

Federal Prison Industries, Inc.: a public corporation with six directors, operating under the Bureau of Prisons of the U.S. Department of Justice, which has charge of industrial enterprises and vocational training in federal penal institutions   (DAP)

federal question: case with a major issue involving the U.S. Constitution or statutes. The jurisdiction of the federal courts is partly controlled by the existence of a federal question

Federal Reserve Board: a federal reserve agency created by and operating under the Federal Reserve Act of 1913. It conducts the affairs of the Federal Reserve System. It is composed of seven members   (LEV)

Federal Security Agency, the first: was established by the President's Reorganization Plan 1 on April 25, 1939 (53 Staf. L. 1424), to place under one administration the agencies which had as their major purpose the promotion of social and economic security, educational opportunity, and health. The units were the U.S. Employment Service, the Office of Education, the Public Health Service, the National Youth Administration, the Social Security Board, and the Civilian Conservation Corps. The first administrator was Paul Vories McNutt who took office on July 13, 1939, and who served until Sept. 13, 1945. His salary was $12,000 a year. On April 11, 1953, the Federal Security Agency became the Department of Health, Education and Welfare   (FAMOUS)

Federal Tort Claims Act: Title IV of the Legislative Reorganization Act of 1946. Under its provisions the federal District Courts were authorized to render judgments on claims against the United States because of property damages or personal injury or death caused by the negligence of a government employee. Administrative agencies were empowered to make out-of-court settlements on claims under $1,000. The heads of federal agencies were required to submit annual reports to Congress of all claims made under the law. The U.S. government was made liable in respect of claims tried in the District Courts, including costs. Employees of the government were exempted from any action by claimants in the event of District Court action. The decisions of the District Courts were made reviewable on appeal in the Courts of Appeal or in the Court of Claims of the United States. The Attorney General was authorized to arbitrate, compromise, or settle any claim, after its institution, with the consent of the court. A one-year statute of limitations was laid down on claims not exceeding $1,000. The law contained many exemptions. These included claims arising out of loss or miscarriage of postal matters, assessment or collection of taxes or customs, damages inflicted by a quarantine, false representation, imprisonment, slander, false arrest, libel, deceit or interference with contract, and those arising in a foreign country or out of the activities of the military forces in time of war, or of the Tennessee Valley Authority   (DOAH)

Federal Trade Commission: a federal agency which administers and enforces federal laws pertaining to price fixing, monopolies, and unfair trade practices   (LEV)

feeder: a device that supplies ammunition to a weapon; it is usually actuated by an automatic or semiautomatic mechanism   (DWMT)

feet per second: the unit of measurement used to indicate the velocity or speed of a projectile   (DWMT)

feigned accomplice: an individual who pretends to act with others in the planning or commission of a crime for the purpose of discovering their plans or evidence against them

Feiner v. New York, 340 U.S. 315, 95 L. Ed. 276, 71 S. Ct. 303 (1951): a conviction affirmed under a New York statute that made it illegal to engage in disorderly conduct which might cause a breach of peace

fellatis, fellation: sexual stimulation of the penis with the mouth

felon: a term derived from the legal classification of crimes as felonies and misdemeanors. The former category includes those crimes regarded as the more heinous which usually involve confinement in a State or Federal prison or death as punishment. A felon is therefore one who commits a felony or who habitually commits felonies (DOS)

felonious: (1) malignant, malicious (2) done with intent to commit a crime

felony: usu. a grave offense punishable by death or imprisonment in a penitentiary; a crime more serious than those defined as misdemeanors

femicide: the killing of a woman

fence: (1) to sell stolen goods (2) a receiver of stolen property

fence alarm: any of several types of sensors used to detect the presence of an intruder near a fence or any attempt by him to climb over, go under, or cut through the fence (TDIAS)

Ferri, Enrico (1856-1928): Ferri, a student of Lombroso, expanded on the ideas of his teacher by claiming that social, economic, and political, as well as biological, factors are involved in the causes of crime. In his book *The Criminal Sociology* he advocated restitution and other concepts of sociology as methods for dealing with crime and criminals

feticide: destroying a fetus; criminal abortion

fetus: an unborn animal or human in the womb. In humans, the developing child is referred to a fetus from the end of the third month until birth (LEV)

fiction: (1) nonfactual writings; novels (LEV) (2) (law) the assumption of a thing as being factual regardless of its truthfulness (LEV)

fiduciary: one authorized to act for another

field: (1) the space or area in which there exists a force such as that produced by an electrically charged object, a current, or a magnet (TDIAS) (2) a set of one or more characters treated as a unit of data. Used for the organization of data on punched cards where enough columns are assigned to each item to handle the longest case likely to occur. Similarly applied to character-addressable processors, although often called "variable word" (ADPS)

Fieldcom: Field Computer, a hypothetical processor used to illustrate the features of and programming for a processor with character-addressable storage that handles data as fields (ADPS)

fieldmark: an indication of the left-hand character for an item of data in FIELDCOM. Commonly called "wordmark" even though data are organized as fields (ADPS)

field name: a symbolic name the programmer gives a field of data; an absolute address assigned during program assembly (ADPS)

field of fire: the area which a weapon or a group of weapons may cover effectively with fire from a given position (DWMT)

field shifting: the adjustment of the address of a field to left or right to shorten or to realign the item of data (ADPS)

file: one or more records concerning people, things, or places that are closely related and handled together for processing (ADPS)

file analysis: a study of file characteristics to locate file redundancies or similarities and to list documents affecting a file and data elements contained in a file (ADPS)

file charges: to formally and officially bring criminal charges against someone (LEV)

file label: a record placed before (and after) the records on tape to indicate their nature, when written, when to use, and how long to retain the file (ADPS)

file maintenance: modification of a file to incorporate changes that do *not* involve arithmetical operations—for example, insertions, deletions, transfers, and corrections (ADPS)

filemark: a mark placed after the last record in a file and its trailer label on tape to indicate end of the file. May be followed by another file. The last file on a reel is followed by trailer label, filemark, and reelmark (ADPS)

file processing: modification of a file to incorporate changes that involve arithmetical operations—for example, issues, receipts, returns, and losses of stock items (ADPS)

final: a term used in classifying fingerprints. In the classification formula it appears at the extreme right on the classification line and above the line. It is determined by ridge counts in the little finger. The right is used if it has a loop, if not, the left is used if it has a loop. If neither have a loop but each has a whorl a ridge count between delta and core is made in the right hand (LEV)

finder: a viewer through which the picture to be taken may be seen and centered (MPPF)

finding: a conclusion of fact certified after inquiry by a judicial or other body (DAP)

fine: a sentence requiring that the offender pay an amount of money to the state

fine-grain developer: a developer of low potential which prevents the clumping of silver grains to form a mottled image (MPPF)

fine-grained: applied to a negative with very little granularity: one which may be enlarged from 7 to 10 diameters or more with satisfactory quality (MPPF)

fine sight: the adjustment of the sight of a gun so that only the tip of the front sight can be seen through the notch of the rear sight (DWMT)

fingerprint, latent: a chance fingerprint left accidentally or otherwise on a surface (LEV)

fingerprint camera: a fixed-focus camera with built-in lights used to photograph fingerprints, stamps, and other small objects (MPPF)

fingerprint classification: a system of classifying fingerprints according to the patterns of the friction ridges on the fingertips. This is done by the use of a definite formula (LEV)

fingerprint conviction, the first: was obtained by the New York Police Department, which arrested Caesar Cella, alias Charles Crispi, for burglary on March 8, 1911. Latent fingerprints found at the scene of the crime were introduced as evidence. He was convicted and sentenced to the New York County Penitentiary by Judge Otto Alfred Rosalsky in General Sessions Court, New York City, on May 19, 1911 (FAMOUS)

fingerprint patterns: the configuration of the friction ridges on the fingers is called a pattern. There are basically three patterns: arches, loops, and whorls. These basic patterns are subdivided as follows: Arch: plain arch; tented arch. Loop: radial loop; lateral loop; ulnar loop; central pocket loop; twin loop. Whorl: plain whorl. In addition to the three basic types of fingerprints there is a catchall or nondescript pattern called accidentals (LEV)

fingerprint system, the first police department to adopt: was the St. Louis (Mo.) Metropolitan Police Department, which on Oct. 28, 1904, adopted the Henry method to fingerprint persons arrested on serious charges. John M. Shea was the first to qualify as a fingerprint expert connected with any police service. He became associated with the St. Louis Metropolitan Police Department,

May 1, 1899, and was appointed Superintendent of the Bertillon System, Sept. 14, 1903. He remained in office until his death, July 17, 1926 (FAMOUS)

fingerprints: also referred to as dactyloscopy. The prints or impressions produced by the friction ridges of the inner surface of the fingertips. The impressions may be left accidentally or otherwise on objects touched by the fingers or may be taken by two methods: (1) rolled—the fingertips are rolled on a freshly inked surface and then rolled on a white paper; (2) plain—the fingertip is pressed on an inked surface without rolling and the print is made on a light-colored surface (LEV) John Vucetichi, born 1858, is considered the "father of fingerprinting." His system generally followed the "Galton-Henry" system. Vucetichi categorized four basic types of prints: (1) arches, (2) those with a triangle on the right side, (3) those with a triangle on the left side, (4) those with a triangle on both sides. The first four letters of the alphabet were used to create a formula for classification—approximately one million combinations are possible. The first state prison to take fingerprints of its prisoners was Sing Sing Prison, Ossining, N.Y., which commenced taking impressions on March 3, 1903

(FAMOUS)

fire: (1) the discharge of a gun, launching of a missile, or the like (DAP) (2) the projectiles or missiles fired (DAP) (3) to discharge a weapon (DWMT)

fire adjustment: the correction of the elevation and direction of a weapon or the regulation of the explosion time of its projectile that ensures that the projectile will strike or burst at the desired point. Fire adjustment for automatic weapons is an operation which is continuous from the instant the first rounds reach the vicinity of the target until the command "cease firing" is given (DWMT)

fire detection system: a thermostatic or photo-electrical system for detecting the presence of abnormal fire or heat (LEV)

firearm: (1) in a general sense, a gun (DWMT) (2) specifically, a small arm, such as a pistol or rifle, designed to be carried by an individual (DWMT)

firearms examination: crime laboratory examination of a firearm and/or projectile, cartridge cases, and shotgun shells. The usual object of such examination is to determine whether such bullets, cartridges, or shells were fired in a certain gun (LEV)

firearms range: a place or area suited for use to fire weapons in practice and to teach the use of firearms (LEV)

firepower: (1) the amount of fire which may be delivered by a position, unit, or weapon style (DWMT) (2) the ability to deliver fire (DWMT)

firetrap: a structure which due to interior arrangement, contents, lack of private protective equipment, and/or inadequate exits is considered likely to contribute to a major loss of life in the event of a fire (LEV)

fire wall: a wall or partition built or provided to prevent the spread of fire (LEV)

firing pin: a device used in the firing mechanism of a gun, mine, bomb, fuze, projectile, or the like which strikes and detonates a sensitive explosive to initiate an explosive train or a propelling charge (DWMT)

firing pin impressions: marks made on the base of a cartridge case or shotgun shell by the firing pin. Such impressions are utilized by the crime laboratory in determining whether a certain cartridge or shell was fired in a specific weapon (LEV)

firing range: a firearms practice

field or area; a specially designated and/or equipped area for teaching marksmanship and proper handling of firearms. Also called firearms range, pistol range, police range   (LEV)

first offender: one who is prosecuted as a law violator the first time; one who violates the criminal law the first time   (LEV)

firsthand: obtained directly from the original source   (LEV)

fishtailing: the tendency of the rear end of a vehicle to make rapid uncontrolled side-to-side movements while moving forward   (TDPPC)

fixation: (1) an unhealthy mental attachment to something (LEV) (2) an obsession (LEV) (3) formation of a habit (LEV) (4) the process of making soluble the undeveloped silver salts in a sensitized material by immersion in a hypo solution   (MPPF)

fixed focus: a term applied to a camera in which the lens is set permanently in such a position as to give good average focus for both nearby and distant objects
(MPPF)

fixed-point arithmetic: a method of calculation in which operations take place in an invariant manner, without regard for location of the decimal or binary point. This is illustrated by desk calculators or slide rules, with which the operator must keep track of the decimal point, and by many automatic computers, with which the programmer is responsible for the location of the decimal point
(ADPS)

fixed surveillance: a surveillance operated from a fixed or semifixed location such as a building or a parked vehicle   (LEV)

flare: a pyrotechnic item designed to produce a single source of intense light for purposes such as terrain illumination   (DWMT)

flare pistol: a pistol for shooting flares (DWMT); Very pistol or signal pistol. The earliest flare pistols served only to ignite and hold the

flare, which burned in place

flare spot: a fogged area on the developed negative due to the multiple reflection of a strong light source by the several surfaces of the lens elements   (MPPF)

flash gun: the battery case, lamp socket, and reflector used with photoflash lamps   (MPPF)

flash paper: paper which, because of its composition, will burn quickly. In case of a raid or search by the police it can be quickly destroyed. The paper leaves no residue   (LEV)

flash suppressor: a device attached to the muzzle of a weapon which reduces the amount of visible light or flash created by burning propellant gases   (DWMT)

flashtube: a glass or quartz tube, usually wound in helical shape, containing two electrodes and filled with xenon or other inert gases at a very low pressure; used as the light source in flash units and photographic stroboscopes
(MPPF)

flat: the expression denoting lack of contrast in a print or negative
(MPPF)

flatness of field: the quality of a lens which produces sharpness of image both at the edges and at the center of the negative   (MPPF)

fleet administrator: an individual concerned with carrying out a set of policies provided by an organization which controls a number of vehicles   (TDPPC)

flintlock: a lock for a gun or pistol. Invented early in the seventeenth century, it consists of a cock that holds a piece of flint. When the flint in the cock strikes against a piece of steel (called the "frizzen"), it creates a shower of sparks that ignite the priming powder in the pan, which in turn fires the charge. This system was employed until superseded by the percussion lock early in the nineteenth century. Students differentiate between the French or "true" flintlock and a number of other mechanisms that employ the same general principle for producing a spark, e.g., the English lock, snaphaunce, miquelet lock, etc. (DWMT)

floating-point arithmetic: a method of calculation which automatically accounts for the location of the decimal or binary point. This is usually accomplished by handling the number as a signed mantissa times the radix raised to an integral exponent. For example, the decimal number 88.3 might be written as $+.883 \times 10^2$; the binary number $+.0011$ as $+.11 \times 2^{-2}$ (ADPS)

flog: to whip or beat someone with a lash, whip, or switch (LEV)

floodlamp: in general, any lamp or lighting unit producing a broad beam or flood of light; colloquially used as a contraction for photoflood lamp (MPPF)

floor trap: a trap installed so as to detect the movement of a person across a floor space, such as a trip wire switch or mat switch (TDIAS)

flow chart: a systems-analysis tool consisting of a graphical representation of a procedure (ADPS)

Floyd, Charles Arthur ("Pretty Boy") (*1901-1934*): born: Atkins, Oklahoma; alias: Jack Hamilton. Record: Between 1925 and his death by FBI agents on 10/22/34 he was credited with 8 robberies and 13 murders in the mid-western states. Six of the murders occurred in the Kansas City Massacre in which Pretty Boy was claimed to have been a machine gunner

fluoroscope: a machine for seeing shadows projected upon a fluorescent screen by objects placed between a beam of x-rays and the screen (LEV)

fluoroscopy: examination made with a fluoroscope (LEV)

f-number: a number used in a system to show the size of the opening of the shutter; lens opening; diaphragm opening (LEV)

focal length: the distance between the center of the lens and the point at which the image of a distant object comes into critical view. The focal length of a thick lens is measured from the emergent nodal point to the focal plane (MPPF)

focal plane: the plane at which the image is brought to a critical focus. In other words, the position in the camera occupied by the film emulsion (MPPF)

focal plane shutter: a shutter which operates immediately in front of the focal plane. A shutter of this type usually contains a fixed or variable-sized slit in a curtain of cloth or metal which travels across the film to make the exposure (MPPF)

focus: (1) to bring the lens of a camera to such a position that the object to be photographed will be clearly defined (LEV) (2) to adjust a camera or microscope so as to see the object clearly (LEV)

focusing cloth: a black cloth used to cover the camera while focusing so that the image on the groundglass may be more easily seen (MPPF)

focusing hood: a collapsible tube shading the groundglass of a camera so that a focusing cloth is not needed (MPPF)

focusing magnifier: a lens through which the image on the groundglass is viewed through for critical focusing (MPPF)

focusing negative: a negative containing geometrical patterns which is temporarily substituted for the picture negative when focusing an enlarger (MPPF)

focusing scale: a graduated scale on a lens or a camera, permitting focusing on a given subject by estimating its distance from the camera and setting a pointer to correspond (MPPF)

focusing screen: a sheet of groundglass on which the image is focused (MPPF)

foil: thin metallic strips which are cemented to a protected surface (usually glass in a window or door) and connected to a closed electrical circuit. If the protected material is broken so as to break the foil, the circuit opens, initiating an alarm signal. Also called tape. A window, door, or other surface to which foil has been applied is said to be taped or foiled   (TDIAS)

foil connector: an electrical terminal block used on the edge of the window to join interconnecting wire to window foil   (TDIAS)

folding camera: a camera having a collapsible bellows so that it may be closed for carrying   (MPPF)

following too close: in highway traffic one vehicle follows another at such a short intervening distance that the driver of the vehicle following is unable to avoid colliding with the vehicle in front when it suddenly stops or slows   (LEV)

Food and Drug Administration (FDA): a division of the Department of Health, Education and Welfare which is charged with the enforcement of federal pure food, drug, cosmetic, and other laws and for this purpose maintains an inspection service to detect adulterated or misbranded goods. If those charged with violations of the law fail to desist voluntarily, the agency may cite them for prosecution to the Department of Justice. The agency also conducts research to determine the effect of all new drugs and to protect consumers against toxic or other potentially dangerous ingredients in foods, drugs, cosmetics, pesticides, and other articles of commerce   (DAP)

footage: (1) the length in lineal feet—measurement (LEV) (2) the number of feet of exposed film in a movie camera   (LEV)

foot-candle: the intensity of light falling on a surface placed one foot distant from a point light source of one candle power   (MPPF)

foot line: one of the elements of the walking picture. It shows the angle at which each foot is placed down   (LEV)

foot patrol: patrol duties done by an officer on foot, usually confined to a designated area   (LEV)

footprint: the imprint or impression of a foot or the shoe a person is wearing   (LEV)

foot rail: a holdup alarm device, often used at cashiers' windows, in which a foot is placed under the rail, lifting it, to initiate an alarm signal   (TDIAS)

foray: a raid, or excursion, to plunder   (LEV)

force: (1) the degree and power of effective action (LEV) (2) an organization or group equipped for action   (LEV)

force, reasonable: the amount or degree of force which can be reasonably used by persons in protecting themselves or others; the force which can be used by law enforcement officials in the conduct of their duties, as authorized by law. The general rule is that an officer can use force no greater than that which is necessary for the purpose. To effect an arrest an officer may use reasonable force to overcome resistance   (LEV)

forcible entry: to enter on the lands or other property of another by the use of force or fear and without the free consent of the owner or possessor of such property. Law enforcement officer is legally given the right to forcibly enter the property of another after announcing his identity and purpose to make an arrest if his entry has been refused or obstructed (LEV)

forcible rape: sexual intercourse against the consent of the victim

forcing: continuing [photographic] development beyond the normal time in an effort to secure more detail   (MPPF)

forcing cone: the tapered beginning of the lands at the origin of the rifling of a gun tube. The forcing cone allows the rotating band of the projectile to be gradually engaged by the rifling, thereby centering the projectile in the bore   (DWMT)

Ford Foundation: organized in Michigan as a nonprofit organization in 1936. It receives and administers the expenditure of funds for scientific, educational, and charitable purposes in the public interest. The Foundation's funds are spent to support research studies and other activities on social human needs rather than the physical. Its assets in 1964 were almost $2,500,000,000. It operates offices in Detroit, New York, and Pasadena (DOAH)

foreclosure: act of barring a mortgagor's fight to redeem mortgaged property; act of foreclosing a mortgage (LEV)

foreground: generally, that part of a scene closer to the camera than the main subject (MPPF)

forensic: relating to the courts or the judiciary (LEV)

forensic medicine: the study or application of the field of medicine as used in judicial or court matters (LEV)

forensic pathologist: a medical doctor, specialized in pathology, who conducts examinations to determine the cause of death in suspected homicide cases and who is in a position to testify to his findings in a court of law. He also makes pathological examinations on persons who have been injured or are suffering from disease and the findings are useable in legal proceedings (LEV)

forensic science: science as applied and used in judicial matters (LEV)

forfeiture: a punishment for the illegal use or possession of specific property, by which one loses to the government his rights and interest in that property; the loss of goods or other property as punishment for the commission of a crime (LEV)

forgery: the making or altering of a document or other writing in order to defraud. *See* Operation Bernhard

fork: (1) a bifurcation of a ridge line in a fingerprint pattern (LEV) (2) a line branching into two lines (LEV)

form of complaint:
State (or Commonwealth) of

_____, County of _____, to wit: A. B. upon oath, complains that on the _____ day of _____, A. D. _____, C. D., in the county of _____, in said state (or commonwealth), (or in the county aforesaid), did feloniously steal, take, and carry away one overcoat, of the value of twenty-five dollars, of the goods and chattels of the said A. B. (the person who is the owner). The said A. B. therefore, prays that the said C.D. may be apprehended, and held to answer the said complaint and to be further dealt with according to law.
Dated this, the _____ day of _____, A. D., _____.
(Signed) A. B.
State (or Commonwealth) of _____, County of _____, to wit: I, X. Y., a justice of the peace, of the county aforesaid, do certify that on this day, in said county, personally appeared before me the said A. B., whose name is signed to the foregoing complaint, dated on this _____ day of _____, A. D., _____, and being duly sworn, deposes and says that the facts stated in said complaint are true.
Given under my hand this _____ day of _____, A. D., _____.
X.Y.,
Justice of the Peace.
Ordinarily, any person knowing the facts is competent to make a complaint if he is capable of understanding the nature of an oath or affirmation, and so competent to testify, for it is the wrong against the public, and not against the individual, that is to be considered and punished. (24 N.Y. Supp. 727) (CDTP)

form of warrant of arrest:
State (or Commonwealth) of _____, County of _____, to wit: To the Sheriff or any Constable of said County:
Whereas, A. B. has this day made complaint and information on oath before me, X. Y., a justice of the peace of the county aforesaid, that C. D., on the _____ day of _____, A. D., _____, in said

county, did feloniously steal, take, and carry away one overcoat, of the value of twenty-five dollars, of the goods and chattels of the said A. B.

These are therefore to command you (or now, therefore, you are commanded) forthwith to apprehend and bring before me, or some other justice of said county, the body of the said C. D., to answer said complaint, and to be further dealt with according to law.

Given under my hand and seal, this _____ day of _____, A. D., _____.

X.Y.,
(Seal) Justice of Peace.
(CDTP)

format: (1) the arrangement of output for printing: page numbering, headings, vertical and horizontal spacing, minor, major, and page totals, etc. (ADPS) (2) the layout or physical arrangement of writings (LEV)

formula: a list of ingredients and quantities necessary to compound a photographic solution (MPPF)

fornication: illegal sexual intercourse between unmarried persons. If one of the parties is married the act is adultery (LEV)

Fortran: *Formula Translating* system; consists of a language and translator designed for programming problems expressed in a mathematical-type language (ADPS)

Foster v. California, 394 U.S. 440, 22 L. Ed. 2d 402, 89 S. Ct. 1127 (1969): the Court, 5–4, through Mr. Justice Fortas, in his pre-*Wade* line-up, held that what the police officers did in conducting the line-ups was "so unnecessarily suggestive and conductive to irreparable mistaken identification as to be a denial of due process under the Fourteenth Amendment." (The opinion points up how not to conduct a line-up.) (ILECJ)

four-time loser: one who has been convicted of a crime four times and thus subject to conviction under the habitual criminal act in some states (LEV)

fracas: a melee; fight; brawl; noisy disturbance; altercation (LEV)

frame: (1) the physical make-up or structure of a person, especially in reference to the bone structure. In descriptions of persons the terms large, medium, or small frame are used (LEV) (2) the group of bits across magnetic tape, usually seven, consisting of one from each row that make up a character; also, five, six, seven, or eight punches across punched-paper tape (ADPS)

frangible bullet: a brittle plastic or other nonmetallic bullet used for firing practice which, upon striking a target, breaks into powder or small fragments without penetrating. Frangible bullets are usually designed to leave a mark at the point of impact (DWMT)

frangible grenade: an improvised incendiary hand grenade consisting of a glass container filled with a flammable liquid, with an igniter attached. It breaks and ignites upon striking a resistant target. Sometimes called a "Molotov cocktail" (DWMT)

franking and penalty privileges: means by which official material is sent by way of the United States Postal Service without paying for postage beforchand. Certain officials of Congress and government, including the Vice President use this privilege for various reports and official correspondence. The payment is made for this service by money appropriated by Congress. The executive branch of government and its agencies use the penalty privilege without prepayment of postage for sending official matter through the mail. There is a printed clause on each item that cites the penalty for using this privilege privately and each division pays the regular postal rates for the proper amounts on the mail.

FRAT: Free Radical Assay Technique. A proprietary device for detecting the presence of drugs of abuse. Manufactured by Syva Corporation, 3221 Porter Drive, Palo Alto, CA 94304 (LEV)

fratricide: the act of killing or murdering one's brother (LEV)

fraud: that method of exploitation or domination in which the purposes of the exploiter or dominator are imposed on the exploited or dominated by deceiving them, or by concealing from them the real purposes of the exploiter or dominator. *Cf.* coercion (DOS) Frazier v. Cupp, 394 U.S. 731, 22 L. Ed. 2d 684, 89 S. Ct. 1420 (1969): in this pre-*Miranda* decision (controlled by *Escobedo* v. *Illinois*), in a unanimous decision by Mr. Justice Marshall for the first time since *Miranda*, the Court sanctions some trickery in obtaining a confession. (This opinion should be read very narrowly, however, as the Court clearly implies that the result might have been different if *Miranda* had been applicable. It is difficult to visualize how there could be a knowing and intelligent waiver of rights, after they have been given, when an investigator turns to deception to get a statement) (ILECJ)

free run: as applied to guns, the travel of a projectile from its original position in the gun chamber until it engages with the rifling in the gun bore (DWMT)

freeway: expressway; a limited access, multilane road or highway (LEV)

freeway patrol: the law enforcement function concerned with the management and surveillance of traffic on a freeway. This function may include rendering assistance, accident investigation, traffic direction, and traffic law enforcement. It may be accomplished with automobile, motorcycle, or aircraft patrol (TDPPC)

Fresnel lens: a lens consisting of a small central plano-convex lens surrounded by a series of prismatic rings; also known as an echelon lens (MPPF)

Freudian: pertaining to the theories of Freud

friction, coefficient of: the amount of friction on a roadway surface as determined in calculating the speed of a vehicle as shown by skid marks. Speed and weight of the vehicle are factors as well as the surface that the vehicle was travelling upon. The coefficient of friction is also referred to as the Drag Factor (LEV)

friction ridges: the ridges of the skin on the palms and palmar side of the fingers. Similar ridges are found on the sole of the feet and the lower side of the toes. The prime function of the ridges is to afford friction with surfaces and objects touched by these parts of the body. These ridges are the means by which fingerprints are formed (LEV)

frilling: the detachment of the emulsion from its support around the edges; happens most often in hot weather because of too much alkali in the developer (MPPF)

frisk: a pat-down search, less than a full search, of a suspect

front sight: a metallic bead, blade, post, or the like, attached on the muzzle end of carbines, pistols, revolvers, rifles, shotguns, and other similar items as a sighting device. It may be provided with a hood or protective wings (DWMT)

fruit of the poisonous tree: a term used by the courts to denote evidence tainted as the result of it being derived from evidence obtained illegally or in such fashion that it was inadmissible. If certain evidence was obtained as the result of an illegal search and, based upon information secured by the search, other evidence was located elsewhere, the latter evidence is also inadmissible, even though properly obtained, and as the courts say it was tainted (LEV)

fruits of a crime: any material objects obtained through criminal acts

F-stop: the number or symbol on a scale indicating the size of the opening of the shutter of a camera. The size of the opening is a factor in the exposure of the film. The larger the opening, the smaller is the F-stop number   (LEV)

fugitive: (1) one who flees, or cannot be located, by law enforcement officers, to avoid arrest, incarceration or questioning concerning an alleged violation of the law (LEV) (2) one wanted for crime who goes outside the state or the territorial jurisdiction of the court   (LEV)

Fugitive Felon Acts: Acts of Congress, 1932 and 1934, which make it a federal offense to travel in interstate or foreign commerce in order to avoid: (a) prosecution, (b) confinement after conviction, or (c) giving testimony, where under the laws of the State, the offense charged is a felony (or in New Jersey, a high misdemeanor)   (DAP)

fugitive from justice: (1) a person who has fled from the state in which he is accused of having commited a crime in order to avoid arrest and punishment (DAP) (2) a person who has fled from the state in order to avoid giving testimony in a criminal prosecution. See extradition   (DAP)

Fugitive Interception Network Design (F.I.N.D.): a plan established by the Philadelphia Police Department to prevent the escape of felons from the scene of major crimes   (LEV)

fugitive slave laws: statutes passed by Congress in 1798 to 1850. These laws covered the return of slaves who escaped from one state and were found in another state or territory.

fugitive warrant: an arrest warrant issued for a person wanted for a violation of the criminal law in another state or jurisdiction; a warrant for a fugitive from justice   (LEV)

full aperture: the maximum opening of a lens or lens diaphragm   (MPPF)

full automatic: a weapon that provides continuous fire as long as the trigger is depressed, as distinguished from semiautomatic   (DWMT)

full sight: an aim in which all the front sight is seen through the rear sight   (CDTP)

Fuller, Melville Weston (1833–1910): b. Augusta, Maine. United States Chief Justice from 1888–1910. Known as a strict constitutionalist who declared the Income Tax law of 1894 unconstitutional, he also served as arbitrator in the Venezuelan boundary controversy between Great Britain and Venezuela. He served as a member of the Hague court of arbitration from 1900 to 1910.

Fuller v. Alaska, 393 U.S. 80, 21 L. Ed, 2d 212, 89 S. Ct. 61 (1968): the court held in a per curiam opinion that Lee v. Florida (1968), which overruled Schwartz v. Texas (1952), is to apply prospectively: "(t)he exclusionary rule is to be applied only to trials in which the evidence is sought to be introduced after the date of our decision in Lee." (Dissents were filed by Justices Black and Douglas.)   (ILECJ)

Fuller v. Oregon, 416 U.S. 40, 40 L. Ed. 2d 642, 94 S. Ct. 2116 (1974): the Court in a very narrow holding says probation may be conditioned on repayment of the cost of prosecution   (ILECJ)

function: as applied to law enforcement vehicles, the use, duty, activity, or requirement of a law enforcement system that can be provided by a vehicle. These functions may include traffic patrol, undercover work, crime patrol, highway patrol, moving surveillance, emergency road service, transporting prisoners and noncriminal personnel, communications carrier, patrolman's office, and high-speed pursuit   (TDPPC)

fundamental fairness: the basic principle that crime prevention and control methods must be democratic and fair

fundamental law: (1) the constitution; organic statutes or laws which are intrinsically superior to the ordinary law of a state or which the courts regard as law of superior obligation (DAP) (2) Natural law, which is sometimes deemed to be morally if not juridically superior to positive law (DAP)

furlough: overnight or longer leave granted to the inmate of a correctional facility

Furman v. Georgia, 408 U.S. 238, 92 S. Ct. 2726, 33 L. Ed. 2d 346 (1972): in this decision, relating to the existing death penalties in Georgia and Texas, the Court held that, "the imposition and carrying out of the death penalty in these cases constitutes cruel and unusual punishment in violation of the Eighth and Fourteenth Amendments." Although the decision effectively invalidated all death penalties as they were then applied, nine opinions were written resulting in confusion as to what, if any, conditions would render the death penalty valid

fuse: (not to be confused with "fuze") an igniting or explosive device in the form of a cord, consisting of a flexible fabric tube and a core of low or high explosive. Used in blasting and demolition work and in certain munitions (DWMT)

fusilade: the simultaneous or rapid firing of firearms (DWMT)

fuze: (1) a device with explosive components designed to initiate a train of fire or denotation in an item of ammunition by means of hydrostatic pressure, electrical energy, chemical action, impact, mechanical timing, or a combination of these. Excludes "fuse" (DWMT) (2) a nonexplosive device designed to initiate an explosion in an item of ammunition by an action such as continuous or pulsating electromagnetic waves, acceleration or deceleration forces, or piezoelectrical action (DWMT)

fuze safety: two terms have been commonly used to describe the safety built into a fuze to prevent premature functions at the time of employment and to provide that required safety in transportation. One term, "bore safety," is strictly applicable only to fuzes used in artillery or mortar projectiles or rockets and refers to the provision of means to prevent functioning while in the bore of the gun or in the launching tube. Such fuzes are said to be "boresafe." "Detonator safety" is the second term and may relate to fuzes for any application. It refers to the provision of means to prevent functioning of the succeeding element(s) of the explosive train if the detonator functions while the fuze parts are in the safe position. Such a fuze is said to be "detonator-safe." In general the terms are interchangeable with respect to artillery, mortar, and rocket fuzes, but "bore-safety" applies only to those types of fuzes (DWMT)

G

gag: something placed over or in a person's mouth to prevent talking or making noise (LEV)

gag law: any law abridging freedom of speech, or of the press, or the right of petition (DAP)

gag rule, the first: was adopted May 26, 1836, by the House of Representatives, which voted 117 to 68 that "and, whereas it is extremely important and desirable that the agitation of this subject should be finally arrested, for the purpose of restoring tranquility to the public mind, your committee respectively recommended the adoption of the following additional resolution: Resolved that all petitions, memorials, resolutions, propositions, or papers, relating in any way, or to any extent whatever, to the subject of slavery, or the abolition of slavery, shall without being either printed or referred, be laid upon the table, and that no further action whatever shall be had thereon" (FAMOUS)

Gagnon v. Scarpelli, 411 U.S. 778, 36 L. Ed. 2d 656, 93 S. Ct. 1756 (1973): the court through Justice Powell held, 8-1, that ". . . a probationer, like a parolee, is entitled to a preliminary and a final revocation hearing, under the conditions specified in *Morrissey.*" Further, that where "special circumstances" exist (the discarded Betts' rule) the state authority may be required to assign counsel at the hearing (ILECJ)

Galante, Carmine (1910-   ): considered to be one of the most important American Mafia leaders today, Galante is a powerful figure among the East Coast families. He is currently serving a 20-year sentence for conspiracy to violate narcotic laws

Gall, Franz Joseph (1758-1828): a European anatomist, Gall is credited with developing the doctrines of phrenology. He believed that head conformations were directly related to personality characteristics of individuals

gallery load: a cartridge loaded lightly for use inside a building (LEV)

Gallo, Joseph (1929-1972): as a member of the Gambino family in New York, Gallo was killed in 1972 when he tried to unseat Joseph Profaci as a leader in the Profaci faction of the East Coast power structure of the Mafia

gallon (gal.): a unit of liquid measure used in the United States and the British Empire; an American gallon contains 128 ounces, the British Imperial gallon contains 160 ounces (MPPF)

gallows: a structure used for hanging criminals (LEV)

Galton, Francis (1812-1911): an English scientist and criminologist, Galton was a pioneer in the field of fingerprint science. Although he didn't develop a workable classification system, his work greatly aided Sir Edward Henry in his developments in this area of criminology

galvanometer: an instrument for measuring small amounts of electricity. Used on some types of lie detectors (LEV)

Gambino, Carlo (1902-   ): a leader of one of the five New York Mafia families and a member of the powerful syndicate commission which controls the national organized crime scene

gambling: gambling or playing for money; betting on the result of a game; playing a game of chance for stakes (CDTP)

game: game in the possession, out of season, of a person may be protected by the constitutional immunity from unreasonable search and seizure (200 S. W. 937; C.J. 56, 1167) (CDTP)

game of chance: a game which is determined entirely or in part by luck (CDTP)

game of skill: a game in which superior knowledge or skill gains the victory, and in which little is left to chance (CDTP)

game warden: one who enforces the game laws in a certain area; a wildlife agent (LEV)

gaming: an agreement between two or more persons to play together at a game of chance for a stake or wager which is to become the property of the winner, and to which all contribute. The words "gaming" and "gambling" in statutes are similar in meaning. To constitute gambling, winner must either pay a consideration for his chance to win, or without paying anything in advance stand a chance to lose or win. Gaming is properly the act or engagement of the players; if bystanders or other third persons put up a stake or wager among themselves, to go to one or the other according to the result of the game, this is more correctly termed betting (CDTP)

gamma: a numerical measure of the contrast to which an emulsion is developed (MPPF)

gamma infinity: the maximum contrast to which an emulsion can be developed (MPPF)

gang: a group of persons; a company of persons acting together for some questionable purpose (CDTP)

Garand rifle: the U.S. .30 cal. rifle M1. It was invented by John C. Garand, a Canadian-born American citizen, and was adopted by the U.S. Army in 1936 (DWMT)

garble: an error in transmission, reception, encryption, or decryption which renders a message incorrect or undecryptable (DWMT)

Gardner, Earle Stanley (*1889–1970*): A California lawyer, Gardner received his notoriety through his famous Perry Mason novels. The character of Mason later inspired several movies, radio and television series and over 100 books which made Gardner an extremely wealthy man. He also started "The Court of Last Resort," an organization which aids persons believed to have been wrongfully convicted.

Gardner v. Broderick, 392 U.S. 273, 20 L. Ed. 2d 1082, 88 S. Ct. 1913 (1968): the court held that a policeman who refuses to waive his Fifth Amendment privilege against self-incrimination (sign a waiver of immunity before testifying) cannot be dismissed from office solely because of his refusal. [Mr. Justice Fortas, speaking for the Court, notes that there is a difference between a police officer (a public officer) and a lawyer, stating that had the police officer refused to answer questions . . . without being required to waive his immunity . . . the privilege against self-incrimination would not have been a bar to his dismissal. It can be noted that the Court *may* eventually reject the Fortas' distinction as Mr. Justice Black, concurring in the result, said: "I find in these opinions (*Gardner* and *Uniformed Sanitation Men Association*) a procedural formula whereby, for example, public officials may now be discharged and lawyers disciplined for refusing to divulge to appropriate authority information pertinent to the faithful performance of their offices."] (ILECJ)

garnish: to use a legal action brought by a creditor, whereby the debtor's money is impounded or attached, while in the hands of a third party. The garnishee is warned not to deliver the money or property to the defendant debtor until the law suit is concluded. This is civil action (LEV)

garnishee: attaching money belonging to a debtor (CDTP)

garnishment: a form of attachment that has as its object the appropriation of money or credits in the hands of a third person

Garofalo, Raffaele (*1852–1934*): the third major Italian positivist who developed the concept of "natural" crime. "Natural" crime consists of that conduct which offends the basic moral sentiments of probity (respect for the property of others) and pity (revulsion against the voluntary infliction of suffering on others). In his major work, *Criminology*, Garofalo outlined a theory of punishment which calls for elimination of those individuals who are unable to adapt themselves to civilized life

garote: any method whereby a victim is seized around the throat and strangled   (DWMT)

Garraud, René (*1849-1930*): an advocate of the theory of rational social contracts, Garraud felt that individuals survey the pro and con of their actions and then make their own rational choices. He argued that the principal instrument of social control should be the fear of pain, and that punishment should be the principal method of creating fear to influence the will of the individual

gas bells: bubbles forcing the emulsions from the support, caused by strong chemical action and resulting in minute holes in negative
(MPPF)

gas cylinder: a tube fixed to the barrel of a gas-operated automatic weapon and containing a piston, the movement of which operates the extracting and reloading mechanisms   (DWMT)

gas grenade: the popular name for a chemical grenade, designed to release a war gas. The types of gases released are usually limited to tear gas and other irritants   (DWMT)

gas mask: a mask worn over the face to protect the eyes and to remove gases from the air as it is inhaled   (DWMT)

gas munition: a munition such as a bomb, projectile, pot, candle, or spray tank containing a war gas and a means of release   (DWMT)

gas operated: said of an automatic or semiautomatic weapon that utilizes part of the gas from the explosion in the barrel to unlock the bolt and actuate the loading mechanism   (DWMT)

gas-operated gun: an automatic gun operated solely by gas, utilizing a portion of the gas pressure to act on some form of piston-and-cylinder arrangement. The relative movement, between the piston and the cylinder, drives the bolt to the rear with sufficient force to unlock and open the breech. The gas may be taken from the barrel through a hole drilled in the barrel

at any point between the chamber and the muzzle itself   (DWMT)

gas port: an opening for the passage of gas. The gas cylinder of a gas-operated automatic weapon has gas ports that admit some of the propellant gases from the barrel of the gun   (DWMT)

gas vent: a venthole in a rifle receiver to release excess gas pressures should they develop. Also, the slotted vents in a muzzle brake
(DWMT)

gate: a metal part in the rear of the cylinder of old-pattern revolvers that was turned out to expose the cylinders for loading   (DWMT)

gate keeping: counting heads; keeping records, as of prisoners

Gatling, Richard Jordan (*1818-1903*): American inventor of Gatling multiple-firing gun, precursor of machine gun. His name gave rise to slang word "gat"
(CVDE)

gauge: the unit of bore measurement for shotguns. Originally it referred to the number of solid lead balls of bore diameter that could be cast from 1 lb. of lead; the larger the bore, the lower the number   (DWMT)

gel: a technical and more strictly delimited term for "jelly"; the state of a colloid such as starch or gelatin which has swollen and softened by the absorption of water. *Cf.* imbibition   (FS)

gelatin: a jelly-like by-product produced from bones, hoofs, horns, and other parts of animals (MPPF)

gendarme: a member of an armed police organization such as in France; a police officer in France
(LEV)

general appearance file: a file maintained by law enforcement agencies wherein photographs and descriptions of persons known to have engaged in certain types of crime are maintained   (LEV)

general intent: conscious wrongdoing which is inferred unless expressly denied, as a method of legal proof   (LEV)

general intent—intent presumed from act: where an act is prohibited on pain of punishment, intention on the part of one capable of entertaining intent, and acting without justification or excuse, to do the act, constitutes criminal intent. In such case the existence of the intent is presumed from commission of the act, on the ground that a person is presumed to intend his voluntary acts and their natural and probable consequences. Criminal intent exists when a person intends to do that which the law says is a crime
(CDTP)

general law: a statute expressed in general terms and affecting all places, persons, or things within the territory over which a legislature has power to act, but which may include reasonable classifications or categories, provided that all places, persons or things within each category are treated alike—distinguished from local legislation and special legislation (DAP)

general verdict: a verdict of either "guilty" or "not guilty" (CDTP)

generalized routine: a routine expressed in computer coding designed to solve a class of problems that can be specialized to a specific problem when appropriate values are supplied (ADPS)

generator routine: a generalized skeleton routine that accepts specifications about a particular situation and causes the processor to prepare a specific routine for further use. For example, in a report generator, specifications must be supplied about printer spacing, input file, record format, calculations desired, and format of each output line (ADPS)

genesis: generation, procreation
(CDTP)

Geneva Convention: an international conference of 13 nations held in Geneva, Switzerland in 1864. The participating nations concluded an agreement which established rules for the care of the sick and wounded in war. The agreement provided for the neutrality of ambulance and military hospitals, the non-belligerent status of persons who aid the wounded, and sick soldiers of any nationality, the return of prisoners to their country if they are incapable of serving, and the adoption of a white flag with a red cross for use on hospitals, ambulances, and evacuation centers whose neutrality would be recognized by this symbol. Ultimately, practically every civilized nation adhered to the Geneva Convention. As a result of the persistence of Clara Barton the United States adhered to the agreement in 1884 by the "American Amendment" which simultaneously extended the scope of the American Red Cross to peacetime humanitarian work in connection with floods, earthquakes, and other public disasters
(DOAH)

genocide: the systematic killing of members of a political, racial, or cultural group, or causing such a group bodily or mental harm, or deliberately inflicting conditions of life calculated to bring about their destruction, or imposing measures intended to prevent births within a group to another group, as defined by the United Nations General Assembly, Dec. 11, 1946, in a convention designed to prevent, for the future, horrors like Hitler's anti-Jewish program (DAP)

germane: pertinent; connected to; relevant (LEV)

Gerstein v. Pugh, 420 U.S. 103, 43 L. Ed. 2d 541, 95 S. Ct. 854 (1957): in an opinion that resolves two issues (search and seizure and the assistance of counsel), the Court speaking through Justice Powell, held that the Fourth Amendment requires a judicial determination of probable cause for pretrial restraint of liberty. The court rejected the contention that the prosecutor's decision to proceed by information was enough to satisfy the consti-

tutional requirements   (ILECJ)
gestapo: secret police in Germany
during Hitler's regime   (LEV)
gestation: the period during which
an embryo or fetus is carried in
the uterus of a female
ghetto: a section of a city in which
people (usu. minority group members) live, often because of social,
political, or economic discriminations
ghost: the reflection of an image on
one or more lens surfaces caught
by the negative   (MPPF)
Giambattista della Porta (1536-
1615): may have been the first
criminologist. Made anthropometric measurements in order to
establish a typology. Practitioner
of physiogonomics (interpreting
the significance of relationships
between the body and mind)
(IESS)
Giancana, Sam (1908-1975): one
of the top Mafia bosses in Chicago
until 1975, when he was killed before testifying in front of a Senate
Subcommittee on C.I.A. and Cosa
Nostra links
Gideon v. Wainwright, 372 U.S.
335 (1963): a case in which the
Supreme Court included among
the fundamental rights of persons
guaranteed by the Fourteenth
Amendment the right under the
Sixth Amendment to be represented by counsel when a person
is being tried for a crime in a State
court, including the right of an
indigent defendant to have counsel assigned by the court   (DAP)
gift causa mortis: a gift of personal
property made by a party in the
expectation of death, then imminent   (CDTP)
gift inter vivos: a gift between the
living   (CDTP)
Gilbert v. California, 338 U.S. 263,
18 L. Ed. 2d 1178, 87 S. Ct. 1951
(1967): the court, in a decision
marked by divisiveness similar to
that characterized Wade, restated
the basic principle announced in
Wade and refined it with respect
to testimony that is the "direct result of an illegal line-up." (The

majority also stressed that only a
per se exclusionary rule can be an
effective sanction to assure that
law enforcement authorities will
respect the accused's constitutional right to the presence of
counsel at the critical line-up. The
majority also rejected the contention that the Fifth Amendment
privilege was violated by placing
the defendant in a line-up and
having him repeat phrases used by
the person who committed the
crime at the time he committed
it.)   (ILECJ)
gill: one-fourth of a pint   (CDTP)
Ginzberg v. United States, 383 U.S.
463 (1966): a case in which the
Supreme Court held that publications created and advertised solely
in order to appeal to prurient interests in sex had the characteristics of illicit merchandise and
could not claim the protection of
freedom of the press, though in a
different context (as by sale to
physicians) their distribution
might not have been challenged
(DAP)
Giske v. Sanders, 9 Cal. App. 13
(1908): this early California case
upholds police procedures regarding suspicious persons and ex-
plores the duty of police to discover, detect, and deter crime
(AOJ)
Gitlow v. New York, 268 U.S. 652,
69 L. Ed. 1138, 45 S. Ct. 625
(1925): the Court upheld the validity of New York's criminal
anarchy act of 1902. (The left-
wing members of the Socialist
Party met in convention in New
York City, June 21-24, 1919. The
convention delegates instructed its
executive committee to draft and
publish the Left Wing Manifesto
and adopted Revolutionary Age as
the left wing's official newspaper.
The Manifesto appeared in the
July 5, 1919 issue of the Revolutionary Age and furnished the
basis for the conviction of its business manager, Benjamin Gitlow,
of criminal anarchy in New York.)
(ILECJ)

glassbreak vibration detector: a vibration detection system which employs a contact microphone attached to a glass window to detect cutting or breakage of the glass (TDIAS)

glossy: applied to photographic papers which are heavily coated with gelatin so that they may be ferrotyped (MPPF)

Glueck, Sheldon: an American criminologist, Glueck, with his wife, Eleanor, wrote many articles on the field of criminal character and behavior. His most famous study was a documented case research of 500 criminal careers

glycerin sandwich: a means of making prints from scratched or damaged negatives; they are placed between glass plates coated with glycerin which temporarily fills in the scratches (MPPF)

G-man: a name, originating in the 1930s, for a special agent of the Federal Bureau of Investigation (LEV)

gonorrhea: a venereal disease of the sexual tract, caused by the gonococcus, [sometimes] characterized by profuse discharge, burning and pain, and frequency of urination (CDTP)

Gooding v. Wilson, 405 U.S. 518, 31 L. Ed. 2d 408, 92 S. Ct. 1103 (1972): in a 5-2 opinion by Mr. Justice Brennan, the Court holds unconstitutional a Georgia statute making it an offense to use "opprobrious words or abusive language tending to cause a breach of the peace." Wilson was convicted on two counts of using abusive language to police during a demonstration at an Army headquarters. Justices Powell and Rehnquist did not participate. (The construction given the Georgia statute by the state courts had not limited it to "fighting words" that "have a direct tendency to cause acts of violence by the persons to whom, individually, the remark is addressed," and so it did not come under the narrow exception to the constitutional right of freedom of expression sanctioned by *Chaplinsky* v. *New Hampshire.*) (ILECJ)

goods and chattels: personal property of every kind, as distinguished from real property (CDTP)

good-time allowance: the method whereby an inmate of a penal institution may have his sentence reduced for "good behavior"

Goring, Charles Buckman (*1870–1919*): a British research scientist and prison physician, Goring published a statistical study of 3,000 male convicts entitled "The English Convict," in which he claimed criminal tendencies are related to mental deficiencies and psychological factors rather than physical characteristics, as theorized by Lombroso

government: the exercise of authority in regulating the action of the state (CDTP)

gradation: the range of densities in an emulsion from highlights to shadows (MPPF)

graft: (1) anything inserted into another thing so as to become an integral part of the other, such as a skin graft or bone graft (CDTP) (2) money or valuable privileges gained at the expense of the public or of the public interest, usually by officeholders, employees, or persons who possess political influence, and obtained through actions ranging from downright theft to morally reprehensible acts for which there is no legal penalty (DAP)

graft, honest: a term coined by the famous Tammany Hall chieftain, George Washington Plunkitt, to identify the profit secured by a politician in making use of his foreknowledge of public building and improvement. ... Dishonest graft is payment for non-existent jobs and services to persons who return a portion of the payment to the politician who made it (DOS)

grafter: one who dishonestly acquires gain by violating a trust or by corrupt agreement or connivance (CDTP)

grain: (1) the unit of measurement used to express the weight of a powder charge or a bullet; 437.5 grains equal 1 oz. avoirdupois, and 7,000 grains equal 1 lb. (DWMT) (2) a single piece of solid propellent regardless of size or shape used in a gun or rocket. For the latter, a grain is often very large and shaped to fit the requirements of the rocket. It is termed "propellant grain" (DWMT) (3) used in speaking of individual silver particles or groups of particles in the emulsion which, when enlarged, become noticeable and objectionable (MPPF)

gram; gramme: See metric units

grand jury: a jury of inquiry who are summoned and returned by the sheriff to each session of the criminal courts, and whose duty is to receive complaints and accusations in criminal cases, hear the evidence on the part of the state, and find bills of indictment in cases where they are satisfied a trial ought to be had. They are first sworn, and instructed by the court. This is called a "grand jury" because it comprises a greater number of jurors than the ordinary trial jury or "petit jury." At common law, a grand jury consisted of not less than 12 nor more than 23 men, and this is still the rule in many of the states, though in some the number is otherwise fixed by statute; thus in Oregon and Utah, the grand jury is composed of 7 men; in South Dakota, not less than 6 nor more than 8; in Texas, 12; in Idaho, 16 to 23; in California, 19; in New Mexico, 21 (CDTP)

grand jury, charging: a grand jury that must decide whether or not to ratify the prosecutor's request for a formal charge against a defendant

grand jury, investigatory: the grand jury for a court with the authority to conduct investigations into possible crimes

grand larceny: See larceny. Grand larceny is larceny of property where the value of the property stolen exceeds the amount fixed by statute in the different states. Often includes larceny from the person and larceny of specific kinds of property (CDTP)

graphology: the study of handwriting for the purpose of determining the character of the writer (LEV)

grapnel: a device with one or more hooks for seizing things. Many times used in water to locate a drowned body or other objects (LEV)

gratis: free; without reward or consideration (CDTP)

gratuity: a gift or present (CDTP)

gray scale: a monochrome strip of tones ranging from pure white to black with intermediate tones of gray. The scale is placed in a setup for a color photograph and serves as a means of balancing the separation negatives and positive dye images, and is cropped from the finished print (MPPF)

grease gun: the nickname given to the U.S. .45 cal. submachine gun M3 and M3A1 used in WW II and the Korean conflict (DWMT)

Green, Edward (1822-1866): the first bank robber in the United States, on Dec. 15, 1863; Green was caught and executed for murdering the bank teller

Gregory v. City of Chicago, 394 U.S. 111, 22 L. Ed. 2d 134. 89 S. Ct. 946 (1969): Chief Justice Warren, in a short opinion, reversed Gregory's conviction. He said, "this is a simple case," concluding that since there was no evidence that the petitioner's conduct was disorderly, the march was protected by the First Amendment. (In effect, the petitioners were arrested for disobeying a law that did not exist until they were commanded to disperse. Justices Black and Douglas, concurring to reverse, thought the case to be of far greater importance than the majority's treatment of it indicated. There is a critical need, they contended, for some "narrowly drawn law" that can reconcile the rights of citizens to propagandize their views and protest through the medium of marches and demonstrations and the interest of government in regulating speech-connected conduct.) (ILECJ)

grenade: a small explosive or chemical missile, originally designed to be projected from special grenade launchers, usually fitted to rifles or carbines. Grenades may be classified in a broad sense as hand grenades or rifle grenades. Many varieties and variations of these have been used, including a number of improvised ones (DWMT)

grid: (1) an arrangement of electrically conducting wire, screen, or tubing placed in front of doors or windows or both which is used as a part of a capacitance sensor (TDIAS) (2) a lattice of wooden dowels or slats concealing fine wires in a closed circuit which initiates an alarm signal when forcing or cutting the lattice breaks the wires. Used over accessible openings. Sometimes called a protective screen. *See also* burglar alarm pad (TDIAS) (3) a screen or metal plate, connected to earth ground, sometimes used to provide a stable ground reference for objects protected by a capacitance sensor. If placed against the walls near the protected object, it prevents the sensor sensitivity from extending through the walls into areas of activity (TDIAS) (4) two sets of parallel lines intersecting at right angles and forming squares. The grid is superimposed on maps, charts, and other similar representations of the earth's surface in an accurate and consistent manner to permit identification of ground locations and the computation of direction and distance to other points. The term is also used in giving the location of a geographic point by grid coordinates (DWMT)

grid search: a technique for searching crime scenes, usually out-doors, whereby an area which has been previously searched by the strip method is again searched after dividing the area into lanes or zones running at right angles to such plots used in the strip search (LEV)

Griffin v. California, 380 U.S. 609, 14 L. Ed. 2d 106, 85 S. Ct. 1229 (1965): the Court held (6–2) that the Fifth Amendment forbids a state prosecutor's comment on failure of a defendant to explain evidence within his knowledge and bars an instruction from the court that such silence may be evidence of guilt. (This holding broadens the meaning of *Malloy* v. *Hogan*, 378, U.S. 1.) (ILECJ)

Griffin v. Illinois, 351 U.S. 12, 100 L. Ed. 891, 76 S. Ct. 585 (1956): the Court held 5–4 that the due process and equal protection clauses of the Fourteenth Amendment require that all indigent defendants be furnished a transcript for an appeal. (Strictly speaking, there was no opinion of the Court as Mr. Justice Black announced the Court's judgment in a four-man opinion.) (ILECJ)

grip: (1) one of a pair of wooden or plastic pieces designed to be attached by threaded fasteners to the two sides of the frame of a weapon, such as a revolver or bayonet. It is shaped to fit the hand and to provide a formed gripping surface to hold the weapon (DWMT) (2) also, the part of a sword or dagger grasped by the hand (DWMT)

groove diameter: the diameter of a bore of a gun as measured from the bottom of one groove to the bottom of the opposite groove (DWMT)

grooves: the spiral depressions in the rifling of a gun. They impart a spinning motion to a projectile which stabilizes it in flight (DWMT)

gross: (1) the whole; total (CDTP) (2) flagrant (CDTP)

gross negligence: apparent failure to exercise care demanded by cir-

cumstances (LEV)
Grossman, Ex parte, 267 U.S. 87 (1925): a case in which the Supreme Court, relying upon earlier British and American practice, ruled that criminal contempt of a federal court is an offense against the United States and, as such, comes within the pardoning power of the President (DAP)

groundglass: a screen at the back or top of the camera upon which the image may be focused (MPPF)

groundglass screen: a translucent screen mounted in the back or top of a camera, upon which the image formed by the lens can be observed (MPPF)

guaranty: a promise or undertaking by one person to answer for the payment of some debt or performance of some contract in case of default by another person (CDTP)

guardian: one who has legally the care and management of the person or the estate, or both, of an infant, lunatic, or incompetent person (CDTP)

guardian ad litem: a guardian appointed for the purpose of a law suit (CDTP)

guerrilla: member of a group or band who carries on harassment activities against the enemy by raiding supply bases, etc., many times behind enemy lines. Not considered an official part of the military establishment (LEV)

guillotine: a machine commonly used in medieval times with two upright posts surmounted by a crossbeam grooved so that a weighted and oblique-shaped knife blade falls swiftly and with force when the cord by which it is suspended is released

guilt: being wrong; having committed an offense in violation of a criminal law (LEV)

guilt by association: the idea which has sometimes been embodied in statutes that a person's guilt is prima facie determined by his membership in an organization stigmatized as criminal or subver-sive regardless of his knowledge of the aims and activities of the organization, or of his own active involvement (DAP)

guilty: having done something wrong or showing guilt (LEV)

gun: (1) in general, a piece of ordnance consisting essentially of a tube or barrel and used for throwing projectiles by force, usually the force of an explosive, but sometimes that of compressed gas, a spring, etc. The general term embraces such weapons as are sometimes specifically designated as guns—howitzers, mortars, cannons, firearms, rifles, shotguns, carbines, pistols, and revolvers (DWMT) (2) specifically, a gun (sense 1) with a relatively long barrel (usually over 30 cal.) and relatively high initial velocity, capable of being fired at low angles of elevation (DWMT) (3) a discharge of a cannon in a salute, such as a signal or the like—for example, a salute of 17 guns; the evening gun (DWMT) (4) to fire upon with guns (DWMT) (5) to advance the throttle or apply full power to an engine or motor (DWMT) (6) any device for igniting flashlamps or flash powder (MPPF) (7) the gunstock for supporting small cameras with greater firmness (MPPF)

gun book: a log that records the history of the operations and inspections of a particular gun (DWMT)

gun chamber: the part of a gun that receives the charge (DWMT)

gun control laws: federal, state, and local laws which regulate the importation, manufacturing, distribution, sale, purchase, or possession of firearms. The Alcohol, Tobacco, and Firearms Division of the U.S. Treasury Department had jurisdiction over the federal laws (LEV)

gunfire: the use of such things as artillery, rifles, and small arms, as distinguished from the use of bayonets, swords, torpedoes, and bombs (DWMT) gunmetal: the material from which guns are made. Specifically, a type of bronze (9 parts copper and 1 part tin) once much used for the manufacture of cannons (DWMT)

gunpowder: a term usu. applied to black powder, which is composed of potassium nitrate (saltpeter), charcoal, and sulfur. It consists of 70 to 80 percent saltpeter and 10 to 15 percent of each of the other ingredients. The mixture contains the necessary amount of oxygen for combustion and, when ignited, produces gases that occupy 1,000 to 1,500 times more space than the powder itself   (DWMT)

gunpowder tests: the testing of objects for the presence of gunpowder residues   (LEV)

gunsmith: a person who makes or repairs small firearms; an armorer   (DWMT)

gunstock: the wooden stock in which the barrel and mechanism of a gun are fixed   (DWMT)

H

H & D (Hurter and Drillield) System: a system for measuring film speed. Little used in this country   (MPPF)

habeas corpus [*Lat, lit you have the body*]: a term describing a writ used as an instrument to bring an accused party immediately before a court or judge

habitual criminal laws: many American states and other countries have passed laws which provide increased penalties for offenders with previous criminal records. The provision for the increased penalty is either permissive or mandatory. The habitual criminal law is invoked after conviction of a second, third, or fourth felony. The advocates of such laws believe the increased severity of penalty will eliminate or considerably reduce serious crime. *Cf.* Baumes Law   (DOS)

habitual offender: a persistent violator of law; *also:* an incorrigible criminal. In certain states, under habitual offender acts or so-called Baumes laws, persons convicted of a certain number of felonies, usually four, are sentenced to imprisonment for life   (DAP)

habitual offender statutes: See recidivism statutes

habituation: a psychological dependence upon a substance such as marihuana or tobacco. Withdrawal from such is essentially psychological in nature   (LEV)

hair trigger: a trigger requiring only a light touch for firing   (CDTP)

halation: a blurred effect, resembling a halo, usually occurring around light objects; caused by the reflections of rays of light from the back of the negative material   (MPPF)

half cock: the position of the hammer of a small-arms weapon when it is held by the first cocking notch, with the trigger locked and the weapon relatively safe. It was possible to carry certain types of loaded flintlock weapons in the half-cocked position, fully cocking them before pulling the trigger. When the secondary sear notch became worn, however, the gun was capable of discharging accidentally   (DWMT)

half-loaded: in automatic arms, a half-loaded weapon is one in which the belt or magazine has been inserted and the receiver charged, but in which the first cartridge is not actually in the chamber   (DWMT)

halftones: a term used in speaking of the middle tones lying between the shadows and highlights   (MPPF)

half-way houses: residences in the community for newly released inmates of correctional institutions. These residences, which are usu.

controlled or supported by the state, provide a structured base from which the inmate may make the transition from prison to society   (IC)

halides (or haloids): a chemical term applied to binary compounds containing any of the elements chlorine, bromine, iodine, and fluorine   (MPPF)

hallucination: a subjective perception of something which does not exist   (CDTP)

hallucinogens: hallucinogens make up one of three general categories of dangerous drugs, and are so named because they may produce hallucinations or illusions of the various senses   (LEV)

halogen: iodine, fluorine, chlorine, or bromine

Haloperidol®: a new nonnarcotic, nonaddicting drug for treating and controlling withdrawal symptoms associated with both heroin and methadone addiction   (LEV)

halt: a stop in marching or walking or in any action   (DWMT)

hammer: the part of the mechanism which strikes the primer directly, or strikes the firing pin. In flintlock days, the frizzen was sometimes called a "hammer"   (CDTP)

hammerless: a type of gun with the striking mechanism enclosed within the frame   (DWMT)

hand: a measure of length, four inches long   (CDTP)

Hand, Learned (1872-1961): considered one of the greatest jurists of his day, Hand served over 50 years on the bench as a federal judge. His final post held (1924–1951) was Chief Judge of the Federal Court of Appeals for the Second Circuit

handcuffs: hinged bands, usu. metal, joined by a short chain, which can be locked on the wrists of a person to restrain him (LEV)

handguard: (1) a wooden part on a rifle to protect the shooter's hands from the hot barrel (DWMT) (2) the part of a sword or dagger designed to protect the hand   (DWMT)

handgun: a firearm carried in the hand; a pistol or a revolver   (DWMT)

handling: the stability and control characteristics of a vehicle   (TDPPC)

handprinting: printing by hand letters of the alphabet and arranging them into words. This may be done with a pen, pencil, or other writing instrument. It is contrasted with handwriting. The document examiner cannot make adequate comparisons of handwriting if the known specimens are in handprinting and vice versa   (LEV)

hand weapon: a weapon, such as a pistol, knife, or sword, used with one hand. Distinguished especially from a shoulder weapon, in regard to firearms   (DWMT)

hangfire: slow or delayed detonation or firing, of a cartridge or shotgun shell, in a firearm (LEV)

hanging: a method of capital punishment devised in ancient times and in use at present in many countries. As originally used death came about by strangling, but as now used there is either a drop of about seven feet, or a sudden jerk upward which usually breaks the neck and causes supposedly instantaneous death   (DOS)

harass: to disturb; to molest; to trouble   (CDTP)

hard: a term used to denote excessive contrast [in film]   (MPPF)

hardener: a chemical such as potassium or chrome alum which is added to the fixing bath to harden the gelatin after development. Prehardening solutions may be used prior to development   (MPPF)

Harding, John Wesley (1853-1895): one of the West's most feared gunslingers, Harding was reported to be one of the fastest and most deadly killers of his time

hardtop: an automobile body type having a fixed roof in which the B-pillar does not extend above the windowsill level   (TDPPC)

hardware: the electric, electronic, and mechanical equipment used for processing data; consists of cabinets, racks, tubes, transistors,

wires, and motors   (ADPS)
hard-working: applied to a developer which tends to give high contrast   (MPPF)
Harris v. New York, 401 U.S. 222, 28 L. Ed. 2d 1, 91 S. Ct. 643 (1971): the Court, 5-4, in an opinion by Chief Justice Burger, held that a prosecutor may use illegally obtained confession to prove that a defendant who testifies is lying (The Chief Justice said that an exception to the exclusionary rule of *Miranda* must be made to counter prejurious testimony by a defendant. It should be noted that the defendant's statement was voluntary and there had been some compliance with *Miranda*. The use of a confession for impeachment purposes should not be considered to extend to involuntary confessions which are inadmissable as being untrustworthy.)   (ILECJ)
Harvey v. Mississippi, 340 F2d 263 (1965): the right to legal counsel guaranteed to defendants in criminal cases by the Sixth Amendment, and made applicable to the states under the Fourteenth Amendment, extends to and includes legal assistance, retained or assigned, in misdemeanor trials   (AOJ)
hashish: a narcotic derived from the Indian hemp plant. It may be inhaled, chewed, or smoked in order to produce a type of exhilaration accompanied by the disorganization of the central nervous system   (DOS)
hash total: sums of data items not ordinarily added, such as the stock numbers of units shipped, which are used to control the accuracy of the data at each stage of processing   (ADPS)
Hatch Act of 1939: a law of Congress enacted "to prevent pernicious political activities." Designed to eliminate corrupt political practices, it forbade anyone to intimidate, threaten, or coerce any person in order to influence his vote for a federal office. It further prohibited promise of employment or other advantage for political support, and made illegal the soliciting of political contributions by relief workers and federal executive or administrative employees. The latter were also prohibited from engaging in political management or in political campaigns. Exempted from its provisions were certain policy-determining officials, principally department heads, assistant heads, and the thousands of officers appointed by the President and Senate who determine foreign policy or are engaged in the "nationwide administration of Federal laws." The amendment of 1940 attempted to regulate campaign contributions and expenditures by limiting to $5,000 per annum the contribution of any one person, committee, or corporation in the nomination or election of any candidate for federal office. No political committee may receive contributions or make expenditures in any calendar year in excess of $3,000,000. No firm under contract with a federal agency for supplies or materials may be solicited or may contribute to any political party, committee, or candidate. No corporation or union may contribute to political parties or campaigns. The Act and its amendment of 1940 have proven unsuccessful in eliminating these practices. Expenditures and contributions by individual committees and persons have raised the amounts far beyond those laid down in the law. The law is also known as the Federal Corrupt Practices Act and the Political Activities Act of 1939. Presently, the federal government has not revised either act (DOAH)
Hauptman, Bruno Richard (*1899–1936*): a German immigrant who had been convicted of burglary and armed robbery, he entered the U.S. illegally in 1923. He kidnapped the son of Col. Charles Lindbergh; he was convicted and was electrocuted on April 3,

1936, at the state prison in New Jersey

Haviland, John (*1792-1852*): a famous penal architectural reformer, Haviland built the state prisons in New Jersey and Pennsylvania. He designed such innovations as detached exercise yards, cell doors opening into corridors, and two-story wings

Hawes-Cooper Act: a law enacted by the Congress of the United States and approved by the President Jan. 19, 1929, which became operative after five years. It provided that all prison-made goods entering into interstate commerce are subject to the laws of any State or Territory of the United States to the same extent and in the same manner as prison-made goods manufactured in that State or Territory. It was aimed at the contract, piece-price, and public account systems of prison labor (DOS)

Haymarket Affair: an incident arising out of the eight-hour movement in the 1880s. A meeting was called by anarchist labor leaders and newspaper editors, to be held on May 4, 1886 in Haymarket Square, Chicago, in protest against the shooting of several strikers in a recent labor dispute. Mayor Harrison, police Captain Bonfield, and 180 police attended the meeting. Following the Mayor's departure, and against his advice, the crowd was ordered to leave. A bomb, thrown by an unknown person, exploded and resulted in the deaths of seven persons and injuries to many others. Eight anarchists were arrested and convicted for conspiracy. In 1887, four were hanged. One later committed suicide, and in 1893 Governor Altgeld of Illinois pardoned the remaining two. It has never been determined who threw the bomb, and labor and radical elements have always claimed the Haymarket Affair to have been an anti-labor conspiracy. The movement for the eight-hour day collapsed for a generation, as a result (DOAH)

Haynes v. Washington, 373 U.S. 503, 10 L. Ed. 2d 513, 83 S. Ct. 1336 (1963): the Court held (5-4) that when a confession is "obtained in an atmosphere of substantial coercion and inducements created by statements and actions of state authorities, "it is inadmissible under due process of the Fourteenth Amendment." [The police "coercion" in *Haynes* rested on their refusal to permit the prisoner to contact his wife unless he confessed, and kept him in a technically incommunicado status, even though there was very little to indicate that his statement in fact was unreliable. The Court expressly recognized, at that time, the need for custodial interrogation. "(C)ertainly, we do not mean to suggest that all interrogation of witnesses and suspects is impermissible," said Mr. Justice Goldberg.] (ILECJ)

hazing: harassment by abusive or ridiculous treatment (CDTP)

header label: label recorded on tape preceding the first record in the file to identify the file—file name, date written, and reel number (ADPS)

hearing: a trial; any action before a court or magistrate

hearsay: evidence the witness has learned through others

hearsay rule: the rule of evidence that prohibits the use of hearsay evidence in a criminal case. There are exceptions (LEV)

Hearst, Patricia (*1955-*). the granddaughter of publisher William Randolph Hearst, Patty was kidnapped on February 5, 1974 by the S.L.A. (Symbionese Liberation Army). She became the object of one of the most intensive manhunts ever conducted by the F.B.I. She was finally captured and found guilty of bank robbery of a San Francisco Bank. She is presently released on bail pending appeal decisions

heat sensor: (1) a sensor which responds to either a local temperature above a selected value, a local temperature increase which is at a rate of increase greater than a preselected rate (rate of rise), or both (TDIAS) (2) a sensor which responds to infrared radiation from a remote source such as a person (TDIAS)

heir: a person who inherits or may by law inherit (CDTP)

heir at law: one entitled by law to inherit by descent the real estate of a decedent (CDTP)

helicopter: an aircraft supported in flight by rotating airfoils instead of fixed wings and used for spotting, rescue, evacuation, transport, and general utility. Also called "pinwheel," "eggbeater," "whirlybird," "windmill," "copter," and "chopper" (DWMT)

hematoporphyrin test: a chemical confirmation test for the presence of blood (LEV)

hemorrhage: profuse bleeding; discharge of blood from wounded or ruptured blood vessel (CDTP)

hemostat: a drug or an instrument to stop bleeding (CDTP)

hereditary: descended by inheritance or from an ancestor (CDTP)

herein: in this matter; into this. (LEV)

heretofore: up to this time; before the present (LEV)

hermaphrodite: one with both male and female sexual organs

heroin: one of the opium family isolated in the search for nonhabit forming anesthetics to take the place of morphine. Heroin is a trademark name which has become identified with a white crystalline form of morphine derivative. It is definitely habit-forming and has become one of the most widely used of all narcotics. It produces a quiet, pleasant, dreamlike slumber (DOS)

hesitation marks: when a person commits suicide by cutting, usu. several small cuts are found near the large wound (LEV)

H-field sensor: a passive sensor which detects changes in the earth's ambient magnetic field caused by the movement of an intruder. See also E-field sensor (TDIAS)

high crimes and misdemeanors: offenses against law sufficiently grave to warrant impeachment by the House of Representatives (DAP)

high explosive: any powerful non-atomic explosive characterized by extremely rapid detonation and having a powerful disruptive or shattering effect. Typical examples are trinitrotoluene (TNT), amatol, tetryl, and picric acid (DWMT)

high-explosive plastic: a high-explosive substance or mixture which, within normal ranges of atmospheric temperature, is capable of being molded into desired shapes; also called "plastic explosive" or "PE" (DWMT)

high-key: applied to a print having the majority of its tones light grays and white (MPPF)

high-low limits: maximum and minimum values used for checking the plausibility of data or results. If the limits are exceeded, corrective action may be taken or the item rejected for investigation (ADPS)

high misdemeanor: in some states crimes are classed as misdemeanors and high misdemeanors, the latter carrying heavier penalties (CDTP)

high-power: military and sporting rifles using small caliber bullets driven by a large charge of smokeless powder (CDTP)

high stress conditions: the stresses to which law enforcement vehicles are subjected in functions requiring performance beyond the demands placed on standard vehicles. These stresses may develop from such activities as high speed pursuit, operation at temperature extremes, and extensive operation of vehicle equipment while the engine is idling (TDPPC)

high velocity: as used in connection

with artillery, small arms, and tank cannons, generally accepted to have the following meanings: (1) the muzzle velocity of an artillery projectile of from 3,000 fps. to, but not including, 3,500 fps.; (2) the velocity of small-arms ammunition between 3,500 and 5,000 fps.; (3) the velocity of tank cannon projectiles between 1,550 and 3,350 fps.   (DWMT)

higher-law doctrine: (1) the concept of a law of nature intrinsically superior to positive law (DAP) (2) a declaration that "there is a higher law than the Constitution," made by Senator William H. Seward of New York, an abolitionist spokesman, March 11, 1850, during the debates on the Compromise of 1850   (DAP)

Highfields: See New Jersey Experimental Project for the Treatment of Youthful Offenders

highlights: the brightest parts of the subject, which are represented by the denser parts of the negative and the light gray and white tones of the print   (MPPF)

highway: a principal or main road usually of considerable length, which is used by the public (LEV)

highway patrol: a special State force, known by various names, which enforces motor vehicle and other laws in those States which have not established a State constabulary invested with general law-enforcement powers   (DAP)

highwayman: one who robs and commits crimes of violence on people traveling the public highways   (LEV)

hijack: to take by force goods or merchandise being transported   (LEV)

hijack alert system: a system worked out by trucking concerns, trucking associations, and law enforcement agencies whereby a theft or hijack is immediately reported to designated law enforcement agencies and to a designated trucking association. The latter, per a prearranged schedule, noti

fies certain strategically located trucking companies who in turn notify others until all truckers in a given area are notified. The drivers and other employees search for and report the stolen equipment   (LEV)

Hill v. California, 401 U.S. 797, 28 L. Ed. 2d 484, 91 S. Ct. 1106 (1971): the Court held, unanimously, through Mr. Justice White, that a mistaken pre-*Chimel* arrest of a man fitting the description of an accused whom the police had probable cause to arrest did not render unlawful a contemporaneous search of the accused's entire apartment where the arrestee was found   (ILECJ)

his honor: a title customarily given to a mayor, magistrate, or judge   (CDTP)

hit-and-run: situation where a driver is involved in a traffic accident and thereafter fails to comply with the laws regarding stopping, giving aid, revealing his identity, or notifying the police   (LEV)

Hobbes, Thomas (*1588–1679*): one of the world's greatest philosophers, Hobbes believed in an utilitarian punishment for a violation of the law. Punishment was not to be revengeful and must be in proportion to the crime committed. Hobbes also stated that punishment must be preceded by public condemnation, inflicted by the proper authority, and must have as its end to dispose men to obey the law

Hobbs Act: an act of Congress, July 3, 1947, designed to curb labor racketeering, which imposed penalties on persons found guilty of robbery or extortion when these acts have the effect of obstructing, delaying, or otherwise affecting interstate commerce   (DAP)

Hoc [*Lat*]: this

hold back: to shade portions of an image while printing in order to avoid excessive density; similar to dodge   (MPPF) holdup: a robbery involving the threat to use a weapon   (TDIAS)

holdup alarm device: a device which signals a holdup. The device is usu. surreptitious and may be manually or automatically actuated, fixed or portable   (TDIAS)

holdup alarm system, manual: a holdup alarm system in which the signal transmission is initiated by the direct action of the person attacked or of an observer of the attack   (TDIAS)

holdup button: a manually actuated mechanical switch used to initiate a duress alarm signal; usually constructed to minimize accidental activation   (TDIAS)

Holmes, Oliver Wendell (1841–1935): Associate Justice of U.S. Supreme Court (1902-32). Known as the "great dissenter," he gained the notice of the nation's liberals by his clear, forceful opinions. He believed in respecting human rights more than property rights. His writings (e.g., The Common Law, 1881) are much admired   (CVDE)

holograph: handwritten will

holster: a pocket-type device with a single compartment designed to be worn on a belt or shoulder harness, which may be furnished with it. It is used to carry a pistol, revolver, or the like. Other types of holsters are carried on horseback, usually in front of the saddle   (DWMT)

homicide: any willful killing (e.g., murder and nonnegligent manslaughter)

homicide, excusable: a killing under such circumstances of accident or misfortune that the party is relieved from the penalty annexed to the commission of a felonious homicide   (CDTP)

homicide, felonious: a killing committed under such circumstances as to make it punishable   (CDTP)

homicide, justifiable: a killing committed with full intent, but under such circumstances of duty as to render the act one proper to be performed, such as cases of self-defense, defense of property, officer lawfully enforcing the law   (CDTP)

homo: a human being   (CDTP)

homologous: in chemistry, a homologous series is one of organic compounds each member of which differs from its predecessor by possessing one more carbon atom and associated hydrogen atoms; e.g., the alcohols methanol, ethanol, propanol, butanol, etc.   (FS)

homosexual: one who is attracted sexually to persons of the same sex   (LEV)

honorary: without profit or reward; conferring honor   (CDTP)

hood contact: a switch which is used for the supervision of a closed safe or vault door. Usually installed on the outside surface of the protected door   (TDIAS)

hook: a fingerprint term, also called a spur—a hook-like ridge or small branch emanating from a single ridge line   (LEV)

Hooton, Earnest Albert (1887–1954): an American physical anthropologist, Hooton conducted studies to ascertain whether criminals differ physically from law-abiding citizens of the same race, nationality, and economic status. He believed that biological determinism influenced an individual's criminal tendencies

Hoover, John Edgar (1895-1972): in 1924, Hoover took over the F.B.I., changing it from a scandalous and disorganized office to an impressive law enforcement unit. During the 1930s he started the bureau's list of "the ten most wanted criminals," providing Americans with an accurate description of the top criminals across the country. He died in 1972 after 48 years as Director of the FBI

hostage: a person held as a pledge that certain terms or agreements will be kept (The taking of hostages is forbidden under the Geneva Convention of 1949.)   (DWMT)

hostile: belonging to an enemy; unfriendly; adverse (CDTP)

hot line: a communication channel providing instantaneous communication without switching (DWMT)

hot pursuit: a principle of international law justifying pursuit and arrest of vessels that have infringed the laws of a state, provided such pursuit begins within the territorial waters of the offended state and is continued without interruption. The right of pursuit ceases when the vessel reaches the territorial waters of another state (DAP)

house of assignation: a house of ill fame (CDTP)

house of correction: English institution established in the 16th century for vagabonds, prostitutes, rogues, and the unemployed. In the United States, place of confinement for offenders whose violations of the law are of a minor nature. Usu. for short-term offenders (DOS)

housebreaking: breaking open and entering a house with felonious intent by night or by day (CDTP)

Huber Law: *See* work release

Hudson v. Parker, 156 U.S. 277 (1895): this is an early case reviewing the traditional right to freedom before conviction and the need for release on bail to prepare an adequate defense and to guard against the unnecessary infliction of punishment pending final disposition of the charge of the crime (AOJ)

hue: (1) the name by which we distinguish one color from another: blue, red (MPPF) (2) sound alarm by shouting. The citizens would chase the criminal with shouts and cries (LEV)

hull: the metal portion of a cartridge (LEV)

human relations: an understanding of why people act in a certain manner, how they get along together in a group setting, and the characteristics of persons and groups. The officer in the field is concerned with linking the larger view of human relations to the tasks and functions of the law enforcement agency, particularly as to how organization changes occur, the resulting interaction of individuals in day-to-day situations. A fuller understanding of community organizations and their human elements. *See* community relations (LEV)

hung jury: a jury that is divided in opinion and cannot reach a verdict

Hurtado v. California, 110 U.S. 516 (1884): a case in which the Supreme Court ruled that the protection of the life and liberty of the person afforded by the due-process clause of the Fourteenth Amendment does not require a State to use an indictment or presentment of a grand jury in prosecutions for murder or other offenses but permits the State, after examining and committing the accused through a magistrate's court, to substitute an information for such indictment or presentment (DAP)

hydrate: a salt which contains water in loose chemical combination (FS)

hydrocyanic acid: a water solution of hydrogen cyanide. It is a colorless, extremely poisonous liquid. The odor is bitter. It is also known as muriatic acid (LEV)

hydrodynamics of blood drops and splashes: the patterns, shapes, and sizes of blood drops and splashes produced by factors such as height of fall, direction, and speed of body from which they emanated (LEV)

hydrolysis: decomposition of a compound into two or more simpler ones by the action and addition of water. This may require the action of heat, acids, alkalis, enzymes, etc. (FS)

hydrometer: an instrument used to find the concentration of a single chemical in water. Most common use is in mixing large quantities of hypo (MPPF)

hydroplaning: a condition in which

the tire tread of a moving vehicle loses contact with the road surface, and thus traction, due to a film of water on the road surface   (TDPPC)

hydroquinone: a reducing agent which is widely used in compounding developers for photographic materials   (MPPF)

hyperfocal distance: the distance from the camera, such that if an object at that point is in sharp focus, then all objects from one-half this distance to infinity give satisfactory definition on the groundglass screen   (MPPF)

hypnosis: a condition, resembling normal sleep, brought about by a hypnotist whose suggestions the subject accepts readily   (LEV)

hypnotic drug: a drug which induces sleep similar to that of hypnosis   (LEV)

hypo: a contraction of sodium hyposulfite (sodium thiosulfate). Hypo is used in compounding fixing solutions. These, in turn, are used to make soluble the undeveloped silver salts in an emulsion   (MPPF)

hypodermic: an injection under the skin layer   (CDTP)

hypo test: a method of checking the completeness of washing by running the drippings of wash water from the film or print into various testing solutions; also, commercial solution used to test strength of hypo   (MPPF)

hypothecation: a right which a creditor has in property of his debtor in virtue of which he may cause it to be sold   (CDTP)

hypothesis: a supposition; a proposition or principle which is supposed or taken for granted; something not provided   (CDTP)

hypothetical question: a form of question put to an expert witness after his competency has been established, containing a recital of facts assumed to have been proved, or proof of which is offered in the case and requiring the opinion of the witness thereon.   (CDTP)

hysteria: a psychic condition marked by various symptoms ranging from nervous instability to fits of causeless crying and laughing   (CDTP)

I

I.A.A.I. (IAAI): International Association of Arson Investigators

I.A.C.P. (IACP): International Association of Chiefs of Police, Inc., 11 Firstfield Road, Gaithersburg, MD 20760. Phone (301) 948-0922

ibidem [Lat]: in the same place

I.C.P.C. (ICPC): International Criminal Police Commission

idem [Lat]: the same

Identi-Code Index: a letter-number symbol appearing on each capsule and tablet and on each label of suppositories and of powders for oral suspension. The Identi-Code Index shows the specific product name and its formula. The Identi-Code Index may be obtained from Eli Lilly Company, Indianapolis, IN 46206, Attention: Mr. Allan Gillies, Assistant to the Group Vice-President, Corporate Services and Pharmaceutical Operations   (LEV)

identification: a photograph showing the head and shoulders, both front and side views, of a person   (MPPF)

identification division: the part of a COBOL program in which the programmer gives information to identify the source and object programs   (ADPS)

identification, investigation: in 1930 Congress established a Division of Identification and Investigation and invested it with the duty of collecting crime records and criminal identifications and made it the duty of the division to exchange such records with state, municipal, and prison officials throughout the United States. (U.S. Code, Title 5, Sec. 340) In order to aid the bureau in apprehending criminals who are now at large as fugitives from justice and to insure the swift capture of any who commit crime in the future, the last three sessions of the California legislature appropriated funds sufficient to connect the Bureau of Identification and Investigation with all of the cities in the state by a system of communication known as the teletype; when all cities are connected with these devices the swift apprehension of criminals will be greatly facilitated. The police broadcasting stations and radio-equipped scout cars are another material aid in the apprehension of criminals   (CDTP)

identification number: the number assigned to a person whose fingerprints are on file in an identification bureau of a police agency. The record of this person, showing all arrests, convictions, and dispositions, is shown under this number for that department
(LEV)

identification order (i.o.): the official wanted notice of the FBI issued for persons wanted by the FBI for crime violation. Each is numbered (in sequence), is dated, and has the following information: the criminal charge, name, and aliases of the subject; subject's fingerprints; description and photograph; criminal record, information of caution concerning the subject; and request that the FBI be notified of any information concerning the subject. These are widely distributed to law enforcement agencies, post offices, and government agencies having frequent contact with the public   (LEV)

identification record: criminal record. The record of an individual as maintained in the identification bureau of a law enforcement agency. The identification of the person should be made on fingerprints. It shows the arrests, convictions, and dispositions of the individual   (LEV)

identify: (1) to recognize a person or thing as being the same as a particular person or thing (LEV) (2) in area of physical evidence, to place markings on evidence or place it in marked containers so it can be positively recognized at a later time   (LEV)

id est (i.e.) [*Lat*]: that is

idiot: a person who has been without understanding from his nativity   (CDTP)

I except: an objection registered (by the words "I except") to a ruling, so that the record may show that the exceptor was dissatisfied with the ruling and probably intended to appeal   (CDTP)

igniter: (1) any device—chemical, electrical, or mechanical—used to ignite (DWMT) (2) a specially arranged charge of a ready-burning composition, usually black powder, used to assist in the initiation of a propelling charge (DWMT) (3) a device containing such a composition and used to amplify the initiation of a primer in the functioning of a fuze   (DWMT)

igniting fuze: a fuze designed to initiate its main munition by an igniting action, as compared with the detonation action of a detonating fuze. This type of fuze is suitable only for munitions using a main charge of low explosive or other readily ignitable material
(DWMT)

ignition: the setting on fire of the powder   (CDTP)

ignorance or mistake of fact, common law offenses: at common law, ignorance or mistake of fact, as a rule, exempts a person from criminal liability, if the act done would be lawful were the facts as the actor believes, provided that the ignorance or mistake is not voluntary or due to negligence (CDTP)

ignorance or mistake of fact, statutory offenses: where an offense is defined by statute, whether or not ignorance or mistake of fact exempts a person doing a prohibited act from criminal liability, as at common law, depends upon the language and construction of the statute. Unless the intention is clearly expressed, it must be determined by a construction of the statute, in view of the nature of the offense and the evils to be remedied, and of other matters making the one construction or the other reasonable, whether it was the intention to make knowledge of the facts an essential element of the offense (CDTP)

ignorance or mistake of law: ignorance on the part of the wrongdoer of the law which makes an act criminal is no excuse. If a specific intent is essential to a crime, and ignorance of the law negatives such intent, such ignorance prevents the crime from being consummated (CDTP)

illegal: not legal; against the law; something prohibited by law (LEV)

illegal detention: the unlawful detention of a person when there is not sufficient cause to believe the person has committed a crime for which he could be arrested. Under such conditions a court has ruled that a confession, even though given voluntarily, is not admissible in evidence (LEV)

illegitimate: contrary to law (CDTP)

illegitimate child: a child which is not the issue of a legal marriage (CDTP)

illicit: unlawful; contrary to criminal law; illegal (LEV)

illiterate: a person who cannot read or write (CDTP)

illuminating projectile: a projectile, with a time fuze, that releases a parachute flare at any desired height. It is used for lighting up an area and is popularly called "star shell" (DWMT)

illumination: the illumination at a point on the surface of a body is the intensity of light received, and is expressed as the number of lumens per square foot or the number of foot candles (MPPF)

image: the representation of an object formed by optical and/or chemical means (MPPF)

imbecile: one who is born with a mental capacity which does not go to a higher level than that of an average seven-year-old child as determined by the Binet-Simon Tests (CDTP)

imbibition: literally, the act of absorbing. The process of dye transfer in the wash-off relief process of making color prints (MPPF)

immaterial: not pertinent; not material; not importantly related to the case (LEV)

immigration laws: certain groups of persons such as beggars, felons, prostitutes, physically or mentally diseased persons, contract laborers, and others are excluded by the immigration laws from entrance to the United States. Aliens who enter illegally and are apprehended immediately are returned to the country from which they came at the expense of the steamship company that brought them. Aliens may be deported within three years of the time of entry if they become public charges from causes arising after their entry, and if they desire to return home. They may be deported within five years if they belong to the excluded groups at the time of their entry into the United States. They may be deported at any time upon proof of their advocating the destruction of property or overthrow of the government; or if they are convicted of a crime, and sentenced to prison for moral turpitude; or if they become public charges because of some cause which antedates their entrance into the United States; or if they are found to be connected with illegal traffic in women and children. When there is reason to believe that an individual has gained illegal entry into the United States it is the duty of a local police officer to refer the facts to the U.S. immigration officers. When a case is accepted by the federal authorities the responsibility of the police department ceases. If there happens to be a coincidence of violation of federal and state law, the merits of the case are considered by both local and federal officials to determine in whose jurisdiction action shall be instituted   (CDTP)

immoral: having bad morals; not compatible with good conscience or public morality; contrary to the rules and principles of morality   (LEV)

immunity: (1) exemption of a person from a duty, obligation, service, or penalty (as presidential or diplomatic immunity from judicial process), imposed by law on all others not similarly situated (DAP) (2) exemption from prosecution which is sometimes promised by a prosecutor to a person accused of crime who agrees to "turn state's evidence"—usually used colloquially   (DAP)

immunity, diplomatic: immunity from arrests and other legal involvement which an official diplomat of another country has while in this country   (LEV)

Immunity Act: an act of Congress, 1954, which provided that, in matters of national security, witnesses could be compelled to testify before Congressional committees if, on request of a federal district attorney approved by the Attorney General, immunity from prosecution has been granted by a U.S. district judge. See *Ullmann* v. *United States*   (DAP)

immunity bath: the exemption from prosecution of an excessive number of accused persons, or of principal defendants; the term

originated in 1906 when 16 defendants alleged to have been implicated in a beef trust were exempted from prosecution because they had aided the government in obtaining evidence against other defendants   (DAP)

impact: the force on an object by the projectile, i.e., the force of the bullet on what it strikes   (LEV)

impact-action fuze: a fuze that is set in action by the striking of a projectile or bomb against an object   (DWMT)

impact fuze: a fuze, as for a bomb, in which the action is initiated by the force of impact; sometimes called a "contact fuze"   (DWMT)

impanel: the process of selecting a jury which is to try a cause   (CDTP)

impeach: (1) to accuse, to discredit, or to censure (LEV) (2) to remove a public official from office for reasons of misconduct or illegal activity, by prescribed methods (LEV) (3) in the Congress of the United States, proceedings are started in the House of Representatives by a written accusation called the articles of impeachment which is directed to the Senate where the case is tried   (LEV)

impeaching credit of witness: the credit of a witness may be impeached by the adverse party, by the evidence of persons from his own community who will swear that they know the general reputation of the witness for truth and veracity, that his reputation is bad, and that they would not believe him on oath. In some states the inquiry may be as to the witness's general moral character. (49 Amer. Rep. 218) In most states the impeaching witness may be asked whether he would believe the other witness on oath; but in a few states this question cannot be asked. (88 Ind. 9) In all states the inquiry is confined to general reputation, and specific acts by the witness sought to be impeached cannot be shown. (12 Mass. 586) The impeaching witness may be cross-examined, and may also be impeached in the manner stated above. (9 N.W. 698) Impeaching witnesses cannot, on their examination in chief, give reasons for their belief; but they may be asked their reasons on cross-examination. The party introducing a witness cannot thus impeach him unless the witness has testified adversely to the party calling him as a witness and the party had reason to expect favorable testimony, but a party is not precluded by the testimony of a witness introduced by him from introducing other witnesses who will testify to the contrary (CDTP)

impeachment: provided for in Article 1 of the Constitution. This is the method for removing political and judicial officers before the expiration of their term. In the federal government it is accomplished by the passage of an impeachment resolution by a majority vote of the House of Representatives. Trial of impeachment proceedings is conducted by the Senate in which a two-thirds vote is necessary for conviction. Conviction of impeachment charges leads only to removal from office following which established judicial procedures may be instituted if a crime has been committed. In the states and municipalities legislative impeachment may be supplemented by popular recall. In American history there have been impeachments of one Senator, seven District Court judges, one Supreme Court Justice, one President, one Secretary of War, and one Commerce Court judge. Of these, three District Court judges and the Commerce Court judge were removed   (DOAH)

impeachment of witness: offering proof that a witness who has testified in a judicial proceeding is not worthy of belief; attack on the credibility of a witness   (LEV)

impedance: the opposition to the flow of alternating current in a circuit. May be determined by the ratio of an input voltage to the resultant current   (TDIAS)

impedance matching: making the impedance of a terminating device equal to the impedance of the circuit to which it is connected in order to achieve optimum signal transfer   (TDIAS)

impersonate: pretend to be someone else   (LEV)

implementation: the steps involved in installing and starting successful operation of a system and related equipment. These steps include feasibility study, applications study, equipment selection, systems analysis and design, physical installation, operation, and review   (ADPS)

implied: by implication; inferred; understood   (CDTP)

implosion weapon: a device in which a quantity of fissionable material, less than a critical mass, has its volume suddenly decreased by compression so that it becomes supercritical and an explosion can take place. The compression is achieved by means of a spherical arrangement of specially fabricated shapes of ordinary high explosive which produce an inwardly directed implosion wave, the fissionable material being at the center of the sphere   (DWMT)

impound: to restrain within limits   (CDTP)

imprison: to incarcerate; to lock up a person; to put someone in jail or prison   (LEV)

imprisonment: a sentence imposed upon the conviction of a crime: the deprivation of liberty in a penal institution

imprisonment for debt: detention on civil process for debt, formerly universal but since 1823, when Kentucky abolished it, prohibited or restricted by constitutional provisions in the States. Where it exists it is mostly applied against absconding debtors or those who have deliberately entered into a contract without means of ful-

filling their obligations   (DAP)
impulse: tendency to act without voluntary direction or reflection; action tendency appearing not to be traceable to stimulation (DOS)
impunity: exemption from punishment or penalty   (CDTP)
inadmissible: not proper to be admitted; not allowed   (CDTP)
inadvertent: heedless; careless; negligent   (CDTP)
inalienable: something which cannot be given away, waived, or taken away   (LEV)
inalienable rights: rights which inhere in a person and are incapable of being transferred. Such rights have been claimed under natural law   (DAP)
in articulo mortis: at the point of death   (CDTP)
in camera: a case heard when the doors of the court are closed and only persons concerned in the case are admitted   (CDTP)
incandescent: glowing with heat (as tungsten filament in an incandescent lamp)   (MPPF)
incapable: legally unable to do something. By law certain persons, or persons with defects, are considered incapable of violating the criminal law. Among these are children under certain ages, mental incompetents, and those who act through mistake of fact or in ignorance, etc.   (LEV)
incapacitating chemical agents: incapacitating chemical agents are capable of producing physiological or mental effects that prevent exposed personnel from performing their primary military duties for a significant period of time. There is, however, complete recovery from these effects. The incapacitating agents fall into two general groups: those which produce temporary physical disability, such as paralysis, blindness, or deafness, and those which produce temporary mental aberrations. The incapacitating agents suggest employment where military necessity requires control of

a situation but where there is good reason for not harming the surrounding population or even the troops. They also suggest covert uses either to confuse defense or retaliatory forces or to affect the rationality of an important leadership group at some particularly crucial point   (DWMT)
incapacitating gas: See incapacitating chemical agents
incarceration: imprisonment in a penal institution
incendiary: (1) any chemical agent designed to cause combustion, used esp. as a filling for certain bombs, shells, bullets, or the like (DWMT) (2) short for "incendiary bomb," "incendiary bullet," etc. (DWMT) (3) a person guilty of the crime of arson or the burning of a building   (CDTP)
incendiary bullet: a bullet having an incendiary charge, used esp. against flammable targets (DWMT)
incest: sexual intercourse, either under form of marriage or without it, between persons too nearly related in consanguinity to be entitled to marry   (CDTP)
incident light: a meter reading designed to be held at the subject position, facing the camera, to measure light strength at the subject plane   (MPPF)
incise (1) to cut or gash (CDTP) (2) an incised wound, a wound made by a cutting weapon   (CDTP)
incite: instigate some action; stir up trouble   (LEV)
inciting a felony: the acts by one person to incite or procure another person to incite or procure another person to commit a felony   (LEV)
incognito: in disguise; unrecognized   (LEV)
incompetent: not qualified, or able to do   (CDTP)
incompetent evidence: evidence which is not admissable under the established rules of evidence; evidence which the law does not permit to be presented at all, or in relation to the particular matter,

on account of lack of originality or of some defect in the witness, the document, or the nature of the evidence itself (43 S.W. 578) (CDTP)

incompetent persons: persons who by law have been declared not competent and therefore not responsible for their criminal acts. Such are young children and insane people. This type of person is also dealt with in the laws of evidence, where testimony from such persons is declared incompetent (LEV)

incontestible: indisputable (CDTP)

incorrigibility: the unmanageable or uncontrollable behavior of a child or minor which is generally classified as an act constituting juvenile delinquency, and hence warrants the authorities making the child behaving thus a ward of the juvenile court (DOS)

incorrigible: incapable of being corrected; bad beyond correction (CDTP)

increase twist: a gain twist in a gun barrel (DWMT)

incriminate: to reflect guilt; to impute guilt or violation of the law; to imply illegal activity or guilt; tend to show guilt; to charge with a crime or a fault (LEV)

incrimination: the disclosure of facts that render one liable to criminal prosecution. The accused cannot be compelled to be a witness against himself in a criminal case, but he may waive the privilege and take the stand voluntarily. A witness is immune from being required to incriminate himself in any proceeding, including a Congressional investigation, but he may not withhold facts that merely impair his reputation, nor even incriminating facts if he has been promised immunity from prosecution under the law. See unreasonable searches and seizures; Immunity Act (DAP)

incrimination, self-: compelling a person to be a witness against himself (CDTP)

inculpate: to imply guilt or wrongdoing; to accuse of crime; to involve in illegal or wrongful activity (LEV)

inculpatory: (law of evidence) showing involvement in criminal activity; tending to establish guilt; indicating guilt; reflecting guilt; incriminating (LEV)

inculpatory evidence: that without which a particular fact cannot be proved (Cal. C.C.P. Sec 1836) (CDTP)

incumbrance: with regard to property means a claim, lien, or liability attached thereto (CDTP)

indecency: it is a misdemeanor to expose the person or private parts thereof in any public place, or in any place where others are present (CDTP)

indecent: repugnant; in bad taste; not proper (LEV)

indecorous: violating good manners; contrary to the rules of good breeding (CDTP)

indefinite sentence: a system, not used in the United States, where a person is sentenced without minimum or maximum limitations and the length of time in prison is determined by his behavior and other factors (LEV)

in delicto: at fault (CDTP)

indemnification: compensation for loss or damage sustained because of improper or illegal action by public authority (DAP)

indentured: apprenticed (CDTP)

indeterminate: not settled or fixed; indefinite (CDTP)

indeterminate sentence: a sentence including a maximum and a minimum term for incarceration rather than a definite period. The amount of time served is determined by the paroling authority

Index Crimes: those crimes used by the FBI to determine the incidence of crime in the United States. The statistics appear in the *Uniform Crime Reports*

Index Offenses: the seven types of offenses reported by the FBI in *Uniform Crime Reports:* willful homicide, forcible rape, robbery, burglary, aggravated assault, larceny over $50, and motor vehicle theft

index of refraction: the mathematical expression of the deviation of a light ray entering a given medium at an angle to its surface (MPPF)

index register: a register to which an integer, usually one, is added (or subtracted) upon the execution of certain machine instructions. The contents of a register are used with other instructions to get effective instruction addresses during execution and for counting the performance of cycles. The register may be reset to zero or to any desired number (ADPS)

indictment: a formal written accusation, drawn up by the prosecuting officer of a state and returned as a true bill by a grand jury duly summoned and sworn, which charges one or more persons with having committed a serious offense against the law. *Cf.* information; presentment (DAP)

indigent: destitute (CDTP)

indirect addressing: the operand in an instruction is the address of a storage location containing the address of the desired operand; may be carried two or more stages (ADPS)

indirect evidence: evidence which does not actually prove the facts, but from which they may be presumed or inferred. *See* circumstantial evidence (CDTP)

individualized treatment: a philosophy of corrections which states that each individual is different in the causes of his criminality and in the particular manifestation of his criminality, consequently, corrections should look at the individual's unique cluster of traits and should devise a correctional treatment program based on his needs and deficiencies (POC)

indorsement: a writing on the back of a paper or document relating to the contents of such paper or document (CDTP)

industrial espionage: *See* espionage, industrial

industrial security: security and protection of industry and businesses (LEV)

Industrial Security Organization: American Society for Industrial Security, 404 NADA Building, 2000 K Street, N.W., Washington, D.C. 20006. Phone (202) 338-7676 (LEV)

industrial union: comprises all the workers of an entire industry which may include several different trades or occupations (CDTP)

inebriate: (1) to make one drunk; to intoxicate (LEV) (2) one who is often drunk (LEV)

inequity: unfairness; injustice (LEV)

inert: descriptive of the condition of a munition, or component thereof, which contains no explosive, pyrotechnic, or military chemical agent (DWMT)

inert ammunition: any shell, bomb, grenade, cartridge, rocket, or the like with its explosive charge, fuze, or other component essential to its normal functioning removed. Usu. collective. Ammunition with all explosives removed is usually described as completely inert or totally inert (DWMT)

inertia: Hurter and Driffield termed the exposure, indicated by the intersection of the straight-line part of the characteristic curve with the log exposure axis, the inertia. It is an inverse measure of the speed of the plate (MPPF)

inertia fuze: a kind of impact fuze that functions by inertial force. Upon impact of the projectile to which an inertia fuze is attached, either a striker will fly forward against a primer or detonator, or the primer or detonator will move forward against a fixed firing pin (DWMT)

in extenso: at full length, leaving out nothing (CDTP)

in extremis: at the point of death (LEV)

in facto: in fact; in deed (CDTP)

infamous: shameful or disgraceful. *See* infamous crime (CDTP)

infamous crime: crimes punishable by imprisonment in the state penitentiary

infamous punishment: punishment by imprisonment, also imprisonment at hard labor, particularly if in a penitentiary or state prison; or, sometimes, imprisonment at hard labor regardless of the place of imprisonment (CDTP)

infancy: in criminal law, where the accused has not arrived at such an age as to be able to distinguish between right and wrong (CDTP)

infant: a person who has not reached the age, usually 21 years, at which the law recognizes a general contractual capacity. In some states females become of age at end of 18th year, and statutes of some states make all persons adults upon their marriage. (14 R.C.L. 215, 216, 218, 219) (CDTP)

infanticide: murder of an infant immediately after birth

infernal machine: a "homemade-bomb"; an explosive device made to illegally destroy property or life (LEV)

infinity: (1) a distance so far removed from an observer that the rays of light reflected to a lens from a point at that distance may be regarded as parallel. (2) a distance setting on a camera focusing scale, beyond which all objects are in focus (MPPF)

in flagranti delicto: in the commission of crime; as "caught in flagranti delicto," in the actual commission of the crime (CDTP)

influence, political: the control, influence, or effect that a politician has in the operations of a law enforcement or other organization; the influence of a politician (LEV)

informant: (1) a person who, wittingly or unwittingly, provides information to agent, a clandestine service, or the police (DWMT) (2) in reporting, a person who has provided specific information and

is cited as a source (DWMT)

in forma pauperis [*Lat, lit in the form of a pauper*]: refers to permission to bring legal action without the payment of legal fees

information: (1) an accusation of criminal offense by a public officer such as district attorney. It is an accusation in the nature of an indictment presented by a competent public officer on his oath of office (2) knowledge that was not previously known to its receiver. Information can be derived from data only if the data are accurate, timely, unexpected, and relevant to the subject under consideration (ADPS) (3) (intelligence) unevaluated material of every description, including that derived from observations, reports, rumors, imagery, and other sources which, when processed, may produce intelligence (DWMT)

information flow analysis: a technique for organizing and analyzing the facts obtained about the flow of documents throughout an organization; can be performed manually or on a processor (ADPS)

information system redesign: stresses complete freedom to redesign both management decision rules and the entire data system (ADPS)

informer: a person who intentionally discloses to police or to a security service information about persons or activities he considers suspect, usu. for a financial reward (DWMT)

infra [*Lat*]: below, under

infraction: the violation of a law or contract (CDTP)

infrared light: a light having a wavelength greater than the visible red. It is in the region of 8,000 to 9,000 angstroms. Used in the police laboratory to read writings which have been erased or obliterated and those which are not visible to the naked eye because of a dark background. It is at the opposite end of the spectrum from ultraviolet light (LEV)

infrared (IR) motion detector: a sensor which detects changes in the infrared light radiation from parts of the protected area. Presence of an intruder in the area changes the infrared light intensity from his direction   (TDIAS)

in future: at a future time   (CDTP)

in general: the writ of habeas corpus is a remedy by which a person illegally deprived of his liberty may secure his release   (CDTP)

ingot: a mass of metal cast in a mold   (CDTP)

in initio: [*Lat*]: at the beginning

initialize: preparatory steps required before executing a repetitive cycle in order to get it started correctly; performed initially and not repeated within the program unless the cycle is started afresh   (ADPS)

injunction: an order issued by a court of equity commanding a person to do, or to refrain from doing, an act which would injure another by violating his personal or property rights. A mandatory injunction commands the specific performance of an act; a preventive injunction orders a person to desist from an act already commenced or contemplated; a preliminary, or interlocutory, injunction may be issued when a danger is immediately threatened and there is inadequate opportunity for a court to determine finally the rights of the parties; and a permanent injunction is the final decree of the court. The violation of an injunction is a contempt of court and may be punished by fine or imprisonment   (DAP)

ink eradicator: a chemical solution used for making writings invisible to the eye. By the use of certain laboratory methods such writings can be seen   (LEV)

inked fingerprints: fingerprint impressions taken after the fingertips have been inked, i.e., ink has been applied to the fingertips   (LEV)

in lieu of: in place of

in loco parentis [*Lat*]: in the place of a parent

inmate: one who is institutionalized in a correctional facility

innocent: not guilty of the charge; having done no wrong   (LEV)

in nomine [*Lat*]: in the name of

in personam: (law) a legal action against a particular person   (LEV)

in primis [*Lat*]: in the first place

input: the process of introducing data into the internal storage of the processor   (ADPS)

input-output control system: library routines that a programmer can select and tailor to the application by means of macro instructions and certain facts supplied in the source program for handling input and output for cards, tape, disk, drum, and printer. Involves a description of machine configuration and definition of files   (ADPS)

inquest: a legal inquiry to establish some question of fact; specifically: an inquiry by a coroner and his jury into a person's death where accident, foul play, or violence is suspected as the cause   (DAP)

inquiry processing: relates to electronic data processing computers. Incoming messages trigger a file search to retrieve information   (LEV)

inquisition: a detailed and intensive investigation or inquiry   (LEV)

in re: in the matter of, concerning; used to label judicial proceeding in which there are no adversary parties

in re Debs, 158 U.S. 546 (1895): a case in which the Supreme Court declared that the federal government has authority to protect its interests in the mails and the flow of interstate commerce and that such authority includes the discretionary power of its officers to secure injunctive relief from the courts   (DAP)

in re Gault, 387 U.S. 1, 18 L. Ed. 2d 527, 87 S. Ct. 1428 (1967): in this ground-breaking decision, with one justice dissenting, the Court held that the due process clause of the Fourteenth Amendment applies to proceedings in state juvenile courts to adjudicate

a juvenile a delinquent. (The Court indicates that a juvenile is entitled, in the adjudicatory stage of a juvenile court proceeding, to substantially the same rights that are accorded to an adult in a criminal court. A wide divergence of views have been expressed by legal commentators and juvenile court personnel as to what *Gault* means, and its prospective reach on juvenile courts. One thing that does stand out is that *Gault* requires a complete alteration of the nation's juvenile court system.)
(ILECJ)

in re Neagle: a case involving a federal deputy marshal who, in the performance of a duty imposed upon him by Presidential order, had killed an assailant and had been indicted for murder by a State court. The marshal's transfer from the State to a federal court for trial turned upon the question whether he acted under a "law of the United States." The Supreme Court [135 U.S. 1 (1890)] declared that the order given Neagle had been issued under the President's constitutional authority to see that the laws are faithfully executed and to preserve the peace of the United States, and, as such, was to be regarded as a "law of the United States." *See* In re Debs   (DAP)

in re Winship, 397 U.S. 358, 25 L. Ed. 2d 368, 90 A. Xr. 1068 (1970): the Court held, 5-3, through Mr. Justice Brennan, that the Due Process Clause requires that the conviction of a criminally accused be based upon proof of guilt beyond a reasonable doubt; the same standard applies to the adjudicatory stage of a juvenile delinquency proceeding in which a youth is charged with an act that would constitute a crime if committed by an adult. [Three standards of proof had been recognized in juvenile courts prior to *Winship*. They were (1) beyond a reasonable doubt, (2) by clear and convincing evidence, and (3) by a

preponderance of the evidence.]
(ILECJ)

in rem: a legal action against property   (LEV)

I.N.S. (INS): Immigration and Naturalization Service, under the U.S. Department of Justice

insane: not responsible for, or not guilty of, offenses

insignia: badges or distinguishing marks of office or honor; any characteristic marks or signs
(CDTP)

insolvent: having more debts than one is able to pay; bankrupt
(LEV)

insomnia: inability to sleep
(CDTP)

inspection: the examination of personnel, organizations, activities, or installations to determine their effectiveness and economy of operation, adequacy of facilities, readiness to perform assigned missions, or compliance with directives; the examination of material to determine quality, quantity, or compliance with standards
(DWMT)

inspector: a high-ranking law enforcement officer, who is usually immediately below the head of the agency   (LEV)

instanter: immediately; forthwith; without delay. Courts issue subpoenaes or other orders specifying they are returnable instanter, meaning the person upon whom served should perform, as ordered, immediately

in statu quo: in the former state; in the condition in which it was   (CDTP)

instigate: start; stir up; cause to happen   (LEV)

institutionalized personality: a non-clinical term that refers to an individual who has become so accustomed to existence in an institution that readjustment to life outside the institution is difficult

instruction: (1) a set of characters that defines an operation together with one or more addresses to cause the processor to operate accordingly on the indicated operands. Single, double, and triple address instructions have one, two, and three operand addresses, respectively (ADPS) (2) instructions to the jury during court proceeding

instruction routine: the set of instructions prepared to direct the processor to process data—for example, update master inventory files—or to perform some calculations (ADPS)

insubordination: defiance; resistance to authority; disobedience; willful failure to obey orders; open refusal to obey orders. Insubordination is a basis of disciplinary action in a law enforcement agency (LEV)

insulation: the condition of being so far removed and so well concealed in the organizational structure of a criminal operation that proof of guilt is made difficult. This is a term used to describe the position of the leaders in organized crime (LEV)

insulation, safe: fireproof material used between the outer and inner walls of a vault or safe so as to protect the contents against the effects of heat or fire originating on the outside of the container (LEV)

insurgency: a condition resulting from a revolt or insurrection against a constituted government which falls short of civil war (DWMT)

insurrection: a rebellion, or rising of citizens or subjects in resistance to their government. It shall consist in any combined resistance to the lawful authority of the state (CDTP)

integrate: to bring parts together and make a whole. In recent years has referred to intermixing people of different races, expecially the blacks and nonblacks (LEV)

integrated data processing: a business data system designed as a whole so that data are initially recorded at the point of origin in a form suitable for subsequent processing without manual recopying (ADPS)

intelligence: a function of law enforcement agencies concerned with the acquisition of information related to crime (TDPPC)

intelligence estimate: an appraisal of the elements of intelligence relating to a specific situation or condition with a view to determining the courses of action open to the enemy or potential enemy and the probable order of their adoption (DWMT)

intelligence files: files in which intelligence information is stored in a systematic manner (LEV)

intelligence quotient: designation of a person's mental development by use of a number arrived at by multiplying his mental age by 100 and then dividing this by his age in years (LEV)

intelligence test: a standardized test designed to determine the mental capacity of an individual as compared with criteria which have been developed from testing many people (LEV)

intelligence unit: a unit of a law enforcement agency charged with the duty of obtaining, filing, and dissemination of intelligence information (LEV)

intensification: the process of building up the density of a photographic image by chemical means (MPPF)

intent: (1) design, purpose, or resolve with which a person acts. It is a state of mind and direct proof is barely available. Intent is most commonly derived from the facts presented (2) mere intent to commit a crime is not a criminal violation. An overt act must accompany or follow the intent. The law in some states declares that a person intends to do what he does. Most crimes require intent as an essential element; however, some do not have this requirement, particularly those which are less serious and do not involve moral turpitude. Some crimes, such as theft, require specific intent, others require only general intent, and others may find that constructive intent is sufficient. In cases of culpable negligence and in minor offenses, such as traffic violations, no intent is required (LEV)

intent, specific: there are certain crimes of which a specific intent to accomplish a particular purpose is an essential element, and for which there can be no conviction upon proof of mere general malice or criminal intent. In these cases it is necessary for the state to prove the specific intent, either by direct or circumstantial evidence. (C.J. 16) (CDTP)

intent in cases of negligence: in crimes which consist in neglect to observe proper care in performing an act, or in culpable failure to perform a duty, criminal intent consists in the state of mind which necessarily accompanies the negligent act or culpable omission. The question of criminal negligence most frequently arises in connection with manslaughter, nuisance, escape (CDTP)

inter alia [*Lat*]: among other things

interception of prisoners' mail: the constitutional guaranty does not apply to the interception of a prisoner's mail by the jailor or warden, nor will it prohibit the turning over of such a letter to the prosecuting attorney, for use against the convict, by the warden who had a right to peruse the convict's mail (251 U.S. 15) (CDTP)

intercourse: communication; sexual intercourse is the sex act

interdict: to prevent or forbid

interdiction: the prevention or destruction of, or interference with, enemy movements, communications, and lines of communication, as by gunfire, shelling, or bombing; the action of making it very difficult for the enemy to move from one place to another (DWMT)

interference, restraint, and coercion: an employer who interferes with, restrains, or coerces employees in the exercise of the rights guaranteed to them under the act is guilty of an unfair practice (CDTP)

interior ballistics: the science of the movement of projectiles within the bore of a gun, with the combustion of powder, development of pressure, etc., to determine the effect of such factors as weight, size, shape, rifling, and so forth. Also called "internal ballistics" (DWMT)

interior perimeter protection: a line of protection along the interior boundary of a protected area including all points through which entry can be effected (TDIAS)

interlocutory: temporary; not final. An interlocutory degree is a temporary court order pending the final determination of the case or matter (LEV)

intermediary: a person who is the connecting link or message carrier between other people; go-between (LEV)

intermediate court: a court, known by various names, in a judicial hierarchy falling between the highest, or supreme, tribunal and the trial court. Its jurisdiction is usually appellate, but some States confer original jurisdiction in special cases such as election contests (DAP)

intern: (1) to shut up within a prescribed space (CDTP) (2) (also interne) a student in a field who works with an organization engaged in that type of work (LEV)

internal ballistics: *See* interior ballistics (DWMT)

internal standard: certain methods of analysis which are primarily qualitative can be made quantitative by the addition to the mixture to be analyzed of a known amount of a component not originally present—i.e., an internal standard. The ratio of the magnitudes of the effects produced by any original component and by the internal standard can then be used to measure the amount of the former   (FS)

internally stored program: a program prepared by programmers and converted to a suitable input media—cards, paper tape, magnetic tape—for reading into the processor and storing for execution when data are read in. Instructions in the program itself can be manipulated in much the same way as data and the whole program can be replaced by merely reading in another program
                                (ADPS)

International Association of Arson Investigators (IAAI): address: 20 North Wacker Drive, Chicago, Ill. 60606. Publishes *The Fire and Arson Investigators*   (LEV)

International Brotherhood of Police Officers (IBPO): first nationwide union of policemen, formed at Denver, Colorado, May 25, 1970
                                (LEV)

International Code: a code adopted by many countries to facilitate sight communication between persons of different nations. The code uses some 26 flags, each standing for a letter of the Latin alphabet. They may be used in different combinations, each signifying a certain message, or used as letters to spell out a word or sentence. If flags are not used, the international Morse code is employed   (DWMT)

International Court of Justice: an international tribunal of 15 judges, elected for nine-year terms by the General Assembly and Security Council of the United Nations, which hears and decides justiciable international disputes referred to it by the parties involved and gives legal advice to organs of the United Nations. Its jurisdiction and powers are defined by its statute, to which all member states of the United Nations are parties and to which nonmember states may adhere as

determined by the General Assembly and Security Council. The tribunal, with headquarters at The Hague, succeeded the Permanent Court of International Justice
                                (DAP)

international extradition: by treaties between the United States and most foreign countries, and by acts of Congress in pursuance thereof, provision is made for the extradition of fugitives from justice in special cases. This is a matter in which the states cannot act. A person extradited for one crime cannot be tried for another. By weight of authority, a person can be tried and punished for a crime committed in this country, though he has been forcibly abducted from a foreign country
                                (CDTP)

international law: an inchoate body of rules, classified as laws of peace, war, or neutrality, which deal principally with relationships between governments or one state and subjects of another. Although various usages existed in the relations between peoples of earlier civilizations, modern international law is a product of the European nation-state system. Early jurists, such as Gentilis and Grotius, endeavored to derive an interstate legal system from Roman and mercantile codes, contemporary custom, and reason. As international relationships grew more complex, new customary law developed and old rules were elaborated and interpreted in court decisions and studies by jurists. In the past century new rules have been decreed by states meeting in conferences, and in organizations like the League of Nations and the United Nations and their auxiliary agencies, thereby adding written international law to customary law. Controversies over the existence of international law are due partly to the common misconception that international law defines interstate relations as they ought to be and partly to the absence of a common superior to make it uniform and enforce it. Austinian jurists maintain that law must necessarily be handed down by a sovereign authority and be enforced by courts and police, whereas the test of a rule of international law is its universal acceptance by the community of states and their obedience to its mandates. That international law does not always coincide with international ethics is regrettable but technically irrelevant   (DAP)

international police forces: contingents of military forces of member states placed under United Nations control, as authorized by Article 43 of the U.N. Charter, for the purpose of preserving peace and preventing or resisting aggressive actions   (DAP)

INTERPOL (International Criminal Police Commission): directors of different countries working in co-operation through a central international office. First organized in 1923 with headquarters in Vienna, Austria, it operated until World War II. It was reestablished in 1946 and its headquarters moved to Paris, France, located in the Police Nationale. Among its branches is the International Bureau which works directly with the national bureaus of the participating nations. All participating nations except West Germany use the telegraphic address "INTERPOL." As of 1970 there were 107 nations, representing every continent, which were members. . . . It is a cooperative agency, is a clearinghouse for international exchange of information, doing no investigation itself. The United States joined the group, pursuant to federal legislation, in 1958. The United States Treasury Department is designated as the agency in this country responsible for liaison with INTERPOL   (LEV)

interpretive routine: an executive routine which, during the course of data-handling operations, translates a stored pseudo-code program into a machine code and immediately performs the indicated operations by means of subroutines   (ADPS)

interrogation (1) an inquiry, usually of a simple nature, . . . for which a quick reply is expected; requires the use of random-access equipment (ADPS) (2) an interview in great detail (LEV) (3) to probe with questions, persons believed involved in crime; to question in detail with the purpose of obtaining information relative to the involvement in crime of the person being questioned. The officer should know the requirements of the *Miranda* decision before interrogating   (LEV)

interrogatory: a question; sets of questions in writing intended to be proposed to a witness   (CDTP)

interrupt: the ability of one device to stop the operation of another to indicate readiness to supply or receive data; for example, tape units can interrupt the processor when ready to read or write   (ADPS)

inter se [*Lat*]: among themselves

intersection: point where one thing crosses another; where lines, which are not parallel, cross or where streets cross   (LEV)

interstate: between states. Many of the federal criminal laws are based on interstate commerce, i.e., movement from one state to another   (LEV)

Interstate Commerce Commission (ICC): an independent U.S. government agency whose responsibility is to regulate common carriers engaged in transportation   (LEV)

Interstate Compact for the Supervision of Parolees and Probationers: this agreement, first instituted in 1937, and entered into by all the states by 1951, allows for the supervision of a parolee or probationer in a state other than the state of conviction, provided that the parolee is a resident of that state, that his family lives there, or that the receiving state agrees to accept supervision. Extradition procedural requirements are waived under the Compact (LCC)

interstate extradition [*also called rendition*]: provision is made by the Constitution of the United States, by the acts of Congress in pursuance thereof, and by auxiliary statutes in the different states for the extradition of a person charged, in one state with treason, felony, or other crime, misdemeanor or felony, who shall flee from justice and be found in another state. In order that a person may be extradited, (1) he must be "judicially" charged with a crime in the demanding state, as by indictment or complaint; (2) he must have been in the demanding state, or he cannot have "fled from justice." It is sufficient, however, if, having been in the demanding state, and having committed a crime therein, he departed from it, though for another reason than to escape; (3) a person may be extradited for any crime against the laws of the demanding state. By the weight of authority, a person may be tried for a crime other than that for which he was extradited. By the weight of authority, also, the forcible abduction of a person from another state does not prevent his trial and punishment   (CDTP)

interstate highway: a road or highway located in more than one state. It usually means a highway extending across the nation (LEV)

interstate transportation: transportation or movement between states

interstate transportation of stolen motor vehicle (ITSMV): the federal law forbidding the interstate transportation of a stolen motor vehicle—U.S.C. Title 18; Sections 2311–13   (LEV)

interval timer: a laboratory clock that may be set to ring after a given time has elapsed   (MPPF)

interview: a conversation with a purpose; talking to a person about something   (LEV)

intestate: refers to dying without making a will

in the presence: an offense is deemed to have been committed in the officer's presence, if as a witness he can testify from actual knowledge to every element of the crime (152 Cal. 42)   (CDTP)

intimidate: to put one in fear; to frighten; to use threats or coercion to influence one to act or not to act   (LEV)

in toto [*Lat*]: in the whole; entirely

intoxicating liquors: any liquor used as a beverage, and which, when so used in sufficient quantities, ordinarily or commonly produces entire or partial intoxication; any liquor intended for use as a beverage or capable of being so used, which contains alcohol, either obtained by fermentation or by the additional process of distillation, in such proportion that it will produce drunkenness   (CDTP)

intoxication: it is a broad and comprehensive term having a different meaning to different persons. In the absence of any controlling, the word should be given a reasonable interpretation. It is defined as drunkenness; inebriety; inebriation; poisoning; the act of inebriating; or the state of being inebriated; the act of intoxicating or making drunk; the state of being intoxicated or drunk; the state produced by using too much of an alcoholic liquid, or by the use of opium, hashish, or the like   (CDTP)

Intoximeter: trade name of a device to test breath to determine amount of alcohol in the blood   (LEV)

intrastate: within a state

intrinsic evidence: evidence that is derived from a document and has no explanation   (CDTP)

intrusion: unauthorized entry into the property of another   (TDIAS)

intrusion alarm system: an alarm system for signaling the entry or attempted entry of a person or an object into the area or volume protected by the system (TDIAS)

invalid: null and void; of no force or authority (CDTP)

invasion phase: refers to that part of the development process during which the developer penetrates into the emulsion (MPPF)

inventory of property seized: an inventory of the property taken, made publicly at the place searched and verified in a prescribed manner. A failure to attach to the return an inventory required by statute is not a defect fatal to a warrant. It is merely a failure to perform a ministerial duty

inverse square law: a physical law which states that illumination intensity varies inversely with the square of the distance from a point source of light (MPPF)

investigation: a careful search for facts; examination, inquiry, search (LEV)

investigation, presentence: an official investigation, ordered by a judge or court, subsequent to conviction or a plea of guilty, for the use of the judge or court in arriving at the sentence to be given to the offender (LEV)

investigatory stage: that part of a police investigation during which suspicion has not yet been focused on a particular person or persons

invisible rays: those rays, such as X-rays, ultra-violet, and infra-red, which are not visible to the eye (MPPF)

involuntary manslaughter: is where a person in committing an unlawful act, not felonious or tending to great bodily harm, or in committing a lawful act without proper caution or requisite skill, unguardedly or undesignedly kills another (CDTP)

iodine: a chemical element which, among other things, is used in a crime laboratory to develop fingerprints on paper. The fumes of iodine are used for this purpose (LEV)

ionization smoke detector: a smoke detector in which a small amount of radioactive material ionizes the air in the sensing chamber, thus rendering it conductive and permitting a current to flow through the air between two charged electrodes. This effectively gives the sensing chamber an electrical conductance. When smoke particles enter the ionization area, they decrease the conductance of the air by attaching themselves to the ions, causing a reduction in mobility. When the conductance is less than a predetermined level, the detector circuit responds (TDIAS)

ipse dixit: he himself said it; dogmatism (CDTP)

ipso facto: by the fact itself; by the mere fact; by that very fact (LEV)

ipso jure: by the law itself (CDTP)

iris diaphragm: a lens control composed of a series of overlapping leaves operated by a revolving ring to vary the aperture of the lens (MPPF)

Irish system: a system of punishment developed by Sir William Crofton, which provided for progressive stages in the prison term and for release under supervision before final termination of sentence (DOS)

iron sight: any metallic gunsight, such as a blade sight, as distinguished from an optical or computing sight (DWMT)

irrefutable: impossible to disprove; undeniable; conclusive (LEV)

irrelevant: not related to; not applicable; off the point (LEV)

irresistible impulse: as used in criminal law, it refers to a situation where a person, due to a mental condition, is driven by impulse to do certain acts and his willpower or reasoning is insufficient to prevent it (LEV)

irrevocable: cannot be revoked or withdrawn; cannot be annulled (LEV)

irritant gas: a nonlethal gas that causes irritation of the skin and a flow of tears. Any one of the family of tear gases used for training and riot control. *See* tear gas (DWMT)

Irvine v. California, 347 U.S. 128, 98 L. Ed. 561, 74 S. Ct. 381 (1954): in this famous micro-phone-in-the-bedroom-case, the Court held (5–4), colored by five separate opinions, that the exclusion of illegally seized evidence from a state proceeding was not required by due process of law, no matter how shocking the violation, so long as there was no element of physical coercion. (This case limited the *Rochin* exception to *Wolf* to a situation involving coercion, violence, or brutality to the person. Perhaps never has a court so castigated police misconduct while affirming a conviction based on such misconduct. What law enforcement officers, by large, neglected to take seriously, was the clear warning to them to put their house in order, or face judicially imposed controls. . . .) (ILECJ)

isolated confinement: keeping a prisoner segregated from the other inmates

isotonic saline: a solution of salt having the same osmotic pressure as tissue fluids, in which cells will therefore neither swell through water passing in by osmosis, nor shrink by it passing out   (FS)

isotope: an atom consists of a nucleus of protons and neutrons surrounded by as many electrons as there are protons in the nucleus. This number—the atomic number—determines the chemical properties of the atom (i.e., its identity as an element). Elements composed of atoms having the same atomic numbers but different numbers of neutrons in the nucleus are chemically identical and are known as isotopes. They can be separated by very small differences in their physical properties. There is no inherent connection between the phenomenon of radioactivity and the existence of isotopes, but the terms are often associated because of the theoreti-

cal interest and technical importance of artificially made radio-active isotopes of nonradioactive elements   (FS)

issuance of search warrants: in general, the issuance of search warrants is regulated by constitutional and statutory provisions in the several jurisdictions. The effect of such regulations being that search warrants must be issued by one authorized to do so, upon application made by a proper party in proper form, showing probable cause, supported by oath or affirmation, and sufficiently describing the place to be searched and the thing to be seized (C.J. 56, 1209)   (CDTP)

issuance of warrant: to authorize the issuance of a warrant before indictment, there must be made before the proper magistrate a proper complaint, on oath or affirmation, showing that a crime has been committed, and that there is probable cause to suspect the accused. After indictment, the usual practice is to issue a bench warrant. An arrest under an insufficient warrant is in effect an arrest without any warrant at all, and if a warrant is necessary such arrest is illegal   (CDTP)

issue: (1) children, progeny (CDTP) (2) a single, certain, and material point, deduced from the pleadings of the parties, which is affirmed by the one side and denied on the other; a fact put in controversy by the pleadings; in criminal law, a fact which must be proved to convict the accused, or which is in controversy   (CDTP)

issue of fact: a question of fact to be determined by the jury (CDTP)

issue of law: can be decided only by the court   (CDTP)

itemize: to state in items   (CDTP)

Ivan V. v. City of New York, 407 U.S. 203, 32 L. Ed. 2d 659, 92 S. Ct. 1951 (1972): by way of a summary reversal of a New York Court of Appeals decision, the Court holds that *In re Winship* applies retroactively. (The reasonable doubt standard, because it is an essential of due process and fair treatment, applies to juvenile proceedings in which the youth is charged with an act that would be a crime if committed by an adult.) (ILECJ)

J

jack: an electrical connector which is used for frequent connect and disconnect operations; for example, to connect an alarm circuit at an overhang door   (TDIAS)
jacket: (1) a cylinder of steel covering and strengthening the breech end of a gun or howitzer tube (DWMT) (2) the water jacket on some machine guns   (DWMT)
jail: institution of the incarceration of individuals who have not been adjudicated, or if adjudicated, those who have been convicted of misdemeanor charges or have received sentences of less than one year   (IC)
jail time: credit allowed in a sentence for time the defendant spent in jail awaiting trial or mandate on appeal
jam: (1) of a machine gun or full automatic, semiautomatic, or other firearm, to stick or become inoperative because of improper loading, ejection, or the like (DWMT) (2) to make the transmissions of a radio unintelligible; to make a radio or radar set ineffective, either by the use of countertransmissions or by the use of a confusion reflector   (DWMT)
Jenkins v. Delaware, 395 U.S. 213, 23 L. Ed. 2d 253, 89 S. Ct. 1677 (1969): the court held, 7–1, that Miranda's standards do not apply to post-*Miranda* retrials of cases

originally tried prior to that decision   (ILECJ)
jeopardy: (1) danger; peril; hazard (LEV) (2) the danger of conviction and punishment which the defendant in a criminal action incurs when he is lawfully charged with a crime before a tribunal properly organized and competent to try him. When jeopardy begins may differ slightly among the states; often it is when the petit jury has been impaneled and sworn or if trial is before a judge without a jury, when the first witness is sworn   (LEV)
jimmy: (1) a tool such as a screwdriver, crowbar, tire tool, or other similar instrument, used to pry open doors, windows, etc. (LEV) (2) to pry open a door, window, drawer, etc. with a jimmy (LEV)
John Birch Society: a semi-secret, authoritarian, right extremist organization, founded by Robert Welch, a Massachusetts manufacturer, in Indianapolis, Ind., in 1958, that opposes Communism (its announced purpose), impugns the motives of moderate and liberal leaders, and opposes all forms of internationalism; named for a Georgia "fundamentalist" missionary preacher who was killed by the Chinese Communists following WW II   (DAP)
John Doe: a fictitious name often used when the true name of a defendant is unknown, or to indicate a person for the purpose of argument   (CDTP)
Johnson, 398 P.2D 420 (1965): this California decision extends the right to counsel to a defendant charged with a traffic offense, and cites numerous precedents for considering the right of a defendant to counsel as fundamental in every criminal case, large or small   (AOJ)
Johnson v. Avery, 393 U.S. 483 (1969): this ruling held invalid a prison regulation that forbade the legal assistance of a "jailhouse lawyer" to other inmates, reasoning that if no other legal assistance

was available, such a regulation resulted in a denial of access to the courts

Johnson v. New Jersey, 384 U.S. 719, 16 L. Ed. 2d. 882, 86 S. Ct. 1772 (1966): the Court held (7-2) that the *Miranda* rules apply only to cases in which the trial began after June 13, 1966, and, similarly, that the *Escobedo* rules affect only those cases in which the trial began after June 22, 1964—the respective dates of the two decisions   (ILECJ)

Johnson v. Zerbst, 304 U.S. 458, 82 L. Ed. 1461, 58 S. Ct. 1019 (1938): the court held that the Sixth Amendment includes the right of federal indigent defendants to be furnished counsel (ILECJ)

joint trial: a trial where two or more defendants, charged with the same crime, are tried simultaneously or together   (LEV)

judge: an officer who presides over and administers the law in a court of justice

Judge Advocate General: the chief legal officer of a branch of the military services who has, among other duties, supervision of military justice and of the proceedings of courts-martial and military commissions   (DAP)

judge-made law: (1) the common law as developed in form and content by judges or judicial decisions (DAP) (2) judicial decisions based on tortured constructions of the Constitution, or on the selection of unusual historical and legal precedents, or on unusual definitions of terms in "discovering" the law applying to a given case—used derogatively   (DAP)

judgement: the decision of a court of justice upon an action or suit

judicial notice: an act whereby a court, in conducting a trial or framing its decision, will of its own motion and without the production of evidence recognize the existence and truth of certain facts, having a bearing on the controversy at bar, which are matters of general or common knowledge of every person of ordinary understanding and intelligence. Among such matters are the laws of the states, historical facts, the Constitution, and principal geographical features   (LEV)

judicial powers: the powers of the courts to interpret the laws and constitutions, define the powers of the branches of government, distinguish between the powers of the national government and those of the states, maintain private rights against illegal public encroachment, and void legislative acts. These powers arise either out of constitutional grant or judicial interpretation in the rendering of decisions   (DOAH)

judicial process: the procedures taken by a court in deciding cases or resolving legal controversies

judicial reprieve: early form of judicial action related to modern-day suspended sentence. In order to give the defendant an opportunity to apply for a pardon from the crown, the judge could grant this temporary suspension of judgement or imposition of sentence (LCC)

judicial review: term popularly applied to the power of the Supreme Court to review the constitutionality of the acts of Congress and the states. The power to review federal legislation is not specially conferred upon the court but was assumed by it in the case of *Marbury* v. *Madison*, 1803. The brilliant exposition of Chief Justice John Marshall of the court, in this decision, has laid the groundwork for what has since been wholly accepted in American political and judicial thinking as a proper power of the court   (DOAH)

judiciary: a system of courts; also, the judges collectively. The federal judiciary consists of a Supreme Court, 11 courts of appeal, 90 or more district courts, a Court of Claims, a Court of Customs, and Patent Appeals, and a Customs Court, besides courts in the

District of Columbia and in the territories. In the states there is always one supreme court, sometimes called the Court of Appeals, or the Court of Errors and Appeals; a number of circuit courts with varying titles, holding sessions in every county; and minor courts presided over by justices of the peace or magistrates. Many states also have intermediate courts ranking just below the circuit courts; and specialized criminal courts, probate courts, domestic relations courts, and children's, juvenile, and adolescent courts. Formerly separate courts were organized to administer law and equity, but this distinction has disappeared almost everywhere. Such courts have been merged and in most states both legal and equitable remedies may be used in the same case. *See* constitutional courts (DAP)

Judiciary Act: passed by Congress in 1789, it created the office of Attorney-General, established the Supreme Court as provided in Article 111 of the federal Constitution, and created a series of federal circuit and district courts. The Supreme Court was to be staffed by a chief justice and five associate justices. The act gave to the federal courts the power of the judicial review over the decisions of the state courts with respect to the constitutionality of state or federal legislation. Although not specially conferred upon the Supreme Court the power of judicial review over acts of Congress was assumed by it in 1803 in the case of *Marbury* v. *Madison* on the basis of Section 13 of the law (DOAH)

judo: special ability or technique to physically control or cope with another person; jujitsu (LEV)

jujitsu: method of wrestling or physical combat with no weapons, that uses the weight and strength of an opponent to his disadvantage. Originated in Japan (LEV)

jump: to transfer control by executing an instruction that specifies the location of the next instruction to be executed by the program. Also called "branch" or "transfer." An *unconditional* jump is made to occur whenever the jump instruction is encountered in the program. A *conditional* jump transfers control only if some specified logical condition is satisfied; if the condition is not satisfied, the next instruction is taken in normal sequence (ADPS)

jurat: a certificate evidencing the fact or statement that an affidavit was properly made before a duly authorized officer (CDTP)

juridical: in accordance with law and with due process in the administration of justice; pertaining to the office and functions of a judge (DAP)

juridical days: days in which courts are in session

jurisdiction: range of authority; the administration of justice; authority or legal power to try cases

jurisdiction, federal: matters over which the federal government courts or agencies have control, supervision, or the right to investigate because of being a violation of federal criminal law or because of federal regulations (LEV)

jurisdiction in general: unless extended by statute, a state has jurisdiction only over those crimes committed within its territorial limits and crimes committed by its own citizens abroad. A crime must be prosecuted in the county in which the crime was committed, and it is generally held to have been committed in the county in which it was consummated. Thus, where a blow is struck in one country and a death ensues in another, the offense is generally held to have been committed in the latter; and when a person in one county commits a crime in another by means of an innocent agent, as the post office, the latter county has jurisdiction. The several states have each special statutes governing the subject of prosecuting homicides in the county where the body is found, giving jurisdiction to either county where the crime is committed partly in one county and partly in another, or to either state when the crime is committed partly in one county and partly in another (CDTP)

jurisdictional dispute: a conflict among labor unions for the control of employment in certain types of work or for the exclusive privilege of organizing employees in certain industries or areas (DAP)

jurisprudence: in the strict sense of the term, an act or a technique which comprises the systematized prediction of what the tribunals will do, with the practical aim of facilitating the work of counselors, judges, and other practitioners. In the light of the fact that there can and must be as many different jural techniques as concrete systems of law and corresponding types of inclusive societies, jurisprudence has rightly been characterized as "social engineering" according to particular social conjunctures and needs. Different trends in jurisprudence, viz.: historical, philosophical, analytical, normative, sociological, and realistic jurisprudence, are just different techniques of this analysis of concrete situations in the life of law and society.

Unfortunately, every interpretation of jural technique has manifested, more or less, a tendency to affirm itself also as separated theoretical knowledge of law, and in this way has contributed to the confusion of jurisprudence as a sum of varying techniques with such purely theoretical disciplines, as history of law, philosophy of law, and sociology of law. So arose a misleading enlargement of the term jurisprudence, which came to be conceived not only as an art, but also as science; the confusing of both led to dogmatism (DOS)

jurist: expert, scholar, or writer in law

juror: one who is sworn for or serves on a jury (LEV)

jury: a body of impartial laymen residing within the territorial jurisdiction of a court who are properly empaneled and sworn to render a true answer to a question of fact submitted to them. In U.S. courts the petit, or trial, jury consists of twelve persons, whose verdict must be unanimous in both civil and criminal cases; but jury trial is usually waived in civil cases and may be waived in criminal cases by the accused with the consent of the prosecutor and the trial court. For the trial of criminal cases (other than those involving capital crimes) several States employ fewer than twelve jurors or authorize verdicts by three-fourths or some other fraction. For civil cases a greater number of States have relaxed the requirement as to both the size of the jury and the majority necessary for a verdict, and several States provide for no jury except on the demand of one of the parties. A few States make the jury the judge of both the law and the facts of a case. *See* grand jury (DAP)

jury school, the first: was opened Jan. 16, 1937, by Federal Judge William Clark, U.S. District Court, District of New Jersey, in the Post Office Building, Newark, N.J. The first class was attended by 150 men and women. About 2,500 persons, mostly women, attended the course, designed to acquaint citizens with courtroom procedure and duties of jurors in considering evidence. The school was disbanded Dec. 10, 1937 (FAMOUS)

jury, grand: *See* grand jury

jury panel: a list of persons summoned as jurors for a particular term of court

jury wheel: a device for selecting by lot the names of jurors who are to be summoned to attend a particular court   (DAP)

jus gentium [*Lat*]: a body of law developed by Roman jurists for the trial of cases between Roman citizens and foreigners and provincials; subsequently held by medieval jurists to embody principles of right reason applicable to all human relationships; and invoked by Grotius and others as authority for rules of international law (DAP)

justice: (1) the title of a judge (DAP) (2) the process of adjudication by which the legal rights of private parties are vindicated and the guilt or innocence of accused persons is established (DAP) (3) in Platonic philosophy, the condition of harmony that exists among citizens of a state when each member cooperates in the affairs of the state and occupies a place according to his individual merits   (DAP)

Justice, Department of: an executive department established by Congress in 1870. The Attorney-General is the head of the department although that office was created by Congress in 1789 and became a cabinet position in 1814. The Federal Bureau of Investigation and the Bureau of Prisons are located within the Department   (DOAH)

justice, sporting theory of: the term applied to the contentious method of judicial procedure in criminal trials. In this form of procedure, characteristic of criminal procedure derived from Anglo-Saxon precedents, the prosecution presents all the evidence against the accused, the defense all favorable, while the function of the judge is to act as umpire to see that the game is played fairly according to the rules of procedure laid down in the law and in court decisions   (DOS)

justice of the peace: a subordinate magistrate, usually without formal legal training, empowered to try petty civil and criminal cases, and, in some states, to conduct prelimi-nary hearings for persons accused of a crime, and to fix bail for appearance in court. Justices of the peace are usually elective within a minor civil division, although their jurisdiction normally extends throughout a county. Except in a few States, their compensation is derived from fees, with the result that, in many cases, judgement is for the plaintiff   (DAP)

justifiable homicide: *See* homicide, justifiable

justify: to shift alphanumeric items to put their left (or numeric items to put their right) characters in the corresponding positions (ADPS)

Justinian Code: authored in 529 A.D. by Emperor Justin of the Byzantine Empire, this code became the standard of law in Europe during the Middle Ages. The Code was compiled by selecting all useful sections of all the existing or known codes and constitutions of the time   (LCC)

juvenile court: a specialized court having jurisdiction in cases of delinquent, neglected, or dependent children which seeks to determine the underlying causes of misconduct and provides for reformation through education, healthful activities, or institutional supervision. Juvenile defendants are entitled to be assisted by counsel and to have all the procedural safeguards that are accorded to adult defendants at all stages of police and judicial proceedings against them   (DAP)

juvenile court, the first: was the Juvenile Court of Cook County, known as the Chicago Juvenile Court, authorized April 21, 1899, and opened July 1, 1899, with Richard Stanley Tuthill as judge. On March 3, 1913, cases involving girls were tried by a woman judge, Mary Bartelme. Yearly, about 2,300 children's cases were heard (FAMOUS)

juvenile offender: a person under 16, 18, or (in some States) 20 years of age who has been found guilty of having committed offenses against the law   (DAP)

K

Kastigar et al. v. United States, 406 U.S. 441, 32 L. Ed. 2d. 212, 92 S. Ct. 1653 (1972): the court, 5–2, in opinion by Mr. Justice Powell, upholds the limited immunity the Organized Crime Control Act of 1970 gives witnesses who are compelled to testify before grand juries. "Transactional immunity would afford broader protection than the Fifth Amendment privilege, and is not constitutionally required," the Court declares. (Prosecutors had been waiting more than two years for the Court to settle the constitutional controversy. The federal law had been copied by several states.) (ILECJ)

Katz v. United States, 389 U.S. 347, 19 L. Ed. 2d. 576, 88 S. Ct. 507 (1967): the court with Mr. Justice Black dissenting, held that the Fourth Amendment "protects people, not places," and as a result, eavesdropping carried on by electronic means (equivalent to wiretapping) constitutes a "search" and "seizure" and is subject to the warrant requirements of the Fourth Amendment—overruling *Olmstead* v. *United States*. (This case involved the use of a nonpenetrating listening device to pick up a gambler's end of telephone calls he made from a public telephone booth.)   (ILECJ)

keeper: an acid chemical added to two-solution developers to prevent oxidation of the developing agent   (MPPF)

Kefauver Investigation: an inquiry into organized crime in interstate commerce by the Senate Crime Committee. The five-man committee was established on May 10, 1950 under the chairmanship of Senator Estes Kefauver to investigate illegal operations, the influence of crime on political leaders, the use of criminal funds for business investments, and the bribery of police by criminal elements. Former assistant district attorney of New York, Rudolph Halley, was named chairman of counsel. The first part of the Committee's work was ended April 30, 1951, at which time Senator Kefauver was replaced by Senator Herbert R. O'Conor of Maryland. By Feb. 28, 1951 the committee had interviewed 500 witnesses in New York, Chicago, Kansas City, Philadelphia, Los Angeles, and other large cities. These witnesses included public officers, political leaders, racketeers, and gamblers. In its first report the Committee declared that gambling involved over $20,000,000,000 annually. It recommended the establishment of a national crime commission, a federal ban on interstate transmission of bets and gambling information, a strengthening of federal law enforcement, and an improvement in federal tax laws to reach concealed profits from illegal deals. The committee highlighted the work of national crime syndicates whose control over state and local politics rendered them immune from prosecution. It charged that crime had infiltrated into such legal businesses as real estate, restaurants, laundries, hotels, and nightclubs. In its final report on Aug. 31, 1951 the Committee declared that conditions in the smaller cities were similar to those in large cities, and recommended attacking crime at the local level. It suggested a congressional appropriation of $100,000 to the private National Crime Coordinating Council to aid its work. It also recommended the continuance of crime investigation by other Senate committees and a widespread program of education, increased appropriations for inquiries, stricter enforcement of existing legislation, coordination of the work of private and public crime agencies, and the prohibition of political contributions by racketeers   (DOAH)

Kent v. United States, 383 U.S. 541, 16 L. Ed. 2d. 84, 86 S. Ct. 1045 (1966): the court, dividing 5-4, held that a juvenile court must conduct a hearing prior to the entry of a waiver order transferring jurisdiction to a criminal court. (The opinion is decided on statutory grounds as an interpretation of the District of Columbia *Juvenile Court Act.* The constitutional mandates which emerged later in *Gault* were obviously close to the surface.)   (ILECJ)

Ker v. California, 374 U.S. 23, 10 L. Ed. 2d. 726, 83 S. Ct. 1623 (1963): in the first state case to reach the Court after *Mapp,* dealing with *Mapp's* implication, the Court held (4-4) that searches by state police must conform to federal standards of reasonableness. Mr. Justice Harlan without passing on this question at all, cast the deciding vote to sustain the conviction on the ground the facts of the case showed no violation of "fundamental fairness" by the police. The Court held, further, that "States are not thereby precluded from developing workable rules governing arrests, searches, and seizures to meet the practical demands of effective criminal investigation in the states. . . ." (The lawfulness of petitioners' arrests by Los Angeles, Cal., police officers, was not vitiated by an unannounced entry. Compare Miller v. United States, 357 U.S. 301 1958, wherein an opposite result was reached by the Court with respect to the admissibility in federal courts of evidence seized under similar circumstances.)   (ILECJ)

key: (1) a term used in fingerprint classification. It is obtained by counting the ridges in the first loop appearing in the set of fingerprints. The loop may be either ulnar or radial, and in any finger except the little finger. The thumb may be used (LEV) (2) a field used for identification of a record; a selected element in each record used for sorting records into a desired sequence (ADPT) (3) the prevailing tone of a photograph, as high-key, low-key, medium-key   (MPPF)

keyboard: the whole arrangement of the keys on a card punch, teletype, or other data origination or communication device, consisting of special symbols, numerals, and letters   (ADPS)

keyhole: an elongated hole made by a bullet which is travelling partially or entirely sideways in its flight   (LEV)

key-punch: a typewriter-like machine for recording data on punched cards by punching a code into them, and, often, printing the same data on the cards   (ADPS)

K.G.B. (KGB): in the Soviet Union, the Commission of State Security, an intelligence system for detecting and accumulating information from abroad   (LEV)

kick: (1) the violent backward movement of a gun after it is fired, caused by the rearward force of the propellant gases acting on the gun (DWMT) (2) to move backward under the force of a propelling explosion. In both meanings, also called "recoil"   (DWMT)

kidnapping: federal law enacted in June, 1936, referred to as the Lindberg Act, as it was passed following the Lindberg kidnapping case. The law makes it a crime to carry away a person against his will, transport him interstate, and hold him for ransom, reward or otherwise. The law was later amended to create a presumption of interstate transportation after the victim had been kidnapped for twenty-four hours and not released. Many of the states have kidnapping laws. This is considered a major crime and many laws carry the death penalty, especially if the victim is not released unharmed   (LEV)

kilo: two and two tenths pounds

kilometer: 1,000 meters, 3,280.8 feet

Kirby v. Illinois, 406 U.S. 682, 32 L. Ed. 2d. 411, 92 S. Ct. 1877 (1972): in a 4-4 opinion by Mr. Justice Stewart (Mr. Justice Powell concurring in the result), the Court holds the formal charge—preliminary hearing, indictment, information, or arraignment—is the cutoff point when a person is entitled to have counsel present at a line-up. (The plurality opinion states the *per se* exclusionary rule of *Wade* and *Gilbert* doesn't apply to pre-indictment confrontations. However, wise prosecutors and law enforcement officers will continue to provide counsel at a line-up as very little weight can be given to a 4-4 decision.)   (ILECJ)

kiting, check: a system of building up deposit balances in a number of banks by drawing on a series of banks where small accounts have been opened. The kiter endeavors to gradually increase the amounts for the deposits. It is a scheme or procedure to defraud and is illegal in many states   (LEV)

kleptomania: a desire to steal or appropriate articles. In many cases psychopathic personalities manifesting the impulsive desire to steal come under the heading of fetish-thieves and during the act of stealing receive sexual gratification, sometimes to the point of orgasm   (LEV)

kleptomaniac: a person who steals uncontrollably or by mental compulsion; it is believed to be a mental or emotional disorder which results in compulsive acts of theft; one afflicted with kleptomania   (LEV)

known specimens: items of physical evidence which are obtained from known sources. Handwriting specimens taken from, or known to be the writings of, a person are such. A pistol taken from a person is a known specimen. Contrasted with questioned specimens. A crime laboratory, especially the FBI Laboratory, divides specimens into classes of known and questioned   (LEV)

Kodachrome: a commercial monopack produced by Eastman Kodak Company. It is processed by reversal to produce colored positive transparencies   (MPPF)

Kodalith: trademark of the Eastman Kodak Company for its line of high-contrast photochemical films and developers. Fine for copying spot maps   (MPPF)

Kovacs v. Cooper, 336 U.S. 77, 93 L. Ed. 513, 69 S. Ct. 448 (1949): the Court held that the state or municipality may prohibit on the streets the operation of sound trucks and loud speakers (ILECJ)

Kraeplin, Emil (*1856-1926*): a German physician and psychiatrist, Kraeplin set the first general standards for classifying mental disorders. He categorized a dichotomy based on a high degree of correspondence between mental type and temperament. One of his students, Ernst Kretschmer, carried on his work and became a leader in the field of modern criminal psychology. *See* Ernst Kretschmer

Kretschmer, Ernst (*1888-1964*): a German psychiatrist, Kretschmer thought mental disorders and crime were related. He felt that a psychotic individual should be given medical treatment, not confinement in jails. He is considered the father of psychopharmacology, the science concerned with the relationship of drugs to human behavior

Ku Klux Klan: (1) an organization founded in Tennessee in 1866 to reassert white supremacy in the South. Disguised in white masks and robes, members of the Klan rode at night, terrorizing, whipping, and committing other acts of violence (including murder) against [blacks] who persisted in voting and against their white leaders. After Congress in 1871 passed the Ku Klux Klan Act and the Force Act, the Klan adopted less violent means to accomplish its purpose (2) a national organization founded in 1915, and directed against Catholics, Jews, and foreigners, as well as [blacks], which was influential in several States for a brief period after World War I. The Klan still exists under several different names (DAP)

L

label: in symbolic programming, a name consisting of several alphanumerics (perhaps required to start with an alpha) to serve as an address while writing a source program; absolute addresses are assigned during assembly or compilation (ADPS)

labels: (1) a written or printed sticker on a tape reel or container identifying contents of tape (ADPS) (2) a record on tape describing file content (ADPS)

labor relations: the relations of employer and employee affecting the conditions of labor. As defined in federal and state labor relations acts, and interpreted by the courts, labor relations include matters dealing with wages, hours, tenure, security, hiring, discharge, union organization and activities, representation, and promotion (DOAH)

labor union: a combination or association of workers in some trade or industry, or in several allied trades, which exists for the purpose of securing by concerted action, the most favorable wages, hours, and conditions of labor, and otherwise improving their economic and social status (CDTP)

Laboratory, Law Enforcement Standards: the National Bureau of Standards operates a laboratory, located at Gaithersburg, MD, funded by the National Institute of Law Enforcement and Criminal Justice, to test equipment used in the field of law enforcement. The standards and information are available to law enforcement (LEV)

laches: an unreasonable delay in pursuing a legal remedy, concurrent with resulting prejudice to the opposing party, whereby a person forfeits his rights

lachrymator: a substance which causes severe weeping or tear production of the eyes. Such chemicals are used in tear gas (LEV)

lacing: a network of fine wire surrounding or covering an area to be protected, such as a safe, vault, or glass panel, and connected into a closed circuit system. The network of wire is concealed by a shield such as concrete or paneling in such a manner that an attempt to break through the shield breaks the wire and initiates an alarm (TDIAS)

land camera: camera developed by the Polaroid Corporation about 1950 which makes finished photographs in about 10 seconds by the diffusion-transfer process; also known colloquially as "Polaroid" camera (MPPF)

land diameter: the diameter of a bore as measured from the top of one land to the top of the land opposite (DWMT)

lands: the raised spiral surfaces between the grooves on the inside of a rifled gun barrel. The surfaces of the lands were the original inside surface of the barrel. The grooves are cut in the inside surface of the barrel thus leaving the lands. The purpose of the lands and grooves is to grip the bullet and cause it to rotate as it travels down the barrel (LEV)

language: expressions used to define the operations of a processor (ADPS)

lantern slides: small transparencies, either 2 x 2, 3-1/4 x 3-1/4, or 3-1/4 x 4, intended for projection (MPPF)

lanyard: (1) a cord or thong attached to a pistol butt; it is looped around the neck to prevent loss of the pistol (DWMT) (2) a cord or cable of specific length, usually with a hook on one end and a handle on the opposite end. It is designed to be attached to a component of the firing mechanism of a gun, rocket launcher, smoke-puff discharger, or the like and is used to fire the weapon by remote control (DWMT)

lanyard ring: a ring located on the butt of certain revolvers, or the side of certain saddle carbines, to which a lanyard can be attached (DWMT)

larceny: the unlawful carrying away of property with intent to deprive the owner of its possession. Grand and petite (or petty) larceny are the major classifications. They are differentiated by the amount or value of the property stolen. The amount varies from state to state in the United States (DOS)

lascivious: lewd, lustful

lascivious cohabitation: the act of living together as man and wife and indulging in sexual intercourse while unmarried

laser: (from Light Amplification by Stimulated Emission Radiation) an electrical/optical device for producing a coherent parallel beam of light—that is, one in which the light waves are all in phase. Such a beam can be made much more precisely narrow and parallel than can one of ordinary light (FS)

latent image: the invisible image formed in an emulsion by exposure to light. It can be rendered visible by the process of development (MPPF)

lateral chromatic magnification: refers to the formation of colored images of different sizes in the same plane, of an object removed from the principal axis of the lens (MPPF)

lateral pocket loop: a fingerprint pattern (LEV)

latitude: exposure latitude is the quality of a film, plate, or paper which allows variation in exposure without detriment to the image quality. Development latitude is the allowable variation in the recommended developing time without noticeable difference in contrast or density (MPPF)

laudanum: opium derivative, the drug is a dark brown liquid, used to allay pain or induce sleep (CDPT)

laundry marks: identification marks or numbers put on clothing or other washable materials processed by a public laundry or a laundry doing business for many people. These may be visible or invisible. Such marks may be helpful in a criminal investigation (LEV)

Lavater, Johan Casper (1741-1801): a Swiss scholar and theologian, Lavater published a four-volume work on physiognomy called "Physiognomical Fragments," which made extravagant claims about the alleged relation between facial features and human conduct. His writings were the forerunner to the physical type theory

law: (1) a general rule for the conduct of members of the community either emanating from the governing authority by positive command or approved by it, and habitually enforced by some public authority by the imposition of sanctions or penalties for its violation (DAP) (2) the whole body of such rules, including constitutions, the common law, equity, statutes, judicial decisions, administrative orders, and ordinances, together with the principles of justice and right commonly applied in their enforcement (DAP)

law book, published, the first: was William Penn's *The Excellent Priviledge of Liberty and Property being the birth-right of the freeborn subjects of England*. Containing (1) Magna Charta, with a learned comment upon it; (2) the confirmation of the charters of the Liberties of England and of the Forrest, made in the 35th year of Edward the first; (3) a statute made the 34 Edw. 1. commonly called De Tallageo non concedendo; wherein all fundamental laws, liberties, and customs are confirmed. With a Comment upon it; (4) an abstract of the patent granted by the king to William Penn and his heirs and assigns for the province of Pennsylvania; (5) and lastly, the charter of liberties granted by the said William Penn to the freemen and inhabitants of the province of Pennsylvania and territories thereunto annexed, in America. A book containing 83 pages, was printed by William Bradford in Philadelphia, Pa., in 1687 (FAMOUS)

law, criminal, positivist school of: this is a term applied to legal scholars who in the latter half of the 19th century urged the reform of the criminal law in the light of scientific discoveries concerning the causation of criminal conduct. The impetus was derived from the Comtian positivistic philosophy on the one hand and the researches of the criminal anthropologists on the other. Its leading exponent was the Italian scholar Enrico Ferri and it greatly influenced criminal law reform, particularly on the continent (DOS)

law, poor: an antiquated name still frequently applied to the body of laws governing the administration of public assistance. The name dates from 16th-century England and is best known in relation to the Elizabethan Poor Law of 1603, which consolidated the numerous poor laws passed by Parliament in the century preceding. The name was borrowed by the colonies and continued in use to designate various state laws dealing with relief of poor and dependent persons. Public welfare and public assistance are terms which are gradually replacing the term "poor law." In a wider sense poor law is synonymous with a degrading and short-sighted system of poor relief based upon severe laws of settlement, pauper oaths, standards of relief below that of the poorest paid common laborer, and relief in kind (DOS)

Law, Poor, Elizabethan: a law enacted by the English Parliament in 1603 summarizing and consolidating a variety of laws concerning poor relief passed during the preceding century. The law required the local community to assume responsibility for the care of its own poor, established the principle of settlement and destitution as tests of eligibility for assistance, and decreed that relief could be granted only in return for work in places provided for housing the poor. The principles of public assistance established by the Elizabethan Poor Law governed the administration of relief in England and the United States for over 300 years (DOS)

law enforcement: the field of crime prevention, enforcement of the criminal laws by investigation and apprehension of the offenders, and preserving the peace; persons and/or agencies involved in law enforcement activities. Some include prosecuting officials, criminal courts and corrections in the field of law enforcement (LEV)

Law Enforcement Assistance Administration (LEAA): the agency of the U.S. Department of Justice responsible for administering law enforcement grants and loans under terms of the Omnibus Crime Control and Safe Streets Act of 1968

Law Enforcement Intelligence

Units (L.E.I.U.): an association of law enforcement intelligence officers and units, participated in by officers from some 150 communities, cooperatively exchanging information concerning criminal activities and criminals   (LEV)

law of nations: called international law, and sometimes public law, includes those rules which define and regulate the conduct of Nations in their intercourse with each other. It consists of: (1) a code of what may be called natural law, dictated by the sentiment that nations should have intercourse with each other; (2) a system of unwritten law, depending upon principles of comity or international courtesy; (3) a code of positive law, derived from ancient codes, treaties, judicial decisions, state papers, and the opinions of great writers upon the subject whose experience as statesmen gives their words authority   (CDTP)

laws: the individual items within the broad field of law, natural or manmade. Scientific laws are particular statements of generalized truths, especially those having to do with causative sequence. Juristic laws are the items on the statute books of states, in ordinary usage the current statutes of any particular state. These fall into three main categories: (1) general laws, which apply to all citizens or persons, or to all persons within legally recognized groups or classes, and (2) special laws, enacted for particular purposes, and (3) private laws, passed for the benefit of particular individuals. Scientific laws are divisible into (1) quantitative laws, which are principles or generalizations explaining the aspects of quantity or of metrication within a field of operations, and (2) qualitative laws, which are principles or generalizations explaining the aspects of quality or non-metricization within a field of operations   (DOS)

laws, compilation of U.S., the first: codifying the laws in force was *The Public Statutes at Large of the United States of America,* from the organization of the government in 1789 to March 3, 1845, arranged in chronological order with references to the matter of each act and to the subsequent acts on the same subject, and copious notes of the decisions of the Courts of the United States construing those acts and upon the subjects of the laws with an index to the contents of each volume . . . . The first volume, containing 777 pages, was published in 1845 in Boston, Mass., by Charles C. Little and James Brown. It was edited by Richard Peters. Publication was authorized by act of March 3, 1845 (5 Stat. L. 798), "a resolution to authorize the Attorney General to contract for copies of a proposed edition of the laws and treaties of the United States"   (FAMOUS)

laws, compilation of colonial, the first: was *The Book of the General Lauues and Libertyes concerning the inhabitants of the Massachusetts collected out of the records of the General Court for the several years wherein they were made and established and now revised by the same Court and disposed into an Alphabetical order and published by the same Authoritie in the General Court held at Boston the fourteenth of the first month Anno 1647.* The work was published in Cambridge, Mass., in 1648 and sold by Hezekiah Usher in Boston, Mass.   (FAMOUS)

laws, sumptuary: laws designed to regulate the expenditure of persons for food, clothing, and other consumption goods, especially luxuries; to restrict or forbid the use of certain goods. A common method of control is through taxation   (DOS)

lead: (1) bullets or projectiles in general (DWMT) (2) the action of aiming ahead of a moving target with a gun, bomb, rocket, or torpedo so as to hit the target, including whatever action is necessary to correct for deflection (DWMT) (3) the lead angle (DWMT) (4) the distance between the moving target and the point at which the gun or missile is aimed (DWMT)

leading: the depositing of lead on the surface of the inside of the gun barrel (LEV)

leading question: a question asked a witness during a trial or court proceeding which suggests an answer and thus may elicit an answer which might otherwise not be recalled by the witness. Leading questions are not ordinarily allowed, however under certain conditions leading questions are permissible (LEV)

leader: a strip of film or paper at the beginning of a roll of film which is used for loading the camera or projector (MPPF)

leaf sight: a rear sight for small arms, hinged so that it can be raised for aiming or lowered to keep it from being broken when not in use. A leaf sight often contains a peep sight that can be moved up and down to make adjustments for range. Sometimes two or three leaves of different sizes are hinged on the same pivot to adjust for range (DWMT)

lease: a contract between two parties which specifies the terms and conditions under which one party will obtain the sole use of a product that is owned by the other party (TDPPC)

lease purchase: a particular type of lease contract which provides an option under which the lessee may purchase the item being leased (TDPPC)

leed: the pitch or rate of twist in the rifling of a pistol or rifle barrel (CDTP)

left: groups ranging in opinion from liberals, radicals, socialists, and labor parties to Communists, their common characteristics being advocacy of change, their differ-

ences being not only in degree, but in methods of accomplishing change—so-called because, from the period of the French Revolution, party members belonging to such groups have been seated to the left of the presiding officer as he faces a Continental European legislature (DAP)

Left, New: a designation used by certain activist groups in the United States, active in the late 1960s and early 1970s. They allegedly had as their goals the changing of structure and operations of the government, especially as concerns certain policies relative to war and related activities (LEV)

leg irons: shackles; apparatus consisting of anklets which are secured around each leg of a person and which are connected with a chain. They impede the speed of walking or running by restricting the length of the step and by their cumbersomeness (LEV)

legal: conforming or according to a law

legal counsel for police: attorneys who work and are employed by law enforcement agencies as legal counsellors, advisors, or house counsel (LEV)

legal duty: that which law requires to be done

legal ethics: customs among those in the legal profession involving their responsibilities toward each other, the courts, and their clients

legal evidence: a broad general term meaning all admissible evidence, including both oral and documentary, but with a further implication that it must be of such a character as tends reasonably and substantially to prove the point, not to raise a mere suspicion or conjecture (CDTP)

legal fiction: a condition assumed to be true in law, regardless of its actual truth or falsity—sometimes used by judges so that a new subject for which no rules of law have been formulated may be em-

braced within existing rules of law
(DAP)

legal personality: the legal status accorded a corporation or other artificial person entitling it to hold and administer property, to sue in the courts, and to enjoy many of the rights and assume many of the liabilities of a natural person (DAP)

Legal Points: a monthly publication by the ICAP Police Legal Center, Research Division, Washington, D.C. 20036. Contains valuable information on points of value in the legal field for law enforcement (LEV)

legal provocation: provocation that can be used as a legal defense for an act

legation: the official establishment of the diplomatic personnel of a nation in a foreign country. It is lower in rank than an embassy (LEV)

legislation: laws of general application, enacted by a law-making body

legislative power: the power to make law. Generally the power to make policy. In the federal Constitution this power is delegated to Congress in Article I. Under the separation of powers principle legislative powers are theoretically exercised only by the legislature. In fact the President exercises considerable legislative powers, and the Supreme Court's power of judicial review may be considered a legislative power as well (DOAH)

lens: an optical term applied to a piece of glass which is bounded by two spherical surfaces or a plane and a spherical surface. The term is also applied to a combination of several glass elements, such as a photographic objective (MPPF)

lens board: a detachable board carrying a lens and a shutter, which is fastened to the front of the camera (MPPF)

lens cap: a cover used to protect a lens from dust and damage when not in use (MPPF)

lens hood: a shade to keep extraneous light from the surface of a lens (MPPF)

lens paper: a fine soft tissue paper used for cleaning lenses (MPPF)

lens shade: a detachable camera used to shield the lens from extraneous light rays (MPPF)

lesbianism: Sapphism. Homosexual relations between women (methods, including oral stimulation of the genitals and the wearing of an artificial phallus by one partner). The term is derived from the extreme sensuality of the women of Lesbos, circa 600 B.C., where Sappho, a famous poetess of aristocratic birth, wrote passionate love lyrics and reputedly indulged in erotic relations with her female pupils (DOS)

lessee: the party of a lease contract who is contracting for the sole use of a product owned by another party (TDPPC)

lesser included offense: a separate offense, all of the elements of which are alleged, among other elements, in an offense charged in the indictment

lessor: the party of a lease's contract who owns the product that is being leased (TDPPC)

lethal chamber: a room or place within or adjacent to a prison or jail where prisoners convicted of capital crimes are put to death (DOS)

L.E.T.S. (LETS): National Law Enforcement Teletype System, a cooperative interstate system of information exchange between law enforcement agencies, started in middle 1960s (LEV)

leuco-malachite test: a preliminary test for the presence of blood. A positive test is not conclusive but a negative reaction eliminates blood as being the substance tested (LEV)

level: in COBOL, the status of one data item relative to another, indicates whether one item includes subsequent ones or whether, as reflected in the numbering scheme which must follow certain rules, data items are independent of each other (ADPS)

leverage: the number of instructions compiled in the object program for each instruction written in the source program. From the programmer's viewpoint, leverage is an indication of the power of a programming language and its processor (ADPS)

lex talionis: (1) law of retaliation; for example, "an eye for an eye and a tooth for a tooth" (DOS) (2) in modern times, also the acts of one nation in retaliation for the acts of another. These may include amicable retaliatory acts (DOS)

liaison: contact or connection between groups or individuals (LEV)

libel: (1) the plaintiff's written statement, which is the first proceeding in an admiralty case (DAP) (2) a defamatory writing, picture, or effigy published without lawful justification which imputes to a person the commission of a criminal act, tends to injure him in his trade or profession, or exposes him to ridicule, contempt, or odium. The injured person may bring action for damages. Where malice is shown, the act of publication may constitute a crime (DAP)

liberal: (1) one who is not narrow-minded; a liberal thinker; one who espouses the cause of change (LEV) (2) tolerant (LEV)

library: an organized collection—for example, tape-file library or subroutine library (ADPS)

license: permission by public authority to perform a certain act (as drive a car) or to engage in a business or profession, often granted only after the passing of a qualifying examination or the payment of a fee, or both; and revocable if the terms of the license or the laws or regulations concerning the conduct of the business or profession are violated. Licensing is an administrative device for expediting mainte-

nance of legally stipulated professional or vocational standards or for correction of violations, without the necessity of bringing prosecutions in the courts. The licensee may, however, appeal to the courts to overturn a ruling of the enforcement officers (DAP)

licentious: lustful; debauched; immoral, lewd; lacking moral restraints (LEV)

lid: one ounce of marihuana in a plastic container (LEV)

lie detector: accurately speaking, the "lie detector" consists of a number of instruments combined into one, commonly referred to as a polygraph. It is made up of a cardiograph which records the pulse wave, the sphygmograph which records the blood pressure, the galvanograph which records the galvanic reflex, and the pneumograph which records the respiratory movements. Such involuntary changes in bodily processes as one undergoes when one is questioned concerning a crime are recorded and compared with the record of the same subject made during an initial test period when no questions concerning the crime are asked. Deviations in the readings provide the basis for interpreting whether deception has occurred (DOS)

life cycle costing: a method for comparing the effect of alternative decisions on the cost of an item or project over the term of its useful life. In law enforcement, fleet management (TDPPC)

light fog: the fog produced over an image by accidental exposure of film to extraneous light (MPPF)

light intensity cutoff: in a photoelectric alarm system, the percent reduction of light which initiates an alarm signal at the photoelectric receiver unit (TDIAS)

light trap: a system of staggered passageways of double doors so that a darkroom may be entered or left without light being admitted (MPPF)

limitations of actions: the period of

time after a crime is committed during which an indictment must be presented

limited entry: a notation restricted to yes, no, X, and blank in a cell in a decision table. Conditions and actions are restricted to the stubs of the rows (ADPS)

limited waiver: the limits of the right of the officers to search are only coextensive with particular search consented to; thus a consent to a search of a portion of a structure gives no right to search the whole structure, nor will a consent to search a house for a man permit a search of it for an illicit still; nevertheless, if officers are allowed upon defendant's premises by his consent, and while thereon, observe a felony being committed in their presence, then a search of defendant's premises is authorized. One consenting to search cannot attack the validity of affidavit upon which search warrant was based. (249 S.W. 769; C.J. 56, 1178) Consent to search renders the validity of the search warrant immaterial (273 U.S. 768) (CDTP)

Lindbergh Law: an act of Congress, May 18, 1934, which, under penalties of death or imprisonment, forbids the transportation in interstate or foreign commerce of any person who has been kidnapped and held for ransom. Failure to release a person within seven days after he has been kidnapped creates the presumption that he has been transported in interstate or foreign commerce (DAP)

line: in public administration, that portion of the civil service, from highest officials to office employees and field force, which has the responsibility for carrying out the basic functions for which an administrative department is established—distinguished from staff (planning) and housekeeping (auxiliary) functions (DAP)

line amplifier: an audio amplifier which is used to provide preamplification of an audio alarm signal

before transmission of the signal over the range of signal transmission (TDIAS)

line copy: original material to be copied, containing only black and white areas or lines, without halftones (MPPF)

line of aim: the line from a person's eye, such as that of a gunner or bombardier, through a sight, along which aim is taken (DWMT)

line of elevation: the prolongation of the bore when the piece is set to fire (DWMT)

line of fire: the flight path or paths followed by projectiles fired from a weapon or group of weapons (DWMT)

line of position: the straight line connecting the point of origin with the point of position. The point of origin is usually the gun or a position-finding instrument. Thus, corresponding to the three positions of the target, there are the line of position at observation, the line of present position, and the line of future position (DWMT)

line of sight: the line of vision; the optical axis of an observation instrument; the straight line between an observer's eye and a target or other observed object or spot, along which sight is taken (DWMT)

line of site: the straight line between the origin of the trajectory and the target. It is sometimes called "line of position" (DWMT)

line screen: a finely lined glass screen used in photomechanical reproduction to produce a halftone negative. Often referred to as a halftone screen (MPPF)

line sensor (detector): a sensor with a detection zone which approximates a line or series of lines, such as a photoelectric sensor which senses a direct or reflected light beam (TDIAS)

line supervision: electronic protection of an alarm line accomplished by sending a continuous or coded signal through the circuit. A change in the circuit characteris-

tics, such as a change in impedance due to the circuit's having
been tampered with, will be detected by a monitor. The monitor
initiates an alarm if the change exceeds a predetermined amount
(TDIAS)
line-up, police: a procedure of
placing crime suspects with others, not believed implicated in the
crime, in a line or other position
so that witnesses can view them
for the purpose of making possible identifications. Since 1967, in
the case of U.S. v. Wade, 338 U.S.
218, the court requires that an
attorney for the accused be present during the line-up   (LEV)
link: in communications, a general
term used to indicate the existence of communications facilities
between the two points (DWMT)
link belt: an ammunition feed belt
for an automatic weapon in which
metal links connect the cartridges
and with them form the belt
(DWMT)
linked ammunition: cartridges fastened to one another side by side
with metal links, forming a belt
for ready feed to a machine gun.
As the linked ammunition runs
through the breech mechanism,
the links and cartridge cases
separate   (DWMT)
list: a single series of similar items—
for example, the name of states
and their current census; a one-
dimensional array   (ADPS)
literal: one or more characters used
to represent the value "literally"
expressed   (ADPS)
litmus paper: paper impregnated
with azolitmin, used for testing
solutions; turns red in acid solutions, blue in alkaline baths
(MPPF)
Little Rock riots: disorders at-
tending efforts to desegregate the
Little Rock, Ark., schools under a
court order which, in September,
1957, led President Eisenhower to
send troops to the city to compel
a reluctant governor and citizenry
to permit [black] children to at-

tend public schools previously
reserved for whites   (DAP)
live ammunition: ammunition containing explosives or active chemicals as distinguished from inert or
drill ammunition   (DWMT)
lividity, postmortem: a condition
caused by the draining of the
blood in a dead body. The blood
flows by gravity to the lower parts
of the body and causes a peculiar
discoloration—usually bluish-red.
The condition appears in about
three hours after death. Due to
pressure on the part of the body
touching the surface upon which
the body rests that part does not
assume the discoloration. If the
body is moved after lividity has
developed and is placed in a different position this will be indicated by lividity   (LEV)
Livingston, Edward (1764-1836):
America's greatest penologist, considered to have been the first legal
genius of modern times. Livingston
wrote a system of criminal jurisprudence for the State of Louisiana and subsequently served as
Secretary of State and Minister to
France under Andrew Jackson
load: (1) a single round of ammunition (DWMT) (2) a command to
put ammunition into a gun
(DWMT) (3) to stow supplies into
a boat, vehicle, ship, or aircraft
(DWMT)
loader: a mechanical device which
loads guns with cartridges
(DWMT)
loading angle: the angle of elevation
specified for loading a particular
weapon with its ammunition
(DWMT)
loading gate: a magazine or breech
cover that is hinged and closed except during loading and unloading
operations   (DWMT)
loan shark: one who loans money
at a very high interest rate—usually an unlawful rate   (LEV)
lobbies: private organizations of
special interest groups which seek
to interest legislatures in enacting
or defeating proposed legislation.

The name derives from the habit of the spokesmen of these organizations meeting representatives in the lobbies of legislative halls for the purpose of invoking their aid. The typical methods of lobbying activity have been promises of financial aid, drafting of bills, campaign assistance, and threats of retaliation for failure to support desired legislation. It is well known that bribery and other corrupt practices have also been employed... (DOAH)

local alarm: an alarm which when activated makes a loud noise (*See* audible alarm device) at or near the protected area or floods the site with light or both (TDIAS)

local alarm system: an alarm system which when activated produces an audible or visible signal in the immediate vicinity of the protected premises or object. This term usually applies to systems designed to provide only a local warning of intrusion and not to transmit to a remote monitoring station. However, local alarm systems are sometimes used in conjunction with a remote alarm (TDIAS)

local reduction: the reduction of certain densities of a negative by the local application of a reducer or by rubbing with an abrasive paste (MPPF)

locality of crime against the United States: the Constitution and the acts of Congress provide the right to be tried where the offense was committed. Trials shall be held in the state where the said crime was committed; but, when not committed within any state, the trial shall be at such place or places as the Congress may, by law, have directed; and that persons accused of crime shall have the right to trial by a jury of the state and district wherein the crime shall have been committed, which district shall have been previously ascertained by law; and there are various provisions by act of Congress. Crimes committed on the high seas, or elsewhere out of the jurisdiction of any particular state or district, are to be tried in the district where the offender is first found, or into which he is first brought (Rev. U.S. Statutes 730) (CDTP)

lock: (1) the position of a safety mechanism which prevents a weapon from being fired (DWMT) (2) the fastening device used to secure against accidental movement, as on a control surface (DWMT) (3) to secure or make safe, as to set the safety on a weapon (DWMT) (4) to lock on; to fasten onto and automatically follow by means of a radar beam. Said of a radar set or antenna (DWMT) (5) the part of apparatus of a firearm by means of which the charge is exploded, such as a matchlock, miquelet, percussion lock, wheelock, or flintlock (DWMT)

Locke, John (*1632–1704*): an English philosopher, Locke supposed that men came to an agreement, or a social contract with one another to surrender their individual rights of judging and punishing not to a King, but to the community as a whole. He also advocated that should the sovereign government violate any of the laws, the community has the right to withdraw from him his authority

locking lugs: metal projections on the bolt of a small-arms weapon which cam into recesses cut in the side of the receiver to lock the weapon prior to firing (DWMT)

logical operation: (1) an operation in which a decision affecting the future sequence of instructions is automatically made by the processor. The decision is based upon comparisons between all or some of the characters in an arithmetic register and their counterparts in any other register on a less-than, equal-to, or greater-than basis, or between certain characters in arithmetic registers and built-in standards (ADPS) (2) operations on a word on a character-by-character basis without regard for other characters as in "logical and" and "logical or" operations (ADPS)

logistical supply vehicle: a vehicle, generally a van-type or a station wagon, used to carry extra supplies, special equipment, or emergency equipment for police activities in special situations (TDPPC)

logistics: the area of activity in a police operation pertaining to supplies, equipment and facilities, the maintenance and support of personnel (LEV)

Lombroso, Cesare (*1836-1909*): Lombroso is considered the father of modern criminology and the original spokesman for the positivist viewpoint. In his book *The Criminal Man*, Lombroso maintained that the criminal type can be identified by a number of different physical characteristics. He believed that the victim should be compensated by the criminal and that society should be protected from these degenerate and atavistic criminal types. He also advocated the use of indeterminate sentences, but favored the death penalty as a last resort

long scale: a long-scale or contrast negative is one in which the least dense portion will transmit 50 to 100 times more light than the densest portion. A long-scale or soft printing paper is one requiring 50 to 100 times the barely visible tint exposure in order to produce the deepest black (MPPF)

loop: (1) an electric circuit consisting of several elements, usually switches, connected in series (TDIAS) (2) a fingerprint pattern. It has ridge lines which enter from either side, recurve, touch or pass an imaginary line between delta and core and pass out or tend to pass out on the side from which the ridge or ridges entered (LEV)

Lopez v. United States, 373 U.S. 427, 10 L. Ed. 2d 462, 83 S. Ct. 1381 (1963): a majority of the Court held that the Fourth Amendment did not apply in the absence of a physical trespass when incriminating statements were obtained by an electronic listening device. (In this case an agent of the IRS had a recording device concealed on his person by means of which the defendant's incriminating statements were recorded.) (ILECJ)

lottery: a form of gambling formerly used by several states, cities, and the District of Columbia to finance internal improvements, and now a source of revenue for [various states] and some foreign countries. The sending of lottery tickets through the mails and by other instrumentalities of interstate commerce is prohibited by federal law (DAP)

Louisiana ex rel. Francis v. Resweber, 329 U.S. 459 (1947): a case in which a convicted murderer who had escaped death due to mechanical failure of the electric chair sought to prevent a second attempt at execution on the grounds of double jeopardy and cruel and unusual punishment. The Court held, 5-4, that Louisiana was not violating these standards in proceeding a second time to carry out sentence of death by electrocution (DAP)

low key: the balance of light or dark tones of a photograph. If light tones prevail with few or no dark tones, the photograph is said to be "high key"; if the opposite, "low key" (MPPF)

L.S.D. (LSD): lysergic acid diethylamide, an hallucinogenic drug

lumen: a measurement of light equivalent to that falling on a foot-square surface which is one foot away from a point light source of one candle power (MPPF)

Lumenized: a trademark of the Eastman Kodak Company for an anti-reflection coating applied to lenses and other glass surfaces (MPPF)

luminosity: the intensity of light in a color as measured by a photometer (MPPF) lunar caustic: silver nitrate (MPPF)

lust: sexual appetite; excessive sex desire or craving, esp. that which is satisfied immediately by brutal acts of violence (LEV)

lust murder: sadistically brutal murder. The victim's body generally has been mutilated, especially the sex organs. . . (LEV)

lux: lumens per square meter (MPPF)

lynch: to practice the custom of enforcing certain mores by death or of punishing violations of certain fundamental regional mores, without due process of law. The avenging group is composed of at least two persons. This practice is commonly referred to as lynch law (DOS)

lynch law: the punishment of persons by mob violence without waiting for a trial

M

Mace: trade name for an aerosol irritant projector (LEV)

Machiavelli, Niccolo (1469-1527): an Italian statesman, Machiavelli advocated in his book *The Prince* that it was the duty of the Prince to furnish his subjects an example of moral goodness and patriotism. He felt that in the pursuit of political good, the ends justified the means and his diplomacy took no account of honesty or morals in arrangements with other people as long as it was for the common good of the community

machine gun: a weapon that automatically fires small-arms ammunition, caliber .60 or 15.24mm

or under, and is capable of sustained rapid fire. It can be belt- or link-fed, air- or water-cooled, and recoil- or gas-operated, and it is usually fired from a mount (DWMT)

machine-independent solution: a procedure or program organized in terms of the logical nature of the problem rather than in terms of any data-processing machine used in solving it (ADPS)

machine-oriented language: a language intelligible to a processor with little or no translation—for example, the programs written in WORDCOM and FIELDCOM order codes. Mnemonic order codes on a one-for-one basis and the symbolic addresses need to be converted into absolute addresses (ADPS)

machine pistol: (1) a pistol of full automatic fire (DWMT) (2) a submachine gun. The application of the term in sense 2 has been in use since WWII, deriving from German and Russian words for "submachine gun," Maschinenpistole, (machine pistol) and pistolyetpulemyot (pistol-machine gun), so called because the submachine gun ordinarily uses pistol-type ammunition. *See* submachine gun (DWMT)

machine-processable form: data on a media suitable for machines to accept; commonly magnetic tape, punched cards, or punched tape (ADPS)

machine-readable characters: printed, typed, or written symbols on documents which both people and character-reading machines can read (ADPS)

machine rest: an arrangement to which a firearm is affixed, or on which it rests, when tested for accuracy (CDTP)

Maconochie, Alexander: as head of the British penal colony at Norfolk Island, Maconochie established an early form of parole in 1840. The system rewarded positive behavior and allowed the inmate to earn marks and thereby to progress through a series of confinement stages resulting in conditional freedom with a ticket-of-leave, and finally absolute freedom

macro-instruction: a mnemonic instruction that a programmer writes in a source program to call for a library routine that performs desired functions—for example, open, close, or seek. The programmer specifies conditions in the operand part of the macro to tailor the library routine to the program requirements   (ADPS)

macrophotography: close-up photography; taking of a picture greater than the size of the subject (MPPF)

macroscopic: large enough to be seen with the naked eyes, as contrasted with microscopic, which means invisible without the aid of a microscope   (LEV)

Mafia: a form of organized and generally violent crime, supposed to have originated in Sicily as an unofficial police system on the large estates to protect the owners during the period of disorganization following the Napoleonic invasion, and to have become a distinctly criminal organization when it turned against the owners and became an independent secret group. Its behavior includes tests for admission, and an oath not to refer any controversy to the legal authorities. The Mafia was introduced into the United States in the last part of the 19th century (DOS)

magazine: (1) a structure or compartment for storing ammunition or explosives (DWMT) (2) the part of a gun or firearm that holds ammunition ready for chambering. In sense 2, magazines for small arms may be detachable or non-detachable from the rest of the piece. A box magazine is a detachable magazine in the shape of a rectangular box; a drum magazine is a detachable magazine in the shape of a drum (DWMT) (3) the container holding the film feed and take-up spools of a motion-picture or still camera, also a device for holding and exposing from 12 to 18 sheet films or plates in succession   (MPPF)

magistrate: (1) a public official (DAP) (2) a local official exercising jurisdiction of a summary judicial nature over offenses against municipal ordinances or minor criminal cases   (DAP)

Magna Charta [Lat, great charter]: a constitutional charter of liberties granted by King John of England to his barons, at Runnymede, on June 15, 1215

magnetic alarm system: an alarm system which will initiate an alarm when it detects changes in the local magnetic field. The changes could be caused by motion of ferrous objects such as guns or tools near the magnetic sensor (TDIAS)

magnetic-core storage: a storage device consisting of magnetically permeable binary cells arrayed in a two-dimensional matrix; a large storage unit contains many such matrices. Each core is wire-connected and may be polarized in either of two directions to store one binary digit. The direction of polarization can be sensed by wires running through the core (ADPS)

magnetic-disk storage: a storage device consisting of magnetically coated disks accessible to a read-write arm operating similar to records in an automatic record player. An arm is moved mechanically to the desired disk (unless there is an arm for each disk) and then to the desired track on that disk. The arm reads or writes data sequentially as the disk rotates (ADPS)

magnetic-drum storage: a device that stores data on tracks around a rotating cylindrical drum surfaced with a magnetic coating. A magnetic read-write head is usually associated with each track so that the desired track can be selected by electric switching. Data from a given track are read or

written sequentially as the drum continually rotates (ADPS)
magnetic-ink character recognition: a system using specially-shaped characters printed in magnetizable ink for machine reading; originally developed for commercial check processing (ADPS)
magnetic sensor: a sensor which responds to changes in magnetic field. *See also* magnetic alarm system (TDIAS)
magnetic switch: a switch which consists of two separate units: a magnetically actuated switch, and a magnet. The switch is usually mounted in a fixed position (door jamb or window frame) opposing the magnet, which is fastened to a hinged or sliding door, window, etc. When the movable section is opened, the magnet moves with it, actuating the switch (TDIAS)
magnetic switch, balanced: a magnetic switch which operates using a balanced magnetic field in such a manner as to resist defeat with an external magnet. It signals an alarm when it detects either an increase or decrease in magnetic field strength (TDIAS)
magnetic-tape storage: a storage device consisting of plastic tape or metal coated with magnetic material. A read-write head is associated with each row of bits on tape so that a frame can be read or written at one time as the tape moves past the head (ADPS)
mail and mail carriers: the constitutional guaranty extends to letters, and sealed packages subject to letter postage, in the mail wherever they be. Furthermore, a refusal to deliver mail addressed to a private citizen, without regard to whether it is nonmailable, violates that guaranty. It has been held in Canada that a detective who is a peace officer has the right to search a letter carrier, where he consents to such search, and there is reasonable cause for issuing the search warrant (C.J. 56, 1167) (CDTP)
maim: wilfully inflict upon the person of another an injury which seriously disfigures his person by mutilation thereof, destroys his person or any member or organ of his body, or seriously diminishes his physical vigor by the injury of any member or organ (CDTP)
maintenance: where a person officiously and without just cause intermeddles with and promotes the prosecution or defense of a suit in which he has no interest (CDTP)
major: the rank of an officer in the army; also used in State Police, municipal police and some other law enforcement agencies. It is above the rank of captain and below that of lieutenant colonel. It also denotes great importance, or serious condition (LEV)
major classification: a part of the system of recording fingerprint classifications (LEV)
major division: a fingerprint classification term. Sometimes called "major classification." Applies to classification of the patterns in the thumbs. The symbols are written in capital letters, such as I/O (LEV)
majority: (1) the greater number; more than half (CDTP) (2) the condition of being of full age (CDTP)
making, forging, counterfeiting, etc.: any deed, certificate, or U.S. obligation for the purpose of obtaining and receiving from the U.S. or its agents any money with intent to defraud the U.S. Maximum fine $1,000, maximum jail sentence 10 years (Fed. Pen. Code, Sec. 29) (CDTP)
maladministration: corruption in public affairs
mala in se: crimes have been divided according to their nature, into crimes mala in se and crimes mala prohibita. Mala in se comprises those acts which are immoral or wrong in themselves, such as murder, rape, arson, burglary and larceny, breach of the peace, forgery and the like (CDTP)
mala prohibita: applied to crimes

that are made illegal by legislation

malefactor: a criminal; a wrong-doer; a convict; an outlaw; a hoodlum (LEV)

malevolent: desiring evil for others; evil-minded; ill-intentioned; treacherous (LEV)

malfeasance: commitment of an act forbidden by the moral code or by contract. The doing of an act which one has no right to do and against which a court action may be instituted. Malfeasance is distinguished from misfeasance in that the latter term denotes an improper act which one may lawfully perform. Malfeasance has come to be commonly used in referring to the misconduct of public officials (DOS)

malfunction: incorrect function occurring in equipment (ADPS)

malice: intent to commit a wrong or hurtful act with no reason or legal justification

malice, express: actual malice

malice, general: wickedness; tendency toward wrongdoing

malice, implied: malice implied by the actions of the subject

malice, legal: malice in law

malice aforethought: determination to commit a malicious act

malicious: spiteful or wicked; of malice

malicious act: an unlawful act done through malice

malicious arrest: an arrest made without probable cause

malicious mischief: a crime consisting of wilful damage to or destruction of personal property of another motivated by ill will or resentment toward its owner or possessor (LEV)

malicious prosecution: a judicial proceeding instigated by the prosecutor without probable cause to sustain it

malign: slander

Mallory v. United States, 354 U.S. 449 (1957): a case in which the Supreme Court held that a confession, obtained from a defendant while being detained by arresting officers for an unnecessarily long time (about 18 hours) before being brought before a committing magistrate, was invalid as evidence in a subsequent trial. *Cf. Escobedo* v. *Illinois, Miranda* v. *Arizona* (DAP)

Malloy v. Hogan, 378 U.S. 1, 12 L. Ed. 2d 653, 84 S. Ct. 1489 (1964): the Court held (7-2) that the states, the same as the United States, cannot compel incriminating testimony—thus overruling *Adamson* v. *California*, 353 U.S. 46 (1947). (This decision makes the self-incrimination privilege of the Fifth Amendment applicable to the states though through the due process clause of the Fourteenth Amendment.)

malpractice: the mistreatment of disease or injury through ignorance, carelessness, or criminal intent (CDTP)

maltreatment: improper or unskilled treatment given wilfully or arising from ignorance or neglect, or willfulness

Malum in se: *See* mala in se

malum prohibitum: *See* mala prohibita

manacles: restraining devices such as handcuffs or leg irons (LEV)

management information system: a data-processing system designed to supply management and supervisory personnel with information consisting of data that are accurate, timely, and new (ADPS)

mandamus: a writ issued by a superior court having jurisdiction and directed to a public officer, corporation, individual, or lower court to compel the performance of an act where there is a clear legal duty to act in a certain way. It may be used to compel a public officer to perform ministerial, but not discretionary, acts (DAP)

mandate: an order or command. A directive of a superior court or its judge, to a lower one (LEV)

mandate, writ of: a term which it is said is employed in statutes in the well-recognized sense in which it has been understood at common law. It has been described as a writ issued out of a higher court to compel a lower court to perform any duty imposed on it by law, hence somewhat similar to mandamus   (CDTP)

mandatory: obligatory; required to carry out or execute in obedience to an order   (LEV)

mandatory law: a law which imposes a duty upon some public official, agency, or local government body and requires that it be executed without exercise of discretion and in accordance with the express terms of the law   (DAP)

mandatory sentences: for some crimes, some legislatures have established sentences which cannot be deviated from by the sentencing authority. Often, mandatory minimum terms are established when a form of indeterminate sentencing is in use

mania: violent insanity; unreasonable or excessive desire   (CDTP)

Mann Act: passed by Congress in 1910, it prescribes a heavy fine and imprisonment for any person who transports a woman or girl in foreign or interstate commerce for an immoral purpose. Congress did not, by this law, attempt to prohibit prostitution, inasmuch as it has no constitutional authority to do so. The law is based on Congress's regulatory power over interstate commerce. The prohibition of prostitution within the states is an exercise of the states' police powers reserved to them in the Tenth Amendment of the federal Constitution   (DOAH)

manner of execution: service of a search warrant must conform strictly to the statutory requirements. All legal formalities with respect to executing the search warrant must be complied with. While it has not been held that executing officers cannot properly proceed to execute a search warrant without first exhibiting it, or at least stating its contents, it is also held that no informal statement as to the contents of the warrant is necessary to its execu-

tion, particularly where those in possession of the premises give no opportunity therefor; nor will the fact that the officer making a search under a lawful warrant declines to exhibit his authority to the wife of the accused, render search and seizure unreasonable; and a statute providing that the officer shall, upon going to the place ordered to be searched, or before seizing any property for which he is ordered to make search, give notice of his purpose to the person in charge of the place or who has possession of the place, is merely directory, and a failure to comply therein is not fatal. (26 S.W. 2nd 211) However, although one possessing a valid search warrant has the right of ultimate entry and ultimate search as against a refusal of permission to enter, an entry without notification, or attempted notification, or without the usual formalities precedent to entry into the premises of another by one who is neither a resident or occupant of such house is not authorized. The provision of a statute that officers executing a search warrant may break doors or windows, if after notice of their authority they are refused admission, does not prevent officers executing a warrant from forcing an entrance into a house without notice, where the house is unoccupied. (C.J. 56, 1241) The only safe method of executing these writs is to comply strictly with the requirements of the statute   (CDTP)

manslaughter: homicide resulting from culpable recklessness or negligence

manual: pertaining to or used by the hand   (CDTP)

Mapp v. Ohio, 367 U.S. 643, L. Ed. 2d 1081, 81 S. Ct. 1681 (1961): expressly overruling its 1949 *Wolf* decision, the Court dividing 5–4 (6–3 to reverse) in this bellwether opinion, held that the Fourth Amendment is applicable to the states through the due process clause of the Fourteenth Amendment. (In a concurring opinion, Mr. Justice Black agreed with five of his brethren to reverse Mapp's conviction—bottoming his views on the traditional due process approach—but refused to join with them to incorporate the Fourth under the Fourteenth Amendment.) (ILECJ)

marihuana, marijuana: comes from the leaves and flowering top of the hemp plant—*Cannabis sativa.* When the leaves and flowering top of the female plant are smoked or ingested it produces an intoxicating effect in some persons. Many States have reduced the criminal penalties for individual use and possession (LEV)

marital: belonging to marriage; pertaining to a husband (CDTP)

marked car: a vehicle which is plainly and prominently marked as a police vehicle (TDPPC)

marker: a visual or electronic aid used to mark a designated point (DWMT)

marking evidence: placing identifying marks or writing on physical evidence so it can later be positively identified as that obtained at a specific place, date, and time. It is most important that physical evidence be handled in such fashion that it can later be identified when it is introduced in evidence (LEV)

marks: a term used in describing persons, denoting blemishes on the individuals which are not scars (LEV)

marriage, common law: marriage by reason of cohabitation for an uninterrupted period of seven years. In the absence of any statute to the contrary common law marriage has the same standing before the law as formal marriage. However, the number of states with laws removing legal recognition from common law marriage is increasing; by such laws the wife and children cannot legally claim the husband's name, support, nor inheritance (DOS)

marshal: (1) an appointive officer in each judicial district of the United States who executes the processes of the court and has law-enforcing authority similar to that of a sheriff (2) an officer sometimes attached to a magistrate's court (DAP)

Marshal, United States: an official of the Federal judicial system, whose functions are the following: make arrests of persons charged with federal criminal violations, transport federal prisoners and insure their incarceration pending trial; maintain order in the federal courts; carry out orders of the federal courts; serve processes in the Federal Judicial District for which he is appointed. His duties correspond to those of a sheriff of a county in many respects (LEV)

Marshall, John (*1755-1835*): jurist. Served in Continental army through the Revolution through many major battles; admitted to the bar (1780); member, Virginia executive council (1782-95); member, House of Burgesses (1782-88); Federalist leader; member, U.S. House of Representatives (1799-1800); appointed by Adams U.S. Secretary of State (1800-01) and Chief Justice, U.S. Supreme Court (1801-35); his decisions established the fundamental doctrines of American constitutional laws as evidenced in *Marbury* v. *Madison, McCulloch* v. *Maryland,* and *Gibbons* v. *Ogden*; generally considered the greatest Chief Justice in the history of the Supreme Court (DOAH)

martial law: (1) government by military commanders over the civilian population in designated areas during which military decrees may, as far as necessary, supersede ordinary laws, and military tribunals may supersede the civil courts. Martial law may be proclaimed during war or threatened invasion in the vicinity of actual hostilities where the local government ceases to function (DAP) (2) a qualified form of military control ordered by a State governor during a domestic disturbance or natural disaster (DAP)

mask: (1) to replace characters in the accumulator with characters from a specified location that corresponds to the "ones" position in the mask, which is in a specified location or register (ADPS) (2) a sheet of thin black paper, metal, or celluloid used to secure white margins on a photograph (MPPF)

masking: a corrective measure used in three-color photography to compensate for the spectral absorptive deficiencies in pigments, dyes, and emulsions. This compensation improves the accuracy of color reproduction (MPPF)

masochism: an abnormal inclination which makes pain, or some expression of cruelty, in mild or greater degree, sexually stimulating (DOS)

massacre: intentional and malicious killing of many people or animals; the killing of a large number of people without necessity or mercy (LEV)

Massiah v. United States, 377 U.S. 201, 12 L. Ed. 2d 246, 84 S. Ct. 1199 (1964): the court held (6–3) that no indicted defendant can be interrogated under any circumstances in the absence of his attorney without having his Sixth Amendment right to counsel impaired. A brief per curiam opinion made the Massiah doctrine binding on the states under the Fourteenth Amendment. McLeod v. Ohio, 381 U.S. 356 (1965) (A government informer, in Massiah, concealed a radio transmitter under the front seat of his automobile. He and the petitioner had a lengthy conversation which, unknown to Massiah, was overheard by a government agent over his automobile radio while parked out of sight down the street. Massiah marked a turning point in the Court's philosophy of disposing of confession cases, on the basis, mainly, of the totality of circumstances. So long as the Court was concerned with the

"totality of the circumstances" of a confession in deciding whether or not to reverse a state conviction, no single factor had conclusive impact. The Court shifted its position to a "single factor" rule in Massiah.) (ILECJ)

master file: a file of records containing a cumulative history or the results of accumulation; updated in each file-processing cycle, and carried forward to the next cycle (ADPS)

master record: the official updated record for use in the next file-processing run. The master record is usually on magnetic tape or cards, but a card copy of it may be used as a visual file for reference purposes (ADPS)

match: comparison of keys (of records) that are identical—for example, transaction record and master-file record; also called a "hit" or "strike" (ADPS)

matching network: a circuit used to achieve impedance matching. It may also allow audio signals to be transmitted to an alarm line while blocking direct current used locally for line supervision (TDIAS)

material evidence: See evidence, material

material fact: a fact necessary to the support of a case or defense

material witness: one who possesses information of value in the trial of a criminal case. Proper magistrates may force a witness of this nature to post bond to insure his appearance in the proceedings or in lieu of bond being posted the witness may be detained. The defense also has rights to insure the testimony of material witnesses if circumstances reflect they may be unavailable at the time of the hearing or trial (LEV)

maternal: motherly; pertaining to a mother (CDTP)

mathematical evidence: demonstrative evidence that establishes its conclusions. Laws of probability and statistical computations are questioned mathematical evidence

matic: an alarm system which employs a holdup alarm device, in which the signal transmission is initiated solely by the action of the intruder, such as a money clip in a cash drawer   (TDIAS)

matriarchate: a form of early social organization in which women are alleged to have wielded both political and domestic authority   (DOS)

matricide: the killing or murder of a mother   (CDTP)

matrix: (1) a rectangular array of numbers, subject to mathematical operations, such as addition, multiplication, and inversion, according to specified rules. Any table is a matrix (ADPS) (2) an array of circuit elements, such as diodes, wires, magnetic cores, and relays, arranged and designed to perform a specified function—for example, conversion from one number system to another (ADPS) (3) a gelatin relief image used in the wash-off relief process of color photography   (MPPF)

mat switch: a flat area switch used on open doors or under carpeting. It may be sensitive over an area of a few square feet or several square yards   (TDIAS)

maturity: (1) lawful age (CDTP) (2) the time when a thing becomes due   (CDTP)

Maudsley, Henry (*1835-1918*): a great physician at the age of 21, Maudsley was appointed Medical Superintendent of the Manchester Royal Lunatic Asylum at age 23. At 27 he was editing the *Journal of Mental Science* and at age 34 he was appointed Professor of Medical Jurisprudence at University College in London. Maudsley's influence on forensic matters was mostly through his general publications, esp. through translations which were specifically devoted to the subject. He paid particular attention to the borderline area between insanity and crime. As well as his ability to apply knowledge from other fields to the problem of criminal behavior, he was quite aware of the effect environmental factors had in the causation of crime. He opposed the harsh punishment of criminals, although his argument against unjust punishment suffers through his inability to differentiate control from punishment. In 1847 he published *Responsibility in Mental Diseases*. This work ran to second and third editions in two succeeding years and remains to this day a much-debated work. In this work he demolished a popular notion of that day that a really insane person acts without motive   (DC)

maximum: the greatest possible

maximum depression: the maximum verticle angle below the horizontal at which a piece can be laid and still deliver effective fire   (DWMT)

maximum effective range: the maximum distance at which a weapon may be expected to deliver its destructive charge with the accuracy specified to inflict prescribed damage   (DWMT)

mayhem: intentional maiming or disfiguring the body of another. At common law the term referred generally to an act depriving another of a limb essential for fighting, as an arm or leg, but not an ear since it was assumed to have no value for defensive purposes. Modern statutes make no distinctions on this ground   (DOS)

McAdoo, William (*1853-1930*): lawyer and city magistrate. B. Ireland. Practiced law in New Jersey; member, U.S. House of Representatives (1883-91); appointed by Cleveland, U.S. Assistant Secretary of the Navy; practiced law in New York City; police commissioner (1905-06); chief magistrate (1910-30); largely responsible for a complete reorganization and reform in the municipal court system   (DOAH)

McCarthyism: a habit of branding all except extreme right-wing ideas as Communistic, of indiscriminately leveling false charges of treason, of making new charges instead of furnishing facts, and of attacking the motives of those who questioned the authenticity

of statements—the term arose from the specious charges of Senator Joseph R. McCarthy of Wisconsin, who undermined public confidence in many public officials and private persons until finally censured by the Senate, Dec. 2, 1954   (DAP)
McCray v. Illinois, 186 U.S. 300, 18 L. Ed. 2d 62, 87 S. Ct. 1056 (1967): this 5-4 opinion is important in preserving the informer privilege. A reliable informant's identity generally need not be disclosed on a motion to suppress. (The dissenters in *McCray* center on another point that is extremely important: the question of arrest warrants and when and where they are essential. In earlier decisions—the *Hoffa*, *Lewis*, *Osborn* complex—the Court clarified the acceptable use of the informer.)
(ILECJ)
McCulloh circuit (loop): a supervised single wire loop connecting a number of coded transmitters located in different protected areas to a central station receiver
(TDIAS)
McGautha v. California (together with Crampton v. Ohio, No. 204), 402 U.S. 183 (1971): this is a controlling case on whether the death penalty can be imposed without standards to govern its imposition (due process). It discusses the role of the penalty jury in capital cases and holds that the Constitution requires no more than that trials be fairly conducted and that guaranteed rights of defendants be scrupulously respected   (AOJ)
McKiever v. Pennsylvania (In re Barbara Burrus et al.), 403 U.S. 528, 29 L. Ed. 2d 647, 91 S. Ct. 1976 (1971): Mr. Justice Blackmun for the Court, 6-3, held that the Sixth Amendment does not require trial by jury in state juvenile delinquency proceedings. (After examining past juvenile court decisions, Mr. Justice Blackmun established that the Court had only extended certain fundamental rights to the juvenile, and

concluded that trial by jury was not an essential safeguard to assure procedural fairness. However, a state may adopt a higher standard than that prescribed. For example, Michigan, by a statute, provides that a juvenile "may demand a jury of 6, or the judge...may order a jury of the same number to try the case.")
(ILECJ)
McLeod case: an international incident resulting from an arrest of Alexander McLeod, a Canadian deputy sheriff, in New York in 1840 on charges of murder and arson at the time of the destruction of the ship *Caroline*. The State authorities refused to release him on demand of the British government supported by United States authorities. He was tried and acquitted. To meet such contingencies in the future, Congress empowered federal courts to issue writs of habeas corpus for aliens held by State courts   (DAP)
McNabb v. United States, 318 U.S. 332, 87 L. Ed. 819, 63 S. Ct. 708 (1943): in a 7-1 opinion, in which Mr. Justice Reed did not take part, the Court held that a confession that had been obtained while the suspect was illegally detained under aggravated circumstances—failure to arraign promptly coupled with noncoercive police methods—was inadmissible in a federal court. (This rule became known as the federal "civilized standards" rule. The decision marked the beginning of a period in which the Court formulated new policy for federal criminal trials under the Court's inherent supervisory powers over lower federal courts)   (ILECJ)
M'Naghten Rule: a legal rule or test for holding a mentally ill person responsible for his criminal acts. If the accused knew the difference between right and wrong he is deemed responsible for his acts
(LEV)
meaning of daytime: some courts adopt the so-called "burglary test" of the ability to recognize a

person's features, holding that when such is possible a daytime warrant may be executed even though it is after sundown; while others, to set a clear and easily ascertainable period, limit the daytime to the period between the rising and the setting of the sun, and under this rule a service of a daytime warrant after sunset is invalid (33 Fed. 2nd 639) (CDTP)

meaning of unreasonable search: officers who have lawfully arrested a person may search him and his personal effects as an incident to such arrest. (232 U.S. 392) But they cannot, without a search warrant, search the house of the arrested party, unless the arrest takes place on the premises. (269 U.S. 20) Automobiles are not personal effects, and it was held that an officer might search one without a warrant, if, e.g., he had reasonable cause to believe that it was being used in illegal transportation. (267 U.S. 132) The affidavit in support of a warrant to search a private dwelling must contain supporting facts to show probable cause; affirmation of mere suspicion and belief is not sufficient. (290 U.S. 41) The protection against unreasonable searches and seizures extends to corporations (8 Cal. L. Rev. 347) (CDTP)

mechanical switch: a switch in which the contacts are opened and closed by means of depressible plunger or button (TDIAS)

mechanic's lien: a legal recourse to obtain defaulted payment by attaching equipment

mechanization: stresses the introduction of new equipment processing procedures with the current inputs, files, outputs, and data flows (ADPS)

media: magnetic tape, punched cards, and punched tape used to hold data and used primarily for input and output (ADPS)

median: middle (CDTP)

mediator: one who interposes for the purpose of effecting a reconciliation (CDTP)

medical examiner: a qualified physician appointed to examine or perform autopsies on the bodies of persons who are supposed to have met violent deaths and to investigate the causes and circumstances of death. In some States he has supplanted the coroner (DAP)

medical jurisprudence: the science which treats of the application of medical and surgical knowledge and skill to the principles and administration of the law. It comprises all legal subjects which have a legal aspect (CDTP)

medium-key: applied to a print having the majority of its tones medium grays, with only a small proportion of solid black or pure white (MPPF)

medulla, of hair: the inner portion of a strand of hair. Some hairs have no medulla. The medulla can be continuous or interrupted. It is an important item in the identification of hair (LEV)

megacycle (mc): 1,000,000 cycles

melancholia: a mental disease marked by apathy, mental sluggishness, depression, and indifference to one's surroundings (CDTP)

Mempha v. Rhay, 398 U.S. 128 (1967): in this case, dealing with revocation of probation, the Court affirmed the right to counsel, "at every stage of a criminal proceeding where substantial rights of a criminal accused may be affected." If the accused in probation revocation proceedings is indigent, counsel must be provided for him

menace: (1) a threat; a dangerous situation (LEV) (2) to threaten (LEV) (3) to have a dangerous situation (LEV)

menis: a mouth (CDTP)

meniscus lens: a positive or negative crescent-shaped lens consisting of one concave and one convex spherical surface (MPPF)

mens rea: every crime consists of

two elements, the criminal act or omission, and the mental element or "criminal intent," the mens rea. The mens rea is the particular state of mind which accompanies the particular act defined as criminal. Hence, the mens rea, or mental element of each crime will be different. Thus, in the crime of receiving stolen goods, the mens rea is the knowledge that the goods were stolen; in the case of murder, the mens rea means malice aforethought; in the case of theft, an intention to steal
(DOS)

mental: of the mind

mental deficiency: feeblemindedness; amentia; mental subnormality; mental defectiveness. A state of mental retardation or incomplete development, existing from birth or early infancy, by reason of which one is unable to meet the social expectation of his own society. Mentally deficient persons of the higher grades can be enabled to be self-supporting, but only with exceptional guidance, care, and direction. The mentally deficient as a whole are conventionally differentiated into three grades as follows: (a) the moron, who has an intelligence quotient (I.Q.) of from 50 to 69 or a mental age (M.A.) of from 84 to 143 months. It is this type which is capable of self-support under the terms mentioned above, and the higher grades, or borderline cases, are frequently difficult to distinguish by the layman from normally minded individuals; (b) the imbecile, who has an I.Q. of 25 to 49 or a M.A. ranging from 36 to 83 months. Such a person is capable of protecting himself from elemental dangers, but not of playing an even approximately mature role in society; (c) the idiot, who has an I.Q. of less than 25 or a M.A. of not more than 35 months. Idiots are so lacking in intelligence that they cannot live without constant care and atten-

tion   (DOS)

mental element in crime: criminal intent. Every common law crime consists of two elements, the criminal act or omission, and the mental element, commonly called "criminal intent"   (CDTP)

mentally ill: a condition of mental derangement; insanity   (LEV)

mercantile: pertaining to merchants; commercial   (CDTP)

mercenary: person doing something only for a monetary purpose
(LEV)

mercury fence alarm: a type of mercury switch which is sensitive to the vibration caused by an intruder climbing on a fence
(TDIAS)

mercury switch: a switch operated by tilting or vibrating which causes an enclosed pool of mercury to move, making or breaking physical and electrical contact with conductors. These are used on tilting doors and windows, and on fences
(TDIAS)

mere evidence: evidence which will aid in the proof of the commission of a crime but which does not fall in the evidentiary categories of contraband or the fruits or instrumentalities of a crime
(LEV)

Mere Evidence Rule: a rule of evidence which forbade the legal search for and use in testimony of mere evidence obtained as the result of a search. This rule was abrogated in Warden v. Hayden, 387 U.S. 294; 87 S. Ct. 1642 (1967) and the use of such evidence obtained by a search was allowed
(LEV)

merge: to produce a single sequence of items, ordered to a certain rule, from two or more sequences previously ordered according to the same rule, without changing the items in size, structure, or total number. Merging is a special kind of collating   (ADPS)

merger: the absorption or extinguishment of one estate or contract in another; the uniting of two or more corporations by the transfer of property of all to one of them which continues in existence (CDTP)

merger of offenses: occurs when the same criminal act constitutes both a felony and misdemeanor or where one crime culminates in another (CDTP)

merit system: the method of appointing members of the Civil Service by open competitive examination. Although temporarily instituted by President Grant in 1876 the permanent merit system was not established until the passage of the Pendleton Act in 1883. In 1789, at the beginning of the nation's history, the entire civil service was politically appointed. After the passage of the Pendleton Act, 13 percent were appointed on a merit basis. By 1932 the figure had risen to 80 percent. In 1952 President Truman declared that 93 percent of the Federal service was on a merit basis. Individual merit systems have been put into effect by some of the independent bodies. These include the Federal Bureau of Investigation and the Tennessee Valley Authority. A merit examination may be written, or as in recent developments, it may take the form of a performance, oral, or interview examination. The merit system has spread widely to state and municipal governments, and has been adopted in part by private industry (DOAH)

mescaline: an hallucinogenic narcotic extracted from mescal buttons (LEV)

mesial: middle (CDTP)

mesmerism: hypnotism (CDTP)

mesne: intermediate; intervening (CDTP)

mesne process: as distinguished from final process, this signifies any writ or process issued between the commencement of the action and the suing out of execution. "Mesne" in this connection may be defined as intermediate; intervening; the middle between two extremes (CDTP)

mesne process, writs of: those of which interlocutory proceedings are initiated (CDTP)

metabolism: the system of chemical reactions in a living organism which are essential to, and occur during, life. The substances produced by these reactions are known as metabolites. Hence drugs administered may, after undergoing reactions in the body, be excreted or recovered as their metabolites (FS)

metal fouling: deposits of metal that collect in the bore of a gun. Metal fouling comes from the jackets or rotating bands of projectiles (DWMT)

meter: 39.37 inches

metes and bounds: the boundary lines or limits of a tract of land (CDTP)

methadone: a fine white powder, methadone is a synthetic drug with opiate effects. Although it is addictive its withdrawal is milder than that of opiates. It is used to "detoxify" heroin addicts in that they can withdraw from heroin without the painful reactions. . . . Methadone is under federal regulation. It is also known by the names: amidone, Dolphine®, adanon, methadon, dollies, dolls (LEV)

methamphetamine: a chemical which is related to amphetamine but has more central nervous system activity and correspondingly less effect on blood pressure and heart rate than amphetamines; a drug stimulant (LEV)

method of arrest by officer by virtue of warrant: when making an arrest by virtue of a warrant the officer shall inform the person to be arrested of the cause of the arrest and of the fact that a warrant has been issued for his arrest, except when he flees or forcibly resists before the officer has opportunity so to inform him, or when the giving of such information will imperil the arrest. The officer need not have the warrant in his possession at the time of the arrest, but after the arrest, if the person arrested so requires, the warrant shall be shown to him as soon as practicable   (CDTP)

method of arrest by officer without warrant: when making an arrest without a warrant, the officer shall inform the person to be arrested of his authority and the cause of the arrest, unless the person to be arrested is then engaged in the commission of an offense, or is pursued immediately after its commission or after an escape, or flees or forcibly resists before the officer has opportunity so to inform him, or when the giving of such information will imperil the arrest   (CDTP)

methods and means protected or prohibited—arrests: in general the constitutional guaranty under consideration has no application to, and does not prevent, arrests in accordance with the course of the common law, nor does it apply to the incidental right of officers to search the prisoner after a lawful arrest and to seize such property as is connected with the crime charged, or to search the place of the arrest for such articles. (51 A.L.R. 409) Under such circumstances the immunity does not prohibit a search of the person of one lawfully arrested or his premises, or the vehicle in which he was riding. (153, N.E. 399) Neither does the guaranty extend to a seizure, after such arrest, of any articles, as evidence. (It does not prevent seizure of a weapon or instrument that could enable an escape, 224 S.W. 860.) The Fourth Amendment has no reference to evidence obtained from the person after legal arrest in a proper case with or without a warrant. Removing prisoner's shoes, by force, after a lawful arrest, the shoes corresponding to footprints near the scene of the crime, did

not violate the prisoner's constitutional rights. (167 N.E. 129) Neither does the guaranty extend to seizure of fruits of the crime, or instrumentalities of its commission, whether they be found on the prisoner or on premises under his control, provided they are directly connected with the crime charged. (C.J. 56, 1168) Search of persons and of packages and bags carried in his automobile at the time of arrest does not violate one's constitutional rights. (153 N.E. 398) Property seized in connection with lawful arrest and held as evidence of crime is not within the protection of constitutional provisions as to search and seizure (11 Fed. 2nd 503) (CDTP)

metol: a popular reducing agent, which is sold under trade names such as Elon, Pictol, and Rhodal. The chemical name is monomethylparaminophenol sulfate (MPPF)

meum [*Lat*]: mine

Michigan v. Tucker, 417 U.S. 433, 41 L. Ed. 2d 182, 94 S. Ct. 2357 (1974): in an opinion by Justice Rehnquist, the Court held, 8-1, a witness's testimony against defendant's interest (held not to be the fruits of the poisonous tree) is admissible even though a statement made by the defendant without full *Miranda* warnings led the police to the witness. (The case is important as it is the first departure from the strict adherence to the *Miranda* rules since they were handed down in 1966.) (ILECJ)

microbe: a single-celled organism, either animal or vegetable (CDTP)

microchemistry: the field of chemistry in which minute quantities of substances are involved. In the crime laboratory this branch is essential in analyzing small amounts of material which may be found at the crime scene or elsewhere (LEV)

microdensitometer: a special form of densitometer for reading densities in very small areas; used for studying astronomical images, spectroscopic records, and for measuring graininess in films (MPPF)

micron: a unit of length; 1/1000 of a millimeter; abb.: F (MPPF)

microphotography: taking a photograph through a microscope. Not necessarily using the lens of the microscope, but the lens of the camera (MPPF)

microscope: an optical device having lens, used for magnifying objects which are so small as to be invisible to the naked eye; used to magnify the surface of visible objects to create a more discernible image. The microscope is important in a crime laboratory. The comparison microscope is used to compare questioned and known specimens in the firearms and tool mark types of examinations as well as in other types (LEV)

microscope, comparison: a microscope which has two objectives or lens systems converging into a single field of vision. Two separate objects can be seen simultaneously and thus compared. Among other uses the crime laboratory examines bullets to determine if the markings on them match, thus reflecting that they were fired in the same weapon (LEV)

microscopic dot: a photograph so reduced in size that it approximates the size of the dot over a typed or printed "i." A photograph of a document or other object can be so reduced. The "dot" photograph could be read in World War II by secret agents; it was used for transmitting intelligence information (LEV)

microscopy: investigation by the use of the microscope (LEV)

microsecond: a millionth of a second; "μs" (ADPS)

microwave: extremely short electromagnetic waves used in high-capacity communications networks. Usually subdivided into many channels of various capacity to transmit voice or data messages

at high rates (ADPS)

microwave alarm system: an alarm system which employs radio frequency motion detectors operating in the microwave frequency region of the electromagnetic spectrum (TDIAS)

microwave frequency: radio frequencies in the range of approximately 1.0 to 300 GHz (TDIAS)

middle stages: that part of the criminal justice process during which formal charges are brought, innocence or guilt determined, and sentencing decided

mid-range: (1) the distance between short range and long range (CDTP) (2) type of ammunition with reduced grain, usually associated with competitive firing matches (CDTP)

midriff: the diaphragm (CDTP)

midwife: one who assists in childbirth

mil: 1/1000 of an inch

militant: aggressively warlike; participating in violence (LEV)

military arrests and searches: the Fourth Amendment to the federal Constitution applies to a military order authorizing arrests of civilians discouraging enlistments, although it will not prohibit a reasonable search and seizure made in the execution of a military order authorized by the constitution and laws (C. J. 56, 1168) (CDTP)

military draft: the enforcement by the government of its constitutional right to require all citizens of sufficient age and capacity to enter the military service of the country (CDTP)

military law: a part of our body of law, fully recognized by the civil courts, in force in time of peace as well as in time of war, and is that law which relates to the organization, government, and discipline of the military forces (CDTP)

military offenses: infraction of military rules and regulations (CDTP)

military police: the police force of an army charged with maintaining law, order, and security. They also arrest stragglers and take charge of prisoners during times of war (DWMT)

militia: (1) all able-bodied male citizens, and resident male aliens between the ages of 18 and 45, whether members of the organized militia (National Guard) or not. The States retain power to appoint officers, to train the militia according to the discipline prescribed by Congress, and to call them out for defense and the preservation of order in emergencies. The federal government may provide for their organization, arming, and discipline, and may call them into the national service in time of war or other emergencies (DAP) (2) (colloquial) the National Guard (DAP)

milky: applied to the appearance of incompletely fixed films or plates; also of incorrectly prepared fixing baths (MPPF)

milligram (mg.): 1/1000 of a gram

milliliter (ml.): 1/1000 of a liter, approximately equal to 1 cubic centimeter

millimeter: one thousandth of a meter, or .03937 inch; a measure used in continental Europe to designate caliber (CDTP)

millimicron (m.): 1/1,000,000 of a millimeter, or 1/1000 of a micron

millisecond (ms.): 1/1,000 of a second; 1,000 microseconds

miniature camera: a term more or less generally applied to a camera using film 2¼ x 3¼ inches or less in size (MPPF)

minie-ball: a conical bullet with a cavity in its base which expands from the force of the powder gas and thus fits the grooves of the rifling; named for its inventor, a French officer (CDTP)

minim: 1/480 of a fluid ounce or approximately 1 drop

ministerial officer: an officer who is required to obey the orders of a superior (CDTP)

minor: a person who has not reached the age, usually 21 years, at which the law recognizes a general contractual capacity (14 R.C.L.

216) (CDTP)

minor caliber: in naval terminology, guns and ammunition over .60 cal. and including 3 in. No longer used as an army classification (DWMT)

minority: the smallest number; state of being a minor (CDTP)

minutes: memoranda of what takes place in court, made by authority of the court (CDTP)

Miranda v. Arizona, 384 U.S. 436, 16 L. Ed. 2d 694, 86 S. Ct. 1602 (1966): a majority of the Court (5-4) in this epic decision, imposed upon law enforcement officers a scheme of preinterrogation warnings and advice as federal constitutional prerequisites to the admissibility of confessions and statements in state and federal prosecutions. The court expressly held that the privilege against self-incrimination is available outside of criminal court proceedings and applied to police interrogations of persons "in custody." [It was in *Escobedo*, however, that a constitutional rule was shaped as a springboard to *Miranda*. The main thrust of *Escobedo* is on the right of a suspect to consult with *retained counsel* in the judicial stage of a criminal investigation. This was absorbed into *Miranda* as a very important ancillary rule. Neither the *Escobedo* nor the *Miranda* decisions could have come about, however, if the Court had neglected the homework that it finished in Malloy v. Hogan, 378 U.S. 1 (1964).] (ILECJ)

Miranda warnings: the information which the court in Miranda v. Arizona, 384 U.S. 436, said must be used in warning a person in custody of his rights prior to interrogation about a crime. They are in substance: (1) You have the right to remain silent; (2) Anything you say can be used in a court of law against you; (3) You have the right to have an attorney with you during the interrogation; (4) If you are unable to hire an attorney one will be provided for you without cost; (5) If you waive these rights and furnish information you have the right to stop talking at any time   (LEV)

misappropriate: to wrongfully appropriate; to use wrongfully; to misapply   (LEV)

miscarriage: the giving of birth to a fetus which has been carried less than six months

miscegenation: (1) mixture of races (2) marriage between persons of different races

misconduct in office: negligent, improper, dishonorable, or unlawful behavior on the part of an individual holding a position of public trust which may result in removal from office   (DAP)

misdemeanor: a criminal offense less serious than a felony; usu. punishable by a minor penalty such as a fine or short jail sentence. Also known as *delicta*

misdemeanor complaint: a verified accusation by a person, filed with the proper officer, which charges one or more persons with the commission of one or more offenses, at least one of which is a misdemeanor and none of which is a felony, and which serves to begin a criminal action but which may not, except with the charged person(s)' consent, serve as a basis for prosecution of the offenses charged therein

misfeasance: performance of a lawful act in an improper or illegal manner—contrasting with a malfeasance, which is the performance of a wrong act, and nonfeasance, the omission or neglect of duty

misfeed: failure to supply ammunition properly, especially to a magazine-fed or belt-fed automatic gun   (DWMT)

misfire: (1) failure to fire or explode properly (DWMT) (2) the failure of a primer or the propelling charge of a projectile to function, wholly or in part   (DWMT)

misnomer: a misdescription of the party. The court usually has the right to amend the indictment by inserting the correct name (CDTP)

misprision: (1) the concealment of a crime, as felony, treason (CDTP) (2) in criminal law, a term used to signify every considerable misdemeanor which has not a certain name given to it by law   (CDTP)

misprision, negative: the concealment of something which ought to be revealed   (CDTP)

misprision, positive: the commission of something which ought not to be done   (CDTP)

misprision of felony: the offense of concealing a felony committed by another, but without such previous concert or subsequent assistance to the felon as would make the party concealing an accessory before or after the fact   (CDTP)

misprision of treason: the bare knowledge and concealment of an act of treason or treasonable plot, that is, without any assent or participation therein, for if the latter elements be present the party becomes a principal   (CDTP)

misrepresentation: statement of something as a fact when it is knowingly untrue; a deceiving or misleading statement; a statement made with the intention that another rely on it as truth when it is not true   (LEV)

missile: any object that is, or is designed to be, thrown, dropped, projected, or propelled, for the purpose of making it strike a target   (DWMT)

mission: the task or function assigned to an organization or a person   (TDPPC)

Missouri Plan: a plan used in the State of Missouri for the selection of judges. A commission, composed of a judicial officer serving ex-officio, lawyers selected by lawyers, and laymen selected by the governor, nominates three candidates for the position. The governor appoints one. At the end of the year, this judge goes before the people at a general election where the people vote on the question. If he receives a majority in his favor he serves the remainder of his term at which time he may become a candidate for re-election merely by certifying his wish to have his name placed on the ballot. He is not allowed to contribute financially to or to participate in any political campaign (LEV)

mistakes: blunders by people causing inaccurate results (ADPS)

mistrial: a trial officially terminated by the judge before completion because of some error in the proceedings, such as lack of jursidiction or some other factor provided by law as the basis for such action (LEV)

mitigation: alleviation; abatement; making less rigorous (CDTP)

mittimus: a court order to a peace officer directing him to take a person to jail (LEV)

mnemonic: memory-aiding instruction names—for example, PRT and SUB for "print" and "subtract," respectively, instead of the numeric code used by the machine. Mnemonics codes are converted to machine code during program assembly (ADPS)

mob: a large crowd, particularly one that is violent and disorderly

mobile command post: a vehicle containing communications and other operations control equipment which permits control of an operation to be moved to a temporary location from the normal fixed location (TDPPC)

mobile crime laboratory: a vehicle, usually a van-type, equipped with investigative instruments, equipment, and supplies which can be moved to the site of an investigation for immediate analysis of materials and clues found at the scene of an incident (TDPPC)

mobile office: a function provided by a patrol car or other vehicle for the officer using the vehicle (TDPPC)

mode: the style of operation; for example, paper-tape punches have both letters and figures modes to increase the number of possible characters from 32 (5 channels on tape offers a maximum of 2^5 or

32 characters) to 52 after allowing for control characters common to both models and for shifting characters. Typewriters, for example, have the upper and lower case modes of operation (ADPS)

mode of waiver: while the intent to waive the constitutional immunity must be positively established, the consent upon which a waiver is predicated may be given by actions alone, by words or actions supplementing statements indicating consent, an example of the latter being, where persons in automobile step out to let officers, requesting to do so, search it. (199, N.W. 196) Liquor found by an officer proceeding upstairs with the owner's implied consent is not obtained by illegal search, for an officer is not bound to be dumb and blind when he enters even by consent. (221 N.W. 302) Where defendant stepped back into room as officers entered, officers had right to assume they were entitled to enter. (173 N.E. 599) (CDTP)

Model Penal Code (MPC): a code drawn up by the American Law Institute defining criminal law and suggesting a model sentencing structure

Model Sentencing Act (MSA): a document drawn up by the Advisory Council of Judges of the National Council on Crime and Delinquency (NCCD), outlining a proposed model sentencing structure

modeling: applied to the representation of the third dimension in a photograph by the controlled placement of highlights and shadows (MPPF)

modular: standardization of processor and components to permit combining them in various ways (ADPS)

modulate: conversion of one form of signal to another suitable for transmission over communication circuits. For example, a modulator converts the bits representing a frame of data on punched-paper tape or magnetic tape from the parallel mode to the serial mode for transmission   (ADPS)

modus operandi: a method of identifying one who has committed a crime by examination of the method used in its commission. It is based upon the theory that each professional criminal has a method of committing a crime peculiar to himself. It was devised by Major Atcherley of Yorkshire, England. It is used to supplement the fingerprint method   (DOS)

mold: in field of moulage, the reproduction of an impression made or left by an object   (LEV)

molding: in field of moulage, the process of reproducing the impression of the object   (LEV)

molecular weight: a number proportional to the weight of a molecule, on a scale in which the relative weight 16 is arbitrarily assigned to the oxygen atom   (FS)

molotov cocktail: a fire bomb or hand grenade, usually made with a breakable bottle containing a flammable liquid with a rag wick protruding from the mouth of the bottle. It is used by lighting the wick and throwing the container against an object, causing the bottle to break and thus igniting the fuel   (LEV)

monitor: a device for receiving radio or television transmissions by signals. Used to check on such transmissions by listening or viewing   (LEV)

monitor cabinet: an enclosure which houses the annunciator and associated equipment   (TDIAS)

monitoring station: the central station or other area at which guards, police, or commercial service personnel observe annunciators and registers reporting on the condition of alarm systems   (TDIAS)

monochromatic: a single color   (MPPF)

monogamy: a marriage between one man and one woman

monomania: an obsession with one subject

monopack: another name for integral tripack   (MPPF)

montage: a composite picture made by a number of exposures on the same film, by projecting a number of negatives to make a composite print, or by cutting and pasting-up a number of prints and subsequently copying to a new negative, or by any of a number of similar processes   (MPPF)

Montero, Pedro Dorado (1861–1919): a professor,...he fought ...against traditional criminological ideas and systems,...Briefly, Dorado is the pioneer of the penal sanction as a pure spiritual function   (PC)

moot: unsettled, undecided

moot case: an issue before a court on a pretended controversy, the resolution of which cannot be implemented

moot court: a mock court used by law students to argue moot or pretended cases

moral: according to the standards of society, ethical, good, honest, upright, virtuous   (LEV)

moral evidence: See evidence, circumstantial

moral turpitude: the quality of a crime that characterizes it as malum in se, that is, as inherently vicious and depraved or as offensive to public morals. Persons convicted of a crime involving moral turpitude are debarred from entry under U.S. immigration laws   (DAP)

morale: esprit de corps

Morales v. New York, 396 U.S. 102, 24 L. Ed. 2d 299, 90 S. Ct. 291 (1969): the Court, 7-1, remanded a murder conviction to the state courts for factual findings. (The New York Court of Appeals approved in principle an arrest that did not measure up to a standard of reasonableness based on the totality of circumstances which is all to the good. This is the approach, seemingly, the New York Court followed in Morales. The Supreme Court's remand in Morales still leaves open the constitutionality of New York's stop and frisk legislation with the result that New York's stop and frisk decisions stand as good law in that State until such time as the United States Supreme Court may reach a contrary result.) (ILECJ)

morals cases: investigations or cases involving the morals of persons, individuals and the public, in such matters as prostitution, gambling, organized crime, etc. Large departments frequently have special units to conduct such investigations. The officers must have high moral stamina as many of the people succumb to bribery or in other ways become obligated to persons engaged in such unlawful activities (LEV)

moratorium: a period during which there is a legal right to delay meeting an obligation (CDTP)

mordant: an etching bath used on metal; also a chemical which causes a dye to become insoluble and prevents its washing out (MPPF)

More, Sir Thomas (*1478-1535*): British statesman and author, More wrote in his *Utopia* that criminality is a reflection of society. Utopia was a city where Sir Thomas saw all the policies and institutions governed completely by reason. He also fought for religious freedom, denying the head of state supreme power over religious choice, a fight that cost More his life

mores: morals; manners (CDTP)

Morgan, 78 Supp. 758 (1948): this is an extensive decision on extradition and fugitives (AOJ)

morgue: (1) a public depository or building for temporarily holding bodies for identification and from whence the unknown or unclaimed dead are taken to the Potter's Field (DOS) (2) the files of a newspaper office for storing news clippings and pictures (DOS)

moron: a person of deficient mentality whose intelligence quotient ranges from 50 to 69 and who has a mental range of from 7 to 12 years. The moron is in the highest

classification of mental deficiency (DOS)

morphine: a habit-forming narcotic drug derived from the juice of [the opium] poppy (CDTP)

Morrisey v. Brewer, 408 U.S. 471, 33 L. Ed. 2d 484, 92 S. Ct. 2593 (1972): the Court through Chief Justice Burger, for the first time, establishes the right of a parolee to at least a "simple hearing" before his parole can be revoked (ILECJ)

mortgage: the conveyance of an estate by way of pledge for the security of a debt, and to become void on payment of it (CDTP)

mortis causa [*Lat*]: in contemplation of death, by reason of death

mortuary: a funeral home; an undertaker's establishment; a place where the body is received and kept temporarily before interment (LEV)

motion: a formal application or request to the court for some action, such as an order or rule (LEV)

motion sensor: a sensor which responds to the motion of an intruder. *See also* radio frequency motion detector, sonic motion detector, ultrasonic motion detector, and infrared motion detector (TDIAS)

motive: an impulse or emotion toward action

motive, not intent: motive is not an essential element of crime. A bad motive will not make an act a crime, nor will a good motive prevent an act from being a crime. Motive may, however, tend to show that an act was willful, and done with criminal intent or tend to prove the perpetrator (CDTP)

motor vehicle: a vehicle which is propelled by a motor contained in the vehicle; a self-propelled vehicle (LEV)

motor vehicle, stolen: a self-propelled vehicle which has been stolen. This term is used in federal law concerning stolen vehicles which are transported interstate. The Act is entitled Interstate

Transportation of Stolen Motor Vehicles, U.S. Code, Title 18, Sec. 2311-13 (LEV)

Motor Vehicle Theft Act: an act of Congress, Oct. 29, 1919, which made it a federal offense to transport across a State boundary line a motor vehicle known to have been stolen (DAP)

motor vehicles, interstate transportation of stolen: motor vehicles which are stolen and transported, or caused to be transported, from one state to another or to the District of Columbia. It is a federal violation provided for in 18 USC 231113 (LEV)

mottling: marks which appear on negatives or prints which have not been sufficiently agitated during processing (MPPF)

moulage: a term synonymous to molding and casting in criminal investigative work but which is used in the field of criminal justice to designate certain materials used in molding and casting, sold under trade names. Moulage is cast materials manufactured commercially, consisting of two kinds: (1) for making a negative mold, and (2) for making the positive cast. It will record fine detail (LEV)

mount: the cardboard or paper support to which a print is fastened for display (MPPF)

mountain rescue vehicle: a special type of vehicle designed to function in mountainous terrain and appropriately equipped to conduct the type of rescue operations required in rugged terrain (TDPPC)

mounting tissue: thin sheets of paper impregnated with shellac and used for attaching prints to mounts by application of heat (MPPF)

mounts: (1) metal blocks on a rifle barrel and receiver used for mounting a telescopic sight (DWMT) (2) metal parts of a firearm used for protection and decoration and to affix the barrel, lock, and ramrod to the stock (DWMT)

move: (1) to formally ask for something (LEV) (2) to apply to a court for an order or a rule (LEV)

moving surveillance: a surveillance which is mobile or moving in order to follow the mobile person or vehicle. A moving surveillance may be on foot, by motor vehicle, by common carrier, or a combination of these methods (LEV)

M-Q developer: a developer containing Metol (Elon, Pictol, Rhodol, etc.) and hydroquinone (Quinol) (MPPF)

M-Q register: a register used in conjunction with the accumulator for performing arithmetical operations. For example, in multiplication, the M-Q is first loaded with the multiplier. After multiplication, the M-Q contains the low-order digits of the product; the high-order digits are in the accumulator and the multiplicand remains in its storage location (ADPS)

mug shot: a photograph showing head and shoulders, both side and front views, of a criminal (MPPF)

mulet: (1) to punish by fine (CDTP) (2) to deprive (CDTP)

multiple camera: a camera which makes a number of small photographs on a single large film or plate (MPPF)

multiple offender: a person who has violated the criminal law more than once: repeater; recidivist (LEV)

multiple printing: repeated printing of the same image on successive coatings of sensitizer on one sheet of paper, usually in the gum-bichromate process, to secure greater contrast (MPPF)

multiplexing: (1) a technique for transferring data from several storage devices operating at relatively low transfer rates to one storage device operating at a high transfer rate in such a manner that the high-speed device is not obligated to wait for the low-speed units. The high-speed device is time-shared by offering service to each low-speed device in turn

(ADPS) (2) a technique for the concurrent transmission of two or more signals in either or both directions, over the same wire, carrier, or other communication channel. The two basic multiplexing techniques are time division multiplexing and frequency division multiplexing (TDIAS)

multiplexing, frequency division (FDM): the multiplexing technique which assigns to each signal a specific set of frequencies (called a channel) within the larger block of frequencies available on the main transmission path in much the same way that many radio stations broadcast at the same time but can be separately received (TDIAS)

multiplexing, time division (TDM): the multiplexing technique which provides for the independent transmission of several pieces of information on a time-sharing basis by sampling, at frequent intervals, the data to be transmitted (TDIAS)

multiply field: a field in a character machine used to hold the results of the multiplication operation. A multiply field, which can be located anywhere in storage, must be as long as the multiplier and multiplicand fields plus one character. Initially, the multiplier is copied into the left end of the field and the product occupies the right end after multiplication is completed (ADPS)

multiplying back: a sliding back for view cameras designed to make a large number of negatives in rows on a single plate or film (MPPF)

municipal: pertaining to a city, town, or place having local government (CDTP)

municipal charter: a legislative enactment conferring governmental powers of the state upon its local agencies, generally cities (CDTP)

municipal corporation: a public corporation established as a subdivision of a state for local governmental purposes

municipal court: a minor court authorized by municipal charter or State law to enforce local ordinances and also to exercise the criminal and civil jurisdiction of the peace (DAP)

municipal home rule: a plan whereby a greater measure of political autonomy is allowed a city within the terms of a charter granted by the state legislature. In 1952 more than 16 states had embodied home rule provisions in their constitutions. The home rule charter is forbidden to contain provisions contrary to the Constitution, statutes, or Treaties of the United States, or to the constitution or laws of the state. The general clauses of a home rule charter provide for the incorporation of the city, describe its framework of government, and determine its officers, elections, tenure, and similar details. They also prescribe the city's power over contracts, finances, and other purely municipal functions which are left within its jurisdiction (DOAH)

municipal law: the law of state or nation;. . .its source is the power within the state. "It is a rule of civil conduct prescribed by the supreme power of a state, commanding what is right and prohibiting what is wrong." Sometimes called arbitrary law. It is made by man, founded on convenience, and is dependent upon the authority of the legislative body enacting it. Also, to designate the law applicable to municipalities (CDTP)

municipal law is classified as: (A) criminal law, (B) civil law. Criminal law deals with those offenses against the individual, or the community, which the state recognized as wrongs to society. Crime is an act committed or omitted in violation of a public law either forbidding or commanding it. A wrong which is punished by the sovereign power is a crime (CDTP)

municipal officer: an officer belonging to a municipality; that is, a city, town, or borough—not including a county   (CDTP)

municipal ordinance: a law created by a municipal corporation to define the proper conduct of its affairs or its inhabitants

municipal reform: the attempts to increase popular controls over municipal government for the purpose of weakening or eliminating political machines. Some of the developments in this direction include the use of municipal home rule for larger cities, proportional representation, the short ballot, the county executive plan, and the county manager and city manager systems.   (DOAH)

municipality: a local area of government in the United States. At various times it has taken the forms of parish, borough, town, township, village, county, and city government. In the constitutional system of the United States the municipality is a nonsovereign entity, its powers depending wholly upon state grant. Municipalities may be incorporated or unincorporated. In the former a state charter provides a degree of autonomy with respect to purely local functions. In the latter control is generally exercised by the state legislature operating by means of a local government. The governments of municipalities vary, but consist generally of a legislative in the form of a council, board of trustees or supervisors, or board of selectmen. If there is an executive it is usually a mayor although this office is customarily absent from the county. Other municipal offices include court, police, sheriffs, clerks, and the legal officers   (DOAH)

murder: the killing of a human being

murder, vicarious: if accomplices engage in a crime inherently dangerous to human life and the actions of one or more are sufficiently provocative of lethal resistance and one or more of the accomplices are killed, the sur-

viving offenders may be guilty of murder   (LEV)

Murphy v. Waterfront Commission, 378 U.S. 52, 12 L. Ed 2d 678, 84 S. Ct. 1594 (1964): the Court held that the constitutional privilege against self-incrimination protects a state witness against incrimination under federal as well as state law and a federal witness against incrimination under state law—thus overruling United States v. Murdock, 284 U.S. 41   (ILECJ)

mushrooming: the upsetting or expanding of a bullet on impact   (CDTP)

mute: dumb; speechless   (CDTP)

mutilate: to deprive of some essential part; to render imperfect   (CDTP)

mutiny: insurrection against constituted authority, particularly military or naval authority; concerted revolt against the rules of discipline   (CDTP)

mutual aid: an arrangement between law enforcement agencies in given areas who worked out and accepted an agreement to render assistance to one another on request of the agencies involved   (LEV)

mutual transfer: two or more objects come in contact with one another, and trace evidence from each may be left on the other. This is called "mutual transfer." Such is often the case when one vehicle is struck by a car. Each usually leaves some evidence on the other, such as an exchange of paint traces   (LEV)

muzzle: the front end of a firearm barrel from which the projectile exits; the open end of a firearm barrel   (LEV)

muzzle blast: sudden air pressure exerted at the muzzle of a weapon by the rush of hot gases and air on firing   (DWMT)

muzzle brake: a device attached to the muzzle of a weapon which utilizes escaping gas to reduce recoil and noise   (DWMT)

muzzle burst: the explosion of a projectile at the muzzle of a weapon or at a very short distance from the muzzle (DWMT)

muzzle compensator: a device attached to the muzzle of a weapon which utilizes escaping gas to control muzzle movement (DWMT)

muzzle distance: the distance the front of the injuring firearm was away from the victim when the shot was fired, i.e., the distance between the muzzle and the object shot (LEV)

muzzle flash: a spurt of flame that appears at the muzzle of a gun when a projectile leaves the barrel (DWMT)

muzzle-loader: a weapon that is loaded from the muzzle (DWMT)

muzzle ring: a ringlike molding near the muzzle of a piece (DWMT)

muzzle velocity: the velocity of a projectile with respect to the muzzle at the instant the projectile leaves the weapon (DWMT)

myopia: short- or near-sightedness (CDTP)

N

nalline test: a test used to determine whether or not a person is using narcotics

name of owner or occupant: while it is held in some jurisdictions that the application must name the owner or party in possession, it is also said that the name of the owner or occupant is not absolutely essential to the sufficiency of the affidavit, but he may be named or described as unknown. An affidavit describing a place as occupied by the estate of a deceased person is, of course, insufficient (CDTP)

names: in COBOL, a combination of one to 30 alphanumeric characters containing at least one alpha (although procedure-names may be all numeric) and no blanks, not starting or ending with a hypen. Names are used for conditions, data, procedures, and special purposes (ADPS)

nanosecond: a billionth of a second; a thousandth of a microsecond (ADPS)

napalm: a powder employed to thicken gasoline for use in flamethrowers and incendiary bombs. It is so named because it is made from the aluminum salts of *na*phthenic and *palm*itic acids (DWMT)

narcotic: a drug, which in medical amounts relieves pain, causes sleep, and diminishes sensibilities, but in large doses is a poison. Opium and morphine are two of a large number of narcotics (LEV)

narcotic addict: one who is addicted to the use of narcotic drugs or cocaine (CDTP)

narcotic drugs: (U.S. Code, Title 21, Ch. 6, Sec. 171–215) the Harrison Anti-Narcotic Act has such reasonable relation to the exercise of taxing authority conferred by the constitution that it will not be invalidated because of the motives which may have induced the passage of the act, because its effect is to accomplish another purpose as well as to raise revenue, nor by the fact that traffic in narcotics may be regulated by the police power of the state. (246 Fed. 958) This act is valid not only as a revenue measure, but because opium, coca, and their derivatives are foreign products, which in the interest of the general welfare congress has power to exclude entirely from importation or to regulate traffic therein in this country so that their importations may be traced. License to dispense drugs is a form of tax required not as an exercise of police power, but for the purpose of revenue, (240 Fed. 671) Failure to preserve a duplicate of order for opium is not a true crime, though by arbitrary classification made a felony. (Pen. Code Sec. 335) Novocaine cannot be treated as a derivative of coca leaves. Scienter is necessary element of offense of purchasing narcotics. Delivery of goods to a carrier designated by purchaser of narcotics for transportation from the place of the seller to that of the purchaser passes title, and wrongful sale is at such place. (C.C.A.2) Double registration is required for one acting both as physician and as a dealer. (255 Fed. 332) Every person is prohibited from making even a single sale without having registered and paid the special tax. (285 Fed. 865) Attempt to pay the tax and register, which was defeated by refusal of the government official, was no defense to the charge of possessing the drugs without being registered. (288 Fed. 816) A drug clerk who is not a prescription clerk, and making sales outside scope of employment, must register. One permitting use of office for sale of narcotics is an accessory (C.C.A.2) (CDTP)

narcotic legislation, the first: narcotic prohibitory legislation (state) was chapter 160 enacted by Nevada on March 19, 1965. It stated that "the possession of dangerous drugs without a prescription is punishable as a gross misdemeanor upon first and second conviction and is punishable as a felony upon third conviction, and exempting physicians, dentists, chiropodists, veterinarians, pharmacists, manufacturers, wholesalers, jobbers and laboratories, and exempting ranchers under certain conditions (FAMOUS)

narcotic offenses: illegal acts related to narcotics, such as possession, sale, or use

narcotic peddler: a person who sells narcotic drugs, such as opium, morphine, heroin, and codine,

without a lawful permit. In general usage the name applies to sellers of cocaine also (CDTP)

narcotic prohibition act (federal), the first: was Section 1 of the act of Feb. 9, 1909 (35 Stat. L. 614): "After the first day of April 1909, it shall be unlawful to import into the United States, opium in any form or any preparation or derivative thereof. . .other than smoking opium for medicinal purposes (FAMOUS)

narcotic regulation (federal), the first: was enacted by Congress as part of the McKinley Tariff Act on October 1, 1890 (26 Stat. L. 567). This act provided for an internal revenue tax of $10 a pound upon all smoking opium manufactured in the United States for smoking purposes, and limited the manufactures, the keeping of books, rendering of returns, etc. (FAMOUS)

narcotic regulation (state), the first: was adopted March 10, 1933, by Nevada (FAMOUS)

narcotic tariff, the first: was enacted by the Tariff Act of Aug. 30, 1842 (S Stat. L. 558), which placed a levy of 75 cents a pound on opium. Prior to this act, opium was exempted from duty by the act of July 14, 1832 (4 Stat. L. 583), and the act of March 2, 1833 (4 Stat. L. 629) (FAMOUS)

narcotics patrol: a function of law enforcement concerned with narcotics law violations for which unmarked vehicles are generally used (TDPPC)

Nardone v. United States, 302 U.S. 379, 83 L. Ed. 314, 58 S. Ct. 275 (1937): the Court held that wiretapping was within the "plain mandate" of Section 605 of the Federal Communications Act of 1934. (Justice Roberts asserted that the section prohibited interception and divulgence of telephone conversations.) (ILECJ)

natal: relating to birth (CDTP)

National Army: in the military history of the United States, the divisions made up of men obtained through the Selective Service Act during WWI   (DWMT)

National Automobile Theft Bureau (NATB): a national organization, funded by insurance companies, which is concerned with investigating theft and arson of motor vehicles   (LEV)

National Bomb Data Center: established in 1970 to provide technical information and services to law enforcement agencies relative to bombs and explosives. Data is published which is available to law enforcement agencies. Details of the service may be obtained from the International Association of Chiefs of Police, 11 Firstfield Road, Gaithersburg, Md. 20760
                    (LEV)

National Clearinghouse for Drug Abuse Information, the: an organization operated by the National Institute of Health. It is the focal point agency for federal information on drugs and their abuse. It provides information on request through publications, computerized information service, and refers technical matters to the proper agencies. Its address is: 5454 Wisconsin Avenue, Chevy Chase, Md. 20015   (LEV)

National Commission on Law Observance and Enforcement: a commission created by President Hoover in 1929, composed of ten attorneys and a woman college president. Its purpose was to study crime as a national problem. It was called the Wickersham Commission, after its chairman, George W. Wickersham, former United States Attorney General. It completed its last report, in a total of twelve, in 1931   (LEV)

National Commission on the Causes and Prevention of Violence: created by Executive Order #11412 (by President Johnson) June 10, 1968. Function: investigate and make recommendations pertaining to causes and prevention of violence, with the coopera-

tion of other executive departments and agencies; to report its findings and recommendations not later than one year from June 10, 1968. The term was extended by President Nixon on May 23, 1969 to completion of its report or December 10, 1969, whichever was earlier   (LEV)

National Computerized Criminal History System: inaugurated by and through the NCIC, United States Department of Justice, in 1971. As of November, 1971 approximately fifteen states participated. The goal is to have all fifty states participate. To participate each state must have the following: (1) a computer capable of interfacing with the NCIC computer for the interstate exchange of criminal history information under the management control of a criminal justice agency authorized to function as a control terminal agency; (2) a communication network serving all criminal justice agencies throughout the state; (3) a central state agency capable of processing all fingerprint cards generated in that state and updating the NCIC files; (4) a computerized state criminal history capability certified by the NCIC as meeting national standards
                    (LEV)

National Council on Crime and Delinquency (NCCD): an organization concerned with studying the causes, extent, and means for correcting crime and delinquency in the United States. Its address is 44 East 23 Street, New York, N.Y. 10010   (LEV)

National Council on Organized Crime: an organization created by President Nixon on June 4, 1970 for the purpose of controlling organized crime by coordinated efforts of the various pertinent federal agencies. Attorney General John N. Mitchell was named chairman. Membership composed of the Postmaster General, Secretaries of Labor and Treasury, heads of all federal investigative agencies (LEV)

National Crime Commission (President's Commission on Law Enforcement and Administration of Justice): established by President Johnson on July 23, 1965 to study the whole field of criminal justice, bring comments on its findings and recommendations for its betterment. The study was divided into five task forces: Assessment of the Crime Problem, Police and Public Safety, Administration of Justice, Corrections, and Science and Technology. Its first report, "The Challenge of Crime in a Free Society," was released February 18, 1967. Other reports followed (LEV)

National Crime Coordinating Council: See Kefauver Investigation

National Crime Information Center (NCIC): computer center at headquarters of the Federal Bureau of Investigation, Washington, D.C., which serves terminals in the states of the United States and in Canada. It provides data regarding wanted fugitives, stolen items such as automobile license plates, securities, guns, office equipment, television sets, appliances, etc. It started operating January 27, 1967 (LEV)

National Data Center (National Data Bank): a proposed national center for storage and utilization of information on people and statistics involved in the operations of the criminal justice system in the United States (LEV)

National Firearms Act: an act of Congress, June 26, 1934, which restrained the importation and interstate transportation of sawed-off shotguns, machine guns, and silencers for any type of weapon, and placed a tax on dealers in firearms (DAP)

National Fire Protection Association (NFPA): a nonprofit and technical association formed in 1896 with headquarters at 60 Batterymarch Street, Boston, Mass., devoted to the protection of life and property by fire loss through the development of fire protection standards and public education (LEV)

National Fraudulent Check File: maintained by the FBI Laboratory, this file serves as a "clearinghouse" for information on worthless checks. Worthless checks sent in by law enforcement agencies are searched against reproductions of checks already in the file to determine if the writing, printing, check protector, etc., is identified with that on other checks in the file. If an identification is made a copy of the check is placed in the file for future reference (LEV)

National Guard: the volunteer militia of the States which in 1916 was organized as an auxiliary of the regular army, armed and trained by the federal government, and made subject to federal service in wartime or other emergencies on call of the President. At other times the respective State contingents may be called out by the governor when, in his judgment, the regular police forces are unable to maintain order (DAP)

National Institute of Law Enforcement and Criminal Justice: the research branch of the Law Enforcement Assistance Administration (LEAA). It is federally funded through Omnibus Crime Bill and Safe Streets Act monies. Research projects through the Institute are evaluated, approved, and financed through its national headquarters in Washington, D.C. (LEV)

National Labor Relations Act: this act creates, by its terms, a board which functions in two capacities. It is empowered to deal with cases of unfair labor practices as defined in the act, and to certify either with or without the holding of elections, what unit shall represent employees in their negotiations with employers (49 U.S. Stat. 448-449) (CDTP)

National Motor Vehicle Theft Act: by section 408 of the Federal Criminal Code it is a crime punishable by $5,000 fine, five years imprisonment, or both, to transport or cause to be transported in interstate or foreign commerce any stolen automobile, automobile, truck, automobile-wagon, motorcycle, or any other self-propelled vehicle not designed for running on rails. A like punishment is prescribed for receiving, concealing, storing, bartering, or selling or disposing of any such vehicle knowing the same to have been stolen   (CDTP)

National Safety Council: an organization concerned with improving safety for the American people. Its address is: 425 North Michigan Avenue, Chicago, Ill. 60611, telephone (312) 527-4800   (LEV)

National Stolen Property Act: an act (approved May 22, 1934) to extend the provisions of the National Motor Vehicles Theft Act to other stolen property, such as securities, which includes any note, stock certificate, bond, debenture, check, draft, warrant, travelers check, letter of credit, warehouse receipts, negotiable bill of lading, evidence of indebtedness, in general, any instrument commonly known as a "security." The term "money" shall mean the legal tender of the United States or of any foreign country, or any counterfeit thereof. Whoever shall transport or cause to be transported in interstate or foreign commerce any goods, wares, or merchandise, securities, or money, of the value of $5,000 or more theretofore stolen or taken feloniously by fraud or with intent to steal or purloin, knowing same has been stolen or taken, shall be punished by fine of $10,000 or imprisonment for not more than 10 years, or both. (Sec. 4) Whoever shall receive, conceal, store, barter, sell, or dispose of any goods, wares or merchandise, securities or money, of the value of $5,000, or more; whoever shall pledge or accept as security for a loan, any goods, wares, or merchandise, or securities of the value of $500 or more, which, while moving in or constituting a part of interstate or foreign commerce, has been stolen or taken feloniously by fraud or with intent to steal or purloin, knowing the same to have been stolen or taken, shall be punished by a fine of $10,000, or by imprisonment of not more than 10 years, or both. Any person violating this act may be punished in any district into or through which such goods, wares, or merchandise, securities, or money, have been transported or removed   (CDTP)

nationality: state, quality, or relation of being, or belonging to a nation   (CDTP)

native citizen: a person born within the jurisdiction of the United States   (CDTP)

natural child: an illegitimate child; a child born out of lawful wedlock   (CDTP)

natural law: a set of principles and rules discovered by human reason which, it is supposed, would govern mankind in a state of nature (before positive law existed) or, according to others, would provide rational principles for the government of man in society. It has also been considered a valuable supplement to positive law in setting moral standards by which the conduct of governments may be judged. Natural law theories originated with Stoic philosophers and statesmen. In the 18th century natural law was variously derived from reason, the Bible, and the fundamental principles of the common law   (DAP)

natural laws: are coeval with the existence of man and are such as are just and good in themselves and are binding wherever human beings dwell. All laws derive their force from natural laws   (CDTP)

natural life: the life which ends by natural death   (CDTP)

natural rights: those rights believed to be intrinsic to the individual before the creation of the state.

They were developed in the political philosophy of John Milton, John Locke, and Jean Jacques Rousseau, and modified in America by Jefferson, Samuel Adams, and Paine. In the early Revolutionary period these rights were conceived of as part of the heritage of British constitutionalism, although Paine considered natural rights as independent of political constitutions. As developed in America, natural rights included popular sovereignty, the right of revolution against tyranny, democracy, liberty, the pursuit of happiness, and property rights. Varying emphases on the importance of natural rights have played significant roles in American history. Hamilton, for example, emphasized property rights. Jefferson and Paine emphasized personal civil rights. In the 19th century Calhoun repudiated the entire doctrine of natural rights as unsound (DOAH)

naturalization: the conferring upon an alien of the rights and privileges of citizenship. This is achieved through federal laws administered by the Bureau of Immigration and Naturalization and the Federal Courts (LEV)

nature, purpose and scope of remedy: a search warrant is a legal process, criminal or in the nature of criminal process, and has been likened to a writ of discovery. It is a specific and peculiar remedy, drastic in its nature, and made necessary because of public necessity. It is restricted to cases of public prosecutions, and it has no relation to civil process or civil trials; hence the common law never recognized it as being available to individuals in civil proceedings or as a process for adjudicating civil rights or maintaining mere private rights. It is a police weapon, issued under the police power and is valid exercise thereof. Search warrant proceedings are in no sense criminal actions, and are not of themselves complete proceedings, but can be separate substantial criminal proceedings, but they are not necessarily so; too, they may be auxiliary to the prosecution of some particular offense, and may or may not be followed by criminal prosecution, depending upon the facts disclosed by the proceedings (C.J. 56, 1185) (CDTP)

natus: born (CDTP)

N.B.: abbreviation of nota bene, "take note," "note well" (CDTP)

necessity and nature of return: the failure of an officer to make a return of a search warrant properly issued and served in a certain time will not invalidate it, although return may be made subsequently. It is the duty of the officer, although not so specified by statute, to endorse on a search warrant before or on the return thereof, the manner and time of his execution (268 S.W. 563) (CDTP)

necessity and nature of showing probable cause for issuance: the constitutional and statutory provisions of the various jurisdictions requiring a showing of probable cause therefor before a search warrant can be issued are mandatory and must be complied with. However, it is held that this constitutional inhibition does not command the legislature to establish a definition or formula for determining what shall constitute probable cause; it merely forbids it from authorizing the issuance of search warrants without probable cause (C.J. 56, 1213) (CDTP)

necessity for overt act: the law does not punish mere intention, but requires some overt act in an attempt to carry the intention into execution (CDTP)

necessity of search warrant when search and seizure not incident to arrest: while search warrants are not necessary in all cases to effectuate a lawful and reasonable search and seizure, generally speaking a search warrant is required for a lawful search and seizure, and the right to search without one is the exception, and it has been pointed out that even though an officer may not be compelled to obtain such a warrant, it is, when possible, always advisable for him to do so, both because of the protection it affords such officer, and because searches and seizures without warrants are not in harmony with the traditions of our government (CDTP)

neck: (1) the open end of the cartridge case where the bullet is seated (DWMT) (2) the part of a cannon immediately behind the swell of the muzzle (DWMT)

need to know principle: one is supplied with full information in the particular field in which he is employed but information of a confidential nature in other fields is made known to him when he needs to know it. This principle is used in intelligence work in government and is also used as a means of insulating the leaders in organized crime (LEV)

ne exeat [*Lat*]: that he do not depart (CDTP)

negative: (1) a proposition by which something is denied (CDTP) (2) tending to disprove the opposite (CDTP) (3) a statement that a thing is not true (CDTP) (4) in the field of moulage, the impression left by or a mold made from an object (LEV) (5) a photographic image on film, plate, or paper in which the dark portions of the subject appear light and the light portions appear dark (MPPF)

negative paper: a paper base coated with a negative emulsion, used mainly by photoengravers (MPPF)

negligence: a somewhat flexible term for the failure to use ordinary care, under the particular factual circumstances revealed by the evidence in a lawsuit

negligence and recklessness: neglect in the discharge of a duty or indifference to consequences is in many cases equivalent to a crim-

inal intent. Upon the ground that everyone is presumed to contemplate the natural consequences of his acts, neglect and reckless conduct may be evidence of malicious intent, and negligent performance of a duty imposed by law or assumed by contract or by wrongful act may render the person guilty of such negligence, criminally liable, except in cases in which a specific intent is essential to constitute the crime charged (CDTP)

negligent: culpably careless; doing some things, or omitting to do something, which a person of ordinary prudence would not have done, or omitted to do (CDTP)

negotiable: capable of being transferred to another by assignment or indorsement (CDTP)

negotiable instruments: a written promise or request for the payment of a certain sum

nemo: no one (CDTP)

neo-Lombrosians: criminologists who emphasize psycho-pathological states as causes of crime (DOS)

nepotism: favoritism granted to relatives without due regard for merit; family favoritism. Used esp. to indicate favoritism in placing near relatives into positions whether they are qualified or not (DOS)

nesting: the relationship between the statements contained in two perform statements. The statements included in the second (or "inner") perform statement must be wholly included within or excluded from the first (or "outer") perform statement; they must not partially overlap (ADPS)

net: (1) clear of, or free from, all charges, deductions, etc (CDTP) (2) the exact weight of an article without the container (CDTP)

net gain: excess of receipts over expenditures (CDTP)

network load analysis: in systems analysis, a listing of the flow of messages between stations to develop station characteristics by volumes of documents, frequency of processing, and special time requirements (ADPS)

neurasthenia: nervous breakdown, an exhaustion of the nervous system (CDTP)

neuter: neither masculine nor feminine (CDTP)

neutral: (1) not engaged on or assisting either side (CDTP) (2) without color; gray (MPPF) (3) chemically, a solution which is neither acid nor alkaline (MPPF)

Neutrality Laws: acts of congress which forbid the fitting out and equipping of armed vessels, or the enlisting of troops, for the aid of either of two belligerent powers with which the United States is at peace (CDTP)

neutron activation analysis: a procedure for detecting the presence and amounts of chemical elements in a substance even when present in extremely small quantities (trace elements). Radioactive materials are used in the test. It is useful in crime laboratories for analyzing substances such as poisons, traces of contaminants, and residues on the hands of homicide suspects to determine if a handgun has been recently fired by them (LEV)

new coccine: a red, water-soluble dye used for dodging negatives (MPPF)

New Jersey Experimental Project for the Treatment of Youthful Offenders: this project, commonly known as Highfields, was established in 1950. The philosophy of the institution is that rehabilitation will be greatly facilitated by close interpersonal contact between the boys in the small groups and between the boys and the staff. The program operates on a four-month incarceration program, and recent evaluations of it have been positive (AC)

New Left Movement: organizations active in the late 60s, aggressive in their tactics, leaning toward or embracing the Marxist-Leninist ideology. In 1969, leading proponents of the movement in the United States more clearly established themselves as Marxist-Leninist revolutionaries dedicated to the violent destruction of our society and the principles of free government. Principal organizations of the New Left Movement in 1969 were: Students for a Democratic Society (SDS); Young Socialist Alliance (YSA); Student Mobilization Committee (SMC) (Nationally controlled by communist SWP/YSA members); Socialist Workers Party (SWP); and the New Mobilization Committee to End the War in Vietnam (NMC) (LEV)

newly discovered evidence: evidence of a new and material fact, or new evidence in relation to a fact in issue, discovered by a party to a cause after the rendition of a verdict or judgment therein (58 N.E. 668) (CDTP)

next friend: a person by whom an infant sues (CDTP)

next of kin: nearest in relationship according to the degrees of consanguinity (CDTP)

NICAD: (contraction of "nickel cadmium") a high-performance, long-lasting rechargeable battery, with electrodes made of nickel and cadmium, which may be used as an emergency power supply for an alarm system (TDIAS)

nickname: a name other than a person's real name

nicol prism: a type of prism used to produce polarized light (MPPF)

night court: a criminal court which, in certain cities, sits during the early evening hours for the immediate disposition of petty offenses and the granting or withholding of bail in more serious cases (DAP)

night court, the first: was opened in New York City on Sept. 1, 1907. The first night session of a magistrates' court, the Jefferson Market Court at Ninth Street and Sixth Avenue, was presided over by Charles Nathan Harris. Sessions were held from 8 P.M. to 3 A.M. until Sept. 1, 1910 when cases against men were transferred to Yorkville Court. Cases against women were held in the same building as before. On June 28, 1911, both sessions closed at 1 A.M. On April 21, 1919, the sessions of the Women's Court were changed to day sessions   (FAMOUS)

nighttime: insofar as reasonably practicable, searches should always be executed in the daytime, and if they are to be made at night, the authority must appear in the warrant (268 Fed. 408)   (CDTP)

night watchman: a person who guards or watches [property] during the night   (LEV)

nihil [*Lat*]: nothing

nihilism: (1) total rejection of belief in laws (LEV) (2) use of force and violence against authority or those representing such authority   (LEV)

nil: an abbreviation of nihil

Nineteen Eighty Three: contraction of the title of a civil rights law found in Title 42, U.S. Code, Section 1983, which reads as follows: "Every person who, under color of any State or Territory, subjects, or causes to be subjected, any citizen of the United States or other person within the jurisdiction thereof to the deprivation of any rights, privileges, or immunities secured by the Constitution and Laws, shall be liable to the party injured in an action at law, suit in equity, or other proper proceedings for redress"   (LEV)

nisi [*Lat*]: unless

nisi prius [*Lat*]: unless before

nisi prius court: a court held for the trial of issues of fact before a jury and a single presiding judge   (CDTP)

niter, nitre: potassium nitrate, an ingredient in black powder   (DWMT)

nitrate base: the term used to designate a photographic film base composed of cellulose nitrate. Highly inflammable   (MPPF)

nitrocellulose: an explosive used in the manufacture of smokeless propellants. It is formed by the action of a mixture of nitric and sulfuric acids on cotton or some other form of cellulose. Guncotton is a nitrocellulose with a very high nitrogen content   (DWMT)

nitroglycerin: a chemical, "$C_3H_5(ONO_2)_3$" which is explosive. It is the explosive substance in dynamite. It is an oily, slightly amber-colored liquid which is sensitive to shock   (LEV)

nock: (archery) (1) one of the notches on the ends of the bow for holding the string (MPPF) (2) the notch on the butt end of an arrow to hold the string (MPPF) (3) the notch in a crossbow nut for holding the string when the bow is bent   (DWMT)

nodal points: the points on the axis of a thick lens, such that a ray traversing the first medium, passing through one nodal point, emerges from the second medium in a parallel direction, and appears to originate at a second point   (MPPF)

noise: errors introduced into data in a system, especially in communication channels   (ADPS)

noise enforcement: a function of law enforcement concerned with violations of local noise control ordinances   (TDPPC)

"no knock" law: a law which empowers an officer to enter a home or other place, with a suitable court order, without knocking or announcing his identity, when to do so would imperil the safety of the officer or when evidence might be easily and quickly destroyed or disposed of   (LEV)

nolle prosequi: prosecutor's decision not to initiate or continue prosecution

nolo contendere [*Lat, lit I will not contest it*]: a plea in a criminal action having the same legal results as a plea of guilty

nomen [*Lat*]: a name

nominal: in name only; not real or actual; formal   (CDTP)

nominal damages: a trifling sum awarded to a plaintiff who has sued for damages and shows a breach of duty on the part of the defendant, but no serious loss resulting therefrom (CDTP)

non [*Lat*]: not; no

noncombustible: not subject to combustion under ordinary and normal oxygen content of the atmosphere (LEV)

non compos mentis [*Lat*]: not of sound mind

nonfeasance: omission to do something; not doing what ought to be done (CDTP)

nonflammable: will not burn under conditions normally found in fires (LEV)

non-halation: a light-sensitive material the back of which is coated with a light-absorbing substance which tends to reduce halation (MPPF)

nonjuror: a person who declines to take an oath required in a proceeding (LEV)

non prosequitor [*Lat; abbr. non pros*]: he does not prosecute

nonresident: (1) not residing in the community where employed or in school (LEV) (2) one who lives in another state (LEV)

nonretractable (one-way) screw: a screw with a head designed to permit installation with an ordinary flat bit screwdriver but which resists removal. They are used to install alarm system components so that removal is inhibited (TDIAS)

nonsecretor: a person whose saliva and other body fluids do not contain blood group antigens. It is not possible to type the saliva and other body fluids of such a person into blood type groups (LEV)

non sequitur [*Lat*]: it does not follow

non sui juris [*Lat*]: not his own master

nonsuit: a judgment given against a plaintiff for his failure to establish his case (CDTP)

nonviolence: a policy adopted by an opposition group which refrains from the use of overt force as a matter of principle or ex-

pediency (DAP)

no operation: a "dummy" operation inserted in a program which, depending upon conditions encountered in the program, can be replaced by a specific instruction formed by the program itself. Also sometimes used at intervals throughout a program written with absolute addresses to provide space to write additional instructions with minimum rewriting of other instructions. A "no operation" instruction per se is skipped and not executed (ADPS)

norm, social: standard of behavior within a society

normal: the ordinary or usual condition; average (CDTP)

normal range: a range of values with specified limits set up so that, if results of a particular plan of action fall within the range, the results are considered satisfactory. This concept is used in "exception-principle systems" for reporting only results not within the normal range (ADPS)

normal saline: another term for isotonic saline (FS)

normally closed (NC) switch: a switch in which the contacts are closed when no external forces act upon the switch (TDIAS)

normally open (NO) switch: a switch in which the contacts are open (separated) when no external forces act upon the switch (TDIAS)

Norris-La Guardia Act: the purpose of the act is to regulate, define, and limit the power of the federal courts in labor disputes rather than to broaden, limit, or define the rights of either an employee or employer. It has no application to state courts. The purpose of congress in enacting the Norris-La Guardia Act was to extend further the prohibitions of the Clayton Act (CDTP)

nota bene (N.B.) [*Lat*]: note well

notary public: a public officer authorized to authenticate and certify documents such as deeds, contracts, and affidavits with his

signature and seal   (DAP)
note: a promissory note   (CDTP)
notice: an advice, or written warning, in more or less formal shape, intended to apprise a person of some proceeding in which his interests are involved, or informing him of some fact which it is his right to know and the duty of the notifying party to communicate (CDTP)
notice of purpose and authority: an officer, commonly known as such, and acting within his own precinct, need not show his warrant, but he must do so if requested. An officer or private person arresting without a warrant must give notice of his authority and purpose, unless they are known, or are obvious   (CDTP)
noxious: harmful; unwholesome (CDTP)
nuisance: any establishment or practice which offends public morals or decency or menaces public health, safety, or order which may be summarily abated by a competent police or other administrative officer   (DAP)
null: of no legal or binding force (CDTP)
nulla bona [Lat]: no goods
number base: the base of a number system; that is, a quantity that defines a system of representing numbers by positional notation; the number of digit symbols required by a number system. Examples: decimal system, base 10; octal system, base 8; quinary system, base 5; binary system, base 2   (ADPS)
number of applicants: under a statute requiring two credible affiants for the issuance of a search warrant for the search of a dwelling house it is held that an affidavit sworn to by two parties deemed credible by the magistrate is sufficient in that respect, and under such statute a search warrant for the search of premises other than private dwellings may be based on the affidavit of one witness (C.J. 56, 1212)   (CDTP)

number of witnesses necessary: in trials for treason no one can be convicted unless he pleads guilty, except upon the oath of two lawful witnesses to the same overt act. (Const. U.S. Art. 3) If upon a trial for perjury the only evidence against the defendant is the oath of one witness contradicting the oath on which perjury is assigned, and if no circumstances are proved which corroborate such witness, the defendant is entitled to be acquitted (10 Law Ed. 527) (CDTP)
numbers, obliterated: serial or identification numbers on objects which have been removed or made unreadable by being hammered or punched. Thieves use this technique on such things as guns, motor vehicles, and other items of value which have an identification number, thus making it difficult or impossible to identify the object. The crime laboratories can restore and read such numbers in many instances by use of acid etching or the application of heat (LEV)
numeric: composed of numerals; a number consisting of numerals; the value of a number (as opposed to the characters representing it) (ADPS)
nunquam [Lat]: never
Nuremberg trials: a series of trials conducted by an international military tribunal at Nuremberg, Germany, after World War II, the defendants being party and military officials and other persons intimately associated with the Hitler regime who were accused of violating the laws of war, crimes against humanity, and other international crimes. Trials of the most serious offenders began Nov. 21, 1945, and ended Sept. 30, 1946. Twenty-two defendants were found guilty, of whom 11 were sentenced to be hanged   (DAP)
nymphomania: a condition of very strong sexual desire in females (DOS)

O

oath: a solemn appeal to God or a supreme being as to the truth of a statement. A false oath is punishable as perjury (DAP)

obit [*Lat*]: he died

obiter: something incidental in the opinion, and not the principal question (CDTP)

obiter dictum: a belief or opinion included by a judge in his decision upon a case. *See* dictum

object computer: a computer used to execute an object program in machine language (after being compiled from the problem-oriented language in which it was originally written) and process data; may be the same or a different machine from the source computer (ADPS)

object program: a program in machine language resulting from the translation of a source program by a source computer. For example, a source program writtin in COBOL and compiled into machine language results in an object program ready to run on an object computer (ADPS)

object time: occurring when an object program is to be executed; for example, index registers are initialized with desired values, and constants used in the program are introduced (ADPS)

objective: (1) the physical object of the action taken, e.g., a definite tactical feature, the seizure or holding of which is essential to the commander's plan (DWMT) (2) A lens that is used to form a real image of an object (MPPF)

obligation: specific enforceable duty (LEV)

obligatory: binding in law or conscience; requiring performance or forbearance of some act (CDTP)

oblique: to march at angle of about 45° to the original front (DWMT)

oblique fire: fire placed on a target from a direction diagonal to the long dimension of the target or on an enemy from a direction between his front and his flank (DWMT)

obliterate: to deface; blot out (CDTP)

obscene: offensive to chastity or modesty (CDTP)

obscenity: whatever is considered by opinion, law, or the public authorities offensive to purity of mind, morals, or public taste. Applied to personal behavior, dress, language, works of art, literature, and the stage to cover whatever is considered obscene, lewd, lascivious, filthy, indecent, or disgusting (DOS)

obsolete: old-fashioned; no longer being used; out-moded (LEV)

obstructing justice: it is a misdemeanor at common law (and by statute in many states) to obstruct public or private justice, as by resisting or obstructing an officer in the exercise of his duty, or preventing attendance of witnesses serving lawful process (CDTP)

occurs: in COBOL, describes a sequence of data items of the same format—for example, the items appearing in a list or table. Subscripting is used to refer to a particular item in a procedure statement (ADPS)

o'clock: the position of points on a target when compared to the face of a clock or watch. As the target is viewed from the front it is compared with a clock face held in front of the viewer with the face toward the viewer. Three o'clock position is the right side of a horizontal line drawn through the center of the target; six o'clock is the bottom of the target and in line with a vertical line drawn through the center of the target (LEV)

O.C.R. (OCR): Organized Crime and Racketeering Section of the United States Department of

Justice

octal: (1) pertaining to the number 8 (ADPS) (2) a number system whose base is the quantity 8. The symbols used are 0, 1, ..., 7. The octal and binary number systems bear a convenient relationship to one another because each is an integral power of 2   (ADPS)

ocular: the eyepiece of an optical device, such as a microscope   (LEV)

O.D. (OD): overdose, of narcotics

odds: the proportion existing between two bets   (LEV)

odium: hatred; antipathy   (CDTP)

off-line equipment: equipment *not* connected directly to the central processor but working through an intermediary device. For example, a processor can write output on an on-line magnetic tape that is *later* used as input to an off-line printer for printing reports   (ADPS)

offenders, sex: sex offenders may be divided into two classes, persons committing illegal acts such as rape, sodomy, and indecent exposure, which indicate physical or mental abnormality, and individuals who commit such acts which in themselves do not indicate abnormalities but which have not been declared unlawful, such as solicitation, maintaining disorderly houses (commercial vice), and seduction   (DOS)

offense: (1) a felony or misdemeanor, or a less serious violation of the law of a state (DAP) (2) a breach of international law which Congress is authorized to punish (Constitution, Art. I, Sec. 8)   (DAP)

office: (1) a governmental position which is held by the incumbent by virtue of election, or appointment, or operation of law and not as the result of a contract of employment, and which has legally defined tenure, emoluments, and duties (DAP) (2) an independent agency or the subdivision of such an agency or of a department   (DAP)

of record: duly enrolled and filed in a court of record   (CDTP)

olfactory: relating to the sense of smell   (CDTP)

Olmstead v. United States, 277 U.S. 438, 73 L. Ed. 944, 48 S. Ct. 564 (1928): the court held (5–4) through Chief Justice Taft, that messages passing over telephone wires were not within the protection of the Fourth Amendment, and, for this reason, the Amendment did not apply as there was no physical trespass on premises owned or under the control of the defendant   (ILECJ)

olograph: a document such as a will totally written by the person whose name is signed to it

ombudsman: (1) an individual who operates within the prison institution, but who is ideally independent of both the administration and the inmates. This individual acts as an intermediary between the prison inmates and the staff in airing grievances, investigating them, etc. The creation of this position is a tension-relieving device which allows the inmate to feel he has an outlet for his complaints (AC) (2) one who heads an independent government office which represents the people and investigates citizens' complaints against alleged abuse by government officials in all departments   (LEV)

ominous: foreboding; portentous   (LEV)

omne: all; everything   (CDTP)

Omnibus Crime Control and Safe Streets Act of 1968: (Public Law 90–351) passed by Congress in 1968 and approved June 19, 1968. Also known as the Safe Streets Act and the Omnibus Crime Bill. It created the Law Enforcement Assistance Administration and provided for financial aid to the field of criminal justice in Title I. Title II deals with the admissibility of evidence and confessions; Title III with wiretapping and electronic surveillance; Title IV with firearms regulations; Title

V with disqualification for engaging in riots and civil disorders; Title VI the confirmation of the Director of the Federal Bureau of Investigation; Title VII with unlawful possession or receipt of firearms; Title VIII with providing for an appeal by the United States from decisions sustaining motions to suppress evidence; Title IX with additional grounds for issuing warrants; Title X with prohibiting extortion and threats in the District of Columbia (LEV)

on call: on demand (CDTP)

on-line equipment: equipment connected directly to the central processor to furnish or receive data—for example, card readers, high-speed printers, inquiry stations, and direct-display devices (ADPS)

on-the-scene: at or near the crime scene, contrasted with action taken at police headquarters or at a point distant from the place where the crime occurred. The courts draw a distinction between the two situations and more freedom of action in questioning persons is allowed on-the-scene (LEV)

on-the-scene questioning of suspects: questioning which occurs at or near the crime scene with the purpose of determining what occurred and who might be involved. If the questioning is truly exploratory or investigatory the necessity to warn persons with the *Miranda* requirements is not as strict as when suspects are questioned in a more formal surrounding, especially if the person questioned is not detained or his freedom of movement substantially restricted. See *Miranda* warnings (LEV)

once in jeopardy: applied to an individual charged with an offense who has already been liable to conviction and punishment for the same offense

onerous: (1) oppressive or burdensome (LEV) (2) constituting a liability, a legal burden (LEV)

onus: burden; responsibility (CDTP)

opacity: the resistance of a material to the transmission of light (MPPF)

opal glass: a white, milky, translucent glass used as a diffusion medium in enlargers (MPPF)

opaque: (1) refers to an object which is incapable of transmitting visible light (MPPF) (2) a commercial preparation used to block out certain negative areas (MPPF)

open areas: areas of the [United States] which any Cosa Nostra family can move into and carry on operations (LEV)

open-circuit system: a system in which the sensors are connected in parallel. When a sensor is activated, the circuit is closed, permitting a current which activates an alarm signal (TDIAS)

open court: (1) a court whose sessions may be attended by spectators (DAP) (2) a court which is in session for the transaction of judicial business (DAP)

open-end lease: a type of lease contract which requires periodic payments covering equipment cost, financing costs, and profit to the lessor for a fixed period of time at the end of which the lessee guarantees payment of the predetermined residual value of the equipment to the lessor (TDPPC)

open shop: a business establishment that employs both nonunion and union workers (LEV)

open sight: a rear gunsight having a notch. It is distinguished especially from a peep sight (DWMT)

opening statement: statement first made by the prosecutor to the jury in which he outlines the case, pointing out the general proof which will be offered. The purpose is to give the jury a brief summary of the case so they will be able to understand the evidence (LEV)

operand: any one of the quantities entering into or arising from an operation. An operand may be an indication of the location of the next instruction or a result from computation (ADPS)

operating handle: a handle or bar with which the operating lever of a gun is operated to open and close the breech of the gun (DWMT)

operating lever: a lever device on a gun with which the breech of the gun is opened and closed (DWMT)

operating slide: a mechanism in a Browning machine gun that permits opening the breech for loading, unloading, and clearing out stoppages and closing the breech for firing (DWMT)

operating system: that part of a software package designed to simplify housekeeping programming. May include an input-output control system, sort-merge generators, data-conversion routines, and test routines (ADPS)

operation: (1) a defined action (ADPS) (2) the action specified by a single processor instruction or pseudo-instruction (ADPS) (3) an arithmetical, logical, or transferral unit of a problem, usually executed under the direction of a subroutine (ADPS) (4) a military action or the carrying out of a strategic, tactical, service training, or administrative military mission (DWMT) (5) the process of carrying on combat, including movement, supply, attack, defense, and maneuvers needed to gain the objectives of any battle or campaign (DWMT)

Operation Police Manpower: a program offered to military personnel, prior to their release, as a part of the "Transition Program." It consists of 240 hours of police training which meets the highest mandatory state standards required in the United States (1970). Except for learning local law, ordinances, and procedures, the trainee in this course is equipped for police work. Contact the IACP for more details (LEV)

operational: when used in connection with equipment such as aircraft, vehicles, etc., the term indicating that the equipment is in such a state of repair as to be immediately usable (DWMT)

"Operation Intercept": a program instituted on the United States-Mexico border Sept. 21, 1969, to cut off the flow of narcotics, marihuana, and dangerous drugs into the United States. The program was jointly undertaken by the U.S. Treasury and Justice Departments with the Bureau of Customs, Immigration and Naturalization Service, Bureau of Narcotics and Dangerous Drugs, Coast Guard, Navy, Federal Aviation Administration and General Services Administration participating (LEV)

operations: the activity resulting from planning and controlling the current ongoing activities of a police force. This term may also refer to the office or communications center from which current operations are controlled (TDPPC)

ophthalmic: relating to the eye (CDTP)

opiate: (1) a substance which contains opium or its derivatives (LEV) (2) anything that calms, soothes, or quiets (LEV)

opinion: belief short of knowledge but greater than mere impression. Usu. a person is not allowed to state his opinion in testifying in court, unless he qualifies as an expert in a particular field (LEV)

opinion evidence: the fact that a person is of opinion that a fact in issue, or relevant to the issue, does or does not exist, is admissible only in exceptional cases. A witness must testify to facts, and not state his opinion or conclusion (CDTP)

opium: the dried-out juice obtained from parts of certain poppies; a habit forming drug; a brownish gummy substance similar in appearance to thick molasses, smoked in an opium pipe, the least harmful of narcotic drugs (CDTP) Opium derivatives: morphine, heroin, Dionin®, Dilaudid®, Apomorphine®, metopon, codeine. Synthetic equivalents of opiate drugs: Demerol, Methadone, Dromoran®, Levorphan®, Phenazocine®, Numorphan®, Prinadol®, Narphen®, Winthrocine®, Leritine® (LEV)

opium for smoking—manufacturer: every person who prepares opium suitable for smoking purposes from crude gum opium, or from any preparation thereof, or from the residue of smoked or partially smoked opium, commonly known as "yen shee," or from any mixture of the above, or any of them, shall be regarded as a manufacturer of smoking opium. No person shall engage in the manufacture of opium suitable for smoking purposes who is not a citizen of the United States. All opium prepared for smoking, manufactured in the United States. shall be duly stamped in such a permanent manner as to denote the payment of the internal revenue tax thereon. A tax of three dollars per pound shall be levied and collected upon all opium manufactured in the United States (CDTP)

optical axis: an imaginary line passing through the centers of all the lens elements in a compound lens (MPPF)

optical sight: a sight with lenses, prisms or mirrors that is used in laying weapons, for aerial bombing, or for surveying (DWMT)

optimus: best (CDTP)

oral: uttered by the mouth; spoken, not written (CDTP)

oral evidence: evidence given by the spoken word as contrasted to documentary or real evidence. Sometimes referred to as parol evidence (LEV)

oralism: sexual satisfaction attained by the use of the mouth on the sexual organs (LEV)

order: a communication, written, oral, or by signal, which conveys instructions from a superior to a subordinate. In a broad sense, the terms "order" and "command" are synonymous. However, an order implies discretion as to the details of execution, whereas a command does not (DWMT)

order code: the complete set of instructions that a processor can execute; also called "instruction repertoire" (ADPS)

order nisi: a conditional order (CDTP)

order of recognizance or bail: in New York, an order setting bail or releasing a person on his own recognizance

order to show cause: a court order calling on the other side to give a reason why a prayer of the petitioner should not be granted (CDTP)

ordinance: a law of an authorized subdivision of the state, such as a city or a county (LEV)

ordinary care: the degree of care exercised by ordinarily prudent persons (CDTP)

ordnance: military weapons, ammunition, explosives, combat vehicles, and battle material collectively, together with the necessary maintenance and equipment (DWMT)

Oregon boot: a device placed on the ankle and foot of a person to impede his walking or running. It has been used on convicts working outside of prison, such as on road gangs, and also in transferring prisoners. It consists generally of heavy metal contrivances something like shoes or boots, which are joined by a chain of such length that a person can only take a short step (LEV)

Oregon v. Hass, 419 U.S. 823, 43 L. Ed. 2d 570, 95 S. Ct. 1215 (1975): Justice Blackmun, speaking for the Court, in reversing the Oregon Supreme Court said, "...(T)he shield provided by *Miranda* is not to be perverted to a license to testify inconsistently, or even prejuriously, free from the risk of confrontation with prior inconsistent utterances." (The Court also points out that a state court may impose greater restrictions than the federal constitutional law as interpreted by the United States Supreme Court if it does so on its own law or constitutional provision. The Oregon decision did not rest on either the Oregon Constitution or Oregon state law but rather was based on the Fifth and Fourteenth Amendments.) *See Harris* v. *New York* (ILECJ)

organic: the opposite of functional. A condition is organic when there is a pathological change in the tissue or organ (CDTP)

organic law: the fundamental law or constitution (DAP)

Organization, the: when used in connection with organized crime it refers to the Confederation, Cosa Nostra, the Syndicate, or the Outfit (LEV)

organized crime: (1) "The produce of a self-perpetuating criminal conspiracy to wring exorbitant profits from our society by any means—fair and foul, legal and illegal. Despite personnel changes, the conspiratorial entity continues. It is a malignant parasite which fattens on human weakness. It survives on fear and corruption. By one or another means, it obtains a high degree of immunity from the law. It is totalitarian in its organization. A way of life, it imposes rigid discipline on underlings who do the dirty work while the top men of organized crime are generally insulated from the criminal act and the consequent danger of prosecution." The above definition was worked out by the Oyster Bay Conference on Combatting Organized Crime (1965) (LEV) (2) a continuing, self-perpetuating criminal conspiracy, which operates for a profit motive and thrives on fear and corruption (LEV)

Organized Crime and Racketeering Unit: an agency under the direct administration of the United States Attorney General—to coordinate the functions of federal agencies to cope with members of crime syndicates (LEV)

Organized Crime Control Act of 1970: signed into law by President Nixon Oct. 15, 1970. The law broadens the fight against organized crime, charges the FBI with investigating bombings of, and bombing attempts on, any property of the Federal Government or that of any institution or organization receiving federal financial assistance (LEV)

organoleptic: of testing or identification by means of the senses—commonly smell or taste (FS)

orgy: a festival or ceremonial celebration characterized by a temporary relaxation of customary taboos and restraints, and hence by an excess of singing, dancing, and indulgence of appetite. It is often a magico-religious celebration in honor of a deity, as in the Dionysian and Bacchanalian orgies; not infrequently, especially among primitive peoples, it is an occasion for the relaxation of sex taboos (DOS)

orifice: an opening or aperture (CDTP)

original: in copying, that which is to be reproduced (MPPF)

original evidence: evidence consisting of an original document or object rather than a copy or description

original jurisdiction: the authority of a court to hear and determine a lawsuit when it is initiated

original writ: a mandate of the court, constituting the foundation of the action, and the commencement of a legal proceeding; the first process or initiatory step in prosecuting a suit; also the judicial instrument by which the court commands something, therein mentioned, to be done (C. J., vol. 71) (CDTP)

Orozco v. Texas, 394 U.S. 324, 22 L. Ed. 2d 311, 89, S. Ct. 1095 (1969): Mr. Justice Black, 6–2, states that once an accused is in custody, regardless of where he is in custody, *Miranda* warnings must be given, if a statement, or evidence derived therefrom, is to be admissible. (The State argued that *Miranda* is inapplicable to an interrogation of a suspect in his own bed, in familiar surroundings. The Court said questioning means more than station house questioning. The opinion makes it clear the gun found as a result of questioning the suspect could not be used on a retrial as it would be the fruit of the poisonous tree. *Miranda* does not contain an absolute mandate that its warnings must be given. It does no more than to say that noncompliance will result in the exclusion of a statement. There could well be circumstances when it would be imperative to get information in a hurry, for example, to save a person's life. The statement would be inadmissible, but a life would be saved.) (ILECJ)

orphan: a child bereaved by death of both father and mother; less commonly, one deprived of either parent (CDTP)

orphans' court: a court, so-called in New Jersey, Pennsylvania, Delaware, and Maryland, which has jurisdiction over probate, administration of estates, and guardianship of minors. Called also surrogate's court. *See* surrogate (DAP)

ortho: an abbreviation for orthochromatic (MPPF)

orthochromatic film: a film, the color sensitivity of which includes blue, green, and some of the yellow. Not sensitive to red (MPPF)

orthochromatic rendition: the reproduction of color brightness in their relative shades of gray (MPPF)

orthonon: refers to a film whose color sensitivity includes ultraviolet and blue. Often referred to as "color-blind" film (MPPF)

orthopedics: from the term "straight child." The specialty of medicine which treats diseases, deformities, and injuries of bones, joints, muscles, and spine (CDTP)

os: (1) a term applied to an opening from an opening (CDTP) (2) bone (CDTP)

Osborn, Albert Sherman (*1858–1946*): an American handwriting analyst whose testimony was of substantial importance in the conviction of Hauptmann in the Lindbergh kidnapping case

ossification: formation of bone (CDTP)

osteopathy: treatment by manipulation of the bones, muscles, and nerve centers (CDTP)

ostracism: a form of punishment administered within the group, in contrast with banishment. Neighborly help is forbidden, and even aid by the members of one's family is denied. Often it is accompanied by sneers and contemptuous attitudes, or by complete indifference. Today the attitude of the public towards the ex-convict or the parolee is one of ostracism (DOS)

O.T.B. (OTB): abbreviation for off-track betting. Legalized in New York City where it started operations in April, 1971. Operated under government direction. Replaces or is in competition with the "bookie" (LEV)

other crimes: when a person is being tried for one crime the state cannot prove the commission by him of another crime, in no way connected with the crime charged. But if the other crime was committed as part of the same transaction, and tends to explain or qualify the fact in issue it may be shown. The rule may also be stated thus; that when it is legally permitted to prove a fact such evidence cannot be excluded merely because it tends to prove a crime other than that for which the accused is on trial. Whenever the existence of any particular intention, knowledge, good or bad faith, malice, or other state of mind is in issue, and the commission of another crime tends to prove its existence, the other crime may be shown. (79 N.E. 941) The evidence is admitted for this purpose only, and not to show that the defendant was likely to commit the crime in question (CDTP)

oust: to eject; turn out (CDTP)

ouster: ejection from real property (LEV)

outcast: one who is rejected, put out from home and friends, friendless (LEV)

outlaw: one deprived of the benefits and protection of the law (CDTP)

outlawry: ...in England it was a form of community retaliation against the criminal. The retaliation was of such severity that the criminal seldom escaped death (LEV)

out of court: without a trial; settling a case without a trial (LEV)

output: process of transferring data from internal storage of a processor to some other storage device. A specific output area may be used for organizing data prior to the output operation (ADPS)

outskirts: the outer edge of a town, city, or community; border (LEV)

oval-bore rifling: a bore that is oval shaped, the oval being twisted to give the bullet a spinning motion; this was developed to take the place of lands and grooves. Most rifles with this feature were made by Lancaster of London, about 1850 (CDTP)

ovary: one of a pair of small almond-sized organs in woman, found in the pelvis on either side (CDTP)

over and out: a code phrase used in radio communications to signify that the speaker will break communication, provided the other party has nothing more to say (DWMT)

overdevelopment: the result of permitting film or paper to remain in the developer too long, resulting in excessive contrast or density (MPPF)

overdraw: to take out of an account more than the person is entitled to; to pass a check for a greater amount than the maker has in his account. When done by check the bank may not honor it and return it marked "NSF"—not sufficient funds (LEV)

overexposure: the result of too much light being permitted to act on a negative, with either too great a lens aperture or too slow a shutter speed or both (MPPF)

overflow: in an arithmetical operation, the generation of a quantity that is too large for the capacity of the register or location that is to receive the result (ADPS)

overlap, processing: processor operations performed at the same time by using different parts of the circuitry—for example, read-process-write or any two of these (ADPS)

overshot: a descriptive term for an individual whose upper jaw extends beyond the lower (LEV)

overt: apparent; manifest; obvious; unconcealed; open. Contrasted with covert (LEV)

overt act: in criminal law, an act done in furtherance of a plan, conspiracy or intent. In a criminal conspiracy case mere planning is insufficient to constitute the crime, an overt act in furtherance of the plan must be done; the same applies in a criminal attempt case (LEV)

ovum: the egg that is produced by the ovary every twenty-eight days during a woman's fertile life (CDTP)

oxidation: (1) a chemical reaction which results in the production from an element of a compound with oxygen, or in the transformation of a compound into another containing more oxygen or (which is chemically equivalent) less hydrogen; also increasing the electron deficit of a salt-forming ion (FS) (2) the loss of activity of a developer due to contact with the air (MPPF)

oyez: means "Hear ye" (CDTP)

P

pacifier (flattener): a term for a mixture of water and glycerin used to avoid curling of prints (MPPF)

pacify: to calm down; to quiet someone; to satisfy the demands of a person (LEV)

pack: to combine two or more different items of data into one machine word. For example, the three fields of employee pay number, weekly pay rate, and number of tax exemptions might be stored together in one word. To *unpack* is to separate the individual items for processing by means of shifting or partial-word logic (ADPS)

packages: sale not made in or from original stamped package, and sale by persons who have not registered are separate offenses. (33 Fed. 2nd 142) Concealment and sale of narcotics, though parts of the same transaction, are separate offenses. (283 U.S. 118) Separate sales on different days but not to same party, of narcotics not from original stamped package, held separate offense. (284 U.S. 299) Six separate sales of heroin on different days and in varying quantities, but to the same man, constituted six separate offenses. (67 Fed. 2nd 315) Sale of narcotics from unstamped containers is clearly a violation of the act (274 U.S. 762) (CDTP)

Packard shutter: a trade name for a type of shutter, operated by a rubber bulb and tube, much used on studio cameras (MPPF)

pact: an agreement (CDTP)

paedophilia: *See* pedophilia

pain: a feeling of physical or mental distress causing suffering (CDTP)

paint examination: the examination of paint specimens by a crime laboratory. In cases where a vehicle has struck another object this type of examination may be most helpful. If there has been a mutual transfer of evidence it is well to get specimens of paint near the points of mutual transfer. *See* mutual transfer (LEV)

PAL (Police Athletic League): a program of police officers working with young people of the community (LEV)

Palko v. Connecticut, 302 U.S. 319 (1937): a case in which the Supreme Court ruled that the prohibition of double jeopardy, applicable to U.S. courts under the Fifth Amendment, is not included among the procedural limitations enforceable against State courts under the due-process clause of the Fourteenth Amendment. The test of the applicability of procedural rights secured by that clause is never a formal one but, in the words of Justice Cardozo, depends on whether or not the action against a defendant is "so acute and shocking that our polity will not endure it" (DAP)

pallid: colorless; pale. Descriptive term to denote the appearance of the skin, usually of the face (LEV)

palmistry: telling fortunes, or judging character, by the features of the palm of the hand (CDTP)

palm prints: the ridge impressions, inked or latent, of the palm of the hands (LEV)

palsy: paralysis (CDTP)

pan: (1) the receptacle for the priming powder in a matchlock, wheel lock, or flintlock (CDTP) (2) an abbreviation for panchromatic (MPPF)

pan cover: the lid or plate protecting the priming powder against spilling or wetting (CDTP)

panchromatic film: a film that is sensitive to all colors of the visible spectrum (MPPF)

pander: to pimp (LEV)

panel: schedule or roll containing the names of jurors summoned for service (CDTP) panhandle: to approach people and beg, especially in a public place (LEV)

panic: fear affecting a large number of people so that they lose control of themselves; an overpowering fear; terror (LEV)

Panoptican Plan: model for prison architecture developed by Jeremy Bentham in 1791. The model was circular, with all cells on the outside. It was thought that a guard stationed at the center of the circle could observe all the prisoners on the many-tiered circular structure. Although the idea was not widely adopted, and although it proved much less efficient than hoped for, an example of this structure is still in use in Joliet, Ill. (AC)

panoramic head: a revolving tripod head, so graduated that successive photographs may be taken which can be joined into one long panoramic print (MPPF)

paper-patched bullet: a bullet patched with paper to produce a tighter fit in a rifled barrel and therefore provide a better spinning motion and improved accuracy. The patch also served as a gas seal and reduced lead fouling in the barrel (DWMT)

par: (1) equal (CDTP) (2) the established value of the monetary unit (LEV) (3) equality of the nominal and market value of securities (CDTP)

paraffin test: a technique of coating the hands of a person with melted paraffin. After the paraffin cools and hardens the "glove" is removed by cutting with scissors and the inside surface is treated with a diphenylamine solution. If nitrates or nitrites are present a distinctive color is produced, thus indicating the presence of gun powder residue. This test is not considered reliable due to the prevalence of nitrates and nitrites (LEV)

parallax: the apparent displacement of an object seen from different points. Commonly encountered in photography in the difference between the image seen in the view finder and that actually taken by the lens (MPPF)

parallel: (1) similar; corresponding to; continually equally distant (CDTP) (2) the internal handling of data in groups, all elements of a group being handled simultaneously (ADPS)

parallel operation (of a system): the period of time when the old and new system are operated together in order to prove the logic of the programs and the capability of people and equipment to function properly (ADPS)

paralysis: a loss of the voluntary use of a muscle due to injury to its nerve supply, by disease or accident (CDTP)

parameter: (1) a measurable quantity which can have any magnitude but the magnitude of which in a specific case constitutes an identifying characteristic; e.g., the length of a piece of string, or the cylinder capacity of a motor car (FS) (2) a quantity in a mathematical calculation which may be assigned any arbitrary value (ADPS)

paramour: an illegal or illicit lover. May be man or woman, i.e., a person of either sex may assume the role of husband or wife in having an affair with one of the opposite sex (LEV)

paranoia: abnormal mental condition which is usu. attended by delusions (LEV)

pardon: the administrative power, usually residing in the executive branch, to grant mercy to one convicted of a crime. In addition to the full pardon, a total forgiveness of crimes, the pardoning authority may grant other forms of clemency, such as commutation of sentence, which is the lessening of a sentence, or reprieve, which is the postponement of execution of a sentence (LCC)

Pardon Attorney: an official of the U.S. Department of Justice who considers all applications for federal pardons and makes recommendations for the exercise of presidential clemency (DAP)

pardons: *See* board of pardons (DAP)

paregoric: a drug containing camphor and a small amount of opium which has a soothing effect. The distribution of this drug is restricted by law (LEV)

parens patriae [*Lat, lit father of his country*]: a doctrine by which the government supervises children and other persons who are under a legal disability. It often takes the form of supervision which is analogous to that of a parent

pari-mutuels: a race betting system where the odds and winnings are determined by the total amount wagered in a particular race (LEV)

pari passu [*Lat*]: by or at equal pace; on an equal basis

parity bit: a bit associated with other data bits to get some specified relation, such as an odd or even total number of bits for each character. A parity bit is usually associated with the frame for each six-bit character on tape; also parity bits may be placed at frequent intervals to associate them with the seven rows of bits (six for data and one for parity) along the tape (ADPS)

parity check: a summation check in which the binary digits in a character or word in storage or a character, word, or row on tape, are added (modulo 2) and the sum checked against a single, previously specified digit; for example, a check which tests whether the number of ones is odd or even (ADPS)

parkerize: to impart a dull, relatively rough, rust-preventive finish to a firearm, using powdered iron and phosphoric acid (DWMT)

parlance: manner of speaking; speech; language (LEV)

parole: a penological device which allows the final portion of a sentence of imprisonment to be served outside the prison in the community. Parole is a contrac-

tual agreement between the state's penal authorities and the parolee in which the parolee agrees to certain conditions, including supervision by the parole department, in return for his release. The parolee remains subject to the jurisdiction of the correctional authorities, and may be returned to prison if he fails to abide by the conditions of parole

parol evidence: oral or verbal evidence; that which is given by word or mouth; the ordinary kind of evidence, given by witnesses in court (CDTP)

parole board: an administrative board which by law has charge of granting paroles, and of supervising the parolees. Usu. the board is governed by law as to who may be granted parole, and the length of time parolees remain under its control. Originated by Maconochie for transportees to Norfolk Island as a method of improving discipline, and called ticket-of-leave (DOS)

parole clinic: a facility which provides intensive aid to parolees who require continued mental health services and therapy after release. This facility is usually maintained by a governmental agency, such as mental health services or social services (IC)

parole contract: a statement of the conditions which the parolee is to observe while on parole. Violation of these conditions is ground for the revocation of the parole and for the return of the parolee to the institution (DOS)

parole officer: individual who is responsible for the supervision of those who have been granted parole by the authority

parolee: a prisoner who has been released on parole (LEV)

parricide: the murder of one's father or mother (CDTP)

parry: act to ward off or evade a weapon such as a knife or sword, or a question (LEV)

pars [*Lat*]: a part

partial: (1) inclined to favor one

side or the other (CDTP) (2) of, or pertaining to, a part (CDTP)

partial evidence: that which goes to establish a detached fact, in a series of facts pertaining to the principal fact in dispute

partial fingerprint: a latent fingerprint which is composed of only part of the total finger impression (LEV)

particeps criminis: a guilty participant in a crime (CDTP)

particular writs: in general, the common law writs, of which there were a multitude, generally bore specific Latin names, from their purpose, or from their emphatic words; but there are some English names (C.J., vol. 71) (CDTP)

partition: a division into parts (CDTP)

partition coefficient: when two immiscible liquids are shaken together and any dissolved substance soluble in both is present, its concentrations in the two liquids after separation depend upon a parameter known as the partition coefficient (FS)

party: (1) a person or group of persons constituting one side of an issue, undertaking, or dispute (LEV) (2) the person or persons involved in different sides of a legal action (3) a person or persons constituting one or more sides of a contractual agreement (LEV)

party wall: wall shared by each of the occupiers of the two buildings it separates (CDTP)

pass: (1) succeed or accomplish something (LEV) (2) pronounce (LEV) (3) become unconscious (LEV) (4) cause to circulate or negotiate an instrument of commerce (LEV)

passenger vehicle inspection: a law enforcement function which monitors conformance of passenger vehicles with state or local safety and/or pollution laws and ordinances (TDPPC)

passion: emotion; excitement; fury; lust; strong feeling (LEV)

passive intrusion sensor: a passive sensor in an intrusion alarm system which detects an intruder within the range of the sensor. Examples are a sound sensing detection system, a vibration detection system, an infrared motion detector, and an E-field sensor (TDIAS)

passive sensor: a sensor which detects natural radiation or radiation disturbances, but does not itself emit the radiation on which its operation depends (TDIAS)

passive ultrasonic alarm system: an alarm system which detects the sounds in the ultrasonic frequency range caused by an attempted forcible entry into a protected structure. The system consists of microphones, a control unit containing an amplifier, filters, an accumulator, and a power supply. The unit's sensitivity is adjustable so that ambient noises or normal sounds will not initiate an alarm signal; however, noise above the present level will initiate an alarm (TDIAS)

passport: an official government document issued to a person, certifying his citizenship and authorizing him to travel to other countries with the full protection of the country issuing it (LEV)

pat: a light touch or stroke

pat down: a search of a suspect's outer clothing to check for weapons

patch: (1) a piece of greased cloth or leather which was wrapped around the ball to make it fit the bore more tightly. It was commonly used with muzzle-loading rifles that fired spherical balls and in some dueling pistols (DWMT) (2) a small piece of cotton cloth used to clean the bore of small arms (DWMT)

patent: (1) open; manifest (CDTP) (2) protected by letters patent (CDTP)

paternal: of or pertaining to a father (CDTP)

paternalism: protection and control, like that of a minor child by a parent, exercised by the government over the governed, employer over employee, or in similar relationships (DOS)

paternity: fatherhood; being the father of a child (LEV)

pathogenic: disease-causing

pathologist: a person who is highly educated and trained in pathology, which is the area of medicine dealing with the nature and causes of illness or injury of people (LEV)

pathology: (1) the science dealing with causes, development, and effects of disease (DOS) (2) the diseased or abnormal condition itself. *Cf.* social pathology (DOS)

patricide: the murder or murderer of one's father (CDTP)

patrol: (1) to make the rounds or travel over certain areas, to watch and protect (LEV) (2) men who patrol (LEV)

patrol beat: an area to which a patrol is assigned and for which it has primary responsibility for responding to calls for police assistance (TDPPC)

patrol bus: bus-type vehicle used to transport police officers, prisoners, or other personnel in connection with law enforcement functions (TDPPC)

patrol car: an automobile, usu. modified with "police options" or special equipment, used by law enforcement agencies in performing the patrol function (TDPPC)

patrol district: a geographical area which consists of more than one patrol beat and which may have its own police station and vehicle maintenance facilities (TDPPC)

patrolman: (1) the law enforcement officer who walks a beat or patrols areas by motor vehicle (2) an official rank of a police officer, generally the beginning rank (LEV)

patrol wagon: a van or bus-type vehicle used primarily to transport people from the site of an incident to a police station. Also called prisoner wagon (TDPPC)

patronage, political: the giving of jobs in public offices by politicians; the distribution of public office jobs (LEV)

pattern: (1) the ridge formation on a person's fingers, palms, or feet (LEV) (2) refers to the distribution of the shot charge after leaving the muzzle (CDTP)

pauper: one without means; one supported at the public expense (CDTP)

pawn: turn over possession of something to another as security that money, borrowed from such person, will be repaid in a specified time (LEV)

pawnbroker: person who takes articles as security on loans with interest (LEV)

P.C.R.O. (PCRO): Police Community Relations Officer

P.D. (PD): Police Department

peace bond: a bond or bail fixed by a magistrate to insure that the person bonded will keep the peace and not molest or injure someone against whom he has made threats or endeavored to do harm. In 1970 the peace bond was declared unconstitutional by a Hawaiian court (LEV)

peace officers: this term is variously defined by statute in the different states; but generally it includes sheriffs and their deputies, constables, marshals, members of the police force of cities, and other officers whose duty is to enforce and preserve the public peace (CDTP)

peaceful picketing: Congress approved, on June 24, 1936, an act making it a felony to transport in interstate or foreign commerce persons to be employed to obstruct or interfere with the right of peaceful picketing during labor controversies. Amended in 1939 as follows: (A) That it shall be unlawful to transport or cause to be transported in interstate or foreign commerce any person who is employed or is to be employed for the purpose of obstructing or interfering by force, or threats with (1) peaceful picketing by employees during any labor controversy affecting wages, hours, or conditions of labor, or (2) the exercise by employees of any of the rights of self organization, or collective bargaining. (B) Any person who willfully violates or abets any person in violating any provision of this act, and any person who is knowingly transported in or travels in interstate or foreign commerce for any of the purposes enumerated in this act shall be deemed guilty of a felony, and on conviction fined $5,000 or imprisoned for two years, or both. The provisions of the act do not apply to common carrier (CDTP)

peculation: the wrongful conversion of property in one's custody or control to one's own use; embezzlement (LEV)

pecuniary: relating to money; monetary (CDTP)

pederasty: unnatural sexual intercourse, usu. between a man and a boy; sodomy

pedestrian: person who travels by walking (LEV)

pedometer: device for recording the number of steps taken, which can then be used to compute distance travelled (LEV)

pedophile: one who indulges in pedophilia

pedophilia: sexual perversion in which a child is selected

Peel, Robert (*1788-1850*): as the British Home Secretary, in 1829, Sir Robert Peel introduced into Parliament an act for improving the police in and near the Metropolis [London]. Peel believed that a community needed a protective body of well-selected and trained men in order to prevent crime and other forms of social control. He reformed criminal laws by limiting their scope and reducing unfair penalties. Peel further removed the death penalty from more than 100 offenses. Most important, he established 12 fundamental principles of quality policing which are still applicable today

peeling: a system used by safe burglars, whereby the outer surface of the safe door is peeled off, thus making access to the locking device available (LEV)

peephole: a hole in something such as a wall or door through which a person may look (LEV)

peer: (1) an equal. A trial jury must be composed of persons who are peers (members of the general class) of the accused (DAP) (2) a member of the British House of Lords (DAP)

pelvis: the cavity in the skeleton of many vertebrates formed by the hip bones and adjoining bones (LEV)

pen register: a device placed on the telephone line of a person suspected of making nuisance calls. It records the time and date of each call and the number called. This is then compared with information recorded by the person called and is used to prove that the suspect made such calls (LEV)

penal: of or pertaining to punishment or penalties (CDTP)

penal administration: the maintenance and management of institutions and programs (as probation and parole) for the punishment and correction of criminals. The personnel of such an administration consists of prison and parole boards, wardens, guards, medical, pedagogical, and psychiatric staffs, and probation and parole officers (DAP)

penal codes: many of the states have adopted penal or criminal codes, the purpose of which is to define what acts shall be punished as crimes. In some of them the code is intended to cover the whole law, and no act is a crime unless it is expressly declared so. In others the code does not entirely abrogate the common law insofar as it makes acts crimes, but merely abrogates it as to the acts expressly prohibited, leaving the common law where it is not so supplanted, still in force. Even in those states, however, which have penal codes, and do not recognize

insanity. It was believed that by this system the prisoner would be kept from contamination or from being a contaminating influence and also that he would not be recognized by other inmates after release. This system was borrowed by most European countries, but has entirely disappeared from the one imposing a penalty or punishment for some offense of a public nature or wrong committed against the state (59 S.W. 952) (CDTP)

penal servitude: punishment which consists of confinement and hard labor (CDTP)

penalty: a punishment by fine or imprisonment, or both, inflicted for violation of a law (DAP)

pendens: pending; hanging (CDTP)

Pendleton Act: the civil service reform act passed by Congress, Jan. 16, 1883. See civil service (DAP)

penetration: (1) the insertion of the penis into the female parts; in criminal law, used in the discussion of rape cases (2) usu. expressed in the number of 7/8-inch white pine boards that a bullet will pass through when fired from a specified length of barrel. Sometimes the penetration is expressed in inches (CDTP)

penis: male sex organ

penitentiary: an institution for the imprisonment of convicted offenders

Penn, William: governor of Pennsylvania, 1682–1692. Author of penological reforms known as "The Great Law," which substituted imprisonment at hard labor for the death penalty for a majority of serious crimes (LCC)

Pennsylvania System: the system of imprisonment originating in the Eastern Pennsylvania Prison when it was opened in 1829. It was characterized by having each prisoner confined in a separate cell without contact with any human beings except the warden and chaplain, and by work in the cell to occupy the prisoner primarily to prevent brooding and ultimate

common law crimes, the common law is in force to the extent that it may be resorted to for the definition of crimes which are not defined in the statutes prohibiting them (CDTP)

penal laws: those which prohibit an act and impose a penalty for the commission of it. A penal law is prison system in the United States (DOS)

penology: the field of study concerning the treatment of criminals

pentaprism: a five-sided prism used in single-lens reflex viewing hoods to turn the image right-side-up and laterally correct (MPPF)

peonage: a condition of enforced servitude, by which the servitor is restrained of his liberty and compelled to labor in liquidation of some debt or obligation, real or pretended, against his will (CDTP)

People ex rel. Forsyth v. Court of Sessions, 141 N.Y. 288, 36 N.E. 186 (1894): the New York Court of Appeals upheld the right of the trial court to suspend the imposition of sentence, indicating that such power was inherent in all superior courts of criminal jurisdiction

People v. Anderson, 6 Cal. 3d 628, 100 Cal. Rptr. 152, 493 P. 2d 880 (1972): in this case, the California Supreme Court invalidated the death penalty under its state constitutional provisions against cruel and unusual punishment

People v. Cahan, 44 Cal. 2d 434, 282 P. 2d 905 (1955): the California Supreme Court (4–3) adopted the federal exclusionary rule of the *Weeks* case. (The Court discusses warnings to law enforcement officers on illegal practices in earlier decisions, and, why, to try to deter such conduct, the Court felt impelled in *Cahan* to apply the exclusionary rule to peace officers.) (ILECJ)

People v. Defore, 242 N.Y. 13, 150 N.E. 585 (1926): this decision by Mr. Justice Cardozo (prior to his appointment to the Supreme Court of the United States in

1932) is recognized as the leading case rejecting the *Week*'s exclusionary rule (ILECJ)
People v. Peters, 18 N.Y. 2d 238, 273 N.Y.S. 217, 219 N.E. 2d 595 (1966): for a third time, a majority of the Court upheld the constitutionality of "stop-and-frisk," this time, after New York's legislation had become effective. The United States Supreme Court granted certiorari, 386 U.S. 980 (1967). [In several states law enforcement has been given so-called "stop-and-frisk" authority either by judicial fiat or statute. See, for example, People v. Michelson, 380 P. 2d 658 (Cal. 1963); State v. Dilley, 231 A. 2d 533 (N.J. 1967); legislation enacted in both Massachusetts and Utah in (1967); and, local ordinance on "stop-and-frisk," enacted by the *Detroit* (Michigan) *Common Council*, effective July, 1968.] (ILECJ)
People v. Rivera, 14 N.Y. 2d 441, 201 N.E. 2d 32 (1964); People v. Pugach, 15 N.Y. 2d 65, 204 N.E. 2d 176 (1964): the New York Court of Appeals, by a divided Court, held that "stop-and-frisk" procedures, as applied by the police officers in the two cases, both involving arrests that were made before the adoption of New York's "stop-and-frisk" legislation—could be sustained as constitutionally permissible. (The United States Supreme Court denied certiorari in both cases.) The Court said, in *Rivera*, that, "the evidence needed to make the inquiry is not of the same degree of conclusiveness as that required for an arrest. The stopping of an individual to inquire is not an arrest and the ground upon which the police may make the inquiry may be less incriminating than the ground for an arrest for a crime known to have been committed." "[T]he right to stop and inquire," the Court continued, "is to be justified for a cause less conclusive than that which would sustain an arrest, so the right to frisk may be

justified as an incident to inquiry upon grounds of elemental safety and precaution which might not initially sustain a search.") (ILECJ)

pepperbox: an obsolete type of revolver (pistol) which had a group of barrels which revolved (LEV)

per annum [*Lat*]: by the year

per capita [*Lat*]: by heads; per person; by or for each person (LEV)

per curiam [*Lat, lit "by the court"*]: an opinion of the full court, rather than one of an individual judge

per diem [*Lat*]: by the day

perambulation, writ of: a writ at common law which is issued by consent of both parties, when they are in doubt as to the bounds of their respective states, and is directed to the sheriff, who is commanded to make the "perambulation" with a jury, and to set the bounds and limits between them in certainty (C. J., vol. 71) (CDTP)

percentage of pattern: number of pellet marks in a thirty-inch circle, over a forty-yard range, divided by the number of pellets in the load (CDTP)

percentage supervision: a method of line supervision in which the current in or resistance of a supervised line is monitored for changes. When the change exceeds a selected percentage of the normal operating current or resistance in the line, an alarm signal is produced (TDIAS)

percussion cap: a small metal cup holding fulminate placed on the tube or nipple of a percussion gun; when struck, the sparks enter the barrel through a hole and fire the charge. Also applied to other priming systems, such as the Maynard (CDTP)

peremptory: positive; decisive; absolute; final (LEV)

peremptory challenge: as applied to selection of jurors, challenges which are made without assigning any reason and which the court must allow

peremptory writ: directs the sheriff to cause the defendant to appear in court without any option given him, provided the plaintiff gave the sheriff security effectually to prosecute his claim. The writ was very occasionally in use, and only where nothing was specifically demanded, but only a satisfaction in general; as in case of writs of trespass on the case, wherein no doubt or other specific thing was sued for, but only damages to be assessed by a jury   (CDTP)

perfidious: false to trust; disloyal
(CDTP)

perform: in COBOL, a verb for departing temporarily from the normal sequence of the program to execute some other procedure a specified number of times and return to the normal sequence
(ADPS)

performance requirement: a functional use or need required of a vehicle, defined by the manner in which the vehicle or its systems should respond or react to fulfill the requirement   (TDPPC)

performance standard: a description of the level of acceptable performance of a product, service, or material for meeting the requirements of a given function when measured in accordance with specified procedures and conditions
(TDPPC)

performance test: a test of an applicant's ability to do the tasks required in a position under actual or simulated conditions of employment   (DAP)

perimeter alarm system: an alarm system which provides perimeter protection   (TDIAS)

perimeter protection: protection of access to the outer limits of a protected area, by means of physical barriers, sensors on physical barriers, or exterior sensors not associated with a physical barrier
(TDIAS)

peripheral vision: side vision; the ability to see things other than through direct vision; to see objects and things to the side of

where vision is focused   (LEV)

periphery: outer boundary; external limit   (LEV)

perjury: the intentional making of a false written or oral statement in, or for use in, a judicial proceeding, or any proceeding before a board or official, wherein such board or official is authorized to take testimony. The false statement must be made under oath, or affirmation, and must relate to matters material to the issue or question in controversy. The statement made must be knowingly false, however an unqualified statement of that which one does not know definitely to be true is equivalent to a statement of that which he knows to be false; violation of an oath. The definition varies among the states
(LEV)

permanent: lasting; intended to last indefinitely   (CDTP)

permanent circuit: an alarm circuit which is capable of transmitting an alarm signal whether the alarm control is in access mode or secure mode. Used, for example, on foiled fixed windows, tamper switches, and supervisory lines. *See also* supervisory alarm system, supervisory circuit, and permanent protection   (TDIAS)

permanent protection: a system of alarm devices such as foil, burglar alarm pads, or lacings connected in a permanent circuit to provide protection whether the control unit is in the access mode or secure mode   (TDIAS)

permit: an official paper identifying a person as one who is entitled to exercise some privilege under the law; also a license   (DAP)

perpetrate: to violate a law or do something bad, such as commit fraud; to commit a wrongful act
(LEV)

perpetual: eternal; continuous
(CDTP)

perquisites: something derived from a position or office in addition to the regular salary fee   (CDTP)

per se [*Lat*]: by itself, alone

Perse®: a new drug developed by Dr. Emanuel Revici, a New York biochemist. It is a nonaddictive drug to cure addicts of heroin, barbiturates, and methadone, and has no apparent bad side-effects. To relieve physical addiction decreasing doses of Perse are given; however, the patient still needs psychotherapy. As of May, 1971 the Food and Drug Administration had not certified the drug as safe   (LEV)

persecute: to harass; to annoy; to torment   (LEV)

persistent: existing continuously; chronic   (CDTP)

person: the common law provides only for the searching, under a warrant, of some place or locality as do the statutes in most of the states. However, it is held that the legislature may, without violating either the state or national constitution, authorize the issuance of a warrant to search the person; and such warrants have been provided for by some statutes, both state and federal. (C.J. 56, 1186) When statute specifies the purposes for which search warrants will issue they cannot be issued for other purposes (208 N.Y. 16)   (CDTP)

personal identification: the means by which a person can be identified. This may be by such things as an official card, letter, or driver's license. There is in use a personal identification fingerprint card. Many citizens have their fingerprints taken on such cards and placed on file with government agencies so as to have a personal identification on record   (LEV)

personal liberty laws: enacted by 10 northern state legislatures after the passage of the Compromise Act of 1850. The aim of the laws was to overcome the effects of the fugitive slave provisions of the federal act. They attempted to accomplish this by forbidding their officers to aid in the arrests of fugitive slaves, denying the use of their jails for the detention of such fugitives, and ordering their courts to provide jury trials for all seized [blacks]   (DOAH)

personal property: goods, money, and all movable property (CDTP)

personate: with fraudulent intent, to assume the character and/or identity of another, without the latter's consent, and to gain some advantage or obtain something of value as the result of such impersonation. To pretend to be or assume the identity of another   (LEV)

personation: passing oneself off as another   (CDTP)

personnel security: a program or procedure whereby an organization seeks to protect its technology, materials, or equipment from loss or embezzlement by its own employees and nonemployees who have contact with personnel of the organization. Employees who are considered "not good risks" are precluded from access to certain types of information and materials   (LEV)

person's room: one's room in an apartment house, or boarding house, or in a tourist camp is also under the protection of the guaranties against unreasonable searches and seizures   (CDTP)

perspective: the illusion of three dimensions created on a flat surface   (MPPF)

per stirpes: by stocks or roots; by sources of descent   (CDTP)

perversion: abnormal sexual desires and activities; the obtaining of sexual satisfaction by abnormal methods   (LEV)

pervert: one who has turned away from what is normal, natural or right   (LEV)

pervert, sex: one who engages in some form of sexual deviation or perversion   (LEV)

petit: small   (CDTP)

petit jury: a body at common law of 12 disinterested and impartial men, chosen from the community in which the trial is held, who render a verdict on questions of fact submitted in the trial of a case, later modified in many States by the introduction of women jurors, reduction in number of jurors, especially in civil cases, and provisions for less than unanimous verdicts except in the trial of persons accused of capital crimes; so-called because fewer in number than a grand jury; called also trial jury (DAP)

petit larceny, petty larceny: any larceny which is not grand larceny. See larceny (CDTP)

petition: a formal request submitted to a court requesting action (LEV)

petrography: the study and identification of rocks and their derivatives, such as soil (LEV)

petty: of little value or significance (LEV)

petty jury: petit jury

peyote: a species of small cactus, or the powerful drug decocted therefrom by the Indians of Mexico and the western United States and widely used for medicinal, ceremonial, and religious purposes (DOS)

pH: the acidity or alkalinity of a solution expressed in terms of the hydrogen ion concentration. A neutral solution has a pH of 7.0; an acid solution below this value; and an alkaline solution above it (MPPF)

pharmacognosy: the identification of plant materials used in pharmacy by means of their microscopic appearance (FS)

phase: in chemistry, "any homogeneous and physically distinct part of a system which is separated from other parts of the system by definite bounding surfaces" (Samuel Glasstone, *Textbook of Physical Chemistry*). For example, gin-and-tonic is a one-phase system; oil and vinegar a two-phase; ice, water, and water vapor a three-phase. All solutions and gases are one-phase systems. In a typical rock, there are as many phases as there are separate crystalline minerals (FS)

phase contrast: a type of micros-

copy in which a transparent object is made more visible by arranging for interference to occur between rays which have, and those which have not, passed through the object (FS)

phenobarbital: a barbiturate, white powder, which has hypnotic and sedative properties (LEV)

phenol: a poison or antiseptic—carbolic acid (LEV)

phenolphthalein test: a preliminary test to determine if a stain is blood. If a positive reaction is obtained then further confirmation tests are conducted (LEV)

phobia: an unnatural, abnormal, illogical fear (LEV)

Phoenix House: a narcotic addict rehabilitation establishment. See therapeutic community (LEV)

phony: a fraud, or fake (LEV)

phosphorus: a chemical that ignites spontaneously in air and gives off a dense white smoke. It is widely used as a smoke agent and for incendiary bombs and shells (DWMT)

phot: a unit of luminance; one lumen per square millimeter (MPPF)

photochemical action: a chemical action induced by exposure to light (MPPF)

photoelectric alarm system: an alarm system which employs a light beam and photoelectric sensor to provide a line of protection. Any interruption of the beam by an intruder is sensed by the sensor. Mirrors may be used to change the direction of the beam. The maximum beam length is limited by many factors, some of which are the light source intensity, number of mirror reflections, detector sensitivity, beam divergence, fog, and haze (TDIAS)

photoelectric alarm system, modulated: a photoelectric alarm system in which the transmitted light beam is modulated in a predetermined manner and in which the receiving equipment will signal an alarm unless it receives the properly modulated light (TDIAS)

photoelectric beam type smoke detector: a smoke detector which has a light source which projects a light beam across the area to be protected onto a photoelectric cell. Smoke between the light source and the receiving cell reduces the light reaching the cell, causing actuation   (TDIAS)

photoelectric sensor: a device which detects a visible or invisible beam of light interruption. *See also* photoelectric alarm system and photoelectric alarm system, modulated   (TDIAS)

photoelectric spot type smoke detector: a smoke detector which contains a chamber with covers which prevent the entrance of light but allow the entrance of smoke. The chamber contains a light source and a photosensitive cell so placed that light is blocked from it. When smoke enters, the smoke particles scatter and reflect the light into the photosensitive cell, causing an alarm   (TDIAS)

photoengraving: a method of producing etched printing plates by photographic means   (MPPF)

photoflash bulb: a specially made light bulb or lamp, fired electrically, which gives a brilliant flash for taking photographs where there is not enough natural light. The flash and the camera shutter must be synchronized   (LEV)

photoflash lamp: a light bulb filled with aluminum wire or shreds in an atmosphere of oxygen; the heating of the filament ignites the primer which in turn fires the aluminum, giving a short brilliant flash of light   (MPPF)

photoflood lamp: an electric lamp designed to be worked at higher than normal voltage, giving brilliant illumination at the expense of lamp life   (MPPF)

photogrammetry: the science of mapping by the use of aerial photographs   (MPPF)

photographic storage: (1) miniature facsimile copies of readable documents or of direct output of the processor (ADPS) (2) photo-

graphic copies of data shown on direct-display tubes (ADPS) (3) high-density storage of data in binary form on photographic disks for quick reference purposes   (ADPS)

photogravure: a method of making an intaglio engraving in copper from a photograph, using the gelatin image as an acid resist (MPPF)

photomacrograph: a photograph of an object large enough to be seen by the naked eye but where the lens of the microscope enlarges the size and detail of the object. Such is used in the examination of the cut surfaces of metal wire, etc., i.e., in tool mark examinations or firearm examinations   (LEV)

photomacrography: enlarged photography of small objects by the use of a long bellows camera and a lens of short focal length (MPPF)

photomicrograph: a photograph taken through a microscope of objects so small as to be invisible to the naked eye   (LEV)

photomicrography: photography through a microscope   (MPPF)

photomontage: a picture composed of several smaller pictures (MPPF)

photons: according to the quantum theory any electromagnetic radiation as a wave motion or as a stream of discrete quanta of energy. Photon is the name applied to a quantum of light or other radiant energy of very short wavelength   (FS)

photoregression: the gradual disappearance of the latent image which has not been subjected to development   (MPPF)

photosensitive: material which is chemically or physically changed by the action of light   (MPPF)

photostat: the trade name of a camera which makes copies of documents, letters, drawings, etc., on sensitized paper; also the copies made by means of this camera   (MPPF)

photosynthesis: a synthetic (i.e., building-up) reaction which uses energy reaching the reactants as light (e.g., the production in sunlight of chlorophyll, the green colouring matter of plants) (FS)

phototopography: the mapping or surveying of terrain by means of photography (MPPF)

phrenology: theory and practice based on Gall's hypothesis that mental traits and therefore human character conform to the shape of the human skull and are localized in certain specific brain and skull areas; of significance to sociologists because it was used for vocational and marital guidance before the present vogue of tests and statistical correlations for predictive purposes (DOS)

phrenology book, the first: was *The Outlines of Phrenology* by Johann Gaspar Spurzheim, M.D., of the universities of Vienna and Paris, and a licentiate of the Royal College of Physicians of London. It was published in 1832 by Marsh, Capen and Lyon, Boston, Mass. It was divided into three sections covering general principles of phrenology, special facilities of the mind, and the usefulness of phrenology (FAMOUS)

physical: pertaining to the structure of an organized being (CDTP)

physical description: a description of the physical features of a person, including such things as age, height, weight, race, hair, eyes, complexion, build, etc. (LEV)

physical evidence: real evidence; evidence which by its nature, "speaks for itself"; nontestimonial evidence. Contrasted with oral evidence (LEV)

physical fact: in the law of evidence, a fact the existence of which may be perceived by the senses (CDTP)

physical security: that part of security concerned with physical measures designed to safeguard personnel; to prevent unauthorized access to equipment, facilities, material, and documents; and to safeguard equipment, facilities, material, and documents against espionage, sabotage, damage, and theft (DWMT)

physique: build or structure of the body (LEV)

physique, asthenic: a human physical type characterized by relatively small trunk, long angular body and limbs, and low constitutional vitality. Believed to be associated with schizophrenic mental traits. *Cf.* physique, athletic; physique, pyknic (DOS)

physique, athletic: medium-proportioned human body type with well-developed musculature suggesting the athlete. Athletic physique is one of the three human body types . . . distinguished in an attempt to establish a relationship between personality traits and the type of body structure. *Cf.* physique, asthenic; physique, pyknic (DOS)

physique, pyknic: round, heavy-set human body type with short limbs. One of three types of identified as significant in establishing a consistent relationship between physical and psychological human types. *Cf.* physique, asthenic; physique, athletic (DOS)

pica: a type size, 12 point. This is the larger of the two sizes of type commonly used on typewriters. The other is elite (LEV)

picket: a person who is posted at an approach to a place of employment or who patrols the area in front of or adjacent to the premises of an employer, with whom a union is in dispute, to persuade and otherwise influence workers not to accept employment there, or to influence them to quit working, and to seek to influence the public against patronizing the employer (CDTP)

picketing: the methods used by labor unions in the vicinity of the employer's premises to make public the existence of a labor dispute (CDTP)

pickpocket: a thief who steals money or things from a person's pockets (LEV)

picric acid: trinitrophenol. A high explosive slightly more powerful than TNT used widely in the form of mixtures with other nitro compounds. It has found extensive use in some foreign countries and is also called "melinite" and "lyddite" (DWMT)

pictorial: the layout of headings, columns, totals, blank spaces, etc., used in planning a report for printing (ADPS)

picture: in COBOL, a symbolic description of each data element according to certain rules concerning numerals, alphanumerics, location of decimal points, and length (ADPS)

pigeon dropping: an old and commonly used confidence game where two con-men work together to defraud a victim of money or property. One form is where one operator drops a pocketbook which is picked up by the second who is in company with the victim. It contains some money, usually counterfeit. Arrangements are made to split the money later and the victim is to hold it until then. The victim gives the operator some money or property for security and never sees him again. There are many variations of the game (LEV)

pillage: plundering and carrying off goods or merchandise by force (CDTP)

pimp: a procurer; one who provides for others the means of gratifying lust (CDTP)

pincushion distortion: a term applied to the pincushion-shaped image of a square object when the diaphragm is placed behind the lens (MPPF)

Pinel, Philippe (1745-1826): a French physician, Pinel advocated humane treatment of mentally ill persons and a more empirical study of mental diseases. He stressed the role of passions in mental disease. His well-documented psychiatric case histories are valuable research

pinfire: a type of cartridge ignition system invented in about 1835. The cartridge had a detonating pin outward from the base, and when this pin was struck with the hammer, the inner end struck a fulminate cap within the base of the cartridge (DWMT)

pinholes: tiny clear spots on negative of positive images, caused by dust, air bells, or undissolved chemicals (MPPF)

Pinkerton, Allan [(1819-1884), detective]: born on Aug. 25, 1819, in Glasgow, the son of a police sergeant, Pinkerton emigrated to the U.S. in 1842 and, after a year in Chicago, opened a cooper's shop in Dundee, Ill. Working on a desolate island one day, he discovered a gang of counterfeiters and later led in capturing them. Similar successful exploits followed and in 1846 he was elected deputy sheriff of Kane County. An abolitionist, he converted his shop into a way station for the Underground Railroad. He moved to Chicago when appointed deputy sheriff of Cook County, and joined the police force in 1850. During a series of railway and express robberies, he opened his own firm, the Pinkerton National Detective Agency, a pioneer venture in the country. The agency solved many of the railroad crimes and in 1861 disclosed a plot to assassinate Abraham Lincoln while the president-elect was passing through Baltimore on the way to his inauguration. Plans for Lincoln's journey were changed and the plot failed. At Gen. George B. McClellan's request, Pinkerton organized a secret service in the area of McClellan's command and followed him to Washington to head a department of counterespionage, working in disguise as "Maj. E. J. Allen." He resigned from the department in 1862 and thereafter was an investigator of various claims and frauds against the government. After the Civil War he resumed control of his own detective agency, although after 1869 he relinquished the field work to subordinates. The agency became particularly prominent for its work against labor unions and labor movements, being widely regarded as a tool of the employers for strikebreaking, and the most famous "Pinkerton," James Mc Parlan, was primarily responsible for the coal fields. Pinkerton's files became invaluable to law-enforcement bodies and he published a number of popular accounts of his work, including *The Molly Maguires and the Detectives*, 1877; *Strikers, Communists, Tramps and Detectives*, 1878; *The Spy of the Rebellion*, 1883; and *Thirty Years A Detective*, 1884. He died in Chicago on July 1, 1884. Today, the company provides both detective services and uniformed guard service, especially industrial security (*Webster's American Biographies*)

pins: pieces of iron or steel used to hold the barrel and stock together (CDTP)

pintle: (1) the verticle bearing about which a gun carriage revolves; a pin used as a hinge or axis (DWMT) (2) a hook for catching, sustaining, or pulling. It is mounted on a vehicle so that another vehicle can be attached (DWMT)

pipette: a pointed glass tube for delivering small volumes of liquid. The type used in chemistry delivers an accurately known volume from a graduation mark. The type used in bacteriology, blood grouping, etc., is not graduated and delivers a roughly-known volume, or a chosen number of drops, by compression of a rubber teat (FS)

piquers: persons who use sharp instruments by which they stab their victims, usually female (LEV)

piracy: an act of violence committed at sea by individuals or armed vessels not acting under the authority of a state or of a belligerent or insurgent government (DAP)

pirate: one who commits robbery on the high seas (CDTP)

pistol: (1) in popular usage, any firearm, usually short-barreled, designed to be held and fired in one hand. Pistols came into use early in the 16th century, when the wheel lock first made them practical (DWMT) (2) more precisely, such a firearm in which the chamber is an integral part of the barrel, especially a self-loading pistol, as distinguished from a revolver (DWMT)

pistol carbine: a pistol equipped with a removable buttstock so that it can be used either as a shoulder weapon or as a handgun. Pistol carbines were first used in quantity early in the 19th century. The United States had an official model in 1855 (DWMT)

place or person: officers may not, under the authority of a search warrant, search any place other than that described therein, even though such other place be owned or controlled by the same person; and if they do so, the search is illegal, and "unreasonable" under the constitutional guaranty. (32 A.L.R. 357) There is no right to search the person under a warrant for the search of "shops" and "premises." (51 U.S. 114) The search of a vehicle under a warrant authorizing the search of a building is unlawful, as the search of the person of one not the owner of an automobile, and not in it, under a warrant for the search of the automobile (268 S.W. 1089) (CDTP)

places of habitation: the legal maxim "Every man's house is his castle" applies with all its vigor to the right of search of private dwellings, and such a search without a warrant is unreasonable and abhorrent to our laws. (269 U.S. 20) This includes apartment or room, used as a dwelling, also extends to luggage kept in such rooms. (31 S.W. 2nd 821) Also applies to abandoned dwelling house, or a house from which the dweller is temporarily absent,

without a search warrant (CDTP)
plain arch: a fingerprint pattern in
which the ridges come in from
one side and go out the other
without recurve or turning back
and in which there is a smooth upward thrust of the lines at or near
the center of the pattern (LEV)
plain whorl: a fingerprint pattern.
See whorl (LEV)
plainclothesman: law enforcement
officer, usually a detective, who
works while dressed in civilian
clothes, rather than a uniform
(LEV)
plaintiff: the complaining party in
any legal case
plant security: the protection of a
business or industrial plant from
fire, burglary, sabotage, theft, or
liability (LEV)
plants: physical arrangements made
by arsonists to facilitate the burning of a structure. These may include use of flammable liquids,
laying of "trailers" of combustible
materials, opening of containers,
blocking open of fire doors, and
various devices to cause ignition
by remote control or when the
"fire bug" is not on the premises
(LEV)
plasma, blood: that part of the
blood which is a liquid. The other
part is composed of the blood
cells. Blood plasma is used as a
transfusion (LEV)
plaster of paris: a powdery substance used in police work for
making casts of impressions in the
earth and other soft surfaces.
Such impressions are usually
caused by shoe or tire imprints.
Plaster of paris is composed of
gypsum and can be obtained from
a druggist (LEV)
plastic prints: fingerprint impressions made in a plastic material
such as melted candle wax, putty,
tar, soap, etc. (LEV)
plastic surgery: surgery where
change or restoration of parts of
the body is accomplished (LEV)
plasticized white phosphorus
(PWP): a common ingredient in
incendiary devices, PWP is pro-

duced by melting white phosphorus (WP) and stirring it into cold
water. This produces small granules which are then mixed with a
viscous solution of synthetic rubber. All the granules become
coated with a film of rubber and
thus are separated from one another. This rubbery mass is dispersed by an exploding munition,
but does not break up to the
extent that WP does (DWMT)
plate back: an attachment to certain rollfilm cameras such as the
older Kodaks, the Rolleiflex, etc.,
permitting the use of plates or
sheet film; incorrectly used as a
description of a camera primarily
designed for use with plates; such
cameras are plate cameras, not
plate-back cameras (MPPF)
plate holder: a lightproof holder in
which sensitized plates are held
for exposure in the camera
(MPPF)
Plato (*428-348 B.C.*): a philosopher of ancient Greece, Plato was
one of the most influential think-
ers in the history of Western civili-
zation. In the *Republic,* one of his
most important works, he argued
that the operation of justice cannot be fully understood unless
seen in relation to the idea of the
good, which is the supreme principle of order and truth. Throughout his writings, Plato touched
upon almost every problem which
has occupied subsequent philosophers
platoon system: the division of
policemen or firemen into shifts,
or platoons, each of which is on
duty during certain hours of a
24-hour day (DAP)
plea: the answer which the accused
makes to the charges against him
(CDTP)
plea bargaining: the practice involving negotiation between prosecutor and defendant and/or his
attorney, which often results in
the defendant's entering of a
guilty plea in exchange for the
state's reduction of charges, or in
the prosecutor's promise to rec-

ommend a more lenient sentence than the offender would ordinarily receive. Plea bargaining was allowed by the U.S. Supreme Court in Brady v. U.S., 197 U.S. 742 and by the California Supreme Court in *People* v. *West* (1970)

plea of guilty: confession of guilt in a courtroom

plea of not guilty: plea denying guilt; consequently the burden of proof of guilt rests on the state

plead: to respond to a charge in a criminal court (LEV)

pleadings: pleadings in criminal cases are comparatively simple, and, contrary to popular opinion, reversals of criminal cases on appeal are very infrequent. The pleadings used by the state in felony and some misdemeanor cases are the indictment and the information; affidavits and complaints in misdemeanor cases. And by the defendant, usually an oral plea of "guilty" or "not guilty." Other pleas, such as, "former jeopardy" or "autrefois acquit," "insanity," or "alibi," are available or required in particular states. Pleas in abatement, demurrers, motions to quash the indictment and in arrest of judgement are also available under some circumstances (CDTP)

pledge, legal: a debtor puts up or turns over to the creditor certain property to be held until the debt is satisfied, with title to the property remaining in the debtor. The creditor must have a lien on the property (LEV)

plenary: full; entire; complete (CDTP)

plot: (1) a secret scheme or plan (LEV) (2) to draw, map, or diagram (LEV)

plurality: excess of votes for one person over those for all others (CDTP)

P.M. (PM): (medical) post mortem

poaching: (1) to trespass, especially after game or fish (CDTP) (2) to take illegally game or fish (CDTP)

poena: punishment; penalty (CDTP)

pogrom: a massacre or wholesale slaughter spontaneously generated or incited and organized by a government or ruling class against a group of unarmed persons because of popular hatred or some sort of prejudice. It refers esp. to the large scale killing of Jews in czarist Russia which from time to time was incited and organized by the governing class (DOS)

point: (1) to aim a weapon; to lay a gun on target (DWMT) (2) the tip or foremost part of a projectile (3) the man or group of men who precede an advancing force (DWMT)

point-blank: direct; directly at; straight at a point or spot (LEV)

points of identification: in fingerprints, identical or matching ridge formations on more than one set or copies of fingerprints, as when comparing a latent print with known prints of a person. Eight to 12 matching points of identification are enough to establish that two or more prints were made by the same person; some courts require a minimum of 12 points (LEV)

poison: a substance, which on being applied to the human body, internally or externally, is capable of destroying the action of the vital functions, or of placing the solids and fluids in such a state as to prevent the continuance of life by other than mechanical means (CDTP)

pola screen: a screen which transmits polarized light when properly oriented with respect to the vibration plane of the incident light. When rotated to a 90° angle it will not transmit the polarized light (MPPF)

polar method: also called radial method. A method of sketching an area where it is necessary to record the outline of a broken or irregular line of objects such as a forest (LEV)

polarization: the mathematical physics of light considered as a wave motion makes it necessary to assume that the displacement which constitutes each wave is randomly in all directions perpendicular to the direction in which the light is travelling. After passage through certain materials, or reflection in certain circumstances, the light behaves as if the displacement was then in one direction (plane) only; it is then polarized. The properties of polarized light make it valuable as an illuminant for microscopy in certain circumstances   (FS)

polarized light: light which vibrates on one manner only—in straight lines, circles, or ellipses. Light is commonly polarized by passing a light beam through a Nicol prism or a polarizing screen   (MPPF)

police: an organized body of municipal, county, or State officers engaged in maintaining public order, peace, and safety, and in investigating and arresting persons suspected or formally accused of crime   (DAP)

police, state, the first: were the Texas Rangers, who were authorized by the General Council of the Provisional Government of Texas to organize three Ranger companies in 1835. On Nov. 9, 1935, G. W. Davis was commissioned to raise 20 more men for this new service   (FAMOUS)

police advisory board: a citizens' group organized to react to general police policy matters; sometimes organized on a neighborhood basis

police bureau of criminal alien investigation, the first: was started by the New York City Police Department Dec. 23, 1930. The purpose was to bring to the attention of the U.S. Immigration authorities the undesirable aliens who are subject to deportation under the Immigration Law, either because of their criminal records or their illegal entry into the United States   (FAMOUS)

police bureau of identification, the first: was established by Captain Michael Patrick Evans on Jan. 1, 1884, for the Chicago Police Department. At its inception, only photographs were used. On June 1, 1887, the Bertillon system of identification was adopted and on Nov. 1, 1904, the Sir E. R. Henry system of fingerprinting was added. Evans was in charge of the Bureau of Identification from the inception until time of his death, Oct. 6, 1931   (FAMOUS)

police community relations officer (PCRO): a law enforcement officer working in the field of police-community relations   (LEV)

police connection: the direct link by which an alarm system is connected to an annunciator installed in a police station. Examples of a police connection are an alarm line, or a radio communications channel   (TDIAS)

police court: a municipal tribunal which tries those accused of violating local ordinances or acts as a tribunal for the preliminary examination and commitment of those accused of graver offenses, and is essentially equivalent to the criminal court of a justice of the peace in rural communities   (DAP)

police handling package: a special set of equipment options, such as heavy-duty suspension, for a particular vehicle which is designed to provide the handling characteristics under high-stress conditions required of vehicles used for police functions   (TDPPC)

police inspection of clubs: whether police inspection of social clubs, authorized by ordinance, be unreasonable, and therefore invalid, will depend largely on the manner in which it is conducted and the purposes to be accomplished (224 Pac. 1098)   (CDTP)

police jury: the administrative board of a parish in Louisiana, equivalent to a county elsewhere   (DAP)

police laboratory: a crime laboratory operated for the benefit of law enforcement   (LEV)

police organization and administration: in order to prevent crime and to apprehend criminals, every civilized country maintains an organization of police officers. The most important development of police work has taken place in larger cities. In a number of states, there have grown up organizations of state police, and state departments of identification and apprehension, as well as public and private agencies for crime detection. All of these police agencies, public and private, operate under provisions of law which regulate their organization, operation, and maintenance and which define their powers and duties   (CDTP)

police power: the power of the State to place restraints on the personal freedom and property rights of persons for the protection of the public safety, health, and morals or the promotion of the public convenience and general prosperity. It is a residuary power of the States. It extends over a multitude of subjects, and may involve taking or destroying property (as in the abatement of a nuisance) or debarring a person from pursuing a trade, or forcing him to submit to vaccination; and it may affect the movement of interstate commerce through quarantine regulations, requirements of proper safety devices on trains, and adequate service to a community. The police power is subject to limitations of the federal and State constitutions, and especially to the requirement of due process. The need of the general public for legislation must be relatively great; the inconvenience to the individual must be relatively slight; and the restraints imposed must be adapted to secure the end in view. In balancing these principles, court decisions tend to vary with the judge's knowledge of the social situation which a statute is designed to improve and the probable burden of the restraint on the individual   (DAP)

police review board: a citizens' group composed of representatives of particular ethnic, racial, or other groups whose task is to investigate allegations of police misconduct

police state: a state (as a totalitarian state or one operating under a dictatorship) which confers special powers over the rights of individuals upon its ordinary or secret police, or military, vesting them with discretion to arrest, detain, incarcerate, and sentence individuals without formal trial or forms of law, and which refuses to be bound by established canons of due process, or by the principle that the rights of individuals shall be adjudicated in established courts of justice   (DAP)

police station: a local command post in a police department (DAP)

police station unit: an annunciator which can be placed in operation in a police station   (TDIAS)

police training: training of and for law enforcement personnel (LEV)

police training school, the first: of the Federal Bureau of Investigation, U.S. Department of Justice, was initiated on July 29, 1935. The courses, similar to those given in the training bureau for newly appointed special agents of the Bureau, provide a program of training for local and state law enforcement officials and include subjects under the following headings: scientific and technical; statistics, records, and report writing; firearms training and first aid; investigations, enforcement, and regulatory procedure; police administration and organization. The course of training lasts for a period of 12 weeks and is given without cost to those enrolled. The first class consisted of 23 representatives of local and state law enforcement agencies   (FAMOUS)

police traffic squad, the first: was the famous old "Broadway Squad" of New York City, organized in 1860. This was the first unit of the Police Department to have special functions in the field of traffic regulation. The members of the squad were stationed on the sidewalks along Broadway, from Bowling Green to 59th Street, at the intersections of the cross streets. It was their purpose to escort pedestrians across the streets and to stop traffic while so doing. The pavement of Broadway was of cobble stones and most of the traffic consisted of slow-moving horse-drawn vehicles (FAMOUS)

police wrongs and criminal wrongs: by criminal wrongs the existence of the state is assailed; by police wrongs, only the administration of its economical structure; the first attacks the fundamental institutes of society, the latter only its modes of operation; the first concerns principle, the second concerns procedure (CDTP)

policy: in gaming, a form of gambling in which bets are made on numbers to be drawn in a lottery (CDTP)

politician: one who is involved with politics; a person who runs for public office or who is engaged in politics (LEV)

politics: (1) the discipline of government or of the operation of government (LEV) (2) the actions of those who seek power through public office (LEV)

poll the jury: a procedure in court whereby each juror is asked to state what his verdict was and is required to make it known (LEV)

polyandry: the practice of one woman having more than one husband

polygamy: the practice of having more than one mate

polygraph: most modern polygraphs have three capacities for recording anatomical responses. These are: the pneumograph—for recording respiration; the galvanograph—for recording skin electrical resistance changes; the cardiograph—for recording changes in blood pressure and pulse rate (LEV)

polyphasic: containing or consisting of more than one phase (FS)

pool: in gaming, a combination of stakes, the money from which is to go to the winner (CDTP)

poppy: a flowering plant. Opium is obtained from one type of poppy, usually referred to as the opium poppy (LEV)

popular front: the combination of or grouping together of leftist groups such as communist, socialist, and other similar political parties (LEV)

pornography, hard-core: pornographic material which is more obscene than picturing and describing nude persons (LEV)

poroscopy: the study of the arrangement and individual characteristics of sweat pores as seen in fingerprint impressions as a means of fingerprint identification. These sweat-pore characteristics are especially important when there is only a fragment of the fingerprint impression available (LEV)

portable: capable of being carried; movable (CDTP)

portable duress sensor: a device carried on a person which may be activated in an emergency to send an alarm signal to a monitoring station (TDIAS)

portable intrusion sensor: a sensor which can be installed quickly and which does not require the installation of dedicated wiring for the transmission of its alarm signal (TDIAS)

portrait parle [*Fr, lit "a speaking likeness"*]: a means of recording the descriptions of persons used in France (LEV)

port-warden: a kind of harbor master (CDTP)

positive: (1) in field of moulage, the reproduction of the original object (LEV) (2) meaning the opposite of negative. Any print or transparency made from a negative is termed a positive (MPPF)

positive evidence: evidence that directly proves fact or point in issue

positive law: law consisting of definite rules of human conduct with appropriate sanctions for their enforcement, both prescribed by a human superior or sovereign; defined by John Austin and others of the positive school of jurisprudence which owed much of its inspiration to the French social theorist, Auguste Comte   (DAP)

positive noninterfering (PNI) and successive alarm system: an alarm system which employs multiple alarm transmitters on each alarm line such that in the event of simultaneous operation of several transmitters, one of them takes control of the alarm line, transmits its full signal, then releases the alarm line for successive transmission by other transmitters which are held inoperative until they gain control   (TDIAS)

posse: a company; a force; a body with legal authority   (CDTP)

posse comitatus: (1) the power of the county (DAP) (2) the whole body (under the common law all male persons over 15 years of age) which the sheriff may summon to assist him in law enforcement; also, the body he summons (DAP)

Posse Comitatus Act of 1878: prohibits the use of Army personnel for the purpose of assisting civil authorities in the execution of civil law enforcement   (LEV)

possession: having possession of certain articles prohibited by law constitutes the criminal offense of possession. Possession of narcotics by persons not legally entitled to have them is such a case   (LEV)

possession, writ of: the term is generally employed to designate any writ by virtue of which the sheriff is commanded to place a person in possession of real or personal property   (CDTP)

possible: in firearms target shooting, the making of a perfect score. All the shots are placed in the part of the target having the highest value   (LEV)

post: (1) a position (LEV) (2) a place of assignment for an officer (LEV) (3) to record or make a record of (LEV) (4) afterward in time; following (LEV) (5) post-

mortem (LEV) (6) abbreviation for Commission on Peace Officers Standards and Training, such as in California   (LEV)

post facto [Lat]: after the fact   (CDTP)

post obit [Lat]: after death

posterior: the rear end or hind end   (LEV)

posterity: descendants   (CDTP)

posthumous: occurring after death. A posthumous child [is] one born after death of a father   (CDTP)

postmortem: (1) subsequent to death (LEV) (2) an autopsy   (LEV)

postmortem lividity: See lividity, postmortem

postmortem routine: a routine that either automatically or on demand prints data concerning contents of registers and storage locations after the routine stops in order to assist in locating a mistake in coding   (ADPS)

Poulas v. New Hampshire, 345, U.S. 195, 97 L. Ed. 1105, 73 S. Ct. 760 (1953): the court held that a state or municipality may require a permit to conduct a meeting in a public park   (ILECJ)

Pound, Roscoe (1870-1964): educator and legal scholar. Born in Lincoln, Neb., on Oct. 27, 1870, Pound studied at the Univ. of Nebraska, from which he received a degree in botany in 1888. Continuing his studies he received an M.A. from Nebraska in 1889, then went to Harvard to study law, but he stayed only one year, returned to Nebraska, passed the bar examination in 1890 without a law degree, and practiced law until 1907. In 1890 he also resumed his work in botany at the Univ. of Nebraska, earned a Ph.D. in 1897, and directed a botanical study of the state from 1892 to 1903; he was the discoverer of the rare lichen *Roscopoundia*. He taught law at the university from 1899 to 1903, was dean of the law department from 1903 to 1907, and was a legal advisor to the state government from 1904 to 1907, holding the post of commissioner of uniform state laws. The bifurcation of his career came to an end, for all practical purposes, in 1907, when he joined the law faculty at Northwestern; he taught law at the Univ. of Chicago in 1909–1910, and then joined the Harvard law faculty; he was dean of the Harvard Law School from 1916–1936. Resigning the deanship in 1936, he was given a "roving professorship" as University Professor and taught a variety of subjects until his retirement in 1947. After his retirement, at the age of 77, he continued to be active in many legal, editorial, and educational positions. Among other activities, he spent several years in Taiwan reorganizing the Nationalist Chinese government's judicial system. During his long career he studied, taught, and wrote in many different fields of law. Among his many books were *Readings on the History and System of the Common Law*, 1904; *Readings on Roman Law*, 1906. During his later years he shared with Learned Hand the reputation of being the nation's leading jurist outside the U.S. Supreme Court bench. He died in Cambridge, Mass., on July 1, 1964 (*Webster's American Biographies*)

powder: an explosive in powder form, that is, in small granules or grains, such as black powder or a smokeless propellant of fine granulation. No longer accepted as a general term for a propellant or propelling charge   (DWMT)

powder, black: a propellant for firearms ammunition, composed of charcoal, sulfur, and nitrate of potassium. Was used in years past in firearms ammunition of that period. Has been largely replaced by smokeless powder   (LEV)

powder, residue analysis of: the chemical analysis of the residue of powder particles found on the barrel fired into or in the gun barrel of the suspected weapon   (LEV)

powder, smokeless: a modern gunpowder consisting primarily of nitrocellulose or a combination of nitroglycerin and nitrocellulose   (LEV)

powder, tattooing by: a pattern around a wound caused by gunpowder particles striking the surface of the object fired into (LEV)

powder charge: the charge of powder for propelling a projectile   (DWMT)

powder pattern: the pattern of powder deposited on an object when fired onto by a firearm. At contact range there is little or no powder deposited and what is there is in a small circle. As the distance between the gun muzzle and the object increases the size of the powder pattern increases until a distance is reached where the discharge of powder particles does not reach the object *See* powder pattern test   (LEV)

powder pattern test: a crime laboratory test of garments to determine the pattern of powder residue and thus determine the distance between the muzzle of the weapon and the person shot. It is a useful test in homicide cases, especially where suicide is falsely claimed. Among others, the FBI Laboratory is equipped to conduct this test   (LEV)

powder train: (1) a train, usually of compressed black powder, used to obtain time action in older fuze types (DWMT) (2) a train of explosives laid out for destruction by burning   (DWMT)

powders: the powders used in loading are three types: black, semismokeless, and smokeless. Smokeless powders are divided into two types; the first is known as bulk, meaning that its charge corresponds, or nearly so, in bulk, to the charge of black powder; the second is the dense type, which means that it is denser and of much less bulk   (CDTP)

Powell v. Alabama, 287 U.S. 45, 77 L. Ed. 158, 53 S. Ct. 55 (1932): in this early landmark case on the right to the assistance of counsel, Mr. Justice Sutherland, speaking for the Court, held that the right to counsel, guaranteed in federal prosecutions by the Sixth Amendment, is not binding on the states in noncapital cases, *providing the trial itself was fair*, through the due process clause of the Fourteenth Amendment   (ILECJ) **Powell v. Superior Court, 48 Cal. 2d 705 (1957)**: this is California's leading case upholding the right of a defendant to pretrial discovery of evidence in the possession of police or prosecutor. The opinion notes that a prosecutor's keeping evidence undisclosed is a form of gamesmanship that is inappropriate as the act of a court official preparing a case for court preparation   (AOJ)

power brake: a braking system in which the pressure applied on the brake pedal by the driver to activate the brakes is multiplied by a vacuum power assist system   (TDPPC)

power of attorney: an instrument authorizing a person to act as the agent or attorney of the person granting it   (CDTP)

power of congress: unlike the state legislature the U.S. Congress has no inherent powers, but derives all its powers, including the power to define and punish crimes, from the federal constitution. Under the powers conferred by the constitution it may define and punish crimes in the District of Columbia, and Territories, and other places within the jurisdiction of the federal government   (CDTP)

power of municipalities: by the weight of authority municipal corporations may, by ordinance, prohibit and punish acts which are not prohibited and punishable as misdemeanors under the general statutes of the state, or which may involve a common law offense. In some jurisdictions, however, this power cannot be exercised in absence of express legislative authority   (CDTP)

power steering: a steering system in which the force applied by the driver on the steering wheel to turn the front wheels is multiplied by a hydraulic power assist system   (TDPPC)

practical examination: a civil service examination which seeks to determine training and fitness of an applicant rather than general knowledge and mental aptitude   (DAP)

precedent: decision by a court that may serve as an example or authority for similar cases in the future

precept: (1) a process or warrant (CDTP) (2) a writ directed to the sheriff or other officer directing him to do something   (CDTP)

precinct: (1) a minor division for police administration in a city or ward (DAP) (2) a county or municipal subdivision for casting votes in elections   (DAP)

precipe: a writing containing the particulars of a writ   (CDTP)

precipitan reaction test: a crime laboratory test to determine if blood is of human origin   (LEV)

preempt: move into a field or area and take possession or jurisdiction with priority ahead of others   (LEV)

preemption right: the right given to settlers upon the public lands of the United States to purchase them at the lowest price in preference to all others   (CDTP)

pre-exposure: exposure of a sensitized material to light either during manufacture, or by the user before exposure in the camera, as a means of intensifying the latent image, particularly in shadowy areas   (MPPF)

prefocused: applied to a lamp having a special type of base and socket which automatically centers the filament with respect to an optical system   (MPPF)

pregnant: the condition of a female who has conceived; carrying an unborn child or fetus   (LEV)

prejudice: an opinion or judgment formed concerning something or someone, prior to having or considering all the available facts; usually refers to an unfavorable opinion. A frame of mind based on emotions rather than rationality (LEV)

prejudicial evidence: *See* evidence, prejudicial

preliminary: introductory; that which precedes the main thing (CDTP)

preliminary examination: both at common law, and very generally by statutes in the different states, a person arrested on a charge of crime is entitled to a preliminary examination before a proper magistrate, without unnecessary delay, to determine whether a crime has in fact been committed, and, if so, whether there is probable cause to suspect that he is guilty of its commission. Without such an examination as soon as the circumstances permit, the detention of the accused will be unlawful (CDTP)

preliminary examination in criminal practice: an investigation by ·a magistrate, of a person who has been charged with crime and arrested, or of the facts and circumstances which are alleged to have attended the crime and to fasten suspicion upon the party so charged, in order to ascertain whether there is sufficient ground to hold him to bail for his trial by the proper court (CDTP)

preliminary hearing: a court examination used as a testing-ground for the information brought against a criminal defendant

preliminary jurisdiction: a criminal court has "preliminary jurisdiction" of an offense and may conduct criminal proceedings with respect to the offense when the proceedings lead or may lead to prosecution and final disposition of the case in a court having trial jurisdiction

premeditation: a design formed to commit a crime or do some other act before it is done; delibera-

tion (CDTP)

preparation for act: any fact or evidence tending to show preparations by the defendant to commit the act charged is admissible (CDTP)

preponderance: superiority or majority in quality or quantity

preponderance of the evidence: evidence that is the most impressive or convincing of any offered

prerogative: a privilege; a prior or exclusive right (CDTP)

prescribe: to become invalid because of lapse of time. Sometimes called the "statute of limitations." If prosecution is not started within a certain time the right to prosecute is lost. Usually in capital offenses prescription does not apply or it is a long period of time (LEV)

prescription: (1) acquiring some advantage or title to property by the possession for specified periods of time (LEV) (2) time limitations, provided by law, within which prosecutions must be commenced after the commission of a crime and within which the trial must be started, in criminal matters. *See* statute of limitations (LEV)

presentence investigation: investigation of the personal history of the convicted offender prior to the imposition of a sentence, for the purpose of aiding the sentencing authority in determining the proper disposition. In most states at this time, the presentence investigation is not mandatory. It is most usually conducted by the court's probation service (LCC)

presentence report: a report prepared from the presentence investigation to aid the sentencing authority in passing sentence

presentment: the written notice of a charge issued by a grand jury on its own motion, rather than as an indictment requested by the prosecutor

preservative: (1) something, usually a chemical, added to a substance to prevent it from spoiling or deteriorating (LEV) (2) A chemical—such as sodium sulphite—which, when added to a developing solution, tends to prolong its life (MPPF)

press, freedom of the: guaranteed in the First Amendment of the Constitution. Until 1925 this guarantee was generally considered to apply against infringement by the Congress. As a result of the Supreme Court's decision in 1925 in the case of *Gitlow* v. *New York,* the free press clause of the First Amendment has since been applied against the states as well. The principle of the freedom of the press was originally set down in North America in 1734 in the famous trial of Peter Zenger (DOAH)

pressure: the force exerted in the cartridge chamber and bore of the barrel by the powder gases is known as the pressure. It is designated in pounds per square inch. The amount of pressure permissible in pistol and revolver charges is governed by safety. Fifteen thousand lbs. per square inch represents about the maximum pressure that may safely be used in the best grades of revolvers, and 30,000 lbs. in the high velocity automatics like the Mauser. The method of ascertaining pressures is rather complicated and requires special equipment. The method generally used by the ammunition companies is known as the "Radial System" (CDTP)

pressure alarm system: an alarm system which protects a vault or other enclosed space by maintaining and monitoring a predetermined air pressure differential between the inside and outside of the space. Equalization of pressure resulting from opening the vault or cutting through will be sensed and will initiate an alarm signal (TDIAS)

Preston v. United States, 376 U.S. 364, 11 L. Ed. 2d 777, 84 S. Ct. 881 (1963): a unanimous Court held that an automobile must be searched at the time and place of arrest. (The search of the automobile at the police garage was too remote in time and place and was not, therefore, incidental to the lawful arrest. Later decisions have modified the *Preston* decision.) (ILECJ)

presumption: inference drawn from some fact or group of facts

presumption, legal: the law which provides that the judiciary shall assume certain facts exist from a set of circumstances. These assumptions or inferred acts persist until disproven. *See* presumption, rebuttable (LEV)

presumption, rebuttable: a legal presumption which relieves him in whose favor it exists from the necessity of offering proof; however it can be disproven or rebutted. Such is the presumption of innocence of an accused (LEV)

presumption of innocence—burden of proof: the defendant is presumed to be innocent and the burden is on the state to prove his guilt beyond a reasonable doubt (CDTP)

presumptive evidence: (1) the presumption of incapacity in a minor to act, which is conclusive and irrebuttable (2) evidence which may be disproved or rebutted by other evidence. Presumptions of fact can be determined by the judge from the existing evidence

pretermit: to pass by, disregard, or take no action concerning. In relation to a grand jury, it means that the jury passes a matter before it without finding a "true bill" or a "no true bill." This is brought about by lack of agreement among the grand jurors or by the intentional act of the grand jury. The next grand jury may consider the case (LEV)

pretext: excuse; ostensible reason (CDTP)

pretrial detention: the procedure of not releasing on bond or bail, between arrest and trial, certain dangerous persons. This procedure has been considered by legislative bodies. Congress considered such in H.R. 12806 in 1969. *See* preventive detention   (LEV)

pretrial publicity: publicity about an accused, a criminal case, or the details of an investigation, prior to the trial of persons accused of the crime. This may prevent the accused from obtaining a fair trial and thus creates a real problem   (LEV)

pretrial screens: steps in the criminal justice process to apply quality control to police arrests and prosecutor's charges to reduce the number of unwarranted trials

prevaricate: to depart from the truth; not follow the truth; to lie   (LEV)

preventive detention: laws which allow the magistrate or judge to hold an accused in jail and not release him on bail where evidence is produced that if released he probably would commit other crimes while awaiting trial of the first offense. *See* pretrial detention   (LEV)

prima facie [*Lat*]: at first view; on the first appearance; on the face of it

prima facie case: one in which the evidence in favor of a proposition is sufficient to support a finding in its favor, if all the evidence to the contrary be disregarded (204 S.W. 1061)   (CDTP)

prima facie evidence: evidence that is sufficient to support a fact or group of facts

primary: preliminary; first in order of time; chief   (CDTP)

primary boycott: a combination, agreement, or understanding to refrain from dealing with a person and to advise and persuade others by peaceable means to do likewise   (CDTP)

primary classification: a term used in classifying fingerprints. A numerical value is given to each of the ten fingers. This is written in the classification formula after the major division as 1/1 or whatever the count requires   (LEV)

primary color: any one of the three components of white light—blue, green, and red   (MPPF)

primary election: a method whereby members of a political party select candidates for office to be voted for at an ensuing election   (CDTP)

primary or secondary: primary evidence is that kind of evidence which, under every possible circumstance, affords the greatest certainty of the fact in question. Thus a written instrument is itself the best possible evidence of its existence and contents. It means original or first-hand evidence, the best evidence that the nature of the case admits of; the evidence that is required in the first instance, and which must fail before secondary evidence can be admitted   (CDTP)

primer: a relatively small and sensitive initial explosive-train component which on being actuated initiates functioning of the explosive train and will not reliably initiate high-explosive charges. In general, primers are classified in accordance with the method of initiation, such as percussion, electric, friction, etc. "Primer" is also used to refer to the assembly which ignites propelling charges. The primer of a center-fire cartridge is a detonating mixture located in a small metal cup and exploded by the impact of a firing pin. In flintlock and earlier firearms the primer consisted of fine gunpowder placed in the flashpan and ignited by spark or flame   (DWMT)

primer cup: a small cup holding a primer mixture and other components and used in small-arms cartridges and certain other ammunition   (DWMT)

primer seat: a chamber in the breech mechanism of a gun that uses separate loading ammunition and into which the primer is set   (DWMT)

priming powder: the gunpowder in the pan used to set off the main charge   (CDTP) principal: a person held accountable for a crime. The person who actually commits the crime is a principal. In some states persons who aid or assist in the commission of the crime are considered principals even though they did not actively participate in the commission of it (LEV)

principal, and accessories: parties concerned in the commission of felonies are principals or accessories according as they are present or absent when the act is committed. Principals are either: (1) principals in the first degree, or (2) principals in the second degree. Accessories are either: before the fact, or after the fact (CDTP)

principal in the first degree: a principal in the first degree is the person who actually perpetrates the deed, either by his own hand or through an innocent agent (CDTP)

principal in the second degree: is one who is actually or constructively present, aiding and abetting another in the commission of the deed. (1) He must be present, actually or constructively, and (2) He must aid or abet the commission of the act. (3) There must be community of unlawful purpose at the time the act was committed. (4) Such purpose must be real on the part of the principal in the first degree (CDTP)

principal registration: a system of classifying and identifying fingerprints based on all ten fingers of the hands. It is necessary to have fingerprints of all ten fingers of the hands in order to classify one's prints. It is also necessary to have the same kind of fingerprints in order to search for and locate a duplicate set of fingerprints on file in this type of registration. Provisions are made for amputations in the classifying system. See single-fingerprint registration (LEV)

principal's liability for acts of agent: as a rule, no person is criminally liable for the act of another unless he has previously autho-

rized or assented to it; and consequently a principal is not liable for acts of his agents or servants which he did not authorize or assent to although they are done in the course of the employment (CDTP)

principle: a rule or law; an established truth (LEV)

printer, high-speed: high-speed printing that makes use of rotating print wheels or a chain with raised type faces and fast-acting hammers to press the paper against the desired character at the instant it is in the correct position (ADPS)

printing frame: a frame designed to hold a negative in contact with paper, under pressure, for the purpose of making prints (MPPF)

printing recorder: an electromechanical device used at a monitoring station which accepts coded signals from alarm lines and converts them to an alphanumeric printed record of the signal received (TDIAS)

printing-out paper (P.O.P.): a photographic paper forming a visible image immediately on exposure, without development. It must be fixed, however, for permanence of the image (MPPF)

priority: the state of being first in rank, time, or place; first claim (CDTP)

prison: otherwise referred to as a penitentiary or correctional institution, the prison is an institution which is usually maintained by the state or federal government for the confinement of convicted felons (MC)

prison, discipline in: all those measures used by the prison administration—the grade system, degradation and advancement in grade, privileges and denial thereof, isolation in cell or in solitary cells; "good time," etc.—designed to promote good behavior in the institution (DOS)

prison, industrial: a term more common in Europe than in the United States to designate a pris-

on in which the inmates carry on production of useful articles and with a minimum emphasis upon vocational or other training intended to prepare the discharged prisoner for life in society. The inmates are those who are looked upon as relatively hopeless for reformatory methods. Originally it meant a prison for those sentenced to hard labor as distinguished from those sentenced to simple imprisonment   (DOS)
prison community: social structure, social relationships, and social processes in prison. The quality of staff-staff, inmate-inmate, and inmate-staff relationships; class stratification, informal group life, leadership, and folkways in prisoner society, the role of gossip and public opinion as means of social control; the processes whereby the guards become institutionalized and the inmates "prisonized"—all these aspects are included   (DOS)
prison farms: farms for convicts, of four general varieties: (1) first, the farms which are owned by counties or municipalities where misdemeanants are committed who would otherwise serve short terms in a county or city jail; (2) second, farms run as an auxiliary to state prisons, partially as a means of segregating a special group of offenders, as for example, first offenders, or habitual offenders, and partially for providing meat and vegetables for the prison kitchens; (3) third, privately owned farms or plantations in the South to which the states leased convicts at considerable profit. Such private farms assumed the responsibility for guarding and disciplining the men, and providing their food and shelter in return for their labor. Most of such privately operated farms have been abolished because of abuses; (4) fourth, the prison farms now owned and operated by a number of Southern states, including Louisiana, Texas, and Mississippi, as a basic part of their

prison system. Prisoners are first sent to a receiving center from which they are allocated to the different farms. Usually an attempt is made to place the prisoners on the different farms according to their types   (DOS)
prison labor: as a tool within the correctional institution, labor by inmates has roots in both the retributive and rehabilitative philosophies. Some avow that prison labor should be as hard and unpleasant as possible, while others maintain that it should be useful and should train the inmate in marketable skills. Nearly all agree that it should be financially beneficial to the state. Methods of utilizing prison labor have ranged from a system of leasing prisoners and their labor to private users, to a state-use system in which the state retains control of the prisoner and his labor, and his products are utilized only by the state   (POC)
prison psychosis: characteristic attitudes on the part of some of the inmates due to the rigid system of discipline in many prisons. They become more or less apathetic and dull, or rebellious and violent. Extreme deviations of these sorts have been observed in prisons throughout the world. The longer the period of confinement, the more marked are the reactions. There is little opportunity for initiative, the prison atmosphere is repressive, and the daily program monotonous. Inmates are robbed of will. They compensate by daydreaming and fantasizing, or by marked aggressive behavior which sometimes takes the form of destroying everything in the cell. This kind of prison stupor or aggression has been labelled "prison psychosis." The term is not used in a critical sense   (DOS)
prison reform: prison conditions in colonial America retained medieval characteristics. Punishments included whipping, the stocks, pillories, and ducking. Prisoners

were confined to unsanitary quarters and not segregated as to sex or age. In 1787 the Quakers in Philadelphia organized the Society for Alleviating the Miseries of Public Prisons, the first reform organization in America. In 1791 the first penitentiary was established in Philadelphia. Overcrowded conditions, nevertheless, prevented any serious reform. It was not until the humanitarian revolt of the Jacksonian period that fundamental prison reform was undertaken. In 1824 the Auburn System of silent confinement was established as part of a new system of prison management in Auburn, N.Y. Correction houses and reform schools were founded to meet the special needs of juvenile offenders. By the opening of the Civil War, Auburn-type prisons had been established in all the states except New Jersey and Pennsylvania. The American Prison Association was founded in 1870 to carry out the ideas of such reformers as Enoch C. Wines and Zebulon R. Brockway. These leaders had been strongly influenced by the Irish penal system which maintained the importance of rehabilitation rather than punishment as the aim of imprisonment. In 1877 the New York State Reformatory at Elmira was opened under Brockway's administration to further this experiment. Youthful offenders were separated from hardened criminals and encouraged to reduce their terms through good conduct. Parole and probation were introduced to provide continuing supervision after release. The Elmira plan was quickly adopted in many northern and western states. In the 20th century, psychology, psychiatry, sociology, and medicine have contributed to reform concepts in penology. These new ideals have emphasized occupational therapy, psychiatric care, social work, classification of inmates, the suspended sentence, and compensated labor. Post-release supervision has stressed adjustment to society through the means of employment services, hospitalization, and family care (DOAH)

Prison Reform Society, the first: to bring about changes in prison administration was the Philadelphia Society for Alleviating the Miseries of Public Prisons, formed May 8, 1787, in the German School House on Cherry Street, Philadelphia, Pa., by Philadelphia Quakers. The first president was William White. A similar organization for war prisoners was the Philadelphia Society for Relieving Distressed Prisoners Owing to the War of Independence, organized in 1776 (FAMOUS)

prisoner: one who is confined in a prison; a person under arrest or in custody (CDTP)

prisoner at the bar: defendant on trial

prisoner transportation: a function of law enforcement requiring the movement of persons in custody from one point to another (TDPPC)

prisoners' aid association: private organization designed to aid discharged prisoners with advice about jobs, often providing a place to live while seeking work, giving counsel, and sometimes money or credit (DOS)

prisoner's rights: the legal rights of a prisoner (LEV)

prisonization: the socializing process by which the offender learns the rules and regulations of the institution and the informal rules of the inmate subculture

prisons, overcrowding in: the optimum-maximum number of inmates in a prison is generally considered to be 500. However, most countries throughout the world build much larger prisons. Even with the larger prisons overcrowding is generally found. In only five or six American states are prisons not overcrowded. The percent of overcrowding in the

American prison varies from about 5 percent (Minn.) to over 115 percent (W. Va.). Overcrowding makes the classification and segregation of prisoners difficult, and complicates the problems of discipline, employment, education, and health   (DOS)

prisons, receiving: induction centers for prisoners to which they are sent for assignment to the particular prison or prison facilities which best fit them. Some prison systems have reception prisons; others have reception facilities at larger prisons. A reception center is supposed to enable classification committees to assign each admitted prisoner to the proper custody, work, and education. During his period of reception, often called the period of quarantine, the prisoner is given the preventive and corrective medical attention necessary for induction, is interviewed for his social and criminal background, is examined psychologically, and is processed for identification   (DOS)

privacy, right of: the right to be left alone; to not be interfered with as to conversations or the possession of and use of property   (LEV)

private law: the law which regulates the relations of individuals with each other. *Cf.* public law   (DAP)

private right: a right enjoyed by the individual under law. Many such rights are enumerated in bills of rights of the federal and State constitutions   (DAP)

privilege: a right or advantage granted by law   (LEV)

privileged communications: no husband is compelled to disclose any communication made to him by his wife during the marriage, and no wife is compelled to disclose any communication made to her by her husband during the marriage. No one can be compelled to give evidence relating to any affairs of state, as to official communications between public officers upon public affairs, except with the permission of the officer

at head of department concerned. In cases in which the government is immediately concerned no witness can be compelled to answer any question, the answer to which would tend to discover the names of persons by or to whom information was given as to the commission of offenses. No legal adviser is permitted, whether during or after the termination of his employment as such, unless with his client's express consent, to disclose any communication, oral or documentary, made to him as such legal adviser. The expression "legal adviser" includes lawyers, their clerks, and interpreters between them and their clients   (CDTP)

privy: private; secret   (CDTP)

probable cause: reasonable cause—that which is more than mere suspicion but less than reasonable doubt

probable cause within rule: the "probable cause" itself, which the officer must possess, is a reasonable ground for belief in guilt, which is the same meaning as where the term is used in other connections. Mere suspicion or belief is generally an insufficient justification for such a search, although belief is held to be sufficient under statutes permitting such search where the officer "has reason to believe" that contraband is being transported in the vehicle to be searched (C.J. 56, 1197)   (CDTP)

probable cause, writ of: a writ which in criminal prosecution operates as an order to stay execution pending an appeal   (CDTP)

probable evidence: presumptive evidence   (CDTP)

probate: proving and establishing a will   (CDTP)

probate court: a court having general supervision over probate of wills, administration of estates, and, in some States, empowered to appoint guardians or approve the adoption of minors. *See* surrogate   (DAP) probation: first authorized in the United States in Boston in 1878, this form of judicial disposition was utilized by all the states by 1957. Probation, which has its antecedents in the common law phenomenon of suspended sentence, is a conditional sentence which avoids the imprisonment of the offender provided that he agree to and abide by court-imposed requirements. Supervision by probation officers is always one of these conditions

probation system, the first: without restrictions as to age, in any country in the world, was legally established as a judicial policy by Boston, Mass., in 1878 and Massachusetts in 1880 (FAMOUS)

probation, adult: a modern system of placing adults who have been convicted of penal or criminal offenses under the supervision of trained workers for the purpose of social rehabilitation after suspension of sentence by the court (DOS)

probation officer: the individual responsible for the supervision of those who have been granted probation

probationary period: (civil service) the period (usually six months) during which a newly appointed employee learns his duties and becomes adjusted to his job, or may be dismissed without right of appeal or reinstatement (DAP)

probationer: a person placed on probation (CDTP)

probative value: having value as proof; value of absolute proof (LEV)

probe: an intensive and thorough investigation into a situation of crime or misconduct (LEV)

problem-oriented language: a language designed for solving a particular class of problems—for example COBOL for business and FORTRAN for mathematics. Requires elaborate translation or compiling—each program instruction becomes several machine

instructions—before the program can run on a processor (ADPS)

procedural law: a branch of law which prescribes in detail the methods or procedures to be used in determining and enforcing the rights and duties of persons toward each other under substantive law. *See* substantive law (DAP)

procedural right: the right of a person to have his case determined before a judicial or administrative tribunal according to the forms set forth in a constitution or law. All procedural provisions of the U.S. Constitution must be observed by federal courts but they are not essential to due process of law in unincorporated territories if other methods insuring fairness and impartiality are followed. *Cf.* substantive right (DAP)

procedure: court procedure is a development from custom, while customs have their origin in the habits, mode of life, and special circumstances of the people among whom they prevail. The chief merit of any system of procedure lies in: (1) the generality of its application, (2) the uniformity of its rules, and (3) the certainty of its course. Courts must adhere to established modes of procedure (CDTP)

procedure, criminal: the law pertaining to procedure in the field of criminal law (LEV)

proceeding: action in conducting judicial business in a court or before a judicial officer (LEV)

process: in practice, this word is generally defined to be the means of compelling the defendant in an action to appear in court, or a means whereby a court compels a compliance with its demands (85 S.E. 819-20), and when actions were commenced by original writ instead of, as at present, by writ of summons, the method of compelling the defendant to appear was by what was termed "original process" being founded on the original writ, and so called also to distinguish it from "mesne" or "intermediate" process, which was some writ or process which was issued during the progress of the suit. The word "process" however, as now commonly understood, signifies those forms as instruments called writs. The word "process" is in common law practice frequently applied to the writ of summons, which is the instrument now used for commencing personal actions. (157 N.W. 642) But in the more comprehensive signification it includes not only the writ of summons, but all other writs which may be issued during the progress of the action. These writs which are used to carry the judgments of the courts into effect, and which are termed "writs of execution" are also commonly denominated "final process" because they usually issue at the end of a suit (CDTP)

process in practice: a writ, summons, or order issued in a judicial proceeding to acquire jurisdiction of a person or his property, to expedite the cause, or enforce the judgment (CDTP)

process lens: a highly corrected lens used for precise color-separation work (MPPF)

processing: the chemical treatment of exposed film to form a permanent visible image (MPPF)

processing plan: the interaction of man and machine to process data, produce information, and control operations of the organization. Examples are manual intervention by people to handle situations not planned for, advance planning for automatic handling of all situations, variable treatment of differing situations depending on circumstances, and adaptive systems to adjust to new and unexpected situations as they arise (ADPS)

processor: (1) any device capable of accepting data, applying prescribed processes to them, and supplying the results of these pro-

cesses. Usually internally stored program, but may be externally stored or built-in (ADPS) (2) an internally stored program electronic computer and peripheral equipment used for business data processing (ADPS) (3) a program used in compiling a source program to produce an object ready to execute with data (ADPS)

process-time: the time for translating a source into an object program through the action of a processor program and a computer (ADPS)

proclivity: a strong inclination toward something (LEV)

procurement policy: an expressed or written statement that defines the terms, conditions, and other relevant criteria under which a using body, such as a law enforcement agency, procures goods or services (TDPPC)

procurer: a pimp; one who obtains women to satisfy the sexual desires of men (LEV)

profane: blasphemous; irreverent; secular (CDTP)

profanity: irreverence towards sacred things; particularly, an irreverent or blasphemous use of the name of God; punishable by statute in some jurisdictions (CDTP)

proffer: to offer or present for acceptance (LEV)

profile: a side view photograph or sketch of a person (LEV)

profiteer: one who demands and secures exorbitant profits in the sale of goods, rental, or services (CDTP)

pro forma [*Lat*]: for form's sake, as a matter of form

program: a noun for the automatic solution of a problem. A complete program includes plans for the transcription of data, coding for the processor, and plans for the absorption of the results into the system. The list of coded instructions is called a "routine" (ADPS)

programming: the process of creating a program; includes applications analysis, design of a solution, coding for testing to produce an operating program, and development of other procedures to make the system function (ADPS)

progressive: one who favors the gradual introduction of political and social reforms by government action (DAP)

progressive system: in penology, a prison program patterned after the so-called Irish system. According to the Irish system, instituted by Crofton, a prisoner advanced progressively from initial cell isolation and lack of privileges to congregate life with increasing privileges. Such advancement into a new grade or class was earned by acquiring credits for good behavior, industry, and interest in education. The later phases of progressive advancement were supposed to include minimum custody in an intermediate prison, where self-control could be fostered and the prisoner prepared for the discharge by parole. The system is sometimes called the graded system. It has never been completely followed but many modern prison systems have incorporated phases and general principles of the progressive system, especially the earning of privileges, promotions to jobs of trust, and classification for degree of custody, such as close, medium, and minimum. In general the prison systems which have used the principles embodied in the Irish system do not have the inmate pass through all the stages of custody but classify at admission as to what degree of custody he requires. But he can be reclassified as time and circumstances warrant both upward and downward in custodial level. See Irish system (DOS)

Prohibition: forbidding by law of the sale, manufacture, and transportation of alcoholic liquors as beverages. Prohibition was introduced by the Eighteenth Amendment to the Constitution and took effect on 17 Jan. 1920. The enforcement legislation was the Volstead Act. Prohibition was repealed by the Twenty-first Amendment to the Constitution, which became effective in 1933

Prohibition, U.S. Treasury Department Agents: federal officers who investigated violations of the Volstead Act while it was effective from 1920 to 1933. The Alcohol and Tobacco Tax Division of the Internal Revenue Service, a branch of the U.S. Treasury Department, still has jurisdiction over violations of alcohol, particularly as to the enforcement of tax provisions concerning it (LEV)

prohibition, writ of: in practice, the name of a writ issued by a superior court, directed to the judge and parties of a suit in an inferior court, commanding them to cease from the prosecution of the same, upon a suggestion that the cause originally, or some collateral matter arising therein, does not belong to that jurisdiction, but to the cognizance of some other court (262 S.W. 215-20) (CDTP)

Project Search: System for Electronic Analysis and Retrieval of Criminal Histories. LEAA awarded an initial grant of $600,000 to finance the project and grantee states matched the project with more than $400,000. Grantee states include Arizona, California, Maryland, Michigan, Minnesota, and New York, with participating observer states. The project ran from July 1, 1969 to Aug. 31, 1970 as a pilot project. There were two principal objectives: (a) computerize data from all segments of criminal justice on a standardized basis, furnishing same to participants; (b) develop statistical records and meaningful research data from the files (LEV)

projectile: an object projected by an applied exterior force and continuing in motion by virtue of its own inertia, such as a bullet, shell, or grenade. Also applied to rockets and to guided missiles (DWMT)

projection printing: a method of making prints by projecting the image of the negative on a suitable easel for holding the sensitive paper (MPPF)

proletariat: the working class

promissory note: a written promise, made by one person to another, to pay on demand or at a fixed time, a sum of money (CDTP)

promulgate: to announce formally and officially or make known something; officially to make known such things as laws (LEV)

proof: method of establishing the truth of an allegation; establishment of a fact; evidence when used to establish a fact (LEV)

proof, burden of: *See* burden of proof (LEV)

proof charge: a propellant charge used in the initial firing tests of a gun. For test purposes, it may sometimes exceed normal pressures intended for use in the gun (DWMT)

proof paper: usually a printing-out paper (P.O.P.) which is exposed in contact with the negative to any bright light and does not require a developing solution to make a visible image. The image must be observed in subdued light or it will become dark and eventually disappear (MPPF)

propaganda: any form of communication in support of national objectives designed to influence the opinions, emotions, attitudes, or behavior of any group in order to benefit the sponsor either directly or indirectly (DWMT)

pro parte [*Lat*]: in part

propellant: that which provides the energy for propelling something. Specifically, an explosive charge for propelling a bullet, shell, or the like. Also, a fuel, either solid or liquid, for propelling a rocket or missile (DWMT)

propensity: a tendency toward; a natural inclination; a leaning in the direction of. Pertaining to crimes committed by the accused, other than that for which he is being tried is not admissible for the purpose of showing mere propensity; such evidence is admissible if related to, or is part of, a plan or scheme involving the crime for which the accused is being tried (LEV)

proper evidence: that which can be legally presented in court

proper subjects of search and seizure under warrant: executed contracts; forged instruments; gaming implements; illegal lottery tickets; intoxicating liquors; stolen goods; books; documents; papers and records, if offending, may be seized. (254 Fed. 171) However where papers and documents afford evidence that a felony has been committed, but are not the means of committing it they are immune from seizure, and since they are immune from unreasonable seizure, it has been held that a person's private papers, correspondence, records of his business, and books of account cannot be seized indiscriminately, esp. when they do not come within the purview of the statute authorizing the search warrant. Corporation records which would be evidence against individuals charged with crime may be seized under a search warrant (CDTP)

property rights: as developed in English common law and in the political philosophy of Thomas Hobbes and John Locke it refers to the right of ownership of private property against public restraint. Property rights, in the evolution of Anglo-American law, have become subject to public control when necessary to protect the public welfare. This has become particularly recognized in the area of public utilities such as transportation, power, communication, and water-works. Public restraints are based on a reconciliation of the police power and due process doctrines (DOAH)

proponent: one who makes a proposal; one who puts forward an instrument as a will for probate (CDTP)

proportional reducer: a chemical reducing agent which reduces the silver in the shadows at the same rate as that in the highlights (MPPF)

propound: to set forth; to propose (CDTP)

proprietary alarm system: an alarm system which is similar to a central station alarm system except that the annunciator is located in a constantly manned guard room maintained by the owner for his own internal security operations. The guards monitor the system and respond to all alarm signals or alert law enforcement agencies or both (TDIAS)

props: accessories used to add interest or provide variety in an illustration or a portrait (MPPF)

pro rata [*Lat*]: in proportion

prorogue: to postpone; to adjourn (CDTP)

prosecute: to bring a matter or person into a court of law with a view of obtaining justice according to law (LEV)

prosecuting attorney: a locally elected officer who represents the State in securing indictments and informations and in prosecuting criminal cases before courts; and who, in some states, also advises local officers and boards concerning their legal powers and duties; called also district attorney or State's attorney (DAP)

prosecution: (1) the conduct of a criminal proceeding before a judicial tribunal including all steps from the indictment or information to the final decision (DAP) (2) the party, usually the State, which conducts a criminal proceeding against an accused person (DAP)

prosecutor: one who prosecutes a defendant for a crime on behalf of the government

prosecutor's information: a written statement by a district attorney filed with a local criminal court accusing one or more defendants with the commission of one or more non-felonious offenses. This

accusation serves as a basis for prosecution

prostitute: an individual who engages in sexual intercourse for money

pro tanto [*Lat*]: for so much, to a certain extent

protected area: an area monitored by an alarm system or guards, or enclosed by a suitable barrier (TDIAS)

protected port: a point of entry such as a door, window, or corridor which is monitored by sensors connected to an alarm system (TDIAS)

protection, exterior perimeter: a line of protection surrounding but somewhat removed from a facility. Examples are fences, barrier walls, or patrolled points of a perimeter (TDIAS)

protection device: (1) a sensor such as a grid, foil, contact, or photoelectric sensor connected into an intrusion alarm system (2) a barrier which inhibits intrusion, such as a grill, lock, fence, or wall (TDIAS)

protective signaling: the initiation, transmission, and reception of signals involved in the detection and prevention of property loss due to fire, burglary, or other destructive conditions. Also, the electronic supervision of persons and equipment concerned with this detection and prevention. *See also* line supervision and supervisory alarm system (TDIAS)

prototype: the first complete and working member of a class. The term is especially applied to the first aircraft made of a given model or model series or to the first specimen of a class of weapons or any other piece of equipment, such member or specimen serving, or intended to serve, as the pattern or guide for subsequently produced members of the same class (DWMT)

provisional: of the nature of a provision; temporary; conditional (CDTP)

provocation: incitement to commit-

ting an act
provost marshal: an officer of an army whose duties correspond to those of a chief of police (CDTP)
prowl car: a car used by the police to patrol, usu. equipped with two-way radio whereby communication is maintained with headquarters (LEV)
proximate: close; nearby; side by side (LEV)
proximate cause: something which produces a result that would not otherwise occur
proxy: person appointed to represent another (LEV)
prudent: wise; considering all aspects; "level-headed"; not erratic in thinking (LEV)
prudery: (1) aversion to sex (LEV) (2) modesty, esp. in reference to sex
prurient: having lustful desires or cravings. This word is used in the legal definition of obscene or pornographic material (LEV)
pry bar: a metal bar used by burglars to pry open doors, windows, or other enclosures (LEV)
pseudocode: an arbitrary code, independent of the hardware of a computer for convenience in programming, which must be translated into computer code in order to direct the computer (ADPS)
Psilocybin®: derived from the Psilocybe mushroom. An hallucinogenic narcotic (LEV)
psychedelic: pertaining to unusual or abnormal stimulation of perception or mental alertness. Psychedelic drugs [are] drugs which tend to produce these effects (LEV)
psychiatric: pertaining to the treatment or study of mental disease (CDTP)
psychiatrist: a physician who specializes in psychiatry (LEV)
psychiatry: the branch of medicine dealing with the study and treatment of mental disorders (DOS)
psychic: (1) pertaining to the soul (CDTP) (2) in spiritualism, a person claiming to have the power of writing or conversing in a trance

state (CDTP)
psychoanalysis: a school of psychology specializing in the clinical treatment of individuals with neurotic tendencies. It is based on the theory that many of our desires involving sex are subconsciously repressed early in our lives and can be dealt with only by bringing them out into the open through such methods as free association and dream analysis (DOS)
psychodiagnosis: a method of diagnosis used in investigating the origin and cause of any given disease or unsound condition by examining a patient's mental condition. The diagnosis is accomplished by the application of prescribed psychological tests and an investigation of the patient's past history in regards to its bearing on the present psychic state
psychological fact: in evidence, a fact perceived mentally only (CDTP)
psychology: the science of the mind of humans in all of its aspects (LEV)
psychoneurosis: various forms of mental illness, including melancholia and mania
psychopath: antisocial personality; one who has no feeling of guilt for misdeeds and no love for others; one who is irresponsible for acts; a person with character disorders bordering on insanity (LEV)
psychopathic: relative to mental disorders, diseases; bordering on insanity; pertaining to a character disorder (LEV)
psychosis: refers to a group of more than one mental disorder, drastic in nature, which interferes with organization of the personality and social relationships. It prevents adequate self-control and manifests itself in behavior which is not appropriate or reasonable. It may or may not be connected with organic diseases (LEV)
psychosomatic: pertaining to mind and body and their interreactions, in reference to diseases (LEV)

psychotherapy: treatment of mental disorders by means of psychological principles and methods (LEV)

psychotic: a mentally ill person; one out of touch with reality; one who may be hallucinating and/or delusional. The psychotic is overwhelmed with fear (LEV)

puberty: the first stages of physical maturity of male or female at which they are capable of reproducing. This stage is approximately 14 in boys and 12 in girls (LEV)

public carrier: a common carrier; one who carries persons or freight for hire (CDTP)

public defender: an attorney appointed by the court to represent indigent defendants in criminal proceedings

public law: (1) a general classification of law, the principal branches being constitutional, administrative, criminal, and international law, which is concerned with the organization of the state, the relations between the state and the people who compose it, the responsibilities of public officers to the state, to each other, and to private persons, and the relations of states to one another (DAP) (2) a statute applying generally to persons and places throughout a state. Cf. private law (DAP)

public nuisance: a nuisance which affects the rights, health, safety, or peace of others (CDTP)

public offense: breach of the law protecting the public, as distinguished from an infringement of private rights; a crime (CDTP)

public property: owned by the public, the state, or community (CDTP)

public trial: a trial open to the attendance of the public at large (DAP)

publicity: release of information to the news media pertaining to investigations, individuals, the department, or other things pertaining to law enforcement; information intended to further the cause of oneself, [one's] department, or law enforcement generally. Care must be exercised in releasing publicity, or allowing it to be obtained, pertaining to persons accused or charged with crime, as it may prevent the accused from obtaining a fair and impartial trial (LEV)

puerile: childish; foolish; unworthy of an adult (CDTP)

pull cord for routing radio antenna: a device used to thread a radio antenna cable through a conduit or concealed portions of a vehicle body (TDPPC)

pulling method: a screw-type device with a long handle used by safe burglars to pull the combination wheel and its attached spindle from the safe (LEV)

pump gun: a repeating rifle, especially one with a lever suggestive of a pump handle (CDTP)

punch job, safe: a method of gaining entry to safes by safe burglars. A punch is used to gain entry to a safe (LEV)

punched card: a card of standard size and shape in which data are stored in the form of punched holes. The hole locations are arranged in 80 or 90 columns with a given pattern of holes in a column representing one alphanumeric character. The data content is read by mechanical, electrical, or photoelectrical sensing of the hole positions (ADPS)

punched tape: tape, usually paper, in which data are stored in the form of punched holes in a frame across the tape (ADPS)

punching tool: a tool used by safe burglars to batter away the safe lock and spindle so that the locking bars can be released and the safe opened (LEV)

punishment: in criminal law, any pain, penalty, suffering, or confinement inflicted upon a person by the authority of the law and the judgment and sentence of a court, for some crime or offense committed by him, or for his omission of a duty enjoined by

law   (CDTP)
punishment, capital: the use of the death penalty as punishment for crime. From an estimated 240 crimes punishable by death in the 18th century in England the number has been reduced to three: murder, treason, and interstate kidnapping. At present there are 29 states in the United States which have abolished the death penalty as punishment for crime, although 9 other states have abolished it and since reinstated it. The effectiveness of capital punishment as a deterrent to crime has long been a subject of controversy and in addition humanitarian arguments against the use of the death penalty have carried great weight. Nevertheless, the trend toward the abolition of the death penalty seems to have been reversed in recent years.

In the United States the general methods of execution are by electrocution or hanging. Nevada executes through lethal gas. The chief offense in the United States punishable by execution is premeditated murder. In a few jurisdictions rape, robbery, or burglary are still treated as capital offenses. Treason is also a capital offense
(DOS)
punishment, corporal: bodily pain or suffering inflicted as punishment for crime. *See* punishment, poetic   (DOS)
punishment, cruel and unusual: the Eighth Amendment to the U.S. Constitution says: "Excessive bail shall not be required nor excessive fines imposed, nor cruel and unusual punishment inflicted." Such punishment has been defined by the courts as those things which are cruel and inhuman, especially if such forms of punishment have not been specifically provided for by law, however this is no guarantee that they will not be held to come within this category. The court held that the use of convict guards in a penitentiary came within this classification   (LEV)

punishment, individualization of: corrective treatment of the offender based upon an analysis of the interrelated factors in the background and personality which have led to his conflict with the law. Such treatment is "making the punishment fit the offender" rather than "making the punishment fit the crime"   (DOS)
punishment, infamous: punishment for what is held by society at a given time to be an infamous crime. The U.S. Supreme Court has decided that death, or imprisonment in a state prison for a term of years at hard labor, especially for treason or felony, are infamous punishments (114 U.S. 417, 426, 429) and later that disqualification for office as a punishment for crime is infamous (112 U.S. 76)   (DOS)
punishment, mitigation of: the reduction in severity of a sentence regularly imposed for an offense, because of some special personal aspects of, or surrounding circumstances in, the case   (DOS)
punishment, poetic: a punishment adapted to the particular crime committed.   (DOS)
punitive: involving or afflicting punishment   (CTDP)
punitive damages: the awarding of damages in a tort action to punish the one at fault. This may be in the form of monetary award or in some other form. Not all states allow such damages.   (LEV)
purge: to cleanse; purify; to clear of guilt or imputation   (CDTP)
purloin: to steal
purpose: the primary purpose of a search warrant is to aid in the detection and suppression of crime and to obtain evidence for use in criminal prosecutions, yet it cannot be used solely as a means to secure such evidence, and general exploratory searches and seizures, with or without a warrant, can never be justified. However, the mere fact that property seized may be used as evidence against its owner will not invalidate the

seizure or the warrant under which it was made. The warrant may under some statutes be allowed for the purpose of obtaining evidence of an intended crime. Another function of a search warrant is the restoration to the owner of his property. (C.J. 56, 1185) If issued for illegal purpose the writ will of course be invalid (CDTP)

purpose of criminal law: crimes are prohibited and punished on the ground of public policy, to prevent injury to the public. Injury to the public may include destruction or interference with government, human life, private property, or other valued institutions or interests. Such considerations as desire for vengeance or uncompensability of injury may also be involved (CDTP)

purse snatching: the illegal taking of a purse belonging to another. This crime is usually committed by snatching a purse from an unsuspecting person and running away with it. The purse is usually discarded after its contents have been removed (LEV)

pursuit: a function which involves pursuing and overtaking another vehicle, sometimes at high speeds or under hazardous environmental conditions (TDPPC)

pursuit driving: the technique of driving a vehicle by an officer in pursuit of one fleeing in another vehicle. This requires thought and training (LEV)

pursuit vehicle: a vehicle specially modified to enable police to pursue and overtake another vehicle under emergency conditions (TDPPC)

putative: reputed; supposed (CDTP)

putative father: the one assumed to be father to an illegitimate child

PW: white phosphorous, a standard filling for smoke bombs. Particles of white phosphorus ignite spontaneously by atmospheric oxygen and produce a dense white smoke (DWMT)

pygmalionism: erotic reaction obtained from statues of women (LEV)

pyromania: an unnatural desire to set fires. A mental disorder is involved; sexual reaction is involved in some cases (LEV)

pyromaniac: a pathological fire setter; one who sets fires due to a mental condition which causes him to have a compulsion to do so (LEV)

pyrotechnic pistol: a pistol for firing flares or other firework signals (DWMT)

pyrotechnics: ammunition flares, or fireworks used for signaling, illuminating, or marking targets (DWMT)

Q

qualification: in COBOL, the technique of making a name unique by adding IN or OF and another name, according to certain rules (ADPS)

quartz lens: a special lens used for ultraviolet photography (MPPF)

quasi: similar to; resembling but not the real thing; not genuine (LEV)

quasi-judicial: resembling a judicial action or procedure—applied to the action of an administrative body with limited powers to hold hearings and make decisions affecting the rights of specified persons under the law (DAP)

questioned specimens: physical evidence specimens the origin or ownership of which is unknown as contrasted with known specimens, the origin of which is known. For example a bullet found in the body of a deceased is a questioned specimen whereas one fired from a gun by an officer or a laboratory technician is a known specimen. The FBI Laboratory and some others number the specimens and assign each a Q number, for questioned items, or a K number, for known items (LEV)

questions lawful in cross-examination: when a witness is cross-examined, he may be asked any questions which tend (1) to test his accuracy, veracity, credibility; or (2) to shake his credit, by injuring his character. Witnesses have been compelled to answer such questions, the court has a right to exercise a discretion in such cases, and to refuse to compel such questions to be answered when the truth of the matter suggested would not, in the opinion of the court, affect the credibility of the witness as to the matter to which he is required to testify (CDTP)

quiet errors: errors occurring in manual-mechanical systems that are corrected by people familiar with the situation before the errors spread throughout the system. In automatic systems, this type of error is likely to spread throughout the records before it is discovered and corrected (ADPS)

quoin: a wedge placed under the breech of a gun to elevate or depress it (DWMT)

quorum: a number of the officers or members of any body as is, when duly assembled, legally competent to transact business (CDTP)

quo warranto: a proceeding requiring a person to show by what right he exercised any office or liberty (CDTP)

R

rabble-rouser: one who works up emotional excitement with a group of people (LEV)

racemic: if the molecule of an organic compound has no plane of symmetry, the compound is optically active—i.e., a solution of it "twists" the plane of polarization of polarized light in one direction or the other, according to whether it is the *dextro* (*d*) or mirror-image *laevo* (*l*) form. A mixture of the two forms in equal proportions is optically inactive and is known as racemic (FS)

racist: one who has racial prejudices; one who believes that one or more races is [are] superior to others (LEV)

racketeering: that phase of crime based on the illegal collection of fees for presumed protection. In the 20th century racketeering became an established criminal activity in large cities in the fields of prostitution, gambling, the sale of liquor, and narcotics. Sharp practices such as swindling schemes, the coercive collection of tolls from reputable business men, hijacking, "protection" rackets, slot machine control, and bookmaking were developed in the "easy money" efforts of gangsters. The high point was reached during the Prohibition era when national gangster syndicates ruled over large empires of crime extending to the control of government, labor unions, and industry. Important rackets arose in poultry, laundries, milk, and other industries. The accompaniments of racketeering were bribes, bombings, assassinations, and corruption. Alphonse Capone was the recognized "king" of the underworld. Other prominent racketeers were "Legs" Diamond, "Dutch Schultz," "Waxey" Gordon, Frank Yale, "Lucky" Luciano, "Nocky" Johnson, and Frank Costello. From time to time public drives against racketeering have been undertaken, generally with little success. Among these campaigns have been those of special prosecutor Thomas E. Dewey in New York County, William O'Dwyer in Kings County, and the national investigation of the Kefauver Committee. See Kefauver investigation (DOAH)

racking: moving either the lens board or the camera back to and fro while focusing (MPPF)

radar: (1) any of certain methods or systems of using beamed and reflected radio-frequency energy (radio waves) for detecting and locating objects, for measuring distance or altitude, or for certain other purposes, such as navigating, homing, or bombing (DWMT) (2) the electronic equipment, sets, or devices used in any such system. The term derives from the words "radio detection and ranging" (DWMT)

radar alarm system: an alarm system which employs radio frequency motion detectors (TDIAS)

radar frequencies: the following are radar-band types, frequencies, and typical application: (1) L-band (1,400 megahertz), used for early-warning systems; (2) S-band (3,000 megahertz), used for search, fighter direction, and missile acquisition; (3) X-band (10,000 megahertz), used for gun laying, ground-to-air missile tracking, and ground-to-air missile guidance; (4) KU-band (14,000 megahertz), used for airborne search, air-to-air missile guidance, and blind bombing; (5) KA-band (35,000 megahertz), used for airport ground surveillance, mortar locating, and mapping and reconnaissance (DWMT)

radial cracks in glass: the cracks in broken glass running in spoke-like fashion from the point of force which broke the glass (LEV)

radial loop: a fingerprint pattern (LEV)

radiant energy: a form of energy of electromagnetic character. All light which causes a photochemical reduction is radiant energy (MPPF)

radical: one who advocates immediate and fundamental changes in governments and laws, especially laws relating to economic and social welfare (DAP)

radio bomb: a bomb provided with a radio bomb fuze (DWMT)

radio bomb fuze: an electronic bomb fuze that works in reaction to radio (i.e., radar) waves reflected from the target. This type of fuze may be set to detonate at any desired distance from the ground by use of the Doppler effect (DWMT)

radio control: a guidance system that uses radio-frequency energy to activate certain mechanisms or systems (DWMT)

radio frequency interference (RFI): electromagnetic interference in the radio frequency range (TDIAS)

radio frequency motion detector: a sensor which detects the motion of an intruder through the use of a radiated radio frequency electromagnetic field. The device operates by sensing a disturbance in the generated RF field caused by intruder motion, typically a modulation of the field referred to as a Doppler Effect, which is used to initiate an alarm signal. Most radio frequency motion detectors are certified by the FCC for operation as "field disturbance sensors" at one of the following frequencies: 0.915 GHz (L-Band), 2.45 GHz (S-Band), 5.8 GHz (X-Band), 10.525 GHz (X-Band), and 22.125 GHz (K-Band). Units operating in the microwave frequency range are usu. called microwave motion detectors (TDIAS)

radio proximity fuze: a proximity fuze that uses a radar antenna, the echoes triggering detonation at the right instant   (DWMT)

radio shielding: devices installed in a vehicle to reduce the effect on radio transmission and reception of electromagnetic radiation generated by the vehicle   (TDPPC)

radiochemistry: the branch of chemistry concerned with the manipulation of radioactive substances, with which special techniques and precautions are necessary   (FS)

radiograph: a photograph made with x-ray or by radioactive material   (LEV)

raid: police raid—action by officers who enter and search a place to detect law violations, arrest law violators, or obtain evidence of criminality   (LEV)

railroad police: largest private police group in the United States, numbering about 8,000 in the United States and Canada. Function: protect the property, cargo, and goodwill of the railroads   (LEV)

random access: access to storage under conditions in which each set of data records is directly addressable. Access to data at random—in any desired sequence. More commonly used to mean bulk storage with access within several milliseconds to several microseconds for data at any location   (ADPS)

range: (1) the distance between any given point and an object or target (DWMT) (2) the extent or distance limiting the operation or action of something, such as the range of an aircraft, ship, or gun (DWMT) (3) the distance which can be covered over a hard surface by a ground vehicle, with its rated payload, using the fuel in its tank and in cans normally carried as part of the ground-vehicle equipment   (DWMT)   (4) an area equipped for practice in shooting at targets. In this meaning, also called "target range"   (DWMT)

range finder: a device which will determine the distance between a fixed point and a distant object. Many cameras have a built-in range finder which is used in focusing the camera as to distance. Also called a distance meter   (LEV)

ransom: payment, demanded or made, for the release of a person or persons. Usually the payment consists of a specified amount of money. This is a normal incident involved in kidnapping   (LEV)

rape: the having of unlawful carnal knowledge by a man, of a woman forcibly without her consent, as in the following cases: (1) where her resistance is overcome by actual force; (2) where no actual force is used, but because of her condition, known to the man, she cannot consciously consent; (3) where she is below the age at which she can consent; (4) where her consent is extorted by fear or immediate bodily harm; (5) where her submission is induced by fraud without her intelligent consent; as, where induced by fraud she submits to connection believed to be a surgical operation, or to connection with a man fraudulently impersonating and believed to be her husband. Rape is a felony at common law and under the statutes   (CDTP)

rapid fire: a rate of firing small-arms or automatic weapons that is faster than slow fire but slower than quick fire   (DWMT)

rare earth elements: a group of rare elements closely similar in their chemical properties and forming highly infusible (i.e. "earth"-like) oxides. The best-known member is cerium, the oxide of which was used in gas mantles   (FS)

rate, crime: a measure of the recorded criminality of given geographical areas or population groups expressed in numbers proportionate to a population unit. Such rates may be crude (per 100,000 population), refined (per 100,000 persons capable of committing a crime), or specific (e.g., per 100,000 native-born males, 21-30 years of age). No generally accepted terminology to distinguish different types of rates exists. The unit of "crime" or "criminality" employed in computing these rates varies. *Cf.* crime index, criminal statistics (DOS)

rate of fire: the number of rounds fired per weapon per minute (DWMT)

ratio: (1) the degree of enlargement or reduction of a photographic copy with respect to the original (MPPF) (2) the relation or proportion of one thing or quantity to another (CDTP)

Ray, Isaac (*1807-1881*): considered the most influential American writer on forensic psychiatry during the 19th century, Ray's chief interest throughout his entire lifetime was in the closer application of the law and psychiatry. He is primarily remembered as the author of *The Medical Jurisprudence of Insanity*, which first appeared in 1838, and deals with the legal relations to insanity. It has become a classic, widely quoted and highly influential. In this work he discusses mental diseases in general, idiocy, imbecility, the legal consequences of mental deficiency, and the pathology and symptoms of mania. In 1845 he was appointed Superintendent of the Butler Hospital in Providence, R.I. He remained there as Superintendent until 1867, during which time he spent most of his time at the hospital writing and thinking on medico-legal problems. In 1850 he proposed a *Project of Law Regulating the Legal Relations of the Insane.* He felt that insane persons should not be held responsible for criminal acts unless such acts could be proven not to be the direct or indirect result of insanity. Probably one of the most significant events of Ray's life, which has left its mark upon American jurisprudence, was the

adoption of the so-called New Hampshire Rule. Ray had long taken the position that the McNaughton Rules were inadequate, universally unapplicable, and presented no legal definition of insanity. In lengthy correspondence with Judge Charles Doe of the New Hampshire Supreme Court between 1866 and 1872, Dr. Ray thoroughly convinced Judge Doe that the state was in need of a better test of insanity. The New Hampshire Rule was passed in 1868 and reaffirmed the following year (DC)

reaction time: (1) the elapsed time between the initiation of an action and the required response (DWMT) (2) the time required between the receipt of an order directing an operation and the arrival of the initial element of the force concerned in the designated area (DWMT)

read: (1) to copy, usu. from one form of storage to another, particularly from external or secondary storage to internal storage (ADPS) (2) to sense the meaning of arrangements of hardware or visually readable patterns (ADPS)

read-process-write: to read in one block of data, while simultaneously processed block. Some processors concurrently perform any two of the three operations; others are restricted to concurrent read-write (ADPS)

read-write head: a small electromagnet used for reading, recording, or erasing polarized spots on a magnetic surface (ADPS)

reagent: a chemical used to produce a desired reaction (MPPF)

real evidence: evidence produced by actual inspection of material objects or physical characteristics

real-time operation: processing data in synchronism with a physical process rapidly enough so that results of data processing are useful to the physical operation. Sometimes called "on-line, real-time control" (ADPS)

rear-end collision: a collision where

one vehicle strikes the rear end of another vehicle. Generally the one who collides with the rear end of another vehicle is at fault   (LEV)

rear sight: an item attached to the breech end of, and integral to, a carbine, machine gun, pistol, rifle, or the like. It may be a fixed or adjustable cross blade with a U- or V-shaped notch or aperture, or it may have elevation- and windage-adjustment knobs, slides, and graduated scales and be provided with aperture disks   (DWMT)

reasonable: sensible; logical; what one should expect a person to do. The courts have put much stress on the reasonableness of the officers' actions in searches. If the search was reasonable the courts have upheld it on close questions of law   (LEV)

reasonable cause, probable cause, or good reason to believe: has been held to mean any of the following: (1) when the person resembles the one accused and fails to identify himself as a person who did not commit the felony; (2) when his movements or actions are similar to those of the person suspected; (3) when information is received that the person to be arrested committed a felony, or was in the company of the perpetrator either immediately before or after commission; (4) when the person to be arrested has some of the proceeds of the felony in his possession or has been seen leaving the place where the felony was committed; whenever under the known facts an ordinarily reasonable person would so believe   (CDTP)

rebellion: opposition or resistance to legally constituted government in an organized manner   (LEV)

receiver: (1) the basic unit of a firearm, especially a small arm, which contains the operating mechanism of the weapon and to which the barrel and other components are attached (DWMT) (2) a component specifically designed to intercept and demodulate signals

propagated by a transmitter. Short for "radio receiver" or "radar receiver" (DWMT) (3) one who is legally appointed to take custody of property belonging to others, pending judicial action concerning them   (LEV)

receiving stolen goods: the offense of receiving property that is known to be feloniously, or unlawfully acquired

reception: the indoctrination and classification process which the prison system institutes for a newly received inmate   (IC)

rechamber: to rebore or otherwise alter the chamber of a small arm, normally for the purpose of adapting it to cartridges for which it was not originally designed   (DWMT)

recidivism statutes: laws that provide for increased penalties for persons who commit additional specific crimes after conviction for previous criminal acts

recidivist: a person who commits further crimes after conviction of other crime(s); a repeated offender

reciprocity law: a law which states that the blackening of photosensitive materials is determined by the product of light intensity and time of exposure. Thus intensity is the reciprocal of time and, if one is halved, then the other must be doubled to obtain the same blackening   (MPPF)

recognizance: pledge by an individual found guilty of an offense to refrain from certain acts or appear at a set time (usu. in court)

recoil: the backward movement of a gun or part thereof on firing, caused by the backward pressure of the propellant gases; the distance that a gun or part travels in this backward movement. Recoil, particularly as it pertains to small arms, is popularly called "kick"   (DWMT)

recoil cylinder: the part of a recoil mechanism that contains recoil oil and a recoil piston. The piston is forced through the oil-filled cylinder, forcing the oil through orifices and thus converting the recoil energy into increased temperature of the oil. The gun is returned to battery by a counter-recoil mechanism which stores energy for this purpose, usually in a pneumatic or spring mechanism (DWMT)

recoilless: of a gun, built so as to eliminate or cancel out recoil (DWMT)

recoilless rifle: a weapon consisting of a light-artillery tube of the recoilless type and a very light mount. For the 57mm caliber, the gun is fired from a shoulder mount, thus giving rise to the term "recoilless rifle." The larger calibers are fired from lightweight portable tripod mounts or from light vehicles such as the jeep. Ammunition for all calibers is termed "recoilless ammunition." Recoil is eliminated in these weapons by controlled escape propellant gases to the rear through an opening in the breechblock (DWMT)

recoil-operated: of an automatic or semiautomatic firearm, one that utilizes recoil to throw back or unlock the bolt or slide and actuate the loading mechanism. Applied esp. to certain locked-breech firearms. Recoil-operated weapons are classified as "long-recoil" when the barrel and breechblock or bolt recoil the entire distance together and as "short-recoil" when the breechblock or bolt is unlocked and the barrel is stopped after only a short distance of recoil together (DWMT)

record: (1) the records of a court are the formal history of the proceedings before it, entered by the clerk, and the only evidence of what has been done by the court. They cannot be explained or contradicted (DDTP) (2) an identification record, including arrests and dispositions (LEV) (3) a set of data elements closely related in

the sense that they pertain to the same person, place, or thing (ADPS)

record description: in COBOL, a record is described in terms of the data elements it contains. For each element in a record, a picture is used to specify its level, name, and format (ADPS)

record name: in COBOL, the name given to a record within a file and assigned the level number 01. Data names for elements within a record have lower-level numbers 02, 03, etc. (ADPS)

recorder: an instrument for amplifying very small potential (voltage) fluctuations, and displaying these as a continuous graph on a roll of paper. Used therefore as the recording instrument in any analytical method in which the "signal" is or can be converted to an electric potential—e.g., gas chromatography (FS)

recovery: the gaining or regaining of possession of something which has been stolen (LEV)

rectilinear lens: a lens corrected so that it does not curve the straight lines of the image (MPPF)

recuse: (1) to challenge or object to a judge or other person officially involved in the trial of a case on the grounds that he is prejudiced, or has an interest in the case (LEV) (2) the nonparticipation of a judge or other official or person officially involved in the trial of a case because of personal interest, prejudice, or close relationship with the parties involved (LEV)

redefine: in COBOL, to reuse the same storage area for different data items during program execution by means of appropriate descriptions in the data division (ADPS)

redevelopment: a step in the intensifying or toning procedure when a bleached photographic image is redeveloped to give the desired results (MPPF)

redirect examination: the questioning of a witness, by the party offering him, after the witness has been cross-examined. In a criminal trial the party offering a witness questions him first on direct examination. The opposing party questions him on cross-examination and the first party then questions him on redirect examination   (LEV)

redress of grievances: the correction of abuses in the government of a state. The right of the individual to petition for redress of grievances, one of the oldest of British constitutional rights, is guaranteed in the First Amendment of the Constitution of the United States. Historically such petitions were considered by the British parliament before voting appropriations for governmental services   (DAP)

reducer: a chemical solution used to decrease the all-over density of a negative or print   (MPPF)

reducing agent: the ingredient in a developer which changes the subhalide to metallic silver. Usu. requires acceleration   (MPPF)

reduction: the opposite of oxidation—i.e., the removal of oxygen or addition of hydrogen, or decreasing the electron deficit of a positive ion   (FS)

reed switch: a type of magnetic switch consisting of contacts formed by two thin moveable magnetically actuated metal vanes or reeds, held in a normally open position within a sealed glass envelope   (TDIAS)

reeve: the head law enforcement officer of a district or shire in England many years ago. It was from "shire reeve" that the title "sheriff" evolved   (LEV)

reflection: the diversion of light from any surface   (MPPF)

reflector: any device used to increase the efficiency of a light source. Examples are flashlight and tinfoil reflectors for outdoor pictures   (MPPF)

reflex camera: a camera in which the image can be seen right side up and full size on the groundglass

focusing screen   (MPPF)

reformatory: a correctional institution for youthful offenders (with the implication that their criminal behavior can be reformed)

refraction: the bending of a light ray when passing obliquely from one medium to a medium of different density   (MPPF)

refractive index: it determines the amount of deviation which a ray of light undergoes on passing across the boundary between that substance and another (normally air)   (FS)

refreshing memory: a witness while on the stand and testifying may look at memoranda or even printed documents or any subject for the purpose of aiding his memory and recalling facts   (CDTP)

register: an electromechanical device which marks a paper tape in response to signal impulses received from transmitting circuits. A register may be driven by a pre-wound spring mechanism, an electric motor, or a combination of these   (TDIAS)

register, inking: a register which marks the tape with ink (TDIAS)

register, punch: a register which marks the tape by cutting holes in it   (TDIAS)

register, slashing: a register which marks the tape by cutting V-shaped slashes in it   (TDIAS)

regulation: (1) a rule or instruction to be followed by members of an organization (2) approved, accepted, or specified by the employing agency   (LEV)

rehabilitate: to restore a person or thing to its original state or capacity, e.g., a slum area to a good residential area; a cripple to economic or social usefulness (DOS)

rehabilitation: one of the objectives and goals of corrections. This goal implies that the criminal can be rehabilitated from his antisocial lifestyle into a more productive and acceptable life. The rehabilitative philosophy arose predominantly out of the horror engendered by the conditions present in purely punitive prisons and the lack of positive results in terms of less criminality   (LCC)

reintegration: a philosophy of corrections that stresses the most positive method of re-entry of the offender into the community

release: turn loose; free someone. Conditional release [is] the release of a prisoner from custody with the understanding he will not violate certain rules or the law for a specified period of time on penalty of being returned to custody   (LEV)

release-on-own-recognizance or **(ROR):** the pretrial release of an arrested person on his pledge to reappear for trial at a later date, granted to those who are presumed likely to reappear

relevant evidence: *See* evidence, relevant

remand: to send a prisoner, offender, or accused back to jail or prison   (LEV)

remedial: curative, ameliorative; describes a level of social casework, group work, or custodial care which is above the merely palliative in that the situation of the client becomes better than it was when the treatment was initiated, and may even be brought up within the range of normality   (DOS)

remission: a release; pardon of an offense   (CDTP)

remote alarm: an alarm signal which is transmitted to a remote monitoring station. *See also* local alarm   (TDIAS)

remote station alarm system: an alarm system which employs remote alarm stations usually located in building hallways or on city streets   (TDIAS)

removal proceedings: a procedure used by the Federal judicial system for transferring an accused from one Judicial District to another, prior to his conviction for an offense. After a hearing on the matter a federal judge signs a removal order which authorizes the United States Marshal to transfer the accused to another district   (LEV)

reparation: the provision that a convicted offender make restitution to the victim in accordance with the damage the latter suffered. Thus, one of the conditions of probation in some jurisdictions is that the offender make weekly or periodic payments to the victim for the injury done to persons or property   (DOS)

repeal: the abrogation of a law by the enacting body, either by express declaration or impliedly by the passage of a later act which contains provisions contradictory to the terms of existing law (DAP)

repeater: a gun that can be fired several times without reloading; usu. applied to rifles and carbines   (CDTP)

replenisher: a modified developer solution which is added in small portions to a working developer to keep its properties constant   (MPPF)

replevin: an action in court brought by an individual to recover possessions unlawfully taken or detained

report: (1) the accurate recording of facts, usually in written form. The preparation of accurate and complete reports is one of the most important elements of law enforcement. An officer may be excellent as an investigator, but his total value is no better than his reports. They serve as a permanent record for the use of himself, court, correctional personnel, probation and parole officers, and for law enforcement in other parts of the world (LEV) (2) data-processing output that has high information content; more broadly, any planned and organized output from a system   (ADPS)

report interval: the length of time between the preparation of two or more issues of a corresponding report. For example, monthly operating reports have a report interval of one month and daily sales reports an interval of one day. The interval may be variable in length when events, rather than the passage of time, trigger the preparation of reports—for example, when stock on hand falls below the review quantity or when a manager requests the preparation of a report whenever he thinks it useful   (ADPS)

reporting period: the length of time covered in a report. For example, in year-to-date reports issued each month, the reporting period is 1, 2, 3, . . . , 12 months, while the interval between the issuance of two successive reports remains constant at one month   (ADPS)

reprieve: the temporary postponement of the execution of a sentence, usu. in order for an appeal to be brought

requisition: the demand made by the governor of one state upon the governor of another for a fugitive from justice   (CDTP)

rerun point: one of a set of planned-for points in a program, used so that, if an error is detected between two such points, the problem may be rerun merely by going back to the last rerun point. Rerun points are often three to five minutes apart, so that little time is required for a rerun. All information pertinent to a rerun is kept in standby storage during the time from one rerun point to the next   (ADPS)

rerun routine: a routine designed for use in the wake of a processor malfunction or coding or operating mistake to reconstitute a routine from the last previous rerun point   (ADPS)

res adjudicata, res judicata: the thing is settled by a court of competent jurisdiction; a matter finally decided on its merits by a proper court   (LEV)

rescue vehicle: a vehicle specially equipped for rescue and emergency functions in situations of natural and man-made disasters   (TDPPC)

research: painstaking and careful in-

vestigation of a matter; a studious examination of a problem, with a view of finding facts   (LEV)

research, applied: scientific inquiry directed towards practical use (or application)

research, pure: inquiry directed toward the solution of a scientific problem

reset: to restore a device to its original (normal) condition after an alarm or trouble signal   (TDIAS)

res gestae: events which speak for themselves under the immediate pressure of the occurrence, through the instructive, impulsive, and spontaneous words and acts of the participants, and not the words of the participants when narrating the events; spontaneous words spoken during or immediately after an act of such nature that the speaker did not have time or opportunity to rationalize what was being said. What forms any part of the *res gestae* is admissible as an exception to the hearsay rule   (LEV)

res ipsa loquitor [*Lat*]: the thing speaks for itself

resistance bridge smoke detector: a smoke detector which responds to the particles and moisture present in smoke. These substances reduce the resistance of an electrical bridge grid and cause the detector to respond   (TDIAS)

resolving power: the ability of a lens to record fine detail or of an emulsion to reproduce fine detail   (MPPF)

respondent: the adverse party to an appeal of a case. The one who appeals is called the appellant and the other party the respondent. This is especially so in cases in equity, admiralty, and divorce   (LEV)

response time: time between receipt of information about a crime and arrival of officers at the crime scene   (LEV)

restitution: (1) a sentence requiring the offender to make some sort of repayment to his victim (2) projection printing for the purpose of reducing the variation in the scale of prints (MPPF)

restrainer: any chemical—such as potassium bromide—which, when added to a developing solution, has the power of slowing down the developing action and making it more selective (MPPF)

restraining order: an order, issued by a court of competent jurisdiction, forbidding a named person, or a class of persons, from doing specified acts (LEV)

retaliation: the term applied to private vengeance for wrongs. The avenger was supposed to make the offender suffer as much as the victim had suffered. . . . the term carries the idea that punishment for an injury is of like kind with the injury (DOS)

retard transmitter: a coded transmitter in which a delay period is introduced between the time of actuation and the time of signal transmission (TDIAS)

reticulation: the formation of a wrinkled or leather-like surface on a processed emulsion due to excessive expansion or contracting of the gelatin caused by temperature changes or chemical action (MPPF)

retouching: a method for improving the quality of a negative or print by use of a pencil or brush (MPPF)

retreat to the wall: a phrase that means that a party must avail himself of any reasonable avenue of escape to eliminate the necessity of slaying his assailant

retribution: a corrections theory based on the idea that the main objective of imprisonment is punishment for crimes committed

return: a return in writing must be made by the person to whom the writ is directed. In most states it is required by statute to be verified, though in many states this is not necessary if the person is in the custody of a peace officer (CDTP)

reus: the individual formally accused of a crime

revenge: the infliction of suffering upon the offender by a private individual who has been injured. A broader term than retaliation in that revenge has no limits as to kind or degree of suffering returned upon the offender (DOS)

reversal: (1) the action of an appellate court in rendering judgment in a case under review which has the effect of invalidating a judgment of a lower court or tribunal or of requiring a new trial. Such action is usually based on an error by the lower tribunal in interpreting the law applicable to the case (DAP) (2) a process by which a negative image is converted to a positive. Briefly, a negative is developed, re-exposed, bleached, and redeveloped to form a positive (MPPF)

review: (1) a re-examination of some matter (as the findings of a board or the valuation of property by an assessor) by a higher officer or tribunal (DAP) (2) reconsideration of applicable law in a judicial decision by a higher court (DAP)

review, writ of: a general designation of any form of process issuing from an appellate court and intended to bring up for review the record or decision of the court below. In code practice, a substitute for, or equivalent of, the writ of certiorari (CDTP)

revocation: in application to either probation or parole, this term refers to the withdrawal of the privileges of either, because the behavior of the individual was in violation of the conditions agreed upon. In both instances, a body of case law has developed which defines the constitutional rights the probationer or parolee retains in revocation proceedings

revolver: a firearm with a cylinder of several chambers so arranged as to revolve on an axis and be discharged in succession by the same lock (DWMT)

reward: money or other things of value offered for the identification or capture of persons responsible for unlawful acts (LEV)

Rh-Hr factors: characteristics or factors of blood which aid the laboratory technician in its analysis (LEV)

ribmarks: stress marks shown on the cross section of a piece of broken glass, especially along a radical crack. From an examination of the rib marks it can be determined from which direction the force came which broke the glass (LEV)

ricochet: a glancing, skipping, jumping, or deflection of a moving projectile after striking something at an angle. This occurs when a bullet strikes a surface which does not halt its flight. (An officer should keep this in mind if firing under conditions where a ricochet could be dangerous to life or property.) (LEV)

Rideau v. Louisiana, 373 U.S. 723 (1963): this decision contains a fine discussion of the right of a defendant in a criminal action to a fair trial by unbiased jurors. The petitioner, Rideau, confessed criminal guilt while in jail in response to leading questions of the sheriff before an array of television cameras and sound recorders. The film and sound track was televised locally prior to trial (AOJ)

ridge: (1) the marks or line shown when fingerprints are taken (LEV) (2) top of hills or mountains (LEV)

ridge count: the number of ridges intervening between the delta and the core. Ridges counted must cross or touch an imaginary line from the delta to the core (LEV)

ridge line: referring to a line in a fingerprint pattern, caused by a ridge in the pattern (LEV)

rifle: (1) a firearm having spiral grooves upon the surface of its bore to impart rotary motion to a projectile, thereby stabilizing the projectile and ensuring greater accuracy of impact and longer range. It may fire projectiles automatically or semiautomatically, or successive rounds may be manually loaded. The operation may be gas, recoil, or manual. It is provided with a stock for shoulder firing and may have a sling to aid in carrying and aiming (DWMT) (2) a recoilless breechloading single-shot artillery weapon with a manually operated vented breechlock and a rifle bore. It is fired from various types of ground or vehicular mounts (DWMT) (3) a rifled muzzle-loading cannon of any size (DWMT) (4) to cut spiral grooves (rifling) in the bore of a gun in order to give a spin to the projectile so that it will have greater accuracy of fire and longer range (DWMT)

rifling: the helical grooves cut in the bore of a rifled gun tube, beginning at the front face of the gun chamber (origin of rifling) and extending to the muzzle; also, the operation of forming the grooves in the gun tube. The purpose of rifling is to impart spin to the projectile; if the spin is fast enough, the projectile will be gyroscopically stable and will travel approximately nose first (DWMT)

right of allocution: the right of the defendant to speak in his own defense before judgment is pronounced. See allocution

right-of-way: (1) land on which, and on either side of which, a road, highway, railroad, electric line or pipeline is built (LEV) (2) the right of passage over another's land—a servitude (LEV)

right to bear arms: the right of citizens under the Second Amendment to the Constitution to possess arms in order to provide a militia. The courts have held that this right is not infringed by the Federal Firearms Act, or by statutes in most of the States which make unauthorized possession of lethal weapons a criminal offense (DAP) right to counsel: a fundamental right of an accused person to be represented by an attorney at any stage of a criminal proceeding, including the rights to have an attorney assigned as counsel by the court if the accused is financially unable to pay counsel fees, to consult privately with counsel, and of counsel to have sufficient time to prepare the case. See *Gideon v. Wainwright; Miranda v. Arizona; Scottsboro* cases (DAP)

right to release on bail: at common law it was within the discretion of the magistrate, judge, or court having jurisdiction and power to allow or deny bail in all cases. It could be allowed whenever it was deemed sufficient to insure the appearance of the accused, but not otherwise, and was therefore always allowed in cases of misdemeanor, less frequently in cases of felony, and almost always denied in cases of felony punishable by death. It is now generally declared by the constitutions of the different states, or provided by statute, that the accused shall have an absolute right to give bail in all cases except where the punishment may be death, and even in those cases except where the proof is evident or the presumption great (CDTP)

right wing: that section of any ideological group that tends toward relative conservatism or reactionism; or within a group, that element which supports the least extreme form of the characteristic ideas or principles of the group (DOS)

rights: something which a person is entitled to; privileges which exist in favor of persons. There are several kinds of rights existing in society and recognized in law. The ones most commonly encountered are legal rights and civil rights. The former are those protected generally by law and the latter usually refer to constitutional and/or those covered by the Constitution's Bill of Rights, or legislation and court decisions in this area of law (LEV)

Rights, Bill of: the first ten amendments to the U.S. Constitution, prohibiting the federal government, or in certain amendments the states, from interfering with political liberties, and guaranteeing to persons charged with crime the protections of fair procedure. The Civil War amendments (Thirteenth, Fourteenth, and Fifteenth) are also commonly classed as part of the Bill of Rights. Most state constitutions also include the equivalent of the federal guarantees, and when codified together these are referred to as bills of rights. The phrase was used earlier in England in the course of the struggle between King and Commons, and there characterizes the similar guarantees won by the people (DOS)

rights, civil: the right to vote, seek office, serve on juries, etc. Also the legal guarantees protecting all persons in a democracy from attack on personal liberties (freedom to live, travel, possess property, etc.) either by governmental agents or mobs. Civil rights comprise the guarantees to defendants in courts of law for fair trials, and against discrimination on account of race, religion, or national origin (DOS)

rights and liabilities of parties (lawful arrest): if an arrest is authorized, and is attempted or made in a proper manner, the person making it, if an officer or private person, merely performs his duty, and he incurs no liability as the law throws its protection around him. If the person sought to be arrested resists, he is criminally liable for the resistance. If he resists with force, he is civilly and criminally liable for assault and battery. If he, or a person assisting him, in his resistance, kills the person making the arrest, the homicide is murder. If a person unlawfully departs from custody after he has been legally arrested he is guilty of a misdemeanor known as "escape," and if he breaks from his place of imprisonment, or forcibly escapes, he is guilty of a misdemeanor or a felony, according to circumstances, known as a "prison breach." If third persons interfere in aid of the person sought to be arrested, the bare interference constitutes a misdemeanor or felony; if they use force, they are also guilty of an assault and battery; and if the person making the arrest is killed, they are guilty of murder. If they procure the escape of the person after his arrest, they are guilty of a misdemeanor or felony known as a "rescue."

(CDTP)

rights and liabilities of parties (unlawful arrest): if an arrest or attempt to arrest is illegal, either because there is no authority to arrest at all, or because the arrest is made in an unlawful manner, as, for instance, by the use of unnecessary violence, the person arresting, whether he is an officer or a private person, and whether the arrest or attempt to arrest was made with or without a warrant, is guilty of assault and battery, or false imprisonment, and is both civilly and criminally liable therefor. (22 Amer. Reports 669) An unlawful attempt to arrest or a false imprisonment may be lawfully resisted by any necessary force short of taking life or inflicting grievous bodily harm. (11 S.W. 638) Even when life is taken in resisting, the attempt to arrest or the imprisonment is generally deemed sufficient provocation to reduce the homicide to manslaughter. Within certain limits, third persons, particularly relatives, may interfere to prevent an unlawful arrest or imprisonment. (Clarks Crim. Law 3rd Ed. 272)

(CDTP)

rim-fire: the type of ammunition cartridge which is detonated by the firing pin or other mechanism striking the rim of the cartridge at its head, or base   (LEV)

rimless: said of a cartridge case in which the extracting groove is ma-

chined into the body of the case, with no part of the case extending beyond the body   (DWMT)

ring-and-bead sight: a type of gunsight in which the front sight is a bead or post and the rear sight is a ring   (DWMT)

ring sight: a sight, especially a gunsight, in the shape of a ring or concentric rings, through which aim is taken and range is estimated. Ring sights include the iron type (in which a simple ring or set of rings encloses a cross hair or the like) and the optical type (in which a system of lenses is used to show a series of concentric rings and the bead)

(DWMT)

riot: any use of force or violence, disturbing the public peace, or any threat to use such force or violence, if accompanied by power of execution, by two or more persons acting together, and without authority of law (CDTP)

Riot Act: a statute that originated in England for the purpose of dispersing unlawfully assembled persons. The statute states that, if 12 persons or more are unlawfully assembled and disturbing the peace, they are guilty of a felony if they do not disperse within one hour when ordered to do so by a duly authorized officer

riot-control agent: a chemical that produces temporary irritating or disabling effects when in contact with the eyes or when inhaled

(DWMT)

riot grenade: a grenade of plastic or other nonfragmenting material containing a charge of tear gas and a detonating fuze with short delay. The grenade functions and the gas is released by a bursting action   (DWMT)

riot gun: any shotgun with a short barrel pecially a short-barreled sho⁺ n used in guard duty or to scatter rioters. A riot gun usually has a 20-in. cylinder barrel

(DWMT)

ripping method: a method of opening safes by burglars. A can-opener type tool is used to remove the metal from the top, bottom, back, or side of a safe (LEV)

roadblock: obstruction to passage on a road or street placed in operation by the law enforcement officers, to slow or stop motor traffic, when endeavoring to apprehend criminals or perform other official functions (LEV)

robbery: the felonious taking of personal property in the possession of another, from his person or immediate presence, and against his will, accomplished by means of force or fear. To constitute the crime of robbery, (1) the property must be such as may be the subject of larceny; (2) it must be taken and carried away, as in the case of larceny; (3) it must be taken from another's person, or in his presence and against his will; (4) it must be so taken by violence or by putting in fear; (5) it must be taken with intent to steal (CDTP)

Robinson v. California, 370 U.S. 660, 82 S. Ct. 1417, 8 L. Ed. 758 (1962): in this decision, the Supreme Court held that the Eighth Amendment, barring cruel and unusual punishment, was applicable to the individual states. This is the first instance of its application to the states

Rochin v. California, 342 U.S. 165, 96 L. Ed. 183, 72 S. Ct. 205 (1952): that *Wolf* did not permit state courts to admit all unconstitutionally seized physical evidence, regardless of how outrageous or offensive the police methods employed, was demonstrated in this famous "stomach-pumping" case. (The decision marks the real beginning of the Court's trek to discredit a case-by-case approach to search and seizure to the final step the Court took nine years later in *Mapp* when the Court incorporated the Fourth Amendment under the due process umbrella of the Fourteenth Amendment.) (ILECJ)

rollfilm: a strip of flexible film, wound on a spool between turns of a longer paper strip, for daylight loading into rollfilm cameras (MPPF)

Rosenberg Case: the trial of Ethel and Julius Rosenberg, husband and wife, for espionage. The trial was held in New York in 1951. The Rosenbergs were accused by David Greenglass, Ethel's brother, of selling atomic secrets, which he had stolen, to the Soviets. They were tried, found guilty, and were executed in Sing Sing Prison on June 19, 1953. They were the first civilians to receive the death penalty for wartime espionage and the first Americans to be executed in peacetime for this crime

round: a unit of gun ammunition consisting of a projectile, propellant, igniting charge, and primer. The term may also apply to a piece of rocket ammunition or to a bomb, especially in the phrases "complete round" and "bomb complete round" (DWMT)

rounding: dropping certain less significant digits of a quantity and applying some adjustment to the more significant digits retained. A common round-off rule is to add 5 in the left-most position to be dropped, make the carry (if any), and discard unwanted digits. Thus, π, 3.14159265 . . . , rounded to three decimals is 3.142 (ADPS)

routine: a set of coded instructions arranged in proper sequence to direct the processor to perform a desired operation or series of operations. *See also* subroutine (ADPS)

routine, compiler: a routine that, before the desired computation is started, translates a source program expressed in a problem-oriented language into an object program in machine code. In accomplishing the translation, the compiler may be required to: (1) routine allocate—to assign storage locations to the main routines and subroutines, thereby fixing the absolute values of any symbolic

addresses; (2) routine assemble—
to integrate the subroutines (supplied, selected, or generated) into
the main routine—that is, to
adapt, incorporate, orient; (3)
routine generate—to produce a
needed subroutine from para-
meters and skeletal coding; called
a "generator routine"   (ADPS)
run: the act of processing, under
the control of one or more programs, a batch of transactions—for
example, the inventory receipts,
issues, etc., for the week—against
all the files that are affected to
produce desired outputs consisting of updated files and reports
                          (ADPS)
run, trial: a preliminary run of
transactions against files, but
without producing any outputs,
for the purposes of finding errors
and omissions in the data and determining the correct effect for interrelated events—for example,
substitution of merchandise to fill
priority customer's orders, or pay-
roll calculations involving group
bonus where the composition of
the groups changes frequently. An
actual run is made to update the
records using knowledge gained
from the trial run   (ADPS)
run diagram: a generalized graphic
representation of the files, transactions, and data that are handled
together under program control to
produce an updated file, list of
changes, and errors   (ADPS)
runs, housekeeping: the sorting,
merging, editing, and operating
runs required for file maintenance; the nonproduction runs. In
a limited sense, the set-up and
clean-up parts of a program as
opposed to production processing
                          (ADPS)
rural: pertaining to the country as
distinguished from the city; not in
a city or town   (LEV)
Rush, Benjamin (1745?-1813): or-
ganizer and leader of the Philadelphia Society for Alleviating the
Miseries of the Public Prisons,
which was founded in 1787. Rush
and his organization were influ-

ential in gaining penal reforms,
including the establishment of the
Walnut Street Jail, the first penitentiary   (LCC)

S

sabotage: any act of obstruction of
industrial processes, usu. secret or
covert, committed by individuals
or groups of employees to further
a private interest; either to force
recognition of workers' grievances
and claims (industrial sabotage) or
in wartime to serve the purposes
of a foreign country (political
sabotage). The word is also properly, but not commonly, applied
to employers' limitation of production, or destruction of products, to maintain prices or to
force governmental conces-
sions. . . . Sabotage takes on
varied forms of obstruction, not
only by damage to property, but
by soldiering on the job, by
spreading false rumors or by publicly revealing unfavorable truths
about goods (open-mouthed sabotage), and by increasing costs
through using expensive materials
                          (DOS)
saboteur: one who commits sabotage   (LEV)
Sacco-Vanzetti case: the case of
two aliens who were convicted of
the murder of a paymaster in Massachusetts on April 15, 1920. The
introduction of evidence showing
their radicalism and certain questions of the prosecutor and remarks of the judge created a widespread impression that the defendants were being tried for their
political opinions. After legal resources had been exhausted, Governor Fuller appointed a commission of laymen, who reported that

the trial had been fair. Both defendants were executed on Aug. 22, 1927　(DAP)

sadism: sexual perversion involving torture or cruelty against another to achieve sexual satisfaction

sadist: one who carries out acts of perverse cruelty against another person to satisfy sexual perversion (LEV)

safe: (1) a sturdy box for keeping money and other valuables safe (LEV) (2) of a bomb or ammunition; so constituted and set as not to detonate or function accidentally; in a safe condition (DWMT)

safe deposit boxes: an order authorizing the sheriff to open a safe deposit box rented to a debtor is not an unconstitutional or unwarranted search and seizure (39 A.L.R. 811), but where, in a pending action, only certain stock certificates are identified, an order for the examination of certain boxes, without limitation to those certificates, is unauthorized (286 Pac. 471), although with such a limitation on the search it would not be unconstitutional (286 Pac. 471) (C.J. 56, 1167)　(CDTP)

Safe Streets Act: *See* Omnibus Crime and Safe Streets Act

safelight: a light, the intensity and color range of which are such that it will not affect sensitive materials　(MPPF)

safety: a locking or cutoff device that prevents a weapon or missile from being fired accidentally (DWMT)

safety film: film with a cellulose acetate base; so-called because it burns very slowly　(MPPF)

safety shot: an unordered, duplicate exposure, made in case of damage to one negative in processing　(MPPF)

safing: as applied to weapons and ammunition, the changing from a state of readiness for initiation to a safe condition　(DWMT)

St. Valentine's Day Massacre: the murder of members of a gang of bootleggers in Chicago in 1929.

This act against the "Bug" Moran Gang enabled Al Capone to consolidate his control in the city of Chicago

saline: often used loosely for isotonic saline　(FS)

saliva: the fluid in the mouth that keeps it moist and assists in digestion, secreted by the salivary glands. The crime laboratory can analyze it and determine its type, which has a correlation to the blood type of the individual (LEV)

sallow: having a yellowish unhealthy appearance. Used as a descriptive term in recording a person's physical features　(LEV)

salt: a compound of positive ions (normally of a metallic element) and negative ions of an acid (e.g., sodium chloride, copper sulphate). All true salts are crystalline, the crystals consisting of an ordered lattice of the two sorts of ions. Most salts are also soluble in water, and are present in solution largely or wholly as ions, not as molecules　(FS)

salute: a greeting or sign of courtesy passed between parties, such as gesturing with the hand, firing a cannon, dipping a flag, dipping the wings of an aircraft, etc. (DWMT)

salvage: act of saving; compensation for saving property　(CDTP)

same: (law and business) the identical thing or person previously referred to or mentioned　(LEV)

same act may be both a crime and a tort: in such a case the wrongdoer is amenable both to a civil action by the state and to a civil action by the party he has injured. These two actions are separate and distinct. Neither of them is a bar to the other. The object of the former is to punish as an example. The object of the latter is to compensate the injured party. If the offense committed is a misdemeanor either action may precede the other; or both may be carried on at the same time. In case of a felony the same rule applies generally in this country; but in England and in a few of the states in this country the civil action may not precede the criminal action (CDTP)

sample: a part of a thing presented as evidence of the quality of the whole; a specimen (CDTP)

sampling: statistical, the process or method of drawing a finite number of individuals, cases, or observations from a particular universe. Selecting part of a total group for investigation. Survey procedures having to do with the selection of the sample, collection of information from sample cases, and statistical treatment of findings so as to yield a representative group (DOS)

sampling, random: process of sample selection in which each individual or element in the universe is assured an equal and independent chance of being included. Also called simple sampling and random selection. Should be distinguished from careless, unsystematic, accidental or opportunistic sampling because careful planning and systematic procedure are required to assure random choice (DOS)

sanction: (1) a permission or social approval of any act or form of behavior (DOS) (2) the legal, or other regulatory, provisions for the enforcement of a legal or social imperative, and accordingly the penalty for the violation of such an imperative (DOS) (3) by a peculiar process of inversion, not uncommon in the history of language, a prohibition or proscription. It is in this latter sense that the term has acquired wide vogue in recent years, particularly in connection with international agreements, and the system of enforcement included in the organizational establishment of the League of Nations. In contemporary usage, the phrase, "to apply sanctions," ordinarily means to apply restraints, prohibitions, or

penalties (DOS)

sanctioned: (1) socially permitted or approved (DOS) (2) subject to social, particularly legal or conventional, restraints, prohibitions, or penalties (DOS)

sane: mentally sound (CDTP)

sanitary: designed to secure health; hygienic (CDTP)

sanity: soundness of mind (CDTP)

sanity hearing: a procedure, ordered by the court, or other official, for the purpose of determining whether a person is sane or insane (LEV)

sans [Fr]: without

sapphist: lesbian

satchel charge: a number of blocks of explosive taped to a board fitted with a rope or wire loop for carrying and attaching. The minimum weight of the charge is usually about 15 lb. (DWMT)

satellite processor: a small processor designed primarily for card-to-tape conversion, printing of tape contents, and other selected, high-volume operations. Used to support a large processor to increase its productivity (ADPS)

satisfactory evidence: such evidence as is sufficient to produce a belief that the thing is true; credible evidence; such evidence as, in respect to its amount or weight, is adequate or sufficient to justify the court or jury in adopting the conclusion in support of which it is adduced (80 Cal. 129: 22 Pac. 124) (CDTP)

saturation, of color: a saturated color is one which can be exactly matched by a pure color of the spectrum, or by a mixture of spectrum red and violet. To match an unsaturated color, white or neutral tint must be added to the spectrum color (FS)

satyriasis: abnormal sex craving on the part of the male (LEV)

saving clause: an exception of a special thing out of general things mentioned in a statute (CDTP)

scabbard: a sheath with an open top. It is usu. made of leather, metal, wood, or canvas and is designed to protect edged weapons, rifles, carbines, and submachine guns from the elements and rough usage (DWMT)

scaffold: a platform upon which convicted criminals are executed by being hanged (LEV)

scale: (1) to climb by a ladder, as to scale the ramparts of a fortification (DWMT) (2) in armor, the scales of armor collectively (DWMT) (3) to clean the inside of an old-time cannon by exploding a small quantity of powder in it (DWMT) (4) the ratio between the length of lines on a map or sketch and the distance between points (LEV) (5) scale is the ratio of a linear dimension in the photograph to the corresponding dimension in the subject (MPPF)

scalp: to sell sports or amusement tickets at a price higher than the printed or stated price of the tickets. This is usually an unlawful act (LEV)

scalper: one who sells tickets at prices higher than the official rates

scandal: acts of alleged wrongdoing which bring shame or disgrace on those who commit the acts (LEV)

scatter read-write: a scatter-read operation performed under program control reads a block of data from tape and breaks it up into processable elements that can be placed where wanted in storage. A scatter-write operation picks up the dispersed data elements in storage and writes them on tape as a block (ADPS)

scene: the place where something occurs, i.e., the scene of the crime, or the scene of the accident (LEV)

scent: (1) odor or smell of something (LEV) (2) the means of locating a person (LEV)

Schenck v. United States, 249 U.S. 47, 63 L. Ed. 470, 39 S. Ct. 247 (1919): Mr. Justice Holmes in the Court's opinion enunciated his famous clear and present danger test. (The Court upheld a convic-

tion under Federal Espionage Act of 1917. The well-known words about shouting fire in a crowded theater are used to illustrate a situation in which free speech may be limited.) (ILECJ)

Schiener scale: a European system of speed ratings for films. It is little used in this country. Abbreviation is Sch. (MPPF)

Schmerber v. California, 384 U.S. 757, 16 L. Ed. 2d 908, 86 S. Ct. 1826 (1966): with four justices dissenting, Mr. Justice Brennan, for the majority, held the prosecution can use as evidence in a drunken driving test the analysis of a blood sample taken without the consent of the accused without violating his Fifth, Sixth, and Fourteenth Amendment rights against self-incrimination. (The Court distinguishes between the production of compelled physical evidence, and testimonial compulsion, i.e., words produced by someone's lips.) (ILECJ)

Schneckloth v. Bustamonte, 412 U.S. 218, 36 L. Ed. 2d 854, 93 S. Ct. 2041 (1973): through Mr. Justice White the Court held, 7–2, that warnings are unnecessary as prerequisite to a consent search in a noncustodial situation (ILECJ)

Schwartz v. Texas, 344 U.S. 199, 97 L. Ed. 231, 73 S. Ct. 732 (1952): speaking for the Court, and relying on *Wolf* v. *Colorado,* Justice Minton held that even though wiretapping was illegal (Section 605, Federal Communications Act), evidence so obtained, nevertheless, could be used in a state court (ILECJ)

scienter [*Lat*]: knowingly; with guilty knowledge

scintilla: a spark; atom; the least particle (CDTP)

scintilla of evidence: a spark of evidence. Any material evidence which if true would tend to establish the issue in the mind of a reasonable jury (59 S.E. 641) (CDTP)

scope: the telescopic sight on a rifle (LEV)

scope of remedy: generally speaking the availability of search warrants extends to and embraces all cases in which a primary right to search and seizure may be found in the interest which the public or complainant may have in the property to be seized or in the right to the possession of it, or when a valid exercise of the police power renders possession of the property by the accused unlawful and provides that it may be taken. (C.J. 56, 1186)   (CDTP)

scope of search incidental to arrest of person: incidental to a lawful arrest an officer has the right to search the person of the individual arrested and seize any evidence tending to establish "crime" whether it be the one for which the arrest was made or any other, the cases do not clearly define how far an officer may go, in searching the room, premises, or effects of the person arrested. The following principles, however, are well settled; (a) if the arrest is made outside the home or rooming place of the arrested party the officer has no right to go to the place where he resides and make a search for incriminating evidence; (b) the officers may seize any articles of an incriminating nature visible to them in the rooms where the arrest is made; (c) the officers have no right to search any part of the residence of the person except the room where the arrest is made. To what extent the officers have the right to search cupboards, dressers, and other receptacles in the room where the party is arrested is not entirely clear; some of the cases uphold the right of the officer to make such search (147 N.W. 526), but deny the right to search any other portion of the premises (190 N.W. 721). It has been held that where several conspirators were arrested at the home of one, the officers had the right to go to the home of another and search for evidence
(CDTP)

Scopes, John Thomas: John T.

Scopes, a 24-year-old teacher in Dayton, Tenn., was charged with "undermining the peace and dignity of the state" by teaching his students the Darwinian theory of evolution, that man had descended from the apes. His famous trial is known as "The Monkey Trial"; Scopes was defended by Clarence Darrow but on July 21, 1925 was found guilty and fined $100. The decision was reversed on technical grounds by the Tennessee Supreme Court

Scopolamine®: a drug which produces drowsiness and stupor. It has been used in lie detection work where the suspect is administered the drug which produces a "twilight" sleep. He is questioned while in this condition and allegedly will speak the truth as his inhibitions are removed. The value of this procedure is questionable
(LEV)

Scottsboro Cases: a series of trials between 1931 and 1938 involving eight [blacks] who had been charged with the rape of two women in Scottsboro, Alabama. After conviction and sentence of death at the first trial the case remained pending for six years as a result of nationwide protest. The evidence at the trial was clear that the defendants were innocent of the charges, and many groups and individuals sought retrials on the basis of new evidence. A second trial was ordered by the U.S. Supreme Court in Nov., 1932 and again in 1934 on the grounds respectively that the defendants had been denied adequate counsel and that [blacks] had been excluded from the juries at the three preceding trials. Continued appeals led to a decision in 1938 by the Court denying new trials for four of the defendants. The other four had been released in 1947
(DOAH)

scoundrel: unprincipled person; rascal; person of low repute (LEV)

scrip: evidence of the right to obtain shares in a public company;

warrants or other like orders drawn on the city treasurer or other official (CDTP)

scruples: caution resulting from the desire to do right; conscientiousness (LEV)

scum: a surface layer which forms on pyro developers, and occasionally on chrome-alum fixing-hardening baths (MPPF)

scuttle: to sink (CDTP)

S.D.S. (SDS): Students for a Democratic Society (LEV)

seal: where a statute provides that a search warrant may issue upon an affidavit not bearing the official seal of the officer issuing it, the seal is, of course, unnecessary to a valid issuance. (267 U.S. 498) Under the common law a search warrant if not under seal is void (CDTP)

search: (1) an operation to locate an enemy force known or believed to be at sea (DWMT) (2) a systematic reconnaissance of a defined area, such that all parts of the area pass within visibility (DWMT) (3) to distribute gunfire over an area in depth by successive changes in gun elevation (DWMT) (4) the term "search," as applied to searches and seizures, is an examination of a man's house or other buildings or premises, or of his person, with a view to the discovery of contraband or illicit or stolen property, or some evidence of guilt to be used in the prosecution of a criminal action for some crime or offense with which he is charged. As used in this connection the term implies some sort of force, either actual or constructive, much or little. The term also implies that the object searched for has been hidden or intentionally put out of the way. While it has been said that searching is generally a function of sight, it is held that the mere looking at that which is open to view is not a "search." (C.J. 56, 1154; 297 Fed. 482) (CDTP)

S.E.A.R.C.H. (SEARCH): See Project Search

search, crime scene: a careful search of the area where a crime was committed. It may include adjacent areas and other areas where some evidence is found or action occurred (LEV)

search and rescue: the use of aircraft, surface craft, submarines, and specialized rescue teams and equipment to search for and rescue personnel in distress on land or at sea (DWMT)

search of curtilage or appurtenant premises: being usually considered to be a part of the dwelling house they, like the dwelling house, are not to be searched without a valid search warrant (267 Pac. 758) (CDTP)

search of person: a legal search made of a person. It may be made upon the authority of a search warrant, following arrest without a warrant, following an arrest made under authority of an arrest warrant, or made under the authority of a "stop and frisk" law, if such exists in the state (LEV)

search of places of business: while officers are vested with the same rights as the general public in entering a business establishment, nevertheless, under general rules above stated, a search warrant may be necessary to search an office or store or a room in a plant, and this rule extends to the premises of the business (282 U.S. 344) (CDTP)

search of the instruments of transportation: although automobiles are within the protection of the constitutional guaranty, it does not follow necessarily therefrom that a search of an automobile without a warrant is "unreasonable," for, because of the obvious impossibility of procuring warrants in all cases in time to search such highly mobile possessions as vehicles and boats, the rule of necessity of a warrant for their search is somewhat different in some jurisdictions from that governing ordinary stationary objects (C.J. 56, 1194)

search on return to repair damage: where, after making a search without a warrant, officers return to the premises to fix a door they had broken, and while there make another search, such search is unlawful (226 Ky. 101)   (CDTP)

search warrant: an order in writing issued by a justice or other magistrate, in the name of the state, directed to a sheriff, constable, or other officer, commanding him to search a specified house, shop, or other premises, for personal property alleged to have been stolen, or for unlawful goods, and to bring the same, when found, before the magistrate, and usually also the body of the person occupying the premises, to be dealt with according to the law (CDTP)

search warrant, sufficiency of: a search warrant must conform to the constitutional and statutory requirements under which it is issued. A search warrant must be valid at the time of its issuance, for its validity can never depend upon the manner of its execution. (13 Fed. 2nd 242)   (CDTP)

searches and seizures: incident to arrest, officers had authority to search defendant's person and his premises. Property seized in connection with lawful arrest and held as evidence of crime is not within the protection of constitutional provisions relating to searches and seizure. (11 Fed. 2nd 503) Where officer had reasonable cause to believe that defendants had just made unlawful sale to their agents, such officers had authority to make arrest without warrant and to search defendants and place where the arrest was made. (292 U.S. 635)   (CDTP)

searches and seizures, illegal ab initio: if a search and seizure is illegal at its inception it cannot become legalized by what it brings to light, rather, it must be justified by the steps that precede the search and seizure, which themselves must be lawful in their entirety. Thus, if disclosed as the result of an illegal search, it is not justified by the discovery of contraband, gambling devices, or unlawfully possessed weapons; nor will a subsequent admission or confession of accused legalize a search illegal at its inception. Moreover, if an unlawful search and seizure is commenced, and during its progress or thereafter, a search warrant is procured it will not render valid the search invalid from its inception; nor where property is seized under a void search warrant, can the seizure be legalized by the issuance of a search warrant based on information secured through the first search and seizure. (C.J. 56, 1184)   (CDTP)

searches and seizures of property: at common law, as well as by statute in most states, a magistrate, to recover stolen property or procure evidence of a crime, may issue a warrant directing a search for, and seizure of, property. To authorize the issuance of such a warrant, the same preliminary proceedings are generally necessary as are necessary to procure a warrant of arrest. The requisites of a search warrant are generally the same as the requisites of a warrant of arrest, except as the difference in the purpose of the warrant renders them different   (CDTP)

searching places outside curtilage: it is the general rule that no search warrant is necessary for a lawful search of an open place not within the curtilage or not in close proximity to the dwelling house, or unenclosed grounds not essential to the enjoyment of a dwelling, where a search in no way invades or disturbs the privacy of one's home or his legitimate business. (230 Pac. 279)   (CDTP)

searchlight or flashlight: the use of a searchlight or flashlight, being comparable to the use of a field glass, is not prohibited by the constitutional guaranty   (CDTP)

seat: (1) a support or holder for a mechanism or for a part of one

(DWMT) (2) to fit correctly in or on a holder or in a prepared position, as to seat a fuze in a bomb, a projectile in the bore of a gun, or a cartridge in a chamber (DWMT)

seating: specifically, the distance to which a projectile is rammed into the bore of a cannon, usu. measured from the base of the projectile to the rear face of the breech (DWMT)

S.E.C. (SEC): Securities and Exchange Commission

seclude: to separate from others; to keep apart from others (LEV)

second application: a refusal to discharge under one writ does not prevent another application to a different court, unless there is a statute to that effect; and even then a second writ can be granted on new facts or evidence. (158 S.W. 843) In absence of such a statute, the decision on the first application will be given great weight, and, as a rule would not be disturbed unless new facts were shown. (158 S.W. 843) If a person once discharged on habeas corpus is rearrested upon the original basis, he should be again discharged on a new writ. But he could be subsequently indicted for the offense (CDTP)

second boycott: a combination agreement or understanding to exercise coercive pressure upon a third person to compel him to withdraw or withhold his patronage from the person against whom a boycott is directed, either by threats of withdrawal of business from him or by threats to him of similar injury (CDTP)

second search with same warrant: a warrant once served cannot, of course, be used for the purpose of additional searches; but, where a search is continuous, not having been abandoned or completed, it will not be held void because the officers go over the premises a second time (146 Miss. 593) (CDTP)

secondary classification: a term used in classifying fingerprints. In the classification formula it follows the primary classification and is written as capital letters, as T/W, whatever the classification requires. It is based on the type of pattern in each of the index fingers (LEV)

secondary colors: colors formed by the combination of two primary colors. Yellow, magenta, and cyan are the secondary colors (MPPF)

secondary evidence: is that which is inferior to primary. Thus, a copy of an instrument, or oral evidence of its contents, is secondary evidence of the instrument and contents (Cal. C.C.P. 1892, 1830) (CDTP)

second-hand evidence: hearsay evidence

secret: (1) well-kept information or knowledge concerning a particular thing (LEV) (2) in government service, material or information which if disclosed without authority could result in serious damage to the nation, by endangering the international relations of the country; jeopardizing the effectiveness of a program or policy of great importance to the national defense; exposing important military or defense plans, technological developments of importance to the national defense, or information relative to important intelligence operations (LEV)

Secret Service: a division of the Treasury Department whose principal function is the investigation of crimes against that Department. At its inception in 1864 its special function was the detection of counterfeiters, smugglers, and illegal liquor manufacturers. Following the death of President Lincoln the Secret Service was entrusted with the protection of the persons of the President and his family at the White House and elsewhere. During the two World Wars it was active in investigating plots designed to interfere with the manufacture and shipment of munitions. It has, as part of its work, collected photographs of well-known international criminals, which today number over 5,000. The organization was originally established in 1864 with a brigadier general in charge of a volunteer force   (DOAH)

Secret Service (colonial), the first: was organized by Aaron Burr and Major Benjamin Tallmadge in June 1778 for the United Colonies. It was known as the Headquarters Secret Service and developed into the first organized intelligence department of the Army of the United Colonies. On July 4, 1778, General George Washington in a special order made Burr head of the Department for Detecting and Defeating Conspiracies and ordered him "to proceed to Elizabeth Town to procure information of movements of the enemy's shipping about New York." Information about the activities of the British, however, had been secretly gathered previously by patriotic individuals and societies
                              (FAMOUS)

Secret Service (federal), the first: under the Treasury Department was created by act of June 23, 1860 (12 Stat. L. 102) to suppress counterfeiting in U.S. coins. The act was extended to include counterfeiting of notes, obligations and securities of the government by act of July 11, 1862 (12 Stat. L. 533), and an appropriation act approved July 2, 1864. Since the death of President Lincoln, one of the duties of the Secret Service has been to guard the President and his family. The F.B.I. was created in 1908 under the Department of Justice to supplement the work of the Secret Service
                              (FAMOUS)

secrete: (1) to remove or keep from observation; to hide or conceal (LEV) (2) (biological) a function of certain glands of an animal which create and exude certain fluids   (LEV)

secretor: a person whose saliva contains blood group antigens. In such persons such antigens also appear in the blood and other fluids. *Cf.* nonsecretor   (LEV)

sector: (1) a defense area designated by boundaries within which a unit operates and for which it is responsible (2) one of the subdivisions of a coastal frontier (DWMT)

sector search: same as zone search. *See* zone search   (LEV)

secular: of or pertaining to this world; not spiritual   (CDTP)

secure: (1) to close up a safe, office or building so as to provide security for classified matter (DWMT) (2) to end or wind up an exercise or operation   (DWMT)

secure mode: the condition of an alarm system in which all sensors and control units are ready to respond to an intrusion   (TDIAS)

Securities and Exchange Commission (S.E.C., SEC): a federal agency involved with the registration of security issues, regulation of transactions in securities, and the investigation of fraudulent stock manipulations   (LEV)

security: (1) measures taken by a command to protect itself from espionage, observation, sabotage, annoyance, or surprise (DWMT) (2) a condition which results from the establishment and maintenance of protective measures which ensure a state of inviolability from hostile acts or influences (DWMT) (3) with respect to classified matter, the condition which prevents unauthorized persons from having access to official information which is safeguarded in the interests of national defense (DWMT) (4) the protection of supplies or supply establishments against enemy attack, fire, theft, and sabotage (DWMT) (5) freedom from danger or damage (LEV) (6) a thing deposited or put up as a guarantee for payment of money. Industrial security is a branch of an industrial organization which has the responsibility of safeguarding the physical plant, properties, and products of the organization   (LEV)

security for costs: the security which a defendant in an action may require of a plaintiff who does not reside within the jurisdiction of the court

secus [Lat]: otherwise

sedition: the advocacy of unlawful means of changing the form of government, such as the "overthrow of government by force and violence," or encouragement of the violation of law with the purpose of promoting disloyalty or disaffection to the government   (DOS)

seditious conspiracy: the agreement of two or more persons to act together in promoting unlawful means of changing the government or of encouraging the violation of law for the purpose of promoting disloyalty or disaffection to the government   (DOS)

seduce: cause one to be led astray; to do wrong; to persuade one to engage in illicit sexual relations, especially for the first time (LEV)

seduction: the offense of inducing a woman to consent to sexual intercourse under promise of marriage   (CDTP)

segregation: the part of a prison where inmates are held in solitary confinement as punishment

seismic sensor: a sensor, generally buried under the surface of the ground for perimeter protection, which responds to minute vibrations of the earth generated as an intruder walks or drives within its detection range   (TDIAS)

seizin: possession of lands or chattels   (CDTP)

seizure: (1) the seizing of something in accordance with law. A search carries with it the right of seizure if objects or materials are found which come within the scope of the search. Under certain writs officers make a seizure (LEV) (2) a violent attack caused by such diseases as epilepsy (LEV)

selected-length field: a fixed number of characters selected for each data element; requires filling out shorter data items with zeros or blanks to reach the fixed number. Corresponds to the field assigned to an item during the design of a punched-card layout   (ADPS)

selective absorption: the capacity of a body for absorbing certain colors while transmitting or reflecting the remainder   (MPPF)

selective enforcement: the deploying of police personnel in ways to cope most effectively with existing or anticipated problems. If records reflect that traffic accidents occur most frequently in certain areas at certain times greater numbers of officers are assigned to such areas at the critical times under a program of selective enforcement   (LEV)

selective patrol: See selective enforcement

self-defense: the right to protect one's person or property against injury or destruction. It is used as a legal defense in criminal cases. Some states do not allow the taking of a life to prevent damage or destruction to property but do allow the taking of the life of an assailant where the victim is in danger of loss of life or great bodily harm and the killing is necessary to save himself from such danger, or the killing is done by one who has reasonable cause to believe a violent and forceable felony, involving danger to life or great bodily harm, is about to be committed and that such action is necessary for its prevention. The law on self-defense varies among the states   (LEV)

self-evident: in itself is proof or evidence of a point in question(LEV)

self-incrimination: implication of oneself in crime or wrongdoing; incrimination of oneself. The Fifth Amendment of the U.S. Constitution provides that a person shall not be forced to incriminate himself. This has been interpreted to mean through the spoken word and the furnishing of physical evidence such as fingerprints and blood is not protected by the Constitution   (LEV)

self-loading: of a firearm or gun, utilizing either the explosive gases or recoil to extract the empty case and chamber the next round. Self-loading firearms or guns include both semiautomatic and full automatic types   (DWMT)

self-protection: self-defense; protection of oneself   (LEV)

self-report studies: a modern survey technique designed to measure the number of criminals by asking respondents if they have committed crimes within a specific period. Although their validity may be somewhat suspect even with firm pledges of confidentiality, as many as 91 percent of the respondents surveyed by some studies have admitted one or more criminal acts

semen: the fluid of male animals that contain spermatozoa or the reproductive cells   (LEV)

semi: half

semiautomatic: of a firearm or gun, utilizing part of the force of an exploding cartridge to extract the empty case and chamber the next round, but requiring a separate pull of the trigger to fire each round. Hence, semiautomatic rifle, semiautomatic pistol, semiautomatic weapon, semiautomatic fire, etc.   (DWMT)

semiconscious: not fully conscious; partly conscious   (LEV)

semifixed ammunition: ammunition in which the cartridge case is not permanently attached to the projectile   (DWMT)

seminal fluid: See semen

semper [Lat]: always

Senate crime investigations: the first committee set up specifically to investigate crime was the Kefauver Committee of 1950–1951. The committee was aided by an executive order from President Truman which gave them access to income tax returns. This tax information was the starting point for many investigations. The

committee discovered considerable evidence of the nationwide crime syndicate and its operations. Numerous Senate crime committees have been formed since 1950

senile: characteristic of old age; aged; decrepit   (CDTP)

seniority: as used in industrial relations, is an employment advantage in the matter of the choice of and the right to work in one's occupation on the basis of an employee's length of service   (CDTP)

sense: the means by which we gain knowledge of happenings in the world. The five senses are sight, taste, hearing, touch, and smell. We can testify on information acquired through these senses unless it is in violation of such rules of evidence as "hearsay"   (LEV)

senseless: (1) having no sense—stupid (LEV) (2) unconscious   (LEV)

sensitizers: dyes used in the manufacture of photographic emulsions. Sensitizers can be of two types: one to increase the speed of an emulsion, the other to increase its color sensitivity (MPPF)

sensitometer: a device for producing on sensitized material a series of exposures increasing at a definite ratio. Such a series is needed in studying the characteristics of an emulsion   (MPPF)

sensitometric strip: a series of densities in definite steps   (MPPF)

sensor: (1) a device which is designed to produce a signal or offer indication in response to an event or stimulus within its detection zone (TDIAS) (2) a technical means to extend man's natural senses; a piece of equipment which detects and indicates terrain configuration, the presence of military targets, and other natural and man-made objects and activities by means of energy emitted or reflected by such targets or objects. The energy may be nuclear, electromagnetic (including the visible and invisible portions of the spectrum), chemical, biological, thermal, or mechanical, including sound, blast, and earth vibration (DWMT)

sensual: lustful; having to do with overinvolvement with appetite or sexual pleasure (LEV)

sentence: (1) in COBOL, a sequence of one or more statements specifying one or more operations, according to certain rules, and terminated by a period (ADPS) (2) a judgement pronounced by a court of law; esp., the penalty imposed upon a convicted defendant in a criminal case (DAP)

sentence, flat (straight): a fixed sentence with no maximum or minimum

sentence, indeterminate: a sentence to incarceration with a spread of time between a minimum date of parole eligibility and a maximum discharge date. A completely indeterminate sentence has a minimum of one day and a maximum of natural life (DOS)

sentence, maximum: the longest period of time the prisoner can be held in custody

sentence, minimum: the shortest period of time an offender must spend in prison before becoming eligible for parole

sentence, short: a sentence that runs from a few days to a few months, imposed on petty offenders, who often cannot afford to pay the alternative of a fine, if such is given. Short sentences are usually served in municipal or county jails, except in those few places where special institutions for misdemeanants are maintained (DOS)

sentence, suspended: technically a "sentence," but involving unconditional, unsupervised release of the convicted defendant (DOS)

sentencing councils: a panel of three or more judges sometimes used instead of a trial judge to determine a criminal sentence, in an attempt to make sentencing more uniform

sentencing jury: the trial jury attached to a court that imposes sentence

sentinel: a person charged with standing guard and giving notice of danger when it arrives (DWMT)

sentry: a guard, esp. one who stands at a point where only properly authorized and identified persons are permitted to pass (DWMT)

separation negatives: three negatives, each of which records one of the three colors—blue, green, and red (MPPF)

sepia toning: a process which converts the black silver image to a brownish image. The image can vary considerably in hue, depending on the process, the tone of the original, and other factors (MPPF)

sepulture: burial; interment (CDTP

sequence: in sorting, the ordering of items on an element—for example, records on a selected key—according to some rules that utilize the processor's collation table: alphanumeric—a sequence developed for records containing alphanumeric characters. The exact sequence depends on the binary value assigned to each alphabetic and numeric character—whether alphabetic precedes numeric or vice versa—by the machine designer; numeric—a sequence developed for records with keys containing numerals only; usu. ascending but may also be descending; random—a sequence that is not arranged by ascending or descending keys but which actually may be arranged in an organized fashion. For example, each record may be placed in bulk storage in a location determined by some calculations and repeated in order to get the address and locate the item (ADPS)

sequester: to keep a jury together and in isolation from the public under charge of the bailiff during the pendency of a trial, sometimes called "separation of the jury"; to keep witnesses apart from other witnesses and therefore unable to hear their testimony

sergeant: a police officer whose rank is higher than a patrolman and lower than a lieutenant. The sergeant is the first supervisory officer in ascending the chain of command. An efficient sergeant is an important and vital link in the administrative operation of a department. He is the line officer who is in closest contact with the field operations of a department (LEV)

serial number control: the control of messages by assigning a number from a master list when it first originates and, perhaps, adding a suffix number from a local list for each point the message passes through to its destination (ADPS)

seriatim [*Lat*]: in order; consecutively

serology: the study of the reactions and properties of serum

serum: a clear, slightly amber-colored liquid which separates from blood when it clots (LEV)

service of process: the act of delivering a written summons or notice of a judicial proceeding to the person who will be affected by it

service routine: a routine designed to assist in actual operation of a computer. Includes tape comparison, block location, certain post-mortems, and correction routines (ADPS)

service vehicle: a vehicle used in any support activity other than direct law enforcement, such as a tow truck, administrative vehicle, maintenance vehicle, etc. (TDPPC)

session: a sitting; an actual sitting of a court, legislative body, or other assembly (CDTP)

set: (1) an incendiary fire; point of origin of any incendiary fire (LEV) (2) an interior or exterior scene or part of a scene, together with furniture or natural objects, built in a studio for photography, or on a motion-picture lot (MPPF)

set-off: that which is set against another thing; a counter-demand (CDTP)

sex crimes: crimes committed by sex deviates; crimes committed as the result of abnormal sex manifestations (LEV)

sex deviate: one who performs sex acts in an unnatural or abnormal manner; one who manifests his sex drives abnormally (LEV)

sex maniac: one who is mentally deranged as to matters of sex; a sex pervert who is mentally ill; one who because of mental illness commits brutal sex crimes (LEV)

sex pervert: *See* sex deviate

shadow: to follow closely and secretly; to keep under observation; a physical surveillance (LEV)

shadow area: the darker portions of a picture or the lighter portions of a negative (MPPF)

shadows: a term applied to the thinner portions of a negative and the darker parts of a positive slide or print (MPPF)

shall: (law) denotes mandatory actions or requirements. If the law states something shall be done it is a positive and definite requirement. If the word "may" is used, discretion is allowed. These words are important in criminal law and procedure (LEV)

shanghai: to drug, intoxicate, or knock out in order to put aboard ship as a seaman

sheath: a case or scabbard for a sword or knife blade (DWMT)

sheet films: individual films loaded into separate holders for exposure; usu. on a heavier base than rollfilms and film packs (MPPF)

shell: (1) a hollow metal projectile designed to be projected from a gun, containing, or intended to contain, a high-explosive, chemical, atomic, or other charge (DWMT) (2) a shotgun cartridge or a cartridge for artillery or small arms (DWMT) (3) to shoot at with projectiles. In nomenclature, the term "projectile" is now used in sense 1, and the term "cartridge" in sense 2 (DWMT)

shell case: that part of a cartridge or complete round for holding a charge, primer, and (usu.) projectile; a case. The term "shell case" is applied to the cases of small-arms ammunition as well as to those of cannon ammunition (DWMT)

shell game: a swindling game in which the operator manipulates a pea-sized object under three walnut shells. The victim bets he can tell which shell it is under. He fails because the object is concealed in the crook of the finger of the swindler (LEV)

Sheppard v. Maxwell, 384 U.S. 333 (1966): this decision contains an extensive discussion of the effect of unfair distorted publicity upon the jurors at the time of trial. The decision notes that neither prosecutors, counsel for defense, the accused, witness, court staff, nor enforcement officers coming under the jurisdiction of the trial court should be permitted to frustrate its function by actions or statements threatening the fair trial of the defendant (AOJ)

sheriff: the chief law-enforcement officer of a county who conserves the peace, attends sessions of courts, executes court orders, has charge of prisoners, usu. has the duty of maintaining the jail and feeding its inmates, and in some States collects taxes. He is popularly elective in all States except Rhode Island and is often not re-eligible (DAP)

sheriff's office (S.O.): the department or office operated by the Sheriff of a county or parish. Also correctly termed the Sheriff's department (LEV)

Sherman Act: provides that "Every contract combination in the form of a trust or otherwise, or conspiracy in restraint of trade or commerce, is hereby declared to be illegal." Combinations of labor are included within the terms of this act as are similar combinations of capital. The act makes no distinction between classes. (208 U.S. 274) (CDTP)

shift: (1) to move the characters of a unit of data to the right or left by means of a shifting register. Used to unpack words to isolate data items and to multiply or divide a quantity by a power of the number base (ADPS) (2) Time of day during which a group of people work. In law-enforcement the times of shifts vary but many use a three-shift system: day shift— 6 A.M. to 2 P.M.; swing shift— 2 P.M. to 10 P.M.; graveyard shift—10 P.M. to 6 A.M. (LEV)

shocking power: the force delivered to the projectile on impact; the result brought about through combination of striking energy and penetration (CDTP)

shoddy: (1) refuse from the shearing of woolen goods (CDTP) (2) also, inferior in quality (CDTP)

shoot: (1) to make an exposure (MPPF) (2) to discharge a firearm (MPPF)

short ridge: in fingerprinting a short, broken ridge or line

short round: (1) the unintentional or inadvertent delivery of ordnance on friendly troops, installations, or civilians by a friendly weapon system (DWMT) (2) a defective cartridge in which the projectile has been seated too deeply (DWMT)

short-stop bath: a solution containing an acid which neutralizes the developer remaining in the negative or print before it is transferred to the fixing bath (MPPF)

shot: (1) (a) a solid projectile for cannon without a bursting charge (b) a mass or load of numerous, relatively small lead pellets used in a shotgun, as birdshot or buckshot (DWMT) (2) that which is fired from a gun, as "the first shot was over the target." In sense 1a, the term "projectile" is preferred for uniformity in nomenclature (DWMT) (3) the flight of a missile, as of a rocket (DWMT) (4) injection of narcotics (DWMT)

shot-delay fuze: a type of delay fuze in both bombs and artillery projectiles in which the fuze action is delayed for a short period

of time, normally 0.01 to 0.24 seconds (DWMT)
shot pattern: the dispersion pattern of shot fired from a shotgun; shot separate from one another in flight. The shot pattern is determined by shooting at a target or other surface which will register the impact of the shots when they strike the surface (LEV)
shotgun: a smoothbore shoulder weapon that fires shot pellets or slugs. The usual classes are riot gun, skeet gun, and sporting gun (DWMT)
shotgun shell: (1) a container or capsule, usually made of stiff paper with a brass base, containing primer, powder, wadding, and shot for use in a shotgun (DWMT) (2) a blank shell of this type for use in a cartridge starter (DWMT)
shoulder: (1) in a cartridge case, the tapered portion between the body and the neck (DWMT) (2) the upper part of a sword blade (DWMT) (3) the angle of a bastion between the face and the flank. Also called an "epule" (DWMT) (4) to bring a weapon to the shoulder or to place it aslant on the shoulder, as a pike or a rifle (DWMT) (5) formerly, to arrange troops shoulder to shoulder (DWMT)
shoulder arm: a shoulder weapon (DWMT)
shoulder arms: a command to bring weapons to the shoulder (DWMT)
shoulder weapon: any firearm designed to be braced on or against the shoulder when firing, as a rifle, carbine, automatic rifle, bazooka launcher, etc. (DWMT)
show cause: an order to appear in court and deliver reasons why certain circumstances continue or be allowed or prohibited
show-up: See line-up
shrapnel: (1) strictly speaking, small lead or steel balls contained in certain shells, which are discharged in every direction upon explosion of the shell. The system was invented by Lieut. (later Gen.) Henry Shrapnel in 1784

(DWMT) (2) a popular term for munition fragments (DWMT)
shrewd: intellectual; cunning; sharp; quick-minded (LEV)
shunt: (1) a deliberate shorting-out of a portion of an electric circuit (TDIAS) (2) a key-operated switch which removes some portion of an alarm system for operation, allowing entry into a protected area without initiating an alarm signal. A type of authorized access switch (TDIAS)
shutter: on a camera, a mechanical device which controls the length of time light is allowed to strike the sensitized material (MPPF)
Shuttleworth v. City of Birmingham, 394 U.S. 147, 22 L. Ed. 2d 162, 89 S. Ct. 935 (1969): the Court, in an opinion by Mr. Justice Stewart, found a Birmingham, Alabama ordinance to be unconstitutional on its face. (He observed that the ordinance conferred "virtually unbridled and absolute power to prohibit any 'parade, procession,' or 'demonstration' on the city's streets or public ways." Justice Stewart acknowledged that the conduct regulated was not "pure speech"— it did involve the use of public streets over which the municipality had a right to exercise considerable control. But previous decisions made it clear that picketing and parading may constitute methods of expression protected by the First Amendment.) (ILECJ)
shyster: a lawyer who uses unethical or improper methods in his legal business. A disreputable, dishonest attorney (LEV)
si [Lat]: if
sibling: a sister or brother (LEV)
sic [Lat]: so
side arms: weapons that are worn at the side or in the belt when not in use. The sword, bayonet, automatic pistol, revolver, etc., are side arms (DWMT)
sideswipe: (1) a blow from the side (LEV) (2) to strike with a blow from the side (LEV)

sight: (1) a mechanical or optical device for aiming a firearm or for laying a gun or launcher in position. It is based on the principle that two points in fixed relation to each other may be brought in line with a third. Sights are classified as fixed or adjustable depending on the provision made for setting windage and range, and also according to type. Glass sights comprise all sights which include an optical element, such as a collimator, telescope, periscope, etc. Iron sights are classified as either open or aperture. Aperture sights are those that are sighted through, such as peep, ring, etc. Open sights are all those that are sighted over or at, such as post, bead, notch, etc. Leaf sights are those which can be folded down for protection (DWMT) (2) to aim at a target or aiming point (DWMT) (3) to look through a sighting device to determine the angular direction of a point, either horizontal or vertical, in surveying or navigation, especially the angular position of the sun, a star, or a planet in navigation (DWMT) (4) in armor, an obsolete term for a slit in a visor to permit vision (DWMT)

sight draft: an order for the payment of money drawn by one person or another which is payable on presentation (LEV)

sight leaf: the movable hinged part of a rear sight of a gun that can be raised and set to a desired range or snapped down when not in use (DWMT)

sighting: actual visual contact. It does not include other contacts, which must be reported by type, e.g., radar and sonar contacts (DWMT)

sighting shot: a trial shot, fired to find out whether the sights are properly adjusted (DWMT)

sighting system: a mechanical or optical device for aiming a firearm or for laying a gun in position; all such devices required for a specific weapon or group of weapons (DWMT)

sigillum [*Lat*]: a seal

signal: (1) as applied to electronics, any transmitted electrical impulse (DWMT) (2) operationally, a type of message, the text of which consists of one or more letters, words, characters, signal flags, visual displays, or special sounds with prearranged meanings and which is conveyed or transmitted by visual, acoustical, or electrical means (DWMT)

signal pistol: a pistol designed to fire pyrotechnic signals such as flares (DWMT)

signal security: a generic term which includes both communications security and electronic security (DWMT)

signals, ten-dash: a system of signals used in law enforcement which consists of the numeral "10" followed by other numbers. Such signals have a prearranged meaning. Such signals are used most frequently in radio communications but may be used in other types of oral communicatons (LEV)

signature: the name of a person written by himself (CDTP)

signature of affiant: while the presence of the name of the person making the affidavit, under some statutes, is not a fundamental requirement, the absence of which would render the search warrant illegal, and the absence of affiant's name in a copy of the affidavit, upon which the warrant issued, is not a defect that is fatal to the warrant, yet under a statute requiring that every affidavit be subscribed by affiant and that the certificate of the officer or person before whom it is made must be written separately following the signature of affiant, an affidavit not signed by affiant is void even though the issuing officer's certificate recites that it was subscribed and sworn to before him; and where a deceased affiant did not sign the affidavit, there being nothing to show that he read it or that it was read to him, there was no affidavit at all, and a search

warrant based upon the alleged affidavit was a nullity. The location of the signature below the jurat of the officer will not necessarily vitiate the warrant issued thereon (C.J. 56, 1213)   (CDTP)
signature of issuing officer: as a general proposition a search warrant must be signed by the officer who issues it. Where a search warrant bears the typewritten name of the issuing officer, and no one testifies that the officer had thus signed his name, the warrant is invalid (277 S.W. 1019)   (CDTP)
silence when accused of crime: the silence of defendant when accused of a crime may be shown as an implied admission of guilt (CDTP)
silencer: a device specifically designed to silence the explosive report caused by the discharge of cartridges by a small-arms weapon. It incorporates integral chambers or baffles which allow the gases to expand gradually
(DWMT)
silent alarm: a remote alarm without an obvious local indication that an alarm has been transmitted   (TDIAS)
silent alarm system: an alarm system which signals a remote station by means of a silent alarm
(TDIAS)
silhouette: a photograph which shows only the mass of a subject in black, against a white or colored background   (MPPF)
silhouette target: a firearms target composed of the dark outline of a man with a white background. This is used in the practical pistol course, in rifle practice, and for target practice with other types of weapons
silver nitrate: a chemical, AgNO3, used in photography, and in a crime laboratory for the development of fingerprints on paper
(LEV)
Simmons v. United States, 309 U.S. 377, 19 L. Ed. 2d 1247, 88 S. Ct. 967 (1968): the Court, 6-2, shows its unwillingness to prohibit the use of photographs in apprehending offenders (which also

spares the arrest of innocent suspects), either by its supervisory power or "still less" as a constitutional requirement. (An attorney need not be present at the viewing of photographs. Suggestions are offered on how photographs should be used to identify a suspect.)   (ILECJ)
simple assault: an assault that is not aggravated. *See* aggravated assault
simple contract: a contract not under seal nor record   (CDTP)
simplification: stresses better forms, elimination of useless data, more efficient flows of data, consolidated files, and improvements in existing techniques   (ADPS)
simplified traffic information: in New York, a written complaint by a local peace officer filed with the criminal court charging a person with a traffic violation or traffic misdemeanors
simulated forgery: forgery of writing accomplished by the forger practicing imitating the genuine writing until the forged writing is similar to the genuine   (LEV)
simulation: an experimental analysis of an operating system by means of mathematical or physical models that operate in a time-sequential manner similar to the system itself   (ADPS)
simulator routine: an interpretive routine to enable one processor to interpret and execute instructions and coding designed for another processor   (ADPS)
simultaneous: existing, happening, or done at the same time (CDTP)
sine [Lat]: without
sine die [Lat]: without day; with out a day appointed to appear again   (CDTP)
sine qua non: an indispensable thing; a necessity   (CDTP)
single action: a method of fire in some revolvers and shoulder arms in which the hammer must be cocked by hand, in contrast to double action, in which a single pull of the trigger both cocks and fires the weapon   (DWMT)
single-base powder: a propellant that contains only one explosive

ingredient, normally nitrocellulose. A double-base propellant contains two explosive ingredients, commonly nitrocellulose and nitroglycerin (DWMT)

single circuit system: an alarm circuit which routes only one side of the circuit through each sensor. The return may be through either ground or a separate wire (TDIAS)

single-fingerprint registration: a system of classifying single fingerprints so that single or multiple fingerprints left at the scene of a crime may be identified. Such a file is more effective if the number of fingerprints placed therein is kept small (LEV)

single-stroke bell: a bell which is struck once each time its mechanism is activated (TDIAS)

single weight (SW): applied to a photographic paper with a lightweight stock (MPPF)

siphon: a bent tube or similar device used to empty containers of fluid by atmospheric pressure (MPPF)

siren: a device which makes a piercing sound by means of air, steam, etc., being forced through perforated revolving disks (LEV)

sit-down demonstration: a situation wherein demonstrators sit or lie down, usu. in a place where they will obstruct pedestrian or motor traffic (LEV)

sit-down strike: a situation wherein striking workers stay in the place of employment, without working, for the duration of the strike (LEV)

size error: the size error condition arises in COBOL whenever the number of positions to the left of the assumed decimal point in a computed result exceeds the corresponding positions in the data-name supposed to hold the result (ADPS)

skeleton force: a part of the regular number of officers normally used to operate the department or shift; less than a full complement of officers who carry on an opera-

tion. Also called skeleton crew (LEV)

sketching: the drawing or charting of objects, places, or scenes to show details and/or the relative positions of objects and other evidence (LEV)

skid: a controlled or uncontrolled slide by the vehicle resulting from the loss of friction between the road surface and the tires (TDPPC)

skid marks: the marking or imprints left on a travelled surface by vehicle tires as a result of sliding or skidding. Skid marks are important in the investigation of traffic accidents. Calculations can be made of the direction and speed of a vehicle prior to the accident by examining the skid marks (LEV)

skyjacker: one who illegally hijacks an airplane. The United States Government in 1970 started putting specially trained officers aboard passenger planes which were thought most vulnerable to such hijackers. The officers are called "sky marshals" (LEV)

skylight: a large window, usually inclined and facing north, used as principal light source in certain photographic studios (MPPF)

sky marshals: a group of officers who travel aboard passenger-carrying airplanes to protect against hijackers. They work in a federal program started in 1970 under the direction of Lt. Gen. Benjamin O. Davis, Director of Civil Aviation Security. As of Dec. 23, 1970 a group of specially trained officers started replacing 1,200 marshals then in service (LEV)

slab: the place of rest upon which a dead body is placed in a morgue (LEV)

slander: the oral utterance or publication of a falsehood that is intended to defame a person or injure his reputation. Cf. libel (DAP)

slash: to cut or wound by a sweeping stroke or movement (LEV)

sleuth: an undercover investigator;

a detective   (LEV)
slide: (1) the sliding part of the receiver of certain automatic weapons (DWMT) (2) the sliding catch
on the breech mechanism of certain weapons (DWMT) (3) a positive print on glass, or a film transparency bound between glasses
for projection; also the removable
cover of a sheet-film plate, or
film-pack holder   (MPPF)
slide action: the mechanism of a repeating rifle operated by the
manual movement of a slide under
and parallel to the barrel   (CDTP)
sliding back: a camera so arranged
that half the film may be centered
in front of the lens, so that two
pictures may be taken on a single
sheet of film   (MPPF)
sling: (1) an item made of leather,
webbing, or the like, designed to
be attached to a carbine, mortar,
musket, rifle, rocket launcher,
shotgun, submachine gun, or the
like. Used as a means of carrying a
small-arms weapon and also to
steady the weapon for firing
(DWMT) (2) a weapon consisting
of a piece of leather with a round
hole in the middle and two pieces
of cord about 1 yd. long. When a
smooth stone is placed in the
leather pouch and the cords are
swung rapidly around, the stone
attains considerable speed. When
one of the cords is let go, the
stone travels with a greater force
than could be imparted by merely
throwing it (DWMT) (3) an obsolete term for a small swivel gun
with a long barrel   (DWMT)
slot machines: machines where by
depositing a coin one may secure
the object advertised   (CDTP)
sloven: dirty; not neat in dress,
habits, or appearance   (LEV)
sludge: a chemical precipitate or
impurities which settle to the bottom of the container   (MPPF)
slug: (1) a large piece of lead or
other metal used as a projectile
for firing in a shotgun (LEV) (2)
any bullet fired in a pistol or
other sidearm or shoulder weapon
(LEV)

slum: an area of physical and social
decadence. On the physical side,
the slum is identified by the presence of run-down, over-aged, neglected houses and facilities. On
the social side, it is identified by
poverty, vice, and the various
forms of social disorganization.
The existence or absence of a
slum in any city is determined on
the basis of relative considerations. It may be said that the slum
in any community is where the
poor people and social outcasts
live. In a large city there may be
various types of slums, each of
which may be occupied by a different population or social class
(DOS)
small arms: all arms, including automatic weapons, up to and including those of .60 cal. and shotguns
(DWMT)
small-arms ammunition: ammunition for small arms, i.e., all ammunition up to and including those
of .60 cal. and all gauges of shotgun shells   (DWMT)
small claims court: a special court
which provides expeditious, informal, and inexpensive adjudication
of small contractual claims (DAP)
smoke bombs: smoke bombs have a
three-fold purpose: they are used
for screening the movements of
troops and ships in combat areas;
for creating an antipersonnel effect on troops in the open or in
dug-in positions; and for making
targets. They also have an incendiary effect in that they will set fire
to materials which are easily ignited such as clothing, dry brush,
canvas, etc. The bodies are filled
with plasticized white phosphorus
(PWP) or white phosphorus (WP).
The functioning of a fuze and
burster shatters the bomb on impact, dispersing the filler over a
wide area. Atmospheric oxygen ignites the particles, which produce
a dense white smoke   (DWMT)
smoke detector: a device which detects visible or invisible products
of combustion. *See also* ionization
smoke detector; photoelectric

beam type smoke detector; photo-electric spot type smoke detector; and resistance bridge smoke detector (TDIAS)

smoke grenade: a hand grenade or rifle grenade containing a smoke-producing mixture and used for screening or signaling. It is sometimes charged with colored smoke, such as red, green, yellow, or violet (DWMT)

smokeless: when used in cartridge or propelling-charge nomenclature, the term indicates that the ammunition is relatively smokeless when used in the weapon for which it is intended (DWMT)

smoldering fire: a fire which because of insufficient oxygen burns slowly and creeps along a wall or ceiling. Paints and resins in the wood are incompletely consumed and the room is filled with nauseating black smoke. When fresh air is admitted to the room it will immediately burst into flames (LEV)

smoothbore: having a bore that is smooth and without rifling. Shotguns and mortars are commonly smoothbore (DWMT)

smother: to kill by making breathing impossible; to suffocate (LEV)

smudged fingerprints: the imprint of finger ridges which is distorted—not clearly defined. This may be caused by lateral movements of the fingers while touching the surface on which the print is made, by having dirty or greasy fingers, or by having too much ink on the fingers (LEV)

smuggle: to import or export without paying duty (CDTP)

smuggling: illegal and clandestine shipment of persons or goods into or out of a country in order to evade legal prohibitions against such shipments or the payment of customs duties (DAP)

snapshot: a listing of the contents of storage locations, registers, and indexes at a given instant in time either at intervals during the execution of a program or when it stops running; may be complete or differential to list the contents of only those locations that have changed since the prior snapshot. Useful in program debugging (ADPS)

S.N.C.C. (SNCC): Student Nonviolent Coordinating Committee

sneeze gas: a gas that causes sneezing, specifically, diphenylchloroarsine (DWMT)

sniper: one who shoots at another from a place of hiding (LEV)

sniperscope: (1) a snooperscope for use on a carbine or rifle. An electronic device that permits a rifleman to aim at a target at night without himself being seen. Infrared rays illuminate the target, which is then viewed through a combination telescope sight and fluorescent screen (in which all objects appear as various shades of green). The system was developed by the U.S. Army during World War II. It weighs 32 lb. and has an angle of view of 14° and a range of 125 yd. *See* snooperscope. (DWMT) (2) a device developed during World War I for firing a rifle from a trench parapet without exposing the shooter. It consisted of a periscope attached near the rifle's rear sights and projecting downward into the trench (DWMT)

snooperscope: a hand-carried device combining a source of infrared rays with a viewer; it enables the operator to see in the dark (DWMT)

snorkel: a tube or pair of tubes for air intake and exhaust that can be extended above the surface of the water for operating submerged submarines. The term is now also applied to almost any tube which similarly supplies air for underwater operation, whether it be for material or personnel. This system was developed by Germany in World War II, and the name derives from the German word *schnorchel*, meaning "snout" (DWMT)

sobriety: soberness; degree of soberness; degree of intoxication.

Sobriety gauging device—*see* alcohol (LEV)

social case work: a method of helping people through social services and personal counselling in order to release their capacities and to bring about personal and family adjustments (DOS)

social causation: causation manifesting itself in the sequences of social phenomena. The principle in social relations which justifies the conclusion that a given set of factors or conditions may be expected to be followed by a specified event or condition (DOS)

social constraint: a type of negative social control exercised by authority in the name of the group, subjecting offenders to custody or limitation of freedom supposedly of sufficient rigor to prevent their repetition of offenses (DOS)

social control: the sum total of the processes whereby society, or any sub-group within society, secures conformity to expectation on the part of its constituent units, individuals, or groups. It exhibits two main forms: (1) coercive control and (2) persuasive control. Coercive control emanates from the agencies of law and government, and is accomplished by force or the threat of force. The types of behavior specifically designated for coercive control fall under the general category of crime. Persuasive control operates through all the various agencies and instrumentalities that induce the individual to respond to the standards, wishes, and imperatives of the larger social group. The means of social control are numerous and varied and rest upon the dynamic characteristics of the units to be controlled. The law is the most concrete, explicit, and obvious instrument of social control but by no means the most powerful or comprehensive. Much the greater bulk of social control falls in the persuasive category, and is achieved by such agencies as suggestion, imitation, praise, blame, reward, recognition, and response. When the controlling group is society, social control takes the specific form of societal control (DOS)

social ethics: that approach to ethics which seeks primarily for practical guidance in relation to specific social problems, including the broad issues of political and economic policy and also such questions as sexual morality (DOS)

social justice: the intelligent cooperation of people in producing an organically united community, so that every member has an equal and real opportunity to grow and learn to live to the best of his native abilities. These ideal conditions of justice through social union are essentially those of democracy. They may be briefly and simply stated as follows in the practical terms in which they are being more widely recognized and achieved: (1) for every child a normal birth, a healthy environment, abundant, good food and liberal, appropriate education; (2) for every mature person a secure job adapted to his abilities; (3) for every person an income adequate to maintain him efficient in the position of his highest social service; (4) for every person such influence with the authorities that his needs and ideas receive due consideration by them. With the possibility of economic abundance for all, now in some countries becoming a reality for the first time in history, the above fundamentals of social justice would appear to be no longer impossible (DOS)

social laws: formulations of uniformities of social behavior under similar conditions, the validity of which has been tested by repeated observations and by various logical and heuristic methods. Sociologists of recent years have been less confident in announcing "social laws," most of which have turned out to be unverified social theories, or at most social principles. Distinguished from axioms, which are supposedly universal self-evident truths; from hypotheses, which, like theories and principles, are plausible guesses in respect to causes, origins, and trends, pending demonstration and proof   (DOS)

social legislation: laws designed to improve and protect the economic and social position of those groups in society which because of age, sex, race, physical or mental defect, or lack of economic power cannot achieve healthful and decent living standards for themselves. The term social legislation was coined by William I of Germany in 1881 in a famous speech before the Reichstag urging the adoption of public accident and health insurance (DOS)

social pathology: (1) a study of social disorganization or maladjustment in which there is a discussion of the meaning, extent, causes, results, and treatment of the factors that prevent or reduce social adjustment such as: poverty, unemployment, old age, ill health, feeblemindedness, insanity, crime, divorce, prostitution, family tensions (DOS) (2) the diseased or abnormal condition itself   (DOS)

social psychology: the scientific study of the mental processes of man, regarded as a socius or social being. The distinction between social psychology and any other psychology is essentially abstract and academic, since it is impossible to study any human being entirely detached from social relationships   (DOS)

social reform: the general movement, or any specific result of that movement, which attempts to eliminate or mitigate the evils that result from the malfunctioning of the social system, or any part of it. In its concept and scope, social reform lies somewhere between social work and social engineering. It rises above and beyond the mere alleviation of individual and family hardships, but it does not aim at the sweeping changes in social structure that are involved in social engineering. Social reform is closely affiliated with the ideas of social progress that characterized 19th-century thought in Western culture. It accepted the existing framework of society, and sought to correct the ills that were associated with it. There have been numerous reform movements such as the extension of the electorate, the protection of the less powerful elements in society, and the control of vice   (DOS)

social restraint: negative control exerted within a group; a condition in which some form of restraint is imposed by a group upon its members; or, a form of internal control in which a person is inhibited by cultural requirements or appreciation of the group situation or demands of membership. Distinguished from social constraint, in which there is physical control imposed by law, and (usu.) custodial care (DOS)

social sanction: any threat of penalty or promise of reward set by or for a group upon the conduct of its members, to induce conformity to its rules or laws. Legal sanction is a form of social sanction; but the phrase may also be used, by contrast, to indicate those group sanctions other than legal. *Cf.* sanction   (DOS)

social science: any organized body of knowledge which deals with man's environment, history, and political, economic, or other social institutions; also, such bodies of knowledge considered collectively. Traditionally the methodology of such sciences has been observational, historical, comparative, deductive, and descriptive, but, increasingly, analysis of behavioral data and application of statistical techniques characterize research in the social sciences   (DAP)

Social Security: in the United

States, a system administered by the Social Security Administration. A government agency. It is a system of old-age and unemployment insurance. It also aids those who are blind and disabled. The funds supporting the program are paid by the worker and his employer   (LEV)

Social Security Administration: a federal agency of the United States administering a legally constituted old-age and unemployment insurance program, as well as other programs. *See* Social Security   (LEV)

socialism: a political theory of social reorganization by which it is contended the opportunities of life and the rewards of labor shall be equally apportioned   (CDTP)

Socialist Party: a political party which works to establish and support socialism   (LEV)

society: a group of human beings cooperating in the pursuit of several of their major interests, invariably including self-maintenance and self-perpetuation. The concept of society includes continuity, complex associational relationships, and a composition including representatives of fundamental human types, specifically men, women, and children. Ordinarily, also, there is the element of territorial establishment. Society is a functioning group, so much so as to be frequently defined in terms of relationships or processes. It is the basic, large-scale human group. It is to be sharply differentiated from fortuitous temporary or nonrepresentative groups or aggregations such as a mob, the passengers on a steamship, the spectators at a ball game, or the inhabitants of an army camp   (DOS)

Society for the Prevention of Cruelty to Animals (SPCA): a nongovernmental agency operating in the United States for the prevention of cruelty to animals. It has offices and functions in many principal cities   (LEV)

Society for the Reformation of Juvenile Delinquents: this organization opened the House of Refuge for young offenders in 1825. It was the first institution in the United States whose function was to remove children from the primarily adult jails and prisons   (AC)

sociological law: a statement of scientifically established causal relations and of causal sequences and continuity; a social law that has been proved. *Cf.* law   (DOS)

sociology: the scientific study of the phenomena arising out of the group relations of human beings; the study of man and his human environment in their relations to each other. Different schools of sociology lay varying emphasis upon the related factors, some stressing the relationships themselves, such as interaction, association, etc., others emphasizing the human beings in their social relationships, focusing their attention upon the socius in his varying roles and functions. Whether sociology, as developed hitherto, is entitled to the rank of a science is still a matter of some disagreement, but it is uniformly recognized that the methods of sociology may be strictly scientific, and that the verified generalizations which are the earmark of true science are being progressively built up out of extensive and painstaking observation and analysis of the repetitious uniformities in group behavior   (DOS)

sociopath: a person with a character disorder; an antisocial personality   (LEV)

Socrates [*469–399 B.C.*]: famous for his view of philosophy as a pursuit proper and necessary to all intelligent men, he was one of the great historical examples of a man who lived by his principles, though they ultimately cost him his life. Socrates believed that virtue and knowledge are identical, so no man knowingly does wrong—it is only that he wasn't taught virtue

sodium amytal: so-called truth serum. *See* truth serum (LEV)

sodium thiosulfate: sodium hyposulphite, commonly known as hypo (MPPF)

sodomy: an unnatural form of copulation between human beings; sexual relations between a human being and an animal

soft: a term used in describing prints and negatives which have low contrast (MPPF)

soft-focus: applied to a lens which has been deliberately undercorrected to produce a diffused image; also applied to pictures made with such a lens (MPPF)

soft-focus lens: a special type of lens, used to produce a picture with soft outlines. Such lenses are well adapted to portrait work (MPPF)

software package: the programming aids supplied by the manufacturer to facilitate the user's efficient operation of equipment. Includes assemblers, compilers, generators, subroutine libraries, operating systems, and industry application programs (ADPS)

solar: pertaining to the sun (CDTP)

solar day: from sunrise to sunset (CDTP)

solar month: a calendar month (CDTP)

solarization: the production of a reversed or positive image by exposure to a very intense light (MPPF)

sole: alone, single

sole prints: the prints, impressions or formations of patterns of friction ridges on the sole of the foot (LEV)

solicit: to ask earnestly; to petition (CDTP)

solicitation: it is a crime under the common law to solicit another to commit a felony, although the person solicited refuses to commit it. Courts differ as to whether it is a crime to solicit another to commit a misdemeanor; by the letter it is, if the misdemeanor is of a serious nature. If the crime solicited is committed, the offense of solicitation is merged in the greater offense (CDTP)

solicitor: a practitioner of the law who practices law in a court of chancery (LEV)

solicitor general: in states having no attorney general he is the ranking law officer. Where there is an attorney general the solicitor general is the next ranking law officer under the attorney general (LEV)

solid state: (1) an adjective used to describe a device such as a semiconductor transistor or diode (TDIAS) (2) a circuit or system which does not rely on vacuum or gas-filled tubes to control or modify voltages and currents (TDIAS)

solitary confinement: *See* isolated confinement

solvent: able to pay all just debts (CDTP)

somnambulism: sleep-walking

sonic motion detector: a sensor which detects the motion of an intruder by his disturbance of an audible sound pattern generated within the protected area (TDIAS)

soothsayer: a "fortune teller"; one who predicts things to come (LEV)

sordid: dirty; unclean; filthy; degraded; vulgar (LEV)

sorting: the arranging of records so that they are in ascending or descending sequence for some data element used as a key (ADPS)

sorting, comparison of pairs: to compare the keys of two records and put the record with the smaller-valued key ahead of the other to get the two items into ascending sequence; or to put the smaller behind to get a descending sequence (ADPS)

sorting, digital: a procedure for first sorting the records on the least significant (right-hand) digit in their keys and re-sorting on each higher-order digit until the records are sorted on the most significant digit in their keys. A commonly used punched-card technique (ADPS)

sorting, internal: the sorting of

items contained in internal storage to develop strings preparatory to merge sorting. All items contained in storage can be sorted into sequence and written out as one string, or blocks of items in sequence can be written out and replaced by other input items to build longer strings. Uses the comparison of pairs or a similar scheme   (ADPS)

sorting, merge: to produce a single sequence of records, ordered according to some rule, from two or more previously ordered (or perhaps unordered) sequences, without changing the items in size, structure, or total number. Although more than one pass may be required for complete sorting, during each pass items are selected on the basis of their entire key to build the sequence   (ADPS)

sorting, minor-major: arranging records in sequence on their keys starting with the right-hand digit only on the first pass and continuing to the left with all records used in each pass. Commonly used for punch-card sorting   (ADPS)

sound mind: a mind not in any way affected by insanity or mental defect   (CDTP)

sound sensing detection system: an alarm system which detects the audible sound caused by an attempted forcible entry into a protected structure. The system consists of microphones and a control unit containing an amplifier, accumulator, and a power supply. The unit's sensitivity is adjustable so that ambient noises or normal sounds will not initiate   (TDIAS)

sound sensor: a sensor which responds to sound; a microphone   (TDIAS)

source computer: a computer used to compile a source program as written by a programmer in a problem-oriented language into a machine-language program for running on an object computer. The compilation is done under control of a processor program designed especially for the computer and the two languages involved   (ADPS)

source program: the program as written by a programmer—for example, COBOL—being translated or compiled by a source computer and a translator into an object program in machine language   (ADPS)

Southerland, Edwin H: an American sociologist of the Univ. of Indiana who concerned himself with crime and its causation. In the 1920s he advanced his theories on white-collar crime and his differential association theory, the latter theory which held that crime was learned through interaction with other delinquents. Dr. Southerland conducted considerable research which was extremely important because of the lack of work that had been done up to that time   (DC)

sovereign: supreme power; highest; higher in position than all others   (LEV)

sovereign immunity: a doctrine under which the government and its subdivisions, in the conduct of governmental functions, is immune from civil liability resulting from wrongful acts of its agents. This doctrine does not apply in a situation where the government is engaged in a proprietary function. In 1946 the Federal Tort Claims Act abolished this immunity as pertains to the federal government. Some states have also abolished the immunity. Courts in other states are striking it down   (LEV)

sovereignty: the possession of and right to supreme power   (LEV)

S.P. (SP): State Police or Shore Patrol

S.P.C.A. (SPCA): Society for the Prevention of Cruelty to Animals

Spear, Charles (1801–1863): a Universalist minister of Boston and advocate of prison reform and anti-capital punishment, he helped organize the Society for the Abolition of Capital Punishment in 1844. He published the *Hanfman*

(1845), which the next year became *The Prisoner's Friend*, and came out till 1859. He and his brother John M. Spear, also a Universalist minister, who later became a spiritualist, worked together to help discharge prisoners, and pioneered in what ultimately became parole considerations (DC)

special procedures for crime prevention: a number of ingenious special procedures have been created by law for checking crime, which avoids the use of trial by jury. These include the abatement of nuisances, such as houses of prostitution, gambling resorts, and buildings used for the manufacture or sale of intoxicating liquor. The confiscation of stills, automobiles, and ships used for the manufacture and transportation of liquor and other agencies used for the commission of crime is also accomplished by the use of similar procedure (17 A.L.R. 568; 50 A.L.R. 97) (CDTP)

special verdict: a verdict by which the jury finds the facts only, leaving the judgment to the court (CDTP)

special weapon: any out-of-the-ordinary modern weapon, such as an atomic, radiological, or biological weapon (DWMT)

specific: definite; explicit (CDTP)

specific intent: when a crime consists, not merely in doing an act, but in doing it with a specific intent, the existence of that intent is an essential element. In such case the existence of criminal intent is not presumed from the commission of the act, but the specific intent must be proved (CDTP)

specimen: an item of physical evidence, or that which might be evidence, in a criminal case, especially as concerns items submitted to a crime laboratory. The laboratory may list or record the items as Questioned (Q) Specimens or as Known (K) Specimens, according to the nature of the evidence, i.e., whether it came from a known source. *See* questioned specimens; known specimens (LEV)

spectrograph: a device used for photographing elements of the light spectrum. It is used in the crime laboratory for making a spectrogram, produced when various inorganic substances are examined to determine their composition. It is useful in detecting the presence of minute quantities of materials (LEV)

spectrophotometer: an instrument for comparing the intensities at the corresponding wavelengths of two spectra (MPPF)

spectrum: a colored band formed when white light is passed through a prism or a diffraction grating; it contains all the colors of which white light is composed; plural, spectra (MPPF)

speed detectors: devices or systems used to measure the speed of moving vehicles. *See* radar; vascar (LEV)

speedgun: a device to ignite flashlamps in synchronism with the opening of the camera shutter (MPPF)

speeding: operation of a motor vehicle or other conveyance at a rate of speed in excess of the maximum allowed by law (DAP)

speedy trial: the right to a trial at an early date as guaranteed by the Sixth Amendment of the United States Constitution. In 1970, the United States Supreme Court held that the state did not give the defendant a speedy trial where he was not tried for six years while he was serving a term in a federal prison, during which time the state maintained a detainer against him, and the defendant repeatedly asked for a trial by the state (Dickey v. Florida, 90 S. Ct. 1564) (LEV)

sperm: seminal fluid containing the male reproductive cells; semen (LEV)

spermatozoan [*pl. Spermatozoa*]: male animal reproductive cell contained in seminal fluid (LEV)

spherical aberration: a lens defect which causes rays parallel to the axis and passing near the edge of a positive lens to come to a focus nearer the lens than the rays passing through the center portion (MPPF)

spherical bullet: one that is a round ball (CDTP)

spin: the rotation of a projectile or missile about its longitudinal axis to provide stability during flight (DWMT)

spindle: a part of the combination lock mechanism on a safe. The combination dial fits on the outer end of the spindle and its function is to turn the lock mechanism when the dial is rotated. On some types of safes burglars gain entry by punching or pulling the spindle (LEV)

Spinelli v. United States, 393 U.S. 110, 21 L. Ed. 2d 637, 89 S. Ct. 584 (1969): a 5–3 opinion by Mr. Justice Harlan, in which four of the seven other members of the Court wrote opinions, wound up more or less announcing new probable cause standards for search warrant affidavits in which the affiant had relied upon an informer. [The majority projects a two-pronged test to determine what constitutes probable cause in an affidavit for a search warrant when an informer is used in a showing of probable cause. The Court sets up guidelines on how to show an informant's reliability and on how to show an informant's information is reliable. The Court held Spinelli's reputation to be immaterial in showing probable cause. See, however, *United States v. Harris* (1971), holding reputation evidence can be used.] (ILECJ)

Spinoza, Benedict (1632–1677): a Dutch classical philosopher, Spinoza felt that the natural right of the individual is determined not by sound reason, but by desire and power. Spinoza rationalized in his *Theory of Individuals* that whatever a man wants to do

he will do, in a manner that will maintain his individual identity within society

spinster: a woman who has never been married (CDTP)

spiral cracks in glass: the concentric cracks in glass which has been broken from a force applied against its flat surface. These cracks are comparable to the rim of a wheel and connect the radial cracks which compare to the spokes of a wheel (LEV)

spiral rifling: the cutting of spiral grooves in the surface of the bore of the barrel. Invented about 1520 by G. Koller (or Kollner) of Vienna. This rifling imparts a rotary motion on its longitudinal axis, to the bullet in its passage through the barrel, which is maintained during its flight. This rotation equalizes any defects or irregularities in the form of the bullet and in its density thus tending to keep it in a straight course in its flight (CDTP)

spoils system: the method of awarding public positions and jobs to the elected officials' friends and supporters without regard to public interest or welfare (LEV)

spontaneous declaration: an utterance made as a result of some sudden and/or shocking event such as an accident or crime. See res gestae (LEV)

spoofing: the defeat or compromise of an alarm system by "tricking" or "fooling" its detection devices, such as by short-circuiting part or all of a series circuit, cutting wires in a parallel circuit, reducing the sensitivity of a sensor, or entering false signals into the system. Spoofing contrasts with circumvention (TDIAS)

spool: the reel on which film is wound for insertion into a camera (MPPF)

spot lamp: a type of mushroom-shaped electric lamp having an integral reflector and producing a narrow, concentrated beam of light (MPPF)

spot protection: protection of objects such as safes, art objects, or anything of value which could be damaged or removed from the premises (TDIAS)

spotting: the removal of small blemishes in photographic negatives or prints (MPPF)

spouse: a married person; a husband or wife (CDTP)

spring contact: a device employing a current-carrying cantilever spring which monitors the position of a door or window (TDIAS)

spur: a ridge detail in a fingerprint, also called a "hook." A hook-like ridge or small branch emanating from a single ridge line (LEV)

spurious: not genuine; fictitious (CDTP)

Spurzheim, John Gasper (*1776-1832*): a contemporary of anatomist Franz Gall, Spurzheim brought the concept of phrenology to America. Phrenology is the concept that personality characteristics of individuals are directly related to the conformations of their heads

squatter: one who settles on land without title to do so (CDTP)

squeegee: (1) a strip of flat rubber set in a handle, used to remove excess moisture from prints before drying (MPPF) (2) to press surplus moisture from prints (MPPF)

squib load: (1) a defective load (CDTP) (2) an extremely light-sounding load (CDTP)

Stack v. Boyle, 342 U.S. 1 (1951): this decision contains an excellent review of the proper methods for fixing pretrial bail (AOJ)

stacking swivel: an elongated C-shaped part usually mounted on an axis to permit partial rotation and with facilities for attachment near the muzzle end of a rifle or other shoulder-fired gun. It is used for attachment to two or more other, similar items to form a gun stack (DWMT)

staff: the portion of an administrative organization which has mainly investigative, advisory, or planning functions *Cf.* line (DAP)

staff functions: doing things of an advisory, specialized, or technical nature which are not concerned directly with carrying out the main objectives of the department. Such things involve fiscal matters for the department, personnel hiring and training, planning and research, etc. (LEV)

stakeout: a constant surveillance of an area by police

stall: delay by means of subterfuge or pretext (LEV)

stand: abbreviation for witness stand, chair, or seat in a court (LEV)

standard: an organizational flag (DWMT)

standard-bearer: the person who carries a flag

standard deviation: if a measurement or analysis is repeated several times, the results will not, because of inevitable small experimental errors, be exactly the same in every case. The standard deviation is a quantity which is calculated from their individual departures from their mean value, and which measures their "scatter"— the extent to which they collectively depart from the mean, and presumed, correct value. It can then also be used to predict the probable accuracy of another measurement or analysis made by the same operator using the same method (FS)

Standard Metropolitan Statistical Areas (SMSAs): 212 thickly populated areas in the United States as categorized by U.S. Census Bureau in its 1960 census. These metropolitan areas comprise 313 counties and 4,144 cities, each having its own police force (LEV)

standard muzzle velocity: the velocity at which a given projectile is supposed to leave the muzzle of a gun. The velocity is calculated on the basis of the particular gun, the propelling charge used, and the type of projectile fired from the gun. Firing tables are based on standard muzzle velocity. Also sometimes called "prescribed muzzle velocity"   (DWMT)

standby power supply: equipment which supplies power to a system in the event the primary power is lost. It may consist of batteries, charging circuits, auxiliary motor generators, or a combination of these devices   (TDIAS)

standing: the qualifications necessary for commencing a legal action

standing order: promulgated orders which remain in force until amended or canceled   (DWMT)

star-chamber proceeding: a secret proceeding in which a person is given inadequate or no opportunity to present his case or defend himself, and in which the proceedings are conducted and conclusions reached without observing usual judicial formalities; from the Star Chamber, an ancient court (abolished by Parliament in 1641) which had no jury and was permitted to apply torture   (DAP)

stare decisis [*Lat, lit "let the decision stand"*]: the legal principle of following judicial precedent from earlier cases

state and federal jurisdiction: the constitutional power of congress to enact legislation, define crimes, and provide for their punishment implies the power to enact that such legislation shall be exclusive of the statutes of the states, and if it does so expressly, impliedly the states cannot punish such acts as offenses against the state. Where this is not done, either expressly or by necessary implication, the statute of the state is not superseded by the federal statute, and the same act may be punished as an offense against the United States and also as an offense against the state   (CDTP)

state constitutions: differ materially from the U.S. Constitution. The former constitutes, for the most part, restrictions or limitations of powers; whereas the latter constitutes, for the most part, grants of powers   (CDTP)

state courts: the courts in the vari-

ous states are created, and their jurisdiction is conferred and defined, by statutes, which must be consulted   (CDTP)

state jurisdictions: officers in the various states who have been held to have been empowered to issue search warrants include judges of courts of record, justices of the peace, mayors who are ex-officio justices of the peace or city judges, police judges, recorders, and certain inferior judicial officers. While a clerk of a municipal court, empowered by statute to do so, has been held authorized to issue search warrants, where not properly authorized by statute a clerk of a circuit court or of a municipality may not do so on his own authority; nor may municipal or police judges issue warrants when not properly authorized by statute. Moreover, it has been held that a municipal judge cannot be empowered to issue such warrants by a city ordinance, in the absence of statutory permission (C.J. 56, 1210)   (CDTP)

state legislatures: have the inherent power to prohibit and punish any act as a crime, provided they do not violate the restrictions of the state and federal constitutions; and the courts cannot look further into the propriety of a penal statute than to ascertain whether the legislature had the power to enact it   (CDTP)

state police: an organized professional police force maintained and directly commanded by a State authority for the enforcement of law, the suppression of disorder, the patrolling of highways, and the guarding of public property   (DAP)

statements accompanying acts: whenever any act may be proved, statements accompanying and explaining that act, made by or to the person doing it, may be proved if they are necessary to understand it   (CDTP)

statements inconsistent with present testimony may be proved:

every witness under cross-examination in any proceeding, civil or criminal, may be asked whether he has made any former statement relative to the subject matter of the action and inconsistent with his present testimony, the circumstances of the supposed statement being referred to sufficiently to designate the particular occasion and, if he does not distinctly admit that he has made such a statement, proof may be given that he did in fact make it (CDTP)

statements in the presence of defendant: when the defendant's conduct is in issue, or is relevant to the issue, statements made in his presence and hearing, by which his conduct is likely to be affected, are admissible when he makes no denial (CDTP)

state's attorney: an officer, usu. locally elective within a county, who represents the State in securing indictments and in prosecuting criminal cases; called also prosecuting attorney (DAP)

state's evidence: testimony by a participant in the commission of a crime that incriminates others involved, given under the promise of immunity

statistics: body of methods dealing with the collection, classification, analysis, and interpretation of masses of numerical data; statistical methods; statistical data; groups of numerical facts, observations, or measures (DOS)

status: social position; rank; the state of affairs (CDTP)

status in quo: the state in which anything is (CDTP)

status quo: the situation in which the case was at any given date (CDTP)

statute: a law enacted by or with the authority of a legislature (CDTP)

statute law: an act of the legislature; a particular law enacted and established by the will of the legislative department of government; the written will of the legislature, solemnly expressed according to

the forms necessary to constitute it the law of the state (196 N.Y.S. 491) (CDTP)

statute of limitations: a statute which fixes a period during which existing claims may be collected, judgements enforced, or crimes prosecuted and which, after the lapse of the prescribed period, serves as a legal bar to such actions (DAP)

statutes: the state legislature can punish any act unless restricted by the state or federal constitution. The U.S. Congress has no power to declare and punish crimes except such as is derived from the federal constitution (CDTP)

statutes and ordinances: authorizing the production of books and papers of persons for certain purposes have been held not unconstitutional as violating the guaranty (C.J. 56, 1170) (CDTP)

statutory: pertaining to a law or statute, i.e., a law enacted by a legislative body (LEV)

statutory law: See legislation

statutory rape: sexual intercourse (not necessarily by force) with any female under a certain age determined by statute

stay: a stoppage of proceedings (CDTP)

stay ad interim: a stoppage of proceedings during the meantime (CDTP)

stay of execution: the period during which no execution can issue on a judgement. In criminal cases an order stopping the infliction of penalty imposed by the sentence and judgement (CDTP)

steal: to appropriate or take something of value which is the property of another, without the consent of the owner; to commit theft; purloin (LEV)

stealth: the act of moving carefully without being seen; slyness; secretiveness (LEV)

step length: the distance between the centers of two successive heelprints made by a person walking (LEV)

stereo camera: a camera having two lenses or the equivalent through which the pair of pictures making up a stereogram may be taken simultaneously   (MPPF)

stereoscope: a device containing lenses, prisms, or mirrors, through which a stereogram is seen as a single, three-dimensional picture   (MPPF)

sterling: (1) genuine; pure (CDTP) (2) current money of Great Britain   (CDTP)

stet [*Lat*]: let it stand

stigmata: physical defects or characteristics believed influential in producing criminal conduct. *Cf.* anomalies   (DOS)

still: a distillery; a mechanism for distilling liquids; the distillery used by "moonshiners" for making illegal whiskey   (LEV)

stills: photographs as distinguished from motion pictures   (MPPF)

stimulant: a drug or other substance which increases the physiological processes of the body   (LEV)

stipend: salary; fixed payment for work done   (CDTP)

stipulate: to agree or covenant (An attorney representing one or more parties in a legal action may stipulate certain things as facts without a witness testifying to such.)   (LEV)

stipulation: an agreement between attorneys, representing different parties, to perform or refrain from doing something in connection with a case in progress in court or pending court action   (LEV)

stirring rod: a glass, Bakelite, or hard-rubber rod used to stir photographic solutions   (MPPF)

stock: the wooden part of a firearm; that portion which fits against the shoulder in firing   (CDTP)

stock solution: a concentrated solution which is to be diluted with water for use   (MPPF)

Stoner v. California, 376 U.S. 483, 11 L. Ed. 2d 856, 84 S. Ct. 889 (1964): the Court held (with only Mr. Justice Black dissenting, in part, on other grounds) that the search of defendant's hotel room without his consent and with nei-

ther search nor arrest warrants, violated his constitutional rights, although with the consent of the hotel clerk. (Only the person, *as a general rule*, whose rights are being invaded can waive a constitutional right.)   (ILECJ)

stop: a lens aperture or a diaphragm opening such as f/4, f/5.6, etc.   (MPPF)

stop and frisk: a law operative in many states and upheld by the U.S. Supreme Court in *Terry* v. *Ohio*, authorizing a police officer to pat down a person who is suspected of having committed, is committing, or is about to commit a crime and the officer's life or limb is endangered (392 U.S. 1)   (LEV)

stop bath: preferred term for an acid rinse used following development of paper and films to neutralize them before placement in fixing bath; also incorrectly referred to as short stop   (MPPF)

stop down: to use a smaller aperture   (MPPF)

stoppage: failure to function; a "jam"   (CDTP)

stoppage in transitu: the right of an unpaid seller to stop goods in transit after he has parted with the possession of them   (CDTP)

storage: a device capable of receiving data, retaining them for an indefinite period of time, and supplying them upon command   (ADPS)

storage, addressable bulk: storage with the primary function of augmenting capacity of internal storage for handling data and instructions. Data from addressable bulk storage must be transferred to internal storage in order to use them in operations   (ADPS)

storage, buffer: (1) secondary storage used exclusively for assembly and transfer of data between internal and external storage (ADPS) (2) storage used to facilitate transfer of data between any two storage devices whose input and output speeds are not synchronized   (ADPS)

storage, high-speed: the quickest

access internal storage of a processor; this is composed of magnetic cores in most processors, although some use special cores or thin-film elements for limited amounts of ultra-high speed (ADPS)

storage, internal: storage that is directly accessible to the arithmetic and control units of a computer. It is used for storage of instructions and for data currently being operated upon (ADPS)

storage capacity: number of units of data that can be stored in a device at one time; variously expressed in terms of bits, characters, or words, depending upon the method of organization (ADPS)

storage density: the number of characters stored per unit length or area of storage medium—for example, number of characters per inch of magnetic tape (ADPS)

storage location: a storage position holding one machine word and usually having a specific address; the character position used to address a data field in a character-addressable machine (ADPS)

stored program: a program for instructing a processor how to manipulate data. Generally taken to mean internally stored program in which data and instructions are placed interchangeably in storage. Also covers (1) special-purpose equipment with instructions designed into the circuitry and (2) externally stored programs set up in wiring boards or plug boards for physical insertion into the machine (ADPS)

stored-program computer: a digital computer capable of performing sequences of internally stored instructions, as opposed to calculators on which the sequence is impressed manually. Such computers also usually possess the ability to operate upon the instructions themselves, and to alter the sequence of instructions in accordance with results already calculated (ADPS)

Stovall v. Denno, 388 U.S. 293, 18 L. Ed. 2d 1199, 87 S. Ct. 1967 (1967): a 6-2 majority of the Court in the last of the line-up cases handed down in the 1966-67 term, limited the exclusionary rule to cases involving line-ups held after the June 12 announcement of the decision in *Wade* [The Court changed its posture to a more fundamental fairness approach, in relation to law enforcement, in *Stovall* than it exercised in *Johnson* v. *New Jersey* with respect to retroactivity. *Stovall*, moreover, by way of dictum, makes it clear that counsel at a line-up identification applies to preindictment stages. *Wade, Gilbert,* and *Stovall* expand the *Schmerber* doctrine, Schmerber v. California, 382 U.S. 757 (1966), so that the net effect of the three cases is that one can be compelled against his will to appear in a line-up, to furnish a handwriting exemplar, to put on clothing or, as in *Wade,* to put strips of tape on one's face and, at least inferentially, to speak for voice identification. This latter act, along with possibly other performance such as walking or taking a particular stance, would seem to have limitations.] (ILECJ)

stowaway: one who secretes or conceals himself aboard an airplane, bus, train, or ship, usu. with intent to avoid paying the fare (LEV)

S.T.P. (STP): DOM: an hallucinogenic drug

straight: not retouched; applied to negatives or prints (MPPF)

strain gauge alarm system: an alarm system which detects the stress caused by the weight of an intruder as he moves about a building. Typical uses include placement of the strain gauge sensor under a floor joist or under a stairway tread (TDIAS)

strain gauge sensor: a sensor which, when attached to an object, will provide an electrical response to an applied stress upon the object, such as a bending, stretching, or compressive force   (TDIAS)

strain sensitive cable: an electrical cable which is designed to produce a signal whenever the cable is strained by a change in applied force. Typical uses including mounting it in a wall to detect any attempted forced entry through the wall, or fastening it to a fence to detect climbing on the fence, or burying it around a perimeter to detect walking or driving across the perimeter   (TDIAS)

strait jacket: a strongly made garment which restrains the use of the arms of a person on whom it is put. Purpose: to prevent a violent person from injuring himself or others   (LEV)

strangle: choke; to prevent breathing by applying pressure to the neck; a frequent cause of death   (LEV)

streetwalker: a prostitute, esp. one who solicits business by walking the streets   (LEV)

strike: cease work; refuse to work unless employer agrees to terms   (CDTP)

strikebreaker: a person who aids in breaking a strike by working in the place of strikers or who arranges for others to perform such work   (LEV)

striker: a firing pin or a projection on the hammer of a firearm which strikes the primer to initiate a propelling charge, explosive train, or fuze explosive train   (DWMT)

striking energy: the force of the impact measured in foot-pounds   (CDTP)

strip: to disassemble a piece of equipment, such as a gun, in order to clean, repair, or transport it   (DWMT)

strip search: (1) a search of a crime scene, usu. outdoors, where the terrain to be searched is divided into strips and searched carefully strip by strip. This should be followed by a grid search which consists of dividing the area into strips at right angles to the lines used in the strip search (LEV) (2)

a search of the person where the wearing apparel is removed during which the clothing and body should be thoroughly searched   (LEV)

stripes: chevrons   (DWMT)

strobe unit: a device, electronic in nature, which can be used repeatedly for flashlight source; has the same use and effect as a flash bulb but can be used again without replacing the bulb or light   (LEV)

struck jury: a trial jury of 12 secured by having opposing counsel each strike out 12 names from a list of 48 veniremen and thereafter eliminate 12 more from the list by exercising the right of challenge   (DAP)

structure, of a system: refers to the nature of the chain of command, the origin and type of data collected, the form and destination of results, and the procedures used to control operations (ADPS)

structure flow charts: general flow charts showing types, times, and quantities of input processing, files, and output but not indicating how jobs are performed   (ADPS)

strychnine: a poison, bitter in taste, composed of white crystals, derived from nux vomica and certain other plants. Medical profession uses it in small quantities as a medicine   (LEV)

stud: a projection on a gun for holding another part, such as the "bayonet stud" or the "sight stud"   (CDTP)

Student Nonviolent Coordinating Committee (SNCC): an extremist organization formed in the 1960s. It was formerly under the leadership of Stokely Carmichael and H. Rap Brown. As of 1969 it had developed into a full-blown all-[black] revolutionary organization   (LEV)

stun: to render unconscious or semiconscious; to become confused and mentally upset by actual force or events   (LEV)

stupid: slow-witted; low in intelligence; not exercising normal fac-

ulties; uninteresting (LEV)
sub [*Lat*]: under
sub justice: under or before a judge or court; undetermined (CDTP)
sub nomine [*Lat*]: under the name
sub rosa [*Lat*]: privately
subculture: a smaller group within a larger culture, identifiable by its own values, social norms, etc.
subject: (1) the person under investigation or about whom information is being sought by a peace officer (LEV) (2) (moulage or casting) the object or impression to be reproduced or cast (LEV)
subjects of protection and prohibition: the protection against unreasonable searches and seizures is a guaranty against the unlawful invasion of the privacy of the people, and not a guaranty of a right to remain undisturbed in the possession of specific property. Moreover the protection of this constitutional provision applies only to searches in private places and not to entries into public places. It is to be emphasized that the protection thereby afforded extends to the person, the home, and premises, and it also applies to the office or the place of business, as well as to the possessions and effects of one so protected, including his personal portable effects and his vehicle. It has been held that the term "houses, papers, and possessions" in a constitutional provision is broad enough to include every article and species of property (C.J. 56, 1163) (CDTP)
subjects of search and seizure: search warrants are limited to a search for and seizure of personal property, and give no right to seize or hold real estate or fixtures or immovable property; they have nothing to do with real estate, except the search of it [17 Fed. (2) 151.] (CDTP)
submachine gun: a readily portable machine gun, which can be fired from the shoulder or from the hip. It can be fired full automatic or semiautomatic. It is often referred to as the "Tommy gun,"

which derived its name from the Thompson submachine gun. *See* machine gun (LEV)
suborn: to cause, persuade, or bribe a person to give false testimony while under oath in a judicial matter (LEV)
subornation of perjury: procuring another to commit legal perjury (CDTP)
subpoena: a court order requiring an individual to appear in court as a witness
subpoena ad testificandum: subpoena to testify—the common subpoena requiring the attendance of a witness on a trial, inquisition, or examination (CDTP)
subpoena duces tecum: a judicial order, in writing, commanding a person to produce in court certain documents, papers, or other evidence, which are allegedly pertinent to matters being considered. The term means, "under penalty you shall bring with you" (LEV)
subrogation: the substitution of one person for another insofar as legal claims or rights are concerned (LEV)
subroutine: a set of instructions in machine code to direct the processor to carry out a well-defined mathematical or logical operation; a part of a routine. A calling sequence of a few instructions and factors are used to initialize a subroutine, transfer control to it, and provide for return to the main program after the subroutine execution is complete. Simpler schemes are available in compiler-level languages to go to a subroutine and return to the main program or merely to perform the subroutine and continue the main program. A subroutine is often written with symbolic relative addresses even though the routine to which it belongs is not (ADPS)
subroutine, closed: a subroutine stored outside the routine which refers to it. Such a subroutine is entered by a jump, and provision is made to return to the proper point in the main routine at the

end of the subroutine   (ADPS)

subroutine, library: a standard and proven subroutine which is kept "on file" for use at any time   (ADPS)

subroutine, open: a subroutine inserted directly into the program; it must be recopied at each point where it is needed in a routine   (ADPS)

subscriber's equipment: that portion of a central station alarm system installed in the protected premises   (TDIAS)

subscriber's unit: a control unit of a central station alarm system   (TDIAS)

subscript: an integer used to specify a particular item in a list or table, according to COBOL rules, and consisting of a numeric literal or data-name   (ADPS)

subsecondary classification: a term used in classifying fingerprints. In the classification formula it follows the primary classification and is written in capital letters, such as I/O or whatever the count requires   (LEV)

subsequent conduct or condition of defendant: any conduct or condition of the defendant subsequent to the act charged, apparently influenced or caused by the doing of the act, and any done in consequence of it, by or by the authority of the defendant, may be shown. But self-serving statements or acts cannot be shown by the defendant   (CDTP)

substantial error: a material, as distinguished from a trivial, error   (CDTP)

substantive evidence: that adduced for the purpose of proving a fact in issue, as opposed to evidence given for the purpose of discrediting a witness   (CDTP)

substantive felony: an independent felony; one not dependent upon the conviction of another person for another crime   (CDTP)

substantive law: the part of law that creates, defines, and regulates rights

substantive right: a right to the enjoyment of fundamental privileges and immunities equally with others; distinguished from procedural rights. See procedural rights   (DAP)

substitutionary evidence: evidence allowed as a substitute for original or primary evidence

subterfuge: a strategy used by a person to avoid an unpleasant or difficult situation   (LEV)

subtractive process: a process in color photography, using the colors magenta, cyan, and yellow. Contrasted with additive color process   (MPPF)

subtractive reducer: a reducer which affects the shadows in a negative without noticeably affecting the highlights   (MPPF)

suburb: a place adjacent to a city   (LEV)

suburban: of or pertaining to a suburb; living in a suburb   (LEV)

subversion: demolition; overthrow; destruction; a cause of destruction or overthrow, especially of a government   (LEV)

succumb: (1) to yield; to give in to; to give way (LEV) (2) to die   (LEV)

sue: to bring a lawsuit against another; to commence a legal action   (LEV)

sufficiency of bail: the bail required should be such, and such only, as will be sufficient to insure the appearance of the accused   (CDTP)

sufficiency of warrant: the warrant, to authorize an arrest, (1) must have been issued by a magistrate having jurisdiction; (2) It may, in the absence of statutory restriction, be issued on Sunday, and at any time of the day or night; (3) It must, in some, but not all, jurisdictions be under seal; (4) It must state the offense, and an offense for which an arrest may be made; (5) It must show authority to issue it, as that a complaint on oath or affirmation was made; (6) It must correctly name the person to be arrested, or if his name is unknown, so describe him that he may be identified; (7) It must show the time of issuance; (8) It must be directed to a proper peace officer, either by name or by description of his office; (9) It must direct, and not merely authorize the arrest; (10) It must command the officer to bring the accused before the issuing magistrate or some other magistrate having jurisdiction; (11) Clerical errors and formal defects will not render it insufficient (CDTP)

sufficient evidence: adequate evidence; such evidence, in character, weight, or amount as will legally justify the judicial or official action demanded; according to circumstances, it may be "prima facie" or "satisfactory" evidence, according to the definitions of those terms given above (22 S.E. 142) (CDTP)

sufficient provocation: See legal provocation

suffocate: to kill by depriving one from getting enough air; to smother (LEV)

suffrage: the right to vote (LEV)

sui juris: of his own right; capable of managing one's own affairs (CDTP)

suicide: self-murder; voluntary destruction of oneself by a person of sound mind (CDTP)

suit: prosecution of some claim or demand in a court of justice (CDTP)

Sullivan Act: a law of New York State making it a felony to possess firearms without legal authority (LEV)

summary: (1) done without delay or ceremony; done instantly or quickly; without formality (LEV) (2) (law) instanter; a trial without a jury (LEV)

summary jurisdiction: the jurisdiction of a court to give a judgement or make an order itself, forthwith; e.g., to commit to prison for contempt; to punish malpractice in a solicitor; or, in the case of justices of the peace, a jurisdiction to convict an offender themselves instead of committing him for trial by jury (CDTP)

summons: an official order to appear in court

sunshade: a hood placed over a lens to keep stray light from its surface; similar to lens hood (MPPF)

super [*Lat*]: above; over

superimpose: put one thing on top of another (LEV)

superior court: (1) a court of record or general trial court in some States, superior to a justice of the peace or magistrates' court (DAP) (2) in other States, an intermediate court between the general trial court and the highest appellate court (DAP)

Superior Court Warrant Of Arrest: in New York, a subpoena that a police officer delivers to the defendant

superproportional reducer: a reducing solution which lowers the highlight density faster than it affects the shadow density (MPPF)

supersede: to set aside; annul (CDTP)

supersedeas: a writ containing a command to stay proceedings at law (CDTP)

supersedeas, writ of: a stay of proceedings. The name of a writ containing a command to stay the proceedings at law. It is either expressed, by the issuance of a writ of supersedeas, or implied, by the issuance of a writ, as of certiorari (CDTP)

supervised lines: interconnecting lines in an alarm system which are electrically supervised against tampering (TDIAS)

supervisory alarm system: an alarm system which monitors conditions or persons or both and signals any deviation from an established norm or schedule. Examples are the monitoring of signals from guard patrol stations for irregularities in the progression along a prescribed patrol route, and the monitoring of production or safety conditions such as sprinkler water pressure, temperature, or liquid level (TDIAS)

supervisory circuit: an electrical circuit or radio path which sends information on the status of a sensor or guard patrol to an annunciator. For intrusion alarm systems, this circuit provides line supervision and monitors tamper devices. *See also* supervisory alarm system   (TDIAS)

supplemental: additional; in aid of or to supply defects   (CDTP)

supplementary lens: an attachable lens by which the focal length of a camera objective may be increased or decreased   (MPPF)

supporting evidence: evidence which will bolster and strengthen such evidence as eyewitness testimony, transfer evidence, and statements of the accused. Supportive evidence includes such things as proof of motivation, similarity of modus operandi of other crimes known to have been committed by the accused, the accused having possession of the stolen property, etc.   (LEV)

supra: above; previously referred to   (CDTP)

supreme court, state: usu. the highest court in the state judicial system   (LEV)

Supreme Court, United States: the highest federal court in the United States. Its existence is provided for in Article III of the Constitution, although Congress is given the power to determine the size of the Court. In 1801 the number of justices was reduced to 5, but was increased to 7 in 1807, to 9 in 1837, and to 10 in 1863. In 1869 the number was again reduced to 9, remaining there to date. The Court's jurisdiction is original and appellate, the latter being determined by Congress. In 1925 a law of Congress delegated to the court the power to lay down the terms of its appellate jurisdiction. The Court's original jurisdiction is limited to cases or controversies to which a state or an ambassador, public minister, or consul is a party. In its early history the Court was held in low esteem, but with the chief justiceship of John Marshall in the first third of the

19th century, its prestige and power became outstanding. Under Marshall the Court assumed the power of judical review, maintaining it to this day. Although the Court does not have self-enforcing power, requiring enforcements of its decisions by the executive branch, its decisions have been ignored only three times by American presidents. There are no constitutional qualifications for Court membership, and in its early history politicians and military figures with little legal or judicial training were appointed to it. It is curious to note that of the 12 chief justices only the last 5 have had prior judicial experience. Decisions of the court are rendered by a simple majority vote, although the majority opinion is frequently the work of one member whose thinking affects the Court's policy and doctrine. Members of the Court are appointed for life by the President. They may be removed only by death, resignation, or impeachment. Outstanding members of the Court have been John Marshall, Joseph Storey, Roger B. Taney, Salmon P. Chase, Oliver Wendell Holmes, Louis D. Brandeis, William Howard Taft, Charles Evans Hughes, Benjamin Cardoza, and Harlan F. Stone   (DOAH)

surety: one who undertakes to become responsible for the debt of another; one who binds himself for the performance of some act of another   (CDTP)

suretyship: an undertaking to answer for the debt, default, or miscarriage of another   (CDTP)

surface development: a characteristic of some fine-grain developers, which tend to develop the image mainly on the surface of the emulsion   (MPPF)

surname: the family name; last name   (LEV)

surprise: a procedural pleading available to parties to a trial when something unexpected, unanticipated, and which could not be prevented by due diligence, develops. The side who is disadvantaged by such a development may plead surprise   (LEV)

surreptitious: covert, hidden, concealed, or disguised   (TDIAS)

surrogate: a judicial officer who has jurisdiction over the probate of wills, the settlement of estates, etc.   (CDTP)

surveillance: (1) control of premises for security purposes through alarm systems, closed circuit television (CCTV), or other monitoring methods (TDIAS) (2) supervision or inspection of industrial processes by monitoring those conditions which could cause damage if not corrected. See also supervisory alarm system (TDIAS) (3) police investigative technique involving visual or electronic observation or listening directed at a person or place (e.g., stakeout, tailing suspects, wiretapping, and so on). Its objective is to gather evidence of a crime or merely to accumulate intelligence about suspected criminal activity   (LEV)

survivor: one of two or more persons who lives after the other or others are dead   (CDTP)

suspended sentence: See sentence, suspended

suspense file: the file of transactions or records that are awaiting some anticipated event. For example, rejected transactions are retained in a suspense file for control purposes until corrections are returned for another attempt at processing   (ADPS)

suspension: a temporary stop   (CDTP)

suspension of judgement: where the court pronounces a fine or a prison sentence, and then orders that upon certain condition the payment of the fine and the prison term, or either of them need not be met   (CDTP)

suspicion: (1) the act of suspecting; mistrust, doubt; (2) apprehension without adequate proof

Sutherland, Edward H.: developed the theory of differential association in 1937. The first important modern theory of crime, it maintains that delinquent behavior is learned from one's associates

suture: to sew or stitch together the edges of a cut or wound   (LEV)

swindler: one who defrauds others by cheating and deception or through fraudulent schemes   (CDTP)

swing back: the back of a view camera which can be tilted in both vertical and horizontal planes   (MPPF)

switch: a device within the processor that stores an indication of various conditions encountered during processing—for example, greater than, less than, or equal to following a comparison operation. The switch contents can be tested by a conditional jump instruction to execute appropriate routines in the program   (ADPS)

switchblade knife: a knife the blade of which will open or extrude by a mechanical device, such as a spring   (LEV)

swivel gun: one fired from a swivel mount, on a boat, wall, or animal   (CDTP)

swivels: a link or coupling device which permits either of the attached parts to rotate independently of the other, such as the sling swivels, the stacking swivel, or a swivel ramrod   (CDTP)

symbolic speech: a theory that actions and objects which convey ideas in lieu of oral communication constitute symbolic speech. A person who appeared in public wearing a shirt resembling the American flag was prosecuted for mutilating and defiling the flag. He claimed his actions were protected by the First Amendment of the Constitution. The appellate court did not agree with this theory and his conviction was affirmed   (LEV)

synchro-flash: a term applied to flash photography in which a flash bulb is ignited at the same instant that the shutter is opened, the flash bulb being the primary source of illumination   (MPPF)

synchronizer: a device for synchronizing the shutter of a camera with a flashlamp so that the shutter is fully opened at the instant the lamp reaches its peak intensity (MPPF)

synchro-sun: a term used in flash photography where flashlight and sunlight are used in combination (MPPF)

syndicate: (1) an association of persons authorized to undertake some duty or to negotiate some business (CDTP) (2) a name [usu. capitalized] applied to the Mafia and other organizations whose purpose is to accomplish certain unlawful or questionable objectives. It also applies to legal and legitimate organizations whose activities are joined together for business purposes. *See* Mafia (LEV)

syndicate security: methods of protection used by organized crime

synonymous: having the same or approximately the same meaning (CDTP)

synthetic: artificial; spurious; made artificially by using certain ingredients to make a product which approximates a thing produced by nature (LEV)

synthetic analgesic: a manufactured or synthesized chemical which has the pain-relieving properties of a narcotic (LEV)

syphilis: a venereal disease caused by a microorganism. It is transmitted by direct contact or from birth. It develops through three stages; primary, where a hard *chancre* develops where the infection starts; secondary, where the skin and blood are affected; tertiary, where the whole system is involved. Modern medical treatment is effective against the disease (LEV)

system: any regular or special method or plan of procedure. In a broader context, a system consists of an organization, people, hardware, and procedures that operate together to perform a set of tasks (ADPS)

system analysis: an orderly study of the detailed procedure for collecting, organizing, and evaluating information about an organization with the objective of improving control over its operations (ADPS)

systems design: formulation and description of the nature and content of inputs, files, and outputs in order to show how they are connected by processing procedures and for the purpose of developing a new or improved system (ADPS)

T

table: a dual series of similar items—for example, the names of states, their current census, and one or more prior censuses; a two-dimensional array (ADPS)

tag reader: a device for reading punched or notched tags, plates, and cards pre-punched and attached to physical objects or given to employees and others for identification; also may be used for accepting keyboard input. Examples are garment tag readers used in department stores which also read customer's charge plates and sales clerk's identification cards (ADPS)

tail: to follow a person secretly for surveillance

takedown: the process of taking a gun apart (DWMT)

take-down rifle: a rifle so made that the action and barrel can be easily taken apart thus making it more convenient to carry (LEV)

tales: persons summoned as jurors (CDTP)

talesman: a bystander who is chosen to serve on a jury when the jury is not filled by those who had been summoned for jury duty. The person chosen may be present in court or outside the court (LEV)

tamper device: (1) any device, usu. a switch, which is used to detect an attempt to gain access to intrusion alarm circuitry, such as by removing a switch cover (TDIAS) (2) a monitor circuit to detect any attempt to modify the alarm circuitry, such as by cutting a wire (TDIAS)

tamper switch: a switch which is installed in such a way as to detect attempts to remove the enclosure of some alarm system components such as control box doors, switch covers, junction box covers, or bell housings. The alarm component is often described as being "tampered" (TDIAS)

tangent of an angle: the ratio of the length of the opposite leg to the adjacent leg of a right triangle (MPPF)

tank: a container or mechanical device in which films or plates may be processed, sometimes without the need of a darkroom (MPPF)

tape unit: a device for reading data from magnetic tape and writing new data (after erasing prior data) on tape. Some tape units read in either direction, although they write in only the forward direction. The device also rewinds tape ready for removal and replacement by another reel (ADPS)

tapper bell: a single-stroke bell designed to produce a sound of low intensity and relatively high pitch (TDIAS)

Tarde, Gabriel (1843-1904): philosopher, psychologist, and sociologist as well as a criminologist of international repute. His emphasis on the social origins of crime is a cornerstone of present American criminological theories. His devastating attack on the Lombrosian theory undermined the influence of that school in Europe. In the field of penology, Tarde furnished us with a theory of moral respon-

sibility which is original and capable of practical demonstration (PC)

tattooing: gunpowder patterns; the marks left on the surface of the skin of the person who has been shot at fairly close range. It is caused from the residue of unburned powder in the propellant. From little or no pattern at contact range the design or pattern increases in size with the increase in the distance of the muzzle of the weapon from the body until a distance is reached where none of the particles reach the body. The markings caused by these particles are black or red (LEV)

Teapot Dome Scandal: the Teapot Dome Scandal disclosed corruption in high levels of government shocking the American public. The findings of a senate committee in October, 1923 inquiring into how the rich naval oil reserves at Teapot Dome in Wyo. and Elk Hills and Buena Vista in Cal. were leased to Harry S. Sinclair's Mammoth Oil Co. and Edward L. Doheny's Pan-American Petroleum and Transport Co. led to the prosecution for conspiracy and bribery of U. S. Senator Albert B. Fall, from New York. As Secretary of the Interior in the Harding Administration, he authorized the award of the leases to the two oil companies; he was confined in the New Mexico State Penitentiary at Santa Fe, but a $100,000 fine was never paid. After his release, he survived in relative poverty until 1944

tear agents: tear gases such as CN, CNC, CNS, CNB, BBC, and CS, are used for training and riot control. They cause a flow of tears and irritation of the skin, but rarely produce casualties (DWMT)

tear gas: a substance, usu. liquid, which when atomized and of a certain concentration causes temporary but intense eye irritation and a blinding flow of tears in anyone exposed to it. Also called a "lacrimator" (DWMT)

technique, of a data-processing system: refers to the method used to collect data inputs, to process them, and to convert processed data into reports or other usable form (ADPS)

technique flow charts: specific flow charts showing data and information and the methods proposed for filling them (ADPS)

telecommunication: any transmission, emission, or reception of signs, signals, writing, images, and sounds or information of any nature by wire, radio, visual, or other electromagnetic systems (DWMT)

teledata: a device for introducing parity bits and transmitting over telegraphic circuits data already punched in five-, six-, or eight-channel paper tape. The receiving unit at a distant point checks parity for code accuracy, and reperforates valid data into paper tape (ADPS)

telegraph channel: a low-capacity communication channel with a maximum data-transmission rate of 10 characters per second (ADPS)

telephone channel: a medium-capacity communication channel with a maximum capacity of 300 characters per second (ADPS)

telephone dialer, automatic: a device which, when activated, automatically dials one or more preprogrammed telephone numbers (e.g., police, fire department) and relays a recorded voice or coded message giving the location and nature of the alarm (TDIAS)

telephone dialer, digital: an automatic telephone dialer which sends its message as a digital code (TDIAS)

telephoto lens: a lens of long focal length having a separate negative rear element; it is used to form larger images of distant objects; it is similar in results to a telescope (MPPF)

telescopic sight: a telescope used on a firearm as a sight (DWMT)

teletypewriter: basically an electric typewriter that can be operated manually or by reading and reperforating paper tape; it is connected to a leased or dial-switched telegraph grade circuit for transmitting text and also data messages in readable form (ADPS)

telpack: broad-band communication channels for transmitting data from magnetic tape to magnetic tape or directly between computers at rates up to 60,000 characters a second (ADPS)

temperature scales: for conversion: F to C: subtract 32 and multiply by 5/9; C to F multiply by 9/5 and add 32 (FS)

tender: to offer money in payment of a debt or in fulfillment of a contract (LEV)

tented arch: a pattern where the ridges come in from one side and go out the other side without recurve or turning back and where the "upward" thrust of the lines at or near the center of the pattern is sharp and abrupt (LEV)

terminal resistor: a resistor used as a terminating device (TDIAS)

terminating capacitor: a capacitor sometimes used as a terminating device for a capacitance sensor antenna. The capacitor allows the supervision of the sensor antenna, especially if a long wire is used as the sensor (TDIAS)

terminating device: a device which is used to terminate an electrically supervised circuit. It makes the electrical circuit continuous and provides a fixed impedance reference (end of line resistor) against which changes are measured to detect an alarm condition. The impedance changes may be caused by a sensor, tampering, or circuit trouble (TDIAS)

territorial jurisdiction: the right of a state to exercise exclusive control over (a) all lands within its boundaries, (b) its territorial waters, (c) an extensive portion of the air space over its territory, and (d) all persons or things not covered by diplomatic immunity within any of the foregoing areas (DAP)

terrorism: the use of terror for coercion (LEV)

Terry v. Ohio, 392 U.S. 1, 20 L. Ed. 2d 889, 88 S. Ct. 1868 (1968): the court held, 8-1, a "frisk" may be justified when its purpose is to "discover guns, knives, clubs, or other hidden instruments for assault of the police officer," when a reasonably prudent man in the circumstances would be warranted in the belief that his safety or that of others is in danger. Thus, the essence of the holding is the self-prosecution of the officer. [The Court said that a "pat-down for weapons" (i.e., a frisk) constitutes a "search" within the meaning of the Fourth Amendment.] (ILECJ)

Tessar: a trade name for a type of anastigmat lens composed of two pairs of lens elements; one pair is cemented together, the other pair is separated by an air space (MPPF)

test strip: an exposed strip of bromide or chloride paper containing several different exposures used to determine the correct exposure for printing (MPPF)

testamentary: having to do with a will or testament; obtained by or through a will (LEV)

testimony: evidence given by a witness, under oath or affirmation

testing: examination to determine the real character of a thing in a particular aspect. Acceptance testing for equipment determines capacity and reliability. Program testing determines whether programs do what they are supposed to when used with test, simulated, or live data (ADPS)

Texas Rangers: a semi-military mounted police force first organized in 1836 as a local body of settlers with the purpose of defense against Indian attacks. During the Texas War they were reorganized by General Houston, who built up their strength to a force of 1,600 men. They served in the Civil War as an element of the Confederate Army and were reorganized in the 1870s. As a police force at this time, the Rangers protected hundreds of miles of the Texas frontier against Indians, hold-up men, rustlers, and bandits. They operated without uniforms or standard procedures, being authorized as roving commissions for specific duties. The Rangers were famous for their skill and ability, and exercised great moral influence in the state. Their exploits have served as a source of much dramatic and literary material (DOAH)

texture: applied to showing an object's surface roughness or smoothness in a photograph; often achieved by using light from a direction almost parallel to the surface of the object (MPPF)

therapeutic community: the name of a program engaged in rehabilitation of addicts. Centers are used for this purpose. These are called by various names, including Synonon, Kinsman Hall, Odyssey House, Phoenix House. ... It operates on the principle that ex-addicts can relate to and communicate effectively with addicts (LEV)

thermal burning bar: a device used by burglars for burning safes. It consists of a steel pipe filled with small steel rods and/or rods of other metals. One end of the pipe is threaded and thus can be coupled to an oxygen supply. It is ignited at the open end with a high temperature torch. It is capable of burning through steel, other metals, and even concrete (LEV)

thermocouple: temperature-measuring device which depends on the fact that, in a closed circuit containing two identical junctions between different metals, if the junctions are at different temperatures a current flows in the circuit. In practice, one junction is kept at a low constant temperature (0° C—melting ice) and the other is exposed to the unknown temperature. The electric potential then produced is then proportional to, and can be used to measure, that temperature   (FS)

thin: applied to a weak negative lacking in density in the highlights and detail in the shadows (MPPF)

thin film: an ultra high-speed storage device consisting of a molecular deposit of material on a suitable plate   (ADPS)

third degree: the process of extorting a confession or information from a prisoner by prolonged questioning, the use of threatening words or gestures, or actual violence   (DAP)

Thompson submachine gun: a weapon designed by Gen. John T. Thompson (1860–1940), Director of Arsenals in the United States during World War I. The first prototypes were developed in 1918. There are several models of the Thompson, with the Models 1921 and 1928 manufactured by Colt, and the M1928A1 and the M1 series manufactured by Auto-Ordnance and Savage. The Model 1921 is a retarded-blowback-operated weapon with selective full automatic and semiautomatic fire. The cyclic rate of fire is 800 rounds per minute, and the .45 cal. ACP cartridge provides muzzle velocities of about 920 fps. The length of the weapon (with stock and compensator) is 33.75 in., and it has a barrel length of 10.50 in. without compensator. Available for use with this weapon are 18-, 20-, and 30-round box magazines and 50-round and 100-round drum magazines. The weapon weighs 12 lb. with a 20-round magazine. The Model 1927 is a Model 1921 with an action that permits semiautomatic fire only. The Model 28 is basically a Model 1921 with provisions to reduce the rate of fire from 800 rounds per minute to less than 700 and with simplifications to allow mass production. When

this weapon was adopted as standard with U.S. forces, it became known as the "Thompson .45 cal. submachine gun M1," and finally as the "M1A1"   (DWMT)

thread count: the number of threads per inch in a piece of fabric. This is a factor used by the crime laboratory in the examination and comparison of fabrics   (LEV)

three-quarter: applied to a portrait pose, standing or seated, including the figure approximately to the knees   (MPPF)

throat: (1) the tapered portion of the bore forward of the chamber where it diminishes in cross-section to meet the rifling. In a revolver it is the enlargement of the bore at the breech to facilitate the centering of the bullet in the barrel when it jumps from the cylinder into the bore. Also may be referred to as "leade" (DWMT) (2) in a sword or dagger scabbard, the metal reinforcement around the mouth   (DWMT)

ticket-of-leave: method of conditional release from prison, used in the 1840s by Alexander Maconochie of England and Sir Walter Crofton of Ireland. The ticket-of-leave allowed conditional release from prison

tilt-top: a device attached to a tripod head to permit the camera to be set at various angles in elevation   (MPPF)

time: an application for a warrant must be made within a reasonable time after the commission of the alleged unlawful acts, the period constituting a reasonable time being a judicial question for the court (17 Fed. 2nd 937)   (CDTP)

time exposure: an exposure in which the shutter is opened and closed manually with a relatively long interval between   (MPPF)

time-gamma-temperature curve: a curve of developing time plotted against developed contrast or gamma. The contrast for any given time may be read directly from the curve, or vice versa. The curve applies only for one particular developer and emulsion (MPPF)

time of arrest: in absence of statutory provision to the contrary, an arrest may be made at any time (CDTP)

timer: a special darkroom clock giving audible or visible indication of various time intervals (MPPF)

timing table: that portion of central station equipment which provides a means for checking incoming signals from McCulloh circuits (TDIAS)

tire roll: the tendency of a tire to deflect to the side during a turn so that in extreme cases the tire sidewall, or even the wheel rim, may be in contact with the road surface (TDPPC)

tire tread: the design on the outer surface of a vehicle rubber tire. The marks and impressions made by such tire can be used to identify the tire which made it (LEV)

titanium tetrachloride: a liquid which causes formation of a screening smoke when it is dispersed in air. It may be dispersed by explosive effect or as a mechanically produced spray. The smoke is corrosive and irritating to the nose and throat, but not serious in effect in the concentration usually present in a smoke cloud (DWMT)

titration: the analytical operation of adding a reagent until a reaction is complete and measuring the volume so added (FS)

T.L.C.: thin-layer chromatography (FS)

TNT: trinitrotoluene or trinitrotoluol

t-number, t-stop: a system of marking lens apertures in accordance with their actual light transmission, rather than by their geometrical dimensions as in the f-stop system (MPPF)

tompion: (1) a wooden plug or cover, esp. for the muzzle of a gun (DWMT) (2) a cover for the sight bracket of a gun when the sight is not in place. Also called "tam-pion" (DWMT)

tone: in photography this usually applies to the color of a photographic image or, incorrectly, to any distinguishable shade of gray; to change the color of a photographic image from its natural black to various colors, either by means of metallic salts, or by mordanting certain dyes to the image. Such dyes do not stain the gelatin; note the difference from tinting (MPPF)

tong: See war, tong

toning: a method for changing the color or tone to an image by chemical action (MPPF)

tool marks: marks, scratches, and depressions made by a hard object on another object or substance which is softer than the tool but is rigid enough to retain the marks. A screwdriver will make tool marks on a softer piece of metal with which it forceably comes in contact (LEV)

Top Ten Most Wanted Criminals: a program of the FBI whereby a group of ten persons charged with major crimes are publicized and their photographs and descriptions published. They are each the subject of an Identification Order. This program has proven effective and many wanted persons have been identified by members of the public, which has resulted in their apprehension (LEV)

top secret: in government service, information which is ranked of extreme importance and which if divulged without authority might cause irreparable harm which would bring about a break in diplomatic relations with another country or cause an armed attack upon the nation or its allies, or would compromise military or defense plans or other developments vital to the national defense (LEV)

top speed: the maximum speed of which a vehicle is capable on a straight, smooth, level surface (TDPPC)

torture: [historically,] suffering

caused by various devices employed in ancient times and during the Middle Ages to induce the accused to confess. It was based on the theory that if the guilty suffered sufficiently he would confess his guilt. The trouble with this method of determining guilt or innocence is that it gave advantage to the most insensitive human beings, and often led to confessions by innocent people. Beccaria and the Classical School of penology protested it, and led to its final abandonment   (DOS)

total: the sum of numeric items. A batch total is the sum of all the items handled as a unit for processing, such as a bundle of checks or other documents. A control or proof total is a sum developed at one stage of processing that must be matched at a later stage of processing. A hash or nonsense total is a sum of numeric items not ordinarily added, such as catalogue numbers for items on a customer's order, to help control accuracy during processing   (ADPS)

touch sensitivity: the sensitivity of a capacitance sensor at which the alarm device will be activated only if an intruder touches or comes in very close proximity (about 1 cm or 1/2 in.) to the protected object   (TDIAS)

toxic: poisonous

toxicology: a study or science which pertains to toxic substances, their characteristics, effects, and antidotes   (LEV)

trace elements: minute quantities of chemical elements present in or on objects or materials. The crime laboratory has developed techniques for finding and analyzing such small amounts of chemicals which can be useful in identifying two or more specimens as having come from the same source   (LEV)

trace routine: a [computer programming] routine used to observe how the object program operates while it is being executed   (ADPS)

traced forgery: the forging of writings accomplished by tracing the genuine writings onto another document. This is usually accomplished by placing the genuine document over a lighted glass or other transparent surface and tracing the genuine writings onto a document placed over the genuine writings. A qualified document examiner can detect this type of forgery due to the wavering lines in the forged writings   (LEV)

tracer bullet: a bullet containing a pyrotechnic mixture that is ignited by the exploding powder charge in the cartridge to make the flight of the projectile visible both by day and night   (DWMT)

track: a sequence of binary cells arranged so that data may be read or written from one cell at a time in serial fashion. For example, a track on a magnetic drum is a path one-bit wide around the circumference of the drum; the bits in several tracks make up a character   (ADPS)

tracking: the following of an individual through the entire criminal justice process

traffic law, the first was passed June 27, 1652, by New Amsterdam (New York City): "The Director General and Council of New Netherland in order to prevent accidents do hereby ordain that no Wagons, Carts or Sleighs shall be run, rode or driven at a gallop within this city of New Amsterdam, that the drivers and conductors of all Wagons, Carts and Sleighs within this city (the Broadway alone excepted) shall walk by the Wagons, Carts or Sleighs and so take and lead the horses, on the penalty of two pounds Flemish for the first time, and for the second time double, and for the third time to be arbitrarily corrected therefor and in addition to be responsible for all damages which may arise therefrom"   (FAMOUS)

traffic management: the function

of law enforcement to assist in the orderly flow of vehicles on streets and highways and to enforce the laws regulating vehicle use (TDPPC)

traffic regulation, the first: the first one-way traffic regulation appears to have been issued in New York City on Dec. 17, 1791, when a regulation incidental to a performance at the John Street Theatre requested that "Ladies and Gentlemen will order their Coachmen to take up and set down with their Horse Heads to the East River, to avoid Confusion" (FAMOUS)

trail arms: the command to carry a rifle so that the butt is raised a few inches from the ground and the muzzle and is inclined forward (DWMT)

trailer label: label recorded on tape following last record in a file—number of records on tape and whether the file is continued on another tape (ADPS)

training school: state institutions providing educational and vocational training programs to the inmates, juvenile delinquents

trajectory: the curve traced by a bullet, projectile, missile, bomb, or other object thrown, launched, or trajected by an applied exterior force, the projectile continuing in motion after separation from the force (DWMT)

transaction: event that affects the status of a business—for example, purchase, sale, issue, and collection. Also called "event" (ADPS)

transaction file: the transactions occurring over a period of time and accumulated as a batch ready for processing against the master files that are affected (ADPS)

transceiver: (1) card-reading, modulating, and punching equipment for card-to-card transmission of data over telephone or telegraph grade circuits (ADPS) (2) radio equipment which will transmit and receive radio messages. This may be fixed or mobile (LEV)

transcript: the official description

of a court proceeding recorded by the court reporter

transient: one who comes to a place for a temporary period of time and then moves on (LEV)

transition, rate of: the period of time during which system changes are made or new equipment introduced. The rate is affected by the degree of change, size of the organization, length of time since the last change, and whether the organization has reached a reasonably steady state following the preceding systems change (ADPS)

translator routine: See routine, compiler

translucent: a medium which passes light but diffuses it so that objects cannot be clearly distinguished (MPPF)

transmission: the ratio of the light passed through an object to the light falling upon it (MPPF)

transparency: an image on a transparent base, which must be viewed by transmitted light. Also refers to the light transmitting power of the silver deposit in a negative and is the opposite of opacity (MPPF)

transportation: (1) the carriage or removal of persons or things by a conveyance on land, water, or in the air, e.g., by beast-, human- or animal-drawn sledge or vehicle, boat, railroad, automotive vehicle, or aircraft. Also, the material instruments involved (DOS) (2) a method of punishment originally devised by England for the most hardened criminals. It had a precedent in that country in the practice of outlawry whereby certain persons could escape hanging by abjuring the realm. It first received legislative sanction during the reign of the colonies of North America. When the American Revolution put an end to the practice, transportation to Australia was put into operation in 1787 (DOS)

Transportation Emergency Center, Chemical: for information dealing with hazardous chemicals involved in transportation accidents, *see* Chemtrec (LEV)

transportation thief: one who steals a motor vehicle which is used in the commission of another crime and then usually abandoned (LEV)

transvestism: sexual excitement obtained by wearing the clothing of the opposite sex and playing the role of that sex (LEV)

trap: (1) a device, usu. a switch, installed within a protected area, which serves as secondary protection in the event a perimeter alarm system is successfully penetrated. Examples are a trip wire switch placed across a likely path for an intruder, a mat switch hidden under a rug, or a magnetic switch mounted on an inner door (TDIAS) (2) a volumetric sensor installed so as to detect an intruder in a likely traveled corridor or pathway within a security area (TDIAS)

traverse: (1) a movement to the right or left on a pivot or mount, as of a gun, launcher, or radar antenna (DWMT) (2) to move or point a gun, launcher, radar antenna, or the like to the right or left on its pivot (DWMT) (3) a bank of earth in a trench to protect the occupants from enfilade fire and to localize the effect of shell bursts (DWMT)

traverse method: a method of sketching a scene, esp. an outdoor scene, where distances, contours, and locations of objects need to be shown. It requires the use of a sketchboard, compass, and an alidade (LEV)

tray siphon: a device for washing prints which projects a stream of water into a tray, and simultaneously siphons off an equal amount of hypo-laden water from the bottom of the tray (MPPF)

treason: the definition of and method of conviction for treason are carefully set down in Article III, Section 3 of the federal Constitution. By removing from Congress the power of defining treason the founding fathers sought to guarantee that charges of this heinous crime would not be lightly made. Treason against the United States can consist only in making war against it or assisting its enemies. No person may be convicted of treason except on the testimony of two witnesses to an overt act or on confession in open court. Congress is given the power to declare punishment for treason (DOAH)

trespass: unlawful entry into someone's property

trial: a formal hearing of a case by a court of law

trial, bench: a trial with a judge without a jury

trial by jury: a trial where the verdict is determined by a jury

trial by ordeal: in which the defendant was thrown into cold water; if he sank, he was deemed innocent, if he floated, guilty; if he could walk hoodwinked, unharmed over red hot irons, could drink with impunity the most deadly poisons, he was considered innocent (CDTP)

triangulation method: a method of sketching where the positions of two points are known and the third, which may be inaccessible, is determined by use of a sketchboard, alidade, and compass (LEV)

tribunal: a court or other body in which decisions binding on litigants are made (DAP)

trickle charge: a continuous direct current, usu. very low, which is applied to a battery to maintain it at peak charge or to recharge it after it has been partially or completely discharged. Usu. applied to nickel cadmium (NICAD) or wet cell batteries (TDIAS)

trifurcation: (in fingerprinting) a single ridge line which divides into three lines (LEV)

trigger: a metallic item, part of the firing mechanism of a crossbow or a firearm, designed to release a firing pin or the bowstring by the application of pressure by the finger (DWMT)

trigger guard: a protective device consisting of a curved framework, usu. of metal, on a gun or rocket launcher within which a trigger is located   (DWMT)

trigger housing: an item, usu. of metal, designed to fit into the framework of a carbine, machine gun, pistol, rifle, or the like. It is used to provide a mounting for a trigger   (DWMT)

trigger pull: the resistance offered by the trigger of a rifle or other weapon; the force which must be exerted to pull the trigger. Usu. expressed in pounds   (DWMT)

trigger squeeze: a method of firing a rifle or similar weapon in which the trigger is not pulled, but is squeezed gradually by an independent action of the forefinger   (DWMT)

trimming board: a device consisting of a board, a hinged blade, and a rule placed at right angles to the blade; used for trimming prints   (MPPF)

trip wire switch: a switch which is actuated by breaking or moving a wire or cord installed across a floor space   (TDIAS)

triple extension: applied to a camera whose bellows extension approaches three times the focal length of its lens   (MPPF)

truancy: the offense of a child absenting himself from school without acceptable excuse; habitual absence from school without leave; one of the types of child behavior constituting a strong factor leading to juvenile delinquency, and in most states of the United States specified by law as actually belonging in that category   (DOS)

truancy legislation, the first: the first legislation (state) was "an act to provide for the care and instruction of idle and truant children," enacted by New York on April 12, 1853 (Chapter 185). A fine of $50 was levied against parents whose children between the ages of 5 and 14 were absent from school   (FAMOUS)

truant officer: an employee of a board of education who enforces compulsory school attendance laws; called also attendance officer   (DAP)

truck inspection: the function of law enforcement requiring the on-the-road inspection of vehicles classified as trucks for conformance with laws and regulations   (TDPPC)

true bill: an indorsement made by a grand jury on a bill of indictment submitted by a prosecuting officer when the grand jury finds that sufficient reason exists to bring an accused person to trial   (DAP)

truncate: to cut off by discarding part of a number without rounding. Usu. applied to the low-order (right-hand) digits but may occur for high-order digits under some conditions   (ADPS)

tube: the main part of a gun; the cylindrical piece of metal surrounding the bore. The term "tube" is frequently used in referring to artillery weapons, and "barrel" is more frequently used in referring to small arms (DWMT)

tungsten: a metallic element of extremely high melting point used in the manufacture of incandescent electric lamps. In photography, tungsten is used to refer to artificial illumination as contrasted to daylight. For example, film emulsion speeds are given both in tungsten and daylight   (MPPF)

Tweed, William: as a New York City administrator, "Boss" Tweed formed a tight partnership with corrupt police, judges, and other city officials. It has been estimated that this group robbed the city of $200,000,000 prior to his arrest in 1871. Although Tweed died in jail, he is still considered one of the most successful political crooks of all time

twist, (of rifling): the inclination of the spiral grooves (rifling) to the axis of the bore of a weapon. It is expressed as the number of calibers of length in which the rifling makes one complete turn (DWMT)

two-for-one;   three-for-two: the combined use of the four bits of each numeric character to represent alphabetic characters with six bits each   (ADPS)

two-for-three: the combined use of twelve bits of two alphanumeric characters to represent three numeric characters   (ADPS)

type lines: (in fingerprinting) the two innermost ridges which start parallel, diverge, and surround or tend to surround the pattern area   (LEV)

typology: classification   scheme based on types

U

UL certificated: for certain types of products which have met UL requirements, for which it is impractical to apply the UL listing mark or classification marking to the individual product, a certificate is provided which the manufacturer may use to identify quantities of material for specific job sites or to identify field installed systems   (TDIAS)

UL listed: signifies that production samples of the product have been found to comply with established Underwriters   Laboratories   requirements and that the manufacturer is authorized to use the Laboratories' listing marks on the listed   products   which   comply with the requirements, contingent upon the follow-up services as a check of compliance   (TDIAS)

ulnar loop: a fingerprint pattern   (LEV)

ultimatum: a final proposition or demand which if not met will result in some action, occurrence, or resort to force   (LEV)

ultra vires [Lat]: beyond the legal authority allowed; acts done outside of legal authority. This term is used by courts in their decisions. It would apply in a situation where an officer does an unlawful act, which is beyond or outside of the authority granted him by the law, such as arresting, by an officer, outside of his jurisdiction and where he has no authority to do so. In a tort action brought by the injured person against the officer's employing agency the latter would claim that the acts of the officer were ultra vires   (LEV)

ultrasonic: pertaining to a sound wave having a frequency above that of audible sound (approximately   20,000   Hz).   Ultrasonic sound is used in ultrasonic detection systems   (TDIAS)

ultrasonic frequency: sound frequencies which are above the range of human hearing; approximately 20,000 Hz and higher   (TDIAS)

ultrasonic motion detector: a sensor which detects the motion of an intruder through the use of ultrasonic generating and receiving equipment. The device operates by filling a space with a pattern of ultrasonic waves; the modulation of these waves by a moving object is detected and initiates an alarm signal   (TDIAS)

ultraviolet filter: a filter which transmits ultraviolet light, as used for photography by the reflected ultraviolet light method   (MPPF)

ultraviolet light: light located in the spectrum beyond the violet end of the visible spectrum. Sometimes referred to as "black light." Used in law enforcement to detect certain fluorescent substances such as semen, invisible laundry marks, and other invisible writings. It is at the end of the spectrum opposite infrared light   (LEV)

ultraviolet rays: rays which comprise the visible portion of the electromagnetic spectrum just beyond the visible violet. Ultraviolet wavelengths are comparatively short and therefore disperse more easily than visible wavelengths. This is a factor to be taken into account in high altitude photography since these rays are photographically actinic (MPPF)

unarmed: the condition of a fuze (or other firing device) in which the necessary steps to put it in condition to function have not been taken. It is the condition of the fuze when it is safe for handling, storage, and transportation. The fuze is "partially armed" if some, but not all, of the steps have been taken (DWMT)

unconditional: without any conditions; for example, an unconditional statement is executed whenever it is encountered during a program (ADPS)

underdevelopment: insufficient development; due to developing either for too short a time in a weakened developer or, occasionally, at too low a temperature (MPPF)

underdome bell: a bell most of whose mechanism is concealed by its gong (TDIAS)

underexposure: the result of insufficient light being allowed to pass through the lens to produce all the tones of an image; or of sufficient light being allowed to pass for too short a period of time (MPPF)

underground: an organized group of people who carry on some regular operation without effective discovery by those in authority; the network to which these people belong (DWMT)

underworld: a semi-popular designation for the sub rosa existence of criminal activity, commercialized vice, gambling houses, places trafficking in contraband narcotics, and other interconnected illicit enterprises, such as bootlegging and "numbers racket." The criminal and pseudo-criminal elements constitute an underworld to the extent that association and activity take place outside the bounds of respectable society; hence, forming a sort of pariah caste. An underworld of crime and vice is likely to be a figment of the moral isolation of respectable from disreputable persons quite as much as a product of informal organization and association among the criminal elements (DOS)

Underwriters Laboratories, Inc. (UL): a private independent research and testing laboratory which tests and lists various items meeting good practice and safety standards (TDIAS)

undeveloped lead: a lead, clue, or investigation which remains to be done, which necessitates further investigation or inquiry. Some agencies list the undeveloped leads at the end of the investigative report (LEV)

Unger v. Sarafite, 376 U.S. 575 (1964): this court decision held that there was no violation of due process where the same judge presided at the trial and the contempt hearing of a witness openly critical of judicial control of the trial, despite the fact that a request for a continuance was refused and the offender permitted only five days to prepare for a defense. This decision makes excellent reading for a better understanding of the contempt power (AOJ)

Uniform Code of Military Justice: a comprehensive statement of the laws governing all the armed forces enacted by Congress in 1950, replacing the Articles of War and the Articles for the Government of the Navy, which also provides for a review of decisions of courts martial and for appeals to a newly created United States Court of Military Appeals (DAP)

uniform state laws: model statutes drafted by the Conference of Commissioners on Uniform Laws and enacted without amendment by all or several State legislatures, which are designed to substitute a series of uniform enactments on subjects like bills of lading, negotiable instruments, motor vehicle registration, and liability for accidents for conflicting laws of the states   (DAP)

Uniform System: a system of marking diaphragm aperture used until recently, in which an f/4 lens was marked U.S. 1; f/5.6 was equal to U.S. 2; f/8 equal to U.S. 4; f/11 equal to U.S. 8, etc.   (MPPF)

United Nations Standard Minimum Rules for the Treatment of Prisoners: adopted on Aug. 30, 1955 by the First United Nations Congress on the Prevention of Crime and the Treatment of Offenders, this document provides recommendations for the operation of penal facilities, as well as for the treatment of offenders   (CRP)

United States Attorney: the chief legal officer of the United States in the federal judicial district. He prosecutes violators of crimes against the United States and represents the federal government in civil matters. He acts under the direction of the U.S. Attorney General. There is one in each federal judicial district. His position is appointive. He usually has one or more assistants who have the title Assistant U.S. Attorney   (LEV)

United States Coast Guard: an essentially autonomous unit of the public forces of the United States, subject to the jurisdiction of the Department of Transportation in time of peace and of the Navy in time of war or national emergency. Although it is especially charged with the enforcement of the customs, navigation, and neutrality laws, it serves as a general law-enforcement agency upon navigable waters and high seas and protects life and property at sea   (DAP)

United States Code: a consolidation and codification of all the general and permanent laws of the United States in effect, classified by subject matter under 50 titles, prepared under the direction of the Judiciary Committee of the House of Representatives. A revision has appeared every six years since 1926, and a supplementary volume is issued after each session of Congress. Many of the titles have been enacted as law and, when all have been enacted, the *Code* will constitute legal evidence of all law   (DAP)

United States Commissioner: a federal magistrate. His functions in the federal field are comparable to those in state matters of the justice of the peace. He is not a judge and does not hold court. He may issue certain warrants, act as a committing official, set bail, and bind over for trial. His functions are prescribed by statute   (LEV)

United States Court of Claims: a special court consisting of a chief justice and four associates set up in 1855 with recommendatory powers only, granted jurisdiction in 1866 to decide claims against the government arising under contracts, and empowered in 1946 to decide certain kinds of cases involving torts by government employees   (DAP)

United States Court of Customs and Patent Appeals: a specialized court established in 1909 as the United States Court of Customs Appeals, given its present title and duties in 1929, and consisting of five justices, which reviews (a) decisions of the U.S. Customs Court on classifications and duties on imported merchandise; (b) decisions of the Patent Office on applications for, and interference with, patents and trademarks; and (c) legal questions in findings of the U.S. Tariff Commission concerning unfair practices in import trade   (DAP)

United States Customs Court: a court created in 1890 as the Board of the United States General Appraisers and given its present title in 1926, which consists of nine judges sitting in New York City, and which has sole jurisdiction over the interpretation of tariff laws, the classification of merchandise, and the determination of the dutiable valuation of imported goods. In 1956 it was made a court of record under Article III of the Constitution (DAP)

United States District Courts: trial courts with original jurisdiction over diversity-of-citizenship cases, and cases arising under U.S. criminal, bankruptcy, admiralty, patent, copyright, and postal laws. There are 89 District Courts in the United States and Puerto Rico, each having from one to 24 judges, a total of 303. Normally, one district judge presides over each trial, but three-judge District Courts are necessary for the issuance of injunctions concerning certain subjects. From District Courts the normal course of appeals is to a court of appeals, but some decisions holding statutes unconstitutional, certain criminal cases, and the injunction orders of three-judge District Courts may be appealed directly to the Supreme Court (DAP)

United States Fish and Wildlife Service: a division of the Department of the Interior, dating from the consolidation in 1940 of the Bureau of Biological Survey and the Bureau of Sport Fisheries and Wildlife, which carries on research and wildlife conservation programs and is charged esp. with the preservation of a vigorous fishing industry, the enforcement of international agreements relating to fur seals and commercial fish, and the conservation, for economic and recreational purposes, of various kinds of wild life (DAP)

United States Marshal: a federal law enforcement officer of the federal judicial district. He is appointed by the President and approved by the U.S. Senate and is under the supervision of the U.S. Attorney General. His duties at the federal level are somewhat comparable to that of the sheriff at the county level. His duties include making arrests for federal crimes, maintaining custody of federal prisoners awaiting trial, transporting federal prisoners to and from jail and the courts as well as to and from federal penal institutions, maintaining order in federal courts, and executing the orders of the federal judges. There is one in each federal judicial district. He may have one or more deputies who bear the title Deputy U.S. Marshal. (LEV)

United States Reports: the official printed record of cases heard and decided by the U.S. Supreme Court which usu. include a statement of the essential facts of each case, the opinion of the Court, concurring and dissenting opinions, if any, the disposition made of each case, and occasionally an abstract of counsel's briefs. Originally a series of *Reports*, with volumes numbered consecutively, was issued during the incumbency of each successive court reporter and these are cited as Dallas (1790-1800); Cranch (1801-1815); Wheaton (1816-1827); Peters (1828-1843); Howard (1843-1860); Black (1861-1862); and Wallace (1863-1874). By 1874, when the number of volumes so identified totalled 90, the practice began of eliminating the reporter's name and citing them as *United States Reports* (DAP)

United States Statutes at Large: an official compilation of the acts and resolutions of each session of Congress published by the Office of the Federal Register in the National Archives and Records Service. It consists of two parts, the first comprising public acts and joint resolutions, the second, private acts and joint resolutions, concurrent resolutions, treaties, and Presidential proclamations (DAP)

United States v. Ash, 413 U.S. 300, 37 L. Ed. 2d 619, 93 S. Ct. 1568 (1973): in this opinion by Mr. Justice Blackmun, the Court held, 6-3, that a defendant has no right

to the presence of counsel at a pretrial photographic array conducted by the government for identification purposes. (Remember a state court may set a higher standard. For example, the Michigan Supreme Court, in a unanimous opinion, People v. Jackson, 391 Mich. 323, 217 N.W. 2d 22, 1974, held that photo showups are even less reliable than live line-ups, and that a photographic display should ordinarily not be used. But when they must, in-custody suspects are entitled to counsel whenever witnesses are presented with a photographic display.)   (ILECJ)
United States v. Calandra, 414 U.S. 338, 38 L. Ed. 2d 561, 94 S. Ct. 613 (1974): Justice Powell in a 6-3 opinion says the purpose of the Fourth Amendment exclusionary rule is to deter improper law enforcement conduct. See United States v. Peltier, — U.S. —, 45 L. Ed. 2d 374, 95 S. Ct. 2313 (1975) wherein Justice Brennan in his dissenting opinion repeats this point of view. (In the past, the Court has relied upon three conceptually distinct considerations in support of the rule—the individual's right to the exclusion of evidence, the constitutional role of the judiciary, and the deterrence of unconstitutional police practices. *Calandra* and *Peltier* view the rule solely as a deterrence mechanism.)   (ILECJ)
United States v. Chavez, 416 U.S. 562, 40 L. Ed. 2d 380, 94 S. Ct. 1849 (1974): the Court held (Mr. Justice Douglas with whom JJ. Brennan, Stewart, and Marshall join, concurring in part and dissenting in part) that where application for wiretap order was authorized by Executive Assistant Attorney General rather than Attorney General or specially designated Assistant Attorney General, statutory requirements were not met and evidence obtained under order was properly suppressed; but that where Attorney General

has in fact authorized wiretap application and court order incorrectly identifies Assistant Attorney General as authorizing official does not require that evidence obtained under order be suppressed   (ILECJ)
United States v. Giordano, 416 U.S. 505, 40 L.Ed. 2d 341, 94 S. Ct. 1820 (1974): the Court held (Mr. Justice Powell with whom Chief Justice Burger, Justices Blackmun, and Rehnquist join, concurring in part) that evidence obtained under a wiretap had to be suppressed because the tap was authorized by the Attorney General's executive assistant, not by the Attorney General or a designated Assistant Attorney General as required by Title III of the Omnibus Crime Control and Safe Streets Act of 1968, 18 U.S.C. 2516 (1) (ILECJ)
United States v. Harris, 403 U.S. 573, 29 L. Ed. 2d 723, 91 S. Ct. 2075 (1971): the Court through Chief Justice Burger held, 5-4, that probable cause to search a suspected moonshiner's premises was established by an affidavit based largely on hearsay obtained by the affiant from a "prudent person" who had recent "personal knowledge" of the suspect's illegal whiskey sales and admitted having made several purchases of illegal whiskey from the suspect; magistrate who issued the warrant was entitled to consider, in determining whether probable cause existed, the affiant's knowledge of the suspect's reputation "as . . . a trafficker in non-taxpaid spirits." (Summed up, a policeman's knowledge of a suspect's reputation may be relied on in evaluating the reliability of an informant's tip. The decision, to this extent, modifies *Spinelli* v. *United States.*)   (ILECJ)
United States v. Matlock, 415 U.S. 164, 39 L. Ed. 2d 242, 94 S. Ct. 988 (1974): a majority of the Court through Mr. Justice White upheld the introduction in evidence of materials seized during

the warrantless search of a bedroom because the common law wife of the defendant had consented to the search   (ILECJ)
United States v. Robinson, 414 U.S. 218, 38 L. Ed. 2d 427, 94 S. Ct. 467; Gustafson v. Florida, 414 U.S. 260, 38 L. Ed. 2d 456, 94 S. Ct. 488 (1973): the Court upheld, 6-3, searches incident to full custody arrests in which arrests had been made on traffic code violations. (Some states are requiring higher standards in searches incident to traffic arrests.) (ILECJ)
United States v. United States District Court, Eastern Michigan, 407 U.S. 297, 32 L. Ed. 752, 92 S. Ct. 2125 (1972): the Court, 6-2, in an opinion by Mr. Justice Powell, refuses to approve warrentless bugging of domestic "subversives." Chief Justice Burger and Justice White wrote concurring opinions. Mr. Justice Rehnquist did not participate (The case was one involving Lawrence Plamondon, a member of the White Panthers who was accused of dynamiting a branch office of the Central Intelligence Agency in Ann Arbor, Mich. The Government acknowledged he had been the subject of wiretapping.) (ILECJ)
United States v. Wade, 338 U.S. 218, 18 L. Ed. 2d 1149, 87 S. Ct. 1926 (1967): in a decision marked by a galaxy of concurring in part and dissenting in part opinions, a majority of the Court held that police line-ups constitute a critical stage of the prosecutorial process, and the Sixth Amendment right to counsel attaches at that time, applicable to the states through due process of the Fourteenth Amendment   (ILECJ)
United States v. White, 401 U.S. 745, 28 L. Ed. 2d 453, 91 S. Ct. 1122 (1971): Justice White's opinion approves of warrantless use of informant, and refuses to overrule *On Lee* (1952) and *Lopez* (1963). (The opinion was joined by the Chief Justice and Justices Stewart and Blackmun, and separate concurring opinions were filed by Justices Brennan and Black. Justice Brennan concurred solely on the separate ground that *Katz* should not be applied retroactively, while Justice Black concurred in the result on the grounds that the Fourth Amendment could not be expanded to protect against electronic surveillance. Federal Bureau of Investigation agents testified over objection to incriminating statements made by the defendant and transmitted by an electronic eavesdropping device worn by a government informer. The informer was not available at the trial to testify as to his conversation with the defendant.)   (ILECJ)
universal developer: a developer which will give satisfactory results on films, plates, and photographic papers   (MPPF)
unlawful: contrary to law; illegal
unlawful entry: a less serious type of burglary; entering an open or unlocked building without authority or legal right   (LEV)
unlawful flight to avoid giving testimony: a federal law making it a felony to travel to another state or nation to avoid giving testimony as a material witness in a criminal proceeding in which a felony is charged under the state laws. This is also called the Fugitive Witness Act   (LEV)
unlawful flight to avoid prosecution: a federal law making it a felony for any person charged by a state with violation of a felony, under the state law, to travel to another state or nation for the purpose of avoiding prosecution. It is also called the Fugitive Felon Act   (LEV)
unmarked car: a vehicle which is not marked to identify it as belonging to a law enforcement agency   (TDPPC)
unnatural offense: sodomy or buggery
unoccupied premises and abandoned articles: a search upon un-

occupied premises without a search warrant violates no right of defendants found thereupon violating the law. Likewise the seizure of an article abandoned by accused does not violate the guaranty (265 U.S. 57)   (CDTP)

unreasonable searches and seizures: searches of persons and places and seizure of papers and effects without search warrants properly sworn to, issued by judicial officers, and particularly describing the places to be searched and the persons or things seized. Wiretapping and the use of a stomach pump are considered unreasonable searches; but blood tests for alcohol, and seizures made immediately after a proper arrest when objects wanted as evidence are in plain sight or danger exists that wrongdoers might escape, because of the delay necessary to obtain a warrant, are considered unreasonable. Since 1967, the courts have broadened the range of items that might be seized in a lawful search and used as evidence. The Fourth Amendment prohibits unreasonable searches and seizures, and the provision against self-incrimination in the Fifth Amendment prohibits the use of illegally seized articles as evidence against an accused person   DAP)

unwritten law: a supposed rule that the murder of a wife's paramour, or of a daughter's seducer, is not a criminal offense

urban: relative to towns or cities

urban guerrilla: a term applied to terrorists who, motivated by some political idea, commit arson, bomb, kidnap, murder, and hijack air planes   (LEV)

use of force: all necessary force, even to the taking of life, may be used to effect an arrest or prevent an escape in cases of felony, and all necessary force, short of taking life, may be used, in cases of misdemeanor. In no case can unnecessary force be used   (CDTP)

usury: a charge made since ancient times for the use of money lent to or deposited with an individual or institution, generally computed annually or for fractions of a year. This charge has always aroused resentment because of the high rates imposed and the heavy penalties for defection. It is difficult to determine the criteria of usury because it is fixed by the ethical norms prevailing in a given culture; this is especially true in a liberal economy where transactions are voluntary   (DOS)

utility routines: subroutines for handling machine operations necessary to data processing but not contributing directly to the output—for example, labeling tapes, loading and organizing disks, clearing storage, printing, copying, and converting from one data media to another   (ADPS)

utmost resistance: to resist to the fullest extent. This is a term used in connection with the crime of rape where the law frequently requires that the victim must have resisted to the utmost   (LEV)

utter: to offer a forged instrument as one that is genuine

V

v., vs. [*Lat*] : versus; against

Vacutainer: trade name for a blood collection system used for collecting blood specimens for laboratory testing of blood for alcohol content   (LEV)

vagrancy: except where defined by statute, the behavior of a person without permanent social attachments; aimless wandering of an individual without visible means of legitimate self-support

At common law vagrancy means wandering about from place to place by an idle person who has no visible means of support, and who subsists on charity and does not work, though able to do so. But the connotations of vagrancy have been extended by statutory regulations so as to include other forms of behavior than that cited above. It would appear that vagrancy is the broadest of the categories of offense. To enumerate but a few of the types of conduct for which vagrancy charges have been sustained, the following may be cited: prostitution, gambling, fortune-telling, drunkeness, begging, and many other forms of behavior are deemed socially undesirable, if not dangerous. Though the charge of vagrancy may not be sustained if the alleged offender has regular employment, or is wandering in search of it, it is to be noted that in times of business depression convictions for vagrancy manifest a sharp increase in industrial areas (DOS)

vagrant: an unattached, itinerary, and indigent person. The several types are variously described on the basis of behavior or appearance. For example, "The hobo works and wanders; the tramp dreams and wanders; and the bum drinks and wanders." The hobo, an itinerant worker who may on occasion be a mendicant, is now practically nonexistent. The homeless indigent types change from one period to another and are different in different localities. The vagrant is so identified because he presents a problem to the security of a community because he is homeless, voteless, without local interests and there is strong presumption that he is or may become a delinquent (DOS)

values, initial: the information represented by a data item, arithmetic expression, or conditional expression before manipulation in the object program (ADPS)

vapor pressure: the gas pressure, normally expressed in barometric units (equivalent *millimetres of mercury*), of the vapor above the surface of a liquid. It rises with temperature, and is equal to the atmospheric pressure at the boiling point of the liquid (FS)

variable: in COBOL, a named data item in storage that assumes different values during execution of the object program (ADPS)

variable-length field: the number of characters used for each item of data is just the number needed for it; there is no need to fill the item of data out to a certain length. Item separators indicate the end of each item. Punched-paper tape uses blanks for separators between items in ordinary communication, but an explicit symbol (not a blank) must be used as an item separator for data on tape read into a processor (ADPS)

VASCAR: abbreviation for Visual Average Speed Computer and Recorder. An electronic device, manually activated, which measures quantities of distance and time and computes the resultant speed (LEV)

vault: a place of security, generally built of steel and/or concrete, for safe storage of valuables. There has been constant competition between burglars and businesses. The latter have sought to develop vaults and safes which were burglar-proof and the safe burglars have worked for ways to overcome such protective devices (LEV)

vehicle: (1) a means of conveyance. The self-propelled vehicle is the one of the most concern in law enforcement (LEV) (2) a person in an illegal enterprise who is used by an undercover man to furnish information about the operation and who introduces the undercover man to other persons operating in the enterprise (LEV)

vehicle armor: a missile-resistant material that can be installed on a vehicle to protect its occupants from gunfire (TDPPC)

vehicle identification number (VIN): a permanent and unique number assigned to and placed on each vehicle by an automotive manufacturer for identification purposes. It may indicate the vehicle's model, engine displacement, place and year of manufacturer, and sequence in the manufacturer's production (TDPPC)

velocity: (1) speed at which a thing moves (LEV) (2) the speed of a bullet in flight (LEV) (3) the speed of a projectile, usu. measured in feet per second

vendetta: a feud in which the blood relatives of the person who has been injured or killed take action against the offender or members of his family (LEV)

vendor: one who transfers property, esp. real, through sale

venereal disease: a disease associated with the sexual act; a disease which is spread through sexual intercourse with an infected person. Gonorrhea and syphilis are two of such diseases (LEV)

venire, venire facias: an ancient writ for summoning jurymen (DAP)

venireman: a member of a jury; a juror summoned by a writ of *venire facias*

venue: the locality in which a case is tried

Vera Institute of Justice: a non-profit research organization devoted to the improvement of the administration of criminal justice. It was started in Oct. 1961 in New York by Louis Schweitzer. It started the Manhattan Bail Project (LEV)

veracity: truthfulness (LEV)

verb: in COBOL, an instruction word that specifies one or more operations to be performed by a data processor (ADPS)

verbal: oral; consisting merely of words; spoken words (LEV)

verbatim: the same words in the same order; word for word (LEV)

verdict: the decision of the jury in the trial of either civil or criminal cases (DAP)

Verdugo v. U.S., 402 F. 2d 599 (C.A. Cal. 1968), certiorari denied 402 U.S. 961, 91 S. Ct. 1623, 29 L. Ed. 2d 124 (1971): contra *United States v. Schipani,* 435 F. 2d 26 (C A N Y, 1970), certorari denied 410 U.S. 983, 91 S. Ct. 1198, 28 L. Ed. 2d 334: information obtained under violation of Fourth Amendment rights was considered by the judge in imposing sentence. The sentence was reversed and the defendant returned for resentencing without the consideration of illegal evidence

verify: (1) to prove to be true; to confirm (CDTP) (2) to check, usu. with an automatic machine, one typing or recording of data against another in order to minimize the number of human errors or mistakes in the data transcription (ADPS) (3) in preparing data for a processor, to make certain that data prepared are correct (ADPS)

Vernier Scale: a device used on a camera to indicate distance (MPPF)

vibrating bell: a bell whose mechanism is designed to strike repeatedly and for as long as it is activated (TDIAS)

vibration detection system: an alarm system which employs one or more contact microphones or vibration sensors which are fastened to the surfaces of the area or object being protected to detect excessive levels of vibration. The contact microphone system consists of microphones, a control unit containing an amplifier and an accumulator, and a power supply. The unit's sensitivity is adjustable so that ambient noises or normal vibrations will not initiate an alarm signal. In the vibration sensor system, the sensor responds to excessive vibration by opening a switch in a closed circuit system (TDIAS)

vibration sensor: a sensor which responds to vibrations of the surface on which it is mounted. It has a normally closed switch which will momentarily open when it is subjected to a vibration with sufficiently large amplitude. Its sensitivity is adjustable to allow for the different levels of normal vibration, to which the sensor should not respond, at different locations. *See also* vibration detection system   (TDIAS)

vice, commercialized: as customarily used in sociological studies, the business of prostitution. Prostitution shows varying degrees of commercialization, all the way from independent conduct of prostitution by [women] themselves to exploitation of prostitutes in brothels or syndicated houses of prostitution. In some Oriental countries the business of prostitution has been accepted as an institution. In Western countries, either it has been tolerated as a part of police policy, or it has had illegal status, in which latter instance it has been the object of suppressive measures of law enforcement   (DOS)

vice squad: a special detail of American police, charged with raiding and closing houses of prostitution and gambling resorts. The vice squads are likely to become unusually active in law enforcement campaigns   (DOS)

victim: person who has been kidnapped, swindled, defrauded, robbed, suffered other types of wrong by criminal acts or injured in traffic accident   (LEV)

victimless crimes: crimes without an official victim, such as prostitution or homosexuality

view finder: a viewing instrument attached to a camera, used to obtain proper composition   (MPPF)

vigilante: a member of a group which undertakes to enforce the law and/or maintain morals, without legal authority for such actions   (LEV)

vignetting: underexposure of the extreme edges of a photographic image; occasionally caused by improper design of lenses or too small a sunshade; also sometimes intentionally done in portraiture   (MPPF)

violence: that force which is employed against common right, against law, and against public property   (CDTP)

violent death: unlike natural death it is death resulting from the acts of other humans. It may be caused or hastened by such humans; death resulting from unusual forces   (LEV)

visible light: the small portion of electromagnetic radiation which is visible to the human eye. Approximately the wave lengths from 400 to 700 millimicrons   (MPPF)

visible prints: fingerprints composed of a deposit of a visible substance or stain left by soiled fingers. These may be left by blood, dirt, oil, stains, etc., being on the fingers   (LEV)

visual signal device: a pilot light, annunciator, or other device which provides a visual indication of the condition of the circuit or system being supervised   (TDIAS)

visual surveillance: keeping watch or observing people, places, or vehicles. These may be (a) fixed, where the watchers are located in a stationary or semistationary place of concealment such as a house or a parked vehicle, and (b) a moving surveillance where the person or vehicle is kept under observation by investigators, either on foot or in a vehicle   (LEV)

voice identification: one may become so familiar with the voice of another that the speaker can be identified. In order for testimony on voice recognition to be admissible in court, a foundation must be laid by testimony that the witness has talked by phone or has otherwise heard the person speak and that the witness does recognize the person's voice when he hears it   (LEV)

voiceprint: a spectrographic record of the energy output produced by the sound of words or sounds made by a person when speaking. Allegedly it is distinctive for each person   (LEV)

Vollmer, August (*1876-1955*): Entered law enforcement as a town marshal and served as Berkely, California's first police chief in 1909. Assisted in the creation of the State Bureau of Criminal Identification. Promoted a police school in conjunction with the U. of Calif. in 1916. Was appointed Professor of Police Administration at the U. of Chicago in 1929 accepting a similar position at the U. of Calif. in 1931, resigning in 1938.

voir dire: the preliminary examination of a prospective juror in order to determine his or her qualifications to serve as a juror

Volstead Act: also known as the National Prohibition Act; passed by Congress in 1919. Its enactment was a result of the authorization conferred upon Congress by the Eighteenth Amendment. The law prohibited the manufacture, transportation, and sale of beverages containing more than .5 percent alcohol. It fixed penalties for sales of liquor and provided for injunctions against public places which dispensed liquor in violation of the law. Private stocks bought before the Act went into effect could be retained. The Act was roundly condemned by a large segment of the American people as an invasion of their constitutional rights. One of the most unfortunate consequences of its passage was the development of widespread violations accompanied by gangsterism and crime (DOAH)

Voltaire, Francois Marie Arouet (*1694–1778*): one of the world's greatest philosophers, this Frenchman recommended that there be a reduction of the death and infamy punishments, a means of making all penalties more socially useful, and having a legislation free of outside influences. Voltaire stated that only those acts which are contrary to society's survival should be considered criminal and that all punishments should be proportional to the crime committed

volumetric sensor: a sensor with a detection zone which extends over a volume such as an entire room, part of a room, or a passageway. Ultrasonic motion detectors and sonic motion detectors are examples of volumetric sensors (TDIAS)

vomiting agents: war gases and mob- and riot-control gases, such as DA, DM, and DC. These three vomiting agents are normally solids which, when heated, vaporize and then condense to form toxic aerosols. Under field conditions, vomiting agents cause great discomfort to their victims; when released indoors, they may cause serious illness or death. The vomiting agents are also used for mob and riot control (DWMT)

voyeur: a peeping tom; a peeper; one who gets sex gratification from seeing the sex organs of another, esp. of the opposite sex, or seeing the act of sexual intercourse (LEV)

V.P.C.: vapor-phase chromatography (FS)

W

wad: a felt or cardboard pad used to secure the propellant in place in cartridges. It was used formerly in muzzle-loading cannons and other firearms to retain a charge of powder or to keep the powder and host close (DWMT)

wad cutter: a bullet designed for target shooting and shaped to cut a clean hole in a paper target (DWMT)

wait, lie in: to conceal oneself, or stay hidden, ready to attack. The Louisiana "Attempt" statute provides that lying in wait with a dangerous weapon with intent to commit a crime constitutes an attempt to commit the offense intended (LEV)

walk test light: a light on motion detectors which comes on when the detector senses motion in the area. It is used while setting the sensitivity of the detector and during routine checking and maintenance (TDIAS)

walking line: one of the elements of the walking picture. An imaginary line which in normal and ideal walking fuses with the direction line and runs along the inner sides of both heelprints (LEV)

walking picture: the study of the characteristics of footprints left by a person walking. Included in this study are the direction line, the walking line, and the foot line (LEV)

Walnut Street Jail: erected in Philadelphia in 1773, it was later called a "penitentiary." Unlike previous prisons, this penitentiary received convicted felons from a state-wide area and kept its prisoners at hard labor in solitary confinement. It was expected that prisoners in solitary confinement could meditate upon their evil ways and become penitent. This institution served as a model of humane penal reform which was widely adopted by European penologists. Among the characteristics that were most impressive were the facts that prisoners were paid for their work, men and women prisoners were separated, corporal punishment was forbidden, and religious instruction required

wanton: reckless; malicious; without regard to the rights of others (CDTP)

war, tong: violent conflict between rival Chinese groups or tongs. Such groups or societies in the United States are a transfer from China where they are based upon kinship, district, or other forms of affiliation. They often serve useful purposes in business or social welfare. But through business rivalry, or efforts to control illicit forms of gain in relation to vice, gambling, or the opium traffic, some of the tongs become involved in criminal violence. Membership in the tongs may consist in part of merchants who are forced to join in order to get protection from rival tongs who seek control over their business. Tong wars ensue. *Cf.* racketeer (DOS)

war crimes: during WWII the first statement by the United Nations that war crimes would be punished after the war was made in the Moscow Declaration on Oct. 30, 1943. Subsequently the United Nations Commission for the Investigation of War Crimes was established to compile lists of suspected war criminals. It classified two groups of crimes: those against the nationals of a state, the trial of which was to be held by national courts or military tribunals, and those international in scope, to be tried by special international courts under military law. In Aug. 1945, the United States, England, France, and the Soviet Union adopted a statute for trying the principal Nazi civil and military leaders. These nations established the Nuremberg Tribunal which opened its hearings on Nov. 20, 1945, for the trial of 24 top Nazi leaders. Associate Justice Robert H. Jackson, on leave from the U.S. Supreme Court, was the prosecutor. War crimes had been defined as plotting aggressive war, atrocities against civilians, genocide, slave labor, looting of occupied countries, and the maltreatment and murder of war prisoners. Voluminous evidence was introduced to the trial, and sentence of death was imposed on Oct. 1, 1946 upon Goering, Streicher, Ribbentrop, and eight others. Seven were sentenced to imprisonment. No convictions were handed down against Nazi organizations or the German general staff. On June 3, 1945 trial was opened in Tokyo by an 11-man international tribunal against 28 Japanese indicted as war criminals. On Nov. 12, 1948, sentence was handed down against 25, and on Dec. 23, 1948 former Premier Tojo and six others were hanged in Tokyo after the failure of their appeal to the U.S. Supreme Court. During this period concurrent trials were held in German and Japanese courts which, by 1950, had tried more than 8,000 war criminals and executed 2,000 of them. The number of trials declined thereafter, and by 1952 many appeals by the convicted had resulted in reversals (DOAH)

warden: a minor administrative official (as the warden of a penitentiary or a game or air-raid warden) with duties of guarding, conserving, or protecting persons or property or of law enforcement (DAP)

Warden v. Hayden, 387 U.S. 294, 18 L. Ed. 2d 782, 87 S. Ct. 1642 (1967): in an 8-1 decision, the Supreme Court decided that officials may use as evidence in courts items such as clothing seized by the police in lawful searches of the residences of suspects. The Court, in short, abrogated the "mere evidence" rule. (This decision shows a "shift" in Fourth Amendment emphasis from property to privacy and redounds to the benefit of law enforcement officials as well as their quarry. The police can seize more things, but an accused can challenge more kinds of evil.) (ILECJ)

warning shot: the firing of a weapon in the air or into the ground or street as a warning to a fleeing person that unless he stops the next shots may be directed at him. The purpose is to frighten the running person so he will stop. Many police agencies have a policy against this. It seldom works in stopping the running person and may injure bystanders (LEV)

warrant: a written order issued by a magistrate or court directing an officer to make an arrest or conduct searches or seizures. Constitutional restrictions prevent the issuance of a search warrant except for good cause, duly certified, and the warrant must describe the place to be searched and the person or property to be seized. See unreasonable searches and seizures (DAP)

Warren Commission: appointed in 1963 by President Johnson to investigate the assassination of President John F. Kennedy and the murder of Lee Harvey Oswald, the alleged assassin. Headed by Chief Justice Earl Warren, the Commission included Allen W. Dulles, former head of the CIA; John J. McCloy, former adviser to President Kennedy; Senators Russell and Cooper; and Representatives Boggs and Ford. A report released on Sept. 27, 1964 concluded that Lee Harvey Oswald was solely responsible for the murder of President Kennedy on Nov. 22, 1963. The Commission also recommended major changes in the methods used to protect the life of the President (DOAH)

watch and ward: an early system of law enforcement used in England in the towns and cities. Citizens took turns serving as watchmen (LEV)

watchman's reporting system: a supervisory alarm system arranged for the transmission of a patrolling watchman's regularly recurrent report signals from stations along his patrol route to a central supervisory agency (TDIAS)

watermark: a design worked into certain kinds of paper. It can be seen by holding the paper so it is viewed against a bright light. It is usu. put in the paper by the manufacturer and the manufacturer may be identified by such watermark. This is one of the factors or characteristics of paper determined by a crime laboratory examination of the paper. A lead may be obtained by tracing such paper from the manufacturer through the retailer (LEV)

wavenumber: a number inversely proportional to the wavelength of a radiation, and therefore proportional to the frequency. Commonly used instead of wavelength in specifying infra-red radiation used in spectrophotometry (FS)

weak: applied to a negative which is thin due to underexposure or underdevelopment (MPPF)

weapon: an instrument used in fighting; an instrument of offensive or defensive combat. The term is chiefly used, in law, in the statutes prohibiting the carrying of "concealed" or deadly weapons (CDTP)

wear tables: tables indicating the decrease of muzzle velocity expected as the result of firing a certain number of equivalent rounds. Although tubes may vary considerably from the wear rate indicated in such tables, the tables may be used to correct calibration data between periods of calibration (DWMT)

Weathermen: a militant faction of the Students for a Democratic Society (SDS). It splintered from SDS in June, 1969 at Ann Arbor, Mich. (LEV)

Weeks v. United States, 232 U.S. 383, 58 L. Ed. 652, 341 S. Ct. 341 (1914): the court held unanimously, speaking through Mr. Justice Day, that in a federal prosecution the Fourth Amendment barred the use of evidence secured through an illegal search and seizure (The Court unequivocally declared, moreover, that the Constitution did not protect against unreasonable searches by state officers. The decision's exclusionary rule has been viewed by most legal commentators as a judicially conceived rule of evidence without any basis in either the explicit re-

quirements of the Constitution, or on legislation expressing Congressional policy in the enforcement of the Constitution.) (ILECJ)

Weems v. United States, 217 U.S. 349, 30 S. Ct. 544, 54 L. Ed. 793 (1909): in applying the Eighth Amendment on cruel and unusual punishment, the Supreme Court emphasized that standards of cruelty, etc., must be defined in modern terms, not according to what was cruel at the time of the writing of the Constitution

weight of evidence: the preponderance of evidence

Welch, Joseph Nye (1890–1960) [lawyer]: born in Primghar, Iowa, on Oct. 22, 1890, Welch graduated from Grinnel College in 1914 and from the Harvard Law School three years later. Admitted to the Mass. bar in 1918, he became within a very few years a noted trial lawyer, dealing mostly in civil cases. Welch first gained national fame in 1954 as special counsel for the U.S. Army in the congressional Army-McCarthy hearings of that year. He was appointed counsel for the army on April 2, and the hearings continued from April 22 until June 17. With many of the sessions televised—a recent innovation for congressional committee proceedings—the hearings became one of the most engrossing and sensational spectacles ever offered the American public. Since early 1950 Senator Joseph R. McCarthy of Wisconsin had been making allegations of subversion and treason in places high and low in American life, particularly in the federal government. Early in 1954, by that time chairman of the Senate's permanent investigations subcommittee, he turned his attention to the military, charging that there was a spy ring at work in the Army Signal Corps installation at Fort Monmouth, N.J. Eventually the case boiled down to that of a New York City dentist who had been drafted during the Korean War, promoted to the rank of major, and given honorable discharge, in spite of his having taken the Fifth Amendment when questioned about alleged Communist activities at an earlier period. McCarthy leveled an attack upon the general in command at Fort Monmouth, then at the army itself, alleging that the secretary of the army had concealed evidence of spying. Countercharges against McCarthy and his aides were filed, and the hearings themselves ranged at large over the topic of supposed subversion. For television viewers the affair dissolved into a contest between Senator McCarthy and Joseph Welch. McCarthy revealed himself as a master of vicious invective, irresponsible charges, and pointless vituperation, while Welch remained for the most part calm, logical, and occasionally cutting. Only after McCarthy made a particularly nasty accusation against one of Welch's assistants did the lawyer respond with the most memorable statement to come out of the sessions: "Until this moment, Senator, I think I never really gauged your cruelty or recklessness. . . . Have you no sense of decency?" The hearings were McCarthy's undoing, although he and his staff were cleared of the charges against them. On Dec. 2, 1954, the Senate, by a vote of 67 to 22, passed a resolution of condemnation against him for misconduct, and his influence rapidly faded thereafter. The charges against the dentist were forgotten, and Welch returned to his law practice in Boston a national figure. Five years later he returned to public view playing the part of a trial judge in the 1959 movie *Anatomy of A Murder* He died in Hyannis, Mass. on Oct. 6, 1960. (*Webster's American Biographies*) **wergild**: the worth of a man injured by another according to the man's station in society. The wergild was the amount of compensation the

offender was compelled to pay the injured or his representative in order to compose the difficulty. If the wergild was not paid, private retaliation could then be exercised against the offender and his kin by the injured and his kin (DOS) **what constitutes an arrest**: there must be actual restraint of the person arrested, or else he must submit to the custody of the officer or person arresting. Mere words are not sufficient, there must submit. Merely to say to the person of the accused, or he must submit. To merely say to him he is under arrest is not enough if he does not submit, but it is sufficient if the officer touches him, however lightly (81 Amer. Dec. 672), and it is enough if the officer, being in a room with the accused, tells him that he is under arrest, and locks the door. If the accused afterwards runs off he is guilty of an escape (CDTP) **white collar crime**: a term first used by criminologist Edwin H. Sutherland to cover business crimes such as embezzlement, price fixing, antitrust violations, etc. **white slave traffic—Mann Act**: the act is comprised in Sections 197 to 404 of the Federal Criminal Code. It punishes by the fine of $5,000 or imprisonment for five years or both, any person who knowingly transports or causes to be transported or assists in obtaining transportation for any woman or girl for the purpose of prostitution or debauchery or for any other immoral purpose or with the intent to induce such woman or girl, or who aids in procuring transportation to be used by any such woman or girl, in interstate or foreign commerce. The act includes inducing, enticing, or coercing a woman or girl to go from one place to another in interstate or foreign commerce for immoral purposes. The act received the cooperation of many foreign nations at the Paris conference on May 18, 1904. It has been used as an instrument for blackmail by prostitutes working bordering states and has proven difficult of enforcement though a very effective weapon for the suppression of the vice it was designed to suppress. The importation of women from foreign countries for the purpose of prostitution or for any other immoral purpose is prohibited by the federal law governing aliens and immigration; the law prohibits the traffic and includes within its scope the keeping, controlling, or harboring of any woman imported for such purposes. (U.S. Code, Title 8, Sec. 138) (CDTP)

Whiteley v. Warden, 401 U.S. 560, 28 L. Ed. 2d 306, 91 S. Ct. 1031 (1971): the Court through Mr. Justice Harlan held, 6–3, that a police radio broadcast based on an affidavit insufficient for issuance of an arrest warrant cannot furnish probable cause to arrest the suspect described in the broadcast. (Reasonable grounds requirements in a warrantless arrest are at least as stringent—if not more so—than need be recited in a complaint for issuance of an arrest warrant. See also *Beck* v. *Ohio, Hill* v. *California,* and *Chambers* v. *Maroney.*) (ILECJ)

who may claim immunity: since immunity to unreasonable searches and seizures is a privilege personal to those whose rights thereunder have been infringed, they alone may invoke it against illegal searches and seizures. Thus one cannot complain of an illegal search or seizure of premises or property which he neither owns nor leases nor controls, nor lawfully occupies, nor rightfully possesses, or in which he has no interest (279 Fed. 98; C.J. 56, 1174.) (CDTP)

who may testify: all persons are competent to testify in cases except as follows: if, in the opinion of the judge, he is prevented by extreme youth, disease affecting the mind, or any other cause of the same kind from recollecting the matter on which he is to testify, from understanding the questions put to him, from giving rational answers to those questions, or from knowing that he ought to speak the truth. A witness unable to speak or hear is not incompetent, but may give his evidence by writing, or by signs, or in any other manner in which he can make it intelligible, but such writing must be written and such signs made in open court. Evidence so given is deemed to be oral evidence. Generally a husband or wife cannot be a witness against his spouse, except for a crime committed against him, but the laws on this subject vary in the different states. In most states, by statute, the accused is now allowed to testify in his own behalf, but he cannot be compelled to testify (CDTP)

whole confession must be introduced: where a confession is used against an accused person, the whole confession must be introduced. A confession, like an admission, is always open to explanation by the person against whom it is used (CDTP)

whore: woman of loose morals; a prostitute (LEV)

whorehouse: house of prostitution (LEV)

whorl, plain: a fingerprint pattern which has one or more ridges which make a complete circuit. It has two deltas, between which, when an imaginary line is drawn, at least one recurving ridge is cut or touched (LEV)

Wickersham Commission on Law Observance: a commission under the chairmanship of former Attorney-General George W. Wickersham to canvass the entire question of law observance and enforcement, with specific reference to the prohibition laws. The Commission was appointed by President Hoover in 1929 as a result of the widespread disrespect for law, the increased willingness of the public to condone graft and corruption, and the deficiency in enforcement of the prohibition laws. The report and findings of the Commission confirmed the current impression that enforcement had proved wholly inadequate, that the law was unsupported by public opinion, that it was freely violated, that the general conduct of enforcement agencies dealing with this and other laws was lax and even "lawless," and that corruption was operating in a novel and greater area than ever before. The Commission, however, did not recommend the repeal of the Eighteenth Amendment, a step which was not taken until the adoption of the Twenty-First Amendment in 1933   (DOAH)

wide-angle lens: a lens of short focal length and great covering power used to cover a larger angle of view than a normal lens will include from a given viewpoint
(MPPF)

windage: (1) the deflection of a bullet or other projectile due to wind (DWMT) (2) the correction made for such deflection (DWMT) (3) in ordnance terminology, the space between the projectile of a smoothbore gun and the surface of the bore   (DWMT)

wiretapping: clandestine listening-in to telephonic and other communications by wire. Although the Supreme Court has held that the constitutional prohibition of unreasonable searches and seizures does not extend to wiretapping, Section 605 of the Federal Communications Act, interdicting such activity, has been upheld by the courts and applied to evidence secured by federal and State officers. See *Olmstead* v. *United States*   (DAP)

withdrawing a juror: withdrawing one of the twelve jurors impaneled to try a case. The court may in some jurisdictions resort to this course when through some unexpected cause a trial cannot proceed without injustice to a party
(CDTP)

Witherspoon v. Illinois, 391 U.S. 510 (1968): this case develops the thesis that a state may not entrust the determination of whether a man is innocent or guilty to a tribunal "organized to convict." Rejecting the classic "hanging jury," the majority opinion holds that a state may not entrust the determination of whether a man should live or die (capital crimes) to a jury organized to return a verdict of death, and that a sentence of death cannot be carried out if the jury that imposed or recommended it was chosen by excluding prospective jurors for cause simply because they voiced general objections to the death penalty or expressed conscientious or religious scruples against its infliction   (AOJ)

witness: one who testifies under oath; a person who has knowledge of facts in a case   (CDTP)

wobble: the erratic spin of a bullet in flight causing "keyholing" upon paper target impact ˆ

Wolf v. Colorado, 338 U.S. 25, 93 L. Ed. 1782, 69 S. Ct. 1359 (1949): with Mr. Justice Frankfurter writing for the majority (5-4) the Court subjected the state to the rule against arbitrary intrusions by the police—the essence of the Fourth Amendment. (The majority declined to take the step of enforcing this constitutional protection by banning the illegal evidence. In the 35 years between *Weeks* and *Wolf*, however, the due process clause of the Fourteenth Amendment had gradually acquired new potency, and when the Court considered *Wolf* the result was different. *Wolf* indicated clearly that the Court would reverse a state criminal conviction under due process when police action—in relation to persons suspected of crime—would offend the Court's sense of "fundamental fairness." This case-by-case approach came to an end in

1961 when the Court in its landmark decision in *Mapp* v. *Ohio* divested itself of major responsibility for the enforcement of the Fourth Amendment's right to privacy. It is interesting to note Mr. Justice Black's concurring opinion in *Wolf*—in the light of the Omnibus Crime Control and Safe Streets Act of 1968—wherein he observes that "the Federal exclusionary rule is not a command of the Fourth Amendment, but is a judicially created rule of evidence which Congress might negate.") (ILECJ)

word: a set of characters occupying one storage location; it is treated by the processor circuits as a unit and transported as such. Ordinarily, the control unit treats a word as an instruction whereas the arithmetic unit treats a word as a quantity (ADPS)

word, fixed-length: the number of characters to be handled as a unit as determined by the equipment designer and built into the circuitry (ADPS)

word, key: in COBOL, words that must be included in statements (unless they are in an optional phrase) and correctly spelled to avoid an error in the program (ADPS)

word, optional: in COBOL, words that may be used solely to improve readability, but, if used, must be correctly spelled (ADPS)

word, partial logic: the ability of a processor to select specified bits of characters from a word for processing and ignore others (ADPS)

word, selectable-length: the number of characters assigned by the programmer to each item of data; must be long enough to handle the longest instance of each item that will occur. Spaces not used for a particular item are filled out with zeros if numeric and blanks if alphanumeric (ADPS)

word, variable-length: the number of characters used for an item of data is exactly equal to its length, whether short or long; item separates of which describes an item in

a work area (ADPS)

work release: patterned after Wisconsin's Huber Law, 1913, statutes which provide for work-release, or day-parole, allowing the inmate of a correctional facility to leave the facility during the daytime to work in the community and to return to the facility in the evening. The wages received are usu. utilized in paying for room and board within the facility, for support of dependants, etc.

work study: a program similar to work 'release in which the inmate is allowed to leave the institution to attend school

writ: the word may be employed as referring to a process in civil proceedings; a summons; a written command, under the seal of the court, authorizing, and directing an officer to execute its judgement; the command of the commonwealth to a wrongdoer to answer to the wrong charges against him; the first step taken to bring the party sued before the court; the judicial notice to a debtor that his creditor demands justice; the summons issued after the filing of the petition (C.J., vol. 71) (CDTP)

rators are used to indicate the end of each item (ADPS)

WORDCOM: *word com*puter, a hypothetical processor used to illustrate the features of and programming for a processor with storage organized into words (ADPS)

workhouse: an English institution for the confinement of vagrants, beggars, and paupers. An American institution for short-term offenders. The same as jail (DOS)

working solution: a photographic solution which is ready to use (MPPF)

working-storage section: describes areas of storage where intermediate results and other items are stored temporarily during program execution; consists of a series of record description entries

writ of attachment: a provisional

remedy issued to seize property to make sure that any judgment awarded will be recovered

writ of certiorari: an original writ or action whereby a case is removed from an inferior to a superior court for review. The record of the proceedings is then transmitted to the superior court

writ of error coram nobis: a procedure directing an inferior court to send the record of proceedings before it to a superior court for review. It is the same as an appeal

writ of execution: the writ, order, or process issued to a sheriff, directing him to carry out the judgment of a court

writ of habeas corpus: the usual remedy for a person deprived of his liberty. Its purpose is to test the legality of the restraints on a person's liberty, to make sure he is restrained of his liberty by due process of law, not to discern whether he is guilty or innocent

writ of injunction: a court order directing that a particular activity stop or not be commenced. Disobedience of this order may be punished as contempt of court

writ of mandamus: a writ issued by a court requiring an individual or corporation to execute a specific act described in the writ

writ of mittimus: a written court order directed to the officer in charge of a prison directing that he receive and safely keep an offender

writ of possession: places plaintiff in possession of premises with the assistance of a sheriff

writ of procedendo: a writ addressed by a superior court to an inferior court, directing the latter to proceed to judgement

writ of prohibition: an order or mandate issued by a superior court to prevent an inferior court from determining a matter outside its jurisdiction

writ of supersedeas: a court order or writ by which proceedings are stayed

writ of venire facias: a writ to the sheriff to summon a jury

writ quo warranto: "By what authority?"; a proceeding by which the court inquires into the right of a person or corporation to hold an office, or to exercise a franchise

write: to cause the contents of one or more storage locations to become the contents of other locations after erasing the contents of the location to receive the data; for example, to write a block of data on magnetic tape after erasing the previous contents at the block written   (ADPS)

X

x-ray: to examine or test something with x-ray. This technique is used extensively in the medical field and in some examinations conducted by a crime laboratory (LEV) It was invented by German Professor Wilhelm Röntgen in 1895 by accident; he received the Nobel Prize in 1901 for his works

XYY chromosomes: an abnormal arrangement of the chromosomes in the nucleus of cells which, according to some scientists, produces antisocial behavior in persons having this abnormality. As of 1970 the National Institute of Mental Health reported that no definite conclusions had been reached as to the validity of such claims. This condition is sometimes referred to as "Y chromosomes"   (LEV)

Y

yen shee: the name given by Chinese to the cake that forms in the bowl of the used opium pipe, usu. drunk in wine   (CDTP)

youth: a person from the age of adolescence to full maturity. As a collective term, "youth" refers esp. to young persons of high school age and early college age. Persons aged 15 through 24 are usu. considered the youth group by researchers dealing with census data. The National Youth Administration considered persons aged 16 through 25 as youth eligible for assistance   (DOS)

youth correction authority: an administrative agency for the treatment of convicted youthful offenders. Designed by a committee of the American Law Institute and described in a model act approved by the Institute in 1940, the agency meets many of the demands for reform in penal treatment urged by social scientists and lawyers in recent times. The model act was, with modifications, adopted by California in 1914   (DOS)

Youth Correction Authority Act: a model act, published by the American Law Institute in 1940, which served as an impetus to several state youth authority acts. Among other proposals, the act gave ultimate sentencing authority to an administrative board, and provided for an indefinite commitment until the maximum age of 25   (LCC)

Youthful Offender Act of New York: enacted in 1943, this statute provided that youths, 16 through 18 years old, could, upon recommendation to the court, be tried as youthful offenders, rather than as felons, thus avoiding a criminal conviction   (LCC)

the integral part of a quantity as part of the editing routine before printing   (ADPS)

zone: (1) in processors, two bits used in conjunction with four numeric bits to represent alphanumeric characters. The zone bits may be used separately to represent signs, to identify index registers, and for other purposes (ADPS) (2) for punched cards, the 11 and 12 punches used with numeric punches 1 through 9 to represent alphabetic and special symbols. Zone punches may be used independently to indicate signs and for special purposes   (ADPS)

zone search: a method of searching a crime scene where the area to be searched is divided into sectors and each one is carefully examined. This is also called the "sector search"   (LEV)

zoned circuit: a circuit which provides continual protection for parts of the protected area while normally used doors and windows or zones may be released for access   (TDIAS)

zones: smaller subdivisions into which large areas are divided to permit selective access to some zones while maintaining other zones secure and to permit pinpointing the specific location from which an alarm signal is transmitted   (TDIAS)

zoom lens: a lens which can be varied in apparent focal-length while maintaining focus on a given object; it gives the effect of moving to or from the subject when used on a motion picture camera   (MPPF)

Z

zero suppression: elimination of nonsignificant zeros to the left of